A. Bronson Feldman
Early Shakespeare

A. Bronson Feldman

Early Shakespeare

Editor:
Warren Hope

Laugwitz Verlag

To the Memory of John Thomas Looney

special issue no. 8 of NEUES SHAKE-SPEARE JOURNAL
All rights for this edition reserved by Verlag Uwe Laugwitz,
Matthias-Claudius-Weg 11B, 21244 Buchholz, Germany
www.laugwitz.com

ISBN 9783-933077-54-7

Contents

Prefatory Note

Bronson Feldman, as a student at Philadelphia's Central High School, found that the traditional attribution of the plays and poems of William Shakespeare to Will Shakspere of Stratford-on-Avon distorted our understanding of the work. He was perhaps taught as I was at the same school decades later that Polonius's advice to Laertes represents Shakespeare's philosophy—a ridiculous view that arises from the life of the author as it has been recorded and repeated. In any case, Feldman took up a systematic study of the literature of the authorship question in an attempt to determine the identity of the true author so that Shakespeare's work could be truly understood. He became convinced by the arguments of J. Thomas Looney in his *Shakespeare Identified in Edward de Vere, seventeenth Earl of Oxford*. Although Feldman spent a good portion of the next fifty years of his life, until his death at the age of 68, studying the life, work, and times of Edward de Vere, alias Shakespeare, he never found any reason to change his mind about that conviction.

He is one of the very few Oxfordians who actually earned the Ph. D. in English Literature and with an emphasis on Tudor Drama. His degree is from the University of Pennsylvania where he wrote his doctoral dissertation on the influence of the Dutch War on Tudor Drama. He was required to meet the rigorous standards of such traditional Elizabethan scholars as Conyers Read, the biographer of Sir William Cecil, later Lord Burghley. He also early became associated with Charles Wisner Barrell and the Shakespeare Fellowship. As a result, he was able to combine a thorough academic knowledge of the period with the pioneering work of such followers of Looney as Eva Turner Clark, B. M. Ward, Percy Allen, and Admiral Holland, the Oxfordians who found evidence that supported and enriched Looney's original case. Feldman also became a practicing lay psychoanalyst, having studied under Theodor Reik. This volume represents an attempt to analyze Shakespeare's first ten plays from an Oxfordian and psychoanalytic perspective in the conjectured order of their composition. Feldman had hoped to follow this volume up with a second, to be entitled *Shakespeare Ripening*, and then eventually a third and final one that would have completed the study. Readers interested in how he treated Shakespeare's later works should go to his book-length study entitled *Hamlet Himself* and also his articles on *Othello* and the sonnets that were published in *The American Imago*.

The first chapter in this book was originally published in a slightly different version in 1955 in the *International Journal of Psychoanalysis*. The author wrote and revised some of the later chapters shortly before his death on February 19, 1982. The entire manuscript was prepared on a manual typewriter and frequently proofread and edited. In putting it together for publication I have simply tried to let the author say what he wanted to say and in the way he wanted to say it. I have no wish to rehearse here what I have come to think of as the tragic comedy of errors that kept the book from being published soon after its author's death as originally planned. It is enough to say that I am extremely relieved and pleased that it is being published now. I am convinced that students of Shakespeare will greatly benefit from reading this book, and I hope that some of them will be encouraged by it to pursue similar studies.

Warren Hope

Chapter 1—EARLY ERRORS

Veterem atque antiquam rem novam ad vos proferam.
Plautus: *Amphitruo*.

I

If we could understand the motives that impelled William Shakespeare to the writing of plays, what were the reasons for his giving a whole life of wealthy imagination to the theater, we might come into possession of the main keys to the psychology of the stage itself, of plays, the players, and their public. In the hope of contributing toward this achievement, I have undertaken an intensive analysis of a play by the paramount dramatist which most historians regard as one of the earliest—if not the very first—of his creative efforts in theater, the *Comedy of Errors*. Because of the juvenile character, the crude frivolity, of this drama scholars have not granted it earnest attention. The eyes of psychoanalysis turn the more readily to it precisely because of this juvenile character. We know how the childishness of an artist will betray the deepest secrets of his mind, the unconscious origin of the passions of his life. If it is true that the *Errors* stands the nearest of Shakespeare's works to his infancy, we may look forward to discovering in it the primary springs of his fantasy, the driving forces of all his dramatic work.

Analysis of the comedy is not an easy task, for Shakespeare bequeathed it to us in a palimpsest form. There is plenty of evidence that he revised this product of his youth several times, and it did not reach the press until he had been in his grave many years. We need not be dismayed by the rapid shifts in quality of its stagecraft and the abrupt variations of the style. The changes in the drama will mystify us only when we lose sight of its substance, the farcical plot, which throws over all the sophistications of Shakespeare's mature art, the unmistakable shadow of his novice mind. Scarcely any of his other plays exhibits so hearty an interest in plot as the *Errors*. The plot is the thing in which we shall catch the conscience of the poet.

Shakespeare apprehended this fact, and therefor labored to fill the fabric of the comedy with snares and delusions, ever hopeful of escape from knowledge. With extreme cunning he wrote and rewrote the comedy, turning it into a net of Gordian knots which nowhere present a single loose end to enable us to unravel the purport of the play. At whatever point we select to begin our analysis we are bound to use a sharpness without subtlety, to cut the fabric so that it can be untied with the loving patience it deserves.

Suppose we begin the investigation of Shakespeare's *Errors* with the obvious motive of the farce. Manifestly its purpose is to provoke laughter, extravagant, strenuous, far-fetched laughter, not without tears. The poet means to be merry, like his hero in the middle of the drama, "in despite of mirth" (*Errors*, 3.1.108). With its wild unbelievable story and dreamlike duplication of characters, the comedy aims at delirium. The prime emotion appears to be one of hysteria, as if the author evolved it from a desperate want of hilarity, feeling that he must have merriment or run mad. He does not leave us in doubt about the source of this manic humor, freedom from woe. It functioned for him in the same way that the clown Dromio of Syracuse serves his curious master. "When I am dull with care and melancholy," the master remarks, Dromio "Lightens my humour with his merry jests" (1.2.20-21). Again and again Shakespeare stresses relief from a devouring sorrow as sufficient excuse for his jokes, no matter how ribald or fierce. He seems to have put such hilarity on the plane of athletic sports, considering it precious recreation:

> Sweet recreation barr'd, what doth ensue
> But moody moping, and dull melancholy,
> Kinsman to grim and comfortless despair ... (5.1.78-80)

Below the surface of the comedy, then, we can plainly see the motive of evading melancholy or depression of soul.

The intensity of the poet's depression on the threshold of his *Comedy* may be estimated by the fact that he altered the raw Roman material of the play in order to give it a groundwork of tragedy. For the sake of its sorrowful opening scene Shakespeare sacrificed elements from his Latin source which would have made the plot more plausible.

In the *Menaechmi* of his beloved Plautus, the twins around whom the comedy revolves are separated by a commonplace event. The father takes one to a distant market town and the boy is lost in a crowd. A merchant finds the little Menaechmus and carries him away across the Adriatic sea to Epidamnus. The lad's father dies of grief. Back in their native Syracuse the grandfather, learning of the double loss, and anxious to preserve the memory of the lost boy who was named after him, changes the name of the remaining twin from Sosicles to Menaechmus. The new Menaechmus grows up and travels across the Adriatic hoping to find out what happened to his dear brother. Shakespeare desired more sensational reasons for the parting of the twins. He invented a tempest and a shipwreck to account for it. He refused to let the father die of grief, and increased the old man's torments by parting him from the second son. This boy leaves his father to go in search of a brother whom he has never known. And old Aegeon is compelled, years later, to sail in search of both his sons, across the Mediterranean sea to Ephesus. Shakespeare completes his disruption of the family by having brutal seamen divide the mother from the child she saved in the wreck. In the midst of this welter of narrative we are disappointed to observe that he names the twins Antipholus and fails to elucidate why they have identical names. In stage directions of the first edition of the drama (the folio of 1623) we learn that the Ephesian brother is called *Surreptus*, as in the prolog of Plautus, and his Syracusan twin Erotes; Surreptus means stolen, and Erotes is self-explanatory though not clean Greek. To augment the mystification our dramatist bestows on their twin servants the single name Dromio, a common name for clowns in Roman comedy. Shakespeare would also find fitting the popular association of English clowns with the drum. We know that he got the idea for his two sets of twins from another comedy by Plautus, *Amphitruo*, but the Latin dramatist accounted for his twins here by making one of each pair a god masquerading to delude mortals.

Plautus opened his *Amphitruo* with the statement, from the mouth of the god Mercury, that the play commences as a tragedy. Shakespeare may have been encouraged by this to start the *Errors* in the same manner. But the Roman playwright shows us nothing piteous and terrible like the first scene of Shakespeare's play. Plautus's excuse for the tragic element in his work is that "it is not right to make a play where kings and gods talk entirely comedy." The tragic feature in Shakespeare's work concerns no god nor king, only the poor old merchant Aegeon, who has no parallel in Plautus.

What could have driven Shakespeare to make these radical alterations in his material? Why did he discard the simple disappearance of a twin in a crowd for the barely credible separation at sea? The tempest must have had a special meaning for the dramatist. The central image of Aegeon's tale, the splitting of his ship, must have exerted an irresistible fascination on Shakespeare's mind. He lavished so much imagination on the disaster that he neglected to make clear the reason for calling both of Aegeon's boys Antipholus. The reckless omission of this important detail gives us a glimpse of the hysterical haste with which the poet went to work on his comedy. His reason seems to have been overwhelmed by the images of the storm and the wreck.

He makes the old man speak of his misfortune as "this unjust divorce" (1.1.104). Now, matrimony has often been compared to a sea, and divorce to shipwreck. How conscious of these metaphors the dramatist may have been, we cannot say. It is incontestable however that the thought of divorce was running in his brain when he composed the *Comedy of Errors*. Its central events occur in consequence of an estrangement between the hero, Antipholus of Ephesus, and his wife. And the two Latin plays from which Shakespeare derived the raw stuff of his farce obtain their effects of fun from breaches of marriage.

So far as I am aware, only one of Shakespeare's critics, Frank Harris, recognised that the poet's own alienation from his wife was a stimulus to writing the *Errors*.[1] Unfortunately Harris's conception of the play and its maker raised more riddles than he solved, obscuring the merit of his discovery. He erred in attempting to sift details from the drama to suit his purely imaginary biography of the poet. In this chapter I intend to steer clear of questions of biography, relying for argument exclusively on the text of the play and its literary analogs. By its fruit we shall know the tree.

The "unjust divorce" of Aegeon and his Aemilia is the work of wind, water, and stone, or the caprice of the goddess Fortune, as the venerable traveler affirms. The alienation of Antipholus and his Adriana, on the other hand, is portrayed error, the crux of a series of errors. The marriage of this couple, Shakespeare seems to say, is nothing but a comedy of errors, indeed a mistake from the start. Adriana's sister suspects that Antipholus married her for her riches (3.2). He grew cold to her, if not cruel. Before the action of the play commences, he was in the habit of keeping late hours away from his house. "His company must do his minions grace," Adriana complains, "Whilst I at home starve for a merry look" (2.1.187-188). She accuses him of unkindness, and he charges her with shrewish behavior. Both are right. Yet until the confusions of the comedy begin, we are led to believe, their temperaments have never exploded in hate. For only a week, prior to the day of the drama, Adriana declares near the end, her husband has been behaving strangely.

> This week he hath been heavy, sour, sad,
> And much different from the man he was;
> But till this afternoon his passion
> Ne'er brake into extremity of rage. (5.1.45-48)

From the lips of Luciana and Aemilia, the poet casts the blame for the estrangement of the wife. They rebuke her for "self-harming jealousy," for breaking the peace of her household with wicked thoughts of her husband wandering abroad in alleged pursuit of unlawful love. According to the judgment of these women, her conduct toward Antipholus is enough to explain his melancholy and the "unjust divorce" of their souls.

The dramatist's compassion for the sad Antipholus bears witness for our conviction that Shakespeare identified himself with the outraged husband. He had broken away from his own wife and felt a strong impulse to justify the act on the stage. It could not be shown straitforwardly of course. In the first place the poet was too blind with tears of self-pity to see the naked truth. Moreover he sensed that his wife did not hold a monopoly of the guilt in their disgrace. He had the intelligence and the courage to admit that he had contributed wrongs and miseries to the marriage; but his courage took the peculiar path of confessing his sins under the mask of comedy. Adopting the counsel of his Luciana, "Be not thy tongue thy own shame's orator" (3.2.10), he showed the world his shame by means of a variety of tongues. He discloses his guilt with a mirthy grimace while protesting, in an agony of remorse, that he is innocent. The core of the whole play is an apology for Shakespeare's errors in matrimony. He is not to blame, the drama pleads in its grotesque fashion: nor should the woman in the case be condemned, though discerning persons of her sex might decide that she was responsible. The fact of the matter, Shakespeare evidently wishes us to think, is that the marriage had been wrecked because the bride and the groom did not really know the individuals they wedded. It was a case of mistaken identity.

In some such way, I imagine, the ego of the poet defended itself against his conscience or superego in the supreme court of his unconscious self. I and my woman, the dramatist inwardly contended, have done nothing more damnable than entertain strangers as lovers. She took me in, like Alcmena in *Amphitruo*, thinking that a hero was going to sleep by her side, and in happy ignorance she united with a god. Alas, poor god! He took in holy wedlock what he believed was an angel, and she turned out to be a termagant, at any rate a woman of torturing whims. Nevertheless, as Plautus says, "The god will not allow his sin and fault to fall upon a mortal's head." In our pitiable and ridiculous way we are trying to correct our mistakes. Anyhow, I am.—Thus seeking balm for hurt vanity, and excuses for his marital follies and cruelties, the dramatist contrived his *Comedy of Errors*.

The dramatic process in his oblivion took the shape of a dream-like confusion of identities. He pictured himself as two persons, the husband Antipholus and his double, the unwedded twin, Antipholus of Syracuse (Erotes), who is taken for the husband by his unhappy Adriana. There is nothing here to prove a split in the dramatist's personality. On the contrary, he has retained his ego entire and dealt himself the luxury of an alter-ego.[2] He demonstrates the sort of esteem for himself which makes people say of certain gentlemen, they are too brilliant, they should have been born twins.[3]

The resemblance between the brothers is more than skin-deep. The Duke of Ephesus indicates their true relationship when he exclaims,

> One of these men is genius to the other.
> ...   Which is the natural man,
> And which the spirit? Who deciphers them? (5.1.333-335)

You might term the Syracusan the mirror-self of the straying Antipholus. I see in their relation a survival in the artist of the stage in which our superego first distinguishes itself from the motorsteering mentality called ego, the stage of our struggle to reflect ourselves inside the skull instead of others' eyes, or voices. The Syracusan could well be described as the "genius" or spiritual double of the husband.

On the first appearance of the brother from the west, he reveals himself as a victim of the same inexplicable melancholy that the man from Ephesus suffers from:

> He that commends me to mine own content
> Commends me to the thing I cannot get. (1.2.33-34)

Erotes glows more lyrical in speech, and briefly evinces a tendency to speculative (literally, mirror) thought. On his arrival in Ephesus, weary from a long voyage, he delays his dinner to gratify a wish to look on the town, "Peruse the trades, gaze upon the buildings..." His pleasure in sights and insights leads him to hazards and bewilderment, but nothing can diminish it. He vows that he will "in this mist at all adventures go." (2.2.215)

The Syracusan's intellectual faculties are never so vivid as his carnal ones. He is almost as brutal as his brother. Both of them are quick to beat their servants' skulls for similar audacities. They cherish in common a profound and unfunny antagonism to the woman Adriana. After making her acquaintance for an hour or two, the westerner confesses:

> She that doth call me husband, even my soul
> Doth for a wife abhor. (3.2.157-158)

The Ephesian bursts into a fury against his wife for barring him mysteriously from their home. He orders a rope to be bought with a view to punishing her (4.1). He even threatens to pluck out her eyes (4.3). In short, his soul abhors her too. It is not the reverence for virtue in the twins that shrinks from the shrill lady. Shakespeare does not depict them as patterns of chastity. The Ephesian plays a bold homage to the harlot who runs the Porpentine inn. His brother makes love to Luciana shortly after their first sight of each other, and plans to leave her city the same day. The ego-glamor of this fellow is oddly displayed by the poet in his pretext for abandoning Luciana. Her charms, says he, "almost made me traitor to myself."

> But lest myself be guilty to self-wrong,
> I'l stop mine ears against the mermaid's song. (3.2.162-163)

His scruples do not prevent him from accepting the wifely services of her sister; he lets Adriana labor under the impression that she is performing her duty to her mate. The promptitude of the twins in embracing female hospitality is nearly equaled by their good-will to men, especially men of their station in society. To these singular traits of the twins we should add their mode of showing anxiety as soon as they experience a loss of money. All these touches of nature prove them more than kin.

Incidentally, the poet gives two different statements of their age. In the first scene we learn that the Syracusan journeyed at eighteen in quest of the other. Since then, Aegeon remarks, five summers have passed, or, to be exact, as he is in the final scene, "seven short years." To the father then the twins are twenty-five years old. The mother dates their birthday earlier. "Thirty-three years," she declares, "have I but gone in travail / Of you, my sons" (5.1.402-403) We are sorry to lose the evidence of those she calls "the calendars of their nativity." The two brothers are presented as men of "gravity" and "serious hours," but demeanor is no index to age. Adriana in anger asserts that her mate is "deformed, crooked, old and sere" (4.2.19). But can we trust her testimony in the face of the romance of his twin and her sister Luciana? We cannot even be sure that Dromio of Ephesus tells the truth when he says, examining Dromio of Syracuse, "I see by you I am a sweet-fac'd youth" (5.1.420). The cause of the poet's discrepant chronology lies, I feel sure, in his revision of the play at different stages of his career, and may be of use to biographers.

The name that Shakespeare chose for his ego surrogates is rare in Latin literature and in Greek. He could have derived it from the Greek *Anthology*, varying a poet's spelling. There was a famous artist, a painter, named Antiphilus in the era of Alexander the Great. Possibly the dramatist remembered him when he cloaked his unconscious self as Grecian for the *Comedy of Errors*. I suppose he made the name by a masculine variation of Antiphila, the name of Terence's heroine in *The Self-Tormentor*, whose slave is Dromo. Antiphila, I am told, signifies "mutual love;" it is obdurate Greek to me. The frequent fatality in the choice of names still challenges us to clarify Shakespeare's designation for his doubles. It strikes me that the spelling "Antipholus," not found in Greek, was meant characteristically for a pun. We know how fond our poet was of legerdemain with words; he could truly be termed a pun-addict. Also well known is his conviction that by means of wit and word-wizardry in plays he could purge the stupidities, the intellectual sicknesses of the world.[4] In the light of these facts I suggest that the name of his heroes may be translated to English as anti-follies. The follies he had mainly in mind were sexual. Therefor I propose to interpret their name also as *anti-phallus*. And immediately the idea obtrudes that "Antipholus" naturally occurred to the poet as the name for his primary stage-images as nearly equivalent to Shakespeare. If I am right

in this surmise it would help to explain Shakespeare's failure to record the reason for the twins bearing the same name. The culture of
his soul, his humane development, would not permit him free rein
in self-righteousness. As a fool of Fortune in marriage, he must
have felt uneasy in his posture of justice superior to the fools of the
planet. In the collision between righteous vanity and the woe and
shame of his "unjust divorce" the memory of the latter would suffice to make him oblivious of the motive for naming his protagonist
Antipholus.

The two Dromios, as twin slaves of the brothers Antipholus, all
of precisely the same age, and one a bachelor like his master, could
be viewed as simply burlesques of the aristocratic pair. They share
certain qualities of their respective employers. The married Dromio,
for example, expresses with his scullion Luce the lechery which his
master has subdued and refined. The unmarried servant shows less
carnality than his brother, and more religion and imagination. His
spiritual attributes remind us poignantly of the harping of Paul on
the distinction between the "natural man and the spiritual," in his
epistle to the church in Corinth (1.2.14). Both Dromios were
shaped at first like brutes of *commedia dell' arte*, mere Italian buffoons;
but they developed into beings rich and strange.

Here we are provided a remarkable contrast of Shakespeare's
dramatic method with that of Plautus. The English artist modelled
his Syracusan clown on the role that the god Mercury enacts in *Amphitruo* as the double of the slave Sosia. The English poet transformed the divine Sosia into a human with an unusual talent for
superstition, just as he changed the Jupiter who usurped Amphitruo's bed into a mortal proud of his chastity, with an unusual talent
for philosophy. Between Plautus and Shakespeare, plainly, there was
a progress of reason in religion accompanied by a tremendous re-
striction of libido. The Syracusan twins, with all their fleshly frailty,
are unquestionably more civilised in morals than the Roman gods.
If the Roman dramatist has any advantage over Shakespeare in ethics, you could say that it consists of his superior passion for liberty.
Plautus never lets pass an opportunity to utter his sorrow and ha-

tred at the sight of humanity in chains. To Shakespeare's eyes, at least in youth, the bondage of a Dromio was too light to be taken seriously. He seems to have enjoyed a feudal sense of intimacy between lord and laborer. Antipholus expresses the feudal idea when he warns Dromio not to let "Your sauciness jest upon my love" even if "I familiarly sometimes / Do use you for my fool, and chat with you" (2.2.27). Their relation might be defined as personal anagogically. It is possible that Dromio incarnates the "earthy-gross conceit" which Antipholus deplores in himself (3.2.34), referring to the avidly plausible and vulgar qualities of the genius who created them both.

When Shakespeare wrote the *Comedy of Errors*, he had already brooded long enough over the riddles of human nature, in the "sweet way" he went (like his king Richard the Second) sometimes "to despair," to reach the point Michel de Montaigne did in 1576, when he had the medallion carved for him with the question *Que scais je?* What do I know?

II

The *Errors* contains another set of mental twins, who have eluded the scrutiny of Shakespearean experts and critics too long. It is conceivable that the dramatist himself was not aware of their identity. Their likeness is drawn with so much dexterity and painstaking cleverness that I am inclined to think he intended them to be equals and opposites. He strove cordially to discriminate them, and the opinion of generations of scholars on their portraits is proof that he was too successful. The cost of this success, in my opinion, is the defeat of the dramatist's honest intention, and injustice to the woman whom he sketched twice as the wife Adriana and her sister. There are good reasons for belief that when Shakespeare outlined their characters he wanted, perhaps unconsciously, to limn two aspects or phases of the same lady, his own wife. Luciana would then represent the girl he made his bride, beautiful, tender, and gleaming with extraordinary wisdom; and Adriana would stand for the woman she became, or rather the creature Shakespeare discovered beneath the veil of his bride. In changing her image to the two seemingly alien heroines he surpassed the metamorphoses of his favorite poet, Ovid, whose mythic transformations he constantly reviewed in the "quick forge and working-house" of his oblivion.

The essential identity of the sisters emerges when we compare their personalities in detail. The outstanding trait of Adriana is her shrewishness. Antipholus of Syracuse contrasts her with Luciana primarily because of the unmarried sister's kind and courteous manner, her "gentle sovereign grace" (3.2.159). Next to this quality, he adores her "discourse," or adroitness in conversation. Now Luciana herself, though critical of her sister's headstrong will and attitude to Antipholus, testifies that

> She never reprehended him but mildly,
> When he demean'd himself rough, rude, and wildly. (5.1.87)

Shakespeare presents the shrew as a model of tenderness in the scene where she humors her husband believing him almost insane—"poor distressed soul" (4.4.60). She exhibits her devotion to him in worry over his arrest for debt, which she hurries to pay off despite his torrent of insults. As for Adriana's "discourse," we have every reason to trust her when she affirms that her conversation had been dulled and her wit turned barren by the chill hostility of her husband. "If voluble and sharp discourse be marr'd," says she, "Unkindness blunts it more than marble hard" (2.1.92-93). We are given not one sign that Antipholus ever acted toward her with generosity, except before their wedding, when she was certainly Luciana -like.

The unmarried sister however is by no means exempt from Adriana's defects. She too can pour a swift shrillness of epithets on people who offend her (2.2). Her volubility on occasions can be bluntly evil (3.2). We may trust the judgment of Adriana when she declares her sister will want to "bear some sway" after she weds, and upbraid her husband if he roves from home to linger in sirens' taverns. Apart from temper and talent in talk the girls are supposed to be distinguished by their looks. Adriana speaks as if "homely age" had deprived her of virgin loveliness, but later she avers that a "sunny look" from her husband would rapidly restore her beauty: "he hath wasted it" (2.1.90). If he had never led her to the nuptial altar she might have glittered precisely as alluring as her sister and the hostess of the Porpentine inn, whom Antipholus praises as "Pretty and witty, wild, and yet, too, gentle" (3.1.110). Shakespeare does not tell us how old she and Luciana were. If there is any difference in their ages, it is not enough to cleave their souls asunder. They too are one. (Shakespeare took the liberty of introducing in his play the name of a property in London, the Porpentine, a "messuage" located like many a brothel on the Bankside near the Pike Garden.)[5]

In the names of the two heroines, I suspect, our dramatist informed us, in his paradoxical way, that they are twins. If we take Luciana to mean, as in Latin, "the bright one," by the facile substitution of a tongue-touch for the second consonant in Adriana, we could translate her name, "the dark one." It may also signify in English the lucent or luscious one gone dry. Recalling that Luci in Latin was closely related to Luti (as in the ancient name of Paris) meaning muddy or wet, we see again how the handsome sister parallels Adriana. For my purpose it is unnecessary to render the last syllables of their names more concretely. To the reader who wishes to take them as meaning Anna, I answer, "as you like it."

It is not unlikely that Shakespeare designed these "witches," as Antipholus of Syracuse calls them (3.2.155), to stand for the grand moon goddess of their city, Diana. (The dramatist always refrained from calling the Ephesian by her Greek name Artemis.) The Syracusan worships Luciana as "more than earth divine," hails her "Fair sun," and speaks of her sister as "night." To the writer, according to my surmise, the feminine sun could only be the shining face of the moon. He symbolised her sister by the dark side of Diana. The name of this goddess might be interpreted, without stretching the patience of philology, as meaning "the twofold one." James Frazer has observed that Diana appears in ancient myth like a partner of Janus (Dianus), the two-faced god of Rome.[6] The concept of the twofold deity could have inspired our poet to alter the setting of his *Errors* from Plautus's Epidamnus to Ephesus. Shakespeare was well acquainted of course with the ancient reputation of the metropolis where Paul found Jewish exorcists competing with him, and both Jews and Greeks "who practised magic arts" lucratively (*Acts of the Apostles*, xix, 19). Presumably Shakespeare was tempted to keep the scene in Epidamnus, since that name surely appealed to his passion for puns and devilry. He made the town the birthplace of his heroes (1.1), and the Syracusan brother is told to pretend that he voyaged from there to Ephesus. When he plans to abandon Luciana his servant buys passage on a vessel bound for Epidamnus. At all events the poet used Ephesus to serve his dramatic aims as a metropolis of the damned.

The Epidamnus of Plautus is a town of swindling, sponging and seduction. Shakespeare's Ephesus is a town of deeds more dreadful, infernal crafts, "And many such-like liberties of sin" (1.2.102). Its wenches, according to Dromio of Syracuse, are accustomed to cry "God damn me," which he believes is equivalent to the prayer "God make me a light wench." These girls are therefor worthy to function as ministers of the moon. Dromio argues that their heavenly bodies are hellish: "It is written, they appear to men like angels of light: light is an effect of fire, and fire will burn; ergo, light wenches will burn" (4.3.53-54). But Dromio, like his master, is an enemy of all things pagan, when these confront him in the flesh. For the literate Antipholus the cult of Diana would have poetic charm, with its visions of wildwood nymphs and vestals entranced or dancing by her silver flame. Outside poetry however he would agree with the illiterate Dromio that her religion was witchcraft or else sheer lunacy. Both master and slave are devout Christians—actually Roman Catholics—and according to Christian tradition the sylvan retinue of Diana eventually turned into "goblins, owls, and elvish sprites" (2.2). In the period of Shakespeare a host of scholars were convinced that warlocks and beldames sold to hell still worshiped her: "in the night-time," it is written, "they ride abroad with Diana, the goddess of the Pagans."[7] The divinity receives no worship in Shakespeare's play because he converted Ephesus to a Christian city. Nevertheless we can glimpse her "sovereign grace," divided among the women of the comedy, performing its magic in the afternoon and dusk. She exercises her spells not only through the dextrous Luciana and the sinister Adriana, but also through the unnamed inn-woman Dromio fancies might be "Mistress Satan" (4.3.47).

By the supernal power of sex, which Diana represents, the characters are all flung into craziness. True, this does not occur until the hero Antipholus of Syracuse sets feet in the city. Shakespeare labored hard to impress us with the notion that Antipholus is ever on guard against the spell of sex. How then could he act as the prime mover of its madness in the comedy? My answer is that, despite his piety, he is the "evil genius" of the *Errors*. To each of the women in it his apparition radiates a magnetism of wickedness, of which he is blissfully unaware. His Dromio seems to comprehend this. When Antipholus warns the hostess of the Porpentine, "Avaunt, thou witch!" Dromio dryly remarks: "Fly pride, says the peacock" (4.3.77 -78) Apropos of the peacock, we recall that the bird was a companion of the goddess Juno, in whom Frazer discerned a twin of Diana.[8] So the Syracusan may rightly be regarded as a minion of the moon. Wherever he walks, it looks as if lunacy prevails; no wonder he must ask himself,

> Am I in earth, in heaven, or in hell?
> Sleeping or waking? mad or well-advis'd? (2.2.211-212)

The adventures of Antipholus prove, by theatrical providence, to be "well-advised." He manages to enjoy himself hugely among the Ephesians, and united with Luciana in the end.

The omission of the moon-goddess from Shakespeare's *Errors* was probably dictated by discretion more than religious propriety. The educated subjects of Elizabeth the First were accustomed to hearing the Virgin Queen extolled as the English Diana, and literary allusions to the divinity of the moon were frequently assumed to imply an opinion of her Majesty.[9] Shakespeare apparently endeavored to banish all thought of Elizabeth from the minds attending to his farce. Perhaps he remembered the penalty inflicted on his fore-runner Richard Edwards when that comic dramatist referred to classic Greek personalities in language that was construed as criticism of some Tudor courtiers.[10] Our poet could not afford to have any wit of the royal court construe the function of Diana in his comedy as a joke on the Queen. He described the city of Ephesus, remember, as a hotbed of black magic, swarming with

> Dark-working sorcerers that change the mind,
> Soul-killing witches that deform the body. (1.2.99-100)

If he had introduced the goddess of these magicians in the play, he would have risked damnation as one who hinted that Elizabeth was the mistress of mountebanks and hell-hags.

Insofar as her Majesty is glanced at in *Errors* it is through the glare of the authority of Solinus, the "sweet prince" of Ephesus. This Duke is barely more than an abstraction, law and order incarnate. The first syllable of his name, Sol, would at once ward off suspicion that the poet delineated him as a deputy of Diana, the antagonist of the sun. Solinus will not stand for nonsense and moonshine; he is emblematic of system, a foe of anarchy, indeed a solvent of the superego.

So Shakespeare expelled the magnificent female moon from the *Comedy of Errors*. A quick look at a concordance tells us that the moon is not mentioned there even once. Yet the shadow of the goddess is perceptible in every scene. She glows beyond the heads of the women in their excitement or serenity, and broods tenebrously over the men. When the young Shakespeare wrote the play, in the darkness of his unconscious, he must have offered a mocking reverence to her "whom all Asia and the world worshipeth," and echoed the cry of the silversmiths against the precursor of iconoclasts, Paul: "Great is Diana of the Ephesians!" (*Acts of the Apostles*, xxix, 28)

To the learned of Shakespeare's period Diana was above all the goddess of virginity. Luciana would therefor seem to be a truer embodiment of the Diana ideal than Adriana. Let us not be deceived by this seeming. The emphasis of the poet on the "unviolated honour" of the wife, her horror of the licentious (2.2), her lack of offspring, and the gestures of frigid purity that drove her husband to the Porpentine inn, prove her deserving of a vestal coronet.

Shall we assent to the proof? Is it not also seeming a tissue of ostensible truth? We have seen Luciana portrayed as a temptress, a siren luring the bachelor Antipholus to "self-wrong." Shakespeare in fact makes her an advocate of hypocrisy. In the belief that Antipholus is her brother-in-law, she instructs him to execute his lust by stealth: "Teach sin the carriage of a holy saint; / Be secret-false" (3.2.14-15). The purity of her sister is no less illusory. Some may reject the accusations of her husband—"Dissembling harlot!" "O most unhappy strumpet!" (4.4.102)—as products of fallacy, brought on by the revelation that she welcomed an unknown man in his absence. Those who think so should try to explain the slip of her slave Dromio's tongue when, early in the play, he chats of her husband's delay in coming home: "Why, mistress," he blurts, "sure my master is horn-mad." She responds instantly to the indictment of adultery, emblemed in England often by holding the first two fingers slanted stiff, two palps of vanity over one palm. "Horn-mad, thou villain!" He hastens to correct himself, "I mean not cuckold-mad" (2.1.58-59). From the psychopathology of similar mistakes we can deduce a hint of veracity in Dromio's slip. Apparently his master has behaved like a man stung by fancies of his wife's infidelity long before her afternoon's entertainment. Is it conceivable that the headstrong Adriana had done absolutely nothing to promote these fancies? Hours before he calls her strumpet, she weeping brands herself with the stigma. She calls herself a "stale" of Antipholus. Later, in fantasy of his own sins, she announces:

> I am possess'd with an adulterate blot;
> My blood is mingled with the crime of lust. (2.2.139-140)

Her basis for this self-accusation is a mere metaphor of marriage, that she and her mate are in wedlock one, and his guilt, like his glory, is hers. Under the tones of uxorious indignation we can detect the murmur of submerged sensuality, just as below the chambers of Adriana we find dwelling the kitchen-wench Nell, or Dowsabel, whose lascivious advances frighten Dromio of Syracuse. The acuteness of Shakespeare's satire on the virginal sisters may be seen in the third name he invented for the obscene scullery girl. He also calls her Luce, as if to invite comparison with the chaste yet hypocritic Luciana.

The truth is that the sisters, like the brothers, are impure in heart. Among the paradoxes of the comedy, the confidence they display in their virginity and virtue is perhaps the most absurd. They are all sinners, all fools—what you will: "Smother'd in errors, feeble, shallow, weak" (3.2.35).

III

Our investigation of *Errors* thus far leads to the decision that the comedy was precipitated out of the artist's oblivion by marital troubles and disaster. We have yet to elucidate the problem, what made a gentleman of his intelligence and courage prone to erotic conflict and calamity? How did he ever come to entertain strangers as lovers? His marriage could not have been the first enterprise of this sort. Before he married he must have committed other erotic errors more or less like those he caricatured in his play. In all his affairs of the heart, one feels sure, the blind god Cupid led him blind, quelling his intelligence and flaring up his courage. In the mist of passion he would go at all adventures, no matter what torments and remorse might ensue. The Narcissus in his nature could usually single out somebody to blame for his stumbling and sprawls. If not, there was always fortune to be cursed, or his birth stars.

The reply to our riddle must be hid in the heart of this Narcissus within Shakespeare, the colossal self-love which could project itself into the twin heroes of the comedy and have enough energy left to form their slave-likenesses and the opposite characters ruddily vital and radiant. From the Narcissus pool of his soul he drew the power—and "will in overplus"—to surmount the tragic defeats and comic humiliations of his life. From mysterious fountains in the same pool his ego also drank sweet poison, mistaking the distillation of self-pity for the medicine of self-criticism, and consequently steeping itself in a melancholy that not seldom resembled madness. It was in flight from the peril of dethroned reason that Shakespeare wrote the *Comedy of Errors.* For the play not only endeavors to explain the struggle of the poet's conscience with an event; it struggles to explain the poet, to assist the understanding of the stranger he felt was himself. To love oneself and win self-knowledge: is the feat possible?

So far as Shakespeare had the strength, when he composed *Errors*, to venture the feat—handicapt by his terror of baring himself to taunts and bladelike mental rapine, he did it in meditation and development of his personae, the two Antipholuses. Naturally he endowed them with his admirable traits—his dignity, his noble compassion and candor, his affection for the arts of peace, his grace to women and good-will to men. Dignity or honor obliged him to paint in his less attractive traits—his jealousy and impulse for revenge, his severely controlled lust and ferocity, and the will to lie, slink, steal, mutilate, and kill.

We have already noticed how the Ephesian twin, on being locked out of his house, commands the purchase of a rope to lash his wife, and later, when she brings a doctor for his distraction, threatens with his own nails to pluck out her "false eyes" (4.4.105). In a parallel scene of the *Menaechmi* the slave Messenio threatens to gouge the eyes of some men who are trying to drag his master off as a lunatic. The memory of this probably lurked in Shakespeare's brain when he pictured the half-crazed husband menacing his wife. (Could we call the difference in the two scenes a displacement socially upward?) Antipholus vents his sadistic wrath on Dr Pinch instead, applying fire to his beard, extinguishing the flame with pails of puddled mire, while his servant nicks the doctor with scissors (5). Meanwhile his brother turns thief with the golden chain that the Ephesian wished to give a courtesan to spite his wife. The theft follows the dinner which the Syracusan has obtained from Adriana by turning cheat.

Afterward he and his Dromio scare off the two sisters and the courtesan with naked swords (4.4). These little larcenies and brutalities recompense the twins for their grand refusal to tread the path of unholy dalliance and adultery.

It is curious to see how the bachelor brother treats the house of Adriana like an inn, and makes love to one of the hostesses, immediately before the espoused brother determines to dine at the inn whose mistress Shakespeare merely names Courtesan. In neither episode does the house turn brothel, like the home of Erotium in Plautus, where Menaechmus the newcomer dines with the prostitute at his brother's expense. The wish, which George Meredith styled sentimental, to get pleasure unpaid for is manifestly behind the comic conception of both playwrights. But Shakespeare's horror of indulging the wish robs his play of much humor. He presents Antipholus of Ephesus as a paragon of idealism in morals. "How dearly," says his wife, "would it touch thee to the quick, / Shouldst thou but hear I were licentious." She conjures a vision of him tearing the wedding ring from her finger to "break it with a deep divorcing vow" (2.2.137). Less than two hours later, her husband gives the hostess of the Porpentine the chain he had promised Adriana, and takes or snatches a ring from the Courtesan (4.3). Perhaps Shakespeare considered that a token of second wedlock, a marriage made in hell.

In the poet's self-portraiture his attitude to matrimony reveals a profound and painful ambivalence. Luciana lectures her sister on the divine rights of the male in wedlock and the necessity of obedience in wives. The essence of this sermon runs veritably through all of Shakespeare's dramas, apparently integral to his dogmas of church and state. At the same time he preaches the doctrine that male and female are incorporated at the marital altar into one. By this ritual the wife partakes in the godlike rights of her mate, and therefor can limit or confine them. She can demand obedience from him. Shakespeare recognised the privilege, the sovereignty of the wife, yet could not bring himself to admit it frankly. Instead he tost in childlike anguish between the horns of his dilemma.

The heroines of Plautus, Roman to the core, exhibit a pride of sex, or sense of feminine dignity, unknown to the women of the *Comedy of Errors*. Alcmena refuses to endure her husband's charges of unchastity. She demands her goods and slaves from him and prepares for divorce. The mate of Menaechmus, lacking her lonesome strength, still castigates her husband for his thieving, and summons her father to protect her from outrage. Erotium is stronger: she storms at her double-crossing lover and drives him out of her house. The men in the *Menaechmi* and *Amphitruo* are forced to appease, cajole, and act subservient to their women. This does not debase their virility in cultivated eyes.

Except in the case of the clergy-crowned Aemilia, Shakespeare commands his ladies to act subservient to their men. And even that sublime dame chiefly functions as a guardian of her men, and condemns the woman who troubles their voluptuous peace. The freedom that Aemilia enjoys from sexual bondage is the outcome of her holiness. She is a governess of nuns. For women who did not covet the virgin's gloriole, and who set their hearts on independence, the poet seldom had anything but anger, scorn, and tears.

At the root of his agony seems to burn the irresistible urge to embrace strangers as lovers. His ego, as I conceive it, constantly hunted for objects on whom to shower the surplus of his libido, and invariably learnt that these objects were doomed to be foreigners. Again and again he must have tried to join an alien soul to his own and waked from the dream of friendship or the honeymoon aghast and bewildered by the discovery that he was once more alone with the extremely unfamiliar, marveling like his Antipholus:

> What! was I married to her in my dream?
> Or sleep I now and think I hear all this? (2.2.181-182)

The plot of the *Errors*, if we interpret it truly, will provide us with clues to the mystery of the dramatist's tendencies in love.

Ordinarily when one hears the popular phrase, a man's better half, one thinks it refers to his wife. Sir Philip Sidney employed it in his *Arcadia* as equivalent to true-love. When Shakespeare uses it—or a variant—we cannot tell what he means. Sidney's usage appears to be intended when Antipholus of Syracuse appeals to the stranger Luciana, "mine own self's better part" (3.2.63). Earlier in the comedy we find the phrase aimed differently. Adriana, reproaching the man she fancies is her husband, exalts herself as "better than thy dear self's better part" (2.2.122). If we take this as a boast of superiority to the woman of his heart, we are confronted with an enigma. Who could this rival woman be? Judging by Adriana's jealousy, we might guess it is her husband's courtesan, though the wife yields no sign of having information about the temptress of the tavern. Adriana simply suspects that his eye offers "homage" somewhere (2.1). It is surprising to hear her, suddenly definite about his alleged sin, allude to the rival with the phrase of respect. Presumably Shakespeare designed it here for irony. The rest of Adriana's speech, however, is so earnest and tragic that we feel it imperative to search for a deeper design.

She pleads for compassion to the frostily intellectual Antipholus of Syracuse:

> How comes it now, my husband, O! how comes it,
> That thou art thus estranged from thyself?
> Thyself I call it, being strange to me,
> That, undividable, incorporate,
> Am better than thy dear self's better part.
> Ah, do not tear away thyself from me,
> For know, my love, as easy mayst thou fall
> A drop of water in the breaking gulf,
> And take unmingled thence that drop again,
> Without addition or diminishing,
> As take from me thyself and not me too. (2.2.118-128)

Thus Adriana sees her husband's inner existence as a structure of three parts: himself, a "better part," and herself, the best, the only one she calls estranged.

With the probe of analytic psychology we can comfortably explore the identity of the second person of this trinity, and determine the moment of her mingling with the hero's self. Shakespeare has betrayed her unaware.

The simile Adriana employs for her spouse's original ego, "A drop of water," is familiar to Antipholus, since he employed it in soliloquy for himself. In one of his first utterances in the play he muses:

> I to the world am like a drop of water,
> That in the ocean seeks another drop;
> Who, falling there to find his fellow forth,
> Unseen, inquisitive, confounds himself. (1.2.35-38)

The "breaking gulf" of Adriana's speech recalls the comparison of matrimony to a sea. The ocean of Antipholus he himself compares to the world. It strikes me as a less extensive vastness. Long before Edward Carpenter consciously spoke of sex as oceanic, poets and other visionaries had establisht the likeness in their dreams, and written rapturously about the ocean unaware of its sexual analogy. The real meaning of Antipholus's ocean springs to view in the lines of his soliloquy that follow the mournful image. In these verses the "fellow" he seeks becomes twofold:

> So I, to find a mother and a brother,
> In quest of them, unhappy, lose myself. (1.2.39-40)

The emergence of the mother in the goal of his search may perplex us after reading the reference to his fellow, especially when we remember that father Aegeon had not mentioned the mother as an object of his boy's voyages. No such motive appears in the *Menaechmi*, where the twins' mother, Teuximarcha, is named once and conveniently forgotten. In the *Comedy of Errors* the mother Aemilia plays a majestic and strategic role. Until the last scene, only her Syracusan son reveals a faith that she is still alive, but he reveals it only in these two lines. Shakespeare plainly found the subject too venerable, or extremely touchy.

Readers may seize this occasion to protest that the brother of Antipholus could not be rationally regarded as an object for him in the ocean of sex. Granting they are right, at the hazard of their tolerance, I am tempted to suggest that the "fellow" whom Antipholus yearns to find is in a potent sense feminine. Possibly the quest of the poet's protagonist was for a feminine companion in the body of a man. I am far from the first who beheld in the pulse and drift of our dramatist a strong homoerotic current. But since the comedy discloses no clearer evidence of the current than the lines I have quoted, the well-tempered psychoanalyst will not expect me to pursue the matter. I content myself with pointing out the early attachment of the narcissic personality to lookingglass likenesses of the same sex.[11]

In view of my belief that the Syracusan twin is a "genius" or demon double, it is logical (by the law of folklore) to assume that he is seeking a body, a material form. Insofar as the Ephesian is earthier and more matter-of-fact he performs this material function. But since earth and matter are anciently symbolic of the maternal, I am led to wonder if the "water" Antipholus longs for is not—more than just feminine—motherly?

In consequence of this reasoning we have to translate the quest of Antipholus for reunion with his mother as a dream-journey of desire for rebirth. In dreams, and in dramas too, "Birth is almost invariably represented by some reference to water: either we are falling into water or clambering out of it, saving someone from it or being saved by them, t.i. the relation between mother and child is symbolised"[12] Shakespeare in fact nearly stript away the last web of glamor between our scientific insight and his poetically concealed sperm-drop endeavoring to reach the womb. It will be noted that Adriana speaks of a drop of water falling in and then being taken from "the breaking gulf." To the woman here is hope of ultimate redemption for the "drop." To the discontented Antipholus the falling drop is fated to devastation, to "confound himself." He travels on however, "unseen, inquisitive."

Just as he fancies himself confounded in the sea of the world and losing himself, he looks with fascination on the city of Ephesus and resolves to wander through its labyrinth of streets: "I will go lose myself" (1.2.30). Shakespeare was acquainted with the poetic practice of hailing cities as foster-mothers. Contemporary playwrights, Thomas Watson and Thomas Dekker, lovingly alluded to their birthplace London as a mother. To Shakespeare the metropolis must have seemed a stepmother, with all the charms and criminal appetites of stepmothers in fairytales. For many years London let him starve for love.

At this point the skeptical reader will have ripened for me a cluster of questions. Among the foremost maybe is this: Will the venerable mother Aemilia fit into the equation which Adriana proposes for her distressed mate's ego? In other words, Is that mother his dear self's better part?

From the text of the farce I have extricated but one piece of proof that Aemilia is the true rival of the wife in the mind of her son. In the final act Antipholus of Syracuse, flying from the wife and her compatriots, escapes into the sanctuary over which the long lost Aemilia rules. She and the Syracusan are of course ignorant of each other's identity. Adriana frustrated demands from Solinus solicitude for her marital rights, not knowing the relation of Aemilia to her man: "Justice, most sacred duke, against the abbess!" Her grievance plainly sounds as if the abbess had stolen her beloved. Unconsciously, so to say, Adriana has fathomed the abyss of the Antipholus mind. Old customs of matrimony ordain that a man shall hold his wife ahead of his mother in his valuescale. The spouse is generally judged more valuable in political economy. So the miserable girl is justified in claiming that she is better than her husband's "better part." Love, notwithstanding, laughs at her priority. Safe in the bosom of the priory church the "genius" Antipholus can defy both wife and duke. The genuine Antipholus, by the dictates of the dramatist's reality principle, stays outside the sacred refuge and faces the music of political economy. On his ego wounds the abbess cannot perform the miracles which her "wholesome syrups, drugs, and holy prayers" promise the sprite from Syracuse. With the confidence of maternal power she expects "to make of him (the fugitive) a formal man again." But she is powerless to make a healthy head of a family out of the profane or "natural" son.

A sequel question we have to confront is—How could Aemilia be the "better part" of the twins when one of them lauds Luciana as his better part? The testimony for my answer is scanty and fragmentary, but it is the best we could hope to obtain from the poet at the stage of his self-understanding and self-revelation where he wrote his *Errors*. My answer is twofold. When the Syracusan makes love to Luciana, the poet revels in the illusion that the mother's idol in this interval is demoted in his mind. And in that interval he is eager to entertain a stranger as a lover. The poet's unconscious remains intrinsically unstirred by the gesture of demotion and goes ardently ahead with its drive for the assimilation of Luciana to the image of Aemilia. Whatever real person he had in thought when he conceived the younger lady vanished while the erotic scene was plotted; or rather, her memory dissolved into the familiar and permanent memory of his mother. Luciana could become the "better part" of Antipholus solely by metamorphosis into Aemilia.

At once a vigilant reader will inquire, Does this mean that Aemilia is a simulacrum of the goddess Diana? I think, no. Diana in this drama—insofar as she is visible—is actually a simulacrum of Aemilia. She has been converted from pagan divinity to Christian abbess, from a queen of vestals to a governess of nuns. That is why the influence of the Ephesian moon-female is felt throughout the play. The influence of the mother assumes the mythic incandescence. She is the goal of the Syracusan's voyage, and therefor the driving force of Shakespeare's plot. In the love song of Antipholus to Luciana I find a faint proof of her immanence in the moonshine of the dramatist's soul. He imagines her sister weeping continually till she creates a "flood of tears." Then the lover begs Luciana not to drown him in the flood—not to unite him to Adriana out of pity—since he wants her alone for his love:

> Sing, siren, for thyself, and I will dote:
> Spread o'er the silver waves thy golden hairs,
> And as a bed I'll take them and there lie. (3.2.47-49)

The waves are silver, we know, because the moon beams on them.

By what magic could the golden locks of Luciana fall on her sister's silver tears? Only by identification of the two. This becomes possible if we translate them into aspects or features of one personification of the moon. (Incidentally, we need not take the allusion to the golden hair as more than tribute to the British Queen. Every peruser of our poet is aware that his radical predilection was for very dark hair.)

Antipholus does not dream of reclining on the moon; he visions himself on a white-crested sea. In the dialect of homely reality, he wishes to lie on his mother's breast and suck her milk. We can now comprehend why the two sisters, the bright and the dark, may claim to possess parts of the hero's self. Having persuaded his ego of their semblance to his mother, they gained admission to her shrine in himself and in turn enjoyed his idolatry. In exchange for this reverence they had to give up his love. Loving them signified "self-wrong" to him and internal treason, betraying the maternal deity erected by his ego in childhood. Since the goddess belonged to none but himself, worshipt without prospect or hope of sexual possession, she could reign in his oblivion both as mother and as virgin. This psychic contradiction has its parallel in the cult of Diana, who was revered for her strict and icy chastity and adored for her warm sympathy with women giving birth. In the sanctuary of Diana at Rome her statue displayed many breasts, as if she herself had known the bliss of motherhood.

Aemilia's children are restored to her at the end of the comedy, and Shakespeare downrightly indicates her stature in their twin minds. He denies the daughter-in-law an apology for Antipholus's truculence or a pardon for her faults. For the sake of popular romance he bestowed on Luciana three lines of reassurance of the other brother's love. There is no mistaking the significance of the happy ending. It is joy over the return of the twins to the supreme love of their life. For the sake of this overwhelming attraction one Antipholus is cruel to her rivals, and the other hardens his heart to the allurements of girls. Under the mask of the abbess we discover the secret cause of her son's unjust divorce. From some abysmal temple in his brow her moon-colored idol dominates his sexual tides. She is a jealous goddess, and will have no other mistresses before her. Union with another is iniquity to her, and she is never slow to revenge the sin. In retaliation for her child's efforts toward liberty, to hunt for a new love elsewhere, she flogs his ego from her stronghold in his head, with silver cords.

The wish for maternal pillow and milk brings to the surface of the dramatist's mind the idea of death. In the "glorious supposition" that Adriana's tears and Luciana's hair have been made a bed for him, Antipholus is ready to believe "He gains by death that hath such means to die." In the midst of his ecstasy the thought of extinction becomes sweet to him. Why? The sole reply that occurs to me is that the mother in the dramatist's mind must be a ghost. Whether the woman in whose image he fashioned his matriarch was really in her grave is a question beyond our present interest. Our business is to explain the connexion in Shakespeare's drama of the thoughts of mother and death. The apparition of Aemilia near the final curtain, like a *dea ex machina*, leaves me with an inkling that she is a holy ghost. Her sacredness is strest to a degree no mortals deserved, summoning to consideration the idea that humans have to perish before they can turn angelic or divine.

We can glimpse the fantom nature of the abbess more plainly when a minor individual of the play defines in her presence the background of her home:

> the melancholy vale,
> The place of death and sorry execution,
> Behind the ditches of the abbey here. (5.1.120-122)

The odor of tombs and hecatombs hangs over the happiness of the comedy's last scene. Could such things be close to the mother of the poet's doubles if death was not irrevocably close to the poet's own mother in his thoughts?

Alert perusers of the play will note the curious fact that Shakespeare designates the home of Aemilia an abbey, also a priory. She herself is always called abbess. In view of the poet's passion for paronomasia, we may wonder whether he sensed a likeness between the spirit of the abbess and the abyss, the "vale," behind her house? The airs of both are sublime and malignant, capable of blasting mortal felicity. If our assumption of their likeness is correct we can proceed to unravel some of the most tenacious knots in the tale. The flourishing of that metaphor in the poet's brain would mean that he regarded the matrix not only as a fountain of life—Adriana's "breaking gulf"—but as a desert of death too. This ambivalence of his concepts of the womb, involving the vagina, would account for the antithetical nature of his two heroines, the lucid and cool yet gilded Luciana and the arid and hot yet night-hued sister, each an embodiment of the celestial mother in the dramatist's brain. When he regarded females as distinct personalities (aliens) his endopsychic mother acted as their prototype, the pattern of all strange beauty and wit. When he regarded them as creatures entwined in his destiny (lovers) she acted as their severest critic, and implacable competitor of the whole sex. In her activity as the model of loveliness she fomented tempests in his libido; in polar opposition she obstructed it, lifting before his intellect's eye the rock on which the loves of his life were wrecked.

The rock in the sexual sea on which Aegeon's family-ship was split is specifically a symbol of the male organ which children often believe the mother cherishes within her vulva.[13] The infant mind, detecting the absence of the penis in infant females, commonly concludes that they have lost it, that the instrument of virility was mysteriously excised. The idea that stronger, elder females may have retained it persists, and mothers who evoke in their sons dread by exhibiting masculine qualities frequently appear in their dreams with the organ in full view; or else nightmares show them brandishing emblems of it. By the poetic mechanism of displacement people shift their feelings of dread from the clitoral zone to the mother's, or vampire-woman's, "hard heart." When the stony bosom surprises her children by abruptly yielding milk or kindness, folklore pays tribute to the sublime woman by picturing her on a rock which miraculously lavishes a reviving liquid when struck by a magic wand.

In *Errors* Shakespeare offered tribute to the elemental woman of his dreams by picturing her as an abbess, which may well be englished "she-father." It was the assertion of her masculinity in his unconscious that blocked his attempts to love other women.

Whenever he engaged in sexual union he became acutely aware of the void in the vagina, and suffered the fear of losing his virility. Fantasies of his own castration blazed in his mind. Under the agony of such thoughts his ego prostrated itself before the maternal idol and begged for mercy, repudiating the pursuit of happiness everywhere else. In short, he spiritually castrated himself. Having made himself a eunuch for the goddess's sake, he could approach her bosom with confidence and nestle down to delectable oblivion. We witness a theatrical mimicry of the act in the entrance of Antipholus to his mother's convent. Cut off from his living family, the hero approaches the rock of the church and it opens to admit him, with the promise of "wholesome syrups" and holy whispers for his peace. Secure inside the rock, lulled by his illusion of a Catholic death, he could smile defiantly at remembrance of marital or political economy. Not the legion of hell nor the populace of Ephesus could prevail against the maternal stone. Nevertheless ideas of castration and death were always associated in the poet's head with pangs of cicatrice and mutilation, sights and smells of blood, visions of cadavers and severed skulls. Even in the final felicity of his play the horrible recollection of such things sticks to his poetry.

Shakespeare was probably persuaded to let the last act take place among these ghastly adumbrations by reasons of dramatic economy. He wanted to disclose the brothers' identity and restore them to their parents on the same street where Aegeon was being led to execution for violating the law of Ephesus.

IV

The return of Aegeon to the stage reminds us that we have yet to reckon with his role in the ego of the dramatist. Surely, if the abbess represents an image of Shakespeare's mother, the tragic merchant must somehow stand for his father. Judging by the play, we would suppose that the poet did not live in awe of his mother's husband. Old Aegeon does not glow for us with the flame of ideality. He warms us with embers of a singular humbleness, the emotion of a man who knows how little history he is able to make. Shakespeare spends no poetic ingenuity on him. He seems to have felt for the old man a filial pity, bordering on disdain. Since he often felt similarly toward himself, experiencing failure after failure, the poet unconsciously installed his father in the center of himself, opposite but intimate.

So intimate was their mental valence that it might be deemed identification. There are moments in the speeches of Aegeon when the voice of our poet can be clearly heard—for instance, in the father's story of the calamity that divided his family. The father remarks that when the tempest menaced his ship not far from Epidamnum, the sky conveyed to his thought "A doubtful warrant of immediate death," which he himself "would gladly have embrac'd." We are granted no reason for this gladness in the face of the danger to his wife and babes. It makes sense only if we recall that the sea is a symbol for sex and birth or resurrection, to Shakespeare's oblivion, a mode of reunion with the mother. The poet is thinking of his own wife and offspring when Aegeon reports that the incessant weeping of his wife and the "piteous plainings" of the infants forced him to hunt for means of rescue. Aemilia does not impress us as a lady capable of incessant weeping, but Adriana is almost perpetually in tears. Finally, at the end of Aegeon's tale, it is the son, brooding over the central tragedy of his life, the loss of maternal love, who sighs:

> Thus have you heard me sever'd from my bliss,
> That by misfortune was my life prolong'd,
> To tell sad stories of my own mishaps. (1.1.118-120)

The misery and impotence of the son produce a mirror of the woeful and ineffectual life of the sire, a mirror which leaves out the virtues of the father and the genius of his boy. Barring these features, our verdict is bound to be that Shakespeare's personality was precisely what we should expect from the heir to his father's natural shocks and outrageous fortune.

Naturally the paternal position in the dramatist's mind was not a static one. During remembrance of the father's fulfilment of claims to the mother's labor and love, the radius between Shakespeare's ego nucleus and the paternal image would seem to widen, and sparks of hate cross it. To the boy's way of thinking, the mother belonged to nobody but him. Intruders on their sacred privacy merited all extreme penalties known to savage and child. The father's intrusions were particularly resented, because the world and the mother sanctioned them good or fair. Nobody but the boy appeared to object to the separation of his mother and himself. On such occasions he could contemplate the idea of his father's extinction with a stern joy, the joy of justice done. Doubtless he exhausted his fancy in devising perfect punishments for the old man, according to the law of talion.

The memory of a particular paternal intrusion may have burned in the poet's oblivion when he invented the legend of Aegeon. He sentenced the old man to death for having dared to enter the precincts of the holy city of Ephesus. Mercantile enmity—so runs the legend—incited the city of Diana and Syracuse to proclaim a state of hatred between them. They decreed a halt of their traffic and intercourse, and resolved, as Duke Solinus puts it,

> if any, born at Ephesus,
> Be seen at Syracusan marts and fairs;
> Again, if any Syracusan born
> Come to the bay of Ephesus, he dies. (1.1.16-19)

Aegeon is doomed to decapitation for dropping his anchor in the bay of Ephesus. He can be forgiven only when his sons regain the mother.

Here I will chance the suggestion that the name Syracuse may be interpreted as a pun. Since the dramatist altered the location of his comedy from Epidamnum to Ephesus, but preserved the home of his hero in Syracuse, I felt it necessary to examine the name for a plausible motive for keeping it. Since it is pronounced Syracusa throughout the play, construing it as "Sire-accuser" did not strike me as too fantastic.

It has probably occurred to the merry reader that the name Ephesus may also be a pun. As a city of enchantment and delusive face-making it may have appealed to the poet as a place which effaces true identities of men and women and puts in their stead moon-animated effigies.

If an accusation of Shakespeare's sire prompted the invention of the framework of his plot, another accusation provided the substance of its middle event.

The first scene of Act 3, perhaps the oldest portion of our palimpsest, communicates through its metrical antiquity a major trauma of the poet's childhood.

Antipholus walks to his wife's door and finds himself locked out. His Dromio calls for servant-girls (all having English names) to open the door. The other Dromio, snug within, inquires,

> Dost thou conjure for wenches, that thou call'st for such store,
> When one is one too many? Go, get them from the door.
> (3.1.34-35)

The persons in the house are eating a commonplace meal. With these words of Dromio the dramatist makes us behold a different feast. But not the one evoked by Antipholus in the last act when he charges that his wife "with harlots feasted in my house." The clown inside is informed that his "master" stands without; he pretends to be touched:

> Let him walk from whence he came, lest he catch cold on's feet.
> (3.1.37)

Now analytic psychology conjures up a vision of the child who became William Shakespeare straining at the door of his parents' chamber and clamoring to get in. Maybe his humorous father responded in the Dromio way. Antipholus knocks the barrier hard and listens to Luce the kitchen-girl deride him: "Let him knock till it ache." He rages, "You'll cry for this, minion, if I beat the door down." The droll inside declares that the town is "troubled with unruly boys." Adriana orders the newcomer to go away. Hurt and perplexed he lingers there, unable to comprehend how his woman could be so frozen-hearted when he stood in need of her warmth. In the autumnal gloom of his mood he murmurs, "There is something in the wind, that we cannot get in." His slave replies, "You would say so, master, if your garments were thin. / Your cake here is warm within; you stand here in the cold." The forlorn master wishes he had an iron crow to wrench his way in. Shakespeare has put us in the presence of what Freud named "the primal scene," the first, most painful consciousness of parental lust.

Obscene notions raced through the author's brain as he wrote the scene. He recalled the passage in Plautus where Amphitruo, knowing that his wife is entertaining a stranger, and unable to gain entrance to her quarters, cries out that he will break in the door, and swears to destroy whomever he sees in his path, wife, father, anyone. No sooner does he raise his arm to execute his oath than Jupiter's thunder bursts from the heavens to arrest him. Amphitruo falls flat before the sound of the god. The piety of the Latin poet seems to have stirred Shakespeare to derision of the divine thunder. In the corresponding scene of his comedy the memory of the celestial admonition is evoked by a mere reference to the breaking of wind. The connexion between the anal and the heavenly thunder in our thought, psychoanalysis long ago pointed out.[14] That Shakespeare connected paternal efforts at dictatorship with flatulence, may properly be disputed. There is some ground for maintaining that he associated paternity with wind. The symbolism of the pompous epithet he invented for the sea in the first scene of his play can hardly be comprehended otherwise. He calls it "the always-wind-obeying deep." The resistance of the real sea to air force counted for nothing in his mind when he conceived of the sexual sea, in particular his amorous mother, and his submission to father-force.

The memory of his banishment from the mother's room excited ideas of libidinal rancor and amorphous fears. Death-wishes against her and his father too must have surged in his head at the time of the trauma, and colliding with pulses of incest produced an unvanquishable terror, a terror he never overcame.[15]

A friend, Balthazar, dissuades Antipholus from assaulting the door, trying to console him with the claim that his wife's honor is unviolated:

> — your long experience of her wisdom
> Her sober virtue, years, and modesty,
> Plead on her part some cause to you unknown;
> And doubt not, sir, but she will well excuse
> Why at this time the doors are made against you. (3.1.89-93)

The friend warns him that violent entrance would bring down on his head "vulgar comment," mob ridicule and calumny,

> That may with foul intrusion enter in
> And dwell upon your grave when you are dead;
> For slander lives upon succession,
> For ever housed where it gets possession. (3.1.101-106)

Antipholus calms down, and determines to visit the wild hostess of the Porpentine inn:

> Since mine own doors refuse to entertain me,
> I'll knock elsewhere to see if they'll disdain me. (3.1.120-121)

And so the odd scene ends.

What little master Shakespeare did when he departed from the forbidden chamber, we can reasonably surmise. Unruly boys of genius are as prone as the dullest lads to the frenzy and torpor of masturbation. When he grew up he wreaked a vicarious vengeance on his parents. He contrived in imagination to get his "spirit" inside the coveted dwelling, with all its cakes and ale at his disposal, while his carnal self (in empathy with the father as husband) stayed outside with fever and chills.

Shakespeare never lost the conviction that slander was a family heritage, like a curse among the ancient Greeks. It is my belief, he unconsciously proved it true, by rehearsing again and again, in young manhood and old age, in various disguises, the fatal scenes of his infancy, thus inflicting on his children the iniquity of his parents. This repetition compulsion traverses and threads together all his poems and theatric works.

The sadism of the fantasies Antipholus indulges in after his exclusion reminds me that my summary of Aegeon's death sentence omitted a detail of grave importance psychologically. He is formally condemned because of his inability to pay an exorbitant fine, a thousand marks. The Duke grants him a day in which to collect this money among the Ephesians. By the lucky discovery of his rich sons the old man comes in reach of it, but Solinus releases him from the fine. Money and its worries are never remote from the dramatist's mind. His Syracusan double, in the first act, is fearful that he may lose a thousand marks of his own. In the next act he is portrayed as obsessed with the idea of his gold. In the third he gets the chain his brother had requested and comments on the acquisition with keen pleasure:

> I see a man here needs not live by shifts,
> When in the streets he meets such golden gifts. (3.2.182-183)

Later the Ephesian double is arrested for debt to the goldsmith, and the money for his freedom is given to his twin. We are not told the metal of the Courtesan's ring, but there is no need to know. The poet's obsession with the yellow treasure is manifest without it. We note that he manifests it, not in ordinary conditions of trade, but luxuriously or anxiously. It glitters for him as a gift, fine or debt. One would think he suffered from the craving to obtain it free and a dread of losing it. These emotions generally run high in the syndrome of the melancholiac. Psychoanalysis has linked this terror of poverty with the peculiar fashion of sexuality known as anal-erotic, which frequently exploded in demonstrations of sadism.[16] In melancholy the enthusiasm for excrement characteristic of this kind of carnality appears torn out of its normal context of absorbing interest in byproducts, commodities, stockpiles, profit and thrift. The anal-erotic mood of inward grinding grief serves as regression to earlier mental frames, refuges of the familiar infantile, under the spell of anxiety. In those conditions bowel movements signified gifts or obligations to maternal exactitude. If the child at this stage of libidinal development does not deliver the ordure on demand, or squanders it in caprice, he hazards the loss of maternal love. Conversely, in the oblivion of the chronically sad, the belief that they have lost maternal love may spur their intellects backward to infantile concern for their ordure, as something wantonly spent or else owed. Under the frown of the mother-power in their conscience, their egos writhe in guilt and look forward to doing penance for their financial faults. The result is the dread of penury which we find so active in the melancholy, and which afflicted Shakespeare most of his life.

The first idea that springs to the abbess's mind when she hears of Antipholus's daily gloom is the likelihood that he has lost money: "Hath he not lost much wealth by wrack of sea?" It is perfectly natural for the mother to fret over the disposal of his gold.

We should not let ourselves be fooled by Shakespeare's costuming of his heroes as merchants. His cranium did not carry comfortably the cap of commerce; and he would not have masked his doubles as money-men if he had not been an apprentice in drama emulating Plautus, during a period of some financial distress. The Roman dramatist was not bothered by the morals and manners of the marketplace. He worked for a public of buyers and sellers, who rejoiced in the worship of Mercury, god of traders and thieves. Shakespeare, on the contrary, worked for an audience of spenders and lenders, above all the courtiers of his Queen. Consequently he could not rest content with a hero like Plautus's Menaechmus, who was raised by an Epidamnian exchange dealer and inherited his cheap principles as well as his fortune. Antipholus of Ephesus is a soldier rather than a salesman. He was brought to the city by "that most famous warrior, Duke Menaphon," the uncle of Solinus, and earned the latter's gratitude by serving him in battle, taking deep scars to save his life (5.1.191-194).

In this conception of Antipholus as a warrior I sense one of the infant inventions which Freud named "family romances;"[17] I prefer to term them parentage legends. Nobody understood better than Shakespeare how to spin these daydreams in which children strive to liberate themselves from disappointing and domineering parents by creating imaginary mothers and fathers of nobler blood and more generous chests. In these fantasies they become the foster sons and daughters of monarchs, or else they are changelings, exiled or stolen from royal cradles and raised by poor but honest wretches who bear a weird resemblance to their real fathers and mothers. Shakespeare's transfer of the lost Antipholus to the care of the martial Duke Menaphon, instead of another merchant like father Aegeon, sounds like a parentage legend, and expresses a mild contempt for the old man's occupation.

It is difficult to see how the poet could have dealt with the paternal figure in a manner so supercilious and icy if the old fellow was still alive. The hypothesis that the father was dead for him has no cult to support it. If my interpretation of his personality is true, the stately yet futile old man could never mount in his son's mind to the pedestal of a god. After death he would remain a ghost. When Antipholus of Syracuse greets his father he asks, "Aegeon art thou not? or else his ghost?" The query may be taken as a conventional phrase of amazement on meeting an acquaintance long unseen or lost. There are features in Aegeon which give the word a putrid precision. He pictures his face as concealed

> In sap-consuming winter's drizzled snow,
> And all the conduits of my blood froze up. (5.1.313-314)

His last words in the play are addrest to Aemilia; they contain not one quaver of affection or anticipation of happiness and peace. Instead he is pallidly conscientious, almost accusing, requiring her to tell the fate of the son she carried with her from the unspeakable rock. This duty done, he is mute.

V

The double Antipholus regains the divine Aemilia. "After so long grief, such festivity!" she cries before departing with her family—into the abbey. The felicity of the writer, the actors, and the spectators, in the last episode of the *Errors* is so cordial and uncontrolled that one is reluctant to survey it from the standpoint of cultural analysis. Yet the combination of childish and ghoulish elements in the scene needs to be illumined if we are ever to grasp the psychology of Shakespeare, and ultimately the psychology of the stage, or mummery. Was it necessary for the comedy to conclude in environs redolent of bloody graves? What have these to do with the dominant theme of mistaken identity, the entertainment of aliens as lovers?

My replies to these problems, to which our analysis inevitably leads, can perhaps be given best in the form of a synopsis briefly reviewing what might have happened to William Shakespeare before he could compose the *Comedy of Errors*. Whether the tale I shall unfold corresponds to the facts of the poet's life is a question for future biography to decide. It will suffice for me to point out that no other hypothesis on the play arranges its details in a coherent and rational structure, casting light on all its parts. What once appeared to be discrete and random inspirations, figures of speech, epigrams and exclamations, poetry scattered from a cornucopia without concord or intrinsic sense, now emerges in a network everywhere meaningful, reflecting actual currents of life. By the Freudian dialectic we are able to unearth the method in the dramatist's seeming madness.

First, there was a tempestuous period which culminated in the wreck of Shakespeare's family. During an absence from home, in a strange city, he had violated his marriage oath: he entertained a stranger as a lover. He did it in absolute ignorance of the real lusts that impelled him. The woman of this adventure had unconsciously reminded him of the dark and marvelous stranger who had been his mother.

After the adventure he felt that he had committed a loathsome sin. He thought it was adultery. It was imaginary incest: in a kind of dream he had ascended to his father's place by his mother's breast. The paternal ganglion of his superego grieved and grew angry. As a child Shakespeare had reverenced his father's might: as a boy he had loved him for his athletic prowess and companionship. Always he had feared and hated him as the man whom his mother obeyed. The permanent residue of these emotions in the poet's brain, circling round the memory of his father, agitated him as self-condemnation. Weakness of paternal authority in his youth, the vicissitudes of misfortune he saw the old man undergo, led to a stealthy disdain, and left him secretly glad that he had done the deed. But the mental image of his mother felt polluted and betrayed. He dread her more than any other power in the universe because she could lock him out from love and leave him eternally alone. To escape these punishments he would happily submit to her whips. The permanent residue of these terrors, and the beatitude of their union in erotic pain, circling round the memory of his mother, tortured him exquisitely as self-damnation. With the father's ghost he felt as if he was in purgatory; with her he plunged into hell.

He suffered from extreme masochism, and his narcissic ego declined to bear it. Very likely he was tempted to look for respite or succor in homosexual experiment; his vanity of manliness would subdue that desire. Hunting for avenues of relief, he heard a rumor that his wife was unfaithful to him. The proofs were preposterous but too opportune for his conceit to resist. He wanted a pretext to vent the sadism of his conscience. With barely suppressed exultation he accused his wife of his own transgression, without daring to face her with any witnesses or evidence. He fled from her and her offspring, outraged and sorrowing over his exclusion from her love. Consciously he feared that if he faced her he might do something frightful. Unaware, he perspired with a lust for destruction, which his ego habitually directed on the internal images or external effigies of his parents, because of the scars and frustrations they had imposed on his infant vanity. Sadist ideas evoked unconscious remem-

brance of his anal malice to the mother, the way he had scattered
bowel-gold to her disgust and ire, or refused to pay it forth till she
became peremptory. This remembrance was sharpened by the fact
that the time of his fury against his wife was also a time of pecuniary
pinches.

Still he lavished money on inns and individuals who enjoyed his
flow of talk. Observing that these luxuries only increased his misery,
he retreated to a solitude where his main expenses were sweetly
sour thoughts, tears, and poetry. He may also have been saddened
by the funeral of a friend, for his intellect dwelt fondly on graves
and effigies of the dead. The urge to self-slaughter kindled memories of his passions of guilt and pangs of outcast love at the time his
imagination first confronted the tombs of his father and mother.
His heart felt eaten by remorse; the nerves of his maternal temple
drained vitality from his narcissus pool, just as he had once drained
liquid of life from her breast.

The poet consciously defined the causes of his melancholy as he
knew them in the questions that the abbess asks Adriana concerning
the fugitive Antipholus:

> Hath he not lost much wealth by wrack of sea?
> Buried some dear friend? Hath not also his eye
> Stray'd his affection in unlawful love?
> A sin prevailing much in youthful men,
> Who give their eyes the liberty of gazing? (5.1.49-53)

After the unjust divorce of his wife, in his seclusion of literature and
tranquil contemplation, he remembered two comedies by Plautus
which attracted him as works of art full of semblances and lessons
of his own wicked experience. Turning over the ancient Latin leaves
he discharged a heartful of pity and terror with laughter over their
lusty gods, jealous husbands, and noble but stubborn wives. The
infinitely funny intrigues struck him like a mixture of his own
wishes and accomplishments. Perhaps, with the aid of alcohol, he
fell asleep on his copy of Plautus. Through the laughter and the
slumber he replenisht the libido in his narcissus pool, and energeti-
cally renewed the ego struggle to control the drives of his id.

The source of this new strength is the essence of Shakespeare's genius, and like all genius continues armored like a sphinx to the tools of analytic psychology. The genetics and physiology of narcissism may some day solve the riddle. Meanwhile we have our hands full with the problem of the devices by which the genius's ego manages the id. Shakespeare's ego not only declined to give the pulses of his id the outright ecstasies of sex and destruction they yearned for, he exposed them to the ridicule of the world, distorted of course, transmuted, and "dolled" or puppeted up. Thus they got the sole outlet his conscience and commonsense could afford, thanks to his native gifts of mimicry, melody and eloquence, and his paramount perceptors of contraries, or polarities.

The basic design for his exposure—tantamount to showing off, the plot, probably occurred to him in a dream. He crossed in fantasy the four twins of the *Amphitruo*, with its celestial cuckoldry, and the twins of the *Menaechmi*, with its domestic quarreling, cheating of prostitutes, and final satisfaction of restored brotherhood. He put this combination in a framework of Grecian romance, like those quaint novels of Heliodorus, of *Daphnis and Chloe*, and the *Gesta Romanorum*, in which lovers are divided by storms and wandering children returned to their parents. The outcome of his dream was a farce about himself, on the surface displaying a will to believe that the origin of his troubles was erroneous marriage, the mistaken union of strangers. He stated his plea of innocence according to his habit of paronomasia: "Not mad, but mated; how, I do not know." He put these words on the lips of Antipholus, courting Luciana (3.2.54), and showed their personal significance by repeating the plea from the mouth of Duke Solinus: "I think you are all mated or stark mad" (5.1.282).

Shakespeare was afraid to find out why mating checkmated him. To be mated, in the English of his lifetime, meant not only to be married; a single man mated was one confounded, rendered impotent. Our poet's occasional impotence resulted from incest guilt after mating with a facsimile of his maternal idol. No sooner was he free of one facsimile than, like Antipholus's water-drop, he drifted wildly about "to find his fellow forth," that is to mate again. Like that water-drop he seemed destined to be confounded and lost, forever searching for a mother from whom he was forever in flight. The dream which the *Comedy of Errors* flowered from displaced the passion of his quest, making its object a brother, a fellow-male, the dramatist's material self. Locating him gave the dreamer the pacific illusion that he was no longer estranged from himself. Latent in the dream was an odyssey of a motherless child, who accused his sire of separating him from the beloved, and sailed alone across a sea of sex to a maternal territory, where, by the contrary lights of a lunar mother, he reached at last the goddess of his desire, the mother-in-death.

By the cerebral dramatic method which Freud designated the dreamwork, Shakespeare saw the fiercest of his unconscious wishes fulfilled. He longed to rise to his father's privilege by his mother's breast.

He performed the incest in a variety of ways. (1) He divided himself into doubles, one of whom floats away with the mother when the father's ship is split. (2) His doubles end their vicissitudes in the bosom of the mother's cathedral, itself a symbol of maternity. (3) By identifying himself momentarily with father Aegeon he also attained his heart's wish: (a) he sailed the sea of sex as captain of a family vessel, "giving honor unto the wife, as unto the weaker vessel" (*First Epistle of Peter*, iii, 7); (b) he guided his mast into the forbidden harbor of Ephesus, the town of the great mother-deity Diana. (4) By identifying Ephesus with the mother, the poet presented his double from Syracuse with a chance to lose himself in her midst. (5) In a regression to infantile rivalry with the father over food, he tricked the wife into serving him a meal while the hungry husband fretted outside. The poet puts emphasis on the sweetness of the meal, comparing it to a cake, an emblem of motherly labor (in Latin placenta). (6) He at least made a gesture of amorous promise to the romantic facsimile of his mother whom he named Luciana.

It will be remarked that for each of these scenes symbolic of incest, except the last, the dreamer provided a condign and cruel chastisement, bordering on bloodshed. (1) For floating off with the mother, one double endured not only hardships of storm and wreck but also suffered kidnapping by rough fishermen. (2) For joining the mother in the bosom of her church, the doubles have to bear the sights and smells of its charnel background, a place of capital retribution. (3) For riding the matrix-boat, the son-incorporating Aegeon is wrecked at sea, and for trespassing on the waters of Ephesus, he is menaced with a hangman's ax, a symbolic castration. (4) For losing a twin-self in the Ephesian port, the poet had to pay with the spectacle of the city rioting after the twin, hounding him—with his drawn sword—to a "melancholy vale" and monastery (a house of "eunuchs for the kingdom of heaven's sake," approved in *Matthew* xix, 12). (5) For tricking the mistress of the hero's home, his "natural" self must stand in impotent wrath and cold, an exile from her chest, or her larder. By these brutal exactions the poet mentally redeemed his soul from blame. At the same time he gratified, in the theater of his mind's might, his lust for falling together with his mother and father to extinction, or rather to sanguine chaos and the brink of death. The coalescence of both these lusts of love and devastation took place in the fantasy of returning to the womb of the mother in her tomb.

Having accomplisht his heart's desires in dream, he woke refresht, and broke the long fast of his sadness with gusto and glee. Then, after some earnest reflection on raw material and art, he sat down to write the *Comedy of Errors*. In the affectionate endeavor to justify himself on the stage, he multiplied reasons for the conduct of his puppets, employing a technique analogous to the secondary elaboration of dreams. Next he carried out a tertiary elaboration: he issued his drama-work in a texture to satisfy actors and critics, fulfilling requirements of the contemporary theater. He garnisht the play with coeval allusions, "modern instances," indicated erudition delicately, sprinkled the scenes with extra dirty jokes for the groundlings, "wise saws" and singable lines for students and gentry, and crowned the concoction with passages that bright particular "stars" could sink their histrionic teeth into joyously. Despite rubs and botches, contradiction and extravagance, he knew he had produced a gem comparable to the *Menaechmi* of Plautus, which was said to be that master's earliest drama, or *The Self-Tormentor* of Terence. What a looking glass he held up to our secret idolatry of Eros and Eris, the might that cements and the power that crumbles humanity! What bleeding fragments of his life he carved and morseled before he could set forth this dish fit for the lords!

References

1   Frank Harris, *The Man Shakespeare* (1909) Bk II, ch. 1

2   Compare Carl G. Jung, "A Contribution to the Psychology of Rumour," 1911, in *Collected Papers on Analytical Psychology*, tr. & ed. by Constance Long (New York; Moffat Yard, 1917) 182.

3   See G. Walsh & R. M. Pool, "Shakespeare's Knowledge of Twins and Twinning," in *Southern Medicine & Surgery*, LII (Apr. 1940). The authors support the old belief that one twin usually draws nourishment and merit at the other's expense. Contrary to my opinion of imaginary twins is Morris Brody, "The Symbolic Significance of Twins in Dreams," *Psychoanalytic Quarterly*, XXI (1952), arguing that they represent dreamer and mother, desire for reunion and nourishment.

4   Cp. Jaques's plea for the liberty of motley in *As You Like It*, III, vii; Hamlet's lines on the purpose of playing (*Hamlet*, III, i).

5   Eleanore Boswell, in the *London Times Literary Supplement*, 13 Nov. 1930.

6   J. G. Frazer, *The Golden Bough*, abridged ed. (1942) 165.

7   Reginald Scot, *Discoverie of Witchcraft* (1584), Bk 12, ch iii.

8   Frazer, work quoted, 165.

9   E. C. K. Wilson, *England's Eliza* (Harvard 1939) passim.

10 Richard Edwards, Prologue to *Damon and Pythias* (1587), quoted by E. K. Chambers, *The Elizabethan Stage* (1923) IV, 193.

11 Bronson Feldman, "Stages in the Development of Love," *American Imago*, v 21 (1964) 73-4.

12 Sigmund Freud, *A General Introduction to Psychoanalysis*, tr. by Joan Riviere (1935) 137.

13 Freud, "On the Sexual Theories of Children," *Collected Papers* (1924) II, 65f.

14 Ernest Jones, "The Madonna's Conception Through the Ear," *Essays in Applied Psychoanalysis* (1923) 274f.

15 Compare Ella Freeman Sharp, "From King Lear to The Tempest," *International Journal of Psychoanalysis*, XXVII (1946) 19f.

16 Freud, "Mourning and Melancholia," *Collected Papers*, IV, 163.
17 Freud, "Family Romances," *Collected Papers*, V, 74.

Note: All citations for quotations from Shakespeare's plays in this book refer to Stephen Orgel and A. R. Braunmuller, eds. *The Complete Pelican Shakespeare* (New York: Penguin Books, 1999).

Chapter 2—PORTALS OF DISCOVERY

> A man of genius makes no mistakes. His errors are volitional
> and are the portals of discovery.
> Joyce: *Ulysses*

On New Year's night 1577 the singing children of St Paul's Cathedral, under the direction of Master Sebastian Westcott, acted a play for Queen Elizabeth and her court, named in the accounts of the Revels "The History of Error".[1] Nothing is known about the plot of this drama, but a number of experts on the Tudor theater have guessed from its odd title that it was an early version if not the protoplast of Shakespeare's *Comedy of Errors*. The limping doggerel of the Comedy's least modern lines would have been quite fashionable on the London stages in the days of the lost "History". In those days, also, the royal court favored plays with materials taken from ancient Greek romance, stories of shipwreck and piracy, of lovers tragically separated and miraculously reunited, and children vanished and found again. Shakespeare's fondness for these old Greek stories can be felt in the latest as well as the earliest of his dramatic works. So if the legend of Aegeon and his family formed the plot of "The History of Error," then it might be possible to determine, with a surprising abundance of biographic details, how the *Comedy of Errors* came to be written. Thus we may discover how Shakespeare came to be a dramatist, and the way his mind was working when he entered this sphere of art.

Just as in a dream we find recollection of events and perplexities which the dreamer had experienced the day before, so in the drama we find remembrance of excitements, irritations and comforts which the dramatist had experienced in the days or the months prior to his hours of production. On the assumption that the original of Shakespeare's *Errors* was composed not long before it was selected for the New Year's night entertainment at Hampton Court, we may confidently go hunting for the factors of its creation in the records of the year 1576. I believe that we will find what we are looking for in the adventures at this time of the poet Edward de Vere, Earl of Oxford (1550-1604). The misfortunes and errors of the Earl seem to illuminate practically all the dark passages in the comedy, including a few that psychoanalysis laboring alone would be mystified by.

I

At the beginning of the play Aegeon confronts Duke Solinus, in whose voice, according to our interpretation, resounds the wrath of governmental authority in general and a hint of Queen Elizabeth in particular. He sternly explains to the old merchant the fate to which the law of Ephesus condemns him for daring to come into the city. The Duke burns with indignation telling about the outrages committed by the Duke of Syracuse, Aegeon's home town, against the merchants of Ephesus —

> Our well-dealing countrymen,
> Who, wanting guilders to redeem their lives,
> Have seal'd his rigorous statutes with their blood. (1.1.7-9)

Solinus blames the atrocities done by Syracuse for the "enmity and discord" which have sprung "of late" between his metropolis and the Sicilian city.

The expression "of late" requires our consideration as a potential testimony of the chronology of this play. Is there anything in the history of 1576 that corresponds to this quarrel between the two towns? There is: and the speech of the Duke indicates it plainly by the use of the word "guilders". In assigning the silver money of the Netherlands for legal tender in his make-believe Ephesus, the writer of *Errors* took dramatic advantage of a political dispute that broke out between England and Holland in the spring of 1576. The dramatist also gave utterance thereby to a private rancor toward the Dutch. Edward de Vere had strong reasons for denouncing the Dutch greed and brutality. He was personally involved in the quarrel of the two countries. Contemporary documents present his role in a fairly clear light, and there is little of the comic in it.

On April 10, 1576, after a tour of fifteen months on the continent, De Vere started out from Paris for the short voyage home. He may have rested at Calais on the 12th in order to celebrate his twenty-sixth birthday. Soon after embarking for Dover he crossed the path of three ships of warlike equipment out of the Dutch port of Flushing; they gave his vessel chase and grappled to rob it. The pirates were recognized as men in the service of William the Prince of Orange, who were fighters for the liberty of the Low Countries from Spain. This was not the first time they had dared to lay their ruffian hands on English wealth at sea. It was only the first occasion on which they robbed an earl.

When Oxford's father-in-law, William Cecil, Lord Burghley, the Treasurer of England, heard of the crime he did his best to have the Earl's property restored and the thieves hanged. The Queen's Privy Council sent the Prince of Orange a letter of sharp protest. On April 17 Robert Beal, clerk of the Queen's Council, and the sea captain William Winter sailed to Flushing for the restoration of goods stolen between Calais and Dover. "I find it hard," Burghley declared, "to make a good distinction between anger and judgment for Lord Oxford's misusage, and especially when I look into the universal barbarism of the Prince's force of Flushingers, who are only a rabble of common pirates, or worse, who make no difference whom they outrage."[2] Maurissiere, the French ambassador in London, reported that Oxford had been "stript naked, and only escaped with his life because a Scotsman had recognized him."[3] He thanked the Council for their action on Oxford's behalf, "in whose person surely her Majesty and the realm has taken disgrace." About May 12 a certain Mr Herbert and a Mr Bodenham left Flanders for England, the former fetching "two pistols which were taken from the Count of Oxenforth." On May 31 Orange wrote to the Lord Treasurer from Camp Veer, regretting the injuries to his son-in-law and informing him that several of the mariners accused had already been put in jaul: "and if they are found guilty, will see how unpleasing such actions are to the States," the government of the Netherlands. Among the Foreign State Papers of April 1576 there is a list of names, chiefly Dutch, which are charged to be "the names of such persons as are confessed to have been in the ship that spoiled me."[4] Robert Beal reported to Burghley from Middleburg that his prosecution of the pirates at the court of William the Silent led to the following consolation for Oxford: "three were found, and one imprisoned, and some of his stuff recovered." According to a reliable English observer, only one pirate, named Cantillon, was imprisoned, and he obtained his freedom without any ado of jurisprudence.[5] The Dutch judges were in no humor to hurt their fellow patriots' feelings by gratifying the desire for revenge of a nobleman so unfriendly to their cause as De Vere.

We can glimpse the intensity of the poet's hatred of the revolutionary Hollanders in one adjective with which Duke Solinus in *Errors* brands the people of Syracuse. He declaims to Aegeon of

> the mortal and intestine jars
> 'Twixt thy seditious countrymen and us. (1.1.11-12)

After listening to his tirade against the bloody Duke of Syracuse, one might think that he would have regarded sedition in the Sicilian city with a tolerant or even sympathetic eye.

In the midsummer of 1576 a couple of Dutch residents in the Earl of Oxford's native shire of Essex became particularly loud in contempt for him and his politics, and their eloquence reached the royal Council's ears. On August 21 the Council instructed some magistrates of Essex to investigate. Among the justices called upon was Henry Golding, who belonged to the family of De Vere's mother and had served his father, Earl John. The offending Dutchmen, Walter de Fourde and Basirie Linghoer, were ordered jailed in Colchester "for having spoken lewd words of the Earl of Oxford." They were released the following February, after stating that they were sorry for the "lewd words." They alleged that they had mistaken Oxford for the Earl of Westmoreland, a Roman Catholic rebel against Elizabeth who had fled to Belgium six years before.[6]

In the summer of 1574 De Vere himself had run away from home to Flanders, in the hope of seeing the war in the Low Countries from the Spanish camp. It was rumored that he intended to join the fugitive Earl of Westmoreland and conspire with him for the overthrow of Protestant power in England. The furious Elizabeth despatched a friend of the Earl, Thomas Bedingfield, to bring the runaway back. She knew how long and ardently he had pleaded for his father-in-law's consent to his desire for traveling through Europe and for learning the art of war from its masters on the battlefields there. Neither she nor her chief minister ever took seriously the young man's ambition for a military or naval career. They allowed free scope and occupation for his talents in nothing but dances, masquerades, wit-combats, tournaments, and the games of chivalry. When he returned from his fortnight's escapade in Belgium "showing in himself a mixture of contrary affections"—it needed a good deal of persuasion by Burghley and his deserted daughter, the Countess Anne, together with Oxford's stalwart friend at Court, the Earl of Sussex, to gain her Majesty's forgiveness.[7]

Long after his homecoming he regaled a group of drinking companions with fantastic lies about his warlike adventures in Flanders. He claimed that the Spanish governor, the Duke of Alva, grew so deeply convinced of his genius in arms that he elected him lieutenant general over the whole army of Spain in the Netherlands. In a few days he had dazzled all eye-witnesses with his feats of bravery and the comprehension of siege-craft he had demonstrated against the Dutch. "And so valiantly he behaved himself as he gained great love of all the soldiers."[8]

In view of this fiction we can understand how the author of *Errors* was inspired to change the protagonist he took from Plautus, making Antipholus of Ephesus a soldier instead of a merchant. When Antipholus appeals to Solinus for justice against his wife he reminds the Duke:

> I bestrid thee in the wars and took
> Deep scars to save thy life. (5.1.192-193)

Another reminder of the war in the Low Countries occurs in Act 2, Scene 2, where Dromio of Syracuse indulges in some word-sport on the Dutch term sconce, meaning fort.

Thus the bloody controversy between the imaginary Syracuse and Ephesus turns out to be a fulfilment of Edward De Vere's wish for conflict between London and Flushing. In a manner characteristic of dream-work the poet reversed the geography of the two cities. He transformed the continental seaport Flushing into the island town of Syracuse and magically moved the English capital in the place of continental Ephesus. Another strange reversal appears in his reference to the Duke of Syracuse's "rigorous statutes." Obviously the governor of the metamorphosed Flushing was not modelled in the image of the good-humored and broadminded Prince of Orange, but after his enemy, the Duke of Alva, who tortured and massacred Protestants and heavily taxed and restricted the Catholic merchants in his provinces.

When Shakespeare pictured the Sicilian duke as a tyrant he was well aware that antagonists of Lord Burghley's power in England sometimes called the kingdom regnum Cecilianae.[9] Young Oxford had known his Lordship as a guardian for nine years before he became Cecil's son-in-law, and he always inclined to behave rebelliously toward the elder statesman. After all, Burghley kept him in wardship and didn't settle Oxford's accounts until long after Oxford's majority. He held Burghley mainly to blame for the defeat of his aspirations in the state. So he would naturally be attracted to puns pertaining to the island of Sicily that offered disguise for hostile feelings toward the politics of the house of Cecil.

I would like to suggest, incidentally, that Shakespeare took the name Solinus from the historian Julius Solinus, whose "Excellent and Pleasant Work. Containing the noble actions of human creatures, the secrets and providence of nature, the description of countries, the manners of the people: with many marvelous things and strange antiquities, serving for the benefit and recreation of all sorts of persons," was translated out of Latin by Arthur Golding, the Earl of Oxford's uncle. This book would have drawn the poetic Earl irresistably. Arthur Golding had observed his nephew's fondness for such literature when he was a boy under his tutelage. In 1564 Golding dedicated to the fourteen-year-old De Vere a translation of *The Histories of Trogus Pompeius* in which he said: "It is not unknown to others, and have had experience thereof myself, how earnest a desire your honour hath naturally grafted in you to read, peruse, and communicate with others as well the histories of ancient times, and things done long ago, as also of the present estate of things in our days, and that not without a certain pregnancy of wit and ripeness of understanding." The literary passions of the little Earl stayed with him the rest of his life.

II

Elizabeth granted the unhappy Oxford a license to go abroad without his wife—in January 1575. "She ascertained," said Giovanni Morosini in a letter from Paris to the Signory of Venice, "that he had resolved to depart under any circumstances."[10]

Before he left London his Countess told him she thought she was with child. He answered, William Cecil affirmed over a year later, "he was glad." The news had no effect on the speed of his preparations for sailing to the mainland. He acted indeed as if the lady's pregnancy did not concern him. Dr Richard Masters, the Court physician, reported in a letter to Burghley of March 7, 1575 that the Queen had heard the gallant Earl state openly, "in the presence chamber of her Majesty," that if Countess Anne was with child, it was not his. Her Majesty inquired from Dr Masters "how the young lady did bear the matter." His reply was: "She kept it secret four or five days from all persons, and that her face was much fallen and thin with little colour, and that when she was comforted and counselled to be gladsome and so rejoice, she would cry: 'Alas, alas, how should I rejoice seeing he that should rejoice with me is not here; and to say truth [I] stand in doubt whether he pass upon me and it or not.' And bemoaning her case would lament that after so long sickness of body she should enter a new grief and sorrow of mind."[11] After three years of married life with the erratic Edward the poor girl (she was just nineteen years old) could not feel certain that he would approve of her maternity. She unburdened her heart to her father and he—no doubt vexed by Dr Masters' disclosure—tried to ascertain his son-in-law's true sentiments. He urged the Earl to come home.

In response to Cecil's plea the wayward husband replied from Paris, on March 17: "My Lord, Your letters have made me a glad man, for these last have put me in assurance of that good fortune which you formerly mentioned doubtfully. I thank God therefore, with your Lordship, that it hath pleased Him to make me a father where your Lordship is a grandfather. And if it be a boy, I shall likewise be the partaker with you in a greater contentation. But," he went on obdurately, "thereby to take an occasion to return, I am off from that opinion." He offered a curious rationalization for his longing to continue his travels despite his wife's longing for him. "For now it hath pleased God to give me a son of my own (as I hope it is) methinks I have the better occasion to travel, with whatsoever becometh of me, I leave behind me one to supply my duty and service, either to my Prince or else my country." He boasted that the King of France had given him letters of recommendation to the Sultan at Constantinople, where he fancied that he might spend two or three months. Morosini, the Venetian ambassador in Paris, "knowing my desire to see those parts, hath given me his letters to the Duke and divers of his kinsmen in Venice." In addition he looked forward to visiting some part of Greece. The goal of his heart, however, seems to have been the Italian city whose divinity many unlearned Englishmen still believed to be Venus.

He thanked Burghley for sending him bills of credit and regretted that he still lacked enough for his expenses. Creditors in England persisted in annoying him, though he had assigned revenue from his estates to appease them. "If I cannot yet pay them as I would," he wrote, "yet as I can I will, but preferring my own necessity before theirs."[12] He purchased luxuries and distributed largesse like a prodigal prince.

Oxford had his portrait painted by a Flemish artist (perhaps Lucas van Heere—the portrait is now known as the Duke of Portland's portrait of the Seventeenth Earl of Oxford) and mailed it to his wife, "with kind letters and messages," but Cecil did not preserve the messages. She also received from Paris a gift of two horses for her coach. In May the Earl arrived in Italy. The scholar William Lewin, who had accompanied him from London to Strasburg, informed Burghley on July 4 that he was no longer acquainted with Oxford's moves and plans. He could not tell whether his Lordship had started for Greece or tarried in Italy.

On July 2, 1575 the Countess of Oxford gave birth to a daughter, named after Queen Elizabeth. Her husband did not get the news of his fatherhood until September 24. He was then a resident of Venice, but not so gay as he had expected to be. While inspecting a Venetian galley he hurt his knee. Also, he "found himself somewhat altered by reason of the extreme heats," and became dangerously weak from fever. He wrote his father-in-law that he was glad he had seen Italy but "I care not ever to see it any more." Nevertheless he wanted the Queen to renew his touring license for another summer, his excuse being that sickness had deprived him of "a great deal of travel, which grieves me most seeing my time not sufficient for my desire. I doubt not her Majesty will not deny me so small a favour." For the lonely Anne his sole allusion in this letter is in a phrase, "thanking your Lordship for your good news of my wife's delivery."[13] We can imagine his disappointment on learning that she had not borne a man-child.

III

De Vere visited other Italian cities and came back to Venice in December to enjoy the Carnival. By the middle of the next month he was on his way to France; the Queen declined to let him wander for another year. This may have been the season when the English artillery master Edward Webb witnessed the Earl of Oxford's heroic behavior in Palermo, Sicily, where De Vere proclaimed his readiness to fight a tournament with any gentleman of Italy and unfortunately found none to welcome his challenge.[14] His letters to London in the meantime appear to be mostly chronicles of his troubles over money. He insisted that Burghley sell his lands in order to silence his creditors and make his tour more comfortable. Oxford knew how the idea of selling his inherited estates saddened the Lord Treasurer and increased his anxiety about Anne and the baby Elizabeth. However, "I have no help but of mine own," the Earl declared, "and mine is made to serve me and myself, not mine."

This declaration was made in a letter from Siena (dated January 3, 1576) which conveyed a sharp warning to Cecil not to interfere with his journeying "unless you would have it thus: ut nulla sit inter nos amicitia." The threat of concluding their friendship apparently sprang from Oxford's despair of winning promotion in the service of the Queen and his country. But why should he have brooded over this frustration in the midst of the delights of Italy? "For every step of mine," he complained, "a block is found to be laid in my way." The bitterness of these words must be traced to a profounder cause than politics, since the young man had no grounds for thinking that if he returned promptly to England like a faithful husband and father, and went quietly to work at Court he would not eventually win a post of glory in the government, worthy of his ancestry and ability. Implicit in his complaint about the Treasurer's failure to speed his political advancement was the wish to be free of responsibility to his father-in-law, free from the bonds of matrimony. Burghley seems to have sensed this. Among his papers of the period is a set of notes concerning the Earl's opinion that the infant Elizabeth was not his, and these notes are mysteriously dated January 3, 1576. Internal evidence leads us to deny the date. It may be explained as an unconscious error written in memory of the defiance from Siena.

When Cecil reviewed the Earl's relations with him and his daughter, in some notes of April, 1576 he had forgotten the defiance. His son-in-law, the minister wrote, "never signified any misliking of anything until the 4th of April at Paris, from whence he wrote somewhat that by reason of a man of his, his receiver, he had conceived some unkindness, but he prayed me to let pass the same, for it did grow by the doubleness of servants." The uneasy statesman sent a messenger to Paris in March to hasten Oxford homeward.[15]

Soon after the Earl landed at Dover (April 19) he was greeted by his Catholic cousin, Lord Henry Howard, a learned and clever nobleman who had recently been rescued by Elizabeth from her inquisitors. They suspected him of plotting for the prisoner Queen Mary of Scotland. A wizard of venomous gossip and propaganda, his motto should have been *Fortiter calumniare, aliquid adhaerebit.* Lord Henry made a pastime of furnishing information to Burghley which could make the old man ill, telling him scandalous things that his son-in-law had said in the exclusive circle of his cups. For example, Burghley noted that Oxford had "confessed to my Lord Howard that he lay not with his wife but at Hampton Court (in October 1574), and that then the child could not be his, because the child was born in July, which was not the space of twelve months."[16] The wise minister wrote no comment on this absurdity. He had long ago learnt to anticipate marvels of logic from De Vere. He commanded his son Thomas to ride down from his country estate, over a hundred miles to the north, in order to meet the Earl at Dover and estimate his temper and mood. Sir Thomas reached the port less than two hours after Howard and some others, and saw his brother-in-law close in comradeship with one Rowland York, who had crossed the Channel with him. York was a youthful soldier of fortune: he appears to have fought for the Papacy under the flag of the Earl of Westmoreland and also served Calvinism in the army of the Prince of Orange. He and Howard were certainly major instruments in the secret conversion of Oxford to the Roman faith, which happened about this time. They encouraged him to break with the Cecils and separate from his wife. Sir Thomas Cecil observed no sign of the Earl's cruel intention toward his sister; he "did not understand from him any point of misliking."

The anxious Anne wished to speed to Gravesend to greet her husband on the Thames river. Her father advised her to wait until brother Thomas "should understand her contentation but she thought long to do for my son's answer," said the miserable Burghley, "and looked that my Lord would be come near before she could have word." In a letter to the Queen of April 23, 1576 he described the Countess's eagerness: "upon expectation of his coming so filled with joy thereof, so desirous to see the time of his arrival approach, as in my judgment no young lover rooted or sotted in love of any person could more excessively show the same, with all comeliest tokens." Burghley sent two messengers one after the other to entreat his son-in-law to take Cecil House for his lodging, but the Earl made no reply. Thomas Cecil reported that "he found him disposed to keep himself secretly two or three days in his own lodging." Yet Edward York, Rowland's brother, told young Cecil in confidence that his Lordship would come first to the home of the Cecils; "but he would nobody know thereof. Whereupon," says the elder Cecil, "I was very glad, but his wife gladder." They were deceived. Instead of going to the house of his in-laws on April 20, Oxford suddenly left his Thames barge and alone with Rowland York went to stay at York House.

His father-in-law sent a message of welcome and invited him to come for a visit. He answered that "he meant to keep himself secret there in his lodging two or three days," and then he would have a talk with the Treasurer. His wife sent a servant to announce, "if he should not come that night to her father's house, that then she would come to him, for she desired to be one of the first that might see him. To it he answered neither yea nor nay, but said, 'Why! I have answered you.'" Hearing this Burghley decided that she should not go to him "until we might see how others were suffered to come to him, or he to resort to others." They heard that the Earl's sister, Lady Mary Vere, had gone to greet him, and other relatives and friends. Lord Harry Howard promised to keep Cecil informed of Oxford's actions but the rest of that unforgettable April 20th passed without further news.[17]

Lord Oxford paid his respects to her Majesty but would not consent to his wife's coming to Court. Her father protested, in a

lengthy and pathetic epistle to the Queen already quoted. He absolutely refused to admit that Oxford's accusations against him and
Anne made any sense: "I have not in his absence on my part omitted any occasion to do him good for himself and his causes; no, I
have not in thought imagined anything offensive to him, but con-
trariwise I have been as diligent for his causes to his benefit as I
have been for my own, and this I pronounce of knowledge for myself." Concerning the Countess, he affirmed, "I did never see in her
behaviour in word or deed, nor ever could perceive by any other
means, but that she hath always used herself honestly, chastely, and
lovingly towards him."[18]

The distressed father confided to his diary that Oxford was
"enticed by certain lewd persons to be a stranger to his wife." He
mentioned no names and noted no details, but we know that courtiers talked about the Earl as if he had been crowned with the horns
of cuckoldry, and he did not spurn this insult to his wife. On April
27 the secretive husband communicated with his father-in-law as
follows:

> My Lord, Although I have forborne in some respects, which
> should (be) private to myself, either to write or come unto your
> Lordship, yet had I determined, as opportunity should have
> served me, to have accomplished the same in compass of a few
> days. But now, urged thereto by your letters, to satisfy you the
> sooner, I must let your Lordship understand this much: that is,
> until I can better satisfy or advertise myself of some mislikes, I
> am not determined, as touching my wife, to accompany her.
> What they are—because some are not to be spoken of or written
> upon as imperfections—I will not deal withal. Some that other-
> wise discontented me, I will not blaze or publish until it please
> me. And last of all, I mean not to weary my life any more with
> such troubles and molestations as I have endured; nor will I, to
> please your Lordship, only discontent myself.

He expressed agreement with Cecil's proposal to let Anne live with
her parents "for there, as your daughter or her mother's, more than

my wife, you may take comfort of her; and I, rid of the cumber thereby, shall remain well eased of many griefs." He wished that this could have been done through private conference and not been made "the fable of the world." He wished the most silent handling of her disgrace. And he wished that Burghley should not bother him any further about her.

On April 29 Oxford dispatched another letter known only through his father-in-law's summary of its charges. Lord Oxford listed several of the "mislikes" and "molestations" which had prompted him to divorce his wife without benefit of clergy or the law. First he accused her father of not delivering him money according to his directions. Next he charged that Burghley had treated his followers with severity—and shown one of his letters to the Queen "of set purpose to bring him into her Majesty's indignation." Moreover, Lady Mildred, the Treasurer's wife, had always been De Vere's antagonist and "ever drawn his wife's love from him." In fact "she hath wished him dead"—for reasons never recorded nor surmised. At his country house of Wivenhoe, on the coast of Essex, his mother-in-law "caused a division," he said, by starting a slander that he intended to murder some of his men. Lady Oxford had been "taken away from him at Wivenhoe and carried to London." Finally the Earl announced that "he means not to discover anything of the cause of his misliking" of Anne; "but he will not come to her until he understand further of it."[19] Later the Treasurer copied down more specific accusations of his neglect of Oxford's financial and household interests, and took pains to refute each one.

It cannot be denied that deep antipathy existed between De Vere and his wife's parents. The statesman's avowal that he had never imagined anything offensive to the young poet who had cost him so much irritation and woe can be accepted only as evidence of Cecil's strength in repressing his harsh thoughts. He simply could not do his best to gain his capricious son-in-law important offices · of state, particularly when a royal darling like the Earl of Leicester · and other aggressive politicians were hungry for the jobs. Cecil did petition the Queen for work suitable to the proud youth; he asked her to appoint him her cavalry commander, Master of the Horse. But her Majesty had no curiosity to see what artistic temperament might achieve in the strategic places of her government. As the courtier Gilbert Talbot observed, De Vere's own "fickle head" was the chief impediment to his progress.[20] We can well understand how a woman of Lady Mildred Cecil's austerity and frigid stiffness would have wished for the head's quietus.

None of Oxford's explanations of his conduct will account for the cruelty to his wife and disregard of his infant daughter. Clearly he was unable to confess, or else did not know, the true motives of the divorce. He yearned to believe evil of Anne. He considered himself a forlorn sinner. While permitting ugly rumors and calumnies to circulate about her, he bragged to his Roman Catholic friends of his sexual prowess in Tuscany. "The Countess of Mirandola," he vowed, "came fifty miles to be with him for love." He also told them that the French princess Marguerite de Valois "sent a messenger to desire him to speak with her in her bed chamber."[21] Whether fact or fantasy, these anecdotes disclose a yearning for erotic liberty among the motives that brought the Earl to Latin Europe. He would have attempted to satisfy this yearing at any price. Perhaps his coming to Venice for the Carnival was an effort to achieve the adultery of his dreams. Beyond question, he failed. Then disgust and remorse threatened to consume his mind ("I care not ever to see it any more") and he fled for salvation to the bosom of the Roman Church, the church of his mother. In turning against the Protestant creed of his education, the faith of his father, he unconsciously renewed spiritual bonds with his mother, the Countess Margery, who after the death of Earl John had married the staunch Catholic Charles Tyrrell, a man well known to his Calvinist neighbors for his devotion to the queen they called Bloody Mary. Earl Edward, brooding over his new creed, nursed the conviction that in wedding Anne Cecil, the offspring of heretics, he had done worse than blunder. He felt as if he had violated a sanctuary and blasphemed against the Holy Ghost. (That is why the hero of the comedy of *Errors*, in flight from the pagan termagant Adriana, ends on the breast of his

mother in a medieval priory.) Yet he had not a single rational pretext for sundering his ties with Countess Anne. So he hid himself
guiltily from her. For London eyes he enacted wondrous roles, and
made rimes about them.

> I am not as I seem to be,
>> For when I smile I am not glad;
> A thrall, although you count me free,
>> I, most in mirth, most pensive sad.
> Thus contraries be used, I find
>> Of wise to cloak the covert mind.

So he sang in the *Paradise of Dainty Devices* (1576). Out of solitude he
conjured a globe of dynamic fantoms, proving his likeness to the
Roman hero Scipio,

> That never am less idle, lo, than when I am alone.

IV

We have reached the point in the life of Edward de Vere where,
according to our interpretation of Shakespeare's *Errors*, the moment
of ripeness would have come for the creation of the play.

Behind the hilarity and subdued horror of the drama we detected
"a tempestuous period which culminated in the wreck of Shakespeare's family." His hero, Antipholus of Ephesus, is twenty-five
years of age (by the reckoning of Aegeon in Acts 1 and 5) when the
farce crisis in his own marriage takes place. At precisely the same
age the Earl of Oxford blithely insulted his wife and went for a
pleasure trip in Europe, hardly expecting to return to her.

During an absence from home, in a strange city, he had violated
his marriage oath: he entertained a stranger as a lover. He did it in
absolute ignorance of the real lusts that impelled him. The woman
of the adventure had unconsciously reminded him of the dark and
marvelous stranger who had been his mother. After the adventure
he felt that he had committed a loathsome sin. He thought it was
adultery. It was imaginery incest: in a kind of dream he had ascended to his father's place by his mother's breast.

Our view of the characters Aegeon and Aemilia led us to the conjecture that Shakespeare, when he wrote *Errors*, conceived of his parents as ghosts. Oxford's own father died in August 1562. There is little to connect Earl John with Aegeon except the similar sound of their names, since the Greek merchant is barely more than a figure of extreme old age, without touches of individuality. The person of the Abbess Aemilia shines more lucidly, but she is simply a fantom of ideal motherhood. Shakespeare portrays her as a loving and protecting mother, who had suffered in separation from her children a second birth travail. We have good reason to think that the dramatist's mother did not live up to his ideal. After the funeral of his father, she transferred the twelve-year-old Earl to the care of the state. He became a royal ward, under the guardianship of William Cecil. In April 1563 Countess Margery wrote a letter to Cecil with the purpose of casting off her shoulders the burden of her boy's heritage of debt. She stated that his late father had kept "most secret" from her the sources and distribution of his wealth. Now that Earl John was dead she wished to be exempt from the cares of his estate. "I had rather leave up the doings thereof to my son," she wrote. Let "my son, who is under your charge," have all "the honour or gain (if any there be)" from the father's last will and testament.[22] There is not a breath of affection or concern for the lad in her letter. No document indicates that they ever met again. She lived with her second husband in the home of the first at Castle Hedingham until she died in December 1568. Edward was then eighteen. At the same age Antipholus of Syracuse suddenly went in search of his lost mother. The poet betrays a frosty and hostile attitude to his mother in the last lines spoken by Aegeon. They are spoken to Aemilia and, as we have remarked, bear no sign of love or friendliness. He is pallidly conscientious, almost accusing, requiring her to tell the fate of the son she carried with her in the stormy hour of their parting. This duty done, he is mute.

Death had divided Aemilia and her husband once before the fatal storm off Epidamnum, when she was pregnant with the twins. The merchant's factor in that city had died, and Aegeon had to voyage there leaving his wife for six months. At the end of this time she crossed the sea to join him and then gave birth. The number is significant. We recall that Earl Edward's own child was born six months after he sailed in quest of somebody to love in the place of his own dead "factor" or maker.

Aemilia was named, I think, after Emilia Pia, the champion of femininity in Baldassare Castiglione's classic book on Renaissance nobility—*The Courtier* (1528). It is possible that Shakespeare chose the name for his Abbess because of its likeness to the Latin for a female rival—*aemula*. His mother was in truth the supreme competitor in his heart of every woman he looked at with warm interest. For her sake he regarded any lady who attracted him as a seducer tempting him to chaos and loss. To each his soul responded with the question his Syracusan "genius" asks Luciana (3.2.37-38):

> Against my soul's pure truth why labour you
> To make it wander in an unknown field?

Antipholus of course likes few things better than such truancy, little minding its effect on his soul's verity.

In Aegeon's reference to his wife's anxiety "for the latter born" of their twins (1.1) there may be a hint of the sibling jealousy that the little Earl Edward de Vere experienced toward his sister Mary (just one year older). Aegeon's words appear to reflect a wish that the dramatist's mother had been "more careful" for him than for her other child. The old man tenderly speaks of the child he rescued as "my youngest boy and yet my eldest care." (1.1.134)

Stronger than brotherly jealousy in *Errors* is the expression of sibling love. Antipholus of Syracuse is willing to embrace Luciana as a sister: "Call thyself sister, sweet, for I am thee" (3.2. 66). Dramatically the girl serves as the virgin double or obverse of the sour Adriana. Thus she may stand for the spirit of Anne Cecil before she became the Countess of Oxford. From a biographic point of view she will pass superbly as a picture of Lady Mary Vere. The Earl's sister had a reputation for plain sense and a tongue like a scourge. Yet her sturdy vivacity proved able to inspire an enduring love. Her pity for

Countess Anne and the baby Elizabeth spurred her to take a hand in schemes for reconciling her brother to the woman he abhorred. It is easy to fancy the shrewd Mary lecturing Edward and her sister-in-law, just like Luciana, on the obligations of wedlock. Anne's own sister Elizabeth, afterward Lady Wentworth, played no visible role in the life of De Vere.

Error's merciless treatment of Adriana corresponds to the cruelty of Oxford to his Anna. The husband of the former defames her with a rage of unreason identical with the anger of the Earl:

> Dissembling harlot! thou art false in all;
> And art confederate with a damned pack
> To make a loathsome abject scorn of me. (4.4.102-104)

This confederacy about which Antipholus of Ephesus raves turns out to be the Cecil circle. We are acquainted with Oxford's charge "That his wife was most directed by her father and mother." Indeed Lady Anne had not the heart to employ her womanly weapons to wrest advantages for her mate from the Lord Treasurer. Instinctively she took the side of the Cecils, the Cooks and Bacons (her mother's kin), and other wealthy relatives of plebeian stock who had climbed to power with the Tudor dynasty in their conflicts with the ancient patrician clans, of which her husband was a fiery scion. She must often have gossipt and wept to her folks and their Puritan intimates about his Lordship's eccentric ways and his comradeship with rimers, playwrights, actors, idle soldiers and sailors, and other fellows of ill fame. To stop such gossip he tried to make her give up one of her solitary pleasures, conversation with the Puritan Lady Elizabeth Drury. He proposed no substitutes. He never took his wife into his confidence.

One of his comrades, by the way, was the poet George Gascoigne, a veteran of the Dutch war who had campaigned with Sir Humphrey Gilbert and Rowland York. When Gascoigne came back from the Low Countries in 1574 he produced a poem, "Dulce Bellum Inexpertis," in which he mentioned De Vere as a youth who promised to be a fine warrior: "Young Oxenford, as toward as the best." Now in April 1576 Gascoigne contributed a preface to Gilbert's *Discourse of a Discovery for a New Passage to Cataia.* This pamphlet came out in support of Captain Martin Frobisher's expedition in search of gold and a northwest sea-way to the riches of China. The financiers of the voyage anticipated a vast profit. Michael Lock, the mariner and capitalist, and Dr John Dee, the renowned physician, astrologer and alchemist, both backed Frobisher. The Earl of Oxford had long been familiar with Dee's ideas, and he became interested in the dream of the northwest path to Cathay. Harassed by his creditors, he was easily lured into projects for quick riches. He invested large sums in Frobisher's later efforts to discover the passage. On Thursday, June 7, 1576, the Captain, with two barks and a pinnace, set sail from Gravesend for his first attempt. An allusion to this event, which may decisively date the *Comedy of Errors,* has been seen in the remark of Dromio of Syracuse: "The bark Expedition put forth tonight" (4.3.36).This remark by itself means nothing. It becomes proof of chronology when joined with the likelihood that Shakespeare derived the name of Angelo, the goldsmith in *Errors,* from the goldsmith Agnello who was employed to assay the ore which Frobisher meant to bring home. In harmony with this chronology is the statement (4.1) that Angelo has to pay a sum of guilders due "since Pentecost." By my calendar reckoning, Easter in 1576 fell on Tuesday, April 23 (William Shakespeare's birthday) and Pentecost on June 9, two days after Captain Frobisher began his voyage Chinabound.

The Goldsmith appointed to examine the ore Frobisher transported from the frozen north was John Baptista Agnello, whom Shakespeare transmuted for the workers in St Helens parish, Bishopsgate, near the Earl of Oxford's home.[23]

To finish this digression about Oxford's companions, let me say that Balthasar, the friend of Antipholus, is not distinguished enough dramatically for us to identify him in history; but I believe that the poet named him after Baldassare Castiglione, author of *The Courtier.* One of Oxford's tutors at Cambridge University, Bartholomew Clark, translated Castiglione into Latin, and the Earl wrote a rapturous introduction to the work in 1572. This Latin epistle "more polished even than the writings of Castiglione himself" was extolled years later by the collegian Gabriel Harvey as a witness of De Vere's excellence in literature.[24] It shows how eagerly the Earl studied the art, how earnestly he applied himself to its "delightful industry." What his wife or her parents thought of his endeavors in literature, we cannot tell. The latter probably viewed them as trivialities at best.

In the *Errors* the lonesome Adriana is made the mouthpiece of accusations which were really hurled at Oxford by his foes. She cries out that her Antipholus is deformed and crooked "Stigmatical in making, worse in mind" (4.2.). The words could have come straight from the pen of Lord Henry Howard in 1581, when he strove to set down a record of De Vere's vices, defects, and alleged crimes, in the hope of destroying him. Howard exhausted his arsenal of rhetoric on the former friend, "the botches and deformities of his misshapen life."[25] So far as we know, there was only one feature that, in the eyes of esthetes, might have marred the Earl's good looks. His short stature was not admirable. We have the testimony of another adversary that he had more than the ordinary man's share of beauty. In 1585 Thomas Vavasor sent him a challenge to a duel, beginning "If thy body had been as deformed as thy mind is dishonorable, my house had been yet unspotted."[26] Oxford's vanity certainly surpassed in many ways the self-admiration of all the rest of Queen Elizabeth's nobles and knights. If he had really been blemished in face or shape, would he have dared to write, as he did in the preface to Clarke's Castiglione, that men could not become courtiers who exhibit "some notable defect, some ridiculous trait, or some deformity of appearance"? Nevertheless he did leave critics with the impression that he was not upright in frame. And it seems he was always haunted by a menace of physical distortion. He lived to see his graceful body deformed.[27] Perhaps the injury to his knee in Venice foreshadowed that event, both misfortunes serving as unconscious penalties for his lusts.

> For my best luck leads me to such sinister state,
> That I do waste with others' love, that hath myself in hate.

In the spring of 1576 De Vere was apparently not so much troubled by the possibility of blemish or loss in his anatomy as he was by the conviction that he had lost the jewel of his soul—honor. A disgrace of his family had become the "fable of the world." This was his own explanation for the melancholy that dominates his poems published this year in the anthology *The Paradise of Dainty Devices*. The first of these, displaying more sincerity than artistic merit, is entitled "His good name being blemished, he bewaileth." It proclaims the writer ("E.O.") a man whose spirits, heart, wit and force "in deep distress are drown'd," because of an undefined infamy that had stript him of pride.

> Help crave I must, and crave I will, with tears upon my face,
> Of all that may in heaven or hell, in earth or air be found,
> To wail with me this loss of mine, as of these griefs the ground.
> Help gods, help saints, help spirits and powers that in the heavens
>   do dwell,
> Help ye that are aye wont to wail, ye howling hounds of hell:
> Help man, help beasts, help birds, and worms that on the earth
>   do toil,
> Help fish, help fowl that flock and feed upon the salt sea soil:
> Help echo that in air doth flee, shrill voices to resound,
> To wail this loss of my good name, as of these griefs the ground.

In the *Errors* the dramatist tried to designate the mainspring of his melancholy—or more exactly, his depression—concretely. He presented the Abbess Aemilia guessing the cause of the Ephesian hero's moodiness and thus succeeded in defining three sources of his grieving of which he was most acutely aware. She inquires:

> Hath he not lost much wealth by wrack at sea?
> Buried some dear friend? Hath not else his eye
> Stray'd his affection in unlawful love? (5.1.49-51)

We have already observed how anxiously Earl Edward wrote about money, and the way he suffered from Dutch enterprise at sea in April 1576. When the twin heroes of *Errors* find themselves deprived of gold and prosecuted for debt, we get an adequate glimpse of the poet's own feelings in straits of finance. We have seen in the psychoanalysis of the play how misery over money is rooted in cloacal constraint. So we have no hardship in understanding why George Baker the chirurgeon believed that his *New Jewel of Health*, printed in 1576, would first of all interest the Earl and Countess of Oxford. In it he urgently advised the use of "An oyle drawne out of the excrements of Chyldren" and "An oyle drawne out of Manne's ordure" for different sicknesses. His physics appear to have been retaliatory, fighting disease with distillation of dung or dirt like his master Bombastus Paralsus.

I regret that I have no contemporary facts that cast so helpful a light on the allusion to the burial of a friend. One friend of De Vere, a nobleman and a patron of stage-players, died in 1576. But Walter Devereux, Earl of Essex, died on September 22, in Dublin, Ireland where he had resided on military duty for three years. The "History of Error," in my estimation, was written late in the spring of 1576, maybe in June, a season in which I can discover nothing to warrant the burial reference. Still I feel sure that the dramatist, when he wrote these words, had a recent funeral in mind. Perhaps the verses do not belong to the old *History* but to a revision. On the assumption that they were composed seven years later, I can offer historical explanations of all three, the funeral reference and its two companion questions. This assumption is justifiable by the fact that Shakespeare gives us two different numbers for the age of his twin protagonists, one (25) according to the reckoning of Aegeon, and the other (33) according to the count of mother Aemilia. The first, by our theory, marks the age of the author when he left his wife and travelled in blind search of amorous adventure. Let us glance at what happened to him in his thirty-third year which could have recalled the *Errors* of 1576.

In the spring of 1583 Lord Burghley described his son-in-law as "ruined and in adversity... all crosses are laid against him, and by untruths sought to be kept in disgrace." Earl Edward was then suffering the consequences, in ill fame and physique, of the most violent love affair of his life. The breach with his Countess had at last been repaired but her tears continued to flow, now more woefully than ever. For after their first and only son died on May 7, two days old, her husband's thoughts forever harked back to the unlawful love. He strove to renew it. And in June his very dear friend, Thomas Radcliff, Earl of Sussex, who had heartily backed his ambitions at Court, died. Sussex was buried not far from De Vere's ancestral home and birthplace, Castle Hedingham, a short distance from the tomb of Oxford's ancestors. Earl Edward was residing at the Castle this season, for the last time. In September he sold his family's ancient estate of Earl's Colne, together with its priory, where ten of the Earls of Oxford and their wives were buried. The dramatist, in my belief, remembered this priory and its graves when he erected in poetry the priory of his Mother Aemilia. In 1583 our Earl was badly in need of money. He sold this year no less than five of his lands, and yet never did he wrestle more hopelessly with debt. He invested heavily in Martin Frobisher's final project for gold and a western seaway to the Orient. Captain Edward Fenton returned from the attempt in May 1583 with gloomy news. Spaniards had attacked his three vessels, one of which Oxford himself had bought, and they sank his flagship. Here, more truly than in 1576, the poet could mourn that he had "lost much wealth by wrack at sea." At the same time England's dealings with the Netherlands must have reminded him of his encounter with the Flushing corsairs. Queen Elizabeth became furious on account of the Dutchmen who maintained commerce with Spain while begging for English money and troops to sustain their war of emancipation. She ordered the capture of Holland ships found trading with the enemy empire.[28] Oxford of course approved her assault on Dutch greed. What better time could there be for a revival of the comedy of *Errors?*

While mourning for Sussex the dramatist would have remembered his old friend's years of political feuding with Robert Dudley, Earl of Leicester. On the deathbed Radcliff is said to have warned the gentlemen in his room: "Beware of the Gypsy; you know not the beast so well as I do."[29] The word "beast" in this connection inevitably conjures up the sign of the bear on Leicester's coat of arms. This may be the reason why Shakespeare chose that animal as an emblem of horror in the *Comedy of Errors*, when he made Dromio of Syracuse say that he flies from the kitchen girl Nell "As from a bear a man would run for life" (3.2.153).

V

The years 1576 and 1583 are both important in English theatrical history. Early in 1576 James Burbage, one of Leicester's company of actors, opened in Shoreditch the first English house devoted to plays, the Theatre. Soon afterward the Curtain playhouse went up nearby. In the autumn Richard Farrant, Master of Windsor Chapel, began producing plays in his grand room at Blackfriars, England's first theater within doors, shutting out the sun. The singing boys of Windsor and the Royal Chapel performed here to crowds smaller but more prosperous and refined than those who went to watch grown men act in the sky-exposed Theatre and Curtain and their competitors of the innyards. In the spring of 1583, by royal command, Edmund Tylney, the Master of the Queen's Revels, selected twelve of the best men on London's stages to form a troop for her Majesty. At least one of these stars, John Dutton, came from a company patronized by Edward de Vere. Three months later the Earl of Oxford purchased the lease of a little theater in the former priory of Blackfriars and placed his secretary John Lyly in charge of the plays given there. The troop that Lyly directed seems to have comprised children from the choirs of the Queen's Chapel and St Paul's Cathedral; they were known as "Oxford's Boys." *The History of Error* was conceivably revived for the new company of St Paul's boys, and altered in concord with the poet's experiments with blank verse.

Sebastian Westcott, who directed the singing lads of St Paul's Cathedral in 1576, would have been happy to produce any play that the Earl of Oxford sent him. Westcott too was a secret Catholic. And the Earl's good friend Sussex, among his court functions as Chamberlain of the Queen's Household, had the task of approving the plays which were acted for her pleasure in the Christmas holidays. Sussex enjoyed a strong personal interest in the theater and

reviewed all the dramas that were submitted for the privilege of performance at Court. Thus the Master of the Revels, Thomas Bel-
grave, went to Hampton Court on December 24, 1576, to visit the
Chamberlain and discuss "alteration of the plays," including *The
History of Error* to be shown on New Year's night. On December 29
the boys of Paul's Cathedral quire brought their play to Court for
the Earl of Sussex to revive for two days.[30]

Incidentally, it seems to me that the description of Adam, the
officer of the debtors' prison in Shakespeare's Ephesus (4.2.37-40)
—"A back-friend, a shoulder-clapper," a fellow who "carries poor
souls to hell"—is a palpable hit at a comedian named John Adams,
who had been the star of Sussex's own company in 1576. Adams
endeared himself to Elizabethan audiences by his practice of carrying fellow actors on his back and prancing off the stage while they
pummelled him. Decades after, a player in Ben Jonson's *Bartholomew
Fair* recalled him: "And Adams, the rogue, ha' leap'd and caper'd
upon him, and ha' dealt his vermin about, as though they had cost
him nothing." Experts have supposed that he acted the part of the
clown Adam in *A Looking Glass for London* by Robert Greene and
Thomas Lodge, which was produced by the Queen's men around
1587. The Devil in this play invites Adam to get upon his back, and
the clown cudgels him off the stage. When Shakespeare named the
prison-keeper in *Errors* Adam, he probably meant to permit some
buffoonery of shoulder-slapping in the scene where the officer
comes to arrest Antipholus and Angelo.

One comedian of the *Errors* baffles all endeavors to identify him:
Doctor Pinch, the conjurer, who is so grotesquely tortured at the
close of the play. Shakespeare styles him a schoolmaster but he
gives no proof of such occupation in the comedy. Instead he is portrayed as "a mountebank, a threadbare juggler, and a fortuneteller,"
pretending to be also a healer of souls possessed by devils. The portrait sounds like something the dramatist would have seen in a har-
lequinade in Italy.

The sadistic fantasy of Pinch's fall into the hands of Antipholus
of Ephesus indicates what their creator secretly wished he could do

to his powerful father-in-law. He dared not follow the *Menaechmi* of Plautus to the extent of giving his hero's wife a father and making that old man a target for wild buffoonery. No matter how much he ached to write it, he could not imitate the scene of the Latin playwright in which the unmarried Menaechmus acts insane to free himself from the jealous wife and her father. This scene surely struck Oxford as a ludicrous picture of his own predicament and savage desire. Menaechmus shouts:

> I am beset upon the left by this rabid bitch-woman, and behind her is that stinking goat who ruins innocent citizens with perjury ... Lo! Apollo from his oracle bids me burn her eyes out with flaming torches!

Antipholus of Ephesus also burns to pluck out his Adriana's eyes.

Menaechmus cries out crazily that the god wants him to take the staff of his wife's father (Burghley as the Queen's Treasurer carried a special staff that stands out in his best known portraits) and with this weapon to knock the "bearded, tremulous Titan" to pieces. Menaechmus goes through the motions of goading imaginary chariot horses into trampling down the "toothless lion." Suddenly he drops in a mock-fit and the father hurries off to find a physician for him. Then the "madman" makes his escape.

Dr Pinch in *Errors* takes the places of both father-in-law and physician, and receives a treatment more brutal than any Plautus ever inflicted on his characters. This sort of poetic justice is precisely what might have been expected from the author of Anne de Vere's "unjust divorce." In struggling to justify the ways of his Lordship to man, the dramatist felt driven to be violently unfair to his wife. He executed a comic reversal of their roles. He made her guilty—through ignorance—of refusal to welcome him home. Fancying himself in the position of Plautus's Amphitryon, locked out of his house while his wife makes love to a stranger inside, he lacked the nerve to present his Adriana in the position of the heroine Alcmena, brave though lonesome, longing for her absent man, and pregnant with a child who is destined to reconcile the frantic husband to her.

The *Comedy of Errors* was composed more in anger than in sorrow, and its art suffered in proportion to the artist's craving for vengeance. He wished to act, not reflect. His mood is mirrored in some verses which may have been written by the Earl of Oxford during his marital crisis in 1576:

> What plague is greater than the grief of mind?
> The grief of mind that eats in every vein;
> In every vein, that leaves such clots behind;
> Such clots behind as breed such bitter pain;
> So bitter pain that none shall ever find
> What plague is greater than the grief of mind.

In form, by the way, this stanza imitates the Greek palilogia, which appears in parody in the *Comedy of Errors* (1.2.47-52):

> She is so hot because the meat is cold;
> The meat is cold because you come not home:
> You come not home because you have no stomach;
> You have no stomach, having broke your fast;
> But we, that know what 'tis to fast and pray,
> Are penitent for your default today.

I have no doubt that the dramatist had a proud answer ready for the critics of the technique in his first play. Surely he would have quoted the defense made by the Roman Terence in *The Woman from Andros*, his first comedy, when he spurned the critics who blamed him for mixing two plays by the Greek Menander together, just as Shakespeare mixed two plays by Plautus to concoct his *Errors*. Terence declared that "He wishes rather to rival" Plautus and poets of his kind, with their "fine carelessness, than the obscure and petty pedantry of his detractors." The young aristocrat Shakespeare actually disdained the playwrights who worried over technique and dramatic workmanship, just as he looked down on all creatures busy with handicraft. He was more interested in Torquato Tasso's use of translations from Hellenic romances in his plays than in his theatric skill. From the day when Thomas Underdowne dedicated to him

"The White Ethiopian" by Heliodorus, Oxford's pleasure in those ancient romances did not wane low.

Most likely De Vere was spending his days at taverns and theaters in the months of May and June 1576, when his father-in-law recorded that he not only rejected the company of his wife but stayed away from the Court too, "in respect to avoid his offense." Queen Elizabeth expressed no judgment on the scandal. Her people knew her low opinion of the holy bonds of matrimony, and the peculiar refreshment she got from the spectacle of her courtiers' marriage troubles. Oxford had no cause to fear the wrath for his return to bachelor life. One of the public houses where he tried to forget that he was not a bachelor could have been the Porpentine on the Thames Bankside. It stood near the Pike Garden close to whorehouses and theatres. The mistress of the Porpentine plays an elfish role in the *Comedy of Errors* as a temptress of the unhappy husband Antipholus.[31]

On June 12 the Queen's chief minister appealed to the Earl to give Lady Anne permission to come into his presence at Court and "to do her duty to her Majesty, if her Majesty shall therewith be content." Cecil demanded that the Countess be allowed to answer her husband's insinuations before any judges Elizabeth might be pleased to appoint. Oxford did not see fit to respond. Then the Lord Treasurer let the Queen see how miserable the whole affair made him, and she decided to intervene, to persuade De Vere to act politely toward his wife. On July 10 Burghley tried again, hopeful that "my Lord of Oxford doth now understand that the conception which he had gathered to think unkindness in me toward him was grounded upon untrue reports of others, as I have manifestly proved them." Cecil went on to affirm that whoever would not listen to a "trial of the falsehood" must be thought "furtherers of untruths, and unworthy for my poor goodwill or friendship." Along with this warning he reminded Oxford that he had sent two thousand pounds of his own to help pay the Earl's expenses on the continent.[32] This time De Vere broke his silence; he arranged an interview with the Treasurer on July 12.

At their meeting he admitted that her Majesty had often talked to him for Anne's sake, requesting that she be allowed to come to Court. He promised to allow her, if Burghley would agree—"that she should not come when I was present, nor at any time have speech with me." Moreover, her father must not "urge further in her cause." The great politician apparently thanked Oxford for his generosity and went away without stating what he thought of his son-in-law's conditions.

The next morning the Earl (from a lodging at Charing Cross not his home) dispatched a letter to the Treasurer repeating his terms. "I understand," he wrote, "that your Lordship means this day to bring her to the Court, and that you mean afterward to prosecute the cause with further hope. Now if your Lordship shall do so, then shall you take more in hand than I have, or can promise you. For always I have, and I will still, prefer mine own content before others." He asked Cecil not to take advantage of the promise he had made until he gave his word to respect the conditions. Not until these were observed, said the Earl, "I could yield, as it is my duty, to her Majesty's request, and I will bear with your fatherly desire towards her"—the forlorn Countess. "Otherwise all that is done can stand to no effect."[33]

So the noble orphan pursued his errors and his discoveries.

For always I have, and I will still, prefer mine own content before others... I have no help but of mine own, and mine is made to serve me and myself, not mine.

Some readers may comment on this: How sinister, or how sad. Others: The audacity, the absurdity of it. Apart from the outlooks of morality and art, a psychoanalyst may point out that rarely has the faith of the gifted and spoiled child in his divine right to be first in nurture and first in love been so straight-forwardly declared.

I have surmised that our dramatist completed the first version, the protoplast of his *Errors* in June 1576. No doubt he had already resolved on its production by the company of the choirboys at St Paul's Cathedral, whose theatrical endeavors were conducted by his friend, the clandestine Catholic, Sebastian Westcott. The Earl may have brought the play to Westcott in person or else delivered it by the hand of a secretary, and afterward given his judgment that the piece deserved to be played. After its first performance and stage success, the Queen's Chamberlain, Sussex, who was in charge of the royal theatricals known as the Revels, and the heartiest friend the Earl of Oxford had at court, was persuaded that the farce would be worthy of the eyes of her Majesty during the Christmas revels, and so it came to be acted in the palace at Hampton on January 1, 1577. Like nearly all the plays of the period, it went without an author's name, and nobody seems to have missed it. The dramatist revised it in June 1583 under the spell of blank verse, and probably altered the comedy again before its most famous performance on the night of December 28, 1594, when the law students of Gray's Inn staged it with riotous results. Not until the year 1623, when the writer's dramatic works were first collected for the press, did the *Comedy of Errors* emerge from anonymity. This was its earliest appearance in print. It emerged under the *nom de plume* of William Shakespeare. No man of that name ever claimed it in his lifetime.

References

1 *Documents Relating to the Office of the Revels in the Time of Queen Elizabeth*, ed. Feuillerat (Louvain, 1908) 256.
2 Public Record Office: Baschet Transcripts, bundle 27.
3 *Calendar of State Papers Foreign: Elizabeth*, 1576, no. 735.
4 Journal of Daniel Rogers in *Relations Politiques des Pays Bas et de l'Angleterre, sous le Regne de Philippe II*, ed. Joseph Kervyn de Lettenhove (Brussels; F. Hayes, 1822-1900) viii, 368.
5 John Strype's *Annals of the Reformation* (London; John Wyat, 1709) iv, 84: Lettenhove, op. cit. viii, 396. *Calendar of State Papers Foreign*, 1577, no. 202. *Ibid.*, no. 799. *Ibid.*, 1576, no. 351.
6 *Acts of the Privy Council*, ed Dasent, ix, 192, 292.
7 *State Papers Domestic: Elizabeth*, 1574, xcviii, 2. *Ibid.*, Addenda, xxiii, 62. Harleian Ms. 6991, 50.
8 *State Papers Domestic: Elizabeth*, cli, 45.
9 *Ibid.*, clxxxi , 42. James A. Froude, *History of England* (London, 1870) xii, 132n.
10 *Calendar of State Papers Venetian*, 1575, vii, 527.

11 Lansdowne Ms. 19, 83.

12 Cecil Ms at Hatfield (*Calendar of Salisbury Papers*) ii, 129.

13 *State Papers Domestic*, 1575, no. 209. Cecil Ms. ii, 114.

14 *Edward Webbe His Trauailes*, ed. Arber (London, 1866) 32.

15 *Ibid.* ii, 83, 131.

16 *Ibid.* xiii, 144.

17 Concerning Rowland York, see Feldman, "Othello in Reality," *American Imago*, 11 (Summer 1954) 151 f. Cecil Ms. ii, 131. Lansdowne Ms. 102, 2.

18 Lansdowne Ms. 102, 2.

19 Cecil Ms. ii, 132; xiii, 128.

20 Edmund Lodge, *Illustrations of British History* (London, 1791), ii, 100. Cecil Ms. ii, 171.

21 *State Papers Domestic: Elizabeth*, cli, 46.

22 B. M. Ward, *The Seventeenth Earl of Oxford* (London, 1928) 21-22.

23 Cecil Ms. ii, 128, 133.

24 Eva Turner Clark, *Hidden Allusions in Shakespeare's Plays*, Ruth Loyd Miller, ed (Jennings, LA, Minos Publishing Company 1974) 21 f. Ward, op. cit. 83.

25 *Calendar of State Papers Domestic*, 1581, cxlvii, 41.

26 Ward, *op. cit.* 229.

27 A. B. Feldman, "The Confessions of William Shakespeare," *American Imago*, 10 (Summer 1953) 121, 134.
Allow me to explain here that Edward de Vere's birthday, according to the Old Style medieval Romanist reckoning, fell on April 12. When Pope Gregory XIII reformed the Romanist reckoning in 1582, eleven days were added, and the Earl of Oxford found himself rejoicing over his nativity on April 23, the day of the martyr George, England's patron saint—also the day we celebrate Shakespeare's birthday.

28 Sir Harris Nicholas, *Memoirs of the Life and Times of Sir Christopher Hatton* (London, 1847) 321, Conyers Read, *Mr Secretary Walsingham* (Oxford, 1925) ii, 111.

29 Sir Robert Naunton, *Fragmenta Regalia*, ed. Arber (London, 1870) 30.

30 *Documents ... of the Revels*, 267.

31 Eleanore Boswell, in the *London Times Literary Supplement*, 13 Nov. 1930.

32 Cecil Ms. ii, 170-1; i, 474.

33 *Ibid.*, ii, 135.

Chapter 3—IMAGINARY INCEST

This is the rarest dream that e'er dull sleep
Did mock sad fools withal.

(*Pericles*, 5.1.156-157)

I

A hundred years ago the consensus of researchers in the art of Shakespeare held that the play *Pericles, Prince of Tyre* was not altogether his handiwork. They pointed out that it was excluded from the first collection of his works, the folio of 1623. Not until 1664 did it enter the Shakespeare canon, and then it came in the disreputable company of six apocryphal plays. The printer Edward Blount, who took a leading part in the publication of the first folio, registered *Pericles* in the spring of 1608, but when it arrived, in a spoiled text, on the bookstalls this year another publisher's name appeared on the titlepage. This is regarded as proof that the first editors of Shakespeare's dramas viewed *Pericles* as mainly the product of an alien pen. Still the tradition persisted that the divine Will had worked on the play, and the authority of Tennyson upheld the belief to the extent of numbering the very scenes the master's hand had issued or touched. There was much throwing about of brains over the problem whether he had revised and improved an old romance, or sketched a new drama and left it to some impoverished wit to finish. With the outstanding exception of Georg Brandes, the commentators stood practically unanimous in the opinion that the first two acts—dealing with the incest of King Antiochus—and the two scenes in Act 4 which take place in a brothel must have been written by a hack like George Wilkins, whose novel *The Painful Adventures of Pericles, Prince of Tyre* appeared in 1608, frankly based on "the Play of *Pericles*, as it was lately presented" on the stage. Brandes considered that Wilkins and a collaborator wrote the play and sold it to Shakespeare's troop; it was then, he thinks, submitted to the greater poet, "who worked upon such parts as appealed to his imagination." Traces of his artistry, in the Danish critic's opinion, can be detected in the first two acts, unless they are simply imitations of his style. The brothel scenes, Brandes thought, were surely Shakespeare's work; scholars who denied this were just "pandering to the narrow-mindedness of the clergy man." He agreed that the romance abounded with verses of "feeble drivel," and that Shakespeare's own voice—"in unmistakable and royal power"—breaks in clearly at the start of Act 3, not before. On esthetic rather than moral grounds, Brandes rejected the claim that Shakespeare wrote the opening story of incest.[1]

The majority of scholars in the nineteenth century judged that Shakespeare's labor in *Pericles* was done in the last period of his creative life. They found it impossible to accept the declaration of John Dryden (in 1684) that it was composed at the dawn of Shakespeare's theatrical aspiration:

Shakespear's own Muse her Pericles first bore,
The Prince of Tyre was elder than the Moor:
'Tis miracle to see a first good play...

On the side of Dryden, in the eighteenth century, Edmund Malone once cast the weight of his learning. He argued that "*Pericles* was the entire work of Shakespeare and one of his earliest compositions."[2] Later Malone changed his mind, and suggested that the dramatist had "repaired" an ancient piece, though the crudities of the drama might still be deemed the ebullition of his own novice pen. Most of Malone's fellow experts inclined to Alexander Pope's decision that the whole play was "wretched," unworthy of the sweet singer of the Avon. The revelations by Tennyson of speeches in it comparable to the noblest in *King Lear* and *The Tempest* did not succeed in convincing the masses of nineteenth century playgoers and students that Pope was wrong. Twentieth century critics rigidly supported the Pope decision by viewing the sublime passages in *Pericles* as mere mimicry or plagiarism, echoes of Shakespeare in the final stage of his art. A few of them contended that Shakespeare was really dead when it was performed in 1608 and never could have predicted that thousands would crowd to see and enjoy it, decade after decade, while the Stuart dynasty reigned.

It is my belief that the play, with all its flaws and repulsive features, is truly Shakespeare's handiwork, written first in green youth and renovated in his gray age. Psychoanalysis will bear witness to the veracity of the claim. Later on I will attempt to show at what time and under what emotional necessity the dramatist created this curious romance.

Among Shakespeare's contemporaries there arose at least one man who protested against the fame of the drama. His affectionate friend and severest critic, Ben Jonson, fumed over its blemishes and sneered at the "the loathed stage" that profited from it. One of the last comedies by this great competitor of Shakespeare went down under the scowls of the public, and Jonson dashed off an ode denouncing the age's theatrical appetite (1631):

> No doubt some mouldy tale,
> Like *Pericles*, and stale
> As the shrieve's crusts, and nasty as his fish-
> Scraps out of every dish
> Thrown forth, and rakt into the common tub,
> May keep up the Play-club.

Pericles was certainly a prized item of diet in the "common tub" of the theatre in those aftermath days of the English Renaissance. The verdict of the commons, to be sure, did not spring from their own ethical or esthetic inquiries; it reverberated the fashionable judgment of their superiors. It was the aristocracy that set the seal of public approval on the play. As the Prologue says,

> Lords and Ladies in their lives
> Have read it for restoratives. (1. Cho. 7-8)

Its popularity ended forever with the fall from moral and artistic authority of the class for whom it was composed.

Those who are not revolted today by its grim sport with obscenity will probably damn the drama for its disunity, the puerile episodic structure, the bewildering mixture of fashions in rhetoric, and the phenomenal lack of controlling thought in the sequence of the acts. "The reader will seek in vain," said Brandes, "for any intention—and I do not mean moral, but any fundamental idea in the play."[3] He rightly spurns the conclusion offered by the "chorus," ancient John Gower, that the play presents a contrast between a wicked princess and a virtuous one. The dramatist grants but one isolate glimpse of the wicked princess at the beginning, lets us hear only two lines from her lips. And her tragedy has no necessary connection with the ensuing plot. The story might have begun with the second act, and barring allusion to the incestuous princess made fair theatrical sense. The Prince of Tyre might have been portrayed from the start as a shipwrecked hero seeking fortune and a bride. Why did Shakespeare have to picture him in headlong flight from the wicked lady of Antioch? It may be replied that he pictured his protagonist as he found him in the predicament of hoary legend, for instance in John Gower's *Confessio Amantis* (1393). We still feel impelled to wonder why he thought it imperative to follow the old legend in such ugly detail. He must have known how Geoffrey Chaucer had criticized his friend Gower's version of the story—"so horrible a tale for to read." What attracted the dramatist to the horror of it? That is the question. The answer to this riddle should provide us with the major motive for the composing of *Pericles*, and consequently bring to light the fundamental idea which Brandes missed. The unity of the romance will have to be hunted beyond the range of conscious art or intention, in the sphere of the artist's unconscious. There alone can we find out how a tale so gamey as *Pericles* could sustain a spell on the intelligence of generations, and help "keep up the Play-club," despite the sarcasms of Ben Jonson and his fastidious college followers.

II

The incest motive in the first act of *Pericles* sounds forthrightly from the mouth of the poet Gower, who provides a choral commentary on each act. His excuse for introducing the incest theme is simply that he is following an old tradition: "I tell you what my authors say." (1. Cho. 20) When we examine these authors carefully we soon learn that Shakespeare has not told us what they actually say. He has modified, transfigured, and cut out certain elements of their narratives, and put in significant features entirely his own. There is perhaps no more reliable guide to the endopsychic life of Shakespeare than the study of the way he handled his source materials. In the case of *Pericles, Prince of Tyre*, this study illumines the mind of the dramatist with a heat that many of us may find difficult to bear. This is possibly the main reason for scholastic neglect of the play. The reward of inquiry cannot be said "To glad your ears, and please your eyes," as Gower promises that the drama will. At the end the best we possess is the knowledge of a few pathetic facts. The pathos becomes manifest at once when we compare Shakespeare's treatment of the incest theme with the treatment by his tiresome authors.

The play opens in the city of Antioch in the reign of a king named Antiochus the Great. Old Gower, in the Prologue, tells us that this king had a wife who died leaving one child, a girl (not named). Antiochus became too fond of his heiress, "And her to incest did provoke." At first they felt ashamed of their passion. But custom, says the poet, custom or "long use" led them to reckon it not a sin. In quaint mimicry of Gower's fourteenth-century verse, the dramatist comments on their love:

> Bad child, worse father. To entice his own
> To evil should be done by none. (1. Cho. 27-28)

The beauty and riches of the princess attracted a host of nobles and princes to Antioch in the hope of winning her, in Shakespeare's phrase, "as a bedfellow,/ In marriage pleasures playfellow." (1. Cho. 33-34) Among those who contested for the heiress was young Pericles, the Prince of Tyre.

When he arrived in Antioch he saw the walls of the royal palace garnished with the heads of earlier lovers of the princess. He learnt that they had been cut off because of their failure to solve a certain riddle the king had set down as the sole obstacle on the road to his daughter's heart. Whoever wished her for a bride would have to interpret the riddle truthfully, or submit his neck to the executioner. Pericles was ready to hazard death for her sake. On the starry night of his drama's first scene, eager to try his luck, he confronts the mysterious girl and her strict yet witty father. The nameless one appears clothed like a bride and speaks her only lines, wishing him briefly prosperity and happiness. Then the Prince, after some hyperbolic utterance of his desire for her, and a brave glance at the bloody faces on the palace wall, reads the enigma of Antiochus:

> I am no viper, yet I feed
> On mother's flesh that did me breed:
> I sought a husband, in which labour
> I found that kindness in a father;
> He's father, son, and husband mild;
> I mother, wife; and yet his child:
> How they may be, and yet in two,
> As you will live, resolve it you. (1.1.65-72)

For this doggerel Shakespeare sacrificed the laconic force of the riddle as it stands in the prose of Lawrence Twine's *Pattern of Painful Adventures* (1576): "I am carried with mischief; I eat my mother's flesh; I seek my brother, my mother's husband, and cannot find him"[4] The princes who lost their heads seem to have read the puzzle without comprehending simply because the idea of incest between Antiochus and his daughter was beyond their credulity. They could not trust the sensible and true vouch of their own eyes. The perfervid imagination of Pericles leaps to the solution at once.

He lifts his eyes from the riddle to gaze his last on the princess of Antioch—"this glorious casket stor'd with ill." (1.1.78) He sighs, confessing a residue of desire, but pride and religion will not endure the prospect of union with her. He compares her body to a musical instrument whose strings are false, played before the right moment of her tune. So "Hell only danceth at so harsh a chime." (1.1.85)

To the mighty father he talks in more bitter and evasive vein, generalizing on the sad condition of persons who realize what wrongs their monarchs do and have no strength to do more than meditate about the sins of kings. He concludes that it is good to smother knowledge which might make matters worse, and asks the permission of Anitochus to keep silent on the riddle. His majesty pretends not to understand the hint. He graciously allows Pericles forty days in which to deliver his solution, and walks away with his girl, wishing under his breath that he could take instant possession of the young man's head.

As soon as the king is gone, the solitary Pericles unloads his stifling thoughts about the "foul incest." He suspects that Antiochus apprehended his insight to the truth and will scheme to silence him forever. At once he resolves, "By flight I'll shun the danger which I fear." (1.1.143) That very night he quits Antioch. Before the king hears of the escape he hires the courtier Thaliard to poison the Prince. When the flight is reported Thaliard swears to kill Pericles with a pistol, and sets sail for Tyre.

In fashioning the plot Shakespeare ignored the real history of the country in which he set his opening scene. There exists a Syrian tale of incest about Antiochus the son of the monarch Seleucus, but it deals with a passion for a mother-in-law. Besides, this Antiochus was not the one known to history as the Great. The reign of the Great Antiochus III (223-187 B.C.E.) yields no story remotely resembling the legend that Shakespeare tells. It is narrated as authentic chronicle by Godfrey of Viterbo, a medieval historian from whose *Pantheon* John Gower derived his poetic version of the legend. Godfrey depicted the Prince of Tyre, named Apollonius, as a fugitive from Antiochus III. There is no doubt now that the origin of his history was a Latin novel (also broadcast in the popular *Gesta Romanorum*) which was almost certainly founded on a lost Greek romance. In the Latin text Antioch is described as the "paternal kingdom" (patrium regnum) of the runaway hero.[5] This seems to indicate that the Latin fiction is a partially censored form of the legend. In its beginning Prince Apollonius most likely became the heir of Antiochus by marriage with the wicked daughter. The king's vindictiveness would then have flowed from jealousy not of a suitor but a son-in-law. In order to avoid this spectacle of the good hero living intimately with the incestuous, a Latin scribe would have suppressed the reason for the Tyrian's claim to the kingdom of Antioch. An old French version makes the claim intelligible by portraying Antiochus as a former vassal owing allegiance to the father of Apollonius.[6] Shakespeare expunged every trace of the hero's right to the crown of Antioch—unless we consider the mere appearance of the princess robed like a bride a vestige of the original marriage plot. The process of moral censorship which commenced in the Latin with vacillations emerges in the English playwright with wonderful emphatic distortions.

If the business of the "paternal kingdom" bothered our poet, he was surely more annoyed by the way his authors drew the reaction of "Apollonius" to the disappointment in Antioch. In their narratives the Tyrian retreats from the diplomatically hidden malignance of the king to think of some method to obtain the prize that Antiochus denies him. Having solved the riddle and earned the heiress, Apollonius protests: "I am notwithstanding restrained from her."[7] He determines that he will not rest until he gets the promised reward. Shakespeare's Pericles displays a very different attitude. He runs away to his home in Tyre, and instead of resuming the reins of government goes off to live in lonely idleness, sunk in infinite gloom. Pericles is a poet, not a man of action; obviously created in the image of his maker.

The poor Prince feels not the faintest pulse of gladness for his escape from the den of iniquity in Antioch. Our dramatist tries to excuse his sorrowing by some utterances of patriotic worry over the fate of Tyre if the incestuous king should wage war on the city in order to destroy the Prince who knows his secret. Pericles believes that the mere ostentation of battle from Antioch would scare his Tyrians into ruin. Duteous concern for their welfare, he says, not pity for himself, prompts him to the resolution to continue his flight, to desert Tyre and sail to a country beyond the despot's reach. He confides in none but a wise old courtier named Helicanus. He tells him how he had journeyed to Antioch glowing with hope of a magnificent alliance, from which might spring a child who would bring great joy to his people. This hope had been quenched by the discovery of a horror yonder "as black as incest." Helicanus is a councilor worthy of his Prince. He grieves listening to the anxiety of Pericles about the danger of an Antioch invasion, and agrees that the tyrant would not spare the expense of "public war or private treason" to shut the Prince's mouth. He advises Pericles to go voyaging until Antiochus forgets his anger or dies. Gratified by Helicanus's echo of his own conscience, the Prince of Tyre arranges for a swift and secret departure from the city, leaving the good old man in charge of his state affairs.

If the application of skepticism to the flimsy excuses of Pericles seems to be like breaking a butterfly on an engine, it should be remembered that the butterfly itself is just mechanical. By exposing the theatrical rationalizations of Shakespeare we expect to attain a clear view of the life current below the surface of the plot. It is impossible to accept the patriotic plangency and altruism of his protagonist at their face value. Never before and never after does he manifest a gleam of solicitude for the welfare of Tyre. His heart feels deep pain for one person alone, the forlorn Pericles. This compassion is beautifully communicated, yet the cause of it remains shrouded in an extraordinary suit of solemn black. We are left in the dark with the question why the Prince had to sink into a torpor of melancholy after his escape from the evil charmer of Antioch. The hero himself asks the question:

> Why should this change of thoughts,
> The sad companion, dull-ey'd melancholy,
> Be my so us'd a guest, as not an hour
> In the day's glorious walk or peaceful night—
> The tomb where grief should sleep—can breed me quiet? (1.2.1-5)

One answer that will occur to many of us is that Pericles is sorrowing over the loss of the princess, whom he had vowed he loved. This is a more trustworthy reason for his mood than worry over the chance of an unprovoked attack from Antioch. If the melancholy of

Pericles was induced by his sudden bereavement or break with Antiochus's daughter, why could not their creator say so? There was
nothing wrong in the Prince's chivalrous love for her untarnished
reputation, nothing deplorable in his wish to be the son-in-law of
the mighty Antiochus. Shakespeare gave him every reason to be
happy in his virtue and proud of his wisdom in eluding the snares of
the tyrant. And yet he has stricken his protagonist with unreason-
able grief. The romance did not require it. We can only conclude
that it represents a lapse of art that betrays a private emotion of the
dramatist.

III

We have no trouble recognizing the melancholy of the Prince of
Tyre as the same peculiar grief of mind that afflicts the twin Greek
heroes of the *Comedy of Errors*. In both cases we find a sudden loss
of the beloved after a sojourn in a strange city, then the seeking of
peace of heart by sea. These are of course recurrent themes in ancient Greek romance and favorites of the Elizabethan stage in the
youth of Shakespeare. We want to know the secret reasons for the
dramatist's attraction to these themes, why he built on their foundation the plays which may be regarded as his earliest theatrical work.
What is ancient Greek romance to him, or he to Greek romance,
that he should weep for it? Our answer has already been outlined in
the chapters on the *Comedy of Errors*. We see it confirmed and elabo-
rated in the tragicomedy of *Pericles*.

The source of both plays is the grief of the poet that followed his
estrangement from his wife.

In the *Errors* he produced an apology for his broken marriage,
affirming that his wife was mainly to blame, because she had been
shrewish and a tearful antagonist of his liberty. In a noble effort to
be fair he made out a comic case for her, too. I and my woman, the
dramatist inwardly contended, have done nothing more damnable
than entertain strangers as lovers. She took me in, like Alcmena in
Amphitruo, thinking that a hero was going to sleep by her side, and

in happy ignorance she united with a god. Alas, poor god! He took in holy wedlock what he thought was an angel, and she turned out to be a termagant, at any rate a woman of torturing whim. Incidentally, there appears to be a reference to the comedy by Plautus in Pericles' line: "And if Jove stray, who dares say, Jove doth ill?" (1.1.105)

In *Pericles* the writer presented this fatal break in his life as coming in the act of courtship. He drew himself as the Prince of Tyre, courting a stranger, but one deserving "the embracements even of Jove himself." (1.1.8)—Alcmena's god. In the nameless princess of Antioch we behold a sketch of the poet's bride in starlight. Her father says that Lucina, the goddess of the moon, reigned at her conception: his speech reminds us of the heroine Luciana who, according to our theory of the *Errors*, lyrically represents both the moon and the girl whom Shakespeare made his bride. Luciana's love, Antipholus of Syracuse, had been prepared to desert her after a brief courtship, for no reason except the fancy that in loving her he might be "guilty to self-wrong." Pericles deserts Lucina's princess for a similar but stronger reason.

What did Shakespeare mean by accusing his wife and her father of the crime of incest? I think the accusation was first of all a lurid device to justify the breach between his unhappy Anne and himself. It was another of the dramatist's alibis: his way of stating that their divorce occurred because she had been irrevocably bound to her father's will, because she loved the old despot more than her husband.

While transforming his Anne into a lovely obscurity in a wedding gown and veil, the poet altered the contours of her father until they formed a pattern of abstract tyranny. None of the details he furnished to enliven their allegorical figures could assist us in identifying the real models for the incestuous pair. For in gratifying his personal grudge, by making two oppressors of his conscience the targets of hate on the stage, he had to be careful to protect himself against the peril of his father-in-law's wrath. William Cecil could not have recognized his own image in the cunning and cruel Antiochus.

Cecil knew that political enemies, especially the Roman Catholics among them, hailed him in bitter derision as the uncrowned monarch of England and called the state *regnum Cecilianae.* "Secretary Cecil," Thomas Stukeley declared, "may be called King of England." The Earl of Leicester once remarked that Cecil did not want the Queen to marry since he wished to remain king himself.[8] The anonymous Catholic booklet, *A Treatise of Treasons* (1572), branded him a usurper and a criminal, but failed to draw up a factual indictment. His modern admirers concede that he lacked a strong sense of loyalty to his benefactors and had too large a faith in the power of the rack to wring the truth out of prisoners. If one translates these faults as treachery and tyranny one can understand why our noble poet envisaged him as King Antiochus. The Earl of Oxford had lived with Cecil from the time he was twelve until he became twenty-one, and he often witnessed his Lordship's defects in action within the family. The crafty minister did not scruple to practice espionage on his boy Thomas when the latter was a student in France. He may also have practiced a little household despotism with his two daughters. When his darling Anne was twelve he engaged her to marry Philip Sidney, and disputed for months with Sidney's father over the land and money he expected for their marriage. In February 1571 the Queen elevated him to the barony of Burghley. Though he affirmed himself "the poorest lord in England" he could no longer think of wedding his daughter to a young man of Philip's rank and means. His eye ranged the nobility for a grander catch. In April Edward de Vere took his place in the House of Lords. And on July 22 a humorous observer, Lord St. John, reported: "The Earl of Oxenford hath gotten himself a wife, or at least a wife hath caught him: this is the mistress Anne Cecil; whereunto the Queen hath given her consent, and the which hath caused great weeping, wailing, and sorrowful cheer of those that had hoped to have that golden day." The golden day was December 19. Catholic authors judged the wedding a triumph for the middle-class "heretic rich, who they alleged were conspiring to get control of the kingdom." "Consider," said the author of *A Treatise of Treasons,* "how the Captain Catiline of this conjuration now linketh himself with the noblest and ancientest of your nobility (least in credit, I mean), how strong thereby he maketh himself." The Lord treasurer's admirers will hardly deny that his girl's chances of happiness with the nervous Earl counted for little when he negotiated this alliance.[9]

Shortly after the marriage De Vere began to importune his father -in-law to save his cousin Thomas Howard, Duke of Norfolk, from the penalty for treason, to which he had been condemned for plotting with Queen Mary of Scotland. Howard, the son of Henry, the poetic Earl of Surrey, and Frances de Vere, sister of Edward's father, but had actually been trapt in a web of Cecilian conspiracy, "framed up," as Americans say. On January 20, 1572, Norfolk complained, "My cousin of Oxford is too negligent in his friend's causes." The Duke, locked in the Tower of London, had heard nothing of his kinsman's device—conceived some weeks before the Earl's wedding—to rescue him from prison and convey him by a specially provided ship to Spain. Feverishly Oxford exerted his influence for the sake of his aunt Frances' son; and four times Elizabeth demurred from letting the death warrant go. She told Burghley that the thought of Norfolk's execution was too terrible to her. He advised her against clemency. On March 18 his agent in Antwerp, John Lee, recorded Papist gossip that Oxford had "conceived some great displeasure" against his father-in-law for not using his authority to save the Duke: "whereupon," Lee wrote, "he hath, as they say here, put away from him the Countess his wife." This piece of gossip grew to amazing proportions after Norfolk was beheaded on June 2, 1572. Centuries later the antiquarian Edmund Lodge imagined the young Earl passionately beseeching Burghley to interfere on the Duke's behalf and storming at the minister's refusal—"he would revenge himself by ruining the Countess." He made his threat good, says Lodge, "for from that hour he treated her with the most shocking brutality, and having broken her heart, sold and dissipated the most part of his great fortune."[10] The source of this dramatic gossip has never been traced. We may be confident that Norfolk's brother, Lord Henry Howard, a far more clever conspirator, had a leading hand in the propagation of the tale. Perhaps he heard the original from Oxford's own tongue.[11]

The Earl concealed his feelings on the death of his kinsman. In the ensuing summer he helped to amuse the Queen at his father-in-law's country mansion, Theobalds, and he staged a mock-battle for her Majesty at Warwick on the Avon. The Treasurer and Countess Anne watched his joy in the mimic warfare. On August 24 the King of France and a party of Catholic fanatics in Paris carried out a massacre of Protestants, and when the news arrived in England the whole Court was steeped in gloom. Oxford and his wife went with her Majesty to London where he listened to French refugees' accounts of the tragedy.

He wrote to Burghley a long letter describing how they told of "their own overthrows, with tears falling from their eyes; piteous thing to hear, but a cruel and far more grievous thing we must deem it thought to see." The letter confessed a profound anxiety for the life of his Lordship. "Sith the world is so full of treasons and vile instruments," said De Vere, "daily to attempt new and unlooked for things, good my Lord, I shall affectionately and heartily desire your L. to be careful both of yourself and of her Majesty, that your friends may long enjoy you, and you them." He reminded his Lordship how Edmund Mather had plotted to kill him and the Queen (for Norfolk's sake). Mather, who cursed Elizabeth for desiring "nothing but to feed her own lewd fantasy, and to cut off such of her nobility as were not perfumed and courtlike to please her delicate eye," died horribly for his design. Oxford warned Burghley to prepare for new schemes of assassination. "This estate," he declared, "hath depended on you a great while, as all the world doth judge, and now all men's eyes not being occupied any more on these lost lords, are as it were on a sudden bent and fixed on you, as a singular hope and pillar, whereto the religion hath to lean. And blame me not," De Vere added, "though I am bolder with your L. at this present than my custom is, for I am one that count myself a follower of yours now in all fortunes; and what shall hap to you, I count it hap to myself, or at least I will make myself a voluntary partaker of it."

One may surmise that the Earl protests too much his concern for Burghley's welfare, as if to quiet the inner voice that accused him of wishing his father-in-law a victim like the lords of the Huguenots. "I humbly desire your L.," he goes on, "to pardon my youth, but to take in good part my zeal and affection towards you, as on whom I have builded my foundation, wither to stand or fall. And good my Lord, think I do not this presumptuously, as to advise you that am but to take advice of your L., but to admonish you, as one with whom I would spend my blood and life. So much you have made me yours. And I do protest, there is nothing more desired of me than so to be taken and accounted of you." The writer displayed his good faith by assuring his Lordship that in the leases of his lands and sales of his other properties, "in this as in all other things I am to be governed and commanded at your Lordship's good devotion."[12]

These promises brought Burghley no nearer to the fulfillment of his son-in-law's desire for a place of splendor in the state. On September 22 Oxford wrote again, from Cecil House in Westminster, pleading for a chance to win military honor: "If there were any service to be done abroad, I had rather serve there than at home, where yet some honour were to be got. If there be any setting forth to sea, to which service I bear the most affection, I shall desire your L. to give me and get me that favor and credit... that I might make one." He announced that Lady Anne had departed for the country and he would follow—"as fast as I can get me out of town." They were bound for his house of Wivenhoe in Essex, by the North Sea. From this favorite retreat, the Earl wrote, "I shall be most willing to be employed on the sea coasts to be in a readiness with my countrymen against invasion."[13] No call to arms came to him at Wivenhoe. So he resigned himself to the service of the Muses. He perused with great pleasure his friend Thomas Bedingfield's manuscript translation of Girolamo Cardano's *Consolation* (1542), a work primarily intended for melancholy intellects, and made up his mind to publish it himself, with a letter of introduction and a poem of praise. To let the book lie in "the waste bottoms of my chests," the Earl declared, would have been like committing murder. Eagerly he got *Cardanus Comfort* ready for the press. It came out early in 1573. The Earl's introductory epistle promised that here was a volume to "comfort the afflicted, confirm the doubtful, encourage the coward…" How much benefit he got from its philosophy, it is difficult to tell. His letter to Bedingfield shows that his thoughts gravitated constantly to death, in particular to the graves of loved ones. Wivenhoe was just a few miles from Colne Priory where so many lords and ladies of the house of Vere were buried.

By the autumn of 1573 Oxford had determined to leave his wife in order to voyage to Ireland, where his friend the Earl of Essex commanded the English troops. On November 1 Essex wrote to Burghley asking to be remembered with "your good Countess, your daughter, of whose match I mistrust not but your L. shall in the end receive singular comfort." The Lord Treasurer prevented this change of his son-in-law's horizon, with the result that Oxford commenced an intrigue with men hostile to Burghley's policies, men suspected of being in the pay of Spain. A gentleman adventurer named Ralph Lane kept Burghley in touch with the conspiracy, informing him how to "cut off not only this, but any other advantages that foreign factions may seek to take of [De Vere's] young unstaid mind." Lane felt sorry for the distracted Earl. He hoped that Cecil would help the young man before he risked the fate of Norfolk: "A western Spanish storm," Lane wrote, "may, with some unhappy mate at helm, steer his noble bark so much to the northward" (into the orbit of the Queen of Scots) "that unawares he may wreck, as some of his noblest kind hath done, the more pity of their fault." Lane's testimony indicates that the soldier of fortune, Rowland York, who afterward played a sinister role in Oxford's divorce, was also involved in the earl's dangerous enterprise.[14]

A few months later, Oxford ran away to Belgium, dreaming of military education on the staff of the Duke of Alva, and Thomas Bedingfield was sent to bring him home. These deeds of De Vere make perfectly plain how seriously we must take his avowals of zeal and affection toward the father of his wife.

Nevertheless Lord Burghley would have needed the eye of a clairvoyant or a poet to perceive in the Shakespeare vision of Antioch's royal "bed of blackness" his son-in-law's response to the fact that the Countess Anne was "most directed by her father and mother." He might have sensed the meaning of *Pericles* if he ever saw the drama at Court and detected in the name of the despot of Antioch an intimation that the dramatist conceived him as anti-Oxford.

IV

Let us recall the letter of the earl dated July 13, 1576, in which he promised that if Burghley would abide by the limits he set for Anne's enjoyment of the Court, "I will bear with your fatherly desire towards her." The peculiarity of the preposition towards, where one might have expected for, suggests that when De Vere wrote these words he was already harboring a fantasy of "untimely claspings" between the statesman and his daughter. This illusion would have been strengthened by his reading of *The Pattern of Painful Adventures* by Lawrence Twine, which was licensed for publication on July 17. Perhaps he knew Twine personally, for that author belonged to the same family as the Thomas Twine who dedicated to Oxford in 1573 his *Breviary of Britain*, a book which expressed the hope that the Earl one day would become "the chiefest stay of this your commonwealth and country." *The Pattern of Painful Adventures* retold the sad romance of Apollonius Prince of Tyre. Unquestionably it sent the poet back to John Gower's version of the tale, and so led to the writing of *Pericles*, in my opinion, a short while after the writing of the first *Comedy of Errors*.

We have noticed how Burghley threatened his son-in-law (on July 10) with the absolute loss of his "good will or friendship" if he persisted in crediting the slanders against the Cecil family. The warning must have struck a chord of terror in the heart of De Vere, remembering how mercilessly his Lordship had worked to cut off cousin Norfolk's head. "I am too little" says the Prince of Tyre (1.2.17), to contend with King Antiochus: and in the avowal we listen to the pangs of psychic impotence that the little Earl Edward had to bear when he stood in the presence of the man whom Elizabeth called burly by name and by nature. The bare thought of the politician excited the fear of emasculation which vibrates through almost all the works of Shakespeare.

We see its impact in the opening scene of *Pericles*, in the symbol of the severed heads on the palace of Antioch. They stand for the pride of young sex that dared in ignorance to provoke a father's jealousy. Our Tyrian hero escapes decapitation but only by surrendering his crown. He saves his skin at the price of manliness—in his own phrase, punishing "that before that he (Antiochus) would punish." (1.2.35) It is conceivable that the castration complex of the poet induced him to drop the name Apollonius and call his protagonist Pericles, after the idol of Athenian democracy. The sound of this Greek name may have appealed to our prince of puns as resembling a compound of two homely English words: prick and leese, meaning lose, as in Shakespeare's Sonnet V—

> But flowers distil'd, though they with winter meet,
> Leese but their show

The reader who laughs at this play with words should get acquainted with the experts on Greek etymology who derive the name of the hero of Homer's *Iliad*, Achilles, from the word *acheilos* meaning "lipless." Our poet is said by some commentaries to have changed the name of Apollonius to Pericles after perusal of Sir Philip Sidney's *Arcadia*, a tedius imitation of Grecian romance (1590). One of the chief characters in *Arcadia* is Pyrocles, a young noble who is first seen mounted on a mast at sea, the picture of a shipwreck. Fishermen fail to rescue him; he is captured by pirates, then turns up as a soldier victorious in a battle. He disappears under a spell of violent love and we next encounter him disguised as an Amazon princess! Later Pyrocles takes part in a tournament in the

shape of an "ill-apparelled knight" and wins glory here too. They
say that Sidney drew an ideal picture of himself in the person of Pyrocles. In my opinion, his inspiration for the portrait, which was
written in 1580, came from his remembrance of the play *Pericles* as
he had witnessed it in the winter of 1576-77. Of course the poet
was aware that Pericles suggested the Latin *periculos*, from which we
get the word *perils*. No peril, however, "drew sleep out of his eyes,
blood from his cheeks," like his conception of steel being wielded
against his sex. That is what the fancy of Antiochus's onslaught on
Tyre signified: that is why Pericles could not imagine his countrymen standing firm before the onslaught.

The huge king in truth is a shadow composite of the poet's two
fathers, the one in law and the one his mother married. Certainly
the spell of dread that Lord Burghley cast on Edward de Vere oper-
ated on his nerves the way it did because of the permanent impression made on them first by childhood dread of Lord John, his father in fact. It meant retribution for the incestuous yearning of his
infancy, which emerges in the drama twofold, projected as a crime
on a substitute for his father, and transmuted to an innocent passion for a stranger, a woman unknown and veiled. Shakespeare
turned the tables on the lord of his superego by making him guilty
of the very deed which, as we deduced from the analysis of his *Errors*, excruciated his conscience under the aspect of adultery.

Ultimately, I assume, the nameless princess stands for the dramatist's mother. He loved her distantly and with superstitious terror,
unconsciously convinced that if he came too close he would hazard
a mortal or an incurable wound. Out of that unconscious conviction
the poet's wit evolved this cryptic couplet of *Pericles* (2.2.43-44):

> All love the womb that their first being bred;
> Then give my tongue like leave, to love my head.

The fantom of maternity within him terrified not only by conjuring
visions of his father and lost masculinity. She also raised in his unconscious the notion that she herself possessed the private part of a
man. For his portrait of the princess of Antioch, Shakespeare used

one of the oldest symbols of the organ, the tree. Pericles calls her a "celestial tree," and Antiochus compares her to the golden-fruited Hesperides—"dangerous to be touch'd" (1.1.28-29)—an admonition that points to the germ of the phallic complex in a paternal menace to masturbation.

Afterward the king refers to the Tyrian himself as a fair tree, wishing that he could have his head. In the Prince's soliloquy in the next scene he compares his spirit to "the tops of trees, Which fence the roots they grow by and defend them." Here the word "tops" may look extravagant if we did not realize how acutely the poet suffered, at the time he wrote the play, from hidden anxiety about his penis. Perhaps he thought it had somehow been deprived of vitality everywhere but at the foreskin. I find support for this idea in the emblem selected by Pericles for the pageant of knighthood in the second act:

A withered branch, that's only green at top:
The motto, 'In hac spe vivo.' (In this hope I live.) (2.2.43-44)

The genital anxiety reflected by these verses carried with it an uncommon torment of another amatory zone of the poet, his mouth. Feasting and fornicating were probably so closely joined in his unconscious that they felt like a single process. The reader will recollect what fun he had in *Errors* confusing a dinner with adultery. In the near tragedy of *Pericles* the intertwining of his notions of eating and sexual intercourse produces images of horror. He likens the incest of Antioch to a child's feeding on mother's flesh. The analogy reminds us of the fact, uncovered by psychoanalysis, that poets in general are afflicted with oral erotic distemper.[15] They all begin life with savage cravings of hunger toward their mothers. They wish to eat them up, and imagine that their mothers might turn to rip and swallow them. And they grow, sometimes to venerable age, with the mouth-lust badly subdued, eternally twitching and gaping for its opportunities, and pausing only to despair. Concerning the oral distemper of Edward de Vere, we have the evidence of the courtier Charles Arundel that the Earl retained a memory of having tasted blood in his childhood.[16]

The cannibal impulse has inspired a massive literature, usually in the form of projection on parents. Thus the appetite connected with incest in the first scene of *Pericles* makes its appearance in the fourth scene as a sign of maternal depravity. Here Shakespeare pictures a famine in the seaport of Tarsus, with the people tottering on the edge of bestiality:

> Those mothers who, to nousle up their babes,
> Thought nought too curious, are ready now
> To eat those little darlings whom they lov'd. (1.4.42-44)

Our hero, learning of the starvation in Tarsus, sails from Tyre with a fleet loaded with corn and wins the gratitude of the Cilician city. The king Cleon and his queen Dionyza welcome him as a godsend, but he is unable to accept their hospitality long.

A letter from Helicanus reports that Thaliard, the agent of Antioch, is after him, and immediately the Prince takes to sea again. A tempest overtakes him and his vessel splits. He is the sole survivor, thrown ashore at night on the coast of Africa, near the town of Pentapolis.

Now occurs a comic interlude (2.1). The prince listens to some fishermen discussing life on the sea, in a manner that proves them English clowns in disguise. One, named Patch-breech, expresses fear of the "porpus," which bounces and tumbles in the waves portending to the sailor a wash. The humor of this fisherman's fear, I guess, consists of an allusion to a joke by the famous comedian Richard Tarlton, who seems to have come from the fishing town of Colchester, within walking distance of Oxford's castle of Wivenhoe. Contemporary anecdotes of Dick Tarlton's antics in the Court show him a jester on the side of the Earl, witty at the expense of Lord Burghley, Sir Walter Ralegh, and others whom Oxford feared, envied, and hated. One of his best known jokes was a simple sport with the word *porpoise*, which he confounded with *prepuce*.[17] If our dramatist intended a phallic allusion in Patch-breech's remarks, one could anticipate that he would follow it with a reference to oral ferocity. Patch-breech's next remark is "I marvel how the fishes live in the sea." His master answers: "Why, as men do a-land: the great ones eat up the little ones." (2.1.26-29)

The master goes on to sarcasm against the "whales," the rich misers of his country, so avid for landed property they "never leave gaping till they've swallowed the whole parish, church, steeple, bells, and all." (2.1.33-34) A plain Protestant listening to this bitterness might have taken it as an attack on the people of the age who were seeking to increase their acres and riches (like Shakspere of Stratford later) by enclosure of village commons and rejection of church rights to real estate. On the other hand, to an Englishman who adhered to the Catholic faith (as De Vere did in secret in 1576) the polemic would have sounded like one of those old nursery rimes which, many scholars think, were aimed by the priests against King Henry VIII and the "whales" of the upstart bourgeois aristocracy who profited from his expropriation of the Catholic Church's wealth. Perhaps Shakespeare was remembering "Robbin the bobbin" when he wrote the master-fisherman's lines:

> Robbin the bobbin,
> The big-bellied ben,
> He ate more meat than three-score men;
> He ate the church,
> He ate the steeple,
> He ate the priests,
> And all the people;
> And yet he complained that his belly was not full.[18]

The poet's sentiments on this business of parish property, which under feudal principles were dedicated to the glory of God and charity for the poor, caused him to mix his metaphors. He shifted from whales to bees, wishing that "We would purge the land of these drones, that rob the bee of her honey." His fishermen's fervor has an interesting parallel in an anecdote told by the theologian and antiquary Thomas Fuller. In 1577, Fuller says, the Earl of Oxford presented the rectory of Lavenham, which had long existed within the Earldom's gift, to the Reverend Henry Copinger. He wanted to attach one string to the grant, "this condition, that he should pay no tithes for his park (nearby), being almost half the land of the parish. Mr. Copinger told his Lordship 'that he would rather return the presentation than, by such sinful gratitude, betray the rights of the Church,' which answer so affected the Earl that he replied, 'I scorn that my estate should swell with Church goods.'"[19]

Pericles approaches the fishermen, entreating their charity. He describes himself as a plaything of the waters and the wind, which, like antagonists in a game, knock him helplessly back and forth. These forces, we have seen in the study of the *Comedy of Errors*, symbolize the lady and the lord who were enshrined dynamically in the dramatist's superego. The following episode provides us with an instructive example of his ego's fluctuations between their magnetic poles in his mind. In headlong flight from two figures who stand for the bad aspects of the father and mother Pericles comes to a place where he can adore two figures who stand for their good sides. He meets and falls in love with "the good King Simonides" and his angelic daughter, Princess Thaisa. To be exact, he falls in love with them before their meeting. Hearing the fishermen call Simonides good, and learning that "there are princes and knights come from all parts of the world to just and tourney" for Thaisa's love, he desires to attempt the conquest of the beautiful stranger himself. Then a suit of rusty armor is seen caught in a fishing net. The Prince identifies it as a bequest from his dead father, which luckily did not sink with his ship. Shakespeare lingers affectionately on the memory of his father's will. It consoles him for the grief he had to bear for the unconscious guilt of jealousy. "He lov'd me dearly...." The passage compels attention to the last testament of Lord John de Vere, in which we learn with wonder that he appointed his boy Edward to act as an executor with Sir William Cecil and Sir Nicholas Bacon. Pericles, exulting in the armored guise of his father, goes once more to make love to a strange lady.

V

The king of Pentapolis has the wit, the craft, and a little of the cruelty of the king of Antioch. He commands his daughter with threats ("Do as I bid you, or you'll move me else"—(2.3.71)). He amuses himself by tormenting his future son-in-law, springing a trap to detect his real feelings about Thaisa. The poet presents both monarchs as men more interested in their daughters than in affairs of state. They praise the beauty of these girls in strikingly similar terms. Antiochus says of the nameless one, "Nature this dowry gave, to glad her presence" (1.1.10). Simonides says that "nature gat [Thaisa] For men to see, and seeing wonder at" (2.2.6-7). The author has made both kings widowers. This served the aim of dramatic economy and also executed a kind of vengeance for the Earl of Oxford, whose mother-in-law, you remember, had wished him dead.

The dramatist's own father becomes visible in Simonides only in his postures of kind and godly royalty, shining like the Lord in stained glass. When Simonides acts like a human being he becomes a comic portrait of Oxford's father-in-law, "Yon king's to me like to my father's picture" (2.3.37). He recalls his father sitting at banquet, surrounded by stars like the sun. They reverenced his Majesty like the heavenly bodies worshipt the boy dreamer Joseph in the Bible. For young Shakespeare, to think of his father as a man like other men was sacrilege. It meant thinking of him in the act of procreation, the abandon of sex. He could not endure this. Consequently he stript his mother's lover of worldliness and the flesh and exalted him to godhood, committing with this compliment unconscious "homicide." Gods have been created in the same way before, and since. Simonides ceases to be godlike and a pattern of abstract stateliness when he occupies himself with love matters, in particular the wedding of his daughter. This plainly signified to our poet a degradation, and therefore proper stuff for comedy. He pictured Lord Burghley for his play as a marriage contriver, not unlike his Pandar of Troy in *Troilus and Cressida*. "Few things," Freud observes, "can afford the child greater pleasure than when the grown-up lowers himself to his level," and much of comic ingenuity and hilarity comes from a process of debasement.[20] The child in the playwright enjoyed the levity that William Cecil exhibited on certain occasions, but he could not help looking on it as a descent from splendor, bringing his Lordship down to the plane where the "madcap" Earl was doomed to spend most of his days. One sign of the lowering of Burghley for the purposes of *Pericles* may be seen in the fact that the original legend of Apollonius of Tyre names his royal father-in-law Archistrates or Altistratus, both names indicating lofty rank. Shakespeare declined to give him a name suggestive of highness. I regret that I am unable to guess why he called the king Simonides.

The spiritual identity of the bad girl of Antioch and the good girl of Pentapolis is revealed by their poetic association with the moon, somewhat like the two heroines of *Errors*. We are told that the moon-goddess Lucina governed the conception of the princess without a name. In source-books of *Pericles* the Prince's second love is actually named Lucina. Shakespeare changed it, presumably, because he wanted to avoid suspicion that he was lightheartedy handling English majesty, for poets frequently extolled Queen Elizabeth with the names of pagan goddesses of the moon, Diana, Cynthia, and so on. To name a girl, so eager for wedlock as the child of Simonides after the virgin queen of heaven was sure to strike a subject of Elizabeth as satire on her. Our dramatist prevented anyone from fancying that her Majesty was hinted in Thaisa by describing the latter in terms that were applicable to her Majesty's servants, the Maids of Honor, among whom Anne Cecil once shone. Thus Simonides announces that his girl desires not to marry for a year (2.5.10-11):

> twelve moons more she'll wear Diana's livery;
> This by the eye of Cynthia hath she vow'd.

The personalities of the two princesses have one distinction in common, which may be termed audacity in quietness. Each pursues the enticement of her heart with noiseless willpower. Yet each finds her satisfaction in the fulfillment of her father's will.

Shakespeare gave his protagonist's wife the name of her daughter in John Gower's poem.

On parting from the princess of Antioch, Pericles assured her, "Fair glass of light, I lov'd you and could still...." (1.1.77). He arrives at the feet of Thaisa because she resembled the noble lady of his dreams, the incestuous one. In turning his passion from the nameless lady to the princess of Pentapolis, the dramatist was not simply returning to the past of his love for Lord Burghley's daughter—as I conjecture he did in the *Comedy of Errors*, when his Syracusan hero, repelled by the malignant Adriana, makes love to her sweet virgin sister. The reincarnation of Antiochus's daughter as Thaisa expressed the desire of the poet for renewal of his passion for Anne Cecil, a desire he was reluctant to confess even to himself. He voiced it through the medium of Thaisa's father, who tells her (2.2.46-47):

> From the dejected state wherein he is,
> He hopes by you his fortune yet may flourish.

Nostalgia for the lost love inspired the tournament scene in which Pericles wins the heart of Thaisa by the prowess shown in his father's obsolete armor. This tournament evokes the memory of the "solemn just at the tilt, tourney and barrier" which was held before the Queen at Westminster on the first days of May 1571. The combatants included De Vere, Sir Henry Lee, Charles Howard, Christopher Hatton, as challengers, and against them rode Thomas Cecil, Thomas Bedingfield, and Thomas Knyvet, the last of whom played a fatal role in Oxford's life. All the knights did valiantly, a contemporary records, "but the chief honor was given to the Earl of Oxford."[21] He broke thirty-two lances and scored three direct hits on head and chest, and won a tablet of diamonds. The sight of him galloping in crimson made an amorous impression on a number of Maids of Honor as well as Anne Cecil. Oxford himself was not unimpressed by the vision. When he visited the island of Sicily in 1575 he issued a challenge at Palermo "Against all manner of persons whatsoever, and at all manner of weapons, as tournaments, barriers, with horse and armor, to fight a combat with any whatsoever in defense of his Prince and Country."

The Italians admired his gallantry but none ventured to answer his call.[22] In honor of his wedding with Anne Cecil the poet Giles Fletcher penned a Latin poem that devotes several ardent lines to a picture of the Earl's fiery energy in these mock-duels, his daring and skill, especially his grace in horsemanship.[23] Perhaps it was under the spell of Anne's rapture over his prowess that the noble orphan resolved to make her his wife.

Without his wife young Oxford felt worse than lonesome. He felt impotent, cut off from his true career as a nobleman, with no prospect of ever showing England and the world what a general or admiral he could make. He whose education, in the phrase of Pericles, had been in arts and arms seemed fated to have his genius confined to the arts, moreover those arts considered by men of action barely better than child's play. Contemplating the portrait of his father, who had obviously thrilled the lad Edward indelibly with his experience as a soldier, the poet believed that destiny or fortune had cheated him, ordaining him to a clandestine career with the inkhorn:

> now his son's like a glow-worm in the night,
> The which hath fire in darkness, none in light. (2.3.43-44)

The Earl's melancholy got little relief from the praise he bestowed on himself from the mouth of King Simonides:

> In framing artists art hath thus decreed,
> To make some good, but others to exceed.
> And you're her labour'd scholar. (2.3.15-17)

The king lauds Pericles as the best dancer among the knights at his court, and later calls him "music's master." The Apollonius of Lawrence Twine is said to have skill in all things: he excels with the tennis racquet and the harp. The praise of Pericles, however, is more than a stage application of Twine's text. Dancing and music were arts in which the Earl of Oxford labored to shine. "The Queen's Majesty," wrote Gilbert Talbot to his father, the Earl of Shrewsbury, on May 11, 1572, "delighteth more in his [Oxford's] personage and his dancing and his valiantness than any other." She thought his skill in the coranto, the galliard, and the lavolt worth showing off to French ambassadors. As for music, we learn from the life of England's outstanding composer of this period, William Byrd, that the Earl recognized his genius almost at the start of his career and encouraged it with characteristic generosity. About 1574 Oxford made arrangements to give Byrd the income from his manor of Battleshall in Essex for 31 years. The musician's work as a gentleman of her Majesty's Chapel must have led to their collaboration in theatre. We know that Byrd composed at least one piece for which De Vere supplied the inspiration: "The Earl of Oxford's March Before the Battle." As late as 1591 the Earl's "great affection to his noble science" of music emboldened the Irish composer John Farmer, who sang as a boy in the choir of St. Paul's Cathedral, to dedicate to him *Forty Several Ways of Two Parts in One Made upon a Plain Song*. In 1599 Farmer acknowledged Oxford's patronage with the dedication of his *First Set of English Madrigals*. "So far," he wrote, "have your honourable favours outstripped all means to manifest my humble affection that there is nothing left but praying and wondering."

These madrigals he offered as "remembrances of my service and witnesses of your Lordship's liberal hand, by which I have so long lived." "Without flattery," Farmer declared, persons who knew Oxford were aware that "using this science as a recreation," the Earl had "overgone most of them that make it a profession."[24]

Lord Burghley did not esteem art like Simonides, and never praised his rhapsodic son-in-law as the young man wished that he would. The best that Burghley could say of him—as far as we can judge from his Lordship's extant writings—are the few lukewarm compliments to be found in a letter he wrote to the Earl of Rutland on August 15, 1571, announcing the engagement of his Anne to De Vere. This letter is a fine illustration of Cecil's labor with prose.

"I think it doth seem strange to your Lordship to hear of a purposed determination in my Lord of Oxford to marry with my daughter; and so, before his Lordship moved it to me, I might have thought it, if any other had moved it to me himself. For at his own motion I could not well imagine what to think, considering I never meant to seek it nor hoped of it. And yet reason moved me to think well of my Lord, and to acknowledge myself greatly beholden to him, as indeed I do. Truly, my Lord, after I was acquainted of the former intention of a marriage with Master Philip Sidney, whom always I loved and esteemed, I was fully determined to have of myself moved no marriage for my daughter until she should have been near sixteen, that with moving I might also conclude. And yet I thought it not inconvenient in the meantime, being free to hearken to any motion made by such others as I should have cause to like. Truly, my Lord, my goodwill serves me to have moved such a matter as this in another direction than this is, but having more occasion to doubt of the issue of the matter, I did forbear, and in mine own conceit I could have as well liked there as in any other place in England. Percase your Lordship may guess where I mean, and so shall I, for I will name nobody. Now that the matter is determined betwixt my Lord of Oxford and me, I confess to your Lordship I do honour him so dearly from my heart as I do my own son, and in any case that may touch him for his honour and weal, I shall think him mine own interest therein. And surely, my Lord, by dealing with him I find that which I often heard of your Lordship, that there is much more in him of understanding than any stranger to him would think. And for my own part I find that whereof I take comfort in his wit and knowledge grown by good observation."[25]

Shakespeare had to labor for years before he could imitate with justice the ponderous modesty of this style.

When I copied the great politician's phrase about honoring Oxford like his son, I recalled the warmth of King Altistratus in Lawrence Twine's novel. The king affirms that he loves Apollonius no less "than if he were my natural child." There is no such declaration in Shakespeare's play. Burghley's letter to Rutland indicates the reason why. Nearly ten years after Edward de Vere entered his home as a royal ward he still seemed a stranger to Cecil, and one whose courtship of his daughter he regarded with profound misgiving. Our noble dramatist naturally made Simonides welcome the courtship of the "mean knight" Pericles, for his self-esteem, especially in youth, could not imagine a social inferior being anything but overjoyed at the proposal of alliance by wedlock with him. The play, however, confirms contemporary Court gossip that neither Oxford nor Burghley was the prime mover in the marriage. It was the clever little daughter of the statesman who captivated the Earl and persuaded her father, no doubt with the slowly won assent of Lady Mildred, her mother, that the marriage would be a success and do credit to the house of Cecil. King Simonides is grimly amused by his girl's affirmation that she will have none for her husband but "the stranger knight."

> I like that well: how absolute she's in't,
> Not minding whether I dislike or no. (2.5.19-20)

But he cannot refrain from accusing Pericles of making love to Thaisa behind his back. He denounced him as a liar and traitor, and warns him that unless the Prince frames himself to obey his dictate, he will—do something frightful, he implies; but playfully alters his tone: he will make Pericles and Thaisa man and wife. The king's heavy joke reflects the hostility that Oxford discerned in his father-in-law, and the enmity of the dramatist toward the old man, his paternal imago, his main rival for Countess Anne's love.

In the scene of the knights' feast (2.3) the lovers silently confront each other and the author's oral fervor manifests itself eloquently. Pericles, unable to share in the banquet, says to himself:

> By Jove, I wonder, that is king of thoughts,
> These cates resist me, she but thought upon. (2.3.28-29)

Thaisa makes his thought explicit:

> By Juno, that is queen of marriage,
> All viands that I eat do seem unsavoury,
> Wishing him my meat. (2.3.30-32)

He devours her instead with his eyes.

After their wedding comes news of the death of Antiochus and his daughter, both stricken by lightning as they were riding in a chariot. This punishment for their "heinous capital offense" is not enough. Their shriveled bodies are next endowed with a stench that stops charitable souls from burying them. The chariot seems to be the poet's contribution to the narrative of their fate. Perhaps he was unconsciously remembering the sight of the Lord Treasurer and Lady Anne in a coach, with the very horses that he sent his wife from France.

In Twine's *Pattern* the report from Antioch carries with it the proclamation that the city and its crown now belong to the Prince of Tyre. He and his queen then set sail for Antioch. Shakespeare, on the contrary, steers them to Tyre, without a word of Pericles' right to the realm of Antiochus. His protagonist is incapable of taking a crown defiled by incest and murder.

From the beginning of Act 3 to the end, the poetry of Pericles differs so magnificently from the preceding scenes that many have refused to attribute them to the same hand. A host of critics hail the last three acts for their lyric quality in Shakespeare's master vein. He transfigured the plot along with the verse. The centre of attention becomes the child of Pericles and Thaisa, the girl whom the poet named Marina because she was born at sea. The loving care which he bestowed on her story marks this part of the drama as a labor of his old age, the result of long brooding over the sorrows and re-sponsibilities and blisses of fatherhood. Analysis of the legend of Marina would be out of place here, since our concern is with the dramatist's apprenticeship, the early passions, mistakes and fantasies that made the man called Shakespeare an artist of the stage.

We note that the Prince prays to the moon-goddess Lucina to lighten his wife's birth-pains. He appeals to Lucina with the title "Divinest patroness," making her male and female. Afterward he swears by "bright Diana," tho Lawrence Twine's record of the same incident simply says that he swore an oath. He and Thaisa are parted in the storm—divorced, not by shipwreck, like the father and mother in *Errors*, but by the apparent death of Thaisa and its frightening effect on the sailors who wish her body thrown overboard. In the *Pattern of Painful Adventures* the hero cries distracted over his queen: "What shall I now answer to thy father for thee?" and "Would God thou haddest remained with him at home." Whatever our poet thought of these outcries, he left no echo of them in the play. Thaisa is placed in a chest with spices and gems, and thrown to the waves, which transport her to the city of Ephesus, the scene of the *Comedy of Errors*.

Here the gentle physician Cerimon revives her. (The portrait of Cerimon forms, in my surmise, a tribute by the poet to Dr. George Baker, who attended Lady Oxford in illness and dedicated to her in 1576 his *New Jewel of Health*. Ten years after her death he reprinted it under the title, *The Practice of the New and Old Physic*, with the dedication changed and addressed to the Earl.) At Cerimon's advice the broken-hearted queen becomes a votaress in the temple of Diana. As Twine puts it, she joins the Ephesian moon-deity's "nuns." Among them she grows to the dignity of the abbess Aemilia in *Errors*.

Meanwhile Pericles has sailed to Tarsus, and left his baby daughter in the care of Cleon and Dionyza, whom he had befriended in their time of famine. In a hurry to make peace among the factions of Tyre he returns to his city. (Apollonius, on the other hand, turns merchant and voyages to Egypt for trade. Shakespeare could transform the merchant's son Antipholus to a warrior, but he would not condescend to have his Pericles become a businessman.) At home in Tyre the Prince, in Gower's phrase, "settled to his own desire," as if he had forgotten his daughter.

Cleon and Dyonyza raise Marina with their own daughter Philoten, who looks a wretch by comparison. The jealous mother plots the foreign princess's death, but pirates arrive in time to save the girl from murder. They kidnap her in slavery. (These rogues serve a Spaniard, "the great pirate Valdes," whose name possibly was borrowed from the Spaniard who commanded the siege of Leyden in 1574, when the Earl of Oxford sailed to see the war in the Netherlands.) King Cleon hides his wife's crime by pretending that Marina died.

I think it likely that the poet, in creating the characters of the king and queen of Tarsus, had in mind William and Mildred Cecil. When he abandoned his family in the crisis of 1576 they took charge of his girl's nursing and education. We know that between Oxford and Lady Burghley there existed a state of psychic war. He charged her with provoking contention in his household, desiring his death, and bereaving him of his wife. Drawing her as the cold-blooded Dionyza he was bound to produce a caricature, the product of infantile fear, like the witches (dream-distorted mothers) in fairy-tales.

Marina is carried to Mitylene and sold to a brothel keeper, but she gains her freedom and makes a livelihood with her needle.

Pericles fourteen years after his departure from Tarsus, returns to bring home his daughter. Cleon shows him her monument and the Tyrian, in dumbshow, laments, puts on sackcloth, and leaves in a mighty passion. He wanders, grieving and starving, to the harbor of Mitylene where Lysimachus, the governor, tries to help him. Marina, whom Lysimachus loves, is summoned to assist with her "sacred physic." There ensues a scene of vivid pathos in which Pericles emerges gradually from his dismal introversion to listen to the girl, and he discovers her identity. Worn out by ecstasy, with hallucination of music, he falls asleep; and the goddess Diana rises in his dream to call him to Ephesus:

> Perform my bidding, or thou liv'st in woe;
> Do it, and happy, by my silver bow. (5.1.238-239)

He responds, "Celestial Dian goddess argentine, I will obey thee." The goddess here represents the Queen, who had requested Oxford to let his unhappy wife come to the Court.

At Diana's temple in Ephesus, where Thaisa serves as high priestess, the hero thanks the deity for his good fortune. The scene calls up the memory of a speech in Plautus's comedy *The Glorious Soldier* which must have affected our dramatist deeply. It is the cry of joy of the slave-girl Philocomasium on her coming safe to Ephesus: "Light the fire on the altar that I may gratefully give praises and thanks to Diana of Ephesus and offer her the pleasing odor of Arabian incense. She saved me in the realms of tumultuous dwellings of Neptune, where I was so thrown about by angry waves."

Pericles announces that Marina still lives, and wears the goddess's "silver livery." Thaisa, listening, tries to speak to her husband and faints. "What means the nun?" he wonders. "She dies!" (In Twine's *Pattern* she runs to embrace him but he thrusts her away in disdain.) At last he recognizes his lost wife. And the happy old couple go to prepare for their daughter's marriage with the governor of Mitylene.

Near the end of the play we are informed that the people of Tarsus burnt Cleon and his mate for their abominable deeds. This doom was invented by the poet to parallel the fiery death of Antiochus and his princess.

We are also told that Thaisa's father is dead. In the *Gesta Romanorum*, the king of Pentapolis dies in the arms of the daughter and son-in-law. Twine gives the three a year of felicity together before Altistrates' funeral, and states that Apollonius then "applied himself to execute his father's testament." Our dramatist clearly thought this reunion one too many. He was willing to take Anne Cecil to his arms again, but to embrace her father—no. "Heavens make a star of him!" This pious wish of Pericles on learning of King Simonides' death leads me, in the light of the burning dooms of King Antiochus and King Cleon, the other surrogates of Lord Burghley, to believe that De Vere had a deep dark yearning for the extinction of his father-in-law by fire. It was certainly a consummation devoutly wished for the arch-heretic by many of the Earl's fellow Catholics, whose leaders Burghley hounded, racked, and hanged.

So our dramatist attained in dreamlike fiction the reconcilement he unconsciously wanted with his Anne. In the *Comedy of Errors* he went back in fantasy as a son to the bosom of his dead mother. This time he went as a father to her reincarnation in his wife. In reality, he remained single, solitary and melancholy, sick with self-love.

The romance of *Pericles* endeavored unaware to excuse the failure of the writer to carry out his duties as husband and father. His defense amounted to three old arguments: (1) The Countess cared more for her father than for him. (2) Affairs of state—including religious loyalties—and wild nature—the sea of sex—kept him apart from his family. (3) His child's guardians conspired to prevent him from ever seeing her. A fourth point might be added: The Countess's father blocked the path to reunion by staying alive and powerful. Shakespeare concealed the intellectual poverty of this apology with a fabric of melodious fairy-tale (leaning heavily on his source materials) ornamented with vigorous realism and humor, to which he probably added in the sunset of his art some lines of irony and compassion for the homeless, the poor, the victims of the social order and law. He wrote the drama in moods of self-glorification and self-pity, forgetful of the artist's duty of self-criticism. Years of labored scholarship had to pass before he learnt how to argue his case in the supreme tribunal of conscience and its mimic court of the theatre with the torch of justice directed at his dear self.

Toward the end of 1576, it appears that Oxford attempted to make his wife as comfortable materially as he could, without lowering himself to beg her forgiveness. He granted her the house at Wivenhoe and lodgings at the Savoy in London. Her father said that he "promised the Queen's Majesty to be wholly advised by me"–in economic matters of course. Yet the Earl wished to make the sons of his uncle Geoffrey the inheritors of the Earldom, though the heirs of his uncle Aubrey stood next in lineage to him. Geoffrey Vere's youngsters, Francis and Horace, afterward won reputation on the battlefields of the Low Countries as two of the extraordinary soldiers of the age. Lord Burghley disliked his son-in-law's plan. It was never carried out.

In January 1577 his Lordship sent Oxford another appeal for Anne—"whose grief," he declared, "is the greater and shall always be inasmuch as her love is most fervent and addicted to you, and because she cannot or may not without offense be suffered to come to your presence, as she desireth, to offer the sacrifice of her heart." De Vere's response is unknown. In the winter of 1577, however, his sister Mary and some Protestant friends devised a method to bring him and the Countess together again, knowing he had a strong desire to see his daughter. Unfortunately we have no record of the outcome of their kind plot.[26]

On Sunday, February 17, 1577, the players of Lord Charles Howard of Effingham, who sometimes acted as Chamberlain in the Earl of Sussex's place, presented before the Queen at Whitehall a drama entitled "The History of the Solitary Knight." The office of the Revels furnished armor with "targets," two glass vials, and bread for the performance.[27] For reasons which I trust our survey of *Pericles, Prince of Tyre* has already made plain, I consider "The Solitary Knight" the first version of Shakespeare's romance.

After Lord Charles Howard became the Admiral of England, the star of his troop was the tragedian Edward Alleyn; he listed in an inventory of his costume properties (without date) a pair of spangled French hose that he used in acting "Pericles," which I take to be an older form of the romance performed years later by the Lord Chamberlain's men, Shakespeare's own company.[28]

Dressed in the sparkling, subtle language of Shakespeare's old age, the ancient legend enraptured the aristocracy, which gladly embraced any pompous and pathetic fabrication to justify its neglect—not to mention maltreatment—of the mother country. It did the hearts of the nobility good to see a prodigal orphan of their class, after his flight from the challenge of a stern father and desertion of his people, bringing succor to a foreign folk, showing off his skill in the violence of a dead chivalry, capturing an heiress and losing both her and her child when sheltering and nourishing the family became an ordeal, yet welcomed in the end to the bosom of the mother like a long-lost beloved boy.

References

1   Georg Brandes, *William Shakespeare* (New York 1924) 582.
2   Quoted by W. J. Rolfe, ed. *Shakespeare's History of Pericles* (New York 1905) 14. The distinguished German critic Karl Elze shared Malone's view.
3   Brandes, *op. cit.* 579.
4   *Shakespeare's Library*, ed. John Payne Collier (London 1841) i, 1866.

5   Albert H. Smyth, *Shakespeare's Pericles and Apollonius of Tyre* (Philadelphia 1898) 15.

6   *Ibid.* 78.

7   *Shakespeare's Library*, i, 190.

8   *Calendar of Papal State Papers*, Vol. ii: *Memorial of the Affairs of the Netherlands and the Queen of Scots*, by Thomas Stukeley (1573). Cp. Martin Hume, *The Great Lord Burghley* (London 1898); G.R. Dennis, *The Cecil Family* (Boston, 1914).

9   *Calendar of Rutland Manuscripts* (British Public Record Office), Vol. i. Bernard M. Ward suggested that Lord Henry Howard was the author of the *Treatise of Treasons* (*The Seventeenth Earl of Oxford*: London, 1928, 131n.)

10 John Bayley, *The History and Antiquities of the Tower of London* (T. Cadell, 1825) ii, 473,477. Edmund Lodge, *Illustrations of British History* (London 1888) Vol. i.

11 On the intrigues of Lord Henry, see the Catholic Record Society's biography of his nephew, *The Venerable Philip Howard, Earl of Arundel*, ed. John Pollen and William MacMahon, S.J. (London 1919). For "The Earl of Oxford's Escape Plot," see Francis Edwards, S.J., *The Marvellous Chance: Thomas Howard, Fourth Duke of Norfolk, and the Ridolphi Plot* (London: Hart-Davis, 1968) Appendix 5.

12 Harleian MSS. 6991, fol. 9.

13 Lansdowne MSS. 14, 84, fol. 188.

14 *Calendar of Salisbury Manuscripts*, ii, 68.

15 Cf. A.A. Brill, "Poetry as an Oral Outlet," *Psychoanalytic Review*, 18 (Oct. 1931), 357-378; E. Bergler, *The Writer and Psychoanalysis* (New York 1950) passim.

16 *State Papers Domestic of the Reign of Elizabeth*, cli, 1581.

17 *Tarlton's Jests*, ed. Halliwell (London 1844).

18 Katherine E. Thomas, *The Real Personages of Mother Goose* (Boston 1930) 76.

19 Eva Turner Clark, "Through De Vere Country," *Shakespeare Fellowship News-Letter*, i (Aug. 1940) 3.

20 Freud, "Wit and Its Relations to the Unconscious," in *Basic Writings* (New York 1938) 796.

21 John Stow, *Annals* (1590), ed. Howes (London 1615) 669.

22 *Edward Webbe His Travels*, ed. Arber (London 1868) 32.

23 B.M. Ward, *The Seventeenth Earl of Oxford*, 60.

24 *Ibid.* 203. E.H. Fellowes, *William Byrd* (Oxford 1936) 3.

25 Calendar of Rutland MSS. i.

26 Ward, *op. cit.* 154-6.

27 *Documents Relating to the Office of the Revels*, ed Feuillerat (Louvain 1908) 270. The play may have been the inspiration for the brochure "The Praise of Solitariness" which was registered in July 1577, and seems to be no longer extant.

28 John Payne Collier, ed. *Memoirs of Edward Alleyn* (London: Shakespeare Society, 1841).

Chapter 4—THE LION AND THE LANCE
A Francophile Noble at Cymbeline's Court

The truest manner'd: such a holy witch
That he enchants societies unto him;
Half all men's hearts are his. (*Cymbeline*, 1.6.166-168)

I

Let us wing our imaginations into the past four hundred courses of the sun and behold as clearly as we can the young dramatist Edward de Vere, the seventeenth Earl of Oxford, celebrating his twenty-seventh birthday, on 12 April 1577. I believe he would have begun the day with a solemn breakfast trying to be cheerful with his servants and his sister Mary, whose mind, most likely, was then twinkling and dancing with reflections about her tall admirer Peregrine Bertie, Lord Willoughby. Her brother would have been hardly pleased to observe the little attention she gave his nativity date. Perhaps on this morning they enjoyed the company of their courageous cousins Francis and Robert, whose brains were diligent with schemes for military careers to be made from the civil war in France. They talked of enlisting in the army of the brother of King Henri III, Hercules the Duke of Alencon and Anjou. Seventeen-years-old Francis and fifteen-years-young Robert, the elder sons of Lord Edward's uncle Geoffrey Vere and his bride Elizabeth Hardekin, filled him with pride of blood. He bothered Lord Burghley intensely at this time with plans or dreams to make these lads the heirs of the Oxford earldom and fortune—with its alp-load of debts. Surely he introduced them to his servant Denis Comry, the Frenchman, and Walter Williams, the Welsh daredevil, who also wanted to join the fighting in France. In honor of their comradeship he may have regaled the breakfast with favorite foods from Essex, their home shire. Slices of cheese from the Colne river country, described by John Skelton, the old Poet Laureate:

A cantle of Essex cheese
Was well a foot thick,
Full of maggots quick:
It was huge and great
And mighty strong meat
For the devil to eat.

Warden pies, pears baked in deep dishes colored by saffron from Walden, which had been first cultivated in that community by the Earl's splendid teacher, Sir Thomas Smith "the flower of the University of Cambridge," Richard Eden the traveler and scholar had called him, distinguished among Englishmen for his "singular learning in all the sciences."[1] And they might have eaten heronshaw, the young and expensive marsh bird, which Prince Hamlet declares he can tell apart from a hawk, when the wind is not bewildering. If Oxford could not afford heronshaw, they would have feasted just as joyously on wildfowl from the home country, maybe marle (a kind of snipe), sheldrake or godwit, that some called goodwin (a curlew), or else fish from the Essex coast, bret (turbot) or oxbird, the dunlin or sanderling, crowned by eryngo, the candied root of sea holly, familiar to good gullets of Colchester and Castle Hedingham from the pristine human ages, for their old wives and witches dug up its deep roots, along the northeastern shores of East Anglia, vowing they were God's own kindness for kidney stones.

Young Oxford would have found his nativity dawn blessed among the bookstalls that clustered in those days around Paul's Cathedral, where he would go to hear the children's wonderful singing, the boys whose brilliance in comedies, interludes, romances, enraptured him, and made him laugh until he felt his frailty and wished he had iron ribs.

Or he might have strolled from Oxford House, by the ancient London Stone in Candlewick Street, down thru Eastcheap, and inquired what diet of drama was served at the Bull Inn of Gracechurch Street near the Tower. He would have wondered if the Earl of Leycester's players, headed by James Burbage and his short sons Richard and Cuthbert, offered fare worth his pennies at the lavishly painted Theatre in Shoreditch or its companion playhouse, the Curtain.

He may have crossed London Bridge and gone wandering in Southwark, on the Bankside of the Thames, taking noontide beakers of beverages with bright-witted apprentices of printers near the Cathedral, young fellows like Anthony Munday, eager to learn foreign tongues, and his kinsman William Hall, or unemployed Masters of Arts from Oxford or Cambridge, like John Lyly, toiling at this time on the artifice of stiffly structured prose entitled *Euphues*, later called *The Anatomy of Wit*. As I see De Vere on this day, he would not have been distracted from the ideas that revolved more or less madly behind his brow by winks or warbles from the Dolls and Nells he met, the gay "geese" from the brothels off whose rent the Bishop of Winchester fatly thrived.

I suppose he would have walked to nearby Bermondsey House for a dinner with his dearest friend, Thomas Radcliff, Earl of Sussex, Lord Chamberlain of the royal household, or dined with a small group of friends on the other side of the river at the home of Lord John Lumley. The qualities of Lumley were so unusual in England that even his native friends must have marveled about the tenacity of the traits he inherited from his ancestors of the Lomellini family, who came from Italy to settle in Britain more generations ago than any of his kin could recall. This profoundly devout Roman Catholic cherished wide-ranging interests in classic literature, contemporary painting, and the advancement of medicine and surgery. At the Sussex table or Lumley's the conversation would have been the best to be heard in Europe, concerned primarily with the cruxes of their culture, the major problem of arms and the arts, religion and the realm. They would have discussed the enigmatic personality of Juan Quixada, the bastard son of the Emperor Charles V, to whom Queen Elizabeth had sent Sir Edward Horsey in December 1576 to offer him English soldiers if the States of Netherlands in revolt against the Spanish empire dared to call the French to help them. Relatives of Radcliff and Lumley were prominent among the English Catholic rebels who had resisted the Tudor dynasty. "The rebels swarm about Don John, being come unto him of late the lewd Earl (of Westmoreland), Stukley the Romanist... besides the whole rabble of the rest."[2] So fumed Dr Thomas Wilson from Holland on February 19, 1577. But on March 6 Dr Wilson wrote to Burghley that he would ride with Master Philip Sidney to Louvain to visit Don John, who "surpasses Circe, everyone who comes in contact with him comes to his devotion."[3] Don John strove to convince the Catholics of the Low Countries that he had come, not as a conqueror, but a peacemaker. He fulfilled his promise to remove Spanish troops from the embattled provinces, and governed with none but Italian and German mercenaries, welcoming many a brave Englishman and Scot under his flag. The heroic and wise warrior from Wales, Roger Williams, whose identification with Shakespeare's Fluellen is practically as secure as the equation of William Cecil with Polonius, ended his service with the Spanish general Mondragon in April 1577 and entered the household of King Philip's halfbrother, John. I know of no document connecting the valiant Roger with the jolly Walter Williams by marriage or sanguinity. There is one document revealing that Roger Williams belonged to the Earl of Oxford's group early in 1576: a letter by Sir Francis Vere, dated in November 1605, recalls a curious Briton: "such a man I saw when I was very young at Paris, by reason of the company I kept with Sir Roger Williams and one Denys a Frenchman, followers of my Lord of Oxford's..."[4]

The twenty-seventh birthday of the Earl of Oxford was perhaps wet and saddened by news of the final malady of John Neville, the last Lord Latimer. The fourth Baron Latimer was the son of Dorothy de Vere, a daughter of John, the twelfth Earl of Oxford, who died with his son Aubrey under the royal ax for combatting the crown right of the house of York. John Neville died on April 23, the date assigned to the birth of William Shakspere according to a tradition nobody can trace, but which makes sense only when we remember that the astronomic reckoning of the Roman church changed the date of Edward de Vere's birth to April 23 by the decree of Pope Gregory XIII in 1582.

In my fantasy of Earl Edward's birthday he fell into an after-dinner slumber from which he woke somewhat disquieted. His dream had not turned out altogether triumphant. Maybe memories of money he owed or invested in hazardous undertakings troubled him. His investment in the second expedition of Captain Frobisher to the northwest Atlantic arrived late. Martin Frobisher and his crew left Blackwall on May 26 and sailed to the white wild wilderness of Greenland, which they explored for gold. Oxford wanted gold or silver badly. I am confident that the joy he experienced in watching the prosperity and plaudits of the Children of Paul's Cathedral and the Lord Chamberlain's men, the actors of the Earl of Sussex, when they played his *History of Errors*, and *The Solitary Knight*, was broken, embittered by temptation to share in their gains. The rumor that his Calvinist rival for the love of Anne Cecil, Master Philip Sidney, might marry a daughter of William the Silent, Prince of Protestants in the Low Countries, and obtain the governorship of Zeeland and Holland, would inflame young Oxford but not warm his heart.[5]

Philip returned to the Court on June 8, and his family steward informed Sir Henry Sidney, the war-weary father in Ireland, "Mr Sidney is returned safe into England, with great good acceptation of his service at her Majesty's hands, allowed of by all the Lords to have been handled with great judgment and discretion: and hath been honored abroad in all the Princes' Courts with much extraordinary favor."[6] The worldly welfare of this advocate of Salvation by Grace predestined instead of the medieval mode of Salvation by Good Works, sacraments, penances, charities, would have provided De Vere with plenty to shoot barbed puns and other smart sayings. But these would not make the sunset of April 12 a vision of loveliness for the Earl.

The success of his comedy and romance on the stage paled below the shadow of his knowledge that these plays failed to do justice to the gloomy story of Ned and Nan de Vere. In the *Comedy of Errors* he had ungallantly put the blame for the breach of their marriage on his weak little wife, while protesting to the supreme court of his conscience that the poor girl must not be condemned too infernally for this because she had made her main mistake by marrying a stranger, indeed a demigod. In the romance of *Pericles, the Prince of Tyre* he had presented her once more as a wicked woman, but the victim of a vile father. He needed no profound insight, no probes at all, to realise the Countess was innocent of every charge or insinuation that his kissing cousins, the Howards, and their circle of wine-weltering wits like Charles Arundel and Rowland York, could spray at her name. Yet how could he conceive of her as guiltless of any sin against him without condemning himself as a scoundrel and fool? He searched, he scoured, and he discovered a way to relieve his colossal vanity of the charges mounting against it in his mind. He wrote another romance, this time accusing Anne Cecil's mother of wrecking his marriage. The seed of this play, which I believe with Eva Turner Clark was originally entitled *The Cruelty of a Stepmother*, and is now to be read in the severely revised shape of the play we call *Cymbeline*, could have been planted by a pamphlet, no longer extant, that came from a London press in mid-June, *The Praise and Dispraise of Women*. For that is the central theme of *Cymbeline*.

Lady Mildred (Cecil) had been extolled by Richard Edwards, Master of the Queen's Chapel children in choral and theatrical training, in her girlhood:

> Coke is comely and thereto
> In book sets all her care.
> In learning with the Roman dames
> Of right she may compare.[7]

Her austere countenance appears thru the honesty of Hans Ewouts's paintbrush in the portrait opposite page 34 in Evelyn Read's little volume *Catherine Willoughby* (New York 1964), which displays her coat of arms surmounted by a monstrous Medusa-like face. At Westminster Abbey one may find her effigy and that of the Countess of Oxford on the Burghley monument.

On Sunday, 28 December 1578, Thomas Blagrave, the clerk of the royal Revels, noted in his accounts, "*An history of the creweltie of a Stepmother* (was) shewen at Richmond on Innocentes daie at night enacted by the Lord Chamberlaynes servauntes furnished in this office with sondrey thinges."[8] *Cymbeline,* wrongly titled in the first folio edition of Shakespeare's dramatic works a "Tragedy," still deserves to be subtitled "The Cruelty of a Stepmother." The nameless Queen of the romance remains the power behind the throne and the drama from *Actus Primus* to the concluding word, "Peace." She was a widow when King Cymbeline wedded her, we are never told why. Her soul's desire, the prime motive of her plot, is to marry her son Cloten—called Clotten a half-dozen times in the play, and his head "Clotens Clot-pole" (4.2)—to the King's daughter, the Princess Imogen. Frustrated by Imogen's clandestine wedding with the "poor, but worthy Gentleman" Posthumus Leonatus, the Queen gets revenge by managing the expulsion of Posthumus from Britain, altho her very first words in Scene Two strive to persuade the Princess that she is her generous friend.

No, be assur'd you shall not find me, daughter,
After the slander of most step-mothers,
Evil-ey'd unto you. (1.1.70-73)

However "this Tyrant, such a crafty Devil," "A woman that / Bears all down with her brain," (2.1.52-53) does not live up to her description on the stage. We listen to a Courtier lament,

Alas, poor Princess,
Thou divine Imogen, what thou endur'st,
Betwixt a Father by thy Step-dame govern'd,
A Mother hourly coining plots. (2.1. 55-58)

But the story of the cruel stepmother in *Cymbeline* as it was first printed in 1623 has been transformed, suffered a metamorphosis that made it inferior in theatric significance to the calumny of Imogen by the Italian intruder Iachimo. In revising the romance, the playwright so far forgot his nameless Queen that her beloved son goes to pursue the Princess, hopeful of rape, without telling his mother of his departure from the Court, without any word of farewell. He deserts her at the peak of her power, just after she and he had patriotically (or should we say matriotically?) goaded the King to defy the Roman empire, refusing to pay its British tribute, and made ready for war. Shakespeare could have combined the hunting of Imogen with Clotten's march to meet the Roman invasion. He might have kept the Queen in fascinating suspenseful view by showing her communicating with her militant son, even spying on his chase of the virgin heroine. Alas, the sole version of the romance we have appears to be poverty-stricken. Cymbeline's mistress disappears from the stage in the fifth scene of the third act, almost immediately after we hear her gloating about the doomed Imogen, wherever she may be, "She being down, / I have the placing of the British Crown." Several scenes later, we learn that the mysterious absence of Cloten has convulsed her with a fever of madness. The King grieves:

> My Queen
> Upon a desperate bed, and in a time
> When fearful wars point at me. (4.3.5-7)

Finally, Cymbeline is informed that she has deserted him,

> With horror, madly dying, like her life,
> Which, being cruel to the world, concluded
> Most cruel to her self. (5.5.31-33)

For no clear reason, the Queen at last confest that she married Cymbeline, who is barely better than an imbecile, for ambition of royalty, not love. In fact, she "Abhorr'd your person." He cries out, "She alone knew this," exalted by her skill in dissembling. When he learns how she plotted to poison his daughter, he exclaims;

> O most delicate Fiend!
> Who is't can read a Woman?

Cloten's failure to return to her, he is told, drove her to despair and the shameless revelation of her "purposes." But she died repentant: "The evils she hatch't were not effected." Cymbeline consoles himself: "she was beautiful," says he, "It had been vicious / To have mistrusted her."

Seeking to undo her deadly schemes, and overjoyed by the restoration of his Princess, and the valor of his Britons who have fought Roman legions to a bloody stand-still, he consents to waging peace, and paying tribute to Rome.

Strange as it may seem, the writer of this quaint perversion of history was not afraid to offend his countrymen by showing ancient English heroes submitting to the sovereignty of imperial Rome. In his time Roman Empire meant the "Holy Roman Empire," that is the royal house of Hapsburg, headed by Maximilian II of Austria and his brother-in-law Philip II of Spain. To ordinary English ears of course the name Rome signified the capital of the Catholic Church, whose crowned head claimed to be the viceroy of the Kingdom of Christ. In 1570 Pope Pius V, the last pope to be promoted to sainthood, hurled against Queen Elizabeth his bull of anathema, commanding all English folk faithful to the Kingdom of Christ to throw her monarchy to hell. Seven years after, in June, agents of Burghley's espionage captured the priest Cuthbert Mayne in Cornwall; he had earned immortality by bringing the Pope's bull into England, but for that bravery Burghley arranged for Mayne to be condemned in September 1577 to hanging and quartering.

In 1577 Henry Bynneman printed *The first volume of the chronicles of England, Scotland and Ireland...* from the first inhabiting unto the Conquest, from which our poet probably drew his raw material for *Cymbeline*. Raphael Hollingshead's Cronycle simply copied from the old cloister legends or lies of Geoffrey of Monmouth's *History of the Kings of Britain* and similar unreliable sources. Our dramatist wanted background for his romance from the history of English relations with Rome. So he took the tale of Cymbeline, "a strenuous knight that had been nurtured in the household of Augustus Caesar. He had contracted so close a friendship with the Romans that, altho he might well have with held the tribute from them, yet nevertheless he paid it of his own free will." When he died Cymbeline yielded the helm of the state to his eldest son Guiderius, who refused to send Rome the treasure due. The Emperor Claudius attacked the obstinate island; his general Lelius Hamo killed King Guiderius, whose brother Arviragus became king and forced the Romans to retreat to the coast. Claudius "chose rather to subdue him by prudence and policy than to run the hazard of a doubtful encounter," and offered a peace treaty the Britons welcomed. Arviragus married the princess Genuissa, daughter of the Roman Emperor.[9]

II

On July 12 in a year I forgot to record, an English archeologist, Ridsdill Smith, announced the discovery of a grave on Hertford Heath which contained the ruins of a wheeled vehicle, strips of iron and bronze, a glass bowl and a quantity of pottery. "The things were of such richness and importance," said this researcher in British antiquity, "that clearly they belonged to a chieftain, possibly even King Cunobelin." This chief belonged to the tribe of the Belgi, kin of the courageous Belgae extoled by Julius Caesar in his *Gallic War*. Edward de Vere may have heard about him in boyhood, when he studied Caesar's report on the conquest of Gaul with his uncle Arthur Golding, who translated and published the Martial Exploits in the *Realm of Gallia* in 1565, dedicated to Sir William Cecil. The Earl of Oxford, remember, was a royal ward, probably tutored by Golding when the lad lived with Cecil at his house in the Strand in Westminster. When the Roman general Caius Lucius (there is no Lelius Hamo in *Cymbeline*) greets the British king (3.1.5-7), he calls

> Cassibulan, thine Uncle,
>
> Famous in Caesars praises, no whit less
>
> Than in his feats deserving it.

Caesar called the Briton Cassivellanus; Golding made it Cassibelan in his translation. If little Edward de Vere heard about the barbaric chief Cunobelin, he gave no sign of such awareness, altho some caves in chalk beds of Little Thurrock in Essex were called, as late as 1880, Cunobelin's gold mines.[10]

When Shakespeare composed the protoplastic Cymbeline he had no intention of amusing his public with rusty dusty history. He aimed to convey a political lesson like that of the chronicle-tragedy of *Ferrex and Porrex* or *Gorboduc* by Thomas Norton and Thomas Sackville, later Lord Buckhurst. This play was printed in 1571, "about nine year past" its playing at the Inner Temple law school. The authors hammered its moral metrically yet plain enough:

> These mischiefs spring when rebels will arise
> To work revenge and judge their prince's fact. (5.2)

The Earl of Oxford still despised all the Dutch for lifting heretic arms against Spain, not only the briny brutes who robbed him when he crossed the Channel to Dover in April 1576. He did not wish John Norris and his three hundred English volunteers luck when they sailed to Dunkirk in July 1577 to join the Prince of Orange. Nor was he thrilled in the same month when a Belgian gentleman named De Vers led soldiers of Brabant in battle against the mercenaries of Don John and defeated them. He cordially agreed with Elizabeth when she exhorted Orange and the insurgent States "to submit themselves to their sovereign Lord and King in all humility."[11] One of the curious facts about *Cymbeline* indicating its connexion with the war of William the Silent and Philip the somber is the stage direction calling for "a Dutchman, and a Spaniard" to witness the bet of Posthumus Leonatus on the virtue of his wife (1.3). But they are given nothing to say, in the current text. When Cymbeline, under the warlike spell of his Queen, reminds the Roman officer that his threats arrive at the same time "That the Pannonians and Dalmatians, for / Their Liberties, are now in arms: A Precedent / Which not to read would show the Britons cold" (3.1.72-74), we are reminded of the arguments employed by the Dudleys and Sidneys for British intervention in the Netherlands war. Shakespeare invented the Pannonian and Dalmatian campaign for their freedom; and Eva Turner Clark rightly remarked that the phrase only signified the Belgians and Dutch.[12]

Possibly the poet intended to glorify the Welsh people when he gave the three foremost fighters of his battle of Britain against Rome Welsh names. Yet particular warriors from Wales would be instantly remembered by many a man in his audience when Belarius calls himself Morgan. Few Britons enjoyed sweeter fame than Thomas Morgan in 1577, specially nicknamed "the warrior." He led the first volunteers from the west to serve under the Orange banner. Belarius is presented as a scarred hero of his breed.

Shakespeare invented Belarius and the boys kidnapped from the cradles of their father King Cymbeline, Guiderius alias Polydore (a Greek name!) and Arviragus alias Cadwal (also Welsh). The dramatist wanted these princes and their runaway fosterfather to be mountaineers who would give his fugitive Imogen a resting place, and the road to reconciliation with her husband-hating King. In my judgment, Polydore was shaped in the image of Oxford's cousin Francis, a torrid tempered young man, perfectly capable of killing a Cloten despite the latter's royal blood. Therefore I fancy that our poet made Cadwal in the semblance of Robert Vere, the younger brother. Mourning over what he imagines is the corpse of Imogen, he declares he would rather "Have skip'd from sixteen years of age to sixty" (4.2.199) than seen her thus. Robert Vere was born in 1562; we have no record of his birthday. But we may be sure that Shakespeare defined the characters of the two brothers precisely when he made Belarius wonder

> That an invisible instinct should frame them
> To Royalty unlearn'd, Honor untaught (4.2.177-178)

Perhaps the very name of Arviragus attracted the poet to draw him as a living portrait of Robert, since the first two syllables would recall R. Vere to the Earl. We know too little about his personality, whether he was in reality gentler and more loving than his older brother. Practically all we know about Robert is that he died fighting for the liberty of the Low Countries, the first of the fighting Veres to give his life for that cause. In 1577, however, we find him and Francis, ever loyal to the beliefs of the head of their house, the Earl of Oxford, offering to fight under the flag of the King of France against the Huguenots, for Catholic authority against Calvinistic revolt. The fighting Veres probably never read *The Staff of Chris-*

tian Faith, a Protestant polemic translated from the French by John Brooke of Ashe, and dedicated in 1577 to the Earl of Oxford in vain.

If the Earl glanced over Arthur Golding's translation of John Calvin's *Sermons on the Epistle to the Ephesians*, which Golding completed on January 7, 1577, he did it out of affection for his uncle, not to acquire more insight than he already had into Puritan theories of divine providence and its care for empires and sparrows. He would have been more profoundly interested in the theory of Father Nicholas Sanders that the health and holiness of the Roman faith required the overthrow of the Anglican crown. Father Sanders, whom Oxford admired immensely, pleaded for years, as he declared to William Allen, founder of the English Catholic college in the Netherlands: "The state of Christendome dependethe uppon the stowte assaylying of England."[13] He might as well have been mute. Rome continued to travel the primrosy rottenness of Madrid, which wanted to squander Catholic strength in the Netherlands, wasting on them the silver it stole from Central and South America.

We get an entertaining glimpse of Francis and Robert Vere in this period from letters of the English ambassador Amyas Paulet in France. He wrote to Francis Walsingham on July 10, 1577, from Poitiers, that "the two young Veres, Denny, and Walter Williams, servants to the Earl of Oxford," had "resolved to follow the Duke of Guise into Champagne," supporting his effort to vanquish the Calvinist rebels encouraged by the kingdom of Navarre.[14] On September 24, he sent Walsingham vivid details:

> You desire to be informed if I gave a horse to young Vere. I fear my action has been questioned, and shall not be quiet till I hear the true cause of your motion.
>
> The two young Veres came to this town accompanied by Denny and Williams, and after two or three days the elder Vere and Williams came to me, and Vere told me that he came into this country with intent to serve in the wars, and finding the army of Monsieur [Alencon] broken, and thereby frustrate of his expectation, was constrained to return to Paris. Having no

money to buy horses, he would be obliged to travel on foot, unless I could provide him, and therefore desired me to bestow a horse upon him.

I answered that I had not so many horses as I had servants, and was far from any means to get more, so that I could not spare those that I had. He confessed he was very bold with me upon so small acquaintance (as indeed I had never seen him before), but begged me to do the best for him. I told him that I would be ashamed for the honor of my country and for the reputation of the Earl of Oxford that he should go to Paris on foot, and therefore would provide him with an ambling nag, trusting that he did not look for a horse of service at my hands, which I could not spare.

I caused the horse to be delivered to this gentleman, who sold him the next day, and prayed Mr [Michael] Lock, who was then here, to say nothing of this horse to my Lord of Oxford. The transaction 'doth decipher the disposition of the gentleman.' God send him better company to make him a better man.

It may be said that, knowing his intention to serve of the King's party under the leading of the Duke of Guise, I ought not to have given him any aid. If he had been my kinsman or friend, I would not have failed to dissuade him; but others had been recommended not long before to serve here in like sort by great personages in England, and Mr Lock told me that those only had reputation among the nobility of the Court that sought to serve on the King's side, and therefore, in my single opinion, I had played the fool if I had made a quarrel of this matter. And, to be plain with you, I was not sorry to see some young fellows of no great 'countenance or service' join the King's party...[15]

On November 19 Paulet reported to Walsingham, "Deny and Williams are recommended to Don John by the Duke of Guise, and serve in the Castle of Namur," along with other Englishmen of Papist persuasion.[16] The adventures of the Veres at this moment remain a mystery.

Presumably, Edward de Vere was thinking of going himself with his cousins and servants to France when Robert Dudley, Earl of Leycester, wrote to Burghley on June 13, 1577 ("this foul Thursday"),

> I am sorry my L of Oxford should for any report think any more of going oversea. I can but wish and advise him to take such course in all things as were best and most honourable for him & specially in his consideration toward her Majesty & his country.[17]

Oxford's father-in-law complained about ill health, and decided in mid-July to visit Buxton Wells and drink its medicinal waters. On July 18 the Queen gave him leave to go, and soon he journeyed in the company of his son Thomas and Roger Manners, kinsman of the Earl of Rutland, whose humor was infinitely fed by observation of William Cecil, whom he nicknamed Pondus. The Lord Treasurer told Manners he would travel "with as much speed as my old crazed body will suffer me."[18] Sir Thomas Smith joined them at Buxton in his last desperate attempt to defeat the cancer that was putting him to death. On August 12 Sir Thomas was buried by his home on Theydon Mount in Essex, a short ride from Oxford's birthplace. It is difficult to believe that the Earl would not have been among the friends who attended the funeral, and heard the epitaph Smith wished to be carved on his grave:

> What yearth, or Sea, or Skies contayne,
>> what Creatures in them be,
>> my Minde did seeke to know,
>> the Heavens continually.

In Sir Thomas's will he left to a certain Henry Butler his copy of Geoffrey Chaucer's works. His former pupil must have coveted it.

I should have mentioned in reviewing the portrayal of the Earl's cousins in the roles of the two heroic princes of the play that our dramatist seems to have endowed them with doubles. For Shakespeare invented a pair of brothers for the hero of *Cymbeline*, whom he borrowed from the *Decameron* of Giovanni Boccaccio, the two young men, "who in the Wars o' th' time / Dy'd with their Swords in hand." (1.1.34-35) Oxford must have been tormented with visions of his fighting "brothers" killed in battle far from home. His "prophetic soul," imagining things to come, could not foretell that Francis and his famous younger brother Horace would close long and sanguine careers on their native land and die serenely in bed.

Naturally De Vere drew himself in the drama in the role of Posthumus, a heroic warrior fighting for Britain against foreign tyranny. No matter what politics he pursued at Court, he loved his mother-country and could not bear the thought of Roman boots treading on her. When Posthumus dons the uniform of a Roman toward the end of the play, his purpose is manifestly to seek a death which he believes he merits for having contrived the murder of Imogen. It is pure romance, unlike his passion for the maternal earth and the children of the land, which can be constantly confused with the devotion to the state, church or government, which is called patriotism.[19] Oddly enough, De Vere never appears to have reacted to the thought of a French invasion of Britain with fury. I believe that he regarded the Gallic religion as different in kind, not merely in creed, from the Spanish Catholic faith. He would have been glad to bend his pride and belong to the same church that Montaigne, Michel de L'Hospital and Rabelais worshipt in.

Cymbeline confesses with all the clarity that our poet had in his power that he had parted from his wife unfairly, "enticed," as her father avered, "by certain lewd persons to be a stranger" to her. Oxford knew that he had listened to the obscene suggestions of Rowland York and his cup-companions with alacrity. We can see how readily he believed the York accusation of cuckoldry in the scene where Posthumus the lion-hearted swallows in a flash the proofs supplied by Iachimo in Rome that he had enjoyed the body of Imogen. The Italian liar tells him of her bedchamber tapestry "of silk and silver," picturing Cleopatra meeting Mark Antony on the river Cydnus, the chimney-piece with "Chaste Dian bathing," and so on; then Iachimo reveals the bracelet he got from her arm. And the Briton betrays his utter ignorance of the girl he married: "O no, no, no, 'tis true." He hands over at once the diamond she gave him when he swore. "I will remain / The loyal'st husband, that did e'er plight troth." When a friend tries to convince him the girl whose sweetness and radiance of soul he had extoled so devoutly before had not "bought the name of Whore thus dearly," he takes a breath of reasonableness, expecting evidence that could not be bribed; Iachimo tells of the mole beneath her breast (about which a servant could have told him). The miserable husband howls, he will tear her "Limb-meal": / I will go there and do't, i' th' Court, before / Her Father. I'l do something." Later we listen to him threatening: women,

> I'l write against them,
> Detest them, curse them: yet 'tis greater Skill
> In a true Hate, to pray they have their will:
> The very Devils cannot plague them better. (2.5.32-34)

Probably the dramatist remembered the charge of his halfsister Katherine Windsor against him and sister Mary when he affirmed from the mouth of Posthumus, "We are all Bastards."

> And that most venerable man, which I
> Did call my Father, was I know not where
> When I was stampt... yet my Mother seem'd
> The Dian of that time: so doth my Wife
> The non-pareil of this. Oh Vengeance, Vengeance! (2.5.2-8)

Shakespeare's mind however remained distant from genuine ideas of revenge; he always chose rather to torture himself. In the play his hero follows the just quoted cry with a personal remembrance that admits us for a moment into the dramatist's bedchamber and his wife's privacy:

> Me of my lawful pleasure she restrain'd,
> And pray'd me oft forbearance; did it with
> A prudency so rosy, the sweet view on't
> Might well have warm'd old Saturn;
> That I thought her as chaste as unsunn'd snow. (2.5.9-13)

When Imogen and Posthumus found occasion for these charming exchanges puzzles everyone who has observed with marveling how the poet developed her character thru his absurd plot. He wedded her secretly, keeping her at home with King Cymbeline, while Posthumus took what chances he dared under the watchful jealous eyes of the Queen. In my opinion, Shakespeare betrayed in these lines, or the old verses we find here reformed, how he missed the amorous mood of his Anne. He chastised himself for unkind handling of her, while denouncing her parents for making it impossible, in his conviction, for them to dwell in peace. And he recalled how William and Mildred Cecil had taken pains to engage her to Master Philip Sidney, before they saw their path clear to promoting Nan to Countess of Oxford. Imogen defines her torments tersely:

> A father cruel, and a Stepdame false,
> A foolish suitor... O, that Husband,
> My supreme crown of grief, and those repeated
> Vexations of it.   (1.6.1-5)

How truly these lines accuse the parents of Anne Cecil, as well as the Earl of Oxford, we can tell from one fact. She must have received a quantity of letters from him in the sixteen months of his European tour. Imogen exclaims over her husband's handwriting:

> Oh, learn'd indeed were that astronomer
> That knew the stars as I his characters;
> He'd lay the future open.   (3.2.27-29)

Lord William recorded that on March 17, 1575, "The Earl departed from Paris and wrote to his wife, and sent her his picture and two horses." The "packets" Oxford mailed from Italy to England must have contained numerous messages to her. Lord William and Lady Mildred did not preserve a single letter to her, from anyone.[20]

III

Yet *Cymbeline*, or *The Cruelty of a Stepmother*, conveyed a dream of expectation of the writer, that there could be a road to reconciliation with the Cecils. His desire for reunion with Countess Anne kindled and fortified the hope. He freed her father from responsibility for the rupture of their marriage by demonstrating that Burghley managed to be a shrewd and despotic statesman while cherishing in his "old crazed body" the soul of a simpleton. The figure of Cymbeline, tho rigorously confined in the framework of royalty, evinces folly recalling Lord Polonius of Denmark. Hamlet asserts about the latter, "that great baby you see there is not yet out of his swathing-clouts" (2.2). And there is one contemporary testimony concerning Burghley which luridly illustrates Hamlet's label. The anonymous Catholic polemic against William Cecil and Nicholas Bacon called *A Treatise of Treasons* (1572), claimed for one John Cuthbert, but in the judgment of Bernard Ward and myself, verily the labor of Lord Harry Howard, describes Oxford's father-in-law thus: "authority fawneth on him, and, for everyone least thwart of his superiority, faineth either to be sick for sorrow or lame of the gout, & falleth to sighing & sobbing, crouching & kneeling, weeping & whining like a boy & a babe till his head be stroked & he comforted & called a good son again." The King of Britain in the romance is not remote from such posturing.

At the same time that our dramatist satirised Cecil mildly in the role of Cymbeline, Imogen's father, he transmuted and exalted him as a hero venerable, "an old man, attired like a warrior; leading in his hand an ancient matron, his wife and mother to Posthumus." (Stage direction of 5.4) In fact, Shakespeare subjected the image of Cecil to a metamorphosis making him appear his own father. Otherwise, how can we explain his naming the father of his protagonist *Sicilius*?

True, only the name identified the fantom of Sicilius Leonatus as a ghost meant to stand for Lord Burghley. Our poet warns us of the remoteness of the stage sire from the son by having old Sicilius die while his boy lay in his nameless matron's womb. This mother is no less a stranger to her son; she died so early, he had to be "ript" from her. Naturally the poet did not have William Cecil, the innkeeper's grandson, in mind when he presented Sicilius pouring glory on Posthumus in these terms:

> Great Nature, like his Ancestry,
> 　moulded the stuff so fair:
> That he deserv'd the praise o' th' World,
> 　as great Sicilius' heir.　　　　　(5.4.48-51)

And in the person of Posthumus our author, the descendant of sixteen earls of Oxford, separated his self-respect, or what we may designate his cultural or historic function, from Cecil's pride in the sharpest manner: "Statist though I am none, nor like to be" (2.4.16). Above all else, Burghley wished to be a statist, a politician. Our play however shows only three characters that can be called politicians: the "yellow Iachimo," whose activity flows in romantic ruts rather than affairs of state, tho he does emerge near the end as an army commander, "Siena's brother" (4.2); Cymbeline, bordering on impotence; and his Queen, who "Bears all down with her Brain," we are told, but scarcely see in her cunningest hour. Shakespeare displays her politically as a demagog, piping like a patriot: "Remember, Sir, my Liege, / The Kings, your ancestors, together with / the natural bravery of your Isle..." Especially she rallies the Britons to rise like they did "to master Caesar's Sword, / Made Luds-Town with rejoicing fires bright,/ And Britons strut with Courage" (3.1.16 -32) We are left to wonder why the King deplored her illness "in a time / When fearful Wars point at me" (4.3.6-7). He seems to miss his girl more, "Imogen, The great part of my comfort." As a statist, Cymbeline is outstanding only when he affirms the faith he holds in common with William Cecil, that "bitter torture shall / Winnow the truth from falsehood," a faith he affirms twice (4.3;5.5).

　We are given no clear hint of the age of Posthumus. Imogen reminds her father, "It is your fault that I have lov'd Posthumus: / You bred him as my Play-fellow" (1.2.143-145) Anne Cecil, her father noted on December 5, 1556, was born to him and Lady Mildred (born Cooke) between eleven and twelve at night. So the Countess of Oxford was "some twenty" years old at the time I imagine the original Cymbeline was conceived and staged. Imogen seems to be "Some twenty years" of age, according to the first scene of her story. When the King took the baby Posthumus into his home, he ordered the boy to be trained in "all the learnings that his time / Could make him the receiver of, which he took / As we do air, fast as 'twas ministered..."—growing up a courtier, exactly like the prince Ophelia loved—"A sample to the youngest: to th' more Mature, / A glass that feated them..." The King accuses the princess of aiming "To make my Throne / A Seat for baseness." Among the sins of Queen Elizabeth against Edward de Vere, none perhaps hurt him more profoundly than her angry terming him once a bastard: "for which cause he would never love her, and leave her in the lurch one day."[21]

Mrs Clark perceived that, for the manifest purport of the play, the dramatist landed his Romans at the port of Milford-Haven in Cambria, ancient Wales, but the place name merely disguised the little town he actually envisioned for the secret romance he was staging, Long Melford not far from Cambridge. Long Melford is near Lavenham, a Suffolk territory where most of the land once belonged to the house of Vere. The fighting Veres came from farms nearby. Percy Allen proved that Milford-Haven in *Cymbeline* signified Long Melford from the passage which informs us that Imogen there would be

> happily, near
> The residence of Posthumus; so nigh, at least,
> That though his Actions were not visible, yet
> Report should render him hourly to your ear,
> As truly as he moves. (3.4.148-152)

In the mind's eye this could have meant Castle Hedingham or Oxford's residence by the sea, Wyvenhoe.[22] Close to Lavenham and Long Melford stood the home of John de Vere, the fourteenth Earl

of Oxford, known for the miseries he inflicted on his wife which
Cardinal Wolsey strove to prevent.

We see what I take to be a personal reference in the scene of
Imogen's bedroom, where Iachimo emerges from concealment to
learn that

> She hath been reading late,
> The Tale of Tereus; here the leaf's turn'd down
> Where Philomel gave up.   (2.2.44-46)

Shakespeare does not mention Publius Ovidius Naso, yet we may
be sure that Imogen's volume is the same that Lavinia in *Titus Andronicus* (4.1) views with mute excitement; "so busily she turns the
leaves."

> What would she find? Lavinia, shall I read?
> This is the tragic tale of Philomel.
> And treats of Tereus' treason and his rape.

Young Lucius identifies the book in the tragedy: "Grandsire, 'tis
Ovid's *Metamorphoses;* / My mother gave it me." Our poet's mother's
brother Arthur Golding dedicated his translation of the *Metamorphoses* to the Earl of Leycester from Cecil House in the Strand on
December 23, 1564. William Seres printed the glamorous volume, in
which his fourteen-year-old customer, Edward de Vere, certainly
exerted an artistic hand; or should we say, a boy-magician's hand? In
what many consider the final play by Shakespeare, the beloved book
is quoted or closely paraphrased:

> Ye elves of hills, brooks, standing lakes, and groves,
> And ye that on the sands with printless foot
> Do chase the ebbing Neptune, and do fly him
> When he comes back... .   (5.1)

I think we almost hear the very voice of Anne Cecil de Vere in the
lines of Imogen sorrowing over the departure of Posthumus before

> I could tell him
> How I would think on him at certain hours,

Such thoughts, and such: Or I could make him swear,
The Shes of Italy should not betray
Mine Interest, and his Honour: or have charg'd him
At the sixth hour of Morn, at Noon, at Midnight,
T' encounter me with Orisons, for then
I am in Heaven for him; Or ere I could
Give him that parting kiss, which I had set
Betwixt two charming words, comes in my Father,
And like the Tyrannous breathing of the North,
Shakes all our buds from growing.   (1.3.26-27)

In the passage about meeting spiritually "with Orisons," one feels as if intruding on the soul of the girl baring herself to God for her love. It helps us to understand what Hamlet means when he greets the fair Ophelia with the words,

> Nymph, in thy orisons
> Be all my sins remember'd.

Imogen is granted no opportunity to return "The scriptures of the loyal Leonatus," kept beneath her bodice so that her heart could respond to the rhythm of his writings. She is stronger, more mature than Ophelia, and therefor more mutinous to her despotic father. It is the Princess who reminds herself, like Hamlet, "Against Self-slaughter / There is a prohibition so Divine, / That cravens my weak hand" (3.4). In modern productions of *Hamlet* we are shown the Prince indignantly flinging Ophelia to the ground when she appeals to him with an embrace. The episode may be unconsciously inspired by the actual throwing down of Imogen by her husband when she interrupts the ecstasy of masochism, the "wrath he hath against himself" (2.4), in which he plunges in exposing his unjust rage against his wife. She cannot endure hearing him cry out, "Thou, King, send out / For Torturors ingenious," and "My Queen, my life, my wife: oh, Imogen, Imogen, Imogen," and rushes to reassure him. He will not tolerate any diversion from favorite histrionics; he thrusts her to the floor: "Shall's have a play of this?"

he says, so blinded by his own playacting, he fails to detect that her cry, "Peace, my Lord, hear, hear," was wrung from no "sweet rosy lad" (5.5.228). When Posthumus delivers the eloquent speech, "O Imogen, I'll speak to thee in silence" (5.4.28-29), the author may have been thinking of communion in death; but he betrayed the fact that no poetic language could bridge the gulf between a self-worshiper like Posthumus and the pure-hearted Imogen, between Anne Cecil and Edward de Vere.

He could play the "holy Witch," and "enchant Societies," but he could not overcome his blindness to her radiance.

> He spake of her, as Dian had hot dreams,
> And she alone were cold.   (5.5.180-181)

Her rosiness struck him like a frost. So, unable to comprehend the bliss of her carnal knowledge of the pits and pinnacles of mother-hood (the Countess Anne had five children and lost two), he kept on comparing her to the phoenix, "She is alone, th' Arabian bird" (1.6), a virginal creature which can have no young. His insight into human nature bettered when he met individuals with whom he had more in common. Meanwhile he perused the magnificent folio called Edward de Vere. Iachimo pictures him as a guest in Italy:

>   none a stranger there
> So merry, and so gamesome: he is call'd
> The Briton Reveller.   (1.6.59-60)

Imogen, surprised, recalls the melancholy man (as we know him from *Errors* and *Pericles*, and will behold him again, more analytic of his mood, in *The Merchant of Venice*), she loved and married.

>   When he was here,
> He did incline to sadness, and oft-times
> Not knowing why.   (1.6.61-63)

She does not contradict the calumniator when he asserts or rather inquired, why she should continue suffering the distant insults of Posthumus, who compels her to "Live like Diana's Priest, betwixt cold sheets, / Whiles he is vaulting variable Ramps / In your despite, upon your purse." She is perfectly aware of the spells a "Roman Courtesan" could subdue her Lord with.

The lust of his Lordship suffered from at least two old handicaps. Closest to the surface of his awareness ran the constraint of inward blame for his evil desire. We get this expressed well enough from the lips of Iachimo:

> The heaviness and guilt within my bosom
> Takes off my manhood. I have belied a Lady. (5.2.1-2)

Posthumus renewed his virility in the Roman war because he goes into it play-acting, disguised as a poor soldier, a British peasant, but inwardly resolute to show the valor that can run in his veins after praying, "Gods, put the strength o' th' Leonati in me" (5.1.31). The lion-born: Shakespeare chose this name for his hero, in my belief, having in view his family coat-of-arms of the Viscounts Bolebec, which displays a lion brandishing a broken spear. Presumably the half-disarmed beast was intended to symbolise indomitable courage, lion-heartedness. The self-questioner, the self-tormenting dramatist appears to have been more interested in the broken lance. Perhaps it represented for him the tragic flaw of the Earls of Oxford, the occult weakness that made them all somehow descend into darkness ingloriously. To his vision, I feel sure, the rift in their instrument, which eventually made their music mute, was sexual. The spear signified for Shakespeare the male member. And he retained this illusion to his last breath.

Yet the truth of the matter seems to have fluttered on the tip of his tongue almost every time he used spontaneous metaphors in writing about erotic appetites. Thus Iachimo mingles the imagery of copulation with that of eating when he reminds Posthumus of the Mole under his wife's breast,

> that most delicate Lodging. By my life,
> I kist it, and it gave me present hunger
> To feed again, though full.   (2.4.136-138)

In the sequel scene, poor Posthumus denounces the tongue, without referring to the organ once, as the evilest organ in the human frame.

> Could I find out
> The woman's part in me, for there's no motion
> That tends to vice in man, but I affirm
> It is the woman's part: be it lying, note it,
> The woman's: flattering, hers; deceiving, hers:
> Lust, and rank thoughts, hers, hers. (2.5.19-24)

The poet who fancied Iachimo climbing on Imogen "Like a full Acorn'd Boar, a German one," knew that the German word for mouth, *Maul*, could be punned on to make it a blemish, a Mole. But he remained blind to the madness of his own mouth in the presence of the memory of his mother's bosom, the anger against her for "starving" him, immuring her milk, the fury which he vented on himself out of fear of defying the mighty. This fear and that fury turned into literature when he discovered how he could make believe that he did not need a mother but could produce milk magically for himself—out of black ink. His tongue first tested the magic, making the language and music which became the foundation of his art. Gladly he forgot the tongue, the source of his self pity and his power, and imagined himself a man of the pen, full of phallic feeling, not a mewling infant, after all. I suppose he did not even perceive the metaphor when he made Cloten plot to ravish Imogen with the words, "when my lust hath dined" (3.5.140). The boy Edward de Vere as little Viscount Bolebec early became accustomed to thinking of foining as feeding.

By the way, I must not forget to mention that Shakespeare probably took the name Posthumus from Ariosto's epic comedy *Orlando Furioso* (Book XLII) where a personage is applauded as

> Great Posthumus, to whom a double wretch
> Passas shall there and Phoebus here bequeath.

Just as the poet fondly combines an image of the sun-god and the morning star of Athens in praise of himself, he makes Imogen, mistaking the corpse of Cloten for her husband's, speak of "His foot Mercurial, his Martial thigh" (4.2.300). I view this line as having once been a rebuke to the poet and soldier and imperial messenger George Gascoigne, whose motto widely known was *Tam Marti quam Mercurio*. Another poet and soldier, George Whetstone, claimed to have been "an eye witness of his Godly and charitable End in this world", when Gascoigne "deceased at Stamford in Lincoln Shire, the 7 of October 1577."[23] Many years later the antiquarian Anthony Wood wrote that Gascoigne "made his last exit, or yielded to nature in his middle age, at his house in Walthamstowe" in Essex, "in October or November 1578, and was buried, as I suppose, in the church there." There is no record of such burial. The record of administration of the earthly goods George Gascoyne left at Walthamstowe, a court document of December 2, 1578, does not prove that he died at his home there.[24] In my opinion, Wood's account is a vestige of the Cecil devices that English Catholic runaways in Flanders called "Cicilian tricks,"[25] designed to hide the fact that Gascoigne had gone, in his last sickness, to Stamford, not on government affairs, but family business, of Thomas Cecil and his father William. Thomas dwelt at Burghley House about a mile from Stamford, the ancient town his father came from. Thomas's mother, like William's mother, had served as a tavern keeper's daughter. But his bride Dorothy Neville was the grand-daughter of Dorothy de Vere, and their daughter Diana became the wife of Henry de Vere, the 18th Earl of Oxford. On February 29, 1572, Thomas and Dorothy Cecil rejoiced in the birth of a boy whom they named Edward in a feast at Burghley House. This boy grew to be a great soldier, arduously educated in the craft of war by his relatives the fighting Veres. In October 1576 George Whetstone sent his book *The Rock of Regard* to the press, from his lodgings in Holborn. It contained piety named "The Orchard of Repentance" dedicated to Sir Thomas Cecil "weighing how deeply both my good mother and all her children are bound unto you for received friendships." In the book a section entitled "The Arbour of Virtue" has verses in honor of Mistress A. C., whom I take to be the Countess of Oxford. Whetstone's work lacks biographic interest, however, and literary value.

The character of Iachimo, I have no doubt, is a portrait of

George Gascoigne's fellow volunteer in the military service of William of Orange, Rowland York. This curious scoundrel, the ninth son of Sir John York, seems to have entered history as a volunteer with the Catholic rebels against Queen Elizabeth who threatened to make Mary Stuart queen of their northern shires in 1569. When the Earl of Sussex crushed the revolt, Rowland was forgiven because he was a young fool, and his brother Edward belonged to the retinue of Robin of Leycester. Gascoigne scribbled plenty of rimes about his and York's adventures military and amorous in the Low Countries, published in his chronicle *The Fruits of War* (1575) as part of the larger *Posies of George Gascoigne*. This wastrel joined the frolic ring formed by the Earl of Oxford in defiance of Baron Burghley, a circle dominated by Catholics, who valued York's company for unclear reasons. He won multitudes of admirers by being the first to demonstrate to the English the trick of employing the rapier with a swerve of hand to drive the point below the belt.[26] Reflecting on Rowland's last name and his service years later of betraying an English fort in the Netherlands to the Spaniards, our dramatist would have found it easy to name the villain in *Cymbeline* after Sant' Iago the patron saint of Spain, changing the name to its Italian form. The Earl of Oxford may have met Jacomo Manucci, the Italian who served the English embassy in France in 1578, and thought of him when he named "Siena's brother." Spiritually Iachimo is Norfolk's brother.

IV

There is a document preserved for centuries in the Cecil family archives, which their librarians have entirely failed to understand. They ascribe it by guesswork to Elizabeth Stanley, Countess of Derby, Oxford's eldest daughter. A cursory look at the faults or cruelties it lists informs us that these "Notes by an Ill-Used Wife" were inscribed or dictated by Lady Mildred of Burghley, Oxford's mother -in-law. Here is the grim and homely indictment complete.[27]

At Greenwich no board wages for two grooms, usher, page,

chamber keeper. After the cooks not paid. Horses lent to Smith before the progress. New nags for L13 sent to Theb. unshod, no money to defray.

Knocked up at i o'clock, waked.

Kept out of his chamber at dinner and supper by York and other within.

When Momerancy came no money to buy before he was landed.

Not speak a word nor countenance in father's house.

So many 100 pounds spent of ten thousand came to his hand since marriage.

Never one token of love in gown, button, aigrettes.

A hose-garter asked again.

No pillion to come from Wyvenhoe, but of poor golden fustian.

His man to demand a note of her small plate in her own hand given her; and he never speak himself. Linen spoiled, very fine and damask.

Women ij gotten with child; men entertaining them in chamber and not dare find fault because they were great about him.

iij M. *li.* since Easter lying at Greenwich.

Change of men to keep purse.

These Notes are not dated. The following chronology will help to illuminate the events and individuals to which they allude.[28]

1571 November 1: William Cecil, Master of the Royal Wards, calculated the Earl of Oxford's debt to the state, after nine years of Cecil's management of the boy's estates: "Fine for wardship–2000 pounds;" and "Fine for livery (costs of maintenance)–1257 pounds, 18 shillings, 3/4 pence." Cecil gained appointment as Master of the Wards and Liveries in 1561, "by means whereof he became rich," declared his agent John Clapham in *Certain Observations Concerning the Reign of Queen Elizabeth.*

December 14: Elizabeth ordered the Spanish ambassador Don Guerau Despes to leave England in four days. She wrote to the Duke of Alva, who was ferociously fighting insurgents against Spanish despotism in the Netherlands, "We can no more endure him to continue than a person that would secretly seek to inflame our realm with fire brands". But Don Guerau was allowed to linger in London until January.

December 19: Edward de Vere married Anne Cecil, after payment to the Crown for his "marriage right" as a ward of the Queen.

1572 January 4: The Earl of Oxford wrote his Latin letter prefacing *De Curiali* by his Cambridge University tutor Bartholomew Clerke, a translation of Baldassare Castiglione's *The Courtier*, which had been Englished by Thomas Hoby, who married a sister of Mildred Cecil.

January 16: Thomas Howard, Duke of Norfolk, charged with treason, went on trial. Denied the right to have counsel, he pleaded from 8 in the morning til 8 at night, in vain. Only one witness testified against him, an agent of the Earl of Leycester, his enemy.

February 10: Elizabeth, after signing Norfolk's death warrant at Burghley's urgency, sent for him and said the idea of the Duke's death was too terrible for her.

March 18: John Lee in Antwerp reported to Burghley that English Catholic refugees affirmed the Earl of Oxford was furious with his father-in-law for not having tried to save his dear friend Norfolk (son of Oxford's father's sister Frances) from his doom: "The Earl hath, as they say here, put away from him the Countess his wife."

April 1: After Dutch pirates led by William de la Marck captured by surprise the port of Brill, the city of Flushing uprose and expelled the Spaniards, commencing Europe's first revolution for a modern republic, damned by Cecil as "democracy."

April: The Welsh warrior Thomas Morgan formed a troop of British volunteers to assist in the Dutch revolt. Among them went George Gascoigne and Rowland York.

May 4: Oxford as "Lord Great Chamberlain of England" signed the charter promoting his friend Walter Devereux, Viscount Hertford, to the new earldom of Essex, at Greenwich Palace.

June 2: After the Queen had revoked Norfolk's death warrant three times, she relented and he was beheaded. He made a scaffold avowal to the weeping people that he was innocent of treason and conspiracy, and never had inclined to Papistry since he knew what religion meant. The Duke did not have the least notion that he had been the victim of provocation devices contrived by Burghley to get rid of the old nobility's most popular chief, the leader of the landlords envied and hated by the commercial class.

June 15: The Duc Henri de Montmorenci and Paul de Foix, the French ambassador, celebrated a treaty with England at a Westminster feast, where the Earl of Essex led ten white knights and the Earl of Rutland ten in blue in a tournament of swords on horseback.

June 24: Sir Thomas Smith became Principal Secretary of the Queen's Council.

July 8: Burghley despatched a company of volunteers led by Sir Humphrey Gilbert to Holland (at Dutch expense).

July: Thomas Smith, bastard of the Privy Council secretary, collected colonists in Liverpool to settle hundreds of thousands of Irish acres granted his father.

July 15: Elizabeth appointed Cecil Lord Treasurer.

July 22: She began her summer "progress" or tour of shires, visiting the Theobalds estate of the Cecils in Hertford, where Burghley entertained her and her courtiers for three days. His spouse was seldom amused herself, and never amused others. But she was fond of flowers, and her herbal gardens were excellent, just like the Queen's in *Cymbeline*.

August: Tom Smith arrived in Ireland with his colonial followers dwindled to a hundred men.

August 12: De Vere amused her Majesty with a mock-battle between artificial forts on the Avon river during her visit to the Dudleys at Warwick.

August 17: Montmorenci came to London.

August 18: The Duc dined with the Queen at Warwick castle, and went with her the next day to Kenilworth.

August 24: Queen Catherine de Medici and the Duc de Guise commanded the massacre of the chief Protestants in Paris. Catholic mobs continued killing Huguenots and their children for two days; then came the turn of the French provinces. King Philip of Spain heard the news with repeated bursts of his peculiar laughter. Pope Gregory XIII (the calendar reformer) struck a medal in honor of the slaughter, "Ugonottorum Strages, 1572." Burghley told Bertrand de Fenelon, the French ambassador, that the Paris carnage was the most horrible crime committed in the world since the crucifixion of Christ. Over 70,000 victims were counted. The Court in England mourned, meditated, or secretly gloated over the tragedy.

September 20? Oxford wrote to Burghley of his fears concerning the latter's life, since he was the main "crossbar" to the Romanists in Britain: "I am one, that count myself a follower of yours now in all fortunes." He wished "to admonish you, as one, with whom I would spend my blood and life, so much you have made me yours...."

September 22: Oxford wrote to Burghley, regretting that the Lord Treasurer was so "affaired with the business of the commonwealth" that he could not "recreate" and "repose" with Edward and Anne during their visit to Cecil House in Westminster. The Countess "departed unto the country this day: and myself as fast as I can get me out of town do follow." They journeyed to his North sea coast mansion at Wyvenhoe. Meanwhile, he begged Burghley to win the Queen's consent to his entry in her military service: "If there were any service to be done abroad, I had rather serve there than at home, where yet some honour were to be got; if there be any setting forth to sea, to which service I bear the most affection, I shall desire your L(ordship) to give me and get me that favour and credit. If there be no such intention, then I shall be most willing to be employed on the sea coasts to be in a readiness with my countrymen against any invasion."

September 23: The Queen ended her progress at Windsor castle.

October? Countess Anne wrote to her father requesting employment for her former tutor William Lewin. From Wivenhoe, she recommended him to the Queen for translation of the Latin works of Bishop John Jewel in defense of the Anglican church, which Lewin wanted to do.

October 31: De Vere wrote to her father from Wivenhoe: "Your last letters, which be the first I have received of your Lordship's good opinion conceived towards me, lightened and disburdened my careful mind. And, sith I have been so little beholden to sinister reports, I hope now, with your Lordship in different judgment, to be more plausible unto you than heretofore." He pleaded that Burghley should beware of "backfriends" and "forbear to believe too fast" accusations against his son-in-law. This reminds me of Posthumus's servant grieving about his "too ready hearing" of the "poisonous tongu'd" (3.2.4-5).

November: Captain Gascoigne and Captain York returned to England with others who had served in the Low Countries after shameful experience. The former seems to have done little fighting, but came home prepared to show Holland's state "In Cartes, in Mappes, and eke in Modells made;" and eager to spin yarns about "the bargaine twene a wanton lasse, / And *Edel Bloetts* (noble bloods)," a bargain made with nuns. His poem *Fruits of War* or *Dulce Bellum Inexpertis* is demurely mute on the affair: "Yong Rouland Yorke may tell it better than I."

December 8: William Humberston, surveyor, informed Burghley, he had gone to Wyvenhoe with William Lewin and spoken to Oxenford, "who seemed willing to consent to all things" Cecil's agent could devise for his benefit. Lewin and he went to Colne to sell oaks from Oxford's woods there, for payment of some of the Earl's debts.

1573 January 1: Thomas Bedingfield of Suffolk finished his version of Girolamo Cardano's *Consolation,* philosophy his friend Lord Edward desired. *Cardanus' Comfort* (famed among scholars as "Hamlet's book") was "published by commandment of the right honourable the Earl of Oxenford," with an English introduction and a poem on the poor rewards of poetry by De Vere.

January 14: Thomas Ratcliff, Earl of Sussex, became Lord Chamberlain of the Queen's Household, including in his duties production of "Revels" or plays for the Court. He may have supervised the performance on January 6 (when the Lord Chamberlain William Howard was dying) of the play *Theagenes and Chariclea* by the boys of Paul's Cathedral, directed by their Catholic singing master Sebastian Westcott. The play derived from a romantic Greek tale by Heliodorus, translated into English in 1569 by Thomas Underdowne, who dedicated *An Aethiopian History* to the boy Edward de Vere.

March 19: Rowland York and his comrade Gascoigne sailed again for army employment in the Low Countries.

March 22: Easter festivity at Greenwich.

April 12: De Vere celebrated his twenty-fourth birthday.

April: Colonel Thomas Smith was murdered by Irish servants after the failure of his colony of Clanboy or the Ardes.

April 24: The Privy Council sent a letter to the Mayor and officers of Gravesend to deliver David Wilkins, John Hammon, and "one Denny, a Frenchman," servants of the Earl of Oxford, to London for questioning; "also to warn William Fainte and John Wutton," former servants of Oxford, actually employed by Burghley, to come to the Council, "and to guard them if there be cause."

This appears to be the time when the "ill-used wife" reported to her parents the rancor that her husband inflicted on her. They kept the trivial tragic record, destroying all the "scriptures" he mailed to her in the seventeen years of their woeful wedlock.

May 20: This is the day when, according to the anonymous comic chronicle, *The Famous Victories of Henry V*, Prince Hal and three comrades were accused of having ambushed and robbed two royal receivers of funds going to the Exchequer, at Gads Hill on the road to Rochester. No such date is to be found "in the fourteenth year of the reign of our sovereign Lord King Henry the Fourth," which concluded on 20 March 1413.

1573 May 20: Men hiding in a ditch shot with calivers at William Faunt and John Wotton, servants of the Lord Treasurer, as they crossed Gads Hill on the road from Gravesend to Rochester. Three of the Earl of Oxford's men, Wilkins, Denny and Hammon were charged with attempted robbery and intent to kill.

May 21: Faunt and Wotton wrote from Gravesend lamenting about "our late noble Lord and master, who—with pardon be it spoken—is to be thought as the procurer of that which is done."

May 31: Faunt complained that Oxford's men threatened "our lodging" and he and Wotton had to leave the city: "we find ourselves in no less peril of spoil than before." Later he informed the Lord Treasurer, Oxford's honor was at stake, "of whom publicly to hear complaint of raging demeanour would grieve your honour and myself to make it." Thus the affair peters out and palls in the Privy Council papers.

September 2: Oxford declared: "To determine what my debts are certainly, it is not possible, and because as yet I cannot have the right of them all; but my debts to the Queen's Majesty are these which I have gathered together considered. I have just cause to think that the sum of my debts will be L6000 at the least."

Lady Mildred Cecil's reputation for extraordinary learning she earned more by industry than insight. Sir Anthony Cooke, her father (who died in 1576) trained her and two sisters in classical tongues, needlecraft, and domestic medicine. For home remedies concocted from her abundance of plants, she consulted Sir Thomas Smith, a wizard of "the true Chymique without imposture," as Gabriel Harvey wrote to her son Robert Cecil in 1598, "which I learnt from Sir Thomas Smith not to condemn."[29] In February 1574 Countess Anne murmured to her mother about feeling unusually ill. Smith recommended for her problem a mixture of fennel, angelica water, and other sorcery stuff. On March 7 he wrote to Lady Burghley: "If her Ladyship (Anne) do not find immediate comfort in it, then nature is too feeble. I can say no more but I would be sorry that my Lady of Oxford should miscarry, as if she were two times my own daughter, for diverse causes, and would be as glad to do her good as any living next to your Ladyship."[30] We hear no more of that malady. Smith's letter personally illustrates the lady of *Cymbeline* who is "devilish" familiar with botany and plants of deadliness. Yet she is not the Lady Mildred Cecil, "*eruditam feminam*," to whom Christopher Ocland the school-master of Greenwich, in April 1582, dedicated his Latin eulogy *Elizabetha*. Maybe Cymbeline's nameless Queen would have been recognized on the stage sooner if the poet had not endowed her with the beauty that wicked stepmothers frequently display in fairytales.

Mother Mildred's own portrait, painted by the veracious brush of the Dutch master Hans Ewouts, reveals her as destitute of pulchritude. Below the austere and frosty countenance the artist drew in shade a classic mask which might be interpreted as a head of Medusa!—the she-monster who turned human faces to stone. As a worker for the Master of the Revels at Court, Hans Ewouts proved ability with tools apart from painting, well rewarded for his labors in staging Greek romances for the Queen in 1572-74. The Dutch artist's name disappears from the Revels accounts after 1574, altho he lived until November 1586.[31]

We are sorry that the witty Roger Manners, whose letters to the Earl of Rutland furnish more than a few valuable sidelights on the soul of William Cecil, remained polite and quiet when writing about Burghley's wife and Countess Anne. In October 1577 he told his kinsman about taking the cure at Buxton Wells with Burghley and Smith, and added: "I came by Theobalds, where the two ladies speak great honour of your entertainment of them."[32]

On September 20, 1577, Captain Frobisher sailed into the Cambrian harbor which had been made ready for his ships and expected gold. Our dramatist must have been reflecting on Frobisher's arrival in Milford Haven, and the likeness of its name to the village of Long Melford, where De Veres were once lords of many lands, when he composed *The Cruelty of a Stepmother*.

The temper of *Cymbeline* in its present form indicates that his mind revolved while writing about the events of his abrupt and "unjust divorce" in April 1576. The only record we now have of that fatal month is the scripture of William Cecil. We can hardly reckon Oxford's letter of Friday, 27 April, as a record of the rupture and its motives. It merely says, "I must let your Lordship understand this much: that is, until I can better satisfy or advertise myself of some mislikes, I am not determined, as touching my wife, to accompany her. What they are—because some are not to be spoken of or written upon as imperfections—I will not deal withal."[33] On April 25, Burghley confided in a notebook: "No unkindness known on his part at his departure. She made him privy that she thought she was with child, whereof he said he was glad. When he was certified thereof at Paris he sent her his picture with kind letters and messages... He never signified any misliking of anything until the 4 of April at Paris, from whence he wrote somewhat that, by reason of a man of his, his receivor, he had conceived some unkindness, but he prayed me to let pass the same, for it did grow by the doubleness of servants."

Then Burghley sent for his son Thomas, who rode a long distance to meet his brother-in-law at Dover "within ij hours after my Lord Howard and others, and thither carried my commend and his wife's, and did not understand from him any point of misliking... But my son sent me word that he found him disposed to keep himself secretly ij or iij days in his own lodging, and yet that Edward York told him secretly that his Lordship would come first to my house, but he would nobody know thereof. Thereupon I was glad, but his wife gladder. And the contrary I knew (not omitted) until he was landed (at London), and then my son told me how he did suddenly leave the barge and took a wherry, and only with Rowland York landed about York's house." He arranged for his sister Mary to visit him there, but refused to see poor Countess Anne. Lord Harry Howard promised to keep her father informed about Edward's future acts and plans.[34] On April 29 the Treasurer recorded several grievances of the Earl: "His money not made over to him according to his directions... his followers not favored by me... his letter showed to the Queen of set purpose to bring him into her Majesty's indignation..." The Lord Treasurer protested that he strove to advance the honor of the Earl at Court, vowing that he had suggested the appointment of Oxford as cavalry commander, Master of the Horse. But we get more details of their private miseries. His lady had been "taken away from him at Wivenhoe and carried to London; he means not to discover anything of the cause of his misliking, but he will not come to her until he understands further of it... my wife hath ever drawn his wife's love from him, and that she hath wished him dead... at Wivenhoe she caused a division in his house, and a slander to be raised of him for intention of killing of his men."[35]

Burghley tried to reply to the charges, but prefered to write down none of his answers but the economic, along with tedious trifles. "The marriage had cost the Lord Treasurer from the beginning about 5 or 6 thousand pounds." Moreover he singled out for praiseworthiness in the year "1576. His own good nature." And added a number of sonorous precepts he approved: "Pleasing of Almighty God wherein is contained omnes charitates... The greatest possession that any man can have is honor, good name, good will of many & of the best sort."[36]

Naturally De Vere did not list among his "mislikings" the marked difference in the way the Cecils had treated him and the way they looked and acted to Philip Sidney, whom Lady Mildred must have often lauded as the youth who should have married their Anne. Four years younger than Oxford, Sidney enjoyed good will of many and of the richest sort from the hour that the Spanish tyrant Philip acted as his godfather. The negotiation between Henry Sidney, his father, and Sir William Cecil concerning the wedlock of their children resounded with fondness on both sides, and Cecil's sole reason for not speeding its consummation was Sidney's comparative poverty. Philip's main advantage, in Cecil's eyes, was being nephew to the Queen's favorite, Robert Dudley, the Earl of Leycester. When Philip first came to Court, in November 1575, he was the prospective heir to two Dudley Earldoms, of Leycester and Warwick, the latter belonging to his uncle Ambrose. The whole Protestant aristocracy chuckled and chattered with pride about him. If you wish to see how Shakespeare regarded him in 1577, you cannot do better, in my opinion, than examine the figure of Cloten or Clotten in our play.

A single word might be taken as the key to identification of Cloten with Sidney, a word pronounced "aside" by the Second Lord in disgust at Cloten's brutality and arrogance: "Puppies" (1.2.21). It will be remembered that in the first biography of Sir Philip, by Fulke Greville, Lord Brooke, a quarrel between Oxford and Sidney on a tennis court is described, apparently climaxed in the presence of French nobles, who heard "my Lord scornfully call Sir Philip by the name of Puppy."[37] A major reason for the heat between them was Sidney's opposition to alliance with France by marriage of the Duc d'Alencon with Elizabeth. The Frenchmen "instantly drew all to this tumult, every sort of quarrels sorting well with their humors, especially this. Which Sir Philip perceiving, and rising with inward strength, by the prospect of a mighty faction against him, asked my Lord with a loud voice that which he heard clearly enough before. Who (like an echo that still multiplies by reflections) repeated this epithet of 'Puppy' the second time. Sir Philip, resolving in one answer to conclude both the attentive hearers and passionate actor, gave my Lord a lie impossible (as he avered) to be retorted: in respect all the world knows, Puppies are gotten by Dogs, and Children by Men."[38] The end of this episode will be told elsewhere.

British imperial propaganda has changed the image of Philip Sidney from the self-righteous Calvinist caviler and adorer of Dudley blood, the young man who menaced his father's secretary with knifing on a hasty suspicion that the latter had betrayed his master's mail. We are instructed to see him now as an almost Puritan war hero and martyr, a knight without stain. So it may be difficult to comprehend why Shakespeare should have depicted him as the wicked Queen's son, would-be raper of Imogen. His threatening of the secretary Edmund Molyneux recalls the contention of Cloten, "It is fit I should commit offence to my inferiors" (2.1.28-29). Cloten's patriotism is as genuine as Sidney's, tho you may sense something putrid in the former's readiness to challenge the legions of Rome, and plunge Britain in blood for it. For the necessity of the plot, the poet made the garments of Posthumus fit Cloten perfectly. I do not know if Sidney really was shaped and short like the Earl of Oxford. But there is no disputing about the difference of their characters, or quality as critics and makers of literature. None of Sidney's sonnets, true as they are to the models of Petrarch, stay in our memories like the nine little lines that Cloten commands to be sung to Imogen, "Hark, hark, the Lark at Heaven's gate sings." (In the *First Folio* text they are seven lines. In many a modern edition they are titled wrongly "Cloten's Song." There is nothing to indicate he did more than pay for the cantilation.) This lyric of the lark reminds historians of poetry of Sir Thomas Wyatt's sonnet, "You that in love find luck," where the knight sings,

> Arise, I say, do May some observance...
> As one whom Love lists little to advance.

Chaucer, whom Wyatt emulated with pains, would have loved the lark song. Some scholars believe that Shakespeare emulated John Lyly in these rimes, echoing the song of Trico in the last act of *Campaspe*, which imitates the nightingale, the lark, robin and cuckoo. Since Lyly never wrote two lines of verse comparable to the poetry in *Cymbeline* even remotely, and Trico's lyric chimes in precision of harmony with the Song in our play, I am certain that Lyly's lord and theatrical patron wrote both.

Incidentally, Cloten's remark about his mode of wooing Imogen reminds us of contemporary poetry that testifies to our date for *Cymbeline*. The pugnacious prince announces, "I am advised to give her Musick o' mornings; they say it will penetrate." He perpetrates the priapic pun two more times, telling his musicians, "If you can penetrate her with your fingering, so," and after the Song, "If this penetrate, I will consider your Music the better" (2.4.28-29). The anonymous tragedy *Arden of Feversham*, which is credited by too many as work of Shakespeare, presents the ridiculous murderer Michael making love with the words, "Let my passions penetrate." These words also appear in the posthumous sonnets of Thomas

Watson, friend of Christopher Marlowe, who I believe dashed off *Arden of Feversham*.[39] Watson, in my judgment, was the author of *The Rare Triumphs of Love and Fortune*, which the Queen and her Court probably witnessed in the Christmas of 1581. This playwright copied from *Cymbeline:* his first act presents Jupiter conversing with other gods; a banished courtier brings up a son, named Hermione, in a cave; Hermione marries the King's daughter, named *Fidelia,* like Imogen, despite adversity, and fights a duel with a Cloten-like person, and is exiled. There is even a figure analogous to the old servant Pisanio. The source of *Arden of Feversham* has long been suspected to be the lost play *The History of Murderous Michael* acted at Whitehall on March 3, 1579, by the Lord Chamberlain's company.

V

The excellent analyst of Shakespeare, Samuel Taylor Coleridge, held that *Cymbeline* was written by the master-artist in his youth and done again in his final theatrical years. Many scholars were attracted to Coleridge's theory until some apprehended that, if they were to stick to their Stratford idolatry, they should not crowd comedies, histories, tragedies, into years of his youth which would not bear the weight. The opinion became fashionable that our romance was composed shortly before it was seen at the Globe theater in 1611 by Simon Forman, a quack doctor and astrologer. His diary note about "Cimbalin King of England" is the oldest record of a performance of the play that we have. However we also have evidence that our romance was composed or revised about the same time that Shakespeare wrote *Much Ado About Nothing*. He showed in old stage directions there that *Cymbeline* haunted him, or glowed fresh in his memory. The first stage direction in the comedy (printed in 1600 after innumerable performances) calls for the entrance of "Leonato, Governor of Messina, Innogen his wife..." At the start of the second act, "Enter Leonato, his brother, his wife." This Innogen twice introduced has nothing to say, and nobody ever talks to her. The mystery of the Italian noblewoman—or is she an English wife?—

named after Innogen, the wife of Brute, lengendary lord of Britain, has never been cleared up. But experts are convinced that *Much Ado* came after the composition of *The Shrew*, which I feel confident was written not long after the original play of *Cymbeline*. The experts are also inclined to trace the sources of our romance to a novelet printed in 1560 called *Frederick of Jennen* (Genoa), translated from a German story printed in Antwerp 1518, "Historie von Vier Kaufmännern," the basis of which may be the ninth novelet of the Second Day in Boccaccio's *Decameron*. Shakespeare surely was acquainted with the Italian tale, perhaps had read Antoine Jean Le Macon's translation of the *Decameron* printed in Lyons 1569. He would have been drawn to this story by the very name of its protagonist, Bernabo Lomellini, whom he turned into Posthumus Leonatus. His fellow explorers of philosophy and folklore, the Lumleys, claimed to have stemmed from the Lomellini. Ginevra, the heroine of the Italian story, easily was converted to Imogen. The villain Ambrogiuolo became Iachimo because the former name did not hint of York. But the name taken by Ginevra when she dons a sailor's dress, Sicuran da Finale, possibly invoked in our dramatist her name Fidele. Unless he took it directly from *Fedele and Fortunio*, which was enacted for the royal Court in 1576, adapted from *Il Fedele* by Luigi Pasqualigo, some say by Stephen Gosson. That poetic comedy made a cordial impression on the writer of *The Two Gentlemen of Verona*.

Bernabo, the hero of the Italian tale, would have appealed to our poet for the same reason that he named the hero of *All's Well That Ends Well* Bertram. The first syllable of both names instantly struck him as sounding like his own family name. Perhaps he knew enough Hebrew to remember that nabo resembled in that language the word for a prophetic soul.

We can tell how radically our dramatist revised *The Cruelty of a Stepmother*, long after the spring of 1581, when Elizabeth locked the Earl of Oxford in the Tower of London for having committed certain offenses, such as a declaration while drinking that "My Lord of Norfolk (was) worthy to lose his head for not following his counsel

at Lichfield to take arms," and "That the Catholics were great Ave-
Maria coxcombs, that they would not rebel against the Queen."[40]
These two charges I select from a swarm made by Lord Henry
Howard and Charles Arundel to discredit Oxford, who had accused
them of being enemies of the French alliance, prefering servility to
Spain. Our poet almost lucidly refers to those two in the speech
where Belarius explains how he came to be banished from Cymbe-
line's Court (3.3.60-64):

> then was I as a tree
> Whose boughs did bend with fruit. But in one night,
> A storm, or robbery (call it what you will)
> Shook down my mellow hangings: nay, my leaves,
> And left me bare to weather.

Note that the language used is exactly like that of the sublime Sonnet about the "Bare ruin'd quires, where late the sweet birds sang."
Guiderius tersely remarks on Belarius's downfall: "Uncertain favour." His guardian says,

> My fault being nothing (as I have told you oft)
> But that two Villains, whose false Oaths prevail'd
> Before my perfect Honor, swore to Cymbeline,
> I was Confederate with the Romans. (3.3.65-68)

For the ensuing twenty years his home has been a cavern and the
surrounding woods. The number suggests that *The Cruelty of a Stepmother* might have been changed into *Cymbeline* in the year 1601. This
could account for the appearance of features of the plot, details
about Imogen and Iachimo, in the booklet *Westward for Smelts* by Kit
of Kingston, which the researcher George Steevens stated came out
in 1603, but the Stationers guild did not register it until 1620. The
old play, and its Antwerp source, could have been the inspiration
for the romantic drama acted at Breslau in 1596, "Eine Schöne Historia. Von einem frommen Gottfürchtigen Kauffmann von Padua,
welcher zu Mantua in beysein andere Kauffleite, wegen seines lieben
frommen Weibes Ehr und frömigkeit, sein Hab und Gut werwettet,

gestellt durch Zachariam Liebholdt von Solbergk."[41] (A Pretty Story, Of a pious Godfearing Merchant of Padua, who, in debate with other Traders at Mantua, wagered his Wares for the Honor and piety of his dear religious Wife; presented thru Zachariam Liebholdt of Solber.)

In Edmund Spenser's lively splendid pastoral poems, *The Shepherds Calendar*, registered by the Stationers on 5 December 1579 the immortal Looney detected a reference to the fierce mood of Mildred Cecil toward Edward de Vere.[42] The March eclog of the *Calendar* contains merry talk between shepherds named Willie and Thomalin. The former's fun glances at the repute of a certain Leticia, most likely the Lady Lettice Knollys Devereux, widow of Walter, Earl of Essex, Oxford's friend:

> shall we sporten in delight,
> And learn with Lettice to wax light... ?

Presumably the Earl of Leycester had not let Spenser into the secret of his engagement to marry Countess Lettice in September 1578. Queen Bess did not hear about the wedding until Jehan Simier, the envoy of the Duc d'Alencon, discovered it. Oxford must have perceived by March 1579 that Robin Dudley, his chief rival for the Queen's favor, was enamored by Lettice Devereux, and flung a similar feathery jest at her. For I believe with Looney that Spenser had De Vere in view when he conceived the personality of Willie. The latter promises to keep watch of Thomalin's herd while his friend discourses of love:

> Thomalin, have no care for thy,
> My self will have a double eye,
> Ylike to my flock and thine;
> For alas at home I have a sire,
> A stepdame eke as hot as fire,
> That duly adays counts mine.

I dare say that Spenser composed these rimes not long after watching and listening to the protoplast of *Cymbeline*. When Willie tells how once he heard his father say he caught Love in a fowling net put up for crows that were cruel to a pear tree, we can hear young Oxford narrating the feats of his father. Willie seems to have been a pastoral or folk name Edward de Vere chose merely because in old English *wyll* was a popular mutation of the Anglian "well," meaning a water-spring. And the season Spring, he never forgot, in Latin was *Ver*. The word and the name "Will" became for him an infinite pond of puns.

The Danish critic Georg Brandes recognised that *Cymbeline* and *Pericles* were drawn from the same well or will in seasons nearly sequent. But he stubbornly maintained that the former's defects of diction, plot structure and delineation of characters were not the result of immaturity; quite the contrary, they showed a supreme genius in decay, at all events, extremely tired. Brandes deplored the tendency in both romances to substitute for clean work-worthy dramatic technic some childishly rapid process of explanation.[43] Brandes complained about the use of supernatural intervention, a method of disentangling plots Shakespeare got from Greek romance. He pointed out: "The wicked stepmother in *Cymbeline* corresponds to the wicked foster-mother in *Pericles*. She hates Imogen as Dionyza hates Marina. Pisanio is supposed to have murdered her as Leonine is believed to have slain Marina, and Cymbeline recovers both sons and daughter as Pericles his wife and child... Diana appears to the slumbering Pericles as Jupiter does to Posthumus in *Cymbeline*." Brandes failed to notice that the plot likenesses are proof of the dramatist's addiction to ancient Hellenic novels. He should have detected that the prevalence of Diana in Shakespeare's earliest dramas and the emergence of Jupiter in her stead in our romance marked stages of the poet's struggles for the salvation of his virility.

Samuel Coleridge's son Hartley myopically perceived effects of those conflicts in *Cymbeline*, but rejected compassion for the rigor of his dim perception, since he believed his religion required it. "I never could forgive Posthumus for laying wagers on his wife's chastity," said Hartley. "Of all Shakespeare's jealous husbands, he is the most disagreeable." This critic's psychology taught him, "Such experiments are more excusable in women, whose weakness, whose very virtue, requires suspicion and strong reassurance; but in man they ever indicate a foul, a feeble, and unmanly mind."[44] I wonder what women think of the younger Coleridge's justification for their lack or loss of faith.

He gives no sign of ever being troubled by the violent discrepance between his Stratford idol's devotion to usury and the dogging of debtors and the dramatist's opinion of these pursuits. "Did you but know the City's usuries, / And felt them knowingly," Belarius exclaims to his boys (3.3.45-46). Imogen offers them money for the meat she has taken, and they exclaim:

> *Guiderius.* Money, Youth?
> *Arviragus.* All Gold and Silver rather turn to dirt,
>   As 'tis no better reckon'd, but of those
>   Who worship dirty Gods.   (3.6.52-55)

Posthumus shares their contempt for surplus-pilers, calling on the gods to deal with him as he deserves:

> No stricter render of me than my all.
> I know you are more clement than vile men,
> Who of their broken Debtors take a third
> A sixth, a tenth, letting them thrive again
> On their abatement; that's not my desire.   (5.4.17-21)

What annoys me in the language of *Cymbeline*, sounding alien, even antagonistic, to the tongue of Shakespeare as we hear it in nearly all his other works, is the ring of ugliness, the inclination to coprophily. Permit me to quote from Iachimo (pretending to contrast Imogen with the alleged objects of her husband's desires in Italy):

> Sluttery to such neat Excellence oppos'd
> Should make desire vomit emptiness...
>   unsatisfi'd desire, that Tub
> Both fill'd and running: Ravenging first the Lamb,
> Longs after for the Garbage. (1.6.44-50)

You may protest, it is a scoundrel speaking. But compare the poetry which the dramatist makes the villain in *Othello* illustrate his thoughts with. Look now where morality may not call for verbiage of that kind, to this metaphor from Cadwal (4.3.59-60):

> And let the stinking-Elder, Grief, untwine
> His perishing root with the increasing Vine.

One more example, where the ugly is dragged in for no theatric necessity, from the scene (5.4.114-115) of Jupiter's descent:

> He came in Thunder, his Celestial breath
> Was sulphurous to smell.

Is there another play in which our lover of Ovid merits the nickname of Naso? (Recall how prince Cloten reeks!) No wonder a host of analysts have been convinced that other hands than our author's worked on the plays of his deathward years.

None of us can tell however in what period of his art he wrote the lines that sing to the very heart of democracy:

> *Arviragus.* Are we not brothers?
> *Imogen* (As Fidele). So man and man should be,
>> But clay and clay differs in dignity,
>> Whose dust is both alike.   (4.2.2-5)

In pronouncing my farewell to the wonderful wifely fantom, the original image of Imogen, and her poor Lord Posthumus, a nobler poet than father, I beg the gentle readers to lend me their ears for the sake of a short song found among the voluminous melodies of William Byrd, which I would vow came from the same cranium that gave us the lyric "Hark, Hark, the Lark."

> Awake, mine eyes, see Phoebus bright arising
> And lesser lights to shades obscure descending,
> Glad Philomel sits tunes of joy devising,
> Whilst in sweet notes
> From warbling throats
> The silvan quire
> With like desire
> To her are echoes sending.[45]

References

1   Richard Eden, Preface to *The Art of Navigation* by Martin Cortez (London, 1561) i.

2   Wilson to Walsingham, 19 Feb. 1577, in *Relations Politiques des PaysBas et de l'Angleterre, sous le regne de Philippe II,* ed. Joseph Kervyn de Lettenhove (Brussels; F. Hayez, 1882-1900) ix, 212.

3   Calendar of State Papers Foreign (1577), no. 1308, 1319, 1326.

4   Historical Manuscripts Commission: Calendar of the Manuscripts of the Marquess of Salisbury (London, 1938), vol. 17 (Vere to Robert Cecil, 17 Nov. 1605).

5   Calendar of State Papers Foreign (1577) no. 1440; Lettenhove, *op. cit.* ix, 316.

6   Sidney, Sir Henry, Sir Philip, et al. *Letters and Memorials of State,* ed. Arthur Collins (London; T. Osborne, 1746) i, 193.

7   O. G. Ravenscroft Dennis, *The House of Cecil* (London; Constable, 1914) 20.

8   *Documents Relating to the Office of the Revels in the Time of Queen Elizabeth,* ed. Albert Feuillerat (Louvain; A. Uystpruyst, 1908) 286.

9   *Shakespeare's Holinshed* (1587), ed. Richard Hosley (New York; Capricorn Books, 1968) 4-8. Geoffrey of Monmouth, *History of the Kings of Britain,* trans. Sebastian Evans & Charles Dunn (New York; Dutton, 1958) 79-82.

10   Gerald Massey, *A Book of the Beginnings* (London, 1881) i, 374.

11   Elizabeth Tenison, *Elizabethan England* (Leamington; The Author, 1930-39) iii, 68, 76.

12   Eva Turner Clark, *Hidden Allusions in Shakespeare's Plays,* ed. Ruth Loyd Miller (Jennings, LA, Minos Publishing Co. 1974) 91.

13   Sanders to Allen, 6 Nov. 1577, in Tenison, *op. cit.* iii, 78.

14   Calendar of State Papers Foreign (1577), no. 22.

15   *Ibid.* no. 256.

16   *Ibid.* no. 447.

17   Frederick Chamberlin, *Elizabeth and Leycester* (New York, 1926) 207; Calendar of Salisbury Manuscripts, ii, 154. Spring of 1577 appears to be the season when Oxford contended, according to Charles Arundel in 1581, "that if he should forsake the realm and live in France, Monsieur (Alencon), with the oath of the King his brother, would better house him, and furnish him with better ability and revenue, than ever he had in England." Moreover, Arundel charged, "I heard Rawlie say that the Earl of Oxford told him that Monsieur would give him 10,000 crowns a year, whenever he list to come to France." To the same period probably belongs "His often wishing that Dr Saunders were Pope, for he would (wears?) into the quick; the rest were but *gods* priests. For he would—hedge give a thousand pounds for such a chaplain." Once he announced, "How he loved no man but Doctor Saunders, and that he should

be his doctor, for he was just of his humor, and as he had written, railed, and executed, so he wanted no will to do as much, at Richmond, at Hampton Court, and at every other place." To these charges of Charles Arundel, Lord Harry Howard added in the margin, Oxford had raged, "that by writing against Dr Saunders, he (Howard) had cut his own throat with all the Catholics beyond sea." (State Papers Domestic, 12/151: 49; *ibid.* 12/151: 57.)

18 Calendar of Rutland Manuscripts, i, 112. See Burghley letter to the Earl of Shrewsbury, on whose land the spa flourisht: Edmund Lodge, *Illustrations of British History, Biography & Manners* (London; John Chidley, 1838) ii, 84.

19 On the vital difference between patriotism and matriotism, see A. Bronson Feldman, *The Unconscious in History* (New York; Philosophical Library, 1959) 62 -72. By the way, Brute or Brutus, called the earliest king of Britain, seems to be a product of British preposterosity trying to explain the name of the realm. He was said to be the son of one Sylvius Posthumus, from whom Shakespeare derived the name of his hero, overlooking the legend that Brute killed his father by bad luck.

20 Calendar of Salisbury Manuscripts, xiii, 144.

21 Charles Arundel, in the State Papers Domestic, vol. 151, article 46.

22 Clark, *op. cit.* 91-2. Percy Allen, *The Life Story of Edward de Vere as "William Shakespeare"* (London; Cecil Palmer, 1932) 91-2.

23 Bernard M. Ward, *A Hundreth Sundrie Flowres*, ed. Ruth Loyd Miller (Jennings, LA. Minos Publishing Co. 1975) 303.

24 *Ibid.* 305.

25 Lettenhove, *op. cit.,* ii, 433.

26 William Camden, *The History of the Most Renowned and Victorious Princess Elizabeth* (London; Charles Harper & John Amery, 1675) 397.

27 Calendar of Salisbury Manuscripts, xiv, 19.

28 Documents for the charted dates are listed here.

1572

Sep 20?   Ward, *op. cit. supra,* 72; from Harleian Ms. 69913 fol. 9, 5.

Sept 22   *Ibid.* 73; from Lansdowne Ms. 14: 84, fol. 185.

Oct ?   Strype, *Annals,* iii, 57.

Oct 31   Ward, *op.cit.,* 76; from Lansdowne Ms. 14: 85.

Dec 8   Calendar of Salisbury (Cecil) Ms. xiii, 112.

1573

Jan 14   *Documents Relating to the Office of the Revels....*

Mar 19   George Gascoigne, *Works*, ed. J. Cunliffe (Cambridge University, 1910) i, 359. See also Prouty, *George Gascoigne* (New York; Columbia University, 1942).

Apr 24   *Acts of the Privy Council of England,* ed. John Roche Dasent (London; Eyre & Spottiswoode, 1890-1907) viii, 99.

May 20   Ward, *op. cit.* 91; from State Papers Domestic, xci, 36. Bernard

Ward, "*The Famous Victories of Henry the Fifth:* Its Place in Elizabethan Dramatic Literature," *Review of English Studies,* iv, July 1928. Ward argued that young Oxford wrote this play. Eva Turner Clark favored his view in her *Hidden Allusions.* Pr. Seymour Pitcher, in *The Case for Shakespeare's Authorship of "The Famous Victories"* (London; Alvin Redman, 1961) contended that the horse-holder from Stratford wrote it. My opinion is that a crew of actors like Robert Wilson and Richard Tarleton, who acted in it, and had been intimate with, if not members of, the Earl of Oxford's theatrical troops, patched up this prose, ribaldry, brutality and all. An Earl of Oxford is the only earl in the Victories, but hardly a character, tho none but the three major actors is more vocal. — A whim of mine selects the lost *Theagenes and Chariclea,* or "The White Ethiopian," as the first of Edward de Vere's dramatic enterprises, which he would permit to perish because of its crudity, its pathos of the apprentice. We may estimate the quality of its verse from the song in Thomas Underdowne's translation of Heliodorus, *An Aethiopian History* (2d ed. 1587) reprinted by Ruth Loyd Miller, ed. *Hidden Allusions...* by Eva Turner Clark (page 98). Some scholars claim that this Grecian romance influenced the final scenes of *Cymbeline,* more directly than I have suggested.

Sept 2   Calendar of Cecil Ms. 11, 58; compare Cecil Ms. xiii, 121.

29 Calendar of Cecil Ms. viii, 160.

30 Lansdowne Ms. 19/50.

31 A. B. Feldman, "Hans Ewouts, Artist of the Tudor Court Theatre," *Notes and Queries,* vol. 195 (10 June 1950) 257-8.

32 Calendar of Rutland Ms. i, 115.

33 Ward, *op. cit.* 121; from Cecil Ms. ii, 132.

34 Calendar of Cecil Ms. ii, 131.

35 *Ibid.* ix, f. 8; xiii, 128.

36 *Ibid.* ii, 144.

37 Greville, *The Life of the Renowned Sir Philip Sidney,* ed. Nowell Smith (London, 1907) 63.

38 *Idem.* The decapitation of Cloten was probably conceived at the time De Vere amused Charles Arundel, or chilled his blood, with words over wine about "His savage and unhumayne practice (?) to make away Philip Sidney." The alleged practice may be "His practice to murder Sidney in his bed and to scape by barge with calivers ready for the purpose." (State Papers Domestic (1581) 12/151: 46, 57.) Together with this nonsense went "A practice with R. York for the destruction of M(aster) Walsingham and to set division between him and Lester &c." (*Idem.*)

39 See Bronson Feldman, "Thomas Watson, Dramatist," *The Bard,* i (1977), p. 148, and Feldman's article on the play *Arden* in *The Bard,* (1979).

40 State Papers Domestic 12/151: 46. His contempt for Catholics in England was formulated plainer in "His fancy that the Catholics were good Ave-Mary

cockscombs for yielding their heads, which might be saved by rebels." On which note by Charles Arundel, Francis Southwell endorsed, *"Audivi"* (I have heard).—*Ibid.* 57.

41 Albert Cohn, *Shakespeare in Germany in the Sixteenth and Seventeenth Centuries* (London; Asher, 1865) lvii.

42 J. Thomas Looney, *"Shakespeare" Identified...* ed. Ruth Loyd Miller (Jennings, LA. Minos Publishing Co. 1975) 291.

43 Georg Brandes, *William Shakespeare; A Critical Study* (London; Macmillan, 1898) 590-1.

44 H. Coleridge, *Essays and Marginalia* (London, 1851) i, 166. I am far from an authority on Christianity. Yet unquestionably the creator of *Cymbeline* is closer to the spirit of the "Sermon on the Mount" than the unforgiving Coleridge. Consider the passage, which I take to be an appeal to Burghley for pity toward the religious who dissented from his government:

> *Posthumus* (to the death-expecting Iachimo).
>> The power that I have on you is to spare you;
>> The malice toward you, to forgive you. Live,
>> And deal with others better.
>
> *Cymbeline* Nobly doomed:
>> We'l learn our Freeness of a Son-in-Law:
>> Pardon's the word to all.   (5.5)

By November 1, 1571, when Cecil calculated what Oxford owed the state, the Norfolk inquisition had to be halted on account of Cecil's gout. (Calendar of Cecil Ms. xiii, 104.)

On July 13, 1572, the Earl of Sussex, the noblest of English nobles, who had competed with Cecil for the post of Crown Treasurer, learnt that he would most likely become Chamberlain of the royal Household. On July 15, Burghley became Lord Treasurer. In this office he steadily influenced Sir William Cordell, Master of the Rolls, keeper of accounts of Oxford's debt to the state. Cordell's residence was at Long Melford in Suffolk, where he entertained the Queen in a progress, in August 1578.

In 1573 Bartholomew Clerk, Oxford's tutor at Cambridge, published a polemic, *Fidelis servi subdito infideli responsio, cum examine errorum N. Sanders...* which appears to have had little or no effect on Oxford's admiration of the militant priest.

Perhaps I should warn students: they will find not a word about Cymbeline's mate in "Shakespeare's Cruel Queens" by Thomas H. McNeal (*Huntington Library Quarterly*, Nov. 1958, xxii, 41-50).

45 William Byrd, *Collected Vocal Works*, ed. Edmund Fellowes (London; Stainer & Bell, 1937-50) xii and xvi.

Chapter 5—THE WOMAN TAMER

In quo peccatur eodum punitur.
Old Proverb

I

The restless temper shown by the dramatist in his first plays re-newed his daydreams of adventure in Europe in the spring of 1577. On June 13 Robert Dudley, Earl of Leicester, who was to prove one of the major obstacles to the Earl of Oxford's political progress, told Burghley he was sorry that his son-in-law "should think any more of going over sea."[1] Before the end of the month, however, Oxford's hankering for romance on the continent succumbed to a warmer interest. His sister Mary had fallen in love with Peregrine Bertie (Lord Willoughby), a Protestant of Protestants, and despite the opposition of their families they determined to marry. One of the results of this romance, according to the evidence of several in-quirers, was the first version of Shakespeare's *The Taming of the Shrew*.

According to the Court gossip Robert Brackinbury sent the Earl of Rutland on February 15, 1577, Oxford's sister expected to be a bride in the spring of that year. "This will be a long Lent to Lady Mary Vere," he wrote... "for at Easter *consummatum erit*... there is nothing in the Court but dancing and triumphing by day, and al-most nightly executions... Lord Pembroke is much made of, and lodged in the house; Lord Oxford in the old sort."[2]

De Vere and Bertie were so contrary in character that Lady Mary must have given up the hope of ever making them friends. Pere-grine was a youth of frank speech, a fighting man, with a warrior's conception of happiness. He had hardly a shade of sophistication or tint of histrionics in his nature. The Earl, on the other hand, con-ducted himself as if he moved perpetually before a mirror or a pro-scenium, always elegantly devout to the standard of the courtier set by Baldassare Castiglione.

"Above all things"—so runs the code of Castiglione as summarized in 1580 by the scholar Gabriel Harvey, "it importeth a Courtier to be graceful and lovely in countenance and behavior; fine and discreet in discourse and entertainment; skilful and expert in Letters and Arms; active and gallant in every courtly exercise; nimble and speedy of body and mind; resolute, industrious, and valorous in action as profound and invincible in execution, as is possible; and withal ever generously bold, wittily pleasant, and full of life in all his sayings and doings. His apparel must be like himself, comely and handsome; fine and cleanly to avoid contempt, but not gorgeous or stately to incur envy, or suspicion of pride, vanity, self-love, or other imperfection. Both inside and outside must be a fair pattern of worthy fine and lovely virtue."

When Lord Willoughby took his place in the Queen's circle he joined a group of fellows whose main pleasure was rough sport. In the summer of 1572 the virago Bess Talbot, Countess of Shrewsbury, was "disappointed of young Bertie, where she hoped" to marry Elizabeth Cavendish, her daughter. His boisterous enterprises worried his mother and she appealed to Burghley for help, "entreating him for God's sake to give the young man, her son, good counsel to bridle his youth." She begged his Lordship to send her Peregrine, before his mischief became dangerous, down to the country where his father supervised the family lands.[3] Young Bertie had a wholesome regard for his quietly powerful father; his manners improved.

In many respects he took after his mother, the vivacious and brave Katherine, Duchess of Suffolk. Reflecting on Katherine of Suffolk's character, Sir Richard Morison regretted the contrast between her intellect and her temper as long ago as 1550; "It is a great pity that so goodly a wit waiteth upon so froward a will." Thomas Fuller's *Church History of Britain* extoled what Morison deplored: "a lady of sharp wit," he called her, "and sure hand to thrust it home and make it pierce when she pleased."[4] She was the only child, the daughter of Lord William Willoughby and Dona Maria de Salinas, a Spanish beauty who had come to England in the retinue of Henry

VIII's queen Catherine of Aragon, and defied the King to stay by her deathbed, but she changed from her mother's religion to the reformed faith of the North against which Spain waged war. In girlhood she became the fourth wife of the sparkling Duke Charles Brandon. He died young and after his death she married Richard Bertie, her "gentleman usher," whose father had been governor of Hurst Castle of the south coast. With him she went into exile when Queen Mary Tudor refused to tolerate objectors to the Catholic Church. The misery and heroism of her wanderings with her husband abroad inspired a popular Protestant ballad and a play or two. The actor Thomas Drew wrote one in 1623, *The History of the Duchess of Suffolk*, "which being full of dangerous matter," the Master of the royal Revels and censor of plays Henry Herbert sighed, probably deploring its attacks on Papal politics, "was much reformed by me." During their exile, on October 12, 1556, Peregrine was born at Wesel in Cleves. They named him in memory of their peregrination. He became indeed a traveler all his life.

Peregrine's adoration of Oxford's sister—a lady seven years older than he—came as a shock to the Duchess, but she could not deny her boy his earnest desire. She fretted over the effect of the news on her Richard, with his acrid opinion of the Earl.

"It is very true," Lady Suffolk wrote to Burghley on July 2, 1577, with her usual honesty and humor, "that my wise son has gone very far with my Lady Mary Vere, I fear too far to turn. I must say to you in counsel what I have said to her plainly, that I had rather he had matched in any other place; and I told her the causes. Her friends made small account of me; her brother did what in him lay to deface my husband and my son; beside our religions agreed not; and I cannot tell what more. If she should prove like her brother, if an Empire followed her, I should be sorry to match so. She said that she could not rule her brother's tongue, nor help the rest of his faults, but for herself she trusted so to use her as I should have no cause to mislike her; and seeing it was so far forth between my son and her, she desired my good will, and asked no more. 'That is a seemly thing,' quoth I, 'for you to live on. For I fear that Master

Bartey will so much mislike of these dealings, that he will give little more than his good will, if he give that. Besides, if her Majesty shall mislike of it, sure we turn him (Peregrine) to the wild world.' She told me how Lord Sussex and Master Hatton had promised to speak for her to the Queen, and that I would require you to do the like. I told her, her brother used you and your daughter so evil that I could not require you to deal in it. Well, if I would write, she knew you would do it for my sake; and since there was no undoing of it, she trusted I would, for my son's sake, help now."

The Duchess had heard that the Queen spoke sharply about her for keeping Peregrine away from the Court. Elizabeth said his mother "did it in a stomach against her. But God knows," Lady Suffolk protested, "I did it not so, but for fear of this marriage and quarrels." She informed Burghley that a few days ago a gentleman had approached her with a proposal to wed her son to one Mistress Gaymege, the heiress to a thousand marks' worth of land. She wished Peregrine could be attracted to the latter but understood how difficult it was to swerve his mind from any goal that he wanted wholeheartedly.

On July 14 she wrote once more to the Lord Treasurer, describing the response of her husband to the news of their son's engagement: "wherein your Lordship may perceive his head is troubled, as I not blame him. But," she went on, "if he knew as much as I of my good Lord of Oxford's dealings it would trouble him more. But the case standing as it doth, I mean to keep it from him." She had no words to express her dismay "that my son, in the weightiest matter, hath so forgotten himself to the trouble and disquiet of his friends, and like enough to be his own undoing and the young lady's too. For if my Lord of Oxford's wilfulness come to my husband's ears I believe he would make his son but small marriage... I am dead at my wit's end. And yet I think if her Majesty could be won to like it, I am sure my husband would be the easier won to it, if my Lord of Oxford's great uncourteousness do not too much trouble him."

It is regrettable that Katherine of Suffolk did not leave a dialog or two portraying the Earl's curtness and caprices to her and Lord

Willoughby. Judging by her extant correspondence, we may be sure that it would have been a gem of unpremeditated art.

In November the impetuous Bertie sent his love a letter telling to what lengths her brother was carrying his discourtesy: "I hear (he) bandeth against me and sweareth my death, which I fear nor force not." The only thing Peregrine feared was that the Earl's hostility "should withdraw your affection towards me; otherwise I think no way to be so offended as I cannot defend." He assured Lady Mary that she meant more to him than "self or life," and urged her, "above all things if you wish me well, let nothing grieve you whatsoever you shall heard do hap." He vowed himself hers "more than his own and so till death."[5]

The rumor that Oxford was egging his followers to assault Willoughby transpired to be mere sound and fury signifying nonsense or slander of the Earl. I suspect it came from provocators in the service of Lord Henry Howard, his treacherous cousin, brother of the beheaded Duke of Norfolk. For Oxford in the summer of 1577 was striving to win from the Queen a grant of land that belonged to the Duke's estate. "It is said her Majesty hath promised to give him fee-simple of Rysing," John Stanhope wrote to Burghley on July 25. Lord Harry's twisted smiles and deftly darted rancor cooled the Earl's delight in his erudition and wit.[6] However, his sister's wedding was postponed until after Christmas, because he did not "wholly assent" and the Queen delayed her approval. The Duchess meanwhile developed a hearty affection for Lady Mary, and in December they enjoyed a little plot to bring Lord Edward and his forlorn Countess Anne together again by playing on his desire to see his child Elizabeth. Lady Suffolk observed that the Earl now looked on her and her son with a not ungenial eye.

"I would wish speed," she wrote to Cecil, "that he might be taken in his good mood. I thank God I am at this present in his good favor."

She gave the Lord Treasurer some curious information about his prodigal son-in-law: "I hear he is about to buy a house here in London about Watling Street, and not to continue a courtier as he hath done. But I pray you keep all these things secret or else you may undo those that do take pains to bring it (the reconciliation) to pass if my Lord's counsel should be betrayed before he list himself. And above all others my credit should be lost with him if he should know I dealt in anything without his consent."

Whatever De Vere's plan of quitting the Court may have been, he showed no sign of it during the Christmas holidays. He certainly would not miss the performance of the Children of St. Paul's Cathedral on December 29 at Hampton Court, nor the play by Lord Howard's servants on Twelfth Night (January 5). The merriment of the wedding of Peregrine and Mary took place, I suppose, on the following Sunday, January 12, 1578, perhaps in the green surroundings of Richard Bertie's house in the country. At the feast afterward the delightful Duchess must have remembered and told the Earl about the Christmas entertainment given at Tylsey in 1551 by the Duke of Suffolk, when he and his wards the Willoughbys had the pleasure of witnessing comedies acted by the stage servants of John de Vere, Edward's father. Edward was then a year and nine months old.

The lonely Earl needed merriment. His melancholy had probably been aggravated in June 1577 by the spectacle of Mr. Philip Sidney's reception at the Court after his homecoming from a diplomatic mission in Europe. Her Majesty praised the youthful statesman—Sidney was only twenty-two and her Councilors all said that he had handled his diplomatic duties with great judgment and discretion. Master Philip reported that he had been "honored abroad in all the Princes' courts with much extraordinary favor." This was the same plebeian Sidney who, seven years before, had been a suitor for the hand of Anne Cecil, eclipsed by the courtship of the Earl of Oxford. Now they were talking about his potentiality as a leader in the state.

In July the Earl came into conflict with members of his own Roman Catholic party. He antagonized the Howard family by pleading with the Queen for possession of the manor of Rysing which she had confiscated from his cousin, the Duke of Norfolk, their patriarch who had lost his head. The "unkindness and strangeness" that ensued between him and Norfolk's son, Philip the Earl of Surrey, and Norfolk's brother, Lord Henry Howard, struck Protestant observers as a portent. His alliance with the house of Bertie strengthened the expectation that Oxford would become an anchor against English "Popery," like his uncle Arthur Golding. The Calvinist John Brooke dedicated to him a Huguenot homily, *The Staff of Christian Faith* (registered on 11 February 1577). De Vere's heart was stirred more deeply by the death of his tall friend George Gascoigne, the soldier and poet, on October 7, 1577. Gascoigne came from Walthamstow, Essex, just a few miles from the Earl's native castle of Hedingham. He married a widow from their home county, Bess Breton, and so became the stepfather of the poet Nicholas Breton, to whom we owe the publication of several of Oxford's rimes. The sad occasion of Gascoigne's death probably called to his young friend's mind the Christmas frolics of the law students at Gray's Inn in 1566, when George's famous comedy *Supposes* (adapted from Ariosto) was acted by the youngsters there. De Vere himself became a student of the Inn the following February, enrolling at the same time as Philip Sidney.

The love story of *Supposes* furnished plot material for *The Taming of the Shrew*, as well as the names Petruchio and Licio. Shakespeare directly recalled Gascoigne's play in the speech where the gallant Lucentio tells old Baptista how he courted his younger daughter—"While counterfeit supposes blear'd thine eyne" (5.1.108). Scholars have long been familiar with the fact that the romance of Lucentio and Bianca was inspired by Gascoigne's work. They have yet to be convinced that the love story of Petruchio and his shrew Katherina was inspired by Peregrine Bertie's marriage with Mary Vere.

II

Our primary justification for believing that Lady Mary was the original model for the Shrew comes from a letter by Sir Thomas Cecil on September 25, 1578. In it he reported a quarrel between her and

Peregrine. "I understand," Sir Thomas gossipt, "that my Lady of
Suffolk's coming down from London (to their rural home) was to
appease certain unkindness grown between her son and his wife.
More particularly as yet I cannot write at this time, but I think my
Lady Mary will be beaten with that rod which heretofore she prepared for others. But it is an old saying, *In quo peccatur eodum punitur.*"[7] By the same thing we sinned with, we are punished.... This
reference to the tongue of Oxford's sister is our only witness to her
mastery of a weapon for which the Earl himself was detested and
feared. Unluckily the correspondence of the Cecils has not yielded
any particulars about Peregrine's manner of chastising his mordant-
mouthed bride.

A minor indication of the real persons caricatured in Petruchio
and his Kate is the statement made by the former to her, "I am too
young for you" (2.2.39). Bertie was in fact seven years younger than
his wife.

Katherina's outburst in the same scene on hearing of Petruchio's
motherwit—"A witty mother!"—sounds like a tribute to Kate the
Duchess of Suffolk, in honor of whom perhaps the poet named his
heroine. The temperament of the two Kates had plenty in common.
Of course our poet associated them with the household beast he
detested above all others, and with the hateful goddess of antiquity,
Hecate, whose sylvan embodiment Diana casts her lunar beams
over *The Comedy of Errors* and the happy ending of *Pericles*.

After all, the dramatist's wit could not have rested content with a
single model for his Shrew. We have no way of knowing if he recognized that a man like Lord Willoughby was fated to fall in love
with a lady resembling his mother. But Shakespeare's eye and ear
were too finely tuned to the rhythms of human nature to miss the
likeness between Katherine Bertie and Mary Vere. And looking over
their portraits in his mental gallery he would also have perceived
their likeness to another Kate he knew intimately, Lady Windsor,
his half-sister.

Katherine Vere, the daughter of Earl John by his first wife,
Dorothy Neville, regarded Earl Edward and sister Mary with un-

concealed contempt. In June 1563 she had pulled political and religious wires to have them both branded as illegitimate. Strange as it may seem, she had no knowledge of her father's wedding with Margaret Golding, their mother, on August 1, 1548. It took place very quietly in the village church of Belchamp St. Paul's, Lady Margery's hometown, and the proud Kate was probably away at the time visiting with her noble kinsmen, the Nevilles. Whether they kept her ignorant of the event or she obliterated the memory of it in her hatred of her father's second wife, Lady Katherine persisted in thinking that Edward and Mary Vere were bastards, and she impressed her descendants with that belief. Her own marriage with Lord Edward Windsor proved an unhappy one. He deserted her, and spent the remainder of his days in obscure pilgrimages on the continent. His loyalty to the Catholic Church furnished excellent reasons for considering his marriage curst. And the character of his wife gave him no incentive to shoulder the curse with Christian charity and English humor.

In October 1578, a few weeks after the outbreak of "unkindness" between Oxford's sister Mary and her merry husband, young George Puttenham complained to the Queen's Council about the "shameless conduct" of Lady Windsor and her mother-in-law, whom he (Puttenham) had married for the sake of her widow's fortune. The two women made his life a purgatory. Puttenham went in quest of consolation and a refuge from his domestic disputes. "I have resolved with myself," he wrote, "to employ my time in studies and with conference with the greatest learned men I can find."[8] No doubt, he found both scholarship and sympathy in conversation with the Earl of Oxford, a fellow victim of Lady Windsor's tongue. If Puttenham, as literary researchers contend, is the author of *The Art of English Poesy* (1589), then he paid the Earl a tribute of friendship as well as esthetic criticism in that justly admired book. The *Art* praises those "noblemen and gentlemen of her Majesty's own servants, who have written excellently well as it would appear if their doings could be found out and made public with the rest, of which number is first that noble gentleman, Edward Earl of Oxford."

It seems to me most likely that the marital troubles of Willoughby and Puttenham recorded in the autumn of 1578, and the memories they evoked of the domestic harassments of Edward of Oxford, not to mention the sorrows of Lord Edward Windsor, combined to raise the idea of *The Taming of the Shrew* in the dramatist's head. The mirth stoked up by his imagination of Peregrine Bertie chastising the obstinate Mary with her favorite weapon would have been enough to inspire the comedy. With the convergence of this and the hilarity and hostility toward womankind aroused by Katherine Windsor's persecution of Edward her brother, Edward her husband, and the young stepfather George Puttenham, the farce must have cried to be written. I conjecture that the poet burned with the wish to utter in a publicly agreeable form the desires of sadism which he had long sustained more or less consciously toward his two sisters and his wife. It will be remembered how Antipholus the poor hero of his *Comedy of Errors* had longed for a rope's end to whip his wife, and threatened to pluck out her eyes with his own nails. The brutality of the Prince of Tyre toward the heroine of his romance was probably one of the sinister attractions that led our poet to write his *Pericles*. In the Latin original of that story the Prince is shown striking the girl to the ground with his foot so that her cheek bleeds. Comparison of Antipholus and Pericles with the hero of *The Shrew* persuades us that Petruchio is right when he states that the chief weapon he employs against his wife is mere "kindness" or husbandly zeal. He never assaults her with physical violence. The dominant mood of this comedy evinces an upward thrust of the dramatist's virility from the eunuchoid depression of his earlier plays. This could be credited to the chill and ill feeling that turned him away from the Howards to explore a new friendliness, the brotherhood of the Berties.

Perhaps the Earl had witnessed in Italy a play with the comic framework of *The Shrew* and recalled it while contemplating the matrimonial miseries of his brother-in-law Bertie and Puttenham. At all events, he set to work on a sketch of the comedy and had it well rehearsed by the Children of Paul's Cathedral before Christmas of

1578. I agree with the opinion of Eva Turner Clark that *The Shrew* was first played by these boys at Court on Thursday, January 1, 1579, under the title "A Moral of the Marriage of Mind and Measure." (In a later age it might have been named The Wedding of Whim and Wisdom.)

We are aided in establishing the date of production by the allusion in Act 3 to the comet of 1577. Petruchio's friends stare at his wedding apparel "As if they saw some wondrous monument. Some comet, or unusual prodigy." I accept the suggestion of Admiral H. H. Holland in *Shakespeare Through Oxford Glasses* (London 1924) that the monument parting jaws with awe was the tower rising over London bridge in the winter end of 1577. Also worth our notice are the lines of Scene 1 in this act which mark the time of Lucentio's Latin lesson as a Saturday in winter. The scene of Petruchio's homecoming is clearly set in a season of very cold weather.

III

There is no question that the play is an early one of Shakespeare's. Its numerous allusions to Latin Classics, not always in the best of taste, inform us that we have here a juvenile work. Look for instance at the odd simile drawn from Vergil with which Lucentio voices his affection for his companion Tranio (1.1.151-152) –

> as secret and as dear
> As Anna to the Queen of Carthage was.

This homoerotic speech is not the least of the play's testimonies that Lucentio was made in the image of his creator.

We first see Lucentio rejoicing on his arrival in the university city of Padua, "fair Padua, the nursery of arts." Edward de Vere was no less eager to visit Padua in May 1575 when he arrived in Italy. His beloved teacher Thomas Smith had studied law at the renowned university there. It was the first Italian town he lodged in, which may account for the choice of Padua as the scene of what I believe was Shakespeare's first play with an Italian locality. The Earl viewed

Padua again in November 1575, and there he penned a letter to his
father-in-law urging him to sell Oxford land in order to pay off ever
-increasing debts. Lord Burghley was grieved by his spending of
good English money for Italian frivolities. The Lord Treasurer had
not forgotten how he denied his son Thomas a chance to travel and
study in Italy "by reason," as Thomas's tutor Windebank said, "of
the enticements to pleasure and wantonness there."[9] This very wantonness enhances the attractiveness of Padua to Lucentio. He does
not intend to pursue the liberal arts in the city to the exclusion of
the art of love, particularly as taught by Ovid, Shakespeare's pet
among poets. When Lucentio's father Vincentio pictures his son
squandering money in Padua he exclaims, "While I play the good
husband at home my son and my servant spend all at the university." He sounds like Burghley lamenting his son-in-law's disdain for
husbandry and thrift. We are reminded especially of William Cecil's
complaints in 1562 about the expenses of maintaining his boy Thomas and his tutor Windebank in France. As a lad in Cecil's house
Edward de Vere must have heard these lamentations often, and the
harangues on good husbandry that his guardian delivered with
them.

The gallant Lucentio is introduced to us as a young man in disguise. He has changed his dress to save his life, for shortly after his
arrival in Padua, he informs Tranio, he engaged in a quarrel and—"I
kill'd a man, and fear I was descried." (1.1.229) Our dramatist might
have presented his romantic hero disguised for a reason less som-
bre, for the purpose of eluding creditors or merely playing a collegiate prank. Why did Shakespeare choose to present him as guilty of
manslaughter? If we examine the hero as one fashioned in the image
of his maker, we may be able to understand this. For we know that
the Earl of Oxford himself killed a man when he was seventeen. In
the summer of 1567, Burghley noted in his journal, young De Vere
fatally wounded an undercook employed in Cecil House. The inquest jury blamed the death on the victim, saying that he had run on
a fencing sword held by the Earl. Years later Burghley remarked in a
private paper that he had exerted his authority to get the jury's deci-

sion in favor of the Queen's ward. Oddly enough, there was a rumor around Padua in the summer of 1575 that implicated Lord Oxford in a charge of homicide. The banker Clemente Paretti wrote to
Burghley from Venice on September 23, 1575, that he should not
believe any gossip from Italy antipathetic to the Earl. "It is true,"
Paretti said, "that a while ago at Padua were killed unawares (in a
Quarrel that was amongst a certain congregation of Saffi and students) two noble gentlemen of Polonia, and the bruit ran *Gentiluo-
mini Inglesi*..." but Oxford was innocent.[10] Lucentio is the first of
Shakespeare's heroes to confess himself a murderer. The fact however is not mentioned again in *The Taming of the Shrew*. The unnecessary shadow of blood it introduces brings to mind the landscape of
carnage with which the *Comedy of Errors* concludes.

Incidentally, the Pedant in the play, who counterfeits the father
of Lucentio, stops in Padua to exchange some banking bills for
money (4. 2). We learn that he was once a lodger at the Pegasus inn
in Genoa (4. 4), a city which Oxford visited soon after his own arrival in Padua.

Lucentio (the brilliant) falls in love with Bianca (the white), second daughter of the wealthy Baptista Minola. Within the name of
this beauty I descry the name of Oxford's wife, the abandoned
Anne. (The thought obtrudes that the syllables "Bi" and "ca", between which "an" appears, may stand for the names of Burghley
and Cecil; but this seems too farfetched.) Bianca and Countess
Anne can be identified by the care which the playwright has taken
to portray the education of the heroine. Her father wants both his
girls to learn literature, music and mathematics, especially Latin and
other tongues, an erudition for which Lady Mildred Cecil, the
Countess of Oxford's mother, was much praised. Lord Burghley's
first wife, Mary Cheke, was the daughter of a professor of Greek
and distinguished like her husband for skill in foreign languages.
When Anne Cecil was twelve her parents hired one John Tassel to
teach her French. Presumably her future husband, who resided and
studied in the same house at the time, assisted her in struggles with
grammar and the rest. The popular scene in *The Shrew* (3.1) in which

Lucentio pretends to teach Bianca Latin under the scrutiny of another wooer may well be a sketch of actuality, from the love life of Earl Edward and his Anne. In the period of her tutoring in French, you see, she was being wooed by Master Philip Sidney. In fact her instructor John Tassel was sent to Cecil House by Sidney's father at Lady Mildred's request.[11]

Oxford's own interest in learning languages is manifested by the earliest letter of his in existence, written to Burghley in French at the age of thirteen, also by the first record of books he bought.[12] In June 1578 the learned William Lewin, one of Anne Cecil's teachers, who had accompanied Oxford to France and Germany, wrote a recommendation for a Belgian gentleman who wanted to travel to Antwerp, and lauded him as a servant of Lord Oxford "well furnished with the languages and other good qualities."[13] Naturally his Lordship, depicting himself as Lucentio, would qualify the youth as a superb scholar, "well read in poetry and other books" (1.2) and "cunning in Greek, Latin, and other languages" (2.1.80-81).

Baptista Minola, the Shrew's father, is an extremely prudent man. He vows that Katherina must be married before her more alluring sister, and invites the suitors of his children to bid fortunes for them (2.1). In Gascoigne's *Supposes* father Damonio wishes only to make sure that his daughter will not be wedded to a moneyless lover. "The narrow prying father" Baptista requires a son-in-law wealthy enough to be worthy of the thousands of crowns he expects to pour into his daughter's dowries. Speaking of crowns calls to memory the discovery by Looney of Earl Edward's craving for crowns while in Italy. Oxford borrowed five hundred of the coins from a dealer named Baptista Nigrone. Looney thought the dramatist contrived the name Baptista Minola from this merchant's name and the name of the financier Benedict Spinola, Burghley's adviser on Italian affairs, who supplied most of the funds that the Earl spent on his journeys abroad. Benedict's brother Pasquale aided Oxford with money during his visit to Venice in December 1575. The Spinolas kept Burghley informed about the Earl's movements during his Italian tour. At home in London he had money dealings with another Spinola (unknown to Looney) whose first name was none other than Baptista. Baptista Spinola was a banker well known to the court of Elizabeth and the Queen herself.[14]

There is a casual remark by Katherina on her father's treatment of money in charity which adds to my own confidence that we possess in Baptista Minola a comic portrait of De Vere's father-in-law. She says (4.3.4-6):

> Beggars that come unto my father's door
> Upon entreaty have a present alms;
> If not, elsewhere they meet with charity.

The last line, an afterthought, excites laughter by its abrupt exposure of Baptista's miserliness. It makes me think of the phrase that the comedian Richard Tarlton used for the gate of Burghley's house. He called it "the Lord Treasurer's alms gate, because it was seldom or never opened."[15]

In creating the characters of Bianca and Katherina, the poet repeated his portrayal of the two sisters in his *Comedy of Errors*. His lines on the Italian girls apply precisely to the two Greeks:

> The one as famous for a scolding tongue
> As is the other for beauteous modesty. (1.2.251-252)

Yet before the curtain closes on *The Shrew* we see Bianca betray herself, like Luciana in *Errors*, for a lady of mordant tongue and untender heart. When Hortensio quits her in Act 4 he declares,

> Kindness in women, not their beauteous looks,
> Shall win my love. (4.1.41-42)

Observe how cleverly she joins Lucentio in the erotic sport of beguiling her father. In the final scene she denounces Lucentio, her husband, for betting a hundred crowns on her wifely obedience: "The more fool you for laying on my duty." Plainly the poet enjoys revealing to us how Bianca resembles the Shrew spiritually. Likewise Anne my wife, he seems to have thought, is sister in soul to Katherine, my half-sister, and Mistress Mary Bertie too. In view of this common resemblance, it is interesting to observe that De Vere employed in a poem the same epithet for women that Shakespeare applies to the heroines of *The Shrew*, a term taken from the ancient sport of falconry. De Vere's poem, "If Women Could Be Fair," compares the sex to "haggards," wild hawks.[16] In the comedy Petruchio meditates cheerfully on ways to man his haggard (4.1) and Hortensio calls Bianca "this proud disdainful haggard" (4. 2.39). The word came easily to a poet fond of the aristocratic sports of yore.

IV

Academic erudition holds that Shakespeare took the name of his shrew-tamer from the *Supposes* by Gascoigne. It is more likely that both playwrights went to the same source for the name. They were both acquainted with Petruccio Ubaldino, a gentleman from Italy in the service of the Queen who was famous for his talents in theatrical enterprise. Petruccio came to England about 1540 and made his home in Hallowell Street, among musicians, minstrels and comedians. In January 1566 the parish clerk recorded the marriage of "Peter Onchio Ubaldino, stranger," to Anne Lawrence. His name occurs again and again in the papers of the royal Office of the Revels. Thus we find, in June 1572, a note of payment to "Petrucio for his travail and pains taken" in preparation of a court masque. He was still active in the Revels in the years 1577 and 1578, when the "Moral of the Marriage of Mind and Measure" was staged. Long before he died a London city record described him as a "gentleman belonging to the Court, hath bene here xxxvii (37) yeares."

For the personality of the poet's Petruchio, as we have already pointed out, the conscious model was Peregrine Bertie, Lord Willoughby, who Sir Thomas Cecil predicted would tame his bride's tongue. Inevitably, however, as the dramatist worked on his hero, he drew vitality for him from the fountainhead of all his conceptions of heroism, his ideal of self. Petruchio became a robust and rough image of the Earl of Oxford. He comes from Verona, which to my way of thinking signifies more than the beautiful city in Italy:

it means the one and only Vere. Like Earl Edward, the fellow from
Verona is an orphan, and though a restless adventurer, profoundly
at home in classical literature. He swears to marry Katherina,

> Be she as foul as was Florentius' love,
> As old as Sibyl, and as curst and shrewd
> As Socrates' Xanthippe... (1.2.68-70)

Like De Vere, the shrew-tamer had a vivid acquaintance with "the
swelling Adriatic seas," had heard "lions roaring," and watched the
sea rage like a boar—the animal whose image in little stands on the
Oxford coat-of-arms. Petruchio possesses his creator's faculty for
telling persuasive soldierly thrasonical lies. He brags of having heard
"great ordnance in the fields" and witnessed at least one battley
"Loud larums, neighing steeds, and trumpets' clang." He makes the
boast a short while after he informed his Paduan friends that he had
to leave Verona because his father had died and left him to hunt his
fortune some other place than "at home, where small experience
grows."

Among the dearest of De Vere's daydreams were visions of himself as a conquering warrior, commanding brave troops, and winning magnificent wars. He studied the military art from boyhood
and in the spring of 1570 was privileged to get a small experience of
warfare when Elizabeth consented to let him ride with the Earl of
Sussex on an expedition in the northern shires to terrorize Roman
Catholic rebels. In the summer of 1574 he attempted to gain more
education in the art by suddenly traveling to Flanders where he
hoped to watch the martial mastery of the Duke of Alva at work
crushing Protestant rebels. In a fortnight he was compelled to return to England, bringing for the amusement of his drinking companions in London little more than a garland of illusions about the
soldier's prowess he said he had exhibited in skirmish and siege to
the wonderment of Spanish and Italian veterans.

When *The Taming of the Shrew* was first acted, Peregrine Bertie
knew less about military business than his brother-in-law. Not many
years passed, however, before Lord Willoughby became a veteran

himself and a general more feared by the Spaniards than any English officer of the age.

Naturally it is the voice of the Earl of Oxford that we hear singing through Petruchio's mouth the fragments of popular melodies in the fourth act. Nearly all of Shakespeare's dramatic mouthpieces have the half-melancholy, half-merry habit of singing such fragments to themselves. "It was the friar of orders gray" must have been a charming ballad to the Catholic Earl. The question warbled by his newlywed hero, "Where is the life that late I led?" seems to come from a lyric known as "Lover Late at Liberty," which Clement Robinson printed in his *Handful of Pleasant Delights* in 1584. It is certainly much older; perhaps it is the lost ditty registered in 1566 under the title "A new ballad of one who, misliking his liberty, sought his own bondage through his own folly."

There is a poem in *A Gorgeous Gallery of Gallant Inventions*, entered in the London Stationers' book on 5 June 1577, which goes to the tune of "Where is the life that late I led?" It is entitled "The Lover wounded with his Lady's beauty craveth mercy," and like the other verses in the anthology bears no author's name. It tells the sad story of Dom Diego's love for Ginevra which, like the marriage of Edward de Vere and Anne Cecil, "was by default of light credit on her part interrupted." Diego in despair retired to the Pyrenees and "led a savage life for certain months." Poetically this parallels the lone retreat of De Vere to the scenes of his childhood, the deserted Castle Hedingham, the tombs of his ancestors in Earls Colne, and the house of his "Muses" by the sea at Wivenhoe, reflections of which occur in *Errors* and *Pericles*, "The Solitary Knight." The Spanish knight of the poem is won back by a friend to society and a happy marriage with Ginevra.

Shakespeare gives us no reason for Petruchio's expression of musical regret on his marriage. The dramatist simply "forgot himself" and allowed his unconscious to utter in this moody manner his own wish for bachelor liberty.

The kind scheming of the Duchess of Suffolk and Lady Mary Vere to win the lone Earl back to his Countess, by playing on his curiosity to see his baby daughter, apparently did not achieve its goal.

One detail concerning Petruchio appeals for inquiry. His servant Grumio says that he is about thirty-two years old (1.2.32). Now Willoughby did not reach this age until 1587. I believe the words were written when the dramatist revised the farce, with the determination to make it less subjective, to make the swashbuckling hero more like his brother-in-law than he had looked in the earlier play. The Shrew came out under its present title, I conjecture, in 1587 and inspired the actor Robert Wilson to mimicry in his comedy *The Three Lords and Three Ladies of London*, which is plausibly assigned to the year 1588 (it was printed as an old piece in 1590). One of the funny passages in this play clearly imitates the sham Latin lesson in *The Shrew*. The scene of that lesson enjoyed remarkable popularity among London theatre-lovers and writers. In John Lyly's enormously successful novel *Euphues or The Anatomy of Wit* Camilla makes believe that Philautus is her tutor and gives him a copy of Petrarch to construe a lesson for her. She really wishes him to find a letter in the book. Lyly published *Euphues* toward the end of 1579; "The Marriage of Mind and Measure" entertained the Court at the beginning of this year.

V

The sadistic gladness of our poet over the domestication of Katherina Minola shows us what Oxford longed to do to his wife. He surely longed for the return of the good old days when an Englishman could lawfully rebuke his wife with both hands. In the reign of Henry VIII Justice Brooke had affirmed "that if a man beat an outlaw, a traitor, a pagan, his villein, or his wife, it is dispunishable, because by the Law Common these persons can have no action." By 1568, however, English jurisprudence arrived at the opinion that, "though the civil law giveth man the superiority over his wife, that is not to offend or despise her, but in misdoing, lovingly to reform her."[17] I have no doubt that Oxford consented on principle to this judgment of women's rights. It conformed to the pattern of courtesy toward the sex drawn by Castiglione in *Il Cortegiano*, Oxford realised that defiance of the principle meant a meanness not to be tolerated in one who aspired to the glory of "The Courtier." Nevertheless the Earl indulged in fantasies of killing his Countess—with kindness.

In the reality of wedlock he had behaved quite cruelly to her. As we have seen in our analysis of *Cymbeline*, the Cecil family papers include an anonymous document which delineates somewhat cryptically a few of the ways he tormented her. It is entitled "Notes by an Ill-Used Wife," but appears to be from the quill of mother Mildred Cecil. We can tell that it refers to Oxford because it speaks of residence at his seacoast retreat in Wivenhoe. Here are excerpts from the paper:

> Knocked up at 11 o'clock, waked.
> Kept out of his chamber at dinner and supper by York and other within...
> Not speak a word nor countenance in father's house.
> So many 100 pounds spent of ten thousand come to his hand since marriage.
> Never one token of love in gown, button, aigrettes.
> A hose-garter asked again.
> No pillion to come from Wyvenhoe, but of poor golden fustian.
> His man to demand a note of her small plate in her own hand given her; and he never speak himself. Linen spoiled, very fine and damask.
> Women ii gotten with child; men entertaining them in chamber and not dare find fault because they were great about him.[18]

These notes are not dated but the allusion to York (Rowland York, the soldier of fortune who served with Gascoigne in the Low Countries and stayed with Oxford intimately when he returned to London in April 1576), in the light of the known facts of the Earl's married life, suggest hours of bitterness between Yuletide of 1572 and the spring of 1573.

The catalog of complaints against Edward de Vere was continued by Lord Burghley in April 1576. He wrote that his daughter, prior to the time of her pregnancy, "was in debt for lack of relief. She had been long sick before that. In her sickness when she bred child her charges were great; the like when she was delivered. (Nota: no land assured to his daughter, though he have no other child.)"[19] Cecil recorded more reasons for detesting De Vere on "12th June, 1576. To be remembered."

> "The time now past almost of two months without certainty whereupon to rest arguments of unkindness both towards my daughter, his wife, and me also.
> Rejecting of her from his company.
> Not regarding his child born of her.
> His absence from the Court in respect to avoid his offence, and her solitary lying."

Oxford appears to have maltreated his wife by contemptuous cold neglect, broken by interludes of sarcasm, wild lamentation or self-delighting indignant eloquence, rather than the torrid boorish tricks employed by Petruchio. The Earl multiplied reasons for disliking and divorcing her, but the more he reasoned the less convincing he became. Ridiculously he tried to connect the sweet little masochist Anne Cecil with his Shrew by calling the latter "Kate of KateHall," a title reminiscent of the Cecil mansion of Theobalds, which the Queen's court pronounced as if it was spelt Tybalds, like the notorious cat Tybalt of French fable. By no stretch of the imagination could the Countess Anne be charged with the faults of Katherina Minola. Yet the dramatist, identifying himself with the woman-tamer from Verona, spontaneously fancied the soul of his wife behind the mask of the rough and defiant Kate. In doing so he gave away the secret of the magnetism of her sex for him and the terror it provoked in his heart.

What drew him irresistibly to the women of his life and chilled him when he finally arrived in their arms was their assertion of masculine energy. The infant in him thrilled to the belief that mothers, potential mothers too, were mightier than most men, including his father. Under its spell he felt belittled and emasculated; he became a pathetic child again. We have seen in the analysis of *The Comedy of Errors* how the poet ascribed the wreck of his marriage to a stony maleness he encountered in his mate. He echoes the theme of that play in *The Shrew*, almost in its very words:

> Lucentio. Mistress, what's your opinion of your sister?
> Bianca. That, being mad herself, she's madly mated. (3. 2..243-244)

In *The Taming of the Shrew* Shakespeare adopted a posture of bravado and pretended to aim at the extirpation of the phallic factor in femininity. Katherina warns Petruchio (2.1.213): "If I be waspish, best beware my sting." He responds, "My remedy is then to pluck it out." "Ay," says she, "if the fool could find it, where it lies." He accepts the challenge: "Who knows not where a wasp does wear his sting? In his tail."

The threat of castration materialises in the stage business of taming, with a hysterical declamation on the virtue of continence pronounced by Petruchio to Kate in the privacy of their bedchamber and so unfortunately left out of the play. Her domestication concludes with the avowal, "But now I see our lances are but straws." (5.2.180) The hero's victory over her clitoral complex is symbolized by having his wife offer to put her hand under his foot.

Kate's preaching on the duties of a wife ardently elaborate the ideas on the subject which the poet had proclaimed from the lips of Luciana in his *Errors*. The writer betrays his patrician prejudice and ignorance of the working women of his country by having his heroine talk of the bodies of her sex as "soft and weak and smooth,/ Unapt to toil and trouble in the world." The child in Shakespeare insisted on his thinking of woman thus, the same child whose yearning for and grievance against the maternal bosom he uttered in these lines:

> A woman mov'd is like a fountain troubled,
> Muddy, ill-seeming, thick, bereft of beauty;
> And while it is so, none so dry or thirsty
> Will deign to sip or touch one drop of it. (5.2.148-151)

For modern audiences, with less archaic concepts of woman's place and function, the speech by Kate has been made sufferable by histrionic devices to indicate that she should not be taken seriously. Actresses of the role today deliver her lecture with coy dropping of the eyes or winks and sly smiles. A number of Shakespeare's contemporaries found the lesson of his comedy a little preposterous. John Fletcher made fun of it in his play *The Woman's Prize or The Tamer Tamed*, which was recorded as an old comedy in 1633. In it Petruchio reappears and is taught uproariously the meaning of feminine dignity by a second wife, named Maria. Fletcher's Epilog declares his purpose, "To teach both sexes due equality"—a concept that would have startled his master Shakespeare with its novelty.

But when our dramatist wrote "The Moral of the Marriage of Mind and Measure," or *The Taming of the Shrew*, he was in no mood for ethical controversy on the relations of the sexes. The Induction to *The Taming of the Shrew* discloses the aggressive temper in which he composed the play and states his purpose to, exactly as in *The Comedy of Errors*, a triumphant fight with melancholy. In both cases the combat required the imaginary abuse of his innocent wife, reviling her as a virago. That was the nearest he could come to vengeance on his mother Margaret until he felt ready to draw the portrait of the royal termagant Margaret of Anjou.

It is difficult to part from these pages without glancing again at the influence of the Duchess of Suffolk and her son on the Earl of Oxford's political passions. Clearly the sunshine of their home, Willoughby House in the Barbican district of London, gently altered the course of his soul back to the way it was going in his boyhood under the spell of Arthur Golding and Thomas Smith. He lost his ardor for Dr. Nicholas Sanders, who labored desperately to interest Philip of Spain in his plan to attack England from the Irish flank. Cardinal Ormenetto, the Pope's envoy to Madrid, failed to persuade the despot that "this lady" Elizabeth "is the source of all the mischief in his patrimonial Low Countries, altho in words she pretends the very contrary."[20] Her Majesty was sincere in wanting to end the "mischief" of self-determination in the Netherlands. "To aid the

Low-countries," in her judgment, "is to deal with people that lack a head, and also to encourage subjects against their sovereign lord."[21] She wished that Spanish weaponry would be far from her shores. Peregrine Bertie and his mother shared the popular enthusiasm for the cause of William the Stadtholder, and wished England to join banners with his in the war. In harmony with their temper, Edward de Vere and his friends swung to Orange's side. In December 1577 Roger Williams left the company of Don John at Luxembourg, and shortly after, we find him carrying despatches between Sir Francis Walsingham and the Netherlands, the same Walsingham whom the Queen accused of being good for nothing but to protect heretics. The valiant Welshman found Orange unwilling to employ a former servant of Don John in his army, but Williams somehow proved that he was "greatly devoted" to the Prince.[22] Another Welshman from the circle of Oxford, Walter Williams, also served Walsingham as a messenger, in 1578.[23] Unluckily we have no documents of this time to illuminate for us the roads taken by the would-be warriors of the Vere family. On March 14, 1579, "Alberic de Vere," whom we know better as Oxford's uncle Aubrey, was buried in the parish of Castle Hedingham. John Vere, the eldest son of Oxford's uncle Geoffrey, turned twenty-one, having made up his mind to be simply a country gentleman, caring for his mother. The Earl arranged that they should live close to his birthplace at Kirby or Picards Hall, no more than a mile away. This would have been the proper occasion for a family conference, in which Francis Vere would gain Lord Edward's consent to his journeying along with Captain Francis Allen to experiment in military enterprise in "Polonia." And the Huguenot sage Hubert Languet persisted in warning his young friend Philip Sidney to subdue his aspiration to shine in war. In July 1578 Languet counseled him, "If you marry a wife, and beget children like yourself, you will be a better servant of your country than if you were to cut the throats of a thousand Spaniards or Frenchmen. I am not in this recommending you to idleness or ease—at least if we are to believe the poet who advises any man that wishes plenty of strife to get himself a wife."[24]

References

1 Historical Manuscripts Commission: Calendar of Cecil Ms. ii, 154.

2 Calendar of Rutland Ms. I, iii.

3 Violet A. Wilson, *Queen Elizabeth's Maids of Honour and Ladies of the Privy Chamber* (1922) 138.

4 Calendar of State Papers Foreign, 1547-1553, p. 101; *Dictionary of National Biography*, "Bertie, Catherine."

5 Cecil Ms. ii, 146; ii, 156; Historical Manuscripts Commission: Manuscripts of the Earl of Ancaster, 4.

6 Cecil Ms. ii, 157.

7 B. M. Ward, *The Seventeenth Earl of Oxford* (1928) 155; Sidney Letters and Memorials, 1, 193; Cecil Ms. ii, 469; ii, 156.

8 Louis Thorn Golding, *An Elizabethan Puritan* (1937) 38; *Dictionary of National Biography*, "Windsor"; *Acts of the Privy Council*, ed. Dasent, cxxvi, 16; *The Arte of English Poesie*, ed. G. L. Willcocks & A. Walker (Cambridge 1936) xxii.

9 Calendar of State Papers Domestic (1562), xxv, 58.

10 Burghley Papers, ed. Murdin, 764; Cecil Ms. ii, 114.

11 Cecil Ms. i, 439.

12 Ward, *op. cit.*, 21, 33.

13 Calendar of State Papers Foreign (1578-79), no. 12.

14 Looney, *"Shakespeare" Identified* (1920) 272 [Reprinted in Looney, *"Shakespeare" Identified*, R. Miller, ed, Kennikat Press, Port Washington, N. Y. (1975) 2261; C. W. Barrell, in *The Shakespeare Fellowship Quarterly*, viii (Autumn 1947) 46.

15 *Diary of John Manningham*, quoted by Halliwell, ed. *Tarlton's Jests* (1844) xxx.

16 *The Poems of Edward de Vere*, ed. Looney (1921) 37 [Reprinted in Looney, *"Shakespeare" Identified*, 3rd ed, R. Miller, ed, Kennikat Press, Port Washington, N. Y. (1975) 595].

17 Carroll Camden, *The Elizabethan Woman* (Houston, TX 1952) 116.

18 Cecil Ms. xiv, 19.

19 *Ibid.* ii, 131, 170-1.

20 Thomas McNevin Veech, *Dr. Nicholas Sanders and the English Reformation* (Louvain: Bibliotheque de l'Universite, 1935) 218.

21 *Relations Politiques des Pays-Bas et de l'Angleterre, sous le Regne de Philippe* II, ed. Kervyn de Lettenhove (Brussels: Hayez, 1882-1900) x, 153.

22 Calendar of State Papers Foreign, 1577-78, no. 871, also p. 693.

23 *Ibid.* 584f.

24 *Correspondence of Sir Philip Sidney and Hubert Languet*, trans. Stuart A. Pears (London: William Pickering, 1845).

The Noble Novice: An Interlude

Think not that I by verse seek fame.
Sir Philip Sidney: *Sonnet to Stella*

For knowledge of the development of Edward de Vere's art we have to examine with special care the lyrical writings that preceded his dramatic works and poured out concurrently with them. All his life he produced songs. It would not surprise me to learn that he began writing poetry in boyhood, soon after the famous *Book of Songs and Sonnets* published in 1557 by Richard Tottel (and better known as *Tottel's Miscellany*) came to the little Viscount's hands. Among the leading authors in this anthology none enjoyed a more splendid reputation than Henry Howard, Earl of Surrey, the devoted husband of Edward's aunt Frances Vere, who also wrote verse. For these family connections alone the volume would have been precious to her nephew. His passion for poetry made it a treasured companion of his solitude.

Another sister of his father, Anne, married Lord Edmund Sheffield, a courtier well liked for his sonnets "in the Italian fashion" and his musical skill.

When Earl John de Vere was accused of taking part in conspiracy against Queen Mary Tudor, the poet William Hunnis, who served for both religion and recreation in her Majesty's Chapel, was also accused of a part in the plot. Hunnis may have come early within the Viscount Edward's ken and encouraged him to try verse.

When Earl John died and Edward became a member of Sir William Cecil's household, his uncle Arthur Golding went along as a tutor. From Cecil House on December 23, 1564, Golding issued the first four sections of his immortal translation of Ovid's *Metamorphoses*. Of all the literature young Oxford read, Ovid's book exerted perhaps the deepest influence on his mind. Two years later, on October 31, 1566, Richard Edwards, poet and playwright, Master of the Royal Chapel children, died leaving a collection of his poems which became the basis of the anthology *The Paradise of Dainty De-*

vices, printed ten years after. Here Oxford's first lyrics appeared in print. In November 1566 William Hunnis took Richard Edwards's place as Master of the Chapel, and directed children of the quire in plays deemed worthy of Queen Elizabeth's Yuletide nights. Uncle Arthur completed his only translation of Latin artistry in Barwick, Essex, in 1567. The Earl's first poetry followed in their vein.

Among the servants of the earl at this time was Thomas Churchyard, a tiresome rimester who had served as a page in the home of Edward's uncle Lord Surrey. This indefatigable writer did not remain long in the retinue of De Vere. He entered the more lucrative employment of Christopher Hatton, the Earl's most elegant and malicious rival at Elizabeth's Court.

When Oxford was nineteen he bought from the stationer William Seres an edition of Geoffrey Chaucer, and other books and papers, and "nibs". He revered Chaucer and in the maturity of his own art strove to educate younger English poets in the reverence for reality which distinguishes the ancient bard. The earliest definite testimony of Oxford's efforts in the lyric vein occurs in the dedication that his uncle Arthur wrote for a translation of *The Psalms of David and Others, with M. John Calvin's Commentaries.*

The dedication to his "very good Lord Edward de Vere" is dated October 20, 1571. It urges the Earl to pay grave attention to religion, "to set more store by it than riches… to talk of it afore Kings and great men, to love it, *to make your songs of it*, to remember it night and day." We do not know what songs De Vere made in those days, but the spell exerted on the brain of the boy Viscount Bulbeck by the paramount poetry of the *Bible* is clear. It must have been from the *Tehilim*—Psalms—that he learnt to put the most powerful utterances of his soul into the briefest arcs or flights of his verbal consciousness.

His earliest emergence in a book was with a piece of Latin prose he wrote to advertise his Cambridge teacher Bartholomew Clerke's Latin translation of Baldassare Castiglione's classic of etiquette and wit, *The Courtier.* Clerke's work, *De Curiali sive Aulico*, came from the press of John Day in 1572; the Earl's preface was composed at the

Court on January 5. With youthful eloquence he praised especially the translator's style, and so made clear his own interest in word-wizardry and the melody of language:

> For who is clearer in his use of words? Or richer in the dignity of his sentences? Or who can conform to the variety of circumstances with greater art? If weighty matters are under consideration, he unfolds his theme in a solemn and majestic rhythm; if the subject is familiar and facetious, he makes use of words that are witty and amusing. When therefore he writes with precise and well-chosen words, with skillfully constructed and crystal-clear sentences, and with every art of dignified rhetoric, it cannot be but that some noble quality should be felt to proceed from his work.

Soon after Oxford wrote this, he engaged to persuade the courtier Thomas Bedingfield to allow publication of his translation in English of Girolamo Cardano's *Consolation*, a work of sad philosophy which has been hailed as "Hamlet's Book" for its effect on the tragedy of the Prince of Denmark. *Cardanus' Comfort* appeared in 1573 "by Commandment of the right honorable Earl of Oxenford." De Vere wrote an introduction in the form of a letter "to my loving friend," Bedingfield, and added his first published poem, sending both from "my new country Muses of Wivenhoe." His verses define with scarce adornment the sorrows of the creative mind that "reaps not the gifts of golden goodly muse." The best one can say of these lines is that they ring sincere. We find superior artistry in Oxford's letters of this period which have been preserved in the papers of the Cecil family.

Early in 1573 the first of the Elizabethan anthologies ran from the press of Henry Bynneman, a workman loyal to the interests of Christopher Hatton. This anonymous collection, *A Hundreth Sundrie Flowres* (Imprinted for Richard Smith), consisted of poems scarcely notable for image, rhythm or thought, but deserving a glance for their gossip of courtiers' love affairs. In August 1573 G. T. the collector (probably the poet George Turberville) gave them to his friend H. W. (perhaps Henry Wotton, the author of *A Courtly Con-*

troversy of Cupid's Cautels, 1578), with the warning that they must not
be put in print. H. W. disobeyed, believing that it was better to
please many by "common commodity" than to gratify the private
whim of the writers, "needless singularity." "If the Authors only
repine," he wrote, and learned readers rejoice over their enrichment
of English poetry, "I may then boast to have gained a bushel of
good will in exchange for one pint of peevish choler." He himself
had reaped one advantage from these effusions, a smiling lesson in
the devices of men who had "enchained themselves in the golden
fetters of fantasy." The printer's name was affixed to a foreword
saying that he had discovered nothing wrong with the book—
"unless it be two or three wanton places passed over in the discourse of an amorous enterprise; the which, for as much as the
words are cleanly (although the thing meant be somewhat natural) I
have thought good also to let them pass as they came to me... the
well-minded man may reap some commodity out of the most frivo-
lous works that are written." We can be confident that the industrious Henry Bynneman would never have printed anything without
the approval of his employer Kit Hatton, who did not mind the lus-
ter of an agile seducer the *Flowres* flung on him.

The main amorous enterprise occurs in a novelet in prose by G.
T. and verse by F. I., more amusing than its companion poetry.
"The Adventures of F. I." recounts the adultery of a gentleman calling himself "Fortunatus Infelix" with a lady of a northern country
named Mistress Elionor P., who soon laughed him away for the
love of a rival. Fortunatus Infelix, we learn from the erudite contemporary Gabriel Harvey, was a "posy" or emblem of Christopher
Hatton.[1] To Hatton then could be attributed not only the amors of
F. I. but the seventeen "flowres" signed with the words "Si fortunatus infoelix." One of these poems was dispatched from "Fontaine
belle eau in France," where Hatton seems to have gone for his
health in the summer of 1573. He visited the famous Spa in Belgium, and while traveling in Catholic Flanders seems to have engaged in an intrigue with Lord Henry Howard and George Turberville aimed at the humiliation of Lord Burghley and his Protestant

cronies.[2] Hatton was a bachelor all his life and a multitalented courtier. They say that he danced his way into the Queen's favor by his
skill in the galliard. He deserves more attention as one of the crafti-
est and cruellest of Elizabethan statesmen.

Several of the poems signed with his posy may have been composed for his humor by George Gascoigne. One, a riddle, is said to
be the product of G. G., who plays an erotic role in others of the
series. Forty-five of the hundred are certainly by Gascoigne. In the
season of their publication he was in the Low Countries, acting as
an observer for the English government and occasionally assisting
the Prince of Orange, chief of the Dutch fighters against Spain.
(Together with the *Flowres*, two of Gascoigne's plays, the comedy
Supposes and the tragedy *Jocasta*, were published: "Printed by Henry
Binneman for Richard Smith.")

Some of the better verses in the anthology are signed "Spraeta
tamen vivunt." The author, according to a keen conjecture by Eva
Turner Clark is the learned Thomas Watson, whose posthumous
Tears of Fancy (1594) reproduces, almost word for word, four stanzas
of Flowre 38, called "A Loving Lady being wounded in the spring
time."

There seems to be a satire on De Vere concealed in this song, for
the lady complains that "The lusty *Ver*" (a pun on the Latin for
spring) now behaves strangely toward her. "What plant can spring,"
she wonders, "that feels no force of *Ver*?" Watson too was away
from England when these frivolities were printed. He went to Flanders to enroll in a Catholic school.

An editor of the book, Bernard M. Ward, has argued that the
Earl of Oxford composed the lyrics signed "Meritum petere, grave."
It is conceivable that some of these were inspired by Oxford's marital troubles, in particular the lament of a noble-woman, victim of
slander, which contains these lines:

> In Lofty Walls, in strong and stately towers,
> With troubled mind in solitary sort,
> My lovely Lord doth spend his days and hours,
> A weary life devoid of all disport...

> And I, poor soul, must lie here all alone,
> To tire my truth, and wound my will with moan.

This suggests an affected compassion for the neglected Countess of Oxford. It might have been written by Edward Dyer, an intimate adviser of Hatton, who consulted him about methods of subtle smearing of Oxford's reputation.

The first outbreak of unkindness between De Vere and his wife of which we have record took place three months after their wedding, when another grandson of John de Vere, the fifteenth Earl of Oxford, Thomas Howard, Duke of Norfolk, the son of the poet Surrey, was waiting to be executed as an alleged traitor. The Earl of Oxford, having failed to turn his father-in-law's heart to clemency for Norfolk, let out his anger on Countess Anne. On March 18, 1572, John Lee wrote to Burghley from Antwerp that his son-in-law, "they say here, hath put away from him the Countess his wife." In the "Notes by an Ill-Used Wife" we quoted in the past chapters, we see what tactics of petty revenge the Earl pursued between May 1572 and May 1573. There is a letter of December 1572 by an agent of Burghley reporting a visit on business to De Vere at Wivenhoe. It does not tell whether his wife was with him. The lament of the lady in the *Flowres* may allude to the stately towers of Oxford's mansion by the North Sea or the lofty walls of his Castle Hedingham, nine miles west. In the fall of 1573 relations between him and Burghley's daughter were such that Walter, Earl of Essex felt constrained to write the Lord Treasurer a greeting for "your good Countess, your daughter, of whose match I mistrust not but your Lordship shall in the end receive singular comfort."[3]

Oxford could not be the author of the lyric "An absent lover (parted from his Lady by Sea)" which also bears the motto *Meritum petere, grave*. And other poems with the same Latin signature toy with the initials of George Gascoigne and hint broadly of his passion for Bess Bacon Breton Boyes, the mother of the poet Nicholas Breton.

In October 1574 Gascoigne returned from the Netherlands sorely in need of funds. He wrote a long poem on his military experience, "Dulce Bellum Inexpertis," which ends with a series of rimes addressed to English Earls, extolling without any personal allusion "Young Oxenford as toward as the best." Then in January the daring earl finally sailed to France for his long-desired tour of the continent. During Oxford's absence Gascoigne assumed authorship for *A Hundreth Sundrie Flowres*. He issued an open letter "from my poor house at Walthamstow (Essex) in the forest 2nd Feb. 1575," claiming the volume as his own, and published an enlarged and corrupted ("corrected, perfected") edition under the title *The Posies of George Gascoigne*. He apologized for having offended by lascivious language but denied that any of the poems intended calumny—though "some busy conjectures have presumed to think that the same was indeed written to the scandalizing of some worthy personages." In his *Posies* he left out the two introductory letters by H. W. and G. T., he cut out all remarks about multiple authorship, rearranged the emblems, and shifted the scene and characters of "The Adventures of F. I." to Italy, pretending that he had translated the tale from a writer named Bartello, whom he invented for the occasion. He got the name from "Bartholomew of Bath," the hero of one of his own amorous poems. Gascoigne also omitted the passages in *Flowres* which darted satirically at the Pope and Papists. Ward has cogently contended that Gascoigne did all this at the behest of Christopher Hatton—"Fortunatus Infelix" himself.[4] In 1576, when the Earl of Oxford returned from the continent, the Court of high Commission ordered all copies of *Posies* seized. Gascoigne this year wrote commendatory verses for the second edition of *Cardanus' Comfort* and for George Turberville's *Noble Art of Venery*. He devoted his last months mainly to the composition of social satire in verse and somber moral prose.

Not long after the Earl of Oxford came back from Italy and severed relations with his wife and all the Cecils, another anthology of a hundred poems, very different from its forerunner, came to light. *The Paradise of Dainty Devices* was printed in 1576 by Henry Disle, who had recently been set free from his apprenticeship. He dedicated it to Sir Henry Compton with a note announcing that the contents had been assembled by a certain gentleman "for his private use: who not long since departed this life." Richard Edwards, the Master of the Queen's Chapel, author of the play *Damon and Pythias*, is meant. He probably commenced the anthology long before with the help of Oxford's close friend Lord Thomas Vaux, a devout Catholic (one of whose songs is exploited in *Hamlet*), and Jasper Heywood the gifted Jesuit, translator of the tragedies of Seneca. Thomas Churchyard, Francis Kinwelmarsh—who collaborated with Gascoigne in the tragedy *Jocasta*—and other minor rimers including perhaps Gascoigne, joined the little chorus of didactic and dismal verse. Outstanding among the younger contributors for the vivacity of his rimes is E. O., Edward of Oxford, who I think sponsored the volume. The earl was unquestionably an admirer of Richard Edwards and may have been intimate with him. Edwards is presumably the "person of the Chapel that died," mentioned in the libels of Charles Arundel against Oxford, with whom De Vere said he "had often seen the Devil by conjuring" in the little house in the tournament yard at Greenwich Palace.[5]

The initials E.O. (expanded in the Rawlinson Manuscripts to E. of Oxenford) appear at the close of the following "Dainty Devices:"

"His Good Name being blemished, he bewaileth;"

"The Judgment of Desire"—a merry piece contrasting brightly with the rest of the *Devices*;

"The Complaint of a Lover, wearing Black and Tawny"—a jolly elegy;

"Being in Love, he complaineth" (first printed as from the pen of a Master Bewe);

"A Lover Rejected, complaineth";

"Not Attaining to His Desire, he complaineth";

"His Mind Not Quietly Settled, he writeth this" (echoing his rimes in *Cardanus' Comfort*);

"Of the Mighty Power of Love."

These "devices" of De Vere are not excelled by any others in the *Paradise* and please us by their youthful temper, their grace and honesty. They reveal an author intensely conscious of the problem of setting words to a tune, and yet one resolved to write only of emotions he has experienced in the flesh. His songs are not redolent of a library and scholastic lamp; though compositions dating to Oxford's juvenile years, his poems are still the freshest in the book. William Shakespeare knew many mature moments when he could do no better.

The best of the eight, I suppose, is "Being in Love," in later editions called *Coelum non solum.*

> If care or skill should conquer vain desire,
> Or reason's reins my strong affection stay,
> Then should my sighs to quiet breast retire,
> And shun such signs as secret thoughts bewray.
> Uncomely love, which now lurks in my breast,
> Should cease my grief, through wisdom's power opprest.
>
> But who can leave to look on Venus' face?
> Or yieldeth not to Juno's high estate?
> What wit so wise as gives not Pallas place?
> These virtues rare, each God did yield a mate,
> Save her alone who yet on earth doth reign,
> Whose beauty's string no God can well distrain.
>
> What worldly wight can hope for heavenly hire
> When only signs must make his secret moan?
> A silent suit doth seld to Grace aspire;
> My hapless hap doth roll the restless stone.
> Yet Phebe fair disdaind the heavens above
> To joy on earth her poor Endimion's love.
>
> Rare is reward where none can justly crave,
> For chance is choice where reason makes no claim;
> Yet luck sometimes despairing souls doth save;
> A happy star made Gyges joy attain;
> A slavish Smith, of rude and rascal race,
> Found means in time to gain a Goddess' grace.

> Then lofty Love, thy sacred sails advance,
> My sighing seas shall flow with streams of tears:
> Amidst disdain, drive forth my doleful chance;
> A valiant mind no deadly danger fears.
> Who loves aloft, and sets his heart on high,
> Deserves no pain, though he do pine and die.

This lyric clearly expresses a desire to win the heart of no less a lady than Queen Elizabeth—"her alone who yet on earth doth reign." At first glance it may seem that the poet intended merely the sort of flattering adoration that the Queen liked to receive from all her handsome courtiers. But Oxford was not simply playing the game she was accustomed to. His narcissism led him to believe that "Phebe" might be enchanted to condescend and give herself to the genius of "Endimion." We do not know when the Earl's erotic interest in her Majesty first kindled, but we have evidence that Elizabeth looked on him with an almost amorous eye in July 1571, the very month in which Lord St. John declared, "The Earl of Oxenford hath gotten himself a wife, or at least a wife hath caught him. This is the mistress Anne Cecil, whereunto the Queen hath given her consent."[6] In June 1571 Elizabeth invited the French ambassador Fenelon to go for a stroll with her in the royal park of Westminster in order to witness a salvo of artillery and parade of arquebusiers under the direction of young Oxford. In July she told Fenelon, speaking of a possible alliance with France by her marriage with a French prince, "considering her time of life, she should be ashamed to be conducted to church to be married to anyone looking so young as the Earl of Oxford," who was nearly the same age as Henri de Valois, Duc d'Anjou. She was then examining a crayon portrait of Anjou.[7]

We may be sure that Elizabeth Tudor was well aware that Edward de Vere was descended from feudal blood ranked superior to her own. The Earl could trace his lineage to the loins of King Edward Plantagenet the First.

Edward I & Eleanor, princess of Castille
/
Elizabeth=Humphrey de Bohun,
Earl of Hertford & Essex
/   /
Henry IV=Mary   Margaret=Hugh Courtney,
Earl of Devonshire
/
Hugh=Philippa Archdeacon
/
Joan=Sir Robert de Vere
/
Alice Kilrington=John
/
Elizabeth Trussell= John de Vere, 15th Earl of Oxford
/
Margaret Golding= John, 16th Earl of Oxford
/
Edward, 17th Earl of Oxford

Queen Bess preferred to think of Oxford as too young for her.

So on August 17, 1571, his dear friend the Earl of Sussex wrote to Edward Manners, Earl of Rutland, who had also been a royal ward in Cecil's house: "I doubt not you hear of a marriage concluded between my Lord of Oxford and my Lord of Burghley's daughter."[8] This wedding, Protestants contended, would take away from the Catholic faction at Court two arms they had high hopes for. However, according to the antiquarian William Dugdale, "This Edward, being an entire friend to Thomas, Duke of Norfolk, when he discerned his life in danger upon what was laid to his charge" (conspiring to marry the Scottish Queen and join invading Spanish troops), "earnestly interceded" with Burghley "for the preserving him from destruction; but prevailing not, grew so highly incensed against Burghley, knowing it was in his power to save him, that in great indignation he said he would do all he could to ruin his daughter; and accordingly, not only forsook her bed, but sold and consumed that great inheritance descended to him from his ancestors."[9] Dugdale neglected to tell us from whom he got this large lie. Gilbert Talbot apparently never heard a murmur of it, and he kept his father, the Earl of Shrewsbury, informed about all follies of the Lords and Ladies he met. And on May 28, Sir Thomas Gresham reported to Oxford's father-in-law, he had two thousand marks ready to lend Lord Oxford.[10] In July 1572 the Earl and his Anne shared rooms at her father's country residence of Theobalds on the north side. The Queen slept on the north side, Robert Dudley the Earl of Leycester on the floor above, and Mr. Hatton in the tower chamber over him.[11]

In August, Elizabeth rode down with her nobles to Warwick on the Avon river. She danced at the castle there and afterward enjoyed the spectacle of a mock-battle between two forts using artillery and fireworks. The Earl of Oxford commanded one, Philip Sidney's friend Fulke Greville the other. Her Majesty took great pleasure in the show, particularly the wild fire falling into the Avon and flashing up from its waters. Her gayety was not overclouded when a ball of flame dropt on a house standing on a bridge and set fire to it. Greville and Oxford had a rough time rescuing the man and his wife who were asleep in the house. Four other houses in Warwick suffered from the fireworks, but not much harm. The Queen was grateful to the Earl for his talent in warlike theatrics, and her affection probably increased his discontent at home. Shrewsbury wrote to Burghley on February 21, 1573, that his wife and he wished "good tidings that my Lady Oxford had a great belly."

On May 11, young Talbot wrote news for his father: "My Lord of Oxforth is lately grown in great credit, for the Queen's Majesty delighteth more in his personage and his dancing and valiantness than any other. He presented her Majesty with a rich jewel, which was well liked. I think Sussex doth back him all that he can. If it were not for his fickle head he would pass any of them shortly. My Lady Burghley [the Earl's mother-in-law, Mildred Cooke Cecil] unwisely hath declared herself, as it were, jealous, which is come to the

Queen's ear: whereat she hath been not a little offended with her, but now she is reconciled again. At all these love matters my Lord Treasurer winketh and will not meddle in any way."[12]

When he returned from his flight to Flanders in the summer of 1574, Oxford knew that the Queen was furious with him and yet he approached her "showing in himself a mixture of contrary affections... The one, fearful and doubtful in what sort he shall recover her Majesty's favor because of his offense in departing as he did without license; the other, glad and resolute to look for a speedy good end because he had in his abode so notoriously rejected the attempts of her Majesty's evil subjects, and in his return set apart all his own particular desires of foreign travel, and come to present himself before her Majesty, of whose goodness toward him he saith he cannot count." Watching De Vere's behavior on this occasion, his father-n-law—from whose account we are quoting—must have recognized the little child in the Earl, afraid of going near the mother who will surely punish him and yet mysteriously faithful that she will forgive him afterward heartily. The hysteric character of the Earl emerges vividly in Burghley's description. The Lord Treasurer asked his friend Francis Walsingham, the Queen's Secretary, "to beseech her Majesty that she will regard his loyalty and not his lightness in sudden joy over his confidence in her goodness and clemency, and not his boldness in that which hath offended her."[13] Elizabeth did pardon him because of his refusal to converse with the Roman Catholic fugitives from England who plotted against her in Flanders. He accompanied the Queen on her usual summer "progress" though the shires.

Elizabeth assured the French ambassador: "The most gallant gentleman, and the most accomplished, who dwells today among mortal men is nothing to me if he is not of royal blood and lineage."[14] We have no way of knowing how deeply she enjoyed the Earl of Oxford's companionship. He strove to convince her of his loverly fidelity. When Dr. Richard Masters, in the presence chamber of her Majesty, informed Oxford that he expected Countess Anne to become a mother, the Earl openly replied, "if she were with child it was not his." Elizabeth reminded Dr. Masters of this blurt when the physician reported to her that Anne was indeed with child. The Queen's response to the news bears the signs of fiercely repressed thought. "She arose or rather sprang up from the cushion" and said that the matter concerned Lord Burghley's joy chiefly: "yet I protest to God," she added, "that next to them that have interest in it, there is nobody that can be more joyous of it than I am." Her Majesty acted sympathetic on hearing of the Countess's depression and gloom, and spoke severely about Oxford's attitude to his wife.[15] Nevertheless, the chronicles indicate that the Queen did nothing to restore harmony between Edward and Anne. Sir Thomas Stucley declared, she would never marry for that she cannot abide a woman with child; such women, she saith, "be worse than a sow in farrow."[16]

In July 1577 the Earl gave diligent attention to the Queen and earnestly labored to gain her signature to a certain improvement of his fortune. It was rumored that she had promised him the manor of Rysing, once the property of his first cousin, the Duke of Norfolk. Early in 1578 Elizabeth granted him the desired land: "in consideration of the good, true and faithful service done and given to Us before this time by Our most dear cousin Edward, Earl of Oxford, Great Chamberlain of England, as for divers other causes and considerations moving Us."[17] The nature of Oxford's services to her Majesty remains unknown. Of one thing we may be sure, that her considerations in the deal were exclusively practical. Elizabeth never gave land or money away without exacting a comfortable quick return.

Let us look once more at the *Dainty Devices*. The "Black and Tawny" song depicts with melodious mournfulness the poet forsaken by his "dear dame," an unknown woman who fled from his passion like Daphne ran from the god Apollo and yet tormented him to tears. She yields her love to another, on whose head De Vere imagines a crown of bays, the symbol of a poet laureate. In "A Lover Rejected" he sounds a distinctly individual note:

> With irksome cries bewail thy late done deed,
> For she thou lovest is sure thy mortal foe.

He demands his soul to answer: "And shall I love on earth to be her thrall?/ And shall I sue and serve her all in vain?/And kiss the steps that she lets fall?" No, he cries with jealous anger:

> And let her have her most desire with speed;
> And let her pine away, both day and night,
> And let her moan, and none lament her need.
> And let all those that shall her see
> Despise her state, and pity me.

Then in "Not Attaining to His Desire" he grieves again that the woman he loves is his deadly enemy:

> O cruel hap and hard estate
> That forceth me to love my foe.

He concludes in the last of his eight lyrics that "love is worse than hate, and eke more harm hath done."

Neither Anne Cecil nor Queen Elizabeth can be identified satisfactorily with this beloved foe. The facts of these melancholy poems point to a third adored one. In the writer's unconscious the woman thus desired and mourned unquestionably was his lost mother, who had delivered him, soon after his father's funeral, into the hands of London strangers while she arranged to marry again.

The early lyrics of the Earl of Oxford deserve our special inquiry because of the efforts they reveal he made in order to understand himself. As Stephane Mallarmé said of Hamlet, "He walks reading the book of himself." He wanted to discover the hidden nature of his incurable melancholy, and in these youthful rimes he manifested already the psychology of his mature years:

> I am not as I seem to be,
> For when I smile I am not glad:
> A thrall, although you count me free,
> I most in mirth, most pensive sad.
> I smile to shade my bitter spite.
> * * * *
> Thus contraries be used, I find,
> Of wise to cloak the covert mind.

Clearly the Earl was aware that a fire of hatred—"bitter spite"—
burnt at the core of his sorrowing. In his "covert mind" he nour-
ished a grudge against the world, or rather somebody who had
meant the world to him. Because of this spite, this retaliatory temper, he could not spare love for anyone but his deprived self. He
could see that his own conduct—"thy late done deed"—got him into
trouble with those persons whose love he wished, but the reason
for his conduct eluded him.

> For my best luck leads me to such sinister state
> That I do waste with others' love, that hath myself in hate.

The truth, of course, is that Oxford loved himself; he hated only the
upper crust of his ego, the sore part developed from the introjection
of his parents' images, always instructive, always critical, and punishing his every fault. Since he could not bear to be parted from those
idols, he endured their imaginary inflictions and learnt how to derive pleasure from their cruel care. The poet plainly demonstrates
his mental masochism:

> The more I would weed out my cares, the more they seem to grow;
> The which betokeneth joy forsaken is of me,
> That with the careful culver climbs the worn and withered tree,
> To entertain my thoughts, and there my hap to moan,
> That never am less idle, lo, than when I am alone.[18]

No other author of this period got a comparable felicity from such
self-revulsion.

To compete with *The Paradise of Dainty Devices* the printer Richard
Jones issued *A Gorgeous Gallery of Gallant Invention*s, licensed on 5
June 1577. In the Stationers' Register it has two other titles:
"Delicate Dainties to sweeten lovers' lips withal" and "A Handful
of Hidden Secrets containing therein certain Sonnets and other
pleasant devices pickt out of the Closet of sundry worthy writers
and collected together by R. Williams." No R. Williams appears in
the published *Gallery*. Its editors seem to have been two young
hacks named Owen Roydon and Thomas Proctor; but they must

have obtained the material from socially superior hands. The book shares with *A Hundreth Sundrie Flowres* a fervor for scandal and obviously aims to make laughing-stocks out of people of the Court who somehow annoyed the anonymous authors. That is why no reprints ever came out in Tudor and Stuart times. As poetry it hardly merits a second look. Archaic diction, dreary alliteration, monotonous moralizing and classical allusions without color or vitality—these make up the "Gallant Inventions."

I mentioned in the previous chapter the poem about Diego and Ginevra. Other verses in the *Gallery* seem to refer directly to the marital woes of Oxford. The most striking of these is "A Letter written by a young gentlewoman and sent to her husband unaware (by a friend of hers) into Italy." The tearful lady of these rimes describes herself in terms plainly applicable to the Countess Anne de Vere. She pleads to her "perjured wight" to rescue her from a "most unhappy state.... debar'd our wonted joys." "Italians," she cries, "send my lover home.... Unless you welcome him because he leaves me thus forlorn." She turns then on her husband:

> But all in vain (forgive thy thrall if she do judge awrong);
> Thou canst not want of dainty trulls Italian dames among
> ***
> Remember, most forgetful man, thy pretty tattling child
> ***
> Thou canst not say but that I have of life unchaste been free.

She alludes to his "sudden flight" from home, which deprived her of rest for ten days, and rebukes him for preferring a dream of heroic deeds in the land of the Caesars to his wife's peace of heart.

> What dost thou think in Italy some great exploit to win?
> No, no, it is not Italy as sometimes it hath been:
> Or dost thou love to gad abroad the foreign coasts to view;
> If so, thou hadst not done amiss to bid me first adieu.

The first line of this quatrain suggests that Oxford's hope of winning martial glory in a Venetian sea fight was well known in London. This poem could properly be ascribed to a courtier who hated the Earl, a penman of elegant malice; if not Master Christopher Hatton, then his dear friend Edward Dyer, or perhaps someone in the vicious circle of Lord Henry Howard, Norfolk's brother, Surrey's second son. As early as October 9, 1572, Dyer had counseled Hatton on the way to undermine Oxford's standing in the heart of the Queen. Hate the earl, Dyer wrote, "in the Queen's understanding for affection's sake, and blaming him openly for seeking the Queen's favor... Marry, thus much would I advise you to remember, that you use no words of disgrace or reproach towards him to any; that he, being the less provoked, may sleep, thinking all safe, while you do awake and attend to your advantages."[19] In accord with the Machiavellian plot proposed, Hatton and Dyer would surely have circulated round the Court whatever poems of calumny against De Vere they commanded or came across.

A less intimate chord is sounded by the Gallant Invention , "A Letter sent from beyond the Seas to his Lover persuading her to continue her love towards him." This epistle wakes remembrance of the accusations of unfaithfulness that were whispered about Oxford's wife:

> Suspect not that I do misdoubt your loyalty at all:
> But ponder how that lovers are unto suspicion thrall.

A voice of personal injury rings from "A Gloze of Fawning Friendship," which instantly makes us think of Oxford's misfortune crossing the channel from Calais. It might have come from his own pen, the same hand that listed for the Privy Council in April 1576 "the names of such persons as are confessed to have been in the ship that spoiled me"—mostly Dutch sailors.[20] In spirit and speech the poem bears an astonishing resemblance to Shakespeare's *Timon of Athens*, the tragedy which Eva Turner Clark believed was written in 1576 and staged under the name of "The Solitary Knight."[21] Mrs. Clark's opinion is strengthened by the passion of these lines:

> For having lost my goods on seas, my friends would not abide,
> Yet having need I went to one, of all I trusted most;
> To get relief. He answer'd thus, Go pack, thou peevish post.

The hypocritical and malicious responses of the poet's friends to his cry for help are practically the same as Timon of Athens is treated with in the play: "I have not, I, yet am I griev'd to see thy luckless fate…" The unknown writer, however, does not turn misanthropic because of a few false men. He contents himself with denouncing them.

> Ah fie on fawning friends, whose eyes attentive be
> To watch and ward for lucre's sake, with cap and bended knee:
> Would God I had not known their sweet and sugar'd speech.

The philosopher Walter Whiter long ago observed that several times in Shakespeare "the *fawning obsequiousness* of an animal, or an attendant, is connected with the word *candy*. The cause of this strange association I am unable to discover." Whiter especially pointed out the linking of these two images in *Timon of Athens* (4.3)[22]

On this ground alone then we might ascribe "A Gloze of Fawning Friendship" to Shakespeare, that is, Edward de Vere. But there is nothing to show that the tragic hero Timon was a knight. Pericles of Tyre, on the other hand, presents a pattern of chivalry; he is hailed "The mean knight," and the way he sits solitary is remarked by strangers and friends. Internal evidence, already discussed in my third chapter, in particular the cult of Diana of Ephesus, convinces me that *Pericles* was "The History of the Solitary Knight" that followed "The History of Error" in 1576. The individual complaint in the *Gorgeous Gallery* is a lyrical adumbration of the drama of Shakespeare's old age which indicts the whole human race, on account of the cruelty of his former friends.

Maybe the main thing Edward de Vere learnt from Ovid and Chaucer, and the aristocratic amateurs of the *Book of Songs and Sonnets* by his ill destined uncle Henry Howard, Earl of Surrey, Lord Thomas Vaux and Sir Thomas Wyatt, was to utter his emotions in language resembling as closely as he could make it the colloquial speech of his people whenever they were driven by passion, laboring all the while in brevity, which is not the "soul of wit," merely its frame. He aimed indeed to be epigrammatic, as Looney pointed out, without sacrificing for wisdom's sake and humor the color and vitality of his vision. The man who became William Shakespeare had a perfect ear for music; with this inheritance he united his genius for vocabulary suiting ideas to moods and deeds.

References

1   *Gabriel Harvey's Marginalia*, ed. G.C. Moore Smith (Stratford on Avon: Shakespeare Head, 1913) 166. See also the long Latin lassitude of Harvey's ode to Hatton, "concerning his emblem Felix Infortunatus," in *Gratulationes Valdinenses* (1578), in the *Works of Gabriel Harvey*, ed. Alexander Grosart (London 1884).

2   Concerning the mysterious *Treatise of Treasons*, which defended Thomas Howard, the Duke of Norfolk, against alleged conspiracy of Cecils, Bacons and Cookes, see the best edition of *A Hundreth Sundrie Flowres*, ed. Ruth Loyd Miller, with an Introduction by Bernard Mordaunt Ward (Jennings , La. Minos Publishing Company, 1975) 78-89.Unfortunately Captain Ward never published his proof that Norfolk's brother, Lord Henry Howard, wrote the *Treatise of Treasons*, as mentioned in Ward's biography, *The Seventeenth Earl of Oxford* (London: John Murray, 1928) 131.

3   Lansdowne MS. xvii, 23.

4   Ward's article was originally published in *Review of English Studies*, Jan, 1928, iv, No 13, pp.35-48.

5   *State Papers Domestic* (1581) cli: 46, item 12. Oxford's poems which are cited in this chapter are found in *"Shakespeare" Identified* by J. Thomas Looney, ed. Ruth Loyd Miller (1974), vol. i.

6   Ward, *op. cit.* 61 *Calendar of Rutland Manuscripts*, i, 94.

7   *Depeches de la Mothe Fenelon*, ed. Cooper, iv, 186.

8   *Calendar of Rutland Manuscripts,* i, 96.

9   William Dugdale, *The Baronetage of England* (London 1675) i, 199-200.

10 *A Collection of State Papers...*ed. Murdin, Iii 217.

11 *Calendar of Salisbury (Cecil) Ms.* xiii, 111 (Microfilm of the original Salisbury Ms., i.e. Cecil Papers which are in the collections at Hatfield House, are on deposit at the British Library, London, and at the Folger Shakespeare Library, Washington, D.C.)

12 Edmund Lodge, *Illustrations of British History*, ii, 11 (1838).

13 *State Papers Domestic* (1574) xcviii:2.

14 *Depeches de la Mothe Fenelon*, v, 465; Frederick Chamberlin, ed. *The Sayings of Queen Elizabeth* (London: Bodley Head, 1923) 64.

15 Ward, *op. cit.* 114-115.

16 John Izon, *Sir Thomas Stucley: Traitor Extraordinary* (London 1956) 143.

17 Ward, *op. cit.* 149.

18 This line derives from a famous quotation of Tullius Cicero, in *De Officiis*, from the hero Scipio: Nunquam se minus otiosum esse, quam cum otiosus, nec minus soum, quam cum solus esset. William Cecil liked to let people believe that Tully's Offices went with him, in pocket or bosom, wherever he went. He never expressed an opinion about the Roman rumor that Scipio was the real writer of some comedies the former slave Terence earned fame for.

19 Sir Harris Nicolas, *Life and Times of Sir Christopher Hatton* (London 1847) 18,19 (from Harleian Ms. 787,f.88).

20 *Calendar of State Papers Foreign* (1576), no. 551.

21 See Clark, *Hidden Allusions in Shakespeare's Plays*, ed. Ruth Loyd Miller (Jennings, LA. Minos Publishing Company 1974), 30-46.

22 Walter Whiter, *A Specimen of a Commentary on Shakespeare* (London 1794) eds. Alan Over and Mary Bell (London 1967) 123-127. Whiter has yet to receive adequate credit from the university sages for blazing trails that others got laurels for plowing or paving, but hardly improving.

Chapter 6—VALENTINE AND PROTEUS

> The private wound is deepest: oh time, most accurst:
> 'Mongst all foes that a friend should be the worst?
>
> (*The Two Gentlemen of Verona*, 5.4.72-73)

Prolog

Although *The Two Gentlemen of Verona* came into print with the last of Shakespeare's plays to be publisht, in 1623, there is widespread agreement that he wrote it not long after he engaged in literature for the theater. In the *First Folio* collection it follows *The Tempest*, apparently the latest of his comedies, as if the overseers of the 1623 volume deemed it to be the earliest. Despite the signs of his hand busy at affectionate revision, the comedy fails to convince us, according to the manner of the master, that he worked with mind absorbed in the matter, with his ruddy fidelity to nature, to the truth. Not only slips of his pen remain in the printed play, such as twice referring to Milan as Verona, once as Padua, and having a character enter the stage in the fourth act admired, yet bearing the same name, Sir Eglamour, as one mentioned with curt dismissal in the first. The plot, with its quick dips into the shallow or silly, is worthy of the formally stiff verse, and the nearly painful extraction of jokes. Generation after generation of readers have felt their gorges heave at the hero's swift forgiving of his best friend's treachery a few minutes before the final curtain, and his exorbitant surrender of the girl he loves to the too rapidly repentant traitor who also adores her, followed by the friend's equally rapid abandonment of her in favor of the girl he deserted in the second act. These faults expelled the play from all but academic footlights. They deprived actors with fine voices of several flights of blank-verse melody, gleaming with the golden brevity of Ovid; the famous song for Silvia, put to music perfectly by Schubert, and the fun of the clown Launce and Crab his big dog, hilarity equal to the skill of the noble novice's model, Rabelais. Perhaps more than mistakes of artistry kept the master from yielding his juvenile *Gentlemen of Verona* to the press until it was securely posthumous. I think he could not bear to make it public property while that "private wound" which it laid bare, and caressed, and bled, continued to "grieve my very heart-strings"—just as Julia laments after listening to her renegade lover play his lute for the song "Who Is Silvia?" (4.2.39-53) So long as the story stayed on the stage, poor Shakespeare must have felt it somehow remained purely personal, like a dream, nobody's but his own, understood by himself alone.

I

In *Palladis Tamia or Wits Treasury* the erudite Francis Meres declared in 1598 that "The best for Comedy among us" was Edward, Earl of Oxford, but having paid this tribute to the aristocrat, Meres went on to praise for particular works "William Shakespeare," and put *The Two Gentlemen of Verona* first in his list of Shakespeare's plays, as if he considered it the oldest.

Every investigator agrees that our poet based the framework of his play on a portion of *Diana Enamorada*, a pastoral fiction by Jorge de Montemayor, which came out in Spanish in 1542 and did not attain English printing until 1598. By the latter date the comedy had long been an acquaintance of the London stage. So the question rises for conscientious critics and scholars—How did Shakespeare get to read the Spaniard's *Diana* so that he could use its tale of Felix and Felismena for so many scenes of his comedy? Several scholars have fancied that the English translator, Bartholomew Yong, let him peruse it in the manuscript which he completed in 1582. Unfortunately for these guessers, Yong reports in his Preface that he had only one copy of his *Diana*, and sent it to the printer "very dark and interlined." Others have fancied that Shakespeare acquired the script of "The History of Felix and Philismena," a play since lost, clearly inspired by Montemayor, that Queen Elizabeth's company of players acted for her court in Greenwich Palace on January 3, 1585.

Professor Felix Schelling, for reasons known to none but himself, pronounced Anthony Munday [Mundy], the jack-of-knacks on the stage and in espionage, the author of the lost play. In November 1584 Munday made ready for his London press a little book entitled *Fidele and Fortunio, the pleasant and fine conceited comedy of two Italian Gentlemen.* The prolog of this effort, which has some pallid details in common with Shakespeare's comedy of the two Veronese gentlemen, indicated that it was acted for the Queen and her court, perhaps by a children's troup. The piece is no more than a paraphrase in rime of an Italian play of 1576 called *Il Fedele*, by the not quite forgotten pastoral poet Luigi Pasqualigo. So far forgotten was the paraphraser in 1600 that four lines of his labor appeared in the anthology *England's Parnassus* as poetry by George Chapman, a far different dramatist.

The royal Chamberlain Thomas Radcliff, Earl of Sussex, liked to have Italian poetry and atmosphere in the "revels" he arranged for her Majesty. That may account for the metamorphosis of the Spanish romance into Italianate comedy. However there seems to be no record of a performance of the Verona story to delight Elizabeth.

Friar Bartholome Ponce, at the court of King Philip II in 1559, saw and read the *Diana Enamorada*, which was at that time, he affirmed, "in such favor as I had never seen any book in the vernacular." The English rimer Barnabe Googe included among his *Eglogs, Epitaphs and Sonnets* (London 1562) an episode from the tale of Felismena. The French translation by Nicholas Colin of parts of Montemayor's romance, printed in 1578, found admiration outside France. So I am inclined to the opinion, Eva Turner Clark guessed right when she argued that *"A History of the Duke of Milan and the Marquis of Mantua* showed at Whitehall on St Stephen's day, at night (December 26, 1579), enacted by the Lord Chamberlain's servants," was the love story of Felix and Felismena transformed into the first version of *The Two Gentlemen of Verona*.[1]

But we have no clear notion of the history that Sussex's men played on that Yuletide night. All the Revels records tell us is that his servants were "wholly furnished in this office, some new made and much altered, where one was employed for four new head attires with trains, scarfs, garters, and other attires, 13 ells of Sarcenet,

a country house, a City, and 6 pairs of gloves."[2] I am willing to conjecture that the four dazzling head attires were designed for the
Veronese beauty Julia, her attendant Lucetta, and the Milanese marvel Silvia, who merited two attires because

> She excels each mortall thing
> Upon the dull earth dwelling. (4.2.52-53)

We might have settled the question of the identity of the lost
"history" if "The Duke of Mantua and the Duke of Verona" had
survived, a comedy performed by English traveling actors at the
ducal court of Dresden on May 31 and again on September 4,
1626.[3] A play was indeed preserved in the German language, in a
collection of English Comedies and Tragedies publisht in 1620,
whose main plot closely resembles *The Two Gentlemen of Verona*; but
"Julio and Hippolyta" is, alas, a tragedy, without a marquis or duke.[4]

If Shakespeare's comedy was verily founded or developed from
the vanished play of Milan and Mantua, we can comprehend at once
why he located most of its action in Milan and the forests beyond
Mantua, and why in hasty revision he wrote "Verona" in two passages when he meant Milan. That he intended the male protagonists
in the primary version of his story to dazzle his public as noblemen,
not gentry, we can see from the way the father of one, later called
Don Antonio, is addrest as "your Lordship" (1.3), which might
make his son at least a viscount. This son's dearest friend derived
from blood and rank not less lordly: "from our infancy we have
conversed, and spent our hours together." (2.4.60-61) He aspires
moreover to marry the daughter of the Duke of Milan, who may
have been a Holy Roman Emperor in the original text—and he
does, with the Duke's compliments.

> I doe applaud thy spirit, Valentine,
> And thinke thee worthy of an Empress love.   (5.4.140-141)

It is impossible to reconstruct the original comedy from the folio
edition, although the dramatist kept several lines that show how
crude the old play was. Listen to the lazy boy-servant Speed de-
claiming (2.1.157-160):

> For often have you writ to her: and she in modesty,
> Or else for want of idle time, could not againe reply,
> Or fearing else some messenger, yt might her mind discover,
> Her self hath taught her Love himself, to write unto her lover.

For lilting and stilting like this on fourteen syllables in each line, we have to go back to the *Errors* of Shakespeare and the plays of its days in 1576 and 1578.

As a matter of fact, our poet appears to have gone back to the spring of Roman merriment that evidently never disappointed him, Plautus, in search of suggestion for the comedy he was determined to write. From the same fountain that inspired him to compose the *Errors* he drew his addition to the plot he took from Montemayor's *Diana Enamorada*. In the play by Plautus called the *Bacchides* he found the gallant Mnesilochus entrusting his friend Pistoclerus with a message of love for Bacchis. The former hears that his friend has been kissing a lass with that name, and instantly imagines Pistoclerus has double-crossed him and courted his Bacchis. Poor Mnesilochus denounces modern friendship in terms reminding us of Valentine's anger, dismay and agony over his friend Protheus's love for the demi-divine Silvia.

We have no way of knowing what influence on our play Drusiano Martinelli of Mantua exerted in January 1578, when the Privy Council told the theater-hating magistrates of London that "one Drousiano, an Italian, a commediante and his company," should be allowed to play in the town.[5] I suppose they performed precisely the same sort of erotic frolic and frothy stuff that enraptured Parisians on the "Boulevard des Italiens," the art of gaming for some Columbine's love against her papa Pantaloon's selection of a husband, with the elegant hero letting himself be leeched by a braggart war-veteran and a couple of less costly clowns. *Fedele and Fortunio* or *The Two Italian Gentlemen* shows us an artistic refinement of the plot, done in colloquial English by a clever versifier, with a view to production by a children's troup. The rimes romp and roll by *con brio*, with "that Magnaniminstrelsy," the versifier celebrates in his second

scene, not without flickers of ribaldry that the Queen and her grav-
est Councilors could chuckle over as with soul-satisfaction of the
nutcracking groundlings of the innyards where Drusiano may have
staged his drolleries. Captain Crackstone was remembered long
years after he recited the line *"Basilus* Codpiece for an old *Manus"*
with a sweeping politeness soon after the comedy began, more than
a decade after the funny line denouncing the hero for "tooting on a
beautiful face" was forgotten. But even more than the wit who
wrote those lines, we would like to know the superior artist who
composed the lyric sung by Victoria to her lute by a window in the
second scene:

> If looue be like the flower that in the night,
> > When darknes drownes the glory of the Skyes:
> Smelles sweet, and glitters in the gazers sight,
> But when the gladsome Sun beginnes to rise,
> > And he that viewes it, would the same imbrace:
> > It withereth, and looseth all his grace.
> Why doo I looue and like the cursed Tree,
> Whose buddes appeer, but fruite will not be seen:
> Why doo I languish for the flower I see?
> Whose root is rot, when all the leaues be green.
> > In such a case it is a point of skill:
> > To follow chaunce, and looue against my will.

In the spirit and burning clarity of this song run the rimes spoken
by Victoria afterward, in the very same metrical pattern, and the following speech by her lover Fedele standing in the shadow below:

> Ah poor Victoria, heer it was thy guise,
> To stand and see Fortunio passing by:
> Whose loovely shape hath caught me by mine eyes,
> And meanes to make me prisoner while I dye.
> > To gaze on him was life to mee before:
> > His absence death, because I see no more.
> *Fedele:*
> Oh greedy looue that neuer feeleth glut,

How haue I boasted of Victoria's grace?
With feare at last from fauour to be shut,
And lose the light of such a shining face?
    Shall neither teares, nor toyle, nor broken sleep
    Haue force inough a Ladies looue to keep?

She continues to harp or lute on her desire for Fortunio, which the
lover below her casement is blissfully oblivious of, enchanted as he
is with the poetry soaring in his heart.

I serue a Mistres whiter then the snowe,
Straighter then Cedar, brighter then the Glasse:
Finer in trip and swifter then the Roe,
More pleasant then the Feeld of flowring Grasse.
    More gladsome to my withering Joyes that fade
    Then Winters Sun, or Sommers cooling shade,
Sweeter then swelling grape of ripest wine,
Softer then feathers of the fairest Swan:
Smoother then Jet, more stately then the Pine,
Fresher then Poplar, smaller then my span,
    Clearer then Beauties fiery pointed beam,
    Or Icie cruste of Chrystalles frozen stream.
Yet is shee curster then the Beare by kinde,
And harder harted then the aged Oke:
More glib then Oyle, more fickle then the winde,
Stiffer then Steele, no sooner bent but broke.
    Loe thus my seruice is a lasting sore:
    Yet will I serue although I dye therfore.

The charm of the lyric lauding the beloved is made more poignant
by the sudden descent into bitter execration, and enables me to dare
identification of the poet as the sweetest singer of England, who
was also the most gay and grim epigrammatist of his time. Who else
but Edward de Vere, Earl of Oxford, whom we are accustomed to
call William Shakespeare? Nobody nowadays takes seriously the belief once upheld that the drudging dramatist and plodding poet An-

thony Munday produced those verses. The sole evidence for that belief were the initials A. M. signed to a dedication of the *Two Italian Gentlemen* in 1585. "I commend to your friendly view this pretty Conceit," A. M. wrote to John Heardson, Esquire, carefully refraining from an utterance that would mark him as the author. In "The Epilogue at the Court" M. A. plainly distinguished the dramatist as none of his crew:

> Lest long delay your Highness might offend,
>> Our Writer here thought good his pen to stay:
> Desiring pardon if he did offend,
> In shooting wide, short, o'er, or any way.
>> And for our selves like courtesy we crave:
>> If that his Arrows we mis-placed have.

In my opinion, the paraphraser of Luigi Pasqualigo's comedy was the Master of the Children of the Queen's Chapel, William Hunnis, who publisht under his own name only poems of piety, psalms for a British Bible, *A Hive Full of Honey* ("Hunny") in 1578, *Seven Sobs of a Sorrowful Soul for Sin* (1585), and similar stuff. All scholars consent that he wrote plays for the Chapel Children when he was training them for theatrical exhibition at the Blackfriars playhouse, opened by his fellow quire-master Richard Farrant before December 20, 1576, when Farrant received from Sir William More the lease to the Blackfriars rooms. None of Hunnis's mellifluous merriments has been recognised as his pen-work. I venture to suggest that he wrote all but the songs I have separated from *Fedele and Fortunio* because (1) the man who took the place of Richard Edwards, Master of the Chapel Children, in 1566 must have been pleasantly acquainted with the Earl of Oxford; (2) the songs are not only in the brilliant manner of Oxford's lyrics shown by his contributions to the *Paradise of Dainty Devices* and the later songs likely from his pen alone which were printed in Anthony Munday's translations of long novels of chivalry; they are prophetic of the greater beauty of the poetry signed by the unknown "Shepherd Tonie," whom academic craniums concluded must be Munday because his name was Tony too; (3) Anthony Munday arranged for the publication of *The Two Italian*

Gentlemen, which he seems to have obtained from Blackfriars files. Richard Farrant died in 1580, and his widow Agnes rented the house "to one Hunnis, and afterward to one Newman or Sutton, as far as I remember," Sir William More recorded, "and then to (Hugh) Evans, who sold his interest to the Earl of Oxford, who gave his interest to (John) Lyly."[6] In April 1580 Munday issued a tome of secular sermons, *View of Sundry Examples,* dedicated to William Waters and Doctor George Baker, "gentlemen attendant upon the Earl of Oxford," and proudly he proclaimed himself "Servant" to the Earl of Oxenford. He appears to have attempted the histrionic profession also, unluckily to his chagrin. Oxford may have given him a manuscript of the comedy in question, if he did not get it from Hunnis or Evans or Lyly, when the Blackfriars playhouse had to close, somewhile before the printing of *The Two Italian Gentlemen,* licensed for printing on November 12, 1584.

Let us note once more, A. M.'s dedication of the comedy to John Heardson makes no claim of authorship: "I commend to your friendly view this pretty conceit, as well for the invention as the delicate conveyance thereof, not doubting but you will so esteem thereof as it doth very well deserve, and I heartily desire. As for myself…" he assures Heardson of his good-will and service. The main student of Munday's work remarked that "suspicion is cast on his command of that language" (Italian) by some verses in French quoted in *The Heaven of the Mind* (1603) from Isabella Sforza, whom Munday mistook for the Duke of Milan's sister. His poor knowledge of Italian glares from his romance *Palmerin of England,* Part III, which he composed to please the Earl of Oxford.[7]

Perhaps the strongest Italian influence on the writing of *The Two Gentlemen of Verona* was the spell exerted on our poet's imagination by the dramatic art of Pietro Aretino, Peter of Arezzo, whom multitudes hail as the father of journalism, if not the father of modern pornography. In the first scene of Act 4 of our comedy, we see the hero Valentine meet a group of outlaws who question him about his wandering in the woods beyond Mantua and then invite him to become a member of their company, indeed their commander.

Second Outlaw. Are you content to be our Generall?
      To make a vertue of necessity,
      And liue as we doe in this wildernesse? (4.1.62-64)

Valentine's ludicrous servant Speed urges him, "Master, be one of them: It's an honourable kinde of theeuery."

The *Filosofo* of Aretino (never publisht in English in Shakespeare's lifetime) contains an adventure of the hero named Boccaccio which will strike us as the very source of Valentine's encounter with the outlaws. Act 3 of Aretino's comedy presents poor Boccaccio, plundered and expelled from the house of the beloved Tullia. He meets two robbers, who congratulate him on getting away from her with so little loss, and then invite him to join their gang. The first *"Ladro"* uses the exact words of our dramatist: *"Fa virtu de la necessita!"*[8]

In the prolog of Aretino's *Maresalco*, whose orator shows the audience how he would portray various characters one after the other, we find the rebuke that the clown Costard makes to Nathaniel in *Love's Labour's Lost* (5.2) "A conqueror, and afeard to speak!" and the excuse Costard furnishes the Curate, an unconscious comedian: "but, for Alisander, alas, you see how 'tis, a little o'er-parted." There is also the mimicry of *"Madonna"* the delicate, who "makes two mouthfuls out of one cherry and one from that sole thing. As soon as the aforesaid Ruffiana puts the letter in my hand, I will watch her first in this fashion, and then in such a mode, and then, handling her head like an old slut's, I shall say with fingers in her eyes, I—I shall pay you one of these years? She charms fogs, drinks babies, chases devils; and the paper is ripped and trampled on; I push her up the stairs, and tho swept away from me in front, the pieces of this are recovered and connected in order, and its tenor understood..." Both the romance by Montemayor and Shakespeare's comedy seem to have taken from this torrent of talk the same ingredients. In *The Two Gentlemen of Verona* (1.2) Lucetta hands her mistress Julia a letter from Protheus, which the lady gives her unread, then recalls Lucetta who lets it drop to the floor. She commands her to leave it there, but when Lucetta appeals for the distant lover's sake, Julia works up a rage in which to tear it to pieces. After the girl has gone, she gathers the fragments lovingly. Neither the Spanish novelist nor his English translator present her ripping the letter and restoring it. Shakespeare got this episode from Aretino, or else they were inspired by the same mental picture.

Another Italian author who enchanted our poet when he was meditating on *The Two Gentlemen of Verona*, Girolamo Cardano, appears to have been read to help Shakespeare overcome waves of melancholy that menaced his intellect at the time he began the play. Cardano died on September 21, 1576, when *The Comedy of Errors* was surprising the liveliest brains in England. The same year saw the second edition of *Cardans Comfort*, a translation of his *De Consolatione* (1542) made by Edward de Vere's Essex friend Thomas Bedingfield, which the Earl had publisht early in 1573 with an introduction and some stanzas from his own pen. Influence of De Vere's English prose from the introduction seems to glow in the comedy we are considering. Thus we have the Earl's apology to his friend for printing the translation: "considering the small harm I do to you, the great good I do to others, I prefer mine own intention to discover your volume, before your request to secrete the same," reflected in these lines from Protheus (3.1.4-5):

> My gracious Lord, that which I wold discouer,
> The Law of friendship bids me to conceale.

Oxford's open letter to Bedingfield speaks of someone yearning for "drink to qualify his sore thirst." This reminds us of Lucetta's words in the scene before Protheus's betrayal of his friend (2.7.22): "But qualifie the fires extreame rage." When Shakespeare wrote these words in 1578, Richard le Blanc's translation of *Les livres de Hierome Cardanus... de la subtilite, & subtiles inventions, ensemble les causes occultes, & raisons d'icelles*, was already beginning to fascinate the best brains in France.

II

The Two Gentlemen of Verona commences with a criticism of William Cecil, the Master of the Queen's Wards, for deliberately resisting the desire for travel of the noble orphans whom she entrusted to his care. What specially aroused Cecil's hostility—and clutch on provincial culture—was any longing these young men expressed for sensory education in Italy. What student of the revival of learning and the arts in the sixteenth century has not heard of his notorious advice: "Suffer not thy sons to cross the Alps"? He did not need Thomas Windebank, his son Thomas's tutor, to warn him against sending the lad to the land of Leonardo da Vinci, Ariosto, Castiglione, Michelangelo, Monteverde, "by reason of the enticements to pleasure and wantonness there," not to mention the expense.[9] Shakespeare's appeal at the opening of his play, "Home-keeping youth haue euer homely wits," scraped against Cecil's grain. "To see the wonders of the world abroad " (1.1.2) served no purpose in his concept of aristocratic training. Edward de Vere's father-in-law rejected the opinion of Protheus's father in the comedy: "he cannot be a perfect man, / Not being tryed, and tutord in the world" (1.3.20-21). Shakespeare urged the guardians of patrician youth to

> Put forth their Sonnes, to seeke preferment out.
> Some to the warres, to try their fortuen there;
> Some, to discouer Islands farre away; (1.3.7-9)

these very enterprises almost dominated the horizon of our dramatist when frustration of his ambition drove him to the writing of comedy, after the failure of his application for a place in the front rank of the officers whom the Queen promised to send to the Netherlands, on January 7, 1578, in command of English infantry and cavalry against the finest professional fighters of Europe, the army of Spain. On January 31, Don John of Austria and his valiant subordinate Alessandro Farnese, the prince of Parma, horribly crushed the union of Protestant and Catholic rebels of the Low Countries in the massacre of Gemblours. The Earl of Oxford must have been consumed by curiosity to learn how the Spaniards and their Italian veterans achieved victory with so little loss. At the same time noble minds in London were sparkling with excitement over the plans of Michael Lock, the treasurer of the Cathay Company, and his brave Captain Martin Frobisher, to sail in search of precious metals and a shortcut to China by the frozen sea north of Canada. They lured the Earl of Oxford into lavishing three thousand pounds on this voyage.

Shakespeare probably got the name for Protheus's clown-servant from a pirate connected with the Frobisher expedition named Launce.[10] I suppose he got the name for Valentine's clown-servant from "Spede," the obscure petitioner to the Queen, in April 1579, about some business with Valentine Dale, the English ambassador in Paris.[11] It would be pleasant to know what Dale thought of his namesake in the comedy, and the merit of its romance, for it is clearly the affectionate work of a Francophile.

Both Valentine and Protheus represent essentially none but the man who created them. The latter, whose name evokes the memory of the god in the Odyssey whose form undergoes marvels of metamorphoses, I regard as the writer's spiritual self. He proclaims himself religious in his first speech, a reckoner of Roman Catholic rosary beads. But Valentine views his alter-ego as one more devoted to love-books. And Protheus reveals quickly how well acquainted he is with what "writers say" on the subject of amorous minds. Valentine pronounces him "a votary to fond desire." The phrase recalls at once the song by the "Earle of Oxenforde" which for centuries remained in the so-called Rawlinson Manuscripts, except for a single appearance in print in 1591; it was publisht in *Brittons Bowre of Delights*, mostly verses by Nicholas Breton, whose mother George Gascoigne married. The song is entitled "Of the birth and bringing up of Desire," and only in the Rawlinson Manuscripts can be seen the opening stanza:

> Come hither, shepherd swain!
> Sir, what do you require?
> I pray thee show to me thy name.
> My name is fond desire.[12]

Whether engaged in religion or the pursuit of felicity in the arms of Julia and afterward Silvia, the volatile soul of Protheus may be said, in the Elizabethan terms of the elements believed to be basic in human nature, to have sprung from fire and air. His dearest friend Valentine, on the other hand, has a soul less mutable, more attached to materials, made, in terms of classic anatomy, of moisture and soil. He, rather than Protheus, enjoys the steadfast temperament for which the Duke of Milan praises Protheus:

> You are already loues firme votary ,
> And cannot soone reuolt, and change your minde.   (3.2.58-59)

So when Protheus sends his clown Launce to hunt for Valentine, and the servant finds him downcast in doleful "dump," our poet holds a mirror up to his master, the trickster who demonically snared his friend, telling him that it is not Valentine they see.

> *Protheus.*   Who then? His Spirit?
> *Valentine.*   Neither.
> *Protheus.*   What then?
> *Valentine.*   Nothing.   (3.1.195-198)

When Protheus thinks of winning his friend's beloved Silvia for himself, his imagination vaults immediately to the evil that will gain her most rapidly and forever.

> The best way is, to slander Valentine,
> With falsehood, cowardice, and poore discent:
> Three things, that women highly hold in hate. (3.2.31-33)

Edward de Vere was accustomed to hearing all three accusations, which his half-sister Lady Katherine Windsor flung constantly at him. He surely knew that Girolamo Cardano and Pietro Aretino were likewise condemned as baseborn. The Earl of Oxford saw himself and the Countess Anne, his forsaken wife, in the images of the players of Protheus and his Julia. Observe that the latter calls her former lover "the musician" when she hears the serenade "Who is Silvia?" altho there is no stage direction in the drama that

Protheus was to play under Silvia's window or sing the nocturn. But she is convinced, "He plaies false (father), so false that he grieues my very heart-strings" (4.2). When we recognise Anne Cecil de Vere in the person of Julia we understand at once why she calls her inn host father. And we may hear the voice of her father coming from the Duke of Milan, when he discloses how he has been spying on Valentine and Silvia (3.1.24-27). ·

> This loue of theirs, my selfe haue often seene,
> Haply when they haue iudg'd me fast asleepe,
> And oftentimes haue purpos'd to forbid
> Sir Valentine her companie, and my Court.

Instead the Duke admits, "I gaue him gentle lookes." This fragment of the great confession or autobiography, which we call the Works of William Shake-speare, enables us to comprehend why the play did not run the sunshine of the press in the poet's lifetime. For the same reason he left to evanescent breath in the theater the "confession" of Valentine that he was compelled to leave his homeland

> For that which now torments me to rehearse;
> I kil'd a man, whose death I much repent, ·
> But yet I slew him manfully, in fight,
> Without false vantage, or base treachery.   (4.1.26-29)

What else did our dramatist have in mind when he wrote this, if not the bloody death of the scullion Thomas Brinknell in July 1567, after running into a fencing sword of the young Earl? Less than ten years later, his father-in-law recorded the killing with deformation of facts: "I did my best to have the jury find the death of a poor man whom he killed in my house to be found *se defendendo*."[13] Tom Brinknell was not slain in Cecil's house but in a backyard. The jury's verdict was "*felo de se*"—a sort of suicide.[14]

That Shakespeare intended his two protagonists to strike us like contrary twins may be glimpsed from Valentine's remark: "I knew him as my selfe: for from our Infancie / We haue conuersed, and spent our howres together" (2.4.60-61). Likewise Protheus thinks of

Ovid's great volume in hailing the fantom of his love: "Thou, Iulia, thou hast metamorphis'd me" (1.1.66), and Valentine's servant remembers the same book, translated by Oxford's mother's brother, in looking at Silvia's lover: "you are Metamorphis'd with a Mistris" (2.1.29-30).

Antonio, the father of Protheus, wants his son to join his boyhood companion Valentine in attendance at the court of the Emperor in Milan (1.3). The Emperor never appears in the play presently before us. Nor do we hear anything more about the two nobles' training at the imperial court along the lines of Panthino's assurance that in Milan Antonio's son will "practise Tilts, and Turnaments; / Heare sweet discourse, conuerse with Noble-men, / And be in eye of euery Exercise / Worthy is youth, and noblenesse of birth" (1.3.30-33). The passage induces me to believe that Edward de Vere suffered from envy of his rival Sir Philip Sidney, who, on February 7, 1577, was sent on a journey to the court of the Austrian Emperor Rudolph II. He carried instructions to visit the Duke Hans Casimir of the Palatinate and the Landgraf William of Hessen, and broach to these foes of Catholic politics the plan—one of Lord Burghley's futile maggots—of a union of Protestant princes. This would have relieved England of the burden of aiding the Netherlands against the Emperor's Spanish kinsmen with the might of her Majesty. Thomas Wilson wrote from the Low Countries to Cecil in January, wishing Elizabeth would "send a general over an English army in aid of the States," if the Duc de Guise rode to assist Don John. Wilson expected the Earl of Leycester to lead such an English force.[15] Hope sprang hot for this enterprise on February 15, 1578, when Hubert Languet, Sidney's old friend, wrote to him from Frankfurt, "The rumor is gaining ground here that your Queen has ordered troops to be sent to the help of the Belgians; it is added that the most noble Earl of Leicester will command the forces that are to go."[16] On June 2, 1578, Burghley noted the purpose of the English project: "to temper the French aid, that they usurp not the whole."[17] Among the spies running errands for Cecil and Walsingham in the Low Countries during these months was the former soldier Rowland Yorke, Oxford's faithless friend.[18] Since our poet presented Protheus being sent to join Valentine at the Emperor's court, I imagine that in fantasy he may have wished to win the friendship of Philip Sidney, with whom he had so much in common. The outlaw declaration in favor of Valentine's election to leadership of romantic robbers: "By the bare scalpe of Robin Hoods fat Fryer, / This fellow were a King, for our wilde faction" (4.1.36-37) echoes the rimes of Oxford that lullaby about the price of peace for his spirit:

> Were I a king I might command content;
>> Were I obscure unknown would be my cares,
> And were I dead, no thoughts should me torment,
>> Nor words, nor wrongs, nor love, nor hate, nor fears:
> A doubtful choice of three things, which to crave,
>> A kingdom or a cottage or a grave.[19]

This musing over three choices, which our dramatist developed and expanded into the better half of the plot in *The Merchant of Venice*, has a romantic reflection in the first act of our comedy. The Veronese lady Julia asks for the opinion of her maidservant Lucetta about would-be husbands:

> Of all the faire resort of Gentlemen,
> That euery day with par'le encounter me,
> In thy opinion which is worthiest loue? (1.2.4-6)

They review three applicants for her heart, Sir Eglamour, "a Knight, well-spoken, neat, and fine," rejected for no manifest reason, the rich Mercatio, whose wealth is more attractive than himself, and the gentle Protheus, whom Lucetta favors, for "a womans reason." Courtiers listening to this dialog of the ladies would naturally compare the three different suitors to the princes who courted their Queen. Particularly they would speculate on the chance of her Majesty's conquest by Francois Hercules de Valois, Duc d'Alencon and Anjou, the youngest and the ugliest of the sons of Catherine de Medici, whose personality charmed many women as well as a host of male friends. His partisans at the French Court included men far more interesting, such as Jean de Simier, the eagle-eyed observer of state affairs, the sword-master, and wit who delighted Elizabeth all the days he spent in England appealing for Alencon, and Bussy d'Ambois, whom George Chapman made the hero of two deeply meditated dramas. They were nicknamed the *Male-contents*, because of their dissatisfaction with Alencon's brother, King Henri III, and his peculiar company of mignons, men fond of displaying effeminate manners that concealed immense love of violence. At the beginning of Act 2 of our comedy, we hear the clown Speed remark to his master Valentine, "you haue learn'd (like Sir Protheus) to wreath your Armes like a Male-content." The Earl of Oxford must have folded his arms in the French fashion, for he ardently supported his old friend the Earl of Sussex in the endeavor to unite England and France by wedlock. The Dudleys and Sidneys on the contrary considered that alliance deadly to all they held dear in church and state.

Whim, mere whim suggests that our author was thinking of Alencon as well as himself when he composed the melodious lines, at the end of Act 1,

> Oh, how this spring of loue resembleth
> The uncertaine glory of an April day,
> Which now shewes all the beauty of the Sun,
> And by and by a clowd takes all away. (1.3.84-87)

The prince from France celebrated his birthday on April 25. Edward de Vere was born on April 12, according to the Julian calendar that Pope Gregory XIII changed in 1582 to the calendar we use nowadays, which dates De Vere's birthday on April 23. Alencon was just five years younger than the Earl, who also cherished fantasies of winning the Queen of England for his mate. Oxford may have felt a spiritual kinship with the "Frog," as the Queen nicknamed her French admirer, because poor Hercules appeared to have a double nose, and little Edward seems to have been ridiculed at Court on account of his alleged deformity.

The evidence that Silvia, the Duke of Milan's daughter, stands for Elizabeth draws attention first to her name. Literally in Latin the name signifies Lady of the Woods, and apparently was one of the words chosen by the Romans to hail their deity, the huntress Diana, virgin queen of their savage ancestors (our word savage comes from the Latin for forest, Silva). Like Elizabeth, Silvia is hailed as heavenly blond. When Protheus abandons desire for Julia and resolves to rob his friend of Silvia's affection, he cries,

> At first I did adore a twinkling Starre,
> But now I worship a celestiall Sunne: ...
> I to my selfe am deerer then a friend,
> For Loue is still most precious in it selfe,
> And Siluia (witness heauen that made her faire)
> Shewes Iulia but a swarthy Ethiope.   (2.6.9-26)

I take these lines not only as dismissal of the Countess Anne of Oxford, but also as avowal of the author's exaltation of the auburn-haired Silvia (4.4) as more adorable than the dark girl who seems to have walked into Edward de Vere's life in 1577 and soon became the darling of his destiny: Anne Vavasor, of Copmanthorp, Yorkshire, maid of her Majesty's bedchamber (never maid-of-honor!). Julia could have been converted from an image of Anne Cecil to the swarthy Anne shortly after Shakespeare started his comedy of Verona. (There is no need to tell the alert reader what Verona means to the punster who composed this play, nor to what crest the poet alluded when he made Julia protest (2.7.74), "But truer starres did gouerne Protheus birth.") I believe it was Anne Vavasor, rather than her mistress Elizabeth, whom our poet heard in his mind's ear, upbraiding him as Silvia denounces Protheus: "Thou subtile, periur'd, false, disloyall man" (4.2.96). She became familiar early with his deceptive vows, how his own advice exhilarated him: "Though nere so blacke, say they haue Angells faces" (3.1.103). The dramatist makes Silvia rebuke her second Veronese lover with the strange oath, "by this pale queene of night I sweare," indicating that the moon-divinity customarily standing on the stage and in poetry for Elizabeth shone beyond the Silvia of this speech, who pleads to Protheus:

> Returne, returne, and make thy loue amends. (4.2.100)

He asserts that his former sweetheart has died. The lady he has just serenaded reminds him that she is "bethroth'd" to his friend Valentine. This induces me to fancy that his friend at this point of the play no longer represents in his remoteness Edward de Vere, but indeed a companion of the time of the *Two Gentlemen*. I surmise this gentleman was Oxford's distant cousin Charles Arundel, who frequently dined and drank with the Earl, stimulated him to monologs of his imaginary adventures on the continent, and later had to leave England to escape prosecution as a spy for Spain. Among Arundel's letters of this period are a few to an unknown lady, whom he pretended to adore, who, I feel certain, was the pure-hearted black beauty, reminiscent of Romany, Anne Vavasor. She perplexed and bewildered Edward de Vere with her love of liberty and her virginal pride so that his profound enmity toward women, originating in revolt against his mother, stirred up and smoldered in his soul. Like his Protheus (4.4.88) he seldom left his chamber, "Where thou shalt finde me sad, and solitarie." The result of the dramatist's merging of Anne Cecil and Anne Vavasor in his Julia is startling; while the latter's hair is called "perfect yellow," her skin is described as black! I will leave to others inquiry about Queen Elizabeth's brow and the brow of the Vavasor, which may be provoked by Julia's lines comparing herself to Silvia: "Her eyes are grey as glasse, and so are mine: / I, but her forehead's low, and mine's as high." (4.4.191-192) Of course, our comic genius may have had Anne Cecil in view when he wrote this, not the dark-orbed Anne.

III

In Act 2 Valentine confides to his untrustworthy friend the plan of elopement with Silvia from the tower where her jealous father, the Duke, has virtually imprisoned her. Her dream-dazzled lover reveals "the cunning manner of our flight," descending from her window by "The Ladder made of Cords." Eva Clark detected the likeness between this invention and the escape of Alencon, his valet Cange, and his devoted comrade Simier, from the second storey of the

Louvre palace by a rope-ladder provided by the Duke's sister Marguerite.[20] Listen to her telling about the flight.

> When we consulted upon the means of its accomplishment,
> we could find no other than his descending from my window,
> which was on the second storey and opened to the moat, for
> the gates were so closely watched... He begged me therefor
> to procure a rope for him.[21]

She refers to the day of the escape as a fast-day; it was Friday, the 14th of February, 1578, St Valentine's day. The conception of *The Two Gentlemen of Verona* occurred, I estimate, about a fortnight later, when our dramatist heard the details of the flight, and was inspired to name his hero Valentine.

As we know, the necessity of the plot he contrived for his comedy enabled the Duke, with the help of Protheus, to discover Valentine's ladder and send him in shame on the road to Mantua.

The Duke of Anjou came to his sister Marguerite's chamber that night with Simier and Cange, and she, assisted by her women, let down the rope for him. He descended "laughing and joking over the dirty trick he was playing on the King," their brother. Next Simier went out the window, "in such a fright," and the Duke's servant followed without a fault. The Queen of Navarre ordered her servants to burn the rope.[22] The three fugitives galloped to the abbey of Ste Genevieve, where the brave Bussy d'Ambois waited for them. "By consent of the Abbot, a hole had been made in the city wall, thru which they passed." Again they mounted and went away to Angers, capital of the dukedom of Anjou.[23] Shakespeare seems to have remembered the abbey when he made the appointment of Protheus at "Saint Gregories well" (4.2.83), where he and the Duke of Milan learn of Silvia's flight with Sir Eglamour from "Fryer Patricks Cell." She makes her escape "Out at the Posterne by the Abbey wall" (5.1.9). If we had the lost romance *Galien of France* that Anthony Munday delivered to the Earl of Oxford in 1578, we would see more of such adventures, more or less amorous, in which De Vere endeavored to forget his mundane miseries. Twenty years later, Francis Meres listed *Galien of France* as "hurtful" fiction. Munday himself, in the preface to his *Mirror of Mutability* (1579), regretted that the windy tale did not have "so fully comprised such pithiness of style as one of a more riper invention" might have wished.

The Two Gentlemen of Verona nears conclusion with the warning Silvia gives Protheus—"Thou Counterfeyt, to thy true friend " —

> Read ouer Iulia's heart, thy first best loue. (5.4.46)

Our poet must have sincerely contemplated at this time reconcilement with his deserted Anne. However, on July 18, 1578, Sir Francis Walsingham finished a letter to Lord Burghley, "beseeching that I may be remembered to my lady (Mildred Cecil) and the poor solitary Countess."[24] It would not surprise me to learn that her father delivered the message with the exact words. Just as we discover William Cecil in Polonius, devouring the love-letters of Hamlet to his daughter, so we can see him in old Antonio, Protheus's father, who demands to examine his son's mail, and abruptly commands him to get ready to leave home and travel to Milan:

> Muse not that I thus sodainly proceed;
> For what I will, I will, and there an end. (1.3.64-65)

The despotic parent sketched in the characters of Antonio and the Duke of Milan summons to my remembrance a ghostly figure, the Countess of Oxford Margaret Golding de Vere. She haunts our play in a fantastic manner. No mother is mentioned in the drama except the mother of Protheus's comic servant Launce. In the second act, scene 3, he appears with his big dog Crab, apparently a silent beast whose prototype Shakespeare found in the epic comedy of Rabelais, a dog ungrateful for all the sacrifices his master has made for him, including acceptance of blame for animal misdemeanors. To show the world "the sowrest natured dogge that liues," Launce depicts how the hard-hearted brute behaved when they departed from his parents.

> Ile shew you the manner of it. This shooe is my father:
> no, this left shoe is my father; no, no, this left shooe
> is my mother: nay, that cannot bee so neyther: yes, it is

> so, it is so: it hath the worser sole: this shooe with the
> hole in it is my mother: and this my father: a vengance
> on't, there 'tis... Now come I to my Mother: Oh that she
> could speake now, like a would-woman: well, I kisse her:
> why there 'tis; heere's my mothers breath vp and downe. (2.3.13-28)

No matter how merry this speech makes you, it is undeniable that a bitter note is struck when the sinister shoe is selected to emblem the mother, because "it hath the worser sole." We can conjecture no reason for this sudden condemnation of her except the writer's unforgiving mood whenever her image is conjured up. The word "would-woman" is usually interpreted as meaning "wood wild or mad". The buffoon's mother is portrayed as frenzied with grief at his leaving home. In my judgment, Countess Margaret conducted herself, at her boy's departure from Castle Hedingham, with the same calm, if not coolness, that Crab showed in the pathetic scene pictured by Launce. (Shakespeare never explained why the clown is called a kind of spear.) "Now the dogge all this while sheds not a teare: nor speakes a word: but see how I lay the dust with my teares." (2.3.29-31)

Charles Arundel's mother was also named Margaret. She and Lord Henry Howard were the children of Thomas, the third Duke of Norfolk. The Lord Henry I mean was the Earl of Surrey, who introduced the Italian sonnet into English, changing its rime pattern for comfort in the way that Shakespeare liked it. He was the first English experimenter with the blank verse invented in Italy, but his translations of Vergil in that form fail to evince his lyric gift. Surrey married Frances Vere, daughter of the fifteenth Earl of Oxford, sister of our Edward's father. Literature held little enchantment for Charles Arundel; politics fascinated him far more, perhaps because he found it from infancy inextricable from the magic he constantly confused with religion. He invested perfervidly in amulets, litanies, rosaries, incense and crosses of all kinds. Sometime before the Yuletide of 1580 he angered his cousin of Oxford with utterances of disgust against England's alliance with France, singling out for his rancor "Monsieur," as the Duc d'Alencon was commonly named at Court: "he said there was neither personage, religion, wit or constancy" in the man, "and that for his part he had long since given over that course and taken another way," which was to Spain.[25] Arundel's strong inclination to the church of Rome made him enthusiastic for the Spanish global policy. Naturally he avoided the subject in responding to the charges De Vere made against him. In "A brief answer to my L. of Ox. slanderous accusations" written in April 1583 he began as follows:

> First he accuseth me of hearing mass six years past in A' v'or chamber.[26]

We are not told why he treated Anne Vavasor's name so. Oxford had not been invited to the ceremony; he made the charge "rather upon hearsay than knowledge," Arundel said, but admitted it was true. He insisted, "Ox was never in our company at any mass or (Catholic?) conference, but forgeth out of his own giddy brain what he taketh to be fittest for the speeding of his ancient friends..."[27] In the light of our play's verdict on the perfidious Protheus, we may be able to extricate the grains of truth in the grim paragraph Arundel entitled "Consideration of the Accuser."

> Now would I require of charity and justice that these brief particulars concerning him that chargeth me may be considered. First, that he was never kind to any friend nor thankful to any kinsman in general, & that though he love no man living from his heart, yet of all he most detesteth these that are either merely kind (of his kind) by nature or have deeply bound him by their well deserving... by devising tales and lies he would set one man to kill another, and hath sought my life by undirect devices... [28]

Among the minor accusations Arundel threw at his antagonist in his voluminous polemic, not the least amusing is this: The Earl of Oxford, evidently during tavern talk in which much wine had been drunk, maintained there was "Better defense for bawdery in the Scripture than in Aretino." Cousin Charles located this contention at the Earl's lodging in Westminster, but did not date it.[29]

Expecting that Elizabeth would want to peruse his revelations of the Earl's private remarks about her Majesty, Arundel scoured his memory for any opinion he could discover to the Earl's disgrace. He recalled having heard this audacity of Edward, "that the Queen said he was a bastard, for which cause he would never love her, and leave her in the lurch one day." Presumably her Majesty felt there was more venom sting in the "Railing at Francis Southwell" reported by Arundel, "for commending the Queen's singing one night at Hampton Court, protesting by the blood of God, that she had the worst voice, and did everything with the worst grace that ever any woman did, and that he was never *non plus* but when he came to speak well of her."[30]

In view of Charles Arundel's scarcely concealed attraction to piety, if not the pay, of the Pope, it is strange to find him in the company of Sir Francis Walsingham, when that champion of the Puritans and other rebels against Romanism sailed over the Channel in summer 1578 to visit the Catholic stronghold of Louvain. On August 29 Robert Dudley, Earl of Leycester, wrote to Walsingham, who was still there: "You carried a companion over with you, what hath played the right Jack since he returned. (In the margin of the letter someone scribbled *Cha. Arun.*) When I first heard of his going, I told some of my friends to what end he would go."[31] Burghley commented on the visit to Louvain that it had put "many evil conceits" in the mind of the Queen and many who surrounded her, "that do sting all profession of true religion."[32] With his usual obliquity Burghley named nobody responsible.

There is barely a record to indicate a connexion between the visit to Louvain and the intrigue of Duke Hercules of France with the revolutionary Prince of Orange, William the Silent. In July Walsingham had failed to build barriers between the chief of the Dutch war and Alencon, and the Queen made furious speeches against him. He heard a rumor that he would be hanged on his return to London. He wrote to Thomas Randolph on July 29, "If I may conveniently, I mean, with the leave of God, to convey myself off from the stage and to become a looker on." In the same month the Queen's agent in Antwerp, William Davison, received the encouraging message, "Those who know most about things say the French marriage is the same play that was acted before."[33] Nevertheless the Dudleys and Sidneys became nearly nauseous and noisy when Backqueville and De Quincey the Huguenot arrived at Audley End on July 30 to greet the Queen with a love message from "Monsieur." The Earl of Oxford was with her. They had come from Cambridge University and Saffron Walden, where De Vere was individually entertained by the pedantry and candied tongue of Gabriel Harvey, whose rhetoric and etiquette we can still see strutting in the person of Holofernes in *Love's Labor's Lost*. It is regrettable that we do not know the gentleman about whom William Lewin, once a tutor of Anne Cecil and one of Oxford's companions in France and Germany, wrote to William Davison on June 8. The bearer, said Lewin, having been born in those parts (Antwerp and environs) and having occasion to resort thither from "My Lord of Oxenford," whom he serves in very good place and credit, "being well furnished with the languages and other good qualities," has requested my letters of commendation to you.[34] On August 1, 1578, the partisans of the French alliance received electrifying news of a victory over the Spanish army at Rymenant, led by the Huguenot warrior Bras de Fer (Iron-Arm) and the English commander John Norris. (Francois de la Noue lost his left arm at the battle of Fontenoy. His nickname probably gave Shakespeare the name of his Norway prince in *Hamlet*, Fortinbras.)

Well known even today are the nicknames Queen Bess bestowed on her French suitor and his friend Simier, the Frog and the Ape. (Backwoods and mountains of America echo to the present day the Elizabethan ballad about Alencon's courtship of the Queen, dear to Dixie as "The Frog He Went Acourtin'.") Not so well known are the nicknames that she gave De Vere (the Boar, the Turk), Christopher Hatton (Mutton, Sheep), Walter Ralegh (Water), and Burghley (Leviathan or Spirit), and Leycester (Lids). Our dramatist may have been remembering Burghley's burly attendance on the Queen when he wrote his praise of poetry in *The Two Gentlemen of Verona*:

> For Orpheus Lute was strung with Poets sinewes,
> Whose golden touch could soften steele and stones;
> Make Tygers tame, and huge Leviathans
> Forsake vnsounded deepes, to dance on Sands. (3.2.77-80)

These lines drop from the lips of Protheus, after he has chanted his counsel on the mode of alluring women with intellects:

> You must lay Lime, to tangle her desires
> By walefull Sonnets, whose composed Rimes
> Should be full fraught with seruiceable vowes. (3.2.68-70)

It seems to me that Edward de Vere bequested a pair of such poems, originally aimed at her Majesty's heart, but buried in a long prose novel by Anthony Munday, not printed until 1596, named *Primaleon of Greece.*

> Prince Edward's Song in the Garden
> Before the Princesse Flerida and Her Ladies
>
> Reason and dutie both commaundeth me
> To love and serve the Soveraigne of my life:
> Whose Vertues Times eternall wonders be,
> And sweet appeasers of heart-breaking strife.
> Though day and night my sorrowes doe increase,
> Through my unworthinesse to taste her grace:
> Yet with my soule her heavenly lookes make peace,
> Whereby my thoughts some comfort doe embrace.
> If then ungentle Fate urge not constraint,
> To leave the place where my most comfort is:
> One time or other she may heare my plaint,
> And with kinde pittie helpe whats now amis.
> Be not so cruell to thy servant then,
> For thou shalt find him dutifull and true:
> And to exceed common esteeme of men
> In Loyaltie, and so sweet soule adue.

From *The Famous and Renowned Historie of Primaleon of Greece, Sonne to the Great and Mighty Prince Palmerin d'Oliva, Emperour of Constantinople;* translated out of French and Italian, into English, by A. M. (London: 1619) Part II, xii. Originally printed 1596.

Prince Edward was a suitor for Gridonia, who had vowed to wed none but the man who would kill her father's murderer and deposit the villain's head in her lap. Primaleon performs the service but not before Edward has fallen in love at first sight with his sister Flerida and forgets about Gridonia. He disguises as a gardener to be near his love and gains "the flower of her chastity" by song and a magic cup. He champions her beauty in tournament at Constantinople.

Prince Edward's Second Song in the Garden
To His Divine Mistresse

He that hath spent his time in silent mone,
And ne'er saw merry minute in his life:
To sad conceit makes all his sorrowes knowne,
Who (to forestall pleasures ensuing strife)
    Tells him whole stories of sweete discontent,
    To adde more vigour to his languishment.
In such a Heaven of inward happinesse,
My labouring thoughts are earnestly imployd:
Hating the vulgar tracke of idlenesse,
Wherein so many infant-wits have joyd,
    And finding that it doth such comfort bring,
    Kinde Discontent, I hayle thee as my King.

From *Primaleon of Greece,* Part II, vii. Edward's First and Second Song were reprinted by Mary Patchell in *The Palermin Romances in Elizabethan Prose Fiction* (New York: Columbia University Press, 1947) p. 134-5.

Also note in *Primaleon of Greece,* Part II, chapter xxvii, there glows the breathtakingly lovely lyric best known by its first line, "Beauty sat bathing by a Spring," but here entitled "To Colin Clout"—a song for Edmund Spenser.

Anthony Munday promised *Primaleon of Greece* to the Earl of Oxford in the second part of Pal*merin d'Oliva*, dedicated to De Vere on 9 March 1588.

IV

The song beginning "When wert thou born, Desire?" ordinarily signed E. of Ox. which clearly flowed from the same pen that exprest pity for Protheus as "a votary of fond desire," was warmly applauded by the anonymous analyst who wrote *The Arte of English Poesie* (1589). "Edward, Earl of Oxford," said he, "a most noble and learned Gentleman, made in this figure of response an emblem of desire, otherwise called Cupid, which from his excellency and wit, I set down some part of the verses." That seems to have been the earliest appearance of the song in print. I follow the flock of those who consider the critic who saw it in manuscript was George Puttenham, nephew of Sir Thomas Elyot, the author of *The Governor* (1531). Sir John Eliot, who died in prison for combatting King Charles Stuart's attempts for absolute monarchy, was Puttenham's brother-in-law. This gentleman married Elizabeth Windsor, widow of Baron William, whose eldest son, Edward, married Katherine Neville de Vere, Oxford's half-sister. On October 25, 1578, George apologised to the Privy Council for his failure to make a personal appearance before them. His long letter elaborately reviewed the conduct of Lady Windsor, his wife, whom he described as a virago setting an example for clamor and malice which her children tried trivially to equal.[35] Eluding the sounds and spectacles of the Windsors, Puttenham told Sir John Throckmorton, "I have resolved with myself to employ my time in studies and with conference with the greatest learned men I can find." He made this resolution in 1578, and might have made it after meeting Edward de Vere and reading his rimes.

When Charles Arundel referred to Oxford's lodging at Westminster, it is conceivable that he meant the Earl's apartment in the Savoy "hospital" in the suburb on the borders of Westminster and

London called the Liberty of Lancaster. In the Savoy the Earl provided a residence for the prose craftsman from Canterbury whom he had chosen for his secretary, John Lyly. Here Lyly arranged for the publication of his famous *Euphues: The Anatomy of Wit*, licensed for printing on December 2, 1578. Here he wrote the sequel *Euphues and His England*, dedicated to Edward de Vere. And here he started writing for the theater, his first play being *The Woman in the Moon*, whose Prolog says it is "but a poet's dream, / The first he had in Phoebus' holy bower."

Sixteen years later Gabriel Harvey felt surges of animosity toward Lyly which compelled expression in dreary prose. "They were much deceived in him, at Oxford, and in the Savoy, when Master Absolon lived [William Absolon, like Lyly, came from Canterbury, and served as chief chaplain at the Savoy from August 1576 to February 1585]; that took him only for a dapper and deft companion, or a pert-conceited youth, that had gathered together a few pretty sentences, and could handsomely help young *Euphues* to an old simile; and never thought him any such mighty doer at the sharp."[36] He begged Lyly not to forget "Thy old acquaintance in the Savoy, when young Euphues hatched the eggs that his elder friends laid (surely Euphues was somewhat a pretty fellow. Would God Lilly had always been Euphues, and never Paphatchet)"—the satirist Harvey hated.[37] It is plain that in these two passages the role of Euphues was reversed by the writer from a simile-maker who could be helped to a hatcher of eggs produced by older birds. In the former I find John Lyly assisting Euphues, meaning Edward de Vere; in the second I see Oxford furnishing Lyly's propaganda.

Later, on April 27, 1593, Harvey ventured to attack "Nash, the ape of Greene, Greene the ape of Euphues, Euphues the ape of Envy, the three famous mammets of the press, and my three notorious feudists, [who, he claimed] draw all in a yoke. But some scholars excel their masters... It must go hard but he will improve himself, the incomparable darling of immortal Vanity."[38]

That was as far as Harvey dared to fly a barb by way of deriding the "minion Secretary's" master, sixteen years after he strove to

amuse the Earl of Leycester and his ring of relatives with the doggerel satire on the Earl called *Speculum Tuscanismi*, a looking glass for
mimics of Italian manners.[39]

Lyly appears to have seen only two suggestions in *The Two Gentlemen of Verona* for his own plays. He copied Launce's pun on the
"tied" (his dog) and the tide in *Endimion* (4.2.10), and altered the
line, "Wilt thou reach stars, because they shine on thee?" (from the
Verona play, 3.1) to "Stars are to be look'd at, not reach'd at," in
Campaspe (3.5). The Duke of Milan's line comparing his girl to a star
reminds us of Helena's metaphor of her love: "That I should love a
bright particular star, / And think to wed it" (*All's Well that Ends
Well*, 1.1), and the warning of Polonius to poor Ophelia, "Lord
Hamlet is a Prince out of thy Star, / This must not be" (*Hamlet*, 2.2).

The two novels about Euphues celebrate the ancient Greek ideal
of unselfish friendship between two gentlemen. Nobles and gentry
at the court of Elizabeth held cults of the heroes of yore whose love
for each other was supposed to surpass the love of men for maids.
Among the pairs of legendary male lovers thus idolised were two
alleged Romans called Titus and Gisippus (the latter name apparently a variant of Joseph). Sir Thomas Elyot included their legend in
The Governor, and in the summer of 1561 a London printer licensed a
book bearing their now oblivious names. On February 19, 1577,
Sebastian Westcott, the obstinately Papist teacher of the children
who sang at St Paul's Cathedral, directed them in a performance of
"*The history of Titus and Gisippus* showen at Whitehall on Shrove
Tuesday at night," for the edification of the Queen and her circle.[40]
This play, I suppose, copied Elyot's "wonderful history" of the two
Roman youths, whose "dear religious love" had visible roots in narcissism, for they looked exactly alike, and are presented as almost a
single soul, after Plato's own heart, in two bodies. Titus in *The Governor* admits to his friend, "all blushing and ashamed," that he is enamored of the girl adored by Gisippus. The latter kisses Titus and
casts off his "titles and interest" in that sweet property. Gisippus
goes so far as to contrive the untying of her "girdle of virginity" by
Titus. The Renaissance rejoiced in this illustration of supersensual

friendship as proof of the virtue of the great Greek philosopher of pederasty.

An idea persistently obtrudes in the fringe of my consciousness that Shakespeare intended to provoke waves of laughter at this cult of masculine mutual affection and sacrifice when he first projected the fantasy of Protheus and Valentine. The absurdity of their readiness to give up the loves of Julia and Silvia for the sake of their friendship would make a reasonable comedy if the cult was kept in mind. But it is difficult to smile even at the defiance of Protheus: "In Loue, / Who respects friend?" (5.4.53-54) No fun overtones resound from the grievance of Valentine: "Thou common friend, that's without faith or loue, / For such is a friend now." (5.4.62-63) The poet himself, under the flagellation of his conscience, deprived his comedy of a climax of mirth. I cannot account for this defeat of his frolic artistry except by referring to the friendship of Edward de Vere and Charles Arundel which appears to have been guiltily interrupted in the soul of the Earl by his passion for Anne Vavasor. Here, in my opinion, we have the source of the sorrow voiced by Valentine toward the end of the play:

> The priuate wound is deepest: oh time, most accurst:
> 'Mongst all foes that a friend should be the worst? (5.4.71-72)

Arundel later confided to elder statesmen that Oxford exprest deep happiness on learning that his cunning cousin did not suffer a broken heart from this affair. "Charles," said De Vere to him in an unnamed palace gallery—"after long speeches in secret between him and my cousin Vavisor, who was the means of our meeting, I have ever loved you, and as you have already given me your word to my mistress, so now I crave it myself."[41] It is not easy to make sense out of Charles Arundel's tortuous reports of conversations or events. They conform strictly to Talleyrand's definition of language as a human invention to hide thought.

Arundel seems to have worked on the soul of Edward de Vere in order to exploit all the resources of his earldom for protecting imported priests. "Till lately," the Spanish ambassador Mendoza wrote to his master in Madrid, on 28 December 1578, "there were but few priests left in England, and religion was dying out for want of teachers." Thanks to the "underground" industry of Charles and Lord Harry Howard and their fellow aristocrats, the number of Catholics increased daily, converted by the passionate preaching of missionaries from King Philip's seminary at Douai in Belgium. They traveled thru England disguised in various costumes and enduring hazards heroically. The fortitude of the Jesuits led to many a martyrdom, for the ferocity of Burghley's government against these outlaws never troubled to pay tongue-tribute to the principles of Shakespeare's beautiful monologs and verses on mercy.[42]

The Two Gentlemen of Verona exposed one corner of the poet's heart where he too could be merciless. Perhaps the earliest theatrical resonance of his cruelty toward the exiled, hounded, and contemptuously tolerated survivors of the Hebrew race appears in the speech of Launce telling how he and his dog left home to go away from Verona. Crab, says he, "this cruell-hearted Curre... has no more pitty in him then a dogge: a Iew would haue wept to haue seene our parting" (2.3.9-11). The implication of course is that a Jewish heart is the paragon of the pitiless. Later Launce invites his fellow clown Speed to a tavern, and again is reminded of the remoteness of Hebrews from humanity: "If thou wilt goe with me to the Alehouse: if not, thou art an Hebrew, a Iew, and not worth the name of a Christian." Speed asks, "Why?" Crab's proud possessor replies, "Because thou hast not so much charity in thee as to goe to the Ale with a Christian" (2.5.44-49). Reflecting on these odd blurts by Launce against the people of the Bible, we find it curious that Shakespeare should have given one of Valentine's gallant outlaws the name of "Moyses" (5.3). What prompted the outburst of animosity to Jews? I suspect it was a sermon our dramatist heard, a fulmination of some "subterranean" Jesuit enraged by the brutal treatment of Catholic missionaries at the hands of Walsingham's rack-masters while certain Jews, fugitives from the Holy Inquisition of Spain and Portugal, were allowed to live in England tranquilly, and even practise their Hebrew rituals secretly, so long as they paid lip-loyalty in public to the Christian state. I shall deal with the mysterious Jewry in England that Shakespeare met when we come to the chronicle of *The Merchant of Venice*.

When I surveyed the adoration of masculine friendship in our play I decided to refrain from examining the theme of homosexuality which runs undercurrently in the love-story of Valentine and Protheus. The dramatist permitted no aperture in the plot for the motive to emerge. In privacy however he murmured to Charles Arundel "that when women were unsweet, fine young boys were in season, with so far worse than this," Arundel added, "as it irketh me to remember." He managed to remember several repulsive testimonies, of which I quote the least loathsome: "He stands charged with more particulars touching this matter as his speech to Mr Cornwallis (will bear witness) that he would have a priest to whom he must confess buggery."[43] The keynote of these confessions seems to be struck by the clause "when women were unsweet." Since the Earl of Oxford's rupture of his marriage in April 1576, his lust had experienced a series of disillusionments; he had no outlet but harlots, and hated to resort to the tiresome and almost tasteless creatures, as the *Comedy of Errors* testifies in its oblique way. He also bore a grudge against womankind which Arundel recorded in this form: "He hath a yearly celebration of the Neapolitan malady."[44]

V

On September 4, 1578, the Privy Council went out of its imperial way to grant "A commission for eight carts to carry my Lord of Oxford's stuff from the Court to London." I like to think that these carts were not for the purpose of transporting domestic materials, but for fetching to the metropolis stuff designed for the stage. Only guesswork suggests that the Earl needed the carts for a rehearsal of John Lyly's play of Alexander and the painter Apelles and his love Campaspe. But I believe it was this play the Children of the Chapel Royal enacted for the Court on March 7, 1579 under the title "The History of Loyalty and Beauty." These Children demonstrated their talents in London town before they presented their play at Court. They played at the roofed and windowed Blackfriars theater by candle-light, in conditions dramatically different from those the actors of the innyards and brothel-district playhouses endured under the sun or rain.

On December 24, the Privy Council sent a letter to the Lord Mayor of London, "requiring him to suffer the Children of her Majesty's Chapel, the servants of the Lord Chamberlain (Sussex), the Earl of Warwick, the Earl of Leicester, the Earl of Essex, and the Children of Paul's, and no companies else, to exercise playing within the City, whom their Lordships have only allowed thereunto by reason that the companies aforenamed are appointed to play this time of Christmas before her Majesty."[45] The servants of Ambrose Dudley, the Earl of Warwick, seem to have performed a play that used a truck or two already employed in *The Two Gentlemen of Verona*. On December 26, they acted *The Three Sisters of Mantua*, whose plot required the use of a rope and pulley and a basket. The leaders of this troup, the brothers John and Lawrence Dutton, left the livery of Warwick in the spring of 1580 and became eminent among the histrionic pupils of Edward de Vere.

Shakespeare's plays of this period are graced with some of his most charming songs, but too little care for the understanding of the music that must have been composed for them is evinced by the modern masters of musicology. They are aware that the greatest music maker of the age, William Byrd, enjoyed writing variations for his setting of the song in *Twelfth Night*, "O Mistress Mine." They know that in 1573 or 1574 the Earl of Oxford made a lease to William Byrd, "gentleman" and organist of her Majesty's Chapel, of his manor of Battleshall in Essex, to take place at the death of Aubrey Vere, esquire, or after Aubrey's wife died.[46] In 1575 the Queen granted Byrd and his teacher Thomas Tallis an exclusive license for the printing and sale of music. Lord Burghley found Byrd to be a firm Roman Catholic whom prosecution for "recusancy," or failure to attend the Tudor church, with daylight fidelity to his mother's creed, could not swerve. Aubrey Vere was buried in Castle Hedingham parish on 14 March 1579, but we are sorry to record that Byrd failed to obtain rental benefit from Battleshall. William Irwin gained it from him in a tricky lawsuit. In 1578 he lived sequestered in Harlington, Middlesex. Henry Percy, Earl of Northumberland, whose wife Catherine was the daughter of John Neville, Lord Latimer, grandson of John de Vere, the thirteenth Earl of Oxford, became a patron of Byrd. On February 28, 1579, he begged Burghley to assist the composer economically, "seeing he cannot enjoy that which was his first suit and granted unto him... he is my friend, and chiefly that he is schoolmaster to my daughter in his art." Percy's luck with the Lord Treasurer was extremely poor. In 1584 Burghley imprisoned him in the Tower for sundry intrigues, and not long after, he was found shot in the heart; the government proclaimed him a suicide.

In the mass of manuscripts William Byrd bequested to his country and the world there are numerous poems having no signature. I have no positive proof of their authorship, but since they sound so verily like the lyrics by the Earl of Oxford written in the time of *The Two Gentlemen of Verona* and the dramas that followed it, I will select one for publication here, hoping that the reader hears in its melody the same voice that gently rings in my ear. Observe how boldly, how echo-like, the sonnet is rimed.[47]

> Weeping full sore with face as fair as silver,
>   Not wanting rose nor lily white to paint it,
> I saw a lady walk fast by a river,
>   Upon whose banks Diana's Nymphs all danced.
> Her beauty great had divers gods enchanted,
>   Among the which Love was the first transformed,
> Who unto her his bow and shafts had granted,
>   And by her sight to adamant was turned.
> Alas, quoth I, what meaneth this demeanour,
>   So fair a dame to be so full of sorrow?
> No wonder, quoth a Nymph, she wanteth pleasure,
>   Her tears and signs ne cease from eve tomorrow:
> This lady rich is of the gifts of beauty,
> But unto her are gifts of fortune dainty.

This sonnet sketch appeals to me as a portrayal of the sweet and solitary Anne Cecil de Vere, who could be seen from the Savoy windows whenever she went for a stroll on the Strand or down by the Thames. (The present-day Savoy Theater stands on ground once owned by the house of Cecil in the Strand.) The poetic picture of the forlorn Countess summons to my memory the fact that the first chords of our dramatist clearly sounding a theme of the noblest work of art ever to emerge from the mind of man, the tragedy of *King Lear*, are struck in *The Two Gentlemen of Verona*. We hear them in the lines of the nameless Duke of Milan pronouncing his anger against his girl Silvia:

> She is peeuish, sullen, froward,
> Prowd, disobedient, stubborne, lacking duty,
> Neither regarding that she is my childe,
> Nor fearing me, as if I were her father:
> And may I say to thee, this pride of hers
> (Vpon aduice) hath drawne my loue from her,
> And where I thought the remnant of mine age
> Should have beene cherishe'd by her child-like dutie,
> I now am full resolu'd to...
>   turne her out, to who will take her in:
> Then let her beauty be her wedding dowre;
> For me, and my possessions she esteemes not.   (3.1.68-79)

If we overlook the juvenile verbosity and the plain intention to depict the Duke as a man with no fears of old age, we can discern here the very voice that will cry out more than twenty years later, "I lou'd her most, and thought to set my rest / On her kind nursery."

References

1   Eva Turner Clark, *Hidden Allusions in Shakespeare's Plays*, ed. Ruth Loyd Miller (Jennings, LA; Minos Publishing Company, 1974) 298.

2   *Documents Relating to the Office of the Revels in the Time of Queen Elizabeth*, ed. Albert Feuillerat (Louvain; A. Uystpruyst, 1908) 320.

3   Albert Cohn, *Shakespeare in Germany in the Sixteenth and Seventeenth Centuries* (London; Asher, 1865) cxv.

4   *Ibid.* cxi.

5   *Acts of the Privy Council of England*, ed. John Roche Dasent (London; Eyre and Spottiswoode, 1890-1907) x, 144.

6   Irwin Smith, *Shakespeare's Blackfriars Playhouse* (New York University Press, 1964) 467.

7   Celeste Turner (Wright), *Anthony Mundy* (Berkeley, CA 1928) 145. [*editor:* Turner, followed by Feldman, always writes "Mundy", but we decided to use the common notation "Munday"]

8   John M. Lothian, "Shakespeare's Knowledge of Aretino's Plays," *Modern Language Review*, vol. 25 (October 1930) 415-6.—For valorous endeavors to translate the Italian of Aretino I am obliged to Gino Segre, professor of physics at the University of Pennsylvania, and my brother, Harold Feldman.

9   *Calendar of Salisbury* (Cecil) *Ms at Hatfield*, xxv, 58.

10 *Calendar of State Papers, Domestic* (1566-79), p. 536.

11 *Acts of the Privy Council*, 26 April 1579.—Valentine Dale's impression of Edward de Vere, when the Earl came to Paris in March 1575, is worth noting in view of the judgment on him pronounced by Elizabethan "authorities": "he used himself very moderately and comely, and is well liked as a goodly gentleman." *Calendar of State Papers, Foreign Series*, 1575, no. 42.)

12 J. Thomas Looney, *"Shakespeare" Identified in Edward de Vere, Seventeenth Earl of Oxford*, and *The Poems of Edward de Vere* (Jennings, LA; Minos Publishing Company, 1975) i, 568-9. Hyder Rollins the antiquarian suggested that this poem may have been translated from Philippe Desportes's Amours de Diana (i, 37) or from verses by Panfilo Sassi, also attributed to Serafino Aquilane de' Ciminelli (*Le Rime*, ed. Marie Menghini, 1894; i, 221). George Buchanan the Scottish scholar translated these verses into Latin (*Poemata*, Amsterdam 1687, p. 377) and Thomas Watson adapted them for his *Hekatompathia or Passionate Century of Love*, dedicated to Oxford in 1582, sonnet 22. Alas, I am at a loss of lingual skill to comment on Professor Rollins's rubrics.—Nicholas Britten's first book, *The Pain of Pleasure*, registered for the press on 9 Septmeber 1578, disappeared.

13 *Calendar of Cecil Ms.* ix, f. 92. The Coroners inquest record of the homicide was finally printed in *Hamlet Himself* by Bronson Feldman (Philadelphia; Lovelore Press, 1977) 123f.

14 *Black's Law Dictionary,* 2nd ed (West Publishing Co, 1910) 488.

15 *Calendar of State Papers,* Foreign (1575-77) 490-1.

16 Hubert Languet in *Correspondence of Sir Philip Sidney...* ed. Steuart A. Pears (London; William Pickering, 1845) 137. See *The Correspondence of Philip Sidney and Hubert Languet,* ed. William A. Bradley (Boston, 1912).

17 *Relations Politiques des Pays-Bas et de l'Angleterre, sous le Regne de Philippe* ii, ed. Joseph Kervyn de Lettenhove (Brussels; F. Hayes, 18821900) x, 508.

18 "Journal of Sir Francis Walsingham," ed. C. T. Martin, *Camden Miscellany,* vi, 36.

19 J. Thomas Looney, *op. cit.,* 396-7.

20 Clark, *op. cit.* 299.

21 Marguerite de Valois, *Memoirs,* trans. anonymous (Boston 1899) 195.

22 *Ibid.* 198-9.

23 *Ibid.* 199. The French adventure provides us with the terminus from which to date the writing of the original *The Two Gentlemen of Verona,* and therefore will not be seen in such tomes as *The Reader's Encyclopedia of Shakespeare,* ed. Oscar J. Campbell (New York; Crowell, 1966).

24 *Calendar of State Papers,* Foreign (1578) no. 87.

25 *State Papers Domestic:* 12, 151: 42. (Public Record Office, London.)

26 *State Papers Domestic:* 12, 151: 44.

27 *Ibid.* The Arundel "Answer" gives us a glimpse of the infinite wonder with which Edward de Vere looked at our planet. Speaking of a "painted book" of predictions, Charles observed, "some man of his, as I conceive, thrust upon him under color of a prophecy, to cozen him of crowns, as indeed it was not rare to pick his purse with pretense of novelties and (foreign) fancy accidents."

28 *Idem.*

29 *State Papers Domestic:* 12, 151: 49.

30 *State Papers Domestic:* 12, 151: 46.

31 *Relations Politiques...* op. cit. X, 773.

32 Conyers Read, *Lord Burghley and Queen Elizabeth* (New York; Knopf, 1961) 200.

33 *Calendar of State Papers,* Foreign (1578-79).

34 *Calendar of State Papers,* Foreign (1578) no. 12.

35 *Calendar of State Papers,* Domestic (1578) cxxvi, 16. Compare A. L. Rowse, *Ralegh and the Throckmortons* (London; Macmillan, 1962) 73-4.

36 Gabriel Harvey, *Works,* ed. Alexander Grosart (London; Huth Library, 1884) ii, 128.—In 1573 the Office of the Queen's Receiver recorded arrears of rent due from the Savoy hotel, including 10 pounds, 11 shillings, 8 pence, from the Earl of Oxford for two "tenements" lately occupied by his servants John Harleston and Barnard Hampton. (Lansdowne Ms. 20, f. 73, quoted by W. J. Loftie, *Memorials of the Savoy;* London 1878; 125.) Harleston was a cousin of the Earl by the wedding of Thomas Darcy of Essex to a daughter of "ye littell

E. of Ox." (*Visitation of Essex,* 1558, ed. Metcalfe, p. 45.) Hampton was expert in the Spanish tongue, like Oxford's physician, George Baker.

37 Harvey (1589), *Works,* ii, 124.

38 *Ibid.* i, 222.

39 J. Thomas Looney, *op. cit.* vol. ii, 67.

40 *Documents Relating to the Office of the Revels...* 270, 275.

41 *State Papers Domestic:* 12, 151: 45.

42 James A. Froude, *History of England from the Fall of Wolsey to the Defeat of the Spanish Armada* (1870), xi, 336.

43 State Papers Domestic: 12, 151: 46 and 57.

44 *Ibid.* 151: 46.

45 *Acts of the Privy Council,* x, 436.

46 Edmund H. Fellowes, *William Byrd* (Oxford University Press, 1936) 3. See Katherine Eggar's article on Byrd in the *Musical Times,* 1 January 1929.

47 William Byrd, *Collected Vocal Works,* ed. Edmund Fellowes (London; Stainer & Bell, 1937-50) xiv, xvi. Compare the "Echo Verses" in *The Poems of Edward de Vere, op. cit.* 560-1.

Chapter 7—HELEN OF ROSE-ILION

> The web of our life is of mingled yarn,
> good and ill together: our virtues would
> be proud, if our faults whipt them not,
> and our crimes would despair if they were
> not cherish'd by our virtues.
>
> *Captain G. Dumain.*
> (*All's Well That Ends Well*, 4.3.70-73)

The man who solved the mystery of William Shakespeare's identity, John Thomas Looney (1870-1944), flung a challenge to the priestlike and professorial attendants at the gaudy manger of Stratford-on-Avon which they have not answered yet. In his book of revelations he offered some proof that *All's Well That Ends Well* "might indeed be compendiously described as Boccaccio's story (the plot Shakespeare took from the *Decameron*) *plus* the early life of Edward de Vere."[1] None of the dons who daily in profane rituals adore the Stratford usurer put this opinion to a public test. Firmly persuaded with Sir John Falstaff that "The better part of valor is discretion," they ignored the challenge and rumpled on with their campaign of calumny against Looney and the 'Bard'. So I will go over the evidence again by which the former proved that the play in question runs "as near to biography, or autobiography if our theory be accepted, as a dramatist ever permitted himself to go."[2] Moreover I will fetch to the trial a group of witnesses whom Looney only guessed existed or glimpsed in his prophetic dreams. A few of them were first summoned to testify by Eva Turner Clark in her monumental *Hidden Allusions in Shakespeare's Plays*,[3] others by Percy Allen in lightning-like pages of his various books on the most singular of England's earls.

> Let us from point to point this story know,
> To make the even truth in pleasure flow. (5.3.321-322)

* * * *

I

The love-story Boccaccio told took place first in the kingdom of France in the region of a king unnamed. Shakespeare too left him nameless. Unlike the Italian storyteller, he pictured the king as a close friend of his hero's father, called Count Isnardo of Rossiglione in the tale but nameless in the play. Isnardo's only son Beltramo (correctly translated "Bertram" in Shakespeare's romance) grew up in companionship with the daughter of Gerard de Narbon, the Count's physician. Her name our dramatist changed from Giletta to Helena—perhaps because he had already employed the name Julia for the minor heroine in the comedy he wrote before, and had called the girlfriend Lucetta. He demoted Helena from the wealthy heiress of a famous physician to the comparatively poor child of a doctor who was nevertheless reputed miraculous—perhaps for dramatic effect, to make Helena's love for Count Bertram seem like the sky climbing of the builders of Babel. Our poet's vision was not intent on her possessions; he meant merely to locate her class, two 'estates' below that of his Count of Rossillion. Boccaccio, the illegitimate son of a Lombard moneylender and a Parisian gentlewoman, did not suffer from the blade-edged class consciousness of Shakespeare, who made his heroine sing about her passion for Bertram thus (1.1.86-90):

> I am undone: there is no living, none,
> If Bertram be away. 'Twere all one,
> That I should love a bright particular star,
> And think to wed it, he is so above me
> In his bright radiance and collateral light.

The last three lines were composed when Shakespeare revised *All's Well*, I believe for purposes of romantic as well as comic relief, while preparing his tragedy *Hamlet* for the press (1604). He put the very same metaphor on the lips of Polonius, for once talking laconically, or so he pretends, warning his daughter to beware of her royal love (*Hamlet*, 2.2): "Lord Hamlet is a prince, out of thy star." More than analogy between social grades and celestial orbs was intended

here: the poet cherished an old belief in the divine arrangement of
human affairs according to patterns of the planets or Zodiac. Helena expresses the faith in deploring her birth below humiliating
planets (1.1.181-182):

> we the poorer born,
> Whose baser stars do shut us up in wishes.

The Italian tale refers to many men who were willing to marry her.
Shakespeare granted her not one; nor would he trouble to invent a
single reason for rendering her so undesirable. Boccaccio gave the
orphan kinfolk interested in her future. The dramatist confined her
life entirely to the orbit of Count Bertram, like a poor little moon
revolving around an earth which is evidently attractive to very few
else.

In the source tale Bertram's father dies shortly before the death
of his doctor Gerard. In the drama these events are reversed; the
latter died six months before his lord and friend. The curtains of
Shakespeare's romance open on the solemnity of the young Count
and his mother, "all in black" with their friend Lord Lafew and Helena, getting ready for Bertram's departure to the royal court.

"In delivering my son from me," mourns the Dowager Countess,
"I bury a second husband." Thanks to Freud we can now behold in
these words, starkly echoing the vocabulary of birth, the wish of the
orphan lad to rise to his vanished father's position by the mother's
bedside, a wish doomed to burial in the boy's unhappy head.

"And I in going, Madam, weep o'er my father's death anew; but I
must attend his majesty's command, to whom I am now in ward,
evermore in subjection." (1.1.1-5) His final phrase comes as surprise
to our ears, for its note of revolt has not the least justification in
experience. This dialog of the Dowager and young Rossillion,
Shakespeare invented alone. The *Decameron* never mentioned Bertram's mother.

We can see how the dramatist could identify himself with the
Count in the moment when he read about the death of his noble
father and the boy's leaving home to become a royal ward. Like

Boccaccio's Bertram, the first syllable of whose name turns in a
twinkle to Ver, De Vere was an only son and "a handsome and
charming boy." It may be accidental that the second syllable of the
hero's name echoes the German for *dream*. Count of course is
merely French for Earl. In Act 3, Scene 5, Bertram is called "this
French Earl" and "the young Earl." The "bright particular star" that
Helena thinks of in dreaming of their wedding is the silver mullet
we see shining on Oxford's coat of arms.

After the death of Lord John, the sixteenth Earl of Oxford, on 3
August 1562, less than four months after his son's twelfth birthday,
Edward de Vere also became a royal ward. The funeral of his father
occurred at Castle Hedingham (his will requested burial at Earls
Colne church) on the last day of August "with many mourners in
black; and a great moan made for him." Later the diary writer I have
just quoted thought worthy of record this spectacle: "The iii day of
September came riding out of Essex from [the funeral] of the Earl
of Oxford his father, the young Earl of Oxford, with vii score horse
all in black through London and Cheap and Ludgate, and so to
Temple Bar, and so to [Westminster and the new house of Sir William Cecil, recently appointed Master of the Queen's Wards] between v and vi of the clock at afternoon."[4] Never again would a
hundred and forty gentlemen having steeds ride in united fidelity
and affection for the house of Vere. For the next nine years Earl
Edward lived under the thrifty eyes and prehensile and punitive
hands of the Cecils, and occasionally under the equally sharp orbs
and talented fingers of Queen Elizabeth, "evermore in subjection."
But the Queen was more fun-prone than her Treasurer and Madam
Mildred, his wife.

Whom did the dramatist have in view when he sketched the portrait of the Countess of Rossillion? In kindliness, humor, compassion, and maternal love, she bears at best a distant faint resemblance
to the Countess Margaret Golding de Vere. We know that the
Dowager Countess of Oxford sorrowed with brevity on parting
from her child. She made no warm speech to him as the lady of
Rossillion made to her boy.

> Be thou blest, Bertram, and succeed thy father
> In manners as in shape: thy blood and virtue
> Contend for empire in thee, and thy goodness
> Share with thy birth-right. Love all, trust a few,
> Do wrong to none: be able for thine enemy
> Rather in power than use: and keep thy friend
> Under thy own life's key. Be checkt for silence,
> But never tax'd for speech. What heaven more will,
> That thee may furnish, and my prayers pluck down,
> Fall on thy head. (1.1.61-70)

The wisdom of these lines deserves a leisurely comparison with the blessing and advice Polonius gives his son in *Hamlet*. With what master-skill the poet renders the good sense of each goodby, silently instructing us by their opposite outlooks in the difference between skinflint prudence and lordly generosity. The celebration of the Earl of Oxford's thirteenth birthday on April 12 seems to have reminded Cecil that the last will and testament of the Earl's father had not been probated yet. He wrote to the Countess Margery about it, and here is her reply on April 30, signed M. Oxinford.

"I gathered generally that complaints had been brought to my Lord of Norfolk's Grace and to my Lord Robert Dudley by sundry, that the only let [Hamlet's word for hindrance] why my Lord's late will hath not been proved or exhibited hath been only in me and through my delays.

"I confess that a great trust hath been committed to me of those things which in my Lord's lifetime were kept most secret from me. And since that time the doubtful declaration of my Lord's debts hath so uncertainly fallen out of that... I had rather leave up the whole doings thereof to my son, if by your good advice I may so deal honourably, than to venture further and uncertainly altogether with the will... And what my further determination is touching the will, yet loth to determine without your good advice, for that I mean the honour or gain (if any be) might come wholly to my son, who is under your charge."[5]

Her secretive husband's will, made on 28 July 1562, seven days before he died, was at last 'proved' 29 May 1563. She left not a word of wonder about her boy's health or education, not a word of affection or farewell, among his numerous papers and books. Shortly afterward she quietly married a scion of Essex gentry, Charles Tyrrel, Esquire, a member of the Queen's Gentlemen-Pensioners or bodyguard. We doubt if the orphan Earl attended the wedding. She died on December 2, 1568, and was buried near his forebears' tomb in Earls Colne. Early in the spring of 1570 her second husband died, leaving a will in which he returned "unto the Earl of Oxford one great horse that his lordship gave me"—presumably at Cecil's prompting as a wedding gift.[6]

To give Count Bertram a warm-hearted loving mother, the poet had to look far from his birthplace Hedingham. He found what he wanted, I think, in the shire north of Essex: he made his lady of Rossillion in the image of Katherine Willoughby, the Duchess of Suffolk, mother of Lord Peregrine Bertie, who married De Vere's sister Mary and so became unaware the hero of *The Taming of the Shrew*. To convert the Duchess into the Dowager of Rossillion, all Shakespeare had to do was tone down her tongue, make her temper more temperate. The praises poured at the feet of Bertram's mother by generations of critics were cordially earned by Mary Vere's mother-in-law. I submit in confirmation a letter she wrote to Lord Burghley in April 1580 appealing for royal permission to be granted her son, who felt as if he would go crazy in idleness, to enter the military service of the Netherlands.

"I am ashamed to be so troublesome to your Lordship and others of my good Lords of her Majesty's honourable Council, specially in so uncomfortable a suit as for license of their assent in the absence of my only dear son, in whose company I hoped with comfort to have finished my last days. But... either I must see his doleful pining and vexed mind at home, which hath brought him to such a state of mind and body as so many knoweth and can witness it, or else content myself with his desire to seek such fortune abroad as may make him forget some griefs and give him better knowledge and experience to serve her Majesty and his country at his return. The time he desireth for the same is five years, so as I am never like after his departure to see him again; yet am I loth he should so long be out of her Majesty's realm, wherefore I cannot consent to any more than three years. Oh, my good lord, you have children and therefore you know how dear they be to their parents,—your wisdom also is some help to govern your fatherly affections by...but alas, I a poor woman which with great pains and travail many years hath by God's mercy brought an only son from tender youth to man's estate...in place of comfort I myself must be the suitor for his absence, to my great grief and sorrow...I most humbly beseech her Majesty even for God's sake therefor to give him leave to go to sea and live in all places where it shall please God to hold him, always with the duty of a faithful subject to serve..."[6]

Beside the character of the Count's mother, Shakespeare also added the Lord Lafew, a figure also heartily extolled by students of the play. Nobody doubts that in picturing this nobleman, old yet ever cheerful, shrewd and witty, but excessively fond of his wit, the poet drew from human nature quite familiar to him. Nobody however, except the followers of John Thomas Looney, has dared to point out the British nobleman whom the poet certainly held in gentle satirical view. As soon as we hear the King of France remark about Lafew's loquacity, "Thus he his special nothing ever prologues" (2.1.93) we realise that we are in the presence of a spiritual twin of Lord Polonius, exhibiting none of the Dane's vices, stressing his aged merits and showing him more amiable. The model for both men could have been none other than William Cecil, Lord Burghley, practically the prime minister of the Elizabethan empire, and the Earl of Oxford's father-in-law. Burghley, whom the Queen enjoyed calling "burly," would have enjoyed deciphering his name in Lafew, which everyone rightly reads "La Feu" without comprehending why Shakespeare should have named him 'Fire.' If we remember that English *fire* and *burn* are virtually the same sound as

Grecian *pyr*, we will easily see how the syllable could be transformed to *Bur*. The suffix of his Lordship's title (frequently spelt Burleigh) naturally changed to the La of so many French names. It must have struck Oxford as irresistibly piquant to convert his father-in-law, a statesman trained from infancy to believe that Britain's fate was forever silver-corded to the "house of Burgundy," into a Francophile courtier.

At the risk of making the romance incredible from the start, our poet presented Lafew, the friend of Lord and Lady Rossillion, as one unacquainted with their medical magician Gerard. This awkwardness resulted from the poet's arduous endeavor to portray Lafew as a total stranger to Helena. "Was this gentlewoman the daughter of Gerard de Narbon?" If the poet had not been so anxious-eager to picture them as unknown to each other, he could have devised a reasonable way to introduce his characters and their family situation. By his mistake we are impelled with strong curiosity to examine the relation of Helena to Lafew. There is none in the play except in two passages of goodby: the single line that he pronounces on going away with the Count—"Farewell, pretty lady, you must hold the credit of your father," and the strange, nearly libidinous lines he utters on leaving the girl alone with the king:

> I am Cressid's uncle,
> That dare leave two together. Fare you well. (2.1.98-99)

But if Lafew is Burghley barely disguised, and Bertram is a dream-Vere, then Helena (she is more often named Helen in the play than Helena) must be meant for Anne, William Cecil's daughter, whose marriage to the Earl of Oxford made her appear in his imagination incarnate Hell. Writing that allusion to Cressida's uncle, the prototype of pandars, the author had no purpose but to blame his father-in-law for the fatal union with little Anne. He worked exactly the same accusation in his five-act fantasy of *Troilus and Cressida*, transforming the heroine's uncle, the traditional Pandaros, until none but the blindest would fail to recognize old William Cecil in him.

The temperament of Bertram's forlorn lover, whom Coleridge hailed as "the loveliest of Shakespeare's characters," is adequately

described in the first scene of *All's Well that Ends Well*. Everyone
seems to speak to her half lovingly, half pitifully. "Little
Helen" (1.1), "sweet Helen" (5.3.) Looney observed, clearly represents the deserted young mother whom Ambrose Dudley, Earl of
Warwick, sent greetings in his letter to her father on 20 October
1578 which calls her "the sweet little Countess of Oxford."[7] If she
had lived to hear or read the verses depicting the way Helen delighted in mutely watching the Count thru endless minutes, Anne
would have remembered many a day of joyous peace at Cecil
House, when the orphan Earl was busy with his books or performing one of the tasks his excellent tutors had assigned him.

> 'Twas pretty, though a plague,
> To see him every hour, to sit and draw
> His arched brows, his hawking eye, his curls
> In our heart's table. (1.1.94-97)

A portrait of the artist as a young prig! well aware that he was
watched, admired, worshipt by the child of the Master of the Wards.
Those brows and curls and that predatory bird's eye are still to be
seen in the picture of De Vere painted in Paris in March 1575 by
the Fleming Lucas van Heere and mailed across the Channel to his
lonely wife.[8]

In the play Bertram listens to the King talk with a sad joy about
the Count's father. Shakespeare could not resist adorning his *Decameron* material with this digression, shaped, I suppose, from reminiscence he heard mostly at the fireside of his Queen's chief minister.
Cecil probably remarked many times how alike "in manners and in
shape" Lord Edward and John of Oxford were.

> Youth, thou bear'st thy father's face.
> Frank Nature, rather curious than in haste,
> Hath well compos'd thee. Thy father's moral parts
> May'st thou inherit too... (1.2.19-22)

We will take a good look at those "moral parts" by and by. Let us
hear the whole eulogy, which incidentally supplies a kind of organic

stuff for the imperious ghost of Hamlet the elder, who ultimately stands for the very same man.

> I would I had that corporal soundness now
> As when thy father and myself in friendship
> First tried our soldiership: he did look far
> Into the service of the time, and was
> Discipled of the bravest. He lasted long,
> But on us both did haggish age steal on,
> And wore us out of act. It much repairs me
> To talk of your good father; in his youth
> He had the wit which I can well observe
> Today in our young Lords: but they may jest
> Till their own scorn return to them unnoted
> Ere they can hide their levity in honour.
> So like a Courtier, contempt nor bitterness
> Were in his pride, or sharpness; if they were,
> His equal had awak'd them, and his honour,
> Clock to itself, knew the true minute when
> Exception bid him speak, and at this time
> His tongue obey'd his hand. Who were below him,
> He us'd as creatures of another place,
> And bow'd his eminent top to their low ranks,
> Making them proud of his humility,
> In their poor praise he humbled. Such a man
> Might be a copy to these younger times;
> Which followed well would demonstrate them now
> But goers backward. (1.2.24-48)

Looney touched a vital spot in Shakespeare's world-outlook when he affirmed that here we have the voice of one mind most critical of his country's approaching culture of capitalism—"not only the aristocrat but also a man who felt out of touch with the new and less chivalrous order then emerging from the protestant middle classes, where individualism and personal ambition were less under the discipline of social principles than in the best manifestations of the departing feudal ideals."[9] The trouble with this interpretation is that it overlooks the precise point, theme, or moral what you will—of *All's Well that Ends Well*. What else does the drama tell or teach us if not the ethical superiority of Helen, the doctor's daughter, sweet small epitome of the rising Protestant burgess class, over Bertram, offshoot of chivalry (strictly speaking, the horse-breeding class) graced by perishing arms and arts, and beautiful, glistering, corrupt-cored, the last fruit of feudalism? In fact the play might be compendiously described as a nobleman's satire on the departing feudal ideals. If Looney had said, instead of "man," *boy*, we would positively echo his statement, but it is necessary to note, as Looney himself was the first to observe, that the retrospection of the sick old King gives us in reality only the patriotic emotion, the father-worship of Shakespeare in beardless youth. The verses present the fantom of his father as he once wished to love and laud him all his days. However, Edward de Vere's motto (apparently chosen when he had his first portrait painted) was *Vero nihil verius*—Nothing truer than truth—Verity.[10] The young Earl of Oxford never wearied, as Gilbert Talbot informed his mother, the Countess of Shrewsbury, of letting the world understand that he came "of that ancient and Very family of the Veres."[11] In becoming a man, I feel absolutely sure, he painfully acquired the facts about his father, and knew when he penned the King's lines that he was composing the swansong of a lad's illusion. Sunken among beakers full of nostalgia his intellect might slide backward to legends about his father and forefathers; but it would always be too infernally vain of its learning in history, and his "hawking eye," to forget that they were lies, white lies, candy lies, nevertheless untruths.

For instance, take the story repeated by Gervase Markham in the quaint tome entitled *Honour in His Perfection* (1624) about John de Vere's encounter with a wild swine in France. In 1544 this Earl of Oxford attended King Henry VIII in the deadlock of war with the French when they besieged the English garrison of Boulogne. The Earl brought many soldiers with him from Essex, and doubtless spent a few exciting winter weeks at Boulogne observing the valor of his brother-in-law, Henry Howard, Earl of Surrey, more famous today for his sonnets and Virgil in blank verse than for his brilliant war work in France. John de Vere, according to all available contemporary accounts, did nothing in particular at the siege, but did it well enough. "By reason of his warlike disposition," Markham scribbled, almost in an ecstasy of flattery, "he was invited to the hunting of a wild boar, a sport mixed with much danger and deserving the best man's care for his preservation and safety. Whence it comes that the Frenchmen, when they hunt this beast, are ever armed with light arms, mounted on horseback, and having chasing staves like lances in their hands. To this sport the Earl of Oxford goes; but no otherwise attired than as when he walked in his own private bedchamber, only a dancing rapier by his side; neither any better mounted than on a plain English Tracconer, or ambling hag. Anon the boar is put on foot (which was a beast both huge and fierce), the chase is eagerly pursued, many affrights are given, and many dangers escaped. At last the Earl, weary of the toil or else urged by some other necessity, alights from his horse and walks alone by himself on foot; when suddenly down the path in which the Earl walked came the enraged beast, with his mouth all foamy, his teeth whetted, his bristles up, and all other signs of fury and anger. The gallants of France cry unto the Earl to run aside and save himself; everyone holloed out that he was lost, and (more than their wishes) none there was that durst bring him succour. But the Earl (who was as careless of their clamours as they were careful to exclaim) alters not his pace, nor goes an hair's breadth out of his path; and finding that the boar and he must struggle for passage, draws out his rapier and at the first encounter slew the boar. Which, when the French nobility perceived, they came galloping in unto him and made the wonder in their distracted amazements some twelve times greater than Hercules' twelve labours, all joining in one, that it was an act many degrees beyond possibility... But the Earl, seeing their distraction, replied: 'My Lords, what have I done of which I have no feeling?... Why, every boy in my nation would have performed it. They may be bugbears to the French: to us they are but servants...' And so they returned to Paris with the slain beast, where the wonder did neither decrease nor die, but to this day lives in many of their old annals."[12]

This gay cock-and-boar tale has the pictorial matter-of-fact manner requisite to a good lie. But hunting the boar would be easier than hunting for it in any "old annals" French or British. The detail of the animal's transportation to Paris, instead of Boulogne, the sole possible scene for such a feat, betrays the artifice of the tale. More curious are the details of the dancing rapier and the bedchamber dress. John de Vere attained no reputation as a dancer; his son did. We shall hear Count Bertram in *All's Well* expressing fury because he is allowed to wear a sword only for show in dances. As for the bedroom attire, I see in it the garment which the child Edward appears to have considered for some strange reason the most characteristic his father wore. Consequently Hamlet the elder makes his last apparition in his own private bedchamber, and his son at the sight cries in amazement, "My Father in his habit, as he lived." Edward de Vere, I feel sure, made the boar story up.

John de Vere would naturally have desired his son to preserve his memory first of all in his majestic soldier costume. Many a contemporary of the seventeenth Earl of Oxford must have recalled the sixteenth in resplendent armor, doing his duty as Lord Lieutenant of Essex, reviewing shire troops or supervising shore defense. He seems however to have made a stronger impression on his countrymen as an unlucky amorist or explorer of love.

At the age of seventeen, in July 1536, John Bulbeck, as his father called him—each heir of the Earldom was titled Viscount Bulbeck—married Dorothy Neville, a girl of the bluest blood flowing in old Catholic (far from merry) England. Their wedding took place at a former monastery named Holywell in the Shoreditch precinct of London; each of these places became notorious in their children's lifetime because of the brothels and theatres that sprang up around them. The marriage was really an alliance between the philoprogenitive fifteenth Earl of Oxford and Dorothy's brother, the Earl of Westmorland. We know next to nothing about the union. They got a daughter, named Katherine in honor of King Henry's fifth wife (the second whom he beheaded). Katherine de Vere grew up to be a mother of Windsors, and she taught her children to detest their cousins Edward and Mary de Vere. In her judgment these two were illicit children, living off privileges to which they had no lawful claim. Her descendants contended in a supreme court that their mother had never married John de Vere. So quietly, so demurely was their ceremony conducted in the parish church of Belchamp St Paul's, six miles from Castle Hedingham![13] The Great Chamberlain of England entered holy matrimony for the second time almost as if he was ashamed of himself, verily like the thief in the *Book of Revelations* (xvi. 15). The minister who presided at the strange wedding did not mention any other witnesses in his church register:

"AᵒDomini 1548... The weddinge of my lorde Jhon De Vere Earle of Oxenforde And Margery daughter of Jhon Gouldhinge Esquire, the first of August."

The last reference to his first wife during her life that can be found in an extant document is a casual inclusion of her name in an account of triviality among the records of King Henry's court dated 17 December 1545. No notice of her death or burial has been located yet. She probably died before the spring of 1547 since in June of that year the banns or church announcements of Lord John's prospect of second marriage had been made twice. But the bride named in his banns was not Margery Golding. According to a letter by Sir Thomas Darcy of June 27 sent to Sir William Cecil, Lord John was desperately in love with "Mistress Dorothy, late woman to my Lady Katherine his daughter," and only stern intervention by the Duke of Somerset, uncle of the boy King Edward VI and his Lord Protector, would rescue the Earl from his folly. What their objections to Mistress Dorothy were exactly or in general, we have not the least inkling. She seems to have been the sister of Edward Green, a gentleman of Little Sampford, tenant of the estates of Grassals and Bloys under the Earl of Oxford—that is all I was able to learn about her. She never emerged from the shade in which the wisdom of King Edward's council condemned her to stay.

Earl John's sister Elizabeth presumably talked his amorous troubles over with her husband Lord Thomas Darcy of Chiche and his kinsman Sir Thomas Darcy. From the latter finally came the suggestion that a marriage should be arranged for poor Oxford with one of the daughters of Lord Thomas Wentworth.[14] The Lord Protector Edward Seymour, Duke of Somerset did not pursue this proposal. Instead he nearly scared the Earl to death with another. On February 1, 1548, a county chronicler of Essex affirms, the King's uncle "out of his extreme avarice and greedy appetite, did, under colour of justice, convent before himself for certain criminal causes John, Earl of Oxenford, and did so terrify him, that to save his life he was obliged to alienate to the said Duke by deed" practically all his wealth in landed property.[15] Every endeavor to determine what "criminal" blames Somerset could threaten the Earl with has so far ended in the darkness where the chronicler left them. By state documents we are merely informed that on February 1 Somerset and Oxford signed an indenture for the wedding of the Duke's son Henry to the Earl's heiress, Katherine. She was destined however to become a Windsor, not a Seymour. Nor did the frightened Oxford have to wed the Wentworth or any girl of the nobility. How he managed the affair, nobody knows, but he could be as stubborn as Count Bertram in *All's Well* when his King insisted that Bertram must marry the royal choice, "a poor physician's daughter" (2.3.114)

In such a business, give me leave to use
The help of mine own eyes. (2.3.106-107)

John coveted a commoner. The choice of his eyes and wits was the daughter of an auditor of the royal Exchequer, maybe the brother of the Golding whom Somerset calls his servant in an order of October 1549 demanding the assembly of the Earl of Oxford's servants for some task said to be required by the Duke's nephew, Edward VI.[16]

On January 22, 1552 Somerset's head fell under the royal ax.

Parliament declared null and void the indenture for marrying Katherine de Vere to Somerset's son. Soon afterward her father got an opportunity to prove that he shared the belief of Sir John Falstaff on the superiority of discretion to raw valor. Henry Neville, Baron Abergavenny, Katherine's cousin, struck the Earl in the presence of the King. For this offense he went for a short while to the Tower of London. But John of Oxford never challenged him to a duel for the blow. In June 1553 he did the Duke of Northumberland a favor by signing approval of his plan to violate the will of Henry VIII and crown Jane Grey, the Duke's daughter-in-law, Queen of England. Within a month he was hurrying to assemble troops in support of the bastardised Mary Tudor's claim to the crown. She rewarded him by an appointment to her Privy Council; however he appears to have lacked the audacity to take such a lofty place. When Mary commenced her private crusade against the Protestants of his county, including some of his most devoted servants, he assisted in hounding and burning them. Manifestly he did so with a reluctant heart. The Queen suspected his show of conversion from her father's Anglicanism to her own Romanism was rank hypocrisy and cowardice. When several of his fellow nobles became entangled in intrigue and conspiracy against her, she suspected him of sympathy with the traitors, and there was court whispering that he stood in danger of losing his lands.[17] Still the Earl eluded his enemies; he lived to stand by Queen Mary's deathbed and celebrate the coming of her sister, the bastardised Elizabeth, to the throne. In the same month, November 1558, he had the happiness of seeing his son, Edward, eight years old, admitted to Queen's College in Cambridge University.

When Duke John of Sweden, the brother of King Eric, arrived in Essex in October 1559 on his way to woo Elizabeth for his brother, he experienced thru the Earl's hospitality and charm an alteration in his own behavior. Sir Thomas Smith wrote to Cecil that the Swede was swiftly learning under Lord Oxford's spell "to leave off his high looks and pontificality." In Sir Thomas's letter we catch a good glance at the very man Shakespeare had in his mind's eye when he pictured Count Bertram's father:

Who were below him,

He us'd as creatures of another place,
And bow'd his eminent top to their low ranks,
Making them proud of his humility,
In their poor praise he humbled.(1.2.41-45)

It was evidently a pleasure for Smith to describe "the love that the gentlemen and the whole country bear to him, whether for the antiquity of his ancestry, or his own gentleness, or the dexterity of these that are about (him), or rather all these."[18] For Christmas recreation the Earl rode with the Prince of Sweden in the valley of the Stour "ahawking, and showed him great sport, killing in his sight both pheasant and partridge, wherein he seemed to take great pleasure."[19] And on New Year's day 1560, when he accompanied the Swede to London and the Court, Lord John and his Countess Margery enjoyed the joy of the Queen over their holiday gifts to her, worth according to Castle Hedingham accounts 15 pounds.[20] And in April 1561, having turned Anglican again, he occupied himself with persecution of Roman Catholics, ferreting out "implements of superstition" near the bedroom of his nabor Lady Wharton. However he engaged in this dirty work only under the urgency of the Queen's minister, Sir William Cecil, and indicated how he really felt about it by pleading for royal clemency toward the Wharton family.[21] The method by which he preferred to fight the power of the Popes was in fact theatrical; he employed John Bale, the future Bishop of Ossory to write plays for his company of actors, making obscene fun as well as enraged propaganda against the Roman Church.

Meanwhile how was John getting along with the pride of the Goldings? No inkling of their actual relation is granted us until after the Earl's death, in the letter I have quoted from her sharp pen. Perhaps there is testimony of his having a desire of distance between them in the document of the town of Ipswich dated June 28, 1562, which mentions a payment of 23 shillings to the "jugler, players, a flute player," who came with John de Vere to entertain Ipswich, twenty miles east of Hedingham. Three days later he made a covenant with Henry Hastings, Earl of Huntingdon, to wed his son Edward to Elizabeth or Mary Hastings, a sister of Earl Henry, if she consented, as soon as Edward attained the age of eighteen.[22] While this marriage would have united the next Earl of Oxford to lineage with a claim to the crown of England, it would also have denied him the privilege his father had enjoyed, to marry only where his heart led. But we never hear of this covenant after John's death which occurred four weeks after. He was only 43 when he died. When the King of France in *All's Well* says of his old friend, "He lasted long," he clearly cherished a standard for the duration of life dear to his creator, certainly not to William Cecil, his creator's father -in-law, who lasted to the age of 68, enjoying decades of "haggish age."

The portrait of the dead Count of Rossillion turns out to be in part, as Looney was the first to recognize, a product of the dramatist's father-worship. Making a god of his father serves for a fairly sure sign that the real man was unknown to the son, or else that the son did not want to become familiar with the man. We deify none but the dead whom we wish to regard as free from the follies if not the ills of the flesh. The old compulsive optimism of *De mortuis nil nisi bonum* blazes the trail to godhood, even if only demigodhood. Shakespeare however, in writing his romance, felt no vocation to exalt his father beyond a modestly ideal manhood. The artist carefully barred in his chest the child's deadly impulse toward deity, its passion for killing carnal and adoring the inhuman, keeping these wild relics of our ape-antiquity constantly in esthetic tether. He uncaged them in his tragedy of the two Hamlets.

To the vicarious fatherhood of the King of France our brave Bertram acts with a spirit worthy of those feudal chiefs who looked on a king as an equal male, privileged to ride in front of their rank when they went to war and command them on the battlefield, but who would not dare command a man of them in his own castle-home. Young Rossillion's independence and courage in the presence of the King has gained him no sympathy and just as much understanding from the cloistral critics, nearly all of whom are bewildered, annoyed, by the clear-eyed Helena's resolution to have this nearly rebel aristocrat for her mate.

Shakespeare followed his Italian text in afflicting the King with a disease, a fistula, that made him weary of life. But he did a hazardous thing in afflicting his French monarch this way, for it was bound to remind Queen Elizabeth of her kindred suffering. Boccaccio's king had the sickness in his chest; Shakespeare left out the location of his king's fistula. In 1579 Mary Stewart was informed by the Countess of Shrewsbury that the English Queen got repeated agonies "from the closing of a fistula" in a leg.[23] The spectacle of Shakespeare's monarch cured by some miraculous medicine inherited by his heroine, unknown to the alchemy available to her Majesty, must have been tormenting to her. She was perhaps induced to pardon the play fistula for the sake of the prospect opened by the poet that someday she might be healed likewise. She may have been encouraged to think so by the Earl of Oxford's enthusiasm for the medical marvels performed by the German "artist" Paracelsus and his pupil Conrad Gesner, whose book *The New Jewel of Health* had been translated by George Baker, with a dedication to the Countess Anne de Vere, Oxford's deserted wife. Baker became "one of the Queen's Majesty's chief chirurgeons in ordinary" in 1599. In honor of his appointment he reprinted *The New Jewel of Health* under the name *Practice of the New and Old Physic*, this time with a dedication to Edward de Vere. Sponsored by the Earl, Baker affirmed,

> it may more easily be defended against sycophants and fault finders, because your wit, learning, and authority hath great force and strength in repressing the curious cracks of the envious and bleating babes of Momus' charms.[24]

By "bleating babes" Baker could have meant only the mummers of the children's theatres, whose writers often seized on contemporary novelties of science and art for purposes of satire. Their comedians would not have resisted the temptation presented by Baker's solemn recommendation in his *Jewel of Health* of a wondrous oil "drawn out of the excrements of children" and another oil extracted from "man's ordure" which he offered as sovren remedy for fistula and other maladies. Baker did not entirely adopt the Paracelsan chemistry but lingered securely in the tradition of Galen, whom the German despised. Shakespeare praised both "artists" in *All's Well.*

Helena's reward for healing her King is a royal grant of her choice of a husband from the noblest bachelors of his court. Of course she picks Bertram, and of course the Count indignantly asks to be excused from enduring in exchange for the royal relief from disease a lifetime of what he feels will be a permanent disgrace from marrying the daughter of a doctor, a leech, belonging to the class that worked for profit, not pride. Realising that she has taken an unkind advantage of her beloved, Helena withdraws her request. But the King, outraged by Rossillion's insolence to his gratitude, demands the Count's surrender and at last obtains it. After the wedding feast, in accord with Boccaccio's plot, Helena is deprived by her husband of the coronal coupling she looked forward to, and he sends her home, promising to see her again, and presumably give her the long coveted love rite, in three days.

II

Shakespeare took from the Italian tale the next phase of his romance, Bertram's running away to take part in a war of Florence against Siena. In the source plot the Count learns of this chance for soldier's glory after his flight to Italy. In the play the King tells his courtiers,

> The Florentines and Senoys are by th'ears,
> Have fought with equal fortune, and continue
> A braving war....
> A certainty vouch'd from our Cousin Austria,
> With caution, that the Florentines will move us
> For speedy aid. (1.2.1-7)

While the emperor of Austria has urged the French king to deny the plea of Florence, and he considers refusal wise,

> Yet for our Gentlemen that mean to see
> The Tuscan service, freely have they leave
> To stand on either part. (1.2.13-15)

Shakespeare's alteration of the war business clearly resulted from his interest in the war of the Flemings against Spain. His quick ear caught at once the likeness between the initial letters of their names and the Italian belligerent cities of Boccaccio's story, and in a flash he saw the latter's war in the Netherlands, particularly the roles played by English volunteers over there.

A truce had been reached in the crusade of the Low Countries in 1577: it came to a bloody end in January 1578. Elizabeth's Catholic "cousin" Don John of Austria, Governor of the Spanish Netherlands, did not have to tell her how he felt about the Flemings' begging her for help. In July 1577 she had allowed Colonel John Norris to land three hundred Englishmen at Dunkirk for service with the Dutch; yet at the same time she adjured the Dutch leader William of Orange and his fellow insurgents "to submit themselves to their sovereign Lord and King," Philip of Spain, "in all humility," because "God would work in the King's heart to forget and forgive all that was past, to remedy all evils present, and provide for the best to come."[24] She and her chief councilors, led by Oxford's father-in-law, despatched the English troops to the Low Countries mainly in determination to prevent French assistance to the Flemings from getting too strong rather than to prevent the Spaniards from reconquering their bequest of Burgundy. Also the rulers of England were not unwilling to see her restless, all too populous and importunate heads reduced in quantity if not in quality by the bloodletting in the Low Countries. They agreed, in short, with Shakespeare that the war might well serve

> A nursery to our Gentry, who are sick
> For breathing, and exploit. (1.2.16-17)

It is in young Bertram's response to the challenge of the Florentine war that we can see the hand of Shakespeare clearly wearing the signet ring of young Oxford. Whether he found his material for *All's*

Well in the original Italian or in William Painter's translation, in his first volume of *The Palace of Pleasure* (1566) the dramatist transmuted it here to self-biography. Here we have the hero aspiring to fight in the battles of Florence and Siena, held back by man-consuming frustration and kept at court with ludicrous excuses:

> I am commanded here, and kept a coil with
> Too young, and the next year, and 'tis too early. (2.1.27-28)

Here we have the Earl Edward de Vere complaining vocally as he had complained in ink to Lord Burghley on January 3, 1576 sending these bitter words from Siena:

> "For having made an end of all hope to help myself by her Majesty's service, considering that my youth is objected unto me, and for every step (slip?) of mine a block is found to be laid in my way, I see it is but vain *calcitrare contra li busse* (to kick against the stings.)"[25]

The immediate cause of Oxford's grievance was the rejection by Burghley and Elizabeth of all his appeals to master the art of war on the fighting in the field, in the Low Countries or in the civil strife of France. The Earl was absolutely convinced that to be or not to be a complete man—he would have said a noble man—depended on whether you learnt or never learnt to be a scholar and a courtier and a soldier. He could not conceive a career for himself without training in arms as he had been trained in arts.

The earliest of his requests for the martial experience which we have on record was heard in February 1569, two months before his nineteenth birthday. We have it from the pen of the French ambassador in London, Bertrand de la Mothe Fenelon (whose figure and behavior as well as his name may have sparkled in the memory of Shakespeare when he created Count Bertram). Fenelon reported to his queen:

> J'entendez, toutes foys, que, ces joures passes, au comte de Oxfort, jeune seigneur, bien estime en ceste court, qui desiroit veoir de la guerre, et inportunoit la dicte Dame de luy donner conge d'aller trouver le prince de Conde, apres plusiers reffuz, elle luy a

respondu qu'elle ne vouloit qu'un tel personnage des siens se trouvat avec ung qui estoit contre son Roy. Dont luy, despuys, deviant avec d'aultres seigneurs de bonne volonte, leur a dict qu'il desireroit que la Royne, sa Mestresse, luy donnast conge d'aller servir le Roy, et qu'il combatroit volontiers contre les rebelles, qui luy faisoient la guerre; de quoy estant taxe, il a este mene devant les seigneurs du conseil, devant lesquelz il s'est monstre si resolu en son opinion, qu'ilz ont estime que cealla venoit d'auleyns pratique des Catholiques, dont luy ont vallu user de quelque riguer; mais, apres leur avoir dict franchement ce que la Royne luy avoit respondu, ilz sont demeurez toutz estonnez, et ne luy ont rien plus replique.[26]

("I hear, with entire trust, that the Count of Oxford, a young noble, well esteemed at this court, who desired to see the war [between the Protestants or Huguenots and the Guisard faction of Roman Catholics] and pleaded with the Lady in question [Elizabeth] to give him consent to seek and join the Prince of Conde, after many refusals, has been answered by her in these days past that she does not want a personage of his standing among her people to join with one who went against his King. Since then, while walking with some other nobles of good will, he told them he would desire the Queen his Mistress to give him permission to go serve the King [Charles IX] and he would willingly combat the rebels who made war on him. Being criticised for this, he was led before the lords of the Council, and showed himself so resolute in his opinion before them that they decided he had been inspired by some encounter with Catholics, for which they deem him deserving of some rigor; but, after he had frankly told them how the Queen had answered him, they remained utterly astonished, and made him no more reply.")

The news of the disaster of the Huguenots at the battle of Jarnac on March 13, 1569, did not apparently cool the ardor of the Earl for military education in France. On March 21 Fenelon wrote to Charles IX,

Vray est que le jeune comte d'Oxfort s'est monstre plusiers jours tout prest, avec ung nombre de jeunes gentis-hommes anglais, pour aller trouver le prince de Conde ou quelque prince d'Alle-maigne, affin de veoir de la guerre, mais il n'en a peu obtenir la permission de la dicte Dame. Bien a semble qu'aulcuns luy conseilloient d'y aller voluntaire, et qu'ilz luy respondaient que pour cella il n'incourroit l'indignation de la dicte Dame; mais en fin elle le luy a deffander expressement et luy a baille lettres pour passer en Irlande. Je ne scay si quelque contraire vent le poulsera, de son gre, a la Rochelle.[27]

("True it is that the young Count of Oxford has for many days shown himself quite ready, with a number of young English gen-tlemen, to join the troops of the Prince of Conde or some prince of Germany [supplying mercenaries for Conde and Coligny] with the aim of inspecting the war, but he could not obtain the least gesture of permission from the Lady alluded to. Truly it seems that some have counseled him to go there as a volunteer, and that they assured him he would not incur for this the indignation of the Lady. But finally she has forbidden him flatly to do so and gave him letters of license for a voyage to Ireland. I do not know if some contrary wind will impel him, to his wish, to the port of Rochelle [the Huguenot naval base].")

Sickness blocked his traveling either to Ireland or insurgent France. In October the French rebels suffered at Montcontour a fiercer de-feat than the veterans under Guise had inflicted on them at Jarnac.

In November the Earls of Northumberland and Westmorland lifted in northern England an insurgent flag of their own, calling for the restoration of the kingdom to the Roman Church. They got dar-ing support from border Scots. Queen Elizabeth and Sir William Cecil moved swiftly to quell them. On November 24 the Earl of Oxford applied to Cecil for a worthy place in the army headed by Thomas Radcliff, Earl of Sussex, riding against the rebels in the north. The whole application is worth perusal for the light it throws on the soul and the style of Edward de Vere at nineteen. (I bring only his spelling and clause spacing up to date).

"Sir. Although my hap hath been so hard that it hath visited me of late with sickness, yet thanks be to God, through the looking to which I have had by your care had over me, I find my health restored and myself doubly beholding unto you both for that and many good turns which I have received before of your part. For the which, although I have found you to not account of late of me as in time tofore, yet notwithstanding that strangeness, you shall see at last in me that I will acknowledge (them crossed out) and not be more at fault with you for them and not to deserve so ill a thought in you that they were ill bestowed on me. But at the present decerning (so) you, if I have done any thing amiss that I have merited your offense, impute to my young years and lack of experience, to know my friends. And at this time I am bold to desire your favor and friendship that you will suffer me to be employed by your means and help in this service that now is in hand, whereby I shall think myself the most bound unto you of any man in this court, and hereafter you shall command me as any of your own. Having no other means whereby to speak with you myself, I am bold to impart my mind in paper, earnestly desiring your Lp. that at the instant as heretofore you have given me your good word to have me see the wars and services in strange and foreign places, sith you could not then obtain me license of the Queen's Mty, now you will do me so much honor as that by your purchase of my license I may be called to the service of my prince and country as at this present troublous time a number are.Thus aiming to importunate you with my earnest suit I commit you to the hands of The Almighty. By your assured friend this 24th of November.

Edward iiii Oxenford[28]

Was there ever such awkward writing, such inhibition of free speech, seen from the fingers of a young man who was already a sophomore master of Latin prose, perhaps French composition, and certainly English prosody? It is painful to contemplate the guilt-twisted intelligence revealed in these would-be courteous, tortuously diplomatic lines. They are still faintly redolent of the hate that the writer struggled so hard to subdue and hide from the eyes and ears of one of the least gullible Englishmen that ever thrived on the sweat and wits of his fellowmen. Only one so vain as Edward of Oxenford, he of the crown-symboled signature, the most narcissic of nineteen-year-old nobles, could have palmed off on William Cecil a missive displaying its infinitely cunning composer trying desperately tongue-tied to be polite and appear not destitute of gratitude. There is a single line in the letter that rings genuine and therefor by contrast with the rest almost melodious: "you have given me your good word to have me see the wars and services in strange and foreign places." The last eleven syllables indicate the blank verse the young writer would be producing within ten years.

Out of his sickbed the poet who would be warrior continued to appeal to his guardian until Cecil relented and opened the first gate to a military career. He instructed Sir William Dansell, the treasurer of the Court of Wards and Liveries, on 30 March 1570: "the Queen's Majesty sendeth at this present the Earl of Oxford into the north parts to remain with my Lord of Sussex, and to be employed there in her Majesty's service," for which Dansell was to give him 40 pounds. Oxford signed a receipt for the money, and Cecil approved payment on April 9 of 145 pounds, 17 shillings and 4 pence for the expenses of the royal ward from January 1 to March 26.[29] Captain Bernard Mordaunt Ward assumed that Oxford was then free to gallop to York where Sussex was getting ready for the grand border raid which he trusted, as he told Cecil on April 10, "before the light of this moon be past to leave a memory in Scotland whereof they and their children shall be afraid to offer war to England."[30] On April 17 the English troops crossed the border at night from three places, the main column under Sussex marching out of Berwick up the valley of the Teviot, "leaving neither castle, town, nor tower unburnt till we came to Jedburgh."[31] Captain Ward described the expedition in detail believing that the hero of his biography, *The Seventeenth Earl of Oxford*, witnessed its exploits, the burning, bombarding, and fighting, until the completion of the cruelties Sussex had promised the Queen.

"We do not know for certain what part Lord Oxford played in the campaign; but his rank and his youth make it probable," Ward is confident, "that he served on Lord Sussex's staff."[32] Not one Tudor document testifies to the presence of Earl Edward in the raid. In the summer of 1570 the herald John Hart paid debts for him amounting to 135 pounds and 9 pence; these dated from March 26 to June 24, and indicate that the gallant Oxford's costs had hardly been affected by the ferocities in Scotland. At the end of September Hart drew up for Cecil another account of the Earl's expenses, covering the period from June 25; their sum was 113 pounds, 11 shillings, 11 pence, connoting minor economies in the past months.[33] If De Vere recollected any experience of war by the side of Sussex in those days, all trace of it has disappeared.

"How long Lord Oxford remained on the Border is not known," Ward regrets, "but he probably returned to London in the late summer or early autumn." The hero-worshiping Ward pictures him riding triumphantly into London, "with four score gentlemen in a livery of Reading tawny, and chains of gold about their necks, before him; and one hundred tall yeomen in the like livery to follow him, without chains, but all having his cognizance of the Blue Boar embroidered on their left shoulder."[34] The glorious company here depicted could have been seen by the Earl of Oxford only in his infancy. The Londoner who supplied this description clearly referred to John de Vere, the sixteenth Earl of Oxford.[35] Captain Ward would have cognized the fact if he had not entranced himself with a vision of Edward de Vere coming home from his first sensations of soldiering.

In 1569 incidentally the French translation of the *Decameron*, by Antoine-Jean Le Macon, was printed at Lyon. Shakespeare seems to have made acquaintance with this translation, which would account for his calling the men of Siena "Senoys" (Sienois) and Santo Giacomo "Saint Jacques" *le grand.*

Edward de Vere married the sweet little Anne Cecil on December 19, 1571, eight months after his coming of age to join the House of Lords. Becoming the son-in-law of the Queen's Lord

Treasurer and closest counselor gave him not the least advantage in his pursuit of a soldier's glory. They suavely restricted his warlike aspirations to tournaments and sports like the mock-siege or fireworks contest between the mimic forts that he and Fulke Greville directed for her Majesty at Warwick Castle on the Avon river near Stratford on the evening of August 18, 1572.[36] In the following month he sent his father-in-law, "my singular good Lord the Lord Burghley," a letter which has been preserved in mutilated condition. It informed his Lordship that Lady Anne, the Countess of Oxford, had left Cecil House in Westminster on the day of the letter, September 22, to go to the country, without taking leave of her father whom her husband had expected home for hours. Myself, Oxford said, "as fast as I can get me out of town do follow *** (the sheet is torn here) for I am content and desire *** (a request to the Queen lost) by it I may shoe myself dutiful to her. If there were any service to be done abroad, I had rather serve there than at home, where yet some honour were to be got: if there be any setting forth to sea, to which service I bear the most affection, I shall desire your L to give me and get me that favour and credit *** that I might make one: Which, if there be no such intention then I shall be most willing to be employed on the sea coasts to be in a readiness with my countrymen against any invasion."[37] The Earl's mind seems to have been dancing on the waves beyond Wivenhoe, the country estate on the coast of Essex where his wife and he were going. But Elizabeth and Burghley not only rejected his suggestion for travel in Europe and Asia minor, which he wished to visit alone. Between himself and Countess Anne had fallen a coolness whose temperature kept dropping despite her attempts to carry out correctly all her conjugal obligations.

The end of spring in 1574 found Oxford in a veritable fever to leave his wife. Reports and rumors of the revolutionary war in the Low Countries against Spain excited his blood so that he could not be quiet. "All our English sailors." Philip Sidney declared on May 28, "have for some time past found employment in the Prince of Orange's ships."[38] The Queen was then staying in seclusion at

Havering Bower, a short ride from Wivenhoe, and her flirtations with Earl Edward were maddening Lady Mildred, the Countess of Oxford's mother. The Queen's coquetry emboldened poor Anne's husband to a point of dangerous liberties. On June 28 the Earl of Shrewsbury's son Gilbert reported to his mother: "The young Earl of Oxford, of that ancient and Very family of the Veres, had a cause or suit that now came before the Queen: which she did not answer so favourably as was expected, checking him, it seems, for his unthriftiness. And hereupon his behavior before her gave her some offense. This was advertised from the Lord Chamberlain (Sussex) to the Lord Treasurer," who evidently advertised it where Gilbert Talbot would hear of it. Lord Burghley was sorry that her Majesty made "such haste" in rebuking the boy. He feared the sequel might breed trouble, "if he were ill counseled," and yielded, as De Vere was quick to do, to the sinister suggestions of his winecup companions, "such heads as himself."[39] Among these evil advisers none stood dearer to the Earl than the soldier of fortune Rowland Yorke. From the house of Lady Yorke in Walbrook, early in July, the poet who wanted to become a general, or an admiral, "took horse," according to courtiers gossip, "and so to Wyvenhoe in Essex and the next night he took ship and coasted over to Flaunders, arryving at Callise."[40] Little Anne, his wife, grieved and could say with Countess Helen of *All's Well* that she was the cause of his escape "from the sportive court, where thou Wast shot at with fair eyes." Those were the same eyes Lord St John alluded to in his letter to the Earl of Rutland announcing Oxford's wedding: "The Earl of Oxford hath gotten him a wife—or at least a wife hath caught him; this is Mistress Anne Cecil; whereunto the Queen hath given her consent, and the which hath caused great weeping, wailing, and sorrowful cheer of those that had hoped to have that golden day."[41]

On July 6 Sir Francis Walsingham confided to Burghley, "I made her Majesty acquainted with my Lord of Oxford's arrival at Calais, who doth not interpret the same in any evil part. She conceiveth great hope of his return upon some secret message." Then the Earl did a more hazardous thing.

In William Cecil's journal July 8 was noted as the day when "The Earl of Oxford departed into Flanders without the Queen's license, and was revoked by the Q. sending the Gentleman Pensioners for him."[42] A letter of the English ambassador in Scotland informs us that Oxford "fled out of England" together with Lord Edward Seymour "and passed by Bruges to Brussels."[43] On July 13 the Earl's old teacher, Sir Thomas Smith, wrote to Burghley: "Of my Lord of Oxford, for my part I can as yet learn no certainty; but it is commonly said that he arrived at Calais and was there very honorably received and entertained, and from thence he went into Flanders. As far as I can yet perceived, her Majesty's grief for him, or towards him, is somewhat mitigated."[44] The Queen went on her customary summer "progress" and "my lady Oxford" accompanied her forlornly, waiting for the return of the Gentleman Pensioner Thomas Bedingfield, who had been despatched to bring the runaway back. Oxford enjoyed Bedingfield's personality and learning. In 1573 he had the pleasure of sponsoring the publication of the Pensioner's version of Geronimo Cardano's sad book *Consolation*. It came out as "Cardanus' Comforte, translated into Englishe. And published by commandment of the right honourable the Earle of Oxenforde." For it De Vere wrote a remarkable introductory letter to the translator, explaining why he disregarded Bedingfield's wish against the broadcasting of his book, and added a poem ("From my new country Muses of Wivenhoe") chanting the sorrow of writers who can never derive from their work the joys of the readers:

> The labouring man that tills the fertile soil,
>   And reaps the harvest fruit, hath not indeed
> The gain, but pain; but if for all his toil
>   He gets the straw, the lord will have the seed.
> ... So he that takes the pain to pen the book
>   Reaps not the gifts of golden goodly muse;
> But those gain that, who on the work shall look,
>   And from the sour the sweet by skill shall choose...

Burghley chose wisely in sending Thomas Bedingfield to the task of persuading the poet to give up his prospect of studying war on the battlefield, and return to his own task of entertaining the Queen with his dancing and wit.

Roman Catholic conspirators at her court spread a claim that Oxford was bound for Bruges in order to join the Earl of Westmoreland, fugitive leader of the northern revolt. Bishop Cox of Ely helped them spread the story on July 20 with an epistle to the Calvinist authorities in Switzerland: "Certain of our nobility, pupils of the Roman pontiff, either weary of their happiness or impatient of the long continued progress of the gospel, have taken flight, some into France, some into Spain, others into different places, with the view of plotting some mischief against the professors of godliness."[45] An agent of Cecil in Antwerp reported to him, "There was a great triumph among the northern rebels (in exile)... when they had heard that the Earl of Oxford was flying, and that the Earl of Southampton had fled to Spain. In a Council held at Louvain it was concluded that the Earl of Westmoreland should ride to Bruges to welcome him, and persuade him not to return, but the Earls did not meet. It were a great pity," said the informer, "such a valiant and noble young gentleman should communicate with such detestable men."[46]

The Earl of Sussex begged the Queen for kindness and understanding when the runaway returned. Burghley wrote to him gratefully on July 15: "I must heartily thank your Lordship for your advertisement of my Lord of Oxford's cause, wherein I am sorry that her Majesty maketh such haste... My Lord, howsoever my Lord of Oxford be for his own part (in) matters of thrift inconsiderate, I dare avow him to be resolute in dutifulness to the Queen and his country."[47] By July 27 Bedingfield and his friend were back in England. Sir Walter Mildmay voiced the opinion of every honest courtier when he declared on that date, "Of my Lord of Oxford's return, I am glad to hear. I trust this little jorney will make him love home the better hereafter. It were a great pitie he shold not go strait, there be so many good things in him, to serve God and his Prince."[48] Oxford's wife and her father went to London on July 29 to meet the errant Earl. The next day they coached down to the Cecil mansion called Theobalds, where Elizabeth kept them waiting for word from her. When Burghley heard that she had descended on Woodstock on August 1, he received good news from Sir Francis Walsingham: "I find her Majesty graciously enough inclined towards the Earl of Oxford, whose peace I think will be both easily and speedily made, for that her Majesty doth conceive that his evidence in his return hath fully satisfied the contempt of his departure." She was particularly pleased by "his honourable and dutiful carriage of himself towards the rebels and other undutiful subjects of her Majesty in that country, and argument of his approved loyalty, which, as opportunity shall serve, I shall not fail to lay before her Majesty by acquainting her with your Lordship's letters."[49] Burghley unpacked his heart in reply.

"Sir, Yesternight your letters came to Master Benigfeld and me signifying her Majesty's pleasure that my Lord of Oxford should come to Gloucester now at her majesty's being there. Whereof he being advertised by us was very ready to take the journey, showing in himself a mixture of contrary affections, although both reasonable and commendable. The one, fearful and doubtful in what sort he shall recover her Majesty's favour because of his offence in departure as he did without license; the other, glad and resolute to look for a speedy good end because he had in his abode so notoriously rejected the attempts of her Majesty's evil subjects, and in his return set apart all his own particular desires of foreign travel to come to present himself before her Majesty, of whose goodness towards him he saith he cannot count. Hereupon he and Master Benigfeld departed this afternoon to London, where the Earl, as I perceive, will spend only two days or less to make him some apparel meet for the Court, although I would have had him forbear that new charge, considering his former apparel is very sufficient, and he not provided to increase a new charge...

"I must be bold by this my letter to require you in my name most humbly to beseech her Majesty that she will regard his loyalty and not his lightness in sudden joy over his confidence in her goodness and clemency, and not his boldness in attempting that which hath offended her."

Burghley's anxiety that his son-in-law should "not repent his dutifulness in doing that which in this time none hath done" spilled as usual in windy damp verbiage. "I think it is sound counsel to be given to her Majesty, that this young nobleman, being of such a quality as he is for birth, office, and other notable valors of body and spirit, he may not be discomforted either by any extraordinary delay or by any outward sharp or unkind reproof...I doubt not but Master Secretary Smith will remember his old love towards the Earl when he was his scholar."[50]

Apparently Elizabeth greeted the apologetic Oxford in her best of humor, making sure that he would remember at least one sting of reprehension for his defiant flight. She probably said nothing of the great expectations he had disappointed by refusing to meet Westmoreland in the Netherlands. The captive Queen of Scotland in Sheffield Castle received from her Romanist admirers at Elizabeth's court the news of De Vere's voyage across the Channel and assurance that he was devoutly on her side in disputes of state. On August 4 she urged the Archbishop of Glasgow in France and the Cardinal of Lorraine, *"Si le conte d'Oxford arrive par de la, advertisez mon cousin de Guise qu'il est ung des plus grands du pays, et catholicque, et amy in secret: et le priez de luy fair bon accueil. Il est folastre et jeune, et cerchera volontiers la jeunesse. Je prie mon dict cousin que luy et ses freres le cherissent, et luy douvent quelques chevaulx, et s'accostent de luy, le menant avec eux passer le temps, et ilz feront pour moy."* (If the Count of Oxford arrives there, let my cousin of Guise know that he is one of the greatest in the land, and Catholic, and a friend in secret; and ask him please to prepare a good reception. He is wanton and young, and goes in quest of youth with pleasure. I pray my said cousin that he and his brothers should cherish him, and favor him with some horses, and act so winningly with him as to lead him to spend the time with them, and they will do this for me.)[51] Unlucky Mary Stewart was deceived about Oxford's religion and love of England because her partisans, the traitors of the Howard and Arundel families, vainly imagined that they understood him and could steer his destiny.

III

All's Well that Ends Well varies from Boccaccio's tale of Beltramo and Giglietta in most dramatic fashion at the point where the hero determines to escape from royal restraint in order to become a man of war. And the difference derives so obviously from the life of the Earl of Oxford that only college dons leading their donqueys would overlook it. The first scene of the second act portrays the seduction of the Count from the Court by volunteers for the "Florentine" (meaning Flemish) camp:

1st Lord, G.	Oh my sweet Lord, you will stay behind us.
Parolles.	'Tis not his fault, the spark.
2nd Lord, E.	Oh, 'tis brave wars.
Parolles.	Most admirable, I have seen those wars.
Rossillion.	I am commanded here, and kept a coil with,
	Too young, and the next year, and 'tis too early.
Parolles.	And thy mind stand to't, boy,
	Steal away bravely.
Rossillion.	I shall stay here the forehorse to a smock,
	Creaking my shoes on the plain masonry,
	Till honour be brought up, and no sword worn
	But one to dance with: by heaven, I'l steal away.
1st Lord G.	There's honour in the theft.
Parolles.	Commit it, Count.
2nd Lord, E.	I am your accessary, and so farewell.
Rossillion.	I grow to you, and our parting is a tortur'd body. (2.1.24-37)

In the original Parolles, I believe, the dramatist incarnated a conception of Rowland Yorke, but I cannot prove it. Rossillion's allusion to a "smock" he had to parade before and dance with has been identified as a sardonic reference to the curious gifts that Philip Sidney and Fulke Greville brought the Queen on New Year's day, 1578. Sidney's mother gave Elizabeth a pair of perfumed gloves with gold buttons containing tiny diamonds, "In odd contrast was her son Philip's present of a cambric smock, its sleeves and collar wrought with black work, and edged with a small bonelace of gold and silver... Sidney and his friend Fulke Greville must have taken counsel together, for Greville also brought a cambric smock, very similarly decorated."[52] De Vere must have made many a merry minute for her Majesty over their questionable taste.

His role in the royal circle was well defined by Gilbert Talbot in a letter to his father written on May 11, 1572: "My Lord of Oxforthe is lately grown in great credit: for the Queen's Majestie deliteth more in his parsonage and his daunsing and valientnes then any other. He presented her Majestie wyth a rych jewell, which was well lyked. I think Sussex doth back him all that he can. If it were not for his fyckle hed he would pass any of them shortly. My Lady Burghley unwisely hath declared herself, as it were, gellous, which is come to the Quenes ear: whereat she hath bene not a litell offended with her, but now she is reconsiled agayn. At all these love matters my Lo Tresurer winketh, and will not meddle in any way."[53] Dear as his daughter was to William Cecil, dearer far was statecraft.

The Queen in the course of "these love matters" experienced no pangs at the spectacle of the Countess of Oxford deprived of her right to dwell with her husband at Court. He seems to have made sweet little Anne do penance on account of his recall. On September 13, 1574, she sighed to Sussex, "I think it long since I saw her Majesty." Now she wished the Lord Chamberlain, Sussex, to prepare Hampton Court lodging for her, reserving three rooms. One of them, "my Lord Howard" informed her, he had occupied, Henry Howard, son of the poet Earl of Surrey, De Vere's uncle. This Howard has not yet obtained his true place in history as perhaps the cleverest in vileness of all Elizabeth's courtiers. At this time the Earl of Oxford felt cordially close to his cousin, spellbound by the honey and venom of his tongue, his infinite cunning in intrigue. "The more commodious my lodging is," Countess Anne said, "the willin-

ger I hope my Lord, my husband, will be to come thither."[54] She
and her father were ignorant of Lord Howard's mouthwork encouraging the estrangement between Edward and Anne. Burghley seems
even to have been convinced that Howard strove to repair the
breach.

At the end of December 1574 Dr. Richard Masters gave De Vere
a surprise: his Countess had sensed an unmistakable quickening in
her womb. The Earl promptly told the physician, "openly in the
presence chamber of her Majesty, viz. that if she were with child, it
was not his." When Dr. Masters verified the conception to the
Queen, she "sprang up from her cushion, and said these words: Indeed, it is a matter that concerneth my Lord's joy chiefly; yet I protest to God that next to them that have interest in it there is nobody
that can be more joyous of it than I am." Her Majesty inquired
"how the young lady did bear the matter. I answered that she kept it
secret four or five days from all persons and that her face was much
fallen and thin with little colour, and that when she was comforted
and counseled to be gladsome and so rejoice, she would cry: 'Alas,
alas, how should I rejoice, seeing he that should rejoice with me is
not here; and to say truth, (I) stand in doubt whether he pass upon
me and it or not;' and bemoaning her case would lament that after
so long sickness of body she should enter a new grief and sorrow of
mind. At this her Majesty showed great compassion... And repeated my Lord of Oxford's answer" to the first evangel of the
child. "I answered that it was the common answer of lusty courtiers
everywhere, so to say."[55] Burghley's secretary put the physician's
account away so that the Cecil family lost it.

On July 2, 1575, seven months after the Earl of Oxford finally
got from the Queen the license he longed for to see the continent
and had sailed to France, the lonely Anne gave birth to a baby girl,
naturally named in honor of Elizabeth. On September 24 De Vere
got the good news in Venice. He sat down to write his father-in-law
a lengthy letter of lamentation over a recent fever and the brevity of
his travels—"which grieves me most, seeing my time not sufficient
for my desire...

"Your Lordship seems desirous to know how I like Italy, what is mine intention in travel, and when I mean to return. For my liking of Italy, my Lord, I am glad I have seen it, and I care not ever to see it any more, unless it be to serve my Prince and country. For mine intention to travel, I am desirous to see more of Germany, wherefor I shall desire your Lordship with my Lord of Leycester, to procure me the next summer to continue my license, at the end of which I mean undoubtedly to return. ... If this sickness had not happened unto me, which hath taken away this chiefest time to travel at this present, I should not have written for further leave, but to supply the which I doubt not her Majesty will not deny me so small a favour."

After a reckoning of money troubles, he reminded Cecil that he had not received the funds from the sale of certain lands. Moreover he complained of brutal treatment of peasants on his estates: "I have understood by my Lord of Bedford, they have hardly dealt with my tenants," and concluded: "Thus thanking your Lordship for your good news of my wife's delivery, I recommend myself unto your favour."[56] When Burghley's report of the Countess's pregnancy reached the Earl in Paris, on March 17, he had replied, "Your letters have made me a glad man, for these last have put me in assurance of that good fortune which you formerly mentioned doubtfully. I thank God therefor, with your Lordship, that it hath pleased Him to make me a father where your Lordship is a grandfather; and if it be a boy I shall likewise be the partaker with you in a greater contentation. But thereby to take an occasion to return, I am off from that opinion; for now it hath pleased God to give me a son of my own (as I hope it is) methinks I have the better occasion to travel, sith whatsoever becometh of me, I leave behind me one to supply my duty and service, either to my Prince or else my country."[57] Like Bertram he could say, "If there be breadth enough in the world, I will hold a long distance." None of the letters he sent from France or Italy which the Cecils preserved contain one word of solace or cheer for his wife. It is difficult to believe he was so brutal as to leave her without a warm word. I prefer to accuse the Cecils of having destroyed any letter by De Vere that would show him in a lovable light. The sole greeting to Anne they kept appears in a swift note to her father insisting on the sale of his lands to speed his journeys: "Thus recommending myself unto your Lordship again, and to my Lady your wife with mine, I leave further to trouble your Lordship."[58] On December 12, 1575, replenished with money from England, he journeyed to Florence, and on January 3, as we have seen, he lingered in Siena reflecting bitterly on the "end of all hope to help myself by her Majesty's service, considering that my youth is objected unto me..." On the next three months of his excursions, the Cecil records preserve a gravelike silence. Then in March we learn he witnessed the Carnival in Lyons and on the last day of the month arrived again in Paris, this time in companionship with William Russell, son of the Earl of Bedford.

From Russell, I suppose, the dramatist George Chapman heard the peculiar remarks that the Earl of Oxford made on that occasion, remarks that Chapman made the text of a tribute to the Earl. The tribute interrupts his tragedy *The Revenge of Bussy D'Ambois* (published in 1613). He put it on the lips of the imaginary hero Clermont (in Act 3, Scene 4).

> ...you make me remember
> An accident of high and noble note,
> And fits the subject of my late discourse
> Of holding on our free and proper way.
> I overtook, coming from Italy,
> In Germany, a great and famous Earl
> Of England, the most goodly fashion'd man
> I ever saw; from head to foot in form
> Rare and most absolute; he had a face
> Like one of the most ancient honour'd Romans
> From whence his noblest family was deriv'd;
> He was beside of spirit passing great,
> Valiant, and learn'd, and liberal as the sun,
> Spoke and writ sweetly, or of learned subjects,

Or of the discipline of public weals;
And twas the Earl of Oxford. And being offer'd
At that time by Duke Casimir the view
Of his right royal army then in field,
Refus'd it, and no foot was mov'd to stir
Out of his own free fore-determin'd course:
I, wondering at it, ask'd for it his reason,
It being an offer so much for his honour.
He, all acknowledging, said 'twas not fit
To take those honours that one cannot quit.
Renel. 'Twas answer'd like the man you have describ'd.
Clermont. And yet he cast it only in the way,
To stay and serve the world. Nor did it fit
His own true estimate how much it weigh'd,
For he despis'd it; and esteem'd it freer
To keep his own way straight, and swore that he
Had rather make away his whole estate
In things that cross'd the vulgar, than he would
Be frozen up stiff (like a Sir John Smith,
His countryman) in common nobles' fashions,
Affecting, as the end of noblesse were,
Those servile observations.

The Sir John Smith of the speech was a military disciplinarian from Oxford's home shire Essex, an old soldier distinguished for his proud stalking and officious furies, who toiled, as Chapman says, "with iron flails to thresh down feathers," his mind tangled in the rules and details of duty so that he could no longer see great goals and principles. Duke Casimir was the lord of the German Palatinate whose army of mercenaries joined the Prince of Conde in 1575 and compelled the Queen of France, Catherine de Medici, and her sons to make the peace of Chastenoy in May 1576. It will be recalled that in March 1569 De Vere had voiced an ambition to join the troops of the Prince of Conde "or some prince of Germany" in the civil wars of France.

In March 1576 however he was not in France to learn soldier-ship. When Conde or some other Huguenot noble invited him to be a guest in the camp of Casimir and inspect his troops in the valley of the Loire, he renounced the honor, knowing that his presence on Huguenot ground would commit his memory in many kingdoms to a cause that was not his country's. Only with his Queen's consent would he salute soldiers abroad. Never did Edward de Vere need to study Dante in order to take to heart the Florentine's wisdom: *Segui il tuo corso e lascia dir le genti* [follow your course, and let the people speak].

When he came back to England he had made up his mind to sunder his marriage. He went to stay at York House, temporarily. He pleaded with Elizabeth for permission to march in the footsteps of his grandfather John de Vere, whose tremendous energy in castle cannonades and battles had hoisted her grandfather Henry Tudor to the English throne. Meanwhile, like his robust friend George Gascoigne, he cheerfully put away his sword and experimented with the pen. "I march amongst the Muses for lack of exercise in martial exploits," Gascoigne explained. Oxford would give the same reason for writing comedies for common buffoons, and romances, called in those days "interludes." He would have spurned the advice that the Huguenot Hubert Languet sent Philip Sidney in July 1578, urging him to "beget children like yourself, you will be a better servant of your country than if you were to cut the throats of a thousand Spaniards or Frenchmen. I am not in this," Languet hastened to add, "recommending to you idleness or ease—at least if we are to believe the poet who counsels any man that wishes plenty of strife to get him a wife." In Oxford's opinion—put on the lips of his hero Rossillion—"War is no strife (compared) To the dark house, and the detested wife." He denied that the baby Elizabeth de Vere was his child. "He confessed to my Lord Howard," his father-in-law noted, "that he lay not with his wife but at Hampton Court," in October 1574. According to Henry Howard's solemn mockery of Burghley, the Earl had sworn, "the child could not be his, because the child was born in July which was not the space of twelve months."[59] As if a scion of the noblest of Roman or Norman families required more than nine months to be born, like the titan of Rabelais' epic farce!

The future Shakespeare spent the years from April 1576 to August 1582 fighting to forget that he was a husband and father. He frequented divines of various creeds, especially Catholics and Calvinists, and heard their critics in grand arguments about the Eternal and Almighty that all agreed was inscrutable. The up-shot of these discussions for the poet appears to have been at least one conviction voiced by his buffoon Lavache: "for young Charbon the Puritan, and old Poysam the Papist, howsome'er their hearts are sever'd in religion, their heads are both one; they may jowl horns together like any deer i' th' herd." (1.3.51-54) Beneath all their controversies he detected spiritual union in the mystery of fatherhood, since not even the wisest of children can verily know their paternal procreant. He chose to name the typical Puritan by vulgar French for Goodmeat because of the clash with Catholics over the right religious diet for Fridays, the latter insisting that the day must be dedicated to Fishlove.

He listened to astrologers like Dr. John Dee debate whether the earth shone in the center of the universe or tilted as a minor star around the sun. He observed the "Wonderful Effects" which the comet of 1577 was claimed to have all over Europe. It was that "Blazing Star" (as pamphleteers termed it) Shakespeare surely had in his mind's eye when he made Helen in *All's Well* compare her passion for Bertram thus:

> That I should love a bright particular star,
> And think to wed it; he is so above me
> In his bright radiance and collateral light. (1.1.88-90)

In 1584 the French linguist John Southern extolled the Earl in his little book *Pandora* for his erudition in astronomy and ancient lore.

> For who marketh better than he
> The seven turning flames of the sky?
> Or hath read more of the antique,
> Hath greater knowledge of the tongues?

In his pursuit of sciences he heard physicians like Dr. George Baker and apothecaries like John Hester debate the values of medicine as practised by the Galenic dogmatists and the empirical Paracelsans who burnt the formers' books. Also he listened to the music of Italian madrigals and the English anthems and airs of William Byrd, whom he encouraged with generous gifts. Also he listened to Rowland Yorke and Charles Arundel and Francis Southwell, all three softly spurred to the treachery by Lord Henry Howard, lure him thru alcoholic hilarities to desire to enlist for a hero's career under the banner of Spain. He heard them slander wedlock and the Cecils, prompting him to revolt, precisely like Parolles: "To th' wars, my boy, to th' wars."

> He wears his honor in a box unseen,
> That hugs his kickie wickie here at home,
> Spending his manly marrow in her arms
> Which should sustain the bound and high curvet
> Of Mars's fiery steed. To other regions...
> A young man married is a man that's marr'd. (2.3.277-281 and 296)

Comic encouragement of this sort enabled De Vere to bear the visions of his Countess and her "single sorrow," that afflicted him between his cups and comedies.

One of the drunken fantasies that Oxford regaled his companions with has been saved for posterity by the pen of Charles Arundel. In 1581 that gentleman remembered how the Earl more than once boasted of having done amazing feats of arms during his short stay in the Netherlands serving under the Spanish flag.

"At his being in Flanders, the Duka of Alba, as he (Oxford) will constantly affirm, grew so much to affect him for the said parts he saw in him, as he made him his lifetenant general over all the army then in the Low Countries, and employed him further in a notable piece of service, where according to his place he commanded and directed the Ambassador of Spain that is now here (Bernardino de Mendoza), Mondragon, Sansio Davila, and the rest of the captains: but these whom I have named, as he will say of all others, were most glad to be commanded by him; and so valiantly he behaved himself as he gained great love of all the soldiers, and in less admiration of his valour of (from) all sorts: and in this journey he passed many straits and divers bridges kept by the enemy, which he let (wrested) them from with the loss of many a man's life... The next day Beningefeld, as the devil would have it, came in upon his posthorse and called him from this service by her Majesty's letters, being the greatest disgrace that any such general received. And now the question is whether this noble general were more troubled with his calling home, or Beningefeld more moved with pity and compassion to behold this slaughter, or his horse more afeared when he passed the bridges at sight of the dead bodies, whereat he started and flung in such sort as Beningefeld could hardly keep his back."[59]

Arundel did not bother to note that the Duke of Alba had retired from duty in the Low Countries long before Oxford's flight there. It is hard to tell what reward he expected from the repetition of such frolic liquor talk. Nevertheless I dare say we owe the scoundrel immortal thanks for his taking the pains to write it down. Nowhere else will we find the fantom of Shakespeare himself, and hear his young imagination at work, his very accents so intimately.

Another liquor-lie that Arundel remembered told of a feud in Genoa that Oxford vowed he had taken a terrific part in: "for the fame that ran through Italy of his service done in the Low Countries under the Duke of Alva, he was chosen and made general of thirty thousand that the Pope sent to the aid of one party; and that in this action he showed great discretion, and government, as by his wisdom the matters were compounded, and an accord made, being more for his glory than if he had fought the battle."

In the third act of *All's Well* our poet presents the Duke of Florence deploring the refusal of France to assist him "in so just a business," exactly as the Prince of Orange deplored the English refusal to send regiments to Flanders in what seemed to him too a holy quarrel. However the Florentine Duke is so delighted to receive

French volunteers like the Count of Rossillion that he makes him at
once commander of the city's cavalry. The new "General of our
Horse" dedicates his life to the pagan god Mars and prays:

Make me but like my thoughts, and I shall prove
A lover of thy drum, hater of love. (3.3.10-11)

What Bertram would have become if he had not been granted the
dignity of the wardrum, we may guess from the account his clown
Lavache gives his mother of the lad's odd behavior after his wedding: "By my troth, I take my young Lord to be a very melancholy
man... Why, he will look upon his boot, and sing: mend the ruff
and sing, ask questions and sing, pick his teeth, and sing. I know a
man that had this trick of melancholy sold a goodly manor for a
song." (3.2.6-9) In the same melancholy or despair the Earl of Oxford sold manors for the sake of his love of theatre and literature.
The clown's description is a sketch from the sad life of the artist
who created him, depicting the habit of singing alone or absent-
mindedly that so many of Shakespeare's heros have.

IV

How devoted the Earl of Oxford was to poetry from his boyhood,
we learn from the oration in Latin verse that the Cambridge scholar
Gabriel Harvey made in July 1578 to celebrate the progress of the
Queen and her court to the University. For Oxford Harvey delivered a eulogy of the "utility and dignity of military matters and warlike exercises" which he contended were deserving of greater love
than pacific arts. His poem pleaded with the Earl: "English poetic
measures have been sung by thee long enough. Let that courtly
Epistle (Oxford's preface to Bartholomew Clerke's *De Curiali sive
Aulico*, a translation of Baldassare Castiglione's *Cortegiano*, published
in London 1571) more polished even than the writings of Castiglione himself, witness how greatly thou dost excel in letters. I have
seen many Latin verses of thine, yes, even more English verses are
extant; thou hast drunk deep cupfuls not only from the Muses of

France and Italy, but hast learned the manners of many men, and the arts of foreign countries... O thou hero, worthy of renown, throw away the insignificant pen, throw away bloodless books and writings that serve no useful purpose; now must the sword be brought into play, now is the time for thee to sharpen the spear and manage great engines of war."[60] De Vere would have joyously gone off to try his talents on horseback with spear and sword against the cavalry of Don John of Austria. But the Queen wanted him always close to her, displaying especially his skill in the lavolta, the coranto and the galliard, with "no sword worn but one to dance with."

Soon after their visit to Cambridge University Elizabeth gave a feast for the messengers sent from France by the Duc d'Alencon (to be precise, Anjou, but England always called him Alencon) to negotiate for his marriage to her Majesty and the collaboration of their realms in the Low Countries. During a dinner, somebody told the Spanish ambassador Mendoza, the Queen became angry over the thrift shown by her Lord Chamberlain, the Earl of Sussex, in furnishing plates. She would have liked the Frenchmen to see her sideboard more gorgeously supplied. Her steward answered that "for many years he had accompanied her and other sovrens of England in their progresses, and he had never seen them take so much plate as she was carrying then. The Queen told him to hold his tongue, that he was a big rogue, and the more good that was done to people like him the worse they got.... The next day the Queen sent twice to tell the Earl of Oxford, who is a very gallant lad, to dance before the ambassadors; whereupon he replied that he hoped her Majesty would not order him to do so, for he did not wish to entertain Frenchmen. When the Lord Steward took him the message the second time he replied that he would give no pleasure to Frenchmen, nor listen to such a message, and with that he left the room. He is a lad who has a great following in the country, and has requested permission to go and serve his Highness (Don John) which the Queen refused; she asked him why he did not go and serve the Archduke Matthias (lord of the Netherlands by request of the Flemish Catholics), to which he answered that he would not go and serve another sovren than his own, unless it was a very great one, such as the King of Spain."[61] The story of Oxford's application for service with her Majesty's "mortal enemy," Don John, was pleasing to the palate of Mendoza and his Most Catholic King, yet a lie they could easily see thru. The courtier who brought it to the Spanish envoy appears to have told the truth about Elizabeth's rebuke to Sussex and the anger it evidently kindled in Sussex's loyal friend Oxford.

About the time of this incident, in August 1578, John Florio issued his first book, entitled with characteristic flourish *First Fruits, which yield Familiar Speech, Merry Proverbs, Witty Sentences, and Golden Sayings*, along with *A Perfect Induction to the Italian and English Tongues*. He dedicated the work to the Earl of Leycester, head of the court faction hostile to Sussex, and members of Leycester's theatrical troup contributed prefatory plaudits. That arch-buffoon Richard Tarlton recommended Florio's book to the London public. A widespread agreement of scholars maintains that in the person of Parolles the author of *All's Well* intended a satire on Florio. I would agree that in the comedian's capacity as a linguist he represents quite jollily the Italian of the "Perfect Induction." As a strutting skinful of words—boasting "I love not many words"—Parolles does indeed caricature Florio, particularly in the scene of his mock-ambush where he begs, "If there be here German or Dane, Low Dutch, Italian, or French, let him speak to me." But Parolles was primarily mocked as a fellow pretending to be warlike, a pseudo-soldier— "Monsieur Parolles the gallant militarist, that was his own phrase, that had the whole theoric of war in the knot of his scarf, and the practice in the chape (tip) of his dagger." There is no testimony extant of John Florio ever posturing as an expert in martial affairs. Consequently I have to view Parolles as only in name and speech satiric to the writer of the *First Fruits*. The bulk and soul of the scoundrel were made in the image of the fortune-hunter Rowland Yorke, who had seen a skirmish or two with the Dutch troops of the Prince of Orange. Burghley must have tried to warn his son-in-law against this "damnable both-sides rogue," who ended his career as a traitor openly in the pay of Spain. Parolles, we are told, "was first smoked (out of his fox-disguise) by the old Lord Lafeu," who assured Bertram, "the soul of this man is his clothes. Trust him not in matter of heavy consequence." But in the summer of 1578 Oxford absolutely refused to believe Rowland Yorke could be a "coward, an infinite and endless liar, an hourly promise-breaker," one who despised him. Originally, therefor I imagine that the poet drew Rosillion's seducer simply as a braggart soldier of the type frequently derided in Italian comedies, modeled after the *miles gloriosus* in Plautus. And in the first version of *All's Well* he acted mainly, I imagine, as a "red-tailed" pimp for Bertram: "a filthy officer he is in those suggestions for the young Earl."

In the third act Shakespeare brings on the stage the second heroine of his romance. "Enter old Widow of Florence, her daughter"—not named till later—and some of their friends to see the Florentine army return victorious with Count Bertram riding in front. In a moment we are informed that the Widow's daughter has been solicited by the Count's gifted companion to yield her virginity to "this French Earl." But she does not need to be warned, "Beware of them, Diana; their promises, enticements, oaths, tokens, and all these engines of lust, are not the things they go under." Diana deserves her name. She is faithful to the end to the goddess of chastity. When Helen enters the city, arrayed as a pilgrim to the shrine of St. James, Diana and her mother offer her the hospitality of their inn. They gossip about Rossillion's departure from France and his bride, and the Widow is inspired to remark: "this young maid might do her a shrewd turn if she pleas'd." Shocked as she is to hear "the amorous Count solicits" Diana "In the unlawful purpose," Helen retains enough *sang froid* to hide her relation to Rossillion, and when his army arrives she inquires, "Which is the Frenchman?" Diana points him out:

> He,
> That with the plume. 'Tis a most gallant fellow.
> I would he lov'd his wife: if he were honester
> He were much goodlier. (3.5.76-79)

At the Widow's inn Helen reveals her identity but still hides from them the challenge that Bertram had flung behind him when he left France: "When thou canst get the ring upon my finger, which never shall come off, and show me a child begotten of thy body, that I am father to, then call me husband: but in such a 'then' I write a Never." Resolved to gain that ring, Helen proposes to the Widow alone that she should get her daughter to consent to the Count's pleas in exchange for the ring, and then arrange for him to tryst unaware with his wife.

After Looney had finished his first demonstration of Shakespeare's identity he came across a history of Oxford's native county that depicted the Earl as the amorous victim of such a trick. Apparently unaware that the plot came from Boccaccio's *Decameron*, the shire historian declared, when the Earl "forsook his lady's bed, the father of Lady Anne by stratagem contrived that her husband should unknowingly sleep with her, believing her to be another woman, and she bore a son to him in consequence of this meeting."[62] The source of this slander has never been disclosed. The oldest printed version of it is found in Francis Osborne's *Historical memories on The Reigns of Queen Elizabeth and King James* (London, Grismond, 1658). According to Osborne, the last daughter of "the last great Earl of Oxford" was born after his "lady was brought to his Bed under the notion of his Mistress, and from such a virtuous deceit she is said to proceed." Who said so? My confident surmise is Lord Henry Howard, the supreme calumny-circulator of the time. I fancy he may have invented the rumor while a spectator at a court performance of our play, or after he had seen the similar contrivance in Shakespeare's *Measure for Measure*. For a hawk's-eye view of Howard's career of almost artistic treachery, look at the references to him in the index to E. M. Tenison's truly heroic chronicles, *Elizabethan England*. Two tacticians of the plot in *Measure for Measure*, Escalus and Mariana, have namesakes in *All's Well that Ends Well*, and the Mariana here is intimate with Diana, whose second name, Capilet, relates her to the heroine of *Romeo and Juliet*.

Count Bertram applies to Parolles his betrayer a curious simile: "has deceived me," he says, "like a double-meaning prophesier." When Shakespeare wrote these words, I conjecture, he held in remembrance how Lord Harry Howard's brother Thomas, the Duke of Norfolk, had deceived himself with wishing to believe an astrological prophecy which had been interpreted as meaning that he would become a lion of England if he courted Queen Mary Stewart. He "made no great account" of the prediction among his kinsmen, including young Oxford, but risked his neck in secret correspondence with the fatal prisoner from Scotland, who agreed to be his bride. The "lion" soon found himself caged in the Tower of London, where he could hear Elizabeth's lions roar every day, and next, as the astrologer had foretold, *"In exaltatione Lunae Leo succumbet."*[63] One of the reasons for Oxford's marriage with Anne Cecil is said to have been his hope that he could win her father to exert influence for the freedom of his cousin of Norfolk.

The memory of these lions in the Norfolk prophecy would augment a strong antagonism to cats in the cranium of Edward de Vere. "I could endure anything before but a cat," Bertram confesses, on learning how willingly Parolles betrays him, and "he is a cat to me", blurting later, "more and more a cat." (4.4.233) That passage induced me to hunting the allusions to cats in a Shakespeare concordance, and I was surprised to find nearly everywhere in his works a fierce aversion to the feline. It must have begun in his brain in earliest childhood, in connexion, I suspect, with some beastliness done by his mother; her image transmuted in his unconscious after saturation in the classics to a fantom of the goddess Hecate, queen of ghosts, the dead who will not stay dead.

Our poet understood that "self-love"—in the pregnant words of Parolles early in the comedy—"is the most inhibited sin in the canon." But he would not admit that his egolatry extended to making himself wear inside the mask and costume of the goddess he detested. Yet Lavache, Rossillion's clown, proclaims his master to be the devil, whom he calls the Black Prince—after the famous medieval prince Edward of England, with whom Edward de Vere must have imagined he had a multitude of qualities in common. The black angel, says the clown, "has an English name."

In the Italian story that Shakespeare may have transported personally from Lyons the Count of Rossillion was "called home by his tenants." Our dramatist ends the war with Siena and sends him back to France with great compliments from the Duke of Florence. And he added the sad detail of Helen's alleged death in a Florentine convent. I am convinced he did this in revising the romance, after the death of little Anne the unfortunate Countess of Oxford, which produced in the dramatist an obsession for scenes resurrecting ill-treated wives from their graves. In *All's Well* he compelled Count Bertram, in penance for the "Deadly divorce" from Helen, to accept a proposal for marriage with a maid who makes no appearance in the play, "fair Maudlin," the daughter of Lord Lafeu. Up to the introduction of her existence, this venerable substitute for Lord Burghley never mentioned that he had a child, nor did anyone else. An exactly similar contrivance dampens the comedy of *Much Ado About Nothing*. But Shakespeare would not let go of the gruesome satisfaction he got from these tricks of his conscience. "So there's my riddle, one that's dead is quick." In the Folio first edition of our play (perhaps the worst printed play in that costly volume), the French King is given the speech, at the moment of Helena's reappearance—

> Is there no exorcist
> Beguiles the truer office of mine eyes?
> Is't real that I see? (5.3.301-303)

Professors of fidelity to the Folio as the sole edition must have little sympathy with Lafeu whose eyes "smell onions" when Helen answers,

> No, my good Lord,
> 'Tis but the shadow of a wife you see,
> The name, and not the thing. (5.3.303-304)

If they reject the testimony of Helen's reply to her Lord as proof that the Folio's *Kin.* should be read *Ber.*, they will spurn with happier speed the suggestion that when the Count swears, "I'l love her dearly, ever, ever dearly," the writer is placing his signature on the vow—E. *Ver.*

V

It seems to me the dramatist was boasting when he presented Parolles lying about Bertram thus: "I knew the young Count to be a dangerous and lascivious boy, who is a whale to virginity, and devours up all the fry it finds." Tudor documents have so far not shown the Earl of Oxford as a man who consumed hymens in numbers, except perhaps verse numbers. He appears to have been indeed a boy with a heart having chambers for hardly more than four women, his mother, his first wife, his second wife, and the girl whose chastity he celebrated and at the same time defamed in *All's Well That Ends Well.* Well, in whose image did he create Diana Capilet? The answer will occur at once to all who have taken the trouble to peruse the life of Edward de Vere: however, the play affords very little to identify her. It tells us that Bertram "found her wondrous cold" at their first interview, that he conducted his wooing every night "With music of all sorts, and songs compos'd to Her unworthiness," declining to leave when chided. We also learn that the widow's lass was nicknamed "Fontybell," and came of "ancient" ancestry, not noble presumably but above the burgess plane. Bertram contends she was "a common gamester to the camp," but she scorns the insult as a woman not to be bought at "common price." On a foundation of such scanty evidence it is impossible to prove that we have in this strange creature the poet's primary sketch of Mistress Anne Vavasor, the lady of Queen Elizabeth's bedchamber who enchanted him. Let us see if contemporary chronicles and logic will help make the sketch a living portrait.

She was born about the year 1560 at Tadcaster in Copmansthorpe, Yorkshire, near the city of York. Her father, Henry Vavasor, and her mother, born Margaret Knyvet, were derived, as the family names indicate, from medieval knighthood, the vassals or "knaves" of barons. In loyalty to family tradition their daughter

Frances became a Maid of Honor at Elizabeth's court and Anne received appointment among the Gentlewomen of her Majesty's Bedchamber, probably several months after her seventeenth birthday, in the spring of 1578.

A certain fatality in the Vavasor blood struck some English antiquarians: "It is observed of this family that they never married an heir, or buried their wives."[64] Anne's mother became a widow on February 15, 1584. Since I date the first writing of the romance of Rossillion nearly six years before, I can account for the poet's presentation of her stage figure as an orphan only by a necessity of his prophetic soul, which had to leave Diana Capilet without a male guardian, just like her prototype in the *Decameron*. Of course the Virgin Queen would not have any attendant in her bedroom who was overtly fond of masculinity. If not as frigid as her Majesty, Anne Vavasor could be "wondrous cold" toward men. Her reputation for harlotry she acquired from the same court circle of Roman Catholic diplomats that secreted the main legends about Edward de Vere, the group who produced the venomous tract printed in Paris 1584 under the title *La Vie Abominable du Comte de Leycester*, translated in Naples in 1585 for the anthology *Flores Calvinistici*, but in English merely named *The Copy of a Letter Written by a Master of Art of Cambridge*. "With our present fairly full information," the researchers of the Catholic Record Society declare, "we can say with some certainty that the editor was Charles Arundel, with assistance of other exiled followers of Mary Stuart."[65] With no less certainty I nominate as Arundel's most acid author Lord Harry Howard, who never joined him in exile. In this tract, aimed at the champion of Protestant militancy in England, the liars state that the Earl of Leycester, lusting after ladies around Elizabeth, "offered to an other of higher place, an hundredth pound lands by the yeare with as many Jewels as most Women under her Majesty used in England: which was no meane bait to one that used traffique in such marchandize: shee being but the leavings of another man before him, whereof my Lord is nothing squemish, for satisfying of his lust, but can bee content (as they say) to gather up crummes when hee is hungry, even in the

very Landry it selfe, or other place of baser quality." The margin of
this obscenity gives the name of the victim as "Anne Vaviser."[66]
Burghley himself in March 1583 denounced her as a "drab."[67] But
he hated her as the woman for whose sake his daughter's husband
persisted in keeping the "Sweet little Countess of Oxford" a prey to
solitary tears. Burghley had mercy only for his son-in-law because
he had been terribly bled "by the drab's friend in revenge, to the
peril of his life."

Only one of the extant poems by Oxford is credited to the
charms of Anne Vavasor. The song however does not sound like
one he would find useful for a wooing serenade at her window.

Verses Made by the Earle of Oxforde

Sittinge alone upon my thoughte, in melancholy moode,
In sighte of sea, and at my back an ancyente hoarye woode,
I saww a faire young lady come, her secret feares to wayle,
Cladd all in colour of a Nun and covered with a vaylle:
Yet (for the day was callme and cleere) I myghte discerne her face,
As one miyghte see a damaske rose hid under christall glasse:
Three tymes with her softe hand full harde on her left syde she knocks,
And syghed so sore as myghte have movde some pittye in the rockes:
Fron syghes, and shedding amber tears, into sweet songe she brake,
When thus the Echo answered her to everye word she spake:

Anne Vavesor's Eccho

O heavens, who was ye first that bredd in me this feavere?   *Vere.*
Whoe was the firste that gave ye wounde whose fearre
                                        I ware for evere?   *Vere.*
What tyrant, Cupid, to mye harme usurpes thy golden quivere? *Vere.*
What wighte first caught this harte, and can from
                                        bondage it deliver? *Vere.*

---

*   The word is "let" in the original prints. To make sense I substitute the old
    word for flax.

Yet who doth most adore this wighte, oh hollowe

caves, tell true?   *You.*

What nymphe deservs his lykinge best, yet doth in sorrow rue? *You.*

What makes him not rewarde good will with some

rewarde or ruthe?   *Youth.*

May I his favour matche with love, if my love will trye?   *I.*

May I require his birthe with faythe? than faithfull will I dy?   <u>I.</u>

> And I that knew this ladye well,
> Said Lord how great a mirakle
> To her how eccho toulde the truthe
> As true as Phoebus orakle.[68]

The lyrics he made for her must have been almost as numerous as the leaves of October woods. In my belief they are to be looked for in the books of writers to whom he was a generous patron, for example, his devoted servant Anthony Munday, whose own attempts at poetry resemble the splendid songs in his books like Hesiod resembled Homer.

All's well that Ends Well admonishes us (2.1.137-138)

> He that of greatest works is finisher
> Oft does them by the weakest minister.

In William Hunnis's play *Fedele and Fortunio, or The Two Italian Gentlemen* (1585), translated from the Italian pastoral *Il Fedele* by Luigi Pasqualigo, there occurs a lyric that neither Munday, Hunnis, nor Pasqualigo could have composed.[69] It was signed "Sheperd Tonie" only to lead the unwary into thinking Anthony made it. Ever since, the academic have deemed him the maker, altho Munday never claimed it, and the last two lines of the song appear in the collection *Englands Parnassus* (1600) over the initials S. G. (standing presumably for Munday's clerical friend Stephen Gosson). I quote the version in *Englands Helicon* (1600).

> I serve Aminta, whiter then the snowe,
> Straighter then Cedar, brighter then the glasse:
> More fine in trip, then foote of running Roe,

More pleasant then the field of flowring grasse.
> More gladsome to my withering ioyes that fade:
> Then Winters Sunne, or Sommers cooling shade.

Sweeter then swelling Grape of ripest wine,
Softer then feathers of the fairest Swan:
Smoother then lint*, more stately then the Pine,
Fresher then poplar, smaller than my span,
> Clearer then Phoebus fierie pointed beame:
> Or Icie crust of Christall frozen streame.

Yet is she curster then the Beare by kind,
And harder hearted then the aged Oake:
More glib then Oyle, more fickle then the wind,
More stiffe then steele, no sooner bent but broake.
> Loe thus my service is a lasting sore:
> Yet will I serve, although I die therefore.

Another pen-name employed by the Earl of Oxford, as early as 1578, was *Willy*, selected, I suppose, not only because it was one of the commonest names in England but also for the sake of its implication of desire. Looney was the first to see in the Willy of Edmund Spenser's *Shepherds Calendar* (listed by London Stationers for printing on December 5, 1579) a representative for Edward de Vere. This shepherd appears only twice in the book, in the March and August eclogs. In the March poem he volunteers to keep a sharp eye on a friend's sheep, having little worry for his own:

> For alas, at home I have a syre,
> A stepdame eke as whott as fyre,
> > That dewly adayes counts mine.

These rimes were the closest that Spenser dared to come in satiric allusion, Looney pointed out, "to the surveillance exercised by Burleigh, and to the irascible Lady Burleigh".[70] The August eclog, Looney showed, provided mild ridicule of the rivalry in riming that Oxford and Philip Sidney amused London intellects with in 1578.

It was an effort on the part of Spenser to make the two courtiers friends. But their versing feud reflected and sparked from the warmer antagonism between Oxford's friend Sussex and Sidney's uncle Leycester, which we have seen provoking conflict with the Queen in the same month.

Oxford wrote a short song beginning "Were I a king," and Sidney made a sour parody of it, "Wert thou a king." In Spenser's poem two shepherds named Willye and Perigot meet and right away the former demands,

> Tell me, Perigot, what shall be the game,
> Wherefore with mine thou dare thy music match?

For "Umpire of their strife," says the alleged editor of the volume, E. K., they choose the genial Cuddy, who plainly stands for Spenser. He consents with pleasure:

> Gin, when ye list, ye jolly shepherds twain;
> Sike a judge as Cuddie were for a king.[71]

The poetic contest that ensues makes us laugh by its spontaneous fun; yet there is more art in the swift melody of the lines than a glance will let you see. But who could take seriously a love song like this?

Perigot.	I saw the bouncing Bellibone.
Willye.	Hey, ho, Bonnybell!
Per.	Tripping over the dale alone:
Wil.	She can trip it very well.
Per.	A chaplet on her head she wore,
Wil.	Hey, ho, chapelet!
Per.	Of sweet violets therin was store,
Wil.	She sweeter than the violet...
Per.	She roved at me with glancing eye,
Wil.	As clear as the crystal glass:
Per.	All as the sunny beam so bright,
Wil.	Hey, ho, the sunny beam!
Per.	Glanceth from Phoebus face forthright.
Wil.	So love into thy heart did stream.

The words are none but Spenser's, but the imagery and music remind us more than once of Oxford's (or Shepherd Tony's) songs.

The strange name of the girl Perigot praises in bad French, meaning to call her Beautiful-good but making us vision instead a pelvic girdle, recalls the name "Fontibell" bestowed for no reason on Diana in *All's Well*. Cuddie declares the contestants equal winners, and diverts them with an elegy by Colin Clout—Edmund Spenser's favorite pastoral name for himself. Willy is delighted.

> For never thing on earth so pleaseth me
> As him to hear, or matter of his deed.

By now it should be clear as crystal that my date for the genesis of *All's Well That Ends Well* is August 1578. When the play got the title it carries in the Folio of Shakespeare's works, we do not know. Many scholars agree that in 1598, when Francis Meres published his *Palladis Tamia: Wits Treasury*, it was the *Love Labours Wonne* which he listed as proof that "Shakespeare among ye English is the most excellent... for Comedy." T. W. Baldwin discovered in 1953 a London bookseller's ledger page of August 1603 which listed among other plays "loves labor won." I agree with Eva Turner Clark that the romance was twenty years old when Meres pedantically echoed the verdict of the noblest nerves in London. She demonstrated that on Tuesday, January 6, 1579, it entertained the royal court at Richmond under the name, *The history of the Rape of the Second Helen*.[72] The company that acted it went unnamed in the "Revels" accounts, but there is no doubt that it was the Lord Chamberlain Sussex's men. His records convey the court's pleasure in the Twelfth Night performance, "well furnished in this office with many things for them."[73] On the night before, Jehan de Simier, messenger from the Duc d'Alencon, entered London, and, before starting his campaign to win the Queen's heart for his master, had the felicity of hearing the early dramatic manners of Will Shakespeare, his reverent and quite unconscious copying from Ovid, his addiction to rimed dialog and letters in sonnet form, his style sometimes going on stilts like the language in Hamlet's little "Mousetrap" tragedy.

In calling his play *The Rape of the Second Helen* it seems he was thinking of the Trojan war (which in the much later *Troilus and Cres-*

sida disguised his ideas of the Anglo-Dutch war with Spain). He remembered how Euripides prevented the carving of Iphigeneia as a
mouthful for the gods by sending a hind in her place to the altar, a
gift from the merciful goddess Artemis, whom the Romans called
Diana. We may be sure that De Vere saw the children of St Paul's
Cathedral play the tragedy of *Iphigenia* for the Queen on December
28, 1571, nine days after his wedding. He also recalled how Euripides created a second Helen from a cloud for Paris to rape and carry
off to Troy so that the real Helen, loyal wife of Menalaos, should
not be blamed for the war.[74] Boccaccio's Florentine virgin who enabled the deserted Countess of Rossillion to recover her husband
merged in our poet's imagination with the nebulous Helen of the
Greek play. Anne Vavasor had not yet yielded herself to the blandishments, songs and rings and things the Earl of Oxford lavished
on her, and all he could embrace on the nights when he wrote his
romance was her ghost. Defeat of his longing for love evidently
made his mind rage in the direction of war. That explains for me the
way his clown Lavache distorts the (lost) ballad of Helen of the *Iliad*:

> Was this fair face the cause, quoth she,
> Why the Grecians sacked Troy?
> Fond done, done fond, was this King Priams joy?
> With that she sighed as she stood,
> With that she sighed as she stood,
> And gave this sentence then,
> Among nine bad if one be good,
> Among nine bad if one be good,
> There's yet one good in ten.

Countess. What, one good in ten? You corrupt the song, sirra.

Clown. One good woman in ten, Madam, which is a purifying o' th'
song: would God would serve the world so all the year, we'd find
no fault with the tithe woman if I were the Parson. One in ten,
quoth a? and we might have a good woman born but for every
blazing star, or at an earthquake, 'twould mend the lottery well. A
man may draw his heart out here a pluck one.[74] (1.3.69-87)

The star to which the cowlike clown (la vache) refers of course was the same astral phenomenon the appearance of Petruchio at his wedding was compared to. A certain T. T. (Thomas Twyne?) publisht in 1578 *A View of Certain Wonderful Effects... of the Comet or Blazing Star*. At the end of July 1578 Cambridge University sages debated for the royal court on the contention that the stars do not govern human destiny. William Cecil, Chancelor of their colleges, acted as moderator. Himself a devout investor in astrology, he made his presence felt only by stopping repetition and tedious discourse.

The dramatist added the allusion to an earthquake, in my belief, when he changed *The Rape of the Second Helen* to *Love's Labours Won*. He coupled the comet of 1577-78 with the vast earthquake of April 6, 1580, as the most impressive global prodigies of the period.

Yet I have not handled the problem of his immediate motivation for writing the strange, if not repellant, romance. What induced him to mediate on this drama, I feel sure, was the tragedy of Helene de Tournon, the obscure beauty from Roussillon in Dauphiny, France, who died young far from home, at Liege in Brabant or Flanders, in the summer of 1578.[75]

Helene de Tournon belonged to the radiant and joyous retinue of Marguerite de Valois, daughter of Catherine de Medici and sister of three French kings, the queen of Henri of Navarre. Marguerite selected the ladies of her escort for brains and talents as well as magnetic countenance. They were far famed as *l'escadrille volante*—the flying squadron (possibly punning on *volante*, which also signifies stealing—of hearts). At the head of the elegant group stood the Princess Roche-sur-Yon. Next to her in noble rank came the Dowager Countess of Roussillon, the lady in charge of Princess Margot's bedchamber, mother of the luckless Helene. She descended from a family related to Queen Catherine. Her castle home was not in the province of Roussillon, east of Navarre, but twenty miles from Tournon, which the Earl of Oxford saw when he traveled north on the river Rhone in March 1576. Tournon is about seventy-five miles south of Lyon, where De Vere rested, and browsed over bookstalls, on his way to Paris.

In the spring of 1578 Queen Marguerite journeyed from Paris to Flanders, pretending to want the medicinal waters of the Spa in Liege, but her real purpose was to advance the ambition of her brother Hercule, Duc d' Anjou. He aimed to wring a princedom of Brabant for himself out of the war in the Low Countries. With her fourteen sirens and company of gentlemen she rode in June from Cambrai to Mons, where she persuaded the governor Lalain to hold the fortress there for her brother, who had promised to defend the region against Spain. A week later Marguerite went to Namur for a visit with Don John of Austria, whose halfbrother Philip had instructed to restore the Netherlands to Spain. She enchanted Don John, who banqueted her with music, and had the aristocrat Ottavio Gonzaga serve them on his knees with wine. The Spanish governor informed his master in Madrid, "Altho this Queen's beauty is more divine than human, she is shaped rather to damn men's souls than to save them." A day later she and her escort sailed up the Meuse to Liege.[76]

"No sooner had the boat left the shore," Marguerite remembered, than Mademoiselle de Tournon fell terribly ill: "this young lady was seized with an alarming malady which caused her, by the great pain that ensued, to scream in the most woeful manner. The physicians maintained the cause was spasms of the heart, which, despite the utmost exertions of their skill, carried her off a few days after my arrival at Liege."

The fate of this Helen of Roussillon would have fascinated the Earl of Oxford to learn every detail of her tragedy he could. The Queen of Navarre tells us that, unnumbered months before, "this young lady, universally admired for her modesty and graceful accomplishments, for which she certainly deserved admiration, attracted the notice of the Marquis de Varenbon," a nobleman then training for the priesthood. He, "violently enamored of the Mademoiselle de Tournon," begged his elder brother for permission to marry Helene. "The young lady's family... readily gave their consent, but his brother refused his, strongly advising him to change his resolution and put on the (priestly) gown."

The girl's mother, "a virtuous and pious lady, thinking she had cause to be offended, ordered her daughter to leave the house of her sister," who was married to Varenbon's brother, and come home to the castle in Roussillon. Helene's mother, "a woman of violent spirit," rigidly justified by her religion, began "continually scolding the poor young lady, so that she was forever with tears in her eyes," because she cherished each of her remembrances of the Marquis's words of adoration. Queen Margot affirms, "there was nothing to blame in the girl's conduct," but her mother relentlessly attacked her affection. Naturally, Helene "wished to get out from under the mother's tyrannic government, and was accordingly delighted with the thoughts of attending me in this journey to Flanders, hoping, as it happened, she should meet the Marquis de Varenbon." Somehow he became a guest of the Don at Namur.

Curiously, "the Marquis, during the whole time we stayed at Namur, showed her not the least attention, and seemed as if he had never been acquainted with her." Proud resentment and profound grief, noted Margot, welled up in the lady's throat, and she downed them with an amazing dignity, "necessarily stifled in her breast," says the Queen. However, when their boat departed from the Don's hospitality, her frail body endured the price of this repression. When they descended from the vessel "the anguish of her mind... stopt her respiration." For eight days she suffered or clung to life, then "she died, to the great grief of her mother, as well as myself."[77]

The love-story of Helene de Tournon surely struck Edward de Vere as strangely resembling his own. He had been passionately attracted to sweet little Anne Cecil, who certainly adored him. Then he had undergone an estrangement, and declined to see her again. Her parents aggravated her grief, scolding her for devotion to his memory, and her weeping was known far beyond her home. The Earl must have wondered what saved her from dying for love. Out of that thought, as I see it, the plot of his play unfolded, in wonderment over poor Anne's courage, and the conquest of her pride by care for him. It reminded him of the *Decameron* tale of Giletta of Narbonne and her self-sacrifice for Beltramo of Rossiglione. Apparently he prefered to review the tale in the French version by Monsieur Macon which came out in Lyon in 1576. It encouraged him to dream of reconcilement with the mother of his Bess. He found only one impediment to their reunion, but that was barely more than a mote in his mind's eye—the icy image of that northern star-eyed lass Anne Vavasor. Did he, in his poverty, under the orb of the virgin queen, have the manhood to melt that chill of the Vavasor chastity?

I surmise that *The Second Helen* contained allusions to Provence as well as the actual fragrance of "Provincial roses"—on actors' shoes perhaps, according to the picture presented by Hamlet (Act 3, Scene 2, line 288)—to remind the Court vividly of the real Rousillon, which the poet with his everlasting passion for punning apparently conceived as Rose-Ilion. This imaginary Troy of roses may have been meant to remind the Queen and England of the antiquarian theory that London was built to be "Troynovant," New Troy.

When John Florio published his *World of Words* in 1598 and dedicated it to the young Earl of Southampton, the Earl of Oxford may have felt inspired to revise *The Rape of the Second Helen* or *Love's Labours Won* as a warning to his friend to beware of Florio's flattery. In forewords to the reader of *A World of Words* the flamboyant Florio denounced satire aimed at him, in particular, "Aristophanes and his comedians" who "make plays, and scour their mouths on Socrates." By that time the Queen's court would scarcely remember why Helen hails Parolles as "monarch" in the first scene, for the demented Italian called the "fantastical Monarcho" who haunted the court in 1578 and died in 1580 would have been a forgotten ghost. But Shakespeare could not resist using the oldfangled meters of the romance in his efforts to perfect *Hamlet.* Hence the appearance of lines in the latter like "Full thirty times hath Phoebus' car gone round," echoing "Ere twice the horses of the sun shall bring" and so on, in *All's Well,* and "Where joy most revels, grief doth most lament" (in *Hamlet*) recalling "Oft expectation fails, and most oft there Where most it promises." Above all, our dramatist felt compelled to repeat himself by granting Helen his Prince's final thought: "All the rest is mute."

References

1 Looney, *"Shakespeare" Identified* (London; Cecil Palmer, 1920) 233-4.
2 Ibid. 459.
3 Published in London by Cecil Palmer as *Shakespeare's Plays in the Order of Their Writing.* (New York: Payson, 1931).
4 *The Diary of Henry Machyn, Citizen and Merchant-Taylor of London, from A.D. 1550 to A.D.1563,* ed. Nichols (London; Camden Society, 1848) 291.
5 Lansdowne Ms. 6, folio 69 quoted by B.M. Ward, *The Seventeenth Earl of Oxford 1550-1604 from Contemporary Documents* (London; John Murray, 1928) 21-2.
6 Samuel Morant, *History and Antiquities of the County of Essex* (1768) ii, 328; Ward, op. cit., 30. and Lansdowne Mss. 25, fo. 39.
7 Looney op. cit. 255. Calendar of Cecil Ms. at Hatfield, II, 220.
8 See frontispieces in Looney and Ward books. The painter's identity is clarified by the Calendar of State Papers, Foreign (1575-1577), p. 35, doc. 835, and E. M. Tenison, *Elizabethan England,* II, plate 24.
9 Looney, op. cit. 233.
10 "My Lord's device," wrote Valentine Dale concerning the motto Oxford had inscribed on his Paris picture,"is very proper, witty and significant." (Ward, 104.)
11 John G. Nichols, *The Progresses & Public Processions of Queen Elizabeth* (London; Nichols, 1823) I, 390.
12 Ward, 7.
13 Calendar of (England) State Papers Domestic 1547-1580, I, No. 45; J.H. Round in *The Ancestor,* iv (Jan. 1903) 24 f.
14 Round, loc. cit.
15 Morant, op. cit. ii, 293 n.
16 State Papers Domestic, IX, no. 4.
17 *Ambassades de Noailles,* V, 319; Calendar of State Papers Venetian, vi, pt. 1, 474.
18 Calendar of State Papers, Domestic, vii, No.2.
19 Calendar of State Papers Foreign, 1559-60, p. 244.
20 Essex Record Office: Hedingham accounts, D/D Pr. 142.
21 Calendar of State Papers Domestic, xvi, 50.
22 Historical Manuscripts Commission: Calendar of Hastings Ms. i, 319. See Hugh Holland, *Shakespeare, Oxford and Elizabethan Times* (London, Archer, 1933)
23 Frederick Chamberlin, *The Private Character of Queen Elizabeth* (London 1921) 68.
24 Ward, op. cit. 205.
25 Ward, 111.
26 *Recueil des Depeches, Rapports, instructions et memoires des Ambassadeurs de France en*

Angleterre, et en Ecosse pendant de XVI siècle, ed. Charles Purton Cooper(Paris 1838)i,197-8.

27 Ibid.i,269-70.

28 Lansdowne Mss. Folio 212, n. 11.

29 State Papers Domestic, Addenda, XIX, 37, 38.

30 Calendar of State Papers, Scotland, p. 110.

31 Lionel Cuthbert Sharpe, *Memorials of the Rebellion of 1569*, 238.

32 Ward, 40

33 State Papers Domestic (loc. cit.) XLX. 39, 40.

34 Ward, 49.

35 John Stow, *Survey of London* (1618), ed. Kingsford (1908) I, 88.

36 Ward, 70-1

37 Lansdowne Ms. 14.84, f. 185. See Ward, 73.

38 *The Correspondence of Sir Philip Sidney and Hubert Languet*, ed. Pears (1845) 66.

39 Nichols, 1oc. cit. supra.

40 Kathleen Le Riche, in *Essex Review* (1952) 189.

41 Calendar of Rutland Ms. (July 1571) i, 94.

42 Harleian Ms. 6991 f. 82. *A Collection of State Papers Relating to Affairs in the Reign of Queen Elizabeth*, ed. Murdin (London, Bowyer, 1759)

43 Calendar of State Papers Foreign, ed. Crosby (1876) 532.

44 Cecil ms. at Hatfield, published by historical Manuscripts Commission, III, 83.

45 *The Zurich Letters*, Ed. Robinson (Cambridge University Press. 1846) 475.

46 State Papers Domestic, Addenda, XXIII. 62.

47 British museum, Cotton Ms. Titus B, 2.298.

48 *Queen Elizabeth and Her Times*, ed. Wright (1838) 507.

49 Harleian Ms. 6991, f. 50; State Papers Domestic, xlv, 59.

50 State Papers Domestic, xcviii, 2.

51 Labanoff, I., 206. *Lettres, Instructions et Memoires de Marie Stuart* (Paris 1844)

52 H.R. Fox Bourne, *Sir Philip Sidney: Type of English Chivalry in the Elizabethan Age* (New York, Putnam, 1891) 140.

53 *Illustrations of British History*, ed. Lodge (1791), ii, 100.

54 Colchester, (Essex) Ms., 150; Ward, 97-8.

55 Lansdowne Ms. 19.83; Ward, 114.

56 Cecil (Hatfield), Ms., Calendar, ii, 114. Ward, 107, 108.

57 Cecil, Ms., 11, 129; Calendar, Ward, 102.

58 Cecil, Ms., Calendar, Xiii, 144; Ward, 115.

59 State Papers Domestic (1581) CLi. 45 (copied with small mistakes in Ward, 99, 100).

60 Harvey, *Gratulationes Valdinenses* (1578) IV, trans. by Ward, 157-8.

61 Calendar of State Papers Spanish (1568-79) 1667.

62 Thomas Wright, *History and Topography of Essex* (1831) I, 517; Looney, op. cit.

280.

63 Calendar of Cecil Ms. i. 524-5; James Froude, *History of England from the Fall of Wolsey to the Death of Elizabeth* (New York, Scribner, 1867) X, 325n.

64 Thomas Fuller, *The History of the Worthies of England*, ed. Nichols (London, Rivington, 1811) iii, 454.

65 Catholic Record Society Publications (London) xxi, 58.

66 *History* (sic) *of Queen Elizabeth, Amy Robsart and the Earl of Leicester*, ed. Frank Burgoyne (London; Longmans, Green, 1904) 49-50.

67 Nichols, *Life and Times of Sir Christopher Hatton* (1847) 321.

68 Bodleian Library, Rawlinson Poetical Ms. 84.11 Ward, 228.

69 My chapter on *The Two Gentlemen of Verona* offers reasons for crediting the royal chapel-master William Hunnis with the comedy *Fedele and Fortunio* rather than Tony Munday, the draper's boy, who was apprentice to the printer John Allde when *The Two Italian Gentlemen* was staged. Hunnis was well known as an author of "Enterludes," printed anonymously.

70 Looney, 346.

71 Ibid. 343.

72 Clark, *Hidden Allusions in Shakespeare's Plays* (New York, Payson & Clark, 1931) 102-6.

73 *Documents Relating to the Office of the Revels in the Time of Queen Elizabeth,* ed. Feuillerot (Louvain, uystpruyot, 1908) 296.

74 I owe this Hellenist explanation of the old title and the Clown's singing about Helen of Troy to Dr. Sidney Halpern (in conversation 26/XII 1967).

75 George Lambinn,*Voyages de Shakespeare en France et en Italie* (Geneva: Librarire E. Droz,). Ruth Loyd Miller called attention to Lambin's revelations in her edition of Eva Turner Clark's *Hidden Allusions* (Jennings, LA Minos Publishing Company, 1974), 120-121.

76 Marguerite de Valois, *Memoires, Poesies et Lettres*, ed. M.F.Guessard (Paris 1842) II,137f. Milton Waldman, *Biography of a Family: Catherine de Medici and her Children* (Boston: Houghton Mifflin, 1936) 210.

77 *Memoirs of Marguerite de Valois, Queen of Navarre,* trans. anon. (Boston, L.C. Page, 1899). This work without copyright may be a (pirated?) edition of Violet Fane's translation of the *Memoirs* (London 1892) which I could not locate.

Chapter 8—PRIM ROADS TO ROSALINE

Young bloud doth not obey an old decree.
We cannot crosse the cause why we are borne:
Therefore of all hands must we be forsworne.

Monsieur Berowne (Love's Labor's Lost, 4.3.213-215)

Collegiate craniums employed to instruct our youth in classics of English literature, especially in plays, have for many years contained a fact that illuminates for us how the mind of the paramount dramatist of all times came to write the strange comedy *Love's Labor's Lost.* The fact is spelled out, for example, in *The Reader's Encyclopedia of Shakespeare* edited by Professor Oscar Campbell of Columbia University, in this way:

> The source of the enveloping action is some lost account of events dealing *(sic)* with a visit of Catherine de Medici (1519-1589) and her daughter Marguerite de Valois, wife of King Henry of Navarre, to Nerac in 1578. The ostensible purpose of the visit was to effect a reconciliation between Henry and Marguerite, who had been separated for years. But the real purpose was to negotiate with the king about Aquitaine.[1]

However this *Encyclopedia* utters not one word to enlighten us about any reasons why the soul of Shakespeare felt so attracted to that serenely forgotten piece of French history that he revolved around it the mildest of his dramas, one bound to bore his average audience and fetch him only a few pence.

Professor Campbell opened his big book with the assurance, "No other author of the Western world has stimulated so much thought among the best minds of each generation, so much research by its most gifted scholars, such keen insight by professional philosophers, so much eloquence by masters of rhetoric, and, alas!, so much tortured ingenuity expended by enthusiasts in support of rival claimants to the authorship of dramas they believe to be falsely attributed to a 'village ignoramus.'"[2]

For several decades I have been among those "enthusiasts" deplored by the Professor. (Usually he and his ilk did not label me so; they preferred the theological stigma of "heretic," if not "blasphemer.") But I could have been convinced there was respectability in their Stratford commerce and cult if they had even once been "stimulated" to a little thought about the motive of making the odd comedy in question. Imagine what they would have us believe: A runaway from his father's trade of butchery or leatherware, a fugitive from marriage with a woman eight years older who had made him a father of three infants, whom he apparently tried to feed by stealing rabbits, young Will Shakspere, who earned his bread and beer doing various unskilled jobs around and on the stage, and made more money by lending and hounding fellows for usury, was drawn to produce a comedy early in his career which he based on a report nobody has ever seen nor heard of, concerning a royal interview in southern France, which inspired the merry and meretricious William to write the exquisite play at least ten, maybe twenty years later! The research by "most gifted scholars" has, alas! failed to furnish them with a single reasonable date for the writing of *Love's Labor's Lost*, desperately confused as they are by the revision of the pleasantry (noted on the titlepage of the 1598 quarto), "As it was presented before her Highnes this last Christmas. Newly corrected and augmented by *W. Shakespere*." (Readers will thank me for rescuing them from the bother of debate with Professor Alfred Harbage, who argued that Shakespeare made the comedy for a company of children to perform in 1588, when all England toiled and growled about the coming of the Spanish Armada to their coast.)

This was the first drama to appear with the name of our prince of poets on the titlepage (spelled, please observe, with a compromise between the way the rogue from Stratford wrote his five or six signatures and the manner of the master's nomenclature on later titlepages—even with a hyphen sometimes). It probably was the play acted for Queen Elizabeth at Windsor castle on Monday evening, December 26, 1597, by the Lord Chamberlain's men, for whose sake the players John Heminges and Thomas Pope received payment from the royal treasury.[3] Evidently they hired a child for the role of Moth the page while employing boys as usual to play the parts of the Princess, her Ladies, and Jaquenetta the Country Wench. Compare the ambiguity of the author's name on the titlepage with the double meaning of the theatrical troop's title: to most English people the Lord Chamberlain would signify at once George Carey, the second Baron Hunsdon, an energetic soldier whom the Queen rewarded near the end of his life by putting him in charge of the imperial household, including the duties of different entertainments; Hunsdon acquired the office in 1597 and must have been mystified by his duties as director of her Majesty's theatrical felicities; he would have been certainly delighted to leave these labors to the Lord Great Chamberlain of England, a veteran of many inventions for the stage, who sponsored an unknown number of theatrical troops, and in 1598 gained honor for his labor as a theatrical writer from Francis Meres, the kinsman of the linguist John Florio and the poet Samuel Daniel. Meres declared in his *Palladis Tamia: Wits Treasury*, shortly after proclaiming "*Shakespeare* among ye English is the most excellent in both kinds for the stage; for Comedy ... for Tragedy..." that "the best for Comedy amongst us bee, *Edward* Earle of Oxforde, Doctor *Gager* of Oxforde, Maister *Rowley* once a rare Scholler of learned Pembroke Hall in Cambridge, Maister *Edwardes* one of her Maiesties Chappell, eloquent and wittie *John Lilly*, *Lodge, Gascoyne, Greene, Shakespeare, Thomas Nash, Thomas Heywood, Anthony Mundye* our best plotter."[4] It is clear that Meres contrived his list according to a scale of social rank and degree, endeavoring to place the authors after Lyly in some chronological order. We have not the faintest notion of what comedies he connected with Edward de Vere, Earl of Oxford. Also it seems to be clear that Meres had never talked with John Lyly or Thomas Nash or Anthony Munday, each of whom had merrily served the Earl of Oxford in stagecraft and literature, about the masterpieces of the mysteriously magnificent "Shakespeare." Meres never printed another word about the greatest writer for the theater, nor evinced any public curiosity about him.

I

Of course *Love's Labor's Lost* was composed and played, both for populace of the theater pits and the students of the lawyers' inns as well as the Queen and her courtiers, long before the Yuletide revival of 1597. By that time Meres was familiar with the fact that the *Two Gentlemen of Verona, Errors, Love labors lost* and *Love labours won*, the *Midsummer night dream*, and the *Merchant of Venice* sufficed to prove Shakespeare "the most excellent... for Comedy," in England any-way. The list indicates that Meres was acquainted with some kind of calendar of their production, in which the comedy we are soon to examine came extremely early, not long after *Errors* and before the Venetian enchantment. We have another contemporary witness to the age of our play, one Robert Tofte, who survives in memory only because of his contribution to this chronology. In 1598 he published a dismal volume of verse called *Alba. The Months Minde of a Melancholy Lover*, in which he exclaimed,

LOVES LABOR LOST, I once did see a Play
Ycleped so, so called to my paine,
Which I to heare to my small loy did stay,
Giuing attendance on my froward Dame,
    My misgiuing minde presaging to me Ill,
    Yet was I drawne to see it gainst my Will.

This *Play* no *Play*, but Plague was vnto me,
For there I lost the Loue I liked most:
And what to others seemde a lest to be,
I, that (in earnest) found vnto my cost,
    To euery one (saue me) was *Comicall*,
    Whilst *Tragick* like to me it did befall.

Each Actor plaid in cunning wise his part,
But chiefly Those entrapt in *Cupids* snare:
Yet all was fained, twas not from the hart,
They seemde to grieue, but yet they felt no care:

Twas I that Griefe (indeed) did beare in brest,
The others did but make a show in lest.

We would cheerfully abandon poor Tofte's rimes to oblivion if his "froward Dame" who compelled him to accompany her to the play had left us a casual letter describing what she had seen and heard on that day she decided to endure the loss of Tofte.

At least fourteen years before the publication of our comedy in quarto, the famous dancing horse Morocco, alluded to in Act 1, Scene 2, whose master Banks had trained to capriole on a stage and count money and dice with a lifted hoof, entertained London. The famous clown Dick Tarlton, who died in September 1588, sick and neglected by his former admirers, made at least one celebrated joke about the marvelous Morocco, but none knows when. I have found one state record of the steed, a notice of November 12, 1584, that Chancelor Walter Mildmay, for some unknown reason, sent both Banks and a horsekeeper, to bring Claude Nau, Mary Stuart's secretary, to Nottingham: "they came into the horse fair at *Lenton*."[5]

Twenty years before *Love's Labor's Lost* came from Cuthbert Burby's press, a crazy Italian whom courtiers named Monarcho, haunted the royal halls wearing "crowns on his shoes," as Thomas Nash reported, and fondly hailed the ships arriving at London docks as his imperial property. In 1580 the rimer Thomas Churchyard gravely wrote "The Phantasticall Monarkes Epitaph" for the book quaintly entitled *Churchyard's Chance*. Shakespeare twice referred to this madman from Italy. In *All's Well That Ends Well*, which I believe was once entitled *Love's Labor's Won*, the bombastard Parolles approaches poor little Helena with the words "Save you, fair Queen." She replies, "And you, Monarch" (1.1.). In the fourth act of *Love's Labor's Lost* the braggart Don Adriano is described in Scene 1, lines 99-100:

This Armado is a Spaniard that keeps here in court,
A Phantasme, a Monarcho, and one that makes sport...[6]

The metaphor would have been most vivid between August 2, 1578, when the princess Marguerite, summoned by her long estranged husband King Henry of Navarre to join him at home, started on her journey to Gascony, and October 2, when she arrived with her mother, Queen Catherine de Medicis, her retinue of beauties called the "flying squadron," and their supervisory Count Biron in the town of Nerac. Before traveling south they visited the renowned Belgian health resort at Spa. The Spanish commander of the territory, Don Juan of Austria—whom Shakespeare caricatured in his comedy as Don Adriano de Armado, Eva Turner Clark conclusively proved in her little book *The Satirical Comedy Love's Labor's Lost* (1933)—nearly captured them. Don John tried to charm and bewitch the princess at his castle in Namur with a banquet and ball-frolic lasting far into the night. But she eluded him and went about her business, which was to assist her ugly brother, the Duke of Anjou, Francois Hercules d'Alencon, in his plot to win control of the Netherlands, starting with Brabant, known as Belgium today. On October 1, when Marguerite, the *escadron volante*, and the Marshal Biron were greeted by festivity of the Huguenot army in Nerac, Don John's dream of conquering England and marrying the captive Queen of Scotland, Mary Stuart, to enthrone himself as emperor of Britain, dissolved. He died of camp pestilence, or poison, it was whispered, frustrated and bitter despite his final victories over the fortresses of Namur and Antwerp soon after Marguerite escaped his reach. She cleverly arranged the entrance of her brother into the city of Mons, and "led captive the hearts of Lalain and his Countess, thus securing the important province of Hainault for the Duke. Don John might, indeed, gnash his teeth with rage, as he marked the result of all the feasting and flattery, the piping and dancing at Namur."[7] After October 1, Don John would hardly have been chosen as a target for sarcasm by a gentleman, not by our noble Shakespeare.

A rumor circulated round Lord Burghley, William Cecil, the Earl of Oxford's father-in-law, that Don Juan perished of syphilis. Burghley would have regarded gossip of that sort proper to subdue the sorrow of Britons over the death of the Christian hero who had headed Spanish galleys, the Pope's fleet, and the Venetian navy to

the terrific defeat of the Turks in 1571. The anniversary of the great
naval victory of Lepanto fell on the sixth day after Don John died.
Shakespeare sings in honor of the Spaniard:

> A man in all the world's new fashion planted,
> That hath a mint of phrases in his braine:
> One, who the musicke of his owne vaine tongue,
> Doth ravish like inchanting harmonie:
> A man of complements whom right and wrong
> Have chose as umpire of their mutinie. (1.1.161-166)

Sir Francis Walsingham, England's spymaster under Lord Treasurer
Cecil, testified that Don John had no equal in Europe "for speech,
wit and entertainment." The eloquence and humor, the scope and
speed of mind displayed by this bastard brother of King Philip of
Spain entranced even enemies. So it was not surprising to behold
both Catholics and Calvinists of the Low Countries consenting to
visions of reconciliation with the Spanish empire under his um-
pireship. The majority of the English Queen's courtiers would agree
with Shakespeare's Berowne that Armado representing the Emperor
Charles's gifted son was "a most illustrious Wight,/A man of fire,
new words, fashion's own Knight." (1.1.174-175) But they might
have been puzzled to see and hear the Spaniard whose very stage-
name reeked of battle smoke and gore, reminding them all of the
Adriatic armada that defeated Turkey at Lepanto, never once delineated as a warrior. We are promised, "This childe of fancie that Armado hight... shall relate

> In high-borne words the worth of many a Knight
> From tawnie Spaine lost in the world's debate. (1.1.169-170)

But never does Adriano allude to the romantic heroes of his homeland. For the purposes of the play, he remains to the end a
"Braggart", a scion from the stock of the *commedia dell' arte* of Italy:
he is constantly named Braggart in the Folio text taken manifestly
from a prompter's copy as well as the printed play.

The barons and burgesses who led the revolt of the Low Countries against King Philip II made one impotent gesture to restore

comradely relations with Madrid. They invited his Vienna cousin, the Archduke Matthias, to become the head of their unhappy provinces. The Austrian accepted the office but behaved ever after like a manling miming a corpselike creature, so reluctant was he to raise fingers to scare or hurt or even defy his kinsman of Spain. When he ventured to exert the military power granted him to end the Philippic siege of Grave, Queen Elizabeth cracked a pun at the Archduke's expense. "Wot you what?" she joked to a secretary. "The Archduke is risen from the grave—without sound of trumpet."[8] Yet she too pursued a policy of appeasement and mollification of Madrid's majesty, in accord with the commercial convictions of her Treasurer, Burghley, who believed that British lucre and bodylard depended on mercantile tranquility in the Netherlands under strong central power of the House of "Burgundy," which we designate Hapsburg today. Philip's sister Maria was the empress of Austria, and she manifested her devotion to Spain by marrying her daughter Anna to her brother. And the main reason for William Cecil's support of the diplomatic games in which princes of France played as lovers of Elizabeth craving the Queen to be their bride was to delay French intrusion and efforts toward sovrenty in the Netherlands. Burghley preferred to see Don John of Austria riding murderously over the Flemings or Dutch. The sorrow of Sir Henry Cobham over the agonies of the Low Countries caught between the millstones of Madrid and Paris left the Lord Treasurer unmoved. On July 23, 1578, for example, Cobham appealed to the Treasurer thus: "This I may truly say, if by her Majesty's credit their want had been supplied, their army had been a long time past in the fields; Don John, driven to have fought, fled or yielded to a peace; and Monsieur d'Anjou clean cast off."[9] The rimer and humorist George Gascoigne interested Burghley more, whom the Treasurer employed as a secret message-carrier and spy on the continent. In October 1576 Gascoigne wrote from Paris concerning "jealousy grows every day greater and greater that France will deal with the Low Countries... The King's reiters (German mercenaries hired by Henri III) march, are already beyond Verdun, which is the direct way to Flanders."[10]

Eminent among those German horsemen were men from the family of Fugger, the chief financiers of the Spanish wars, whom Gascoigne persisted in naming Fuckers in his letters to London. He was in Antwerp at the end of 1576 when the Spanish troops, desperate for want of pay, performed their feat of massacre, rape and plunder in "*queste India d'una citta*," as Bentivoglio of Bologna called it. Three days before the conclusion of those horrors, Don Juan arrived in Luxemburg, disguised as a Moor and slave. In a short while he returned the Spanish army to discipline.

As the illicit child of Charles V and Barbara Blomberg of Regensburg, an obscure but rich burgess's girl, Juan had been educated in Spain by an even more obscure gentleman named Luis de Quixada living near Valladolid. I believe that Miguel Cervantes named the hero of his epic comedy of chivalry turned obsolete in a Christian realm running after money in honor of Don Juan de Quixada. Cervantes had been a volunteer in Don Juan's navy at war with the Turks, and lost the use of his left hand and arm at Lepanto. Even tho this admiral and general and governor of the Netherlands was only thirty three years old when he died, Edward de Vere, Earl of Oxford, surely considered him one of the most enviable of victims, a man destined to be forever famous.

In the very first line of *Love's Labor's Lost* Shakespeare voiced his disdain for the experience of common humanity, and his faith that Fame "all hunt after in their lives." He made Ferdinand the King of Navarre set the goal of noble virility in the grandeur of solitary scholarship, desired by very few mortals, yet known to crown a minority with "honour which shall bate (Time's) sythe's keene edge,"

And made us heyres of all eternitie. (1.1.6-7)

The sequel verses of the King seem to make fun of the hopes and aspirations of almost every noble and gentleman in the world of Shakespeare. They use the vocabulary of men of war, men whose supreme ideal was military, the mastery of kingdoms and empires by good soldiership, by valor, resourcefulness in killing and inventiveness, to extol a life of learning, devoted to the arts, not arms.

> Therefor, brave Conquerours, for so you are,
> That warre against your owne affections,
> And the huge Armie of the world's desires,
> Our late edict shall strongly stand in force,
> Navar shall be the wonder of the world.
> Our Court shall be a little Achademe,
> Still and contemplative in living Art. (1.1.8-14)

Imagine, if you please, how amazed and amused the people who listened to these lines were by the spectacle on the stage, of aristocrats, whose country at the time of the play's composition was convulsed by the fiercest wars in the history of France before the Twentieth century, talking about occupying their days and nights with sheer literature.

The opening scene of the comedy tells us in as plain a language as the dramatist could utter the object, the target of his satire. It was not scholarship, nor intellect under the spell of books and artistry. It was the policy or whim of his Queen to deny her nobles the chance to study the art of war with its masters in the Low Countries or the battlefields of France; it was the insistence of her Majesty that her courtiers confine their talents to skills of tranquility at home. The most militant activity Elizabeth could bear watching them enjoy was riding with lances in contests called tournaments. But when her chief prize winner in these tiltyard sports pleaded with her to allow him to volunteer for the Protestant revolution in France, she warned the Earl of Oxford: "I cannot wish that a man of such note among my people should find himself on the side of one who is fighting against his King."[11] She did not mind the sending of Sir Humphrey Gilbert and two hundred English volunteers led by the valiant Welshman Roger Williams and the gallant or "Italianate" adventurer George Gascoigne to the Netherlands in the spring of 1572 to assist the Flemings in rebellion against Philip of Spain. She risked their necks, not primarily to promote the Dutch republican revolution, but to secure the textile trade of England with the Low Countries. In June 1572 her Privy Council heard a lecture by Lord

Burghley arguing that the encroachment of the French in the maritime towns of Holland and Belgium constituted a threat to Britain, to be resisted at all costs, even if England had to give help to the Spanish despot's servant over there, the Duke of Alba.[12] The English recruits were instructed to keep their eyes on the island of Walcheren, the seaward key to the Netherlands, and restrain their eagerness to test prowess with the Spaniards by maintaining vigilance toward the French. When Alba's professional killers, the best paid soldiers of Europe, came out to skirmish with the newcomers, the Britons battled courageously and well. We have the word of their severe and honest critic, Roger Williams, for that.[13] One of them, Lieutenant Rowland Yorke, distinguished himself in a surprise raid on the enemy's supply wagons.[14] Later he became notorious as a companion of the Earl of Oxford on certain midnights of conviviality, entertaining young De Vere with tales of how he and Gascoigne had found romance with some nuns in the Netherlands during idle hours of their "cut-throat life."[15] When the English troops tried to capture the Spanish fort of Tergoes by a siege in summer, Christobal Mondragon rescued his countrymen by a splendid feat of crossing a narrow ridge submerged in water at ebbtide. Discouraged, the Englishmen returned to the port of Flushing and made up their minds to sail home. Prince William of Orange urged them to stay. They refused; by the end of October they were back in England. Gascoigne went to work on the rimes of *The Fruits of War*, or *Dulce Bellum Inexpertis* (Sweet is war to the inexperienced) which tell at least rapidly, if sometimes wretchedly, the story of how he strove

"to be a soldier in his age,
Mistrusting all the virtues of the mind"

to gain him the livelihood he craved.

The Cambridge University expert on rhetoric Gabriel Harvey made a summary note on his copy of Gascoigne's poem: "A sory resolution for owre Netherland Soldiours. A good pragmatique Discourse; but unseasonable, & most unfitt for a Captain, or professed Martiallist."[16] Nobody reading the swift humorous rimes in that period would have dreamed that it described the earliest English fighting for the principles of freedom from both church and state. Queen Elizabeth, who deserved to be nicknamed Bloody Bess for her persecution of the Catholics and Protestants repelled by her assumption of her father's brag "Vicar of Christ," discerned in the Dutch revolution seeds of a future insurrection against the English throne. She admonished the French ambassador Mauvissiere, on 16 October 1579, that "in the end" her Huguenots, the Puritans, "would want to recognise neither God nor King."[17] John Milton wrote the epic comedy of that uprising in his poem *Paradise Lost*, where the battle litany for democracy is perversely transformed into the song of Satan.

II

There is a royal court story told about Charles Blount, who became the eighth Lord Mountjoy, which illustrates like lightning the point and purpose of *Love's Labor's Lost*. In 1591 Spanish forces commanded by the magnificent fighting Duke of Parma, Alessandro Farnese, invaded Picardy and Bretagne to assist the Catholic League of France in their civil war with King Henri of Navarre. Worried over the security of commerce between the French channel ports and England, Elizabeth sent a small army led by Sir John Norris to support Navarre. Young Charles Blount, eager to study war under the greatest masters of the art, stole away from her Majesty's circle of sycophants and experts in scandal to join Sir John on the coast of France. The angry Queen "sent a Messenger unto him, with a strict charge to the General to see him sent home: when he came into the Queen's presence, she fell into a kind of reviling, demanding how he durst goe over without her leave; Serve me so (quoth she) once more, and I will lay you fast enough for running; You will never leave it untill you are knockt on the head, as that inconsiderate fellow Sidney was; You shall go when I send you, in the mean time see that you lodge in the Court (which was then at White-hall) where you may follow your Book, read and discourse on the Wars."[18]

In *Love's Labor's Lost* Shakespeare presented an imaginary King of Navarre occupying himself and his courtiers precisely as the English Queen advised, instead of concentrating their minds on the grand obligation of all nobles, the protection of their people, the safeguarding of the state, in short, the art of war. In the comedy or rather romance which the poet called for a while *Love's Labor's Won*, known to us now as *All's Well That Ends Well*, he presented his hero, the French earl Bertram, running away from home to study war on battlefields, just as the Earl of Oxford had done in July 1574, when he sailed to Flanders to learn how to be a General. When the furious Elizabeth summoned him back to Britain, she probably ordered him to busy his brain with books. Maybe the gallant Blount was inspired to attempt his two or three flights to France by a vivid performance of *Love's Labor's Won* or *Love's Labor's Lost*?

That both plays were written within the same twelve months of 1578, I feel persuaded, not only by their similarity of themes, but by the location of their scenes in southern France. *All's Well* begins in the country of Count Bertram, Roussillon, next to Navarre. In the comedy we are concerned with, Shakespeare excluded romance by devoting much attention to the money matter dividing the Princess of France from her lover, the King of Navarre. Shakespeare's King declares that since the King of France has failed to pay him an immense sum he had promised, Navarre was driven to take control of certain territory in Aquitaine (2.1.135). Actually King Henri of Navarre had never been paid the dowry that France owed him for wedding Marguerite de Valois. So he seized parts of Aquitaine, certain towns, and to win restoration of the towns and the military support of the Protestant prince for the realm of France governed by Henri III, the Princess Marguerite, as we have seen, traveled in the summer of 1578 southward to Gascony. By that time Queen Elizabeth surely realised how vain were her efforts to bring Don John and William the Silent, prince of Orange, to the table where she could act as "umpire" of their bloody debate. She proposed on January 7, 1578, to serve as mediator, but the terrific victory of Don John and his comrade the Duke of Parma over the rebels at Gemblours on January 31 showed her how Spain would manage without her graceful offices. The Spaniards went on to capture Tirlemont, Louvain, and other strategic cities, and the patriotism of Catholics in the Netherlands ebbed.

On July 7 Francois Hercules de Valois, the Duc d'Alencon, crossed the frontier of Brabant and endeavored to capture the city of Mons by stealth. He publicly vowed that he wanted only "to help this oppressed people, and to humiliate the prince of Spain." Aided by the champions of Dutch freedom, he was able to conduct a long siege there. While maskerading outside Mons in the role of "Defender of the Liberty of the Low Countries," he entertained himself and his mignons, his effeminate admirers, with a passionate courtship of Queen Elizabeth. Indeed he despatched the subtle Jean Simier to make love to her in his name. Simier made life hilarious for her with his "monkey" business. But her counselors would not supply him with the help he required to conquer Mons. The Spanish ambassador in London, Mendoza, informed King Philip that the main result of the French enterprise at Mons that he observed was, "The Queen is now turning her eyes more to your Majesty, and her ministers have commenced to get friendly with me." Mendoza reported this on July 19. Early in December the Duc, always called Alencon in England, tho his brother King Henri III decorated him with the dukedom of Anjou, withdrew his army from Mons and returned to France. The popular English comedian Richard Tarleton must have composed at this time the couplet, now so innocuous in the nursery,

> The King of France, with forty thousand men,
> Went up a hill, and so came downe agen.[19]

Therefor the lines that open the fourth act in *Love's Labor's Lost*, where the Princess watches with wonder a majestic hunter struggling to ride up a slope, could have been composed between July and December of 1578. In the quarto revision of 1598 the Princess is occasionally called Queen, which appears to be a vestige of the old play. And the lines run as follows:

> *Queen.* Was that the King that spurd his horse so hard,
>   Against the steepe uprising of the hill?
> *Boyet.* I know not, but I thinke it was not he.
> *Queen.* Who ere a was, a shew'd a mounting minde. (4.1.1-4)

The reference to a hill, and the pun in "mounting," point to the siege of Mons and the French frustration as the events that inspired Shakespeare to write this passage. Eva Turner Clark was the first to observe the fact. But, alas, it led her to the sad mistake of believing that the poet intended to make fun of Hercules d'Alencon in the person of his Pedant Holofernes, whom he introduced in the comedy only in the fourth act. She rightly recognised an allusion to the militancy at Mons in the dialog of the last act where the Braggart Armado asks the Pedant, "Do you not educate youth at the Charghouse on the top of the Mountaine?" The schoolmaster answers, "Or Mons the hill." "At your sweet pleasure," Braggart says, "for the Mountaine." And the Pedant replies, "I doe *sans question.*" The French phrase, Eva Clark was convinced, certified the caricature of Alencon.[20] However the Duc did not educate youth in the technology of murdering myriads, certainly not at Mons; there was nothing of the Pedant in his nature.

Of course Clark saw as well as many less talented researchers that Holofernes remains in our minds fundamentally as a farcical picture of Gabriel Harvey, the Cambridge University instructor in rhetoric. She should have apprehended that the dialog between the Spaniard and the Pedant was meant by the master dramatist to satirise Harvey's endeavors, with his university Latin verse, to encourage English youth into siding with the French and the Dutch. None was better acquainted with Gabriel Harvey's pompous poem attempting to inspire Edward de Vere with martial ardor against Don John.

In the spring of 1578 a group of German Protestant princes arranged a conference to be held in Schmalkalden on June 7. The Duke Hans Casimir of the Palatinate urged Elizabeth to take part. He was happily preparing troops of mercenaries on foot and horseback to assist the revolt against Spain. She nominated four grave and reverend fellows to go to Germany, but they never went. Gabriel Harvey appears to have hoped that he would be appointed one of their deputies.[21] The little orator was ambitious for political fortune and fame, tired of toiling for extremely humble repute over writings like his *Ciceronianus* (registered for printing in January 1577) and *Rhetor* (licensed in July 1577). Incidentally, he dedicated the former work to William Lewin, who had accompanied the Earl of Oxford on his tour in France and Germany in 1575 and the *Rhetor* to Bartholomew Clerke, whose translation of the brilliant book about courtiers by Baldassare Castiglione into Latin, *De Curiali sive Aulico* (printed by John Day in 1572) was published at the expense of the Earl of Oxford. Edward de Vere's earliest appearance in public as an author was in the preface of this book, "To the Reader— Greeting."[22]

Toward the end of July 1578 Queen Elizabeth and her courtiers made a stately journey or "progress" to Cambridge University. They visited Saffron Walden, the home town of Gabriel Harvey in Essex, and at nearby Audley End (one of England's better preserved castles or manor houses) on July 26 he delivered to her Majesty and Lord Burghley, the Earls of Leycester and Oxford, Philip Sidney and Sir Christopher Hatton, who had recently entranced the Queen by his talent for dancing the galliard together with his multifaceted suppleness in politics, a volume of Latin verses entitled in Greek *Xaire* (Rejoice) *vel Gratulationes Valdinenses*. The Walden Gratulation devoted to Edward de Vere merits our scrutiny as the first eulogy and criticism of the poetic Earl of Oxford in print. Harvey headed it "A heroic address... concerning the combined utility and dignity of military affairs and warlike exercises." I quote from the excellent translation by Captain Bernard Mordaunt Ward.[23]

The pompous poem begins like a flourish of trombones: "This is my welcome; this is how I have decided to bid All Hail! to thee and to the other Nobles."

Thy splendid fame, great Earl, demands even more than in the case of others the services of a poet possessing lofty eloquence.

Thy merit doth not creep along the ground, nor can it be confined within the limits of song. It is a wonder which reaches as far as the heavenly orbs.

O great-hearted one, strong in thy mind and thy fiery will, thou wilt conquer others; thy glory will spread out in all directions beyond the Arctic Ocean; and England will put thee to the test and prove thee to be a native-born Achilles. Do thou but go forward boldly and without hesitation. Mars will obey thee, Hermes will be thy messenger, Pallas striking her shield with her spear shaft will attend thee; thine breast and courageous heart will instruct thee.

For a long time past Phoebus Apollo has cultivated thy mind in the arts. English poetical measures have been sung by thee long enough. Let that Courtly Epistle—more polished even than the writings of Castiglione himself—witness how greatly thou dost excel in letters. I have seen many Latin verses of thine, yea, even more English verses are extant; thou hast drunk deep draughts not only of the Muses of France and Italy, but hast learned the manners of many men, and the arts of foreign countries. It was not for nothing that Sturmius himself was visited by thee; neither in France, Italy, nor Germany are any such cultivated and polished men.

O thou hero worthy of renown, throw away the insignificant pen, throw away bloodless books, and writings that serve no useful purpose. Now must the sword be brought into play; now is the time for thee to sharpen the spear and to handle great engines of war. On all sides men are talking of camps and of deadly weapons; war and the Furies are everywhere, and Bellona reigns supreme. Now may all martial influences support thy eager mind, driving out the cares of Peace.

Pull Hannibal up short at the gates of Britain. Defended tho he be by a mighty host, let Don John of Austria come on only to be driven home again. Fate is unknown to man, nor are the counsels of the Thunderer fully determined. And what if suddenly a most powerful enemy should invade our borders? If the Turk should be arming his savage hosts against us? What tho the terrible war trumpet is even now sounding its blast? Thou wilt see it all; even at this very moment thou are fiercely longing for the fray. I feel it. Our whole country knows it. In thy breast is noble blood, Courage animates thy brow, Mars lives in thy tongue, Minerva strengthens thy right hand, Bellona reigns in thy body, within thee burns the fire of Mars. Thine eyes flash fire, thy countenance shakes a spear. Who would not swear that Achilles had come to life again?

Students of the history of education will remember John Sturmius, the director of the great school of Strasburg, who had aroused his pupils to wonderful feats of learning, not only with their books, but in handicrafts and music and mastery of infinite arts, by organizing them to stage classical plays. The Earl of Oxford went out of the usual way from France to Italy for the sake of conversation with the teacher, who wrote about him with affectionate remembrance in letters to England before he died.

The zeal of Johann Sturm for the cause of the Protestants of France led him into steep debt. He sent a plea for financial help to England, to William Lewin, the Earl of Oxford's fellow-traveler. Lewin replied on September 8, 1576: "I perceive that you inquire respecting the Earl of Oxford, whether he also did not recommend your cause to (Sir Amias) Paulet (the English ambassador to France). But you must know that I diligently interested myself with the Earl, who replied, that he would not only recommend his friend Sturmius to Paulet, but would also request the Earl of Leycester to recommend him in every possible way. He added also, that unless you are relieved from France, he will take care that assistance shall be obtained for you in England; lastly, that he had a most high opinion of you, and had made most honourable mention of you; which things afforded me the greatest pleasure when I heard them, and certainly ought to delight you on being informed of them." Lewin urged the Strasburg schoolmaster to "make much" of Archbishop Grindal "who is so firm and steadfast in friendship; and do not disparage this young Earl, who has so favourable an opinion of you: from both I dare hope everything, while from the one I dare promise everything." He had "heard from the Earl of Oxford" that he and Leycester would plead for Sturmius's sake to Paulet, "but do not yet understand that they have done it."[24] Oxford's ardor for Sturm was not affected in the least by the influence of his kinsmen, Lord Henry Howard and the Arundels, who were swaying him toward the Roman Catholic faith at this time: they hated the Huguenots.

When Oxford was fourteen years old the University of Cambridge gave him a more than ceremonial degree for his mastery of certain arts. He attended lectures at St John's College, where his guardian Sir William Cecil, later Lord Burghley, had acquired a modest fame for his mastery in mischief. Before his twentieth birthday the overseer of his estates paid 2 pounds, 7 shillings, 10 pence, "To William Seres, stationer, for a Geneva Bible gilt, a Chaucer, Plutarch's works in French, with other books and papers" the young Earl desired. And in the autumn of 1570 the protector of his purse spent 4 pounds, 6 shillings, 4 pence, to buy from the stationer William Seres "Tully's (Cicero's) and Plato's works in folio, with other books, paper and nibs."[25] In the same year Gabriel Harvey obtained the degree of Bachelor of Arts from Christ's College in Cambridge. Harvey never forgot how he had profited from young Oxford's admiration of scholarship after their first meeting at the University: "in the prime of his gallantest youth, he bestowed angels (gold coins with an image of archangel Michael on them slaying a dragon) upon me in Christ's College, in Cambridge, and otherwise vouchsafed me many gracious favors at the affectionate commendation of my cousin, M. (Master) Thomas Smith, the son of Sir Thomas, shortly after Colonel of the Ardes in Ireland."[26]

Master Smith was the bastard son of Sir Thomas, who seems to have been the most stimulating instructor that Edward de Vere enjoyed in his boyhood, before the elder Smith became one of Queen Bess's finest diplomats and author of *De Republica Anglorum*. We do not know which of the bewitching Harvey girls Sir Thomas se-

duced, nor when the future Colonel was born. De Vere may have
learned to like the boy Thomas in the spring of 1554, when he entered the household of Lady Philippa Smith to be tutored by her
brilliant husband in his home, Hill Hall on Theydon Mount, Essex.
Lady Philippa, by the way, was the widow of Sir John Hampden, a
gentleman of consanguinity with the first leader of the glorious
revolution that temporarily made England a republic.[27]

Sans question, Shakespeare drew the character of Holofernes for a
comic portrayal of Gabriel Harvey. The Pedant bears no resemblance naturally to his namesake, the Assyrian general of the Jewish
romance of *Judith*. To cast the infamy of the Assyrian oppressor on
the head of the Duke of Parma, whose last name, Farnese, reminded the Flemings of Judith's victim, they called the Duke
"Holofernese."[28] In my conception, Shakespeare chose the name
for Harvey's image in his comedy because he compared the Pedant
to a hollow furnace exuding smokey rhetoric and hot air. Originally
our dramatist must have recalled, in figuring the part of the Pedant,
the pathetic scholar in Francois Rabelais's epic *Gargantua and Pantagruel* who was hired by Gargantua's parents to teach their child:
"they appointed for him a great sophist-doctor called Tubal
Holofernes, who taught him his ABC so well that he could say it by
heart backward." He trained the lad to recite whole books backward, giving scarce attention to his pupil's wavering wishes to understand them. Soon, unfortunately, the sophist-doctor died of the
pox.[29] This type of teacher had been often condemned and mocked
by Sir Thomas Smith, who did not need Talleyrand to teach him
that language might have been invented to hide thought. In July
1549, when the Privy Council sent Secretary Smith to examine
Bishop Bonner about his plots to destroy the government for the
greater glory of his idol the Pope, Smith attacked the prelate for using the English language as a tool for tangling minds, and cheating
the state. He accused Bonner of employing rhetoric tricks,
"quiddities and quirks invented to delay matters."[30] Such devices of
tongue and pen were the chief consolations of Gabriel Harvey for
his intellectual lowliness.

On May 10, 1578, the Queen ended a visit of three days at Theobalds, the luxurious country home of the Earl of Oxford's father-in-law. Lord Burghley or Edward de Vere provided her with lyric entertainment, the most memorable feature of which appears to have been the rimer Thomas Churchyard's praise of Captain Martin Frobisher's voyage to the Arctic Ocean (mentioned in Harvey's Walden welcome to the Earl of Oxford). The Earl fervently believed and invested heavily in Frobisher's effort to find gold or a seaway to Cathay and India past the polar ice. It was the obsession that drove Hamlet mad "north-north-west." On May 13, Elizabeth and her bards, lords and ladies came to stay at Wanstead, the rural retreat of her darling Robin Dudley, Earl of Leycester. The prime amusement here was a softly funny play by her host's nephew, Philip Sidney, *The Lady of May.* In it we find the pedant Rombus, portrayed according to the stereotype of the schoolmaster cut in antiquity, without the warm touches of individuality that endear Shakespeare's Pedant to us. *The Lady of May* is almost entirely bereft of drama, but several phrases from it lingered in the spirit of Shakespeare, notably "all their loving labor of folly" and "long labor lost." After three days at Wanstead the Queen continued her "progress" thru the shires near London. Perhaps the keenest pleasure of the season for her was hunting, killing deer and smaller mammals, like the Princess or "Queen" in Shakespeare's comedy. She delighted in hearing poets compare her to Diana, the virgin divinity of Roman woods, and knew whom Shakespeare had in his mind's eye when he wrote the reference in the play to the moon-goddess Dictynna (4.2.36-48). She may not have known that he was thinking of Arthur Golding's version of Ovid's *Metamorphoses,* where we are flashed a vision of "Dictynna guarded with her train, and proud of killing deer."

Near the end of the Queen's Progress, she basked in the adoration of the city of Norwich, spending a week there watching the industries that multiplied her wealth, and the citizens' laborious festivities. Tom Churchyard, who strove to help them with his showmanship and riming, reported that "the substance of the whole triumph and feasting was in a manner there new to begin, for order was taken there that every day, for six days together, a show of some strange device should be seen."[31] We do not know of any production by the artisans of Norwich of the popular pageant known as the Nine Worthies, a parody of which is presented in our comedy. On August 16 there were Songs for the Queen, and two days later, a Speech delivered by somebody costumed like the god Mercury. This reminds us of the very last lines in our play: "The Words of Mercurie are harsh after the songs of Apollo. You that way, we this way." Then her Majesty enjoyed a pageant of seven female Worthies, among them the heroine of Jewish legend, Judith, the slayer of the Assyrian Holofernes.[32] English folk were very fond of seeing and hearing recitals of their sons in costume making mouth-thunder in the roles of the three famous pagans, Hector, Alexander, Caesar, the three heroic Jews, Joshua, David and Judas Maccabeus, and the three almost mythical Christians, Arthur, Charlemagne, Godfrey of Bouillon, the Crusader. The show pleased Gabriel Harvey as we know from his notebooks: in one of them he merely scribbled a short applause of "The most egregious acts, and admirable exploits of ye Nine Worthies," and in another put the rhetorical question, "Who would not rather be on (sic) of ye Nine Worthyes: then on of ye Seaven Wise masters (of the Greeks)?"[33] Harvey's enthusiasm for the martial mummery clearly provoked Shakespeare to show Holofernes proposing and performing in the Nine Worthies in the last act of *Love's Labor's Lost.*

Among the men instrumental in solemn speech-making before the Queen at Norwich was a clergyman, the Reverend Nathaniel Woods, whose memory, in my opinion, Shakespeare preserved in the comic character of the curate Nathaniel, the companion of Holofernes. On his first appearance in the play, the Reverend Nathaniel pronounces an odd comment on the deer-killing they have witnessed: "Very reverent sport, truly, and done in the testimony of a good conscience" (4.2.1). These words prompt me to suppose that the poet must have been among the noble observers in Norwich when Nathaniel Woods contrived the primitive text of the play he published in 1581, *The Conflict of Conscience.*

Both the quarto and the folio edition of the comedy drop from the breath of Nathaniel a sparkling speech which nearly every reader would deny him and grant to the Pedant. In these words the supreme dramatist mentally embraced the witty little Gabriel, acknowledging a certain singularity of their souls, their imaginations:

> This is a gift that I have, simple, simple, a foolish extravagant spirit, full of formes, figures, shapes, objects, ideas, apprehensions, motions, revolutions. These are begot in the ventricle of memory, nourisht in the womb of a pia-mater, and delivered upon the mellowing of occasion: but the gift is good in those in whom it is acute, and I am thankful for it. (4.2.65-71)

We can tell who really utters that speech from the fact that the Folio printers of 1623 foolishly followed the Quarto printers of 1598, having Holofernes respond to it with praise of the Lord and allusion to "my parishioners," whose sons, he declares, "are well tutor'd by you, and their Daughters profit very greatly under you." (4.2.72-74)

III

Whether the real Nathaniel that evoked in Shakespeare the Curate of his comedy carried a tablet to record epithets, fragrant phrases, clauses with claws, and so on, or not, the real Shakespeare, like his hero Hamlet, kept one in his pocket. It may have developed as a habit of the Earl of Oxford from the days when he studied Ovid with his uncle Arthur Golding. The latter's translation of *The First Four Books of P. Ovidius Naso's Work entitled Metamorphosis* came from Cecil House, where the boy De Vere lived as a royal ward, with a dedication to the Earl of Leycester dated December 23, 1574. The stationer William Seres printed it. And I imagine that uncle and nephew celebrated the publication at Christmas when the Children of the Queen's Chapel enacted for the Court the tragedy of *Damon and Pythias* by their music and drama master, Richard Edwards, whose poems Oxford published in the first book bearing his own, *The Paradise of Dainty Devices* (1576).

When academic and commercial craniums exalted the Stratford malt-monger as the dramatist, they found themselves instantly burdened with the task of fitting his life and labors into the biographic frame of their demigod. Shakspere (whose name was never pronounced in the way we say the writer's, but sounded more like "Shockspoor") practically learnt his art, the professors tried to persuade themselves, from playwrights he aped or copied from, whose works he retaled and retailored for the stage. The eldest of these, according to the experts on Shakspere, was John Lyly. The facts about Lyly are few, yet they suffice to correct the picture of Shakespeare parroting his inferior.

Lyly was four years younger than Edward de Vere. He came from Canterbury, where Peter his father served as chief clerk of the bishopric register. Altho his aunt married John Manwood, the brother of Sir Roger Manwood, chief baron of the state exchequer, a servant of Sir Christopher Hatton and Sir Francis Walsingham, Lyly had little political influence. He earned the Bachelor of Arts degree at Magdalen College, Oxford, granted him on April 27, 1573. But he had to beg Burghley, the Chancelor of Cambridge University, in a Latin letter of hyperbolic flattery, to commend him for a Magdalen College fellowship. (Leycester was the Chancelor of Oxford University.) In that specimen of truly beautiful penmanship, written 15 May 1574, Lyly thanked the thrifty Lord Treasurer for his "munificence." On June 1, 1575, Oxford University gave him the Master of Arts degree. Later he exprest a grudge against the College clergy for delaying his graduation; they blamed him, he claims, for "glancing at some abuses." He worded his grievance exactly like many a penman nursing tenebrous anger against barely chronicled maternity. "Yet may I of all the rest most condemne Oxford of unkindness, of vice I cannot; who seemed to weane me before I could get the teate to suck. Wherein she played the nice mother in sending me into the country to nurse, where I tyred at a dry breast three yeeres, and was at the last enforced to weane myself."[34] [So it appears that Lyly turned writer under the very motivation of milk-mania and along the same psychological path of pathos that the late

Edmund Bergler defined in his key to the creation of literature, *The Writer and Psychoanalysis* (1950).]

It has been alleged, irrationally, that Burghley gave John Lyly an obscure job in the government. William Cecil never hired any writer with an inclination to artistry to work for him, except as a spy. According to John himself, he went to work on his first book, *Euphues: The Anatomy of Wit*, for which he gained the patronage of William West, who was allowed to inherit the barony of his uncle twenty years after his failure in an attempt to poison the old man. Baron De la Warr made the attempt in the same year the Earl of Oxford was born, who became the patron of Lyly's second novel and his plays. This is how Lyly described the birth of his first books; in the dedication of *Euphues and His England*, registered by the stationers on July 24, 1579, but published in 1580:

> I have brought into the world two children; of the first I was delivered before my friends thought me conceived; of the second I went a whole year big, and yet when everyone thought me ready to lie down I did then quicken... My first burthen coming before his time must needs be a blind whelp, the second brought forth after his time must needs be a monster; the one I sent to a Nobleman to nurse, who with great love brought him up for a year, so that wheresoever he wander he hath his Nurse's name in his forehead, where sucking his first milk he cannot forget his master.

Gabriel Cawood got the license to print *Euphues* on December 2, 1578, two years and nine months after Edward de Vere came home from Italy and France, bringing new fashions of language and dress, manners and artistry, wonders of wit. I suggest that John Lyly was among the earliest Englishmen to discern the revival of culture inside the humor and glamor of the *History of Error*, which we call the *Comedy of Errors*, first performed in London in 1576. Perhaps in that very year he met the Earl of Oxford in the printing shop of the Cawoods. In April 1573 John Cawood became the husband of a niece of Sir Thomas Smith. In the same month Oxford heard the news of

the murder of his friend Colonel Thomas Smith, killed by some
Irish workers in his father's colony of the Ardes or Clanboy, a colony that failed dismally. At this time the Earl seems to have been a
resident of the Savoy in the Strand, near his father-in-law's mansion;
at least Oxford paid the rent for two tenements there occupied by
his servants John Hurleston, from a family of soldiers faithful to his
father, and Bernard Hampton, a wizard in Spanish lore, who had
served the Queen's Council as a "sufficient Castilian."[35] And John
Lyly lived in the Savoy in 1578, when, according to Gabriel Harvey,
who knew him well, "young Euphues hatched the egges, that his
elder freendes laide."[36] *Euphues* came from the Cawood press at
Christmas time, and was then, I think, subtitled *The Anatomy of Wit*,
to reap a silver harvest from the intellectual reception of *Love's Labor's Lost*, the strange play deliberately deprived of action, where the
conflict is entirely talk, and the word wit occurs almost fifty times

Did not the comedy deserve the superlatives Gabriel Harvey
piled for the poetic Earl himself in a Latin laudation he wrote in
Thomas Twyne's translation of the *Survey of the World* by Dionysius
Periegetes in 1574?

> Ver animi, corporis, fortunae aeternum
> Imprimisque florentissimae orationis
> pulcherrimum, dulcissimumque Ver.[37]

Thomas Twyne, an Oxford scholar who became a physician, dedicated to Edward de Vere in 1573 *The Breviary of Britain*. Written in
Latin by Humphrey Lhuyd... and lately Englished by Thomas
Twyne, gentleman, because of the perusal "you are accustomed to
do on books of Geography, Histories, and other good learning,
wherein I am privy your honour taketh singular delight ... "[38]

Euphues burnt the usual incense to Elizabeth, hailing her as a
princess of peace, "Against whome neyther forren force, nor civill
fraude, neyther discorde at home, nor conspiricies abroad, could
prevaile." Mildly the book mocked her courtiers—"too experte in
love, having learned in this time of their long peace, every wrinckle
that is to be seene or imagined." Lyly's hero heard that the coast of

Britain was a refuge for "such as have passed thether out of *Belgick* to search booties and to make war."[39]

However in his first play, *Alexander and Campaspe* (published in 1584) I have been able to find only one passage that might be construed as a reference to the Belgian war. The tiny comedian Manes hears that his name foretold he would run away from his master; when he asks why, Psyllus commits this pun: "You know that it is called *Mons, a movendo*, because it stands still... And thou art named Manes, a manendo, because thou runst away" (1.2). Manifestly we have here a jejune joke about the long siege of Mons by the Duc d'Alencon and his comrade Bussy d'Ambois, which in *Love's Labor's Lost* had been regarded more than charitably, as if it illustrated the motto "To the stars despite scars," or *Ad astra per aspera*. Lyly's little sarcasm flickered in the spirit of Tarleton's famous rime. In the Prologue at the Court that we read at the entrance to *Alexander and Campaspe*, you can plainly perceive how Lyly craved to please the Queen, writing in the spirit of her rebuke to Charles Blount: "we, calling Alexander from his grave, seeke only who was his love." The atmosphere of Shakespeare's comedy is reflected in the first scene of *Campaspe*, where Alexander instructs his courtiers: "Whilest armes cease, artes may flourish, and ioyning letters with launces, we endevor to be as good Philosophers as soldiers" (1.1).

The foremost French authority on Lyly's works remarked with relish that "he entered the service of the most brilliant, the most literary, and also the most levity-driven of the lords in the Court of Elizabeth."[40] Yet, while Albert Feuillerat never doubted that the Earl of Oxford had closely supervised the wit and art of John Lyly during the years when he earned the glory that still lingers round his name, the critic persistently credited Lyly with the composition of the poems that dazzle us in his plays. Nobody doubts that Lyly wrote the prose of the eight plays listed as his. When these were staged, the actors included thirty-two songs, which were left out of the original quartos of the comedies, with two exceptions "retained by an oversight, being printed as part of the dialogue... There are strong reasons for looking beyond John Lyly to discover the genius of those songs."[41]

The songs were first printed in Edward Blount's publication "*Six Court Comedies. Often presented and acted before Queen Elizabeth, by the Children of her Majesty's Chapel, and the Children of Paul's. Written by the only rare poet of that time, the witty, comical, facetiously-quick and unparalleled John Lilly, Master of Arts... London, ... 1632.*" The book was dedicated to Viscount Richard Lumley, cousin and heir of Lord John Lumley, the antiquarian and portrait-collector, the noblest friend of the Earl of Oxford next to his own cousins, the warrior Veres. The dedication, signed by Edward Blount, tho written, I feel sure, by the playwright Thomas Dekker, who died in 1632, bursts into poetry: "The spring is at hand, and therefore I present you a Lilly, growing in a Grove of Laurels. For this Poet sat at the *Sun's* table: *Apollo* gave him a wreath of his own Bays, without snatching. The Lyre he played on had no borrowed strings." Remembering how popular among Elizabethans was the Latin pun on *Ver* (spring), we wonder whether the author of this dedication recalled at whose table Lyly acquired his laurels. On a page of temptation To the Reader, "Ed. Blount" affirmed, "Oblivion shall not so trample on a son of the Muses. And such a son, as they called their Darling." (The writer could not resist an allusion to the splendid play, *The Suns's Darling*, recently written by John Ford and Thomas Dekker.) "Our Nation," he added, "are in his debt for a new English which he taught them. *Euphues and His England* began first that language: All our Ladies were then his Scholars; And that Beauty in Court, which could not Parley Euphuism, was as little regarded, as she which now there speaks not French." Frederick Fleay surmised that Dekker wrote all the songs in the *Court Comedies* because the printer included the song from *The Sun's Darling* among the more musical and merry songs, but the former lyric is hardly more than an echo of the poem in *Campaspe* about the nightingale and the lark. Walter Greg contented himself with the proof, "that in the two parts of (Lyly's) lengthy novel (*Euphues*) the only verses introduced are a copy of Latin elegies, and there is nothing either in his prose or verse to suggest that he was gifted with any lyrical aptitude."[42] Greg also pointed out that Blount made his volume out of the latest and most corrupt quartos of the Lyly plays. So the songs reached him from an independent source. My guess is they came from Lord John Lumley's priceless library. His wife, born Elizabeth Darcy, was a granddaughter of Elizabeth de Vere, an aunt of Oxford.

Twice in our comedy Don Adriano calls the child Moth to sing of love—apparently in vain (1.2). Act 3 starts with the Braggart's Boy warbling a tune evidently entitled "Concolinel." Otherwise the comedy contains no songs until the very end, when Shakespeare springs on us the two contrasting chants concerning the cuckoo and the owl, which remind us remotely of the song in *Campaspe* about the birds of the dusk and the dawn. An American scholar noticed that Shakespeare's two melodies recall the song contest in the August eclogue of Edmund Spenser's *Shepherds' Calendar* (1579). Too long ago John Thomas Looney had noticed that Spenser's counterpoint in rime reflected a peculiar feud between Sir Philip Sidney and Earl Edward de Vere, of which we have a vestige in their verses about Oxford's dream of being a king.[43]

IV

Sidney and Oxford may have been rivals in their youth for the favor of Anne Cecil, whom her father had engaged to marry Sidney, but determined to make the bride of the Earl when he found the Queen willing to promote him to the barony of Burghley, probably because Edward desired Anne. The gallant Earl never consented to the opinion of his teacher Sir Thomas Smith uttered at the Court of King Charles IX in April 1565. The French King told Sir Thomas that he loved Queen Elizabeth. "Your Majesty does not know yet what love is," the genial English envoy remarked, "but you will soon go thru it. It is the most foolish, impotent and disrespectful thing possible!" (Smith seems to have been unaware of the young King's lifelong love of his mother, which made affairs with any other females most foolish for him.)

De Vere's name was not linked with a single girl's name until 28 July 1571, when Lord St John informed Edward Manners, Earl of Rutland, who had also been educated in William Cecil's home as a royal ward: "The Earl of Oxford hath gotten him a wife—or at the least a wife hath caught him; this is Mistress Anne Cecil; whereunto the Queen hath given her consent, and the which hath caused great weeping, wailing, and sorrowful cheer of those that had hoped to have that golden day."[44] Earlier in July, the Queen remarked to the French ambassador La Mothe Fenelon that, "considering her time of life, she should be ashamed to be conducted to church to be married to anyone looking as young as the Earl of Oxford." She was examining a crayon portrait of Henri de Valois, the Duc d'Anjou, who had formally offered to make her his wife. The Duke, said she, was nearly the same age as De Vere.[45] What made her think of Oxford in talking with the Frenchman, we cannot tell. In June she had strolled with Fenelon in Westminster park and witnessed a salute of artillery and a review of arquebusiers under the command of Edward of Oxford. Her dialog with Fenelon on this occasion concerned the Anjou proposal, warmly advocated in the Court by Thomas Howard, Duke of Norfolk, "the leader of the ancient nobility," whose father the poetic Henry Howard, Earl of Surrey, had married Oxford's aunt Frances. Norfolk, by the way, had been secretly encouraged by Sir William Cecil to pursue his prospect of marrying Mary Stuart, the fugitive Queen of Scotland.[46] All the courts of Western Europe seem to have heard the rumor that Don John of Austria was jealous of the English Duke. On December 19, 1571, the wedding of Edward and Anne entertained an uncounted crowd of the curious in Westminster Abbey. Fenelon informed the King of France that Elizabeth "took me with her to dine with Lord Burghley, who was celebrating the marriage of his daughter to the Earl of Oxford."[47]

In April 1572, a week before Oxford's twenty-second birthday, he heard the gossip from Paris about the marriage that royalty in France and Navarre arranged for Henri de Bourbon and Marguerite de Valois. Pope Gregory XIII gave his dispensation for the union of the Catholic and the Calvinist after Pius V had absolutely refused. The "sweet little Countess of Oxford," as Leycester's brother Ambrose, the Earl of Warwick, called the new Anne de Vere, suffered from the fury of her husband against her father, who had cold-bloodedly plotted for the Duke of Norfolk's head. Oxford broke away from her, and the civilian dynasty of the Cecils, by voyaging to Belgium at the end of June 1574, ostensibly for the sake of studying warfare at close range. The Queen, raging, sent his friend Thomas Bedingfield, the translator of Italian books dear to Oxford, to fetch the Earl back to idleness, the coquetry of her Maids of Honour, and other games that amused him.

Among the games furnishing fun for the Earl in December 1574 was the unhappy attempt of Norfolk's son Philip Howard, Lord Surrey, his cousin, to seduce Mercy, the sister of Gabriel Harvey. On Sunday, December 26, Gabriel recorded in a diary that "Phil" had vainly tried to ravish Mercy, but her Puritan training succeeded in overcoming the allurements of "Don Jamy," as Philip whimsically called himself.[48] I presume he took this title to honor Saint James of Spain, Iago of Compostella, whose church he wished to kneel in all his life. The miserable romance in Saffron Walden was eclipsed by Lord Philip's martyrdom in prison for conspiring with Rome and Madrid against the Tudor church and state. In 1886 the Vatican elevated him to the "Venerable" sphere and (the last time I inquired) he was well on the way to Sainthood.

On January 7, 1575, with the Queen's license for a tour of Europe, Edward de Vere departed from her Court and went on his way to Paris. When the English ambassador, Valentine Dale, presented him to King Henri III, the former Duc d'Anjou inquired whether he was married. It was the ambassador who answered, "I said he had a fair lady." The French monarch declared they must be "*un beau couple*." Oxford surely thanked him for the compliment, and withdrew. On receiving the news from Burghley in mid-March, that Countess Anne would become a mother in a few months, he wrote letters of somewhat stiff "contentation." He refused to turn back to his wife, and requested funds to support his plans for a visit to Venice, perhaps Constantinople, "and some part of Greece." In the city commonly extolled as sacred to Venus, the Earl learnt about the birth of his daughter Elizabeth on July 2. Lord Burghley deliberately neglected to preserve the letters that Oxford *certainly* wrote to his wife. The letters from the Earl's Italian travels he did preserve tell us nothing about his feelings of fatherhood; they resound with complaints over money, the sale of his lands, his expenses in various towns. The Venetian envoy to France reported his arrival in Paris on April 3, 1576. He landed in London on April 20, and would not say a word to Burghley and his Countess when they approached to embrace him. Lord Harry Howard, the late Norfolk's brother, promised Burghley to keep him informed about Oxford's movements and meditations. However, Cecil, the overseer of England's secret service, never left a single document concerning the "mislikes" and "disgrace" which De Vere lamented the Countess had brought on his head.

The Earl gave her the house in Wivenhoe where he fantasied the Muses came to inspire him by the sea, and also the lodging he rented for her in the Savoy. She preferred to remain, like Niobe or a tearful nun, in her parents' house nearby. The Earl endeavored to submerge his grief of guilt and remorse in various beverages and by writing plays, comedies and romances, alternately, in his lonely Anglo-Italian style. They proved the insight of the Princess in *Love's Labor's Lost* (4.1.30-33):

> And out of question, so it is sometimes,
> Glory grows guilty of detested crimes,
> When, for fame's sake, for praise, an outward part,
> We bend to that the working of the heart.

The Queen and her environers delighted in "The History of the Solitary Knight" (later titled *Pericles, Prince of Tyre*), "A Moral of the Marriage of Mind and Measure" (now named *The Taming of the Shrew*), and "The Rape of the Second Helen" (afterward called *All's Well That Ends well*).[49]

Meanwhile he regaled his drink-companions, the Howards,

Arundels, Southwells and Yorkes, with cascades of dramatic mono-
log, his imaginary adventures on the continent, his opinions on politics or rather politicians, and his beliefs about love and lovers.
Charles Arundel reported several years later a fantasy of Oxford
which he had nearly convinced himself was true: "That the Queen
of Navarre sent a messenger to desire him to speak with her in her
chamber," during his last visit to Paris, I suppose.[50] We may be sure
that the Princess of France who is adored in Act 4, Scene 3, with
the words "O Queene of Queenes," was shaped in the image of
Marguerite of Navarre. But the King Ferdinand of the comedy is
not individual enough to identify with Henri de Bourbon, her warrior husband, or any personality of the period.

Don Adriano is merely a scorn-sketch of Don John, and I derive
his name as Eva Turner Clark did. Shakespeare may have been
thinking of Captain Alfonso Adriano, author of *Della Disciplina Mili-
tare* (1566) when he created Armado. Certainly he had Queen Mary
Stuart in view when he made the character of Armado's country
wench Jaquenetta. Her name may be Englished "Little James," and
recalls at once the captive Queen's father, James V, and her son,
who became the first James to wear the British crown. Jaquenetta
also reminds us of Mary's last husband, James Hepburn, Earl of
Bothwell, who died crazy in captivity. The first scene of our play
alludes to Mary's imprisonment. Jaquenetta, we learn, is kept "as a
vessell of thy Lawes furie, and shall at the least" of royal notice, be
fetched to trial. (1.1.259-262)

In January 1577 Edward Horsey enjoyed an interveiw with Don
John. He told the blond Spaniard that rumors were spreading in
England that his army would quit the Low Countries and try to dis-
embark in Britain for the purpose of liberating Mary from the castle
where Queen Bess kept her. Don Juan smiled and said he had no
such hostile aim in mind. But on April 28 Sir Amias Paulet wrote to
Walsingham that he had learnt from the secretary of the Duc de
Guise, a marriage was devised between Mary and Don John.[51]

More fascinating to our dramatist was the courtship of his
Queen by Hercules d'Alencon, which accounts for many, if not all

the allusions to Hercules the Greek hero and ill-fated lover strewn tantalisingly thru our comedy. When Armado asks in the second scene, "Comfort me, Boy. What great men have been in love?" Moth answers immediately, "Hercules, Master," which makes his master extol "Most sweet Hercules." Later he dampens his own spirit with the suspicion, "Cupid's But-shaft is too hard for Hercules' Clubbe." In the second scene of the fourth act Holofernes is lauded by the innocent Nathaniel with a blindly bawdy pun on his membership in the commonwealth. The Pedant responds with a chastely classical invocation of the Roman god of virility, *Me hercule*. (Oddly, Eric Partridge omitted the word member from the "Comprehensive Glossary" of his book *Shakespeare's Bawdy*, tho he was aware that later lines in the same scene form "one of the most 'greasy' passages in the whole of Shakespeare.")[52] In another scene the "merry madcap Lord" Berowne, having observed his monarch sighing and sonneting for love, laughs at the spectacle: "To see a King transformed to a Gnat?/To see great Hercules whipping a Gigge" (4.3.162-163). Later Berowne redeems his fame for swift-darting dialectic metaphor by praising love as a spur to courage, again conjuring up the namesake of Alencon: "For Valour, is not Love a Hercules?/Still climbing trees in the Hesperides." But at the close of the play, the page Moth among the Nine Worthies assumes the posture of Hercules himself, introduced as an infant by the bookbug because "when he was a babe, a childe, a shrimpe,/Thus did he strangle Serpents in his *Manus*." Apparently the Imp here did something ludicrous with a stage-snake, perhaps mimicking manustrupation, as the word was spelled in *The Anatomy of Melancholy* (1621). By the time our dramatist revised and augmented the play for printing in 1598, that was all he left of its former references to the French hero and the Greek god he was named after.

Everyone consents that the principal character in the comedy, the most lively and attractive, is the noble humorist Berowne, named after the Marshal Armand de Gontaut, Baron de Biron, who fought for a strictly Catholic France against the Huguenots in battles that gained him the rank of grand master of artillery in 1569 and marshal of France in 1577, as well as the Dukedom of Biron. On March 26, 1577, he signed a truce with his adversary Henri of Navarre. When King Henri III was murdered in 1589, by the monk Jacques Clement, Marshal Biron was among the first to uphold the claim of the King of Navarre to the crown of France. As early as August 1570, when he took an energetic part in the treaty of St Germain, he moderated his Catholic loyalty to the extent of granting the Huguenots freedom of conscience but public worship according to their creed only in two towns in each province. On July 26, 1578, the English ambassador Paulet wrote to Walsingham, "Marshal Biron continues in his old seditious humor, and has done enough of late to renew civil troubles in the realm."[53] What precisely this meant, none can say. He did not belong to the faction of "Malcontents" who clustered round the Duc d'Alencon. (Shakespeare refers to them in his comedy, where Berowne calls Cupid "Liedge of all loyterers and malecontents"–3.1.180) Old Biron contributed valiantly to the victories of his Huguenot King before he was killed in the siege of Epernay on July 26, 1592. Nobody ever accused him of being a "merry madcap Lord," and Shakespeare's protagonist resembles him only as any nobleman might. The courtier in the comedy bears the name Berowne for the same reason that Shakespeare changed the name of the hero in *Love's Labor's Won* or *All's Well That Ends Well* from Beltramo to Bertram. In both cases the dramatist gave his favorite personages the first syllable *Ber* for no other reason than its pun potential, its nearness to the Latin name for Spring, of which we are reminded at the end of *Love's Labor's Lost*, when Ver is called on to begin the song of the cuckoo.

The description of Berowne given by his prime charmer Rosaline fits no courtier of Queen Elizabeth better than Edward de Vere.

> Berowne they call him; but a merrier man,
> Within the limit of becoming mirth,
> I never spent an houres talke withall.
> His eye begets occasion for his wit,
> For every obiect that the one doth catch,
> The other turnes to a mirth-moving iest,

> Which his faire tongue (conceits expositor)
> Delivers in such apt and gracious words,
> That aged eares play treuant at his tales,
> And yonger hearings are quite ravished.
> So sweet and voluble is his discourse. (2.1.66-76)

In the final scene Rosaline tells him to his face the chief fault of his merriment.

> Oft have I heard of you, my Lord Berowne,
> Before I saw you: and the worlds large tongue
> Proclaimes you for a man repleate with mockes,
> Full of comparisons, and wounding floutes:
> Which you on all estates will execute,
> That lie within the mercie of your wit. (5.2.825-830)

Perhaps the keenest testimony to aid us in identifying Shakespeare's protagonist may be found in Sir Walter Raleigh's letter to Burghley of May 12, 1583, promising to use his influence with the Queen to restore the Earl of Oxford to imperial generosity:

> And the more to witness how desirous I am of your Lordship's favour and good opinion, I am content, for your sake, to lay the serpent before the fire as much as in me lieth, that, having recovered strength, myself may be most in danger of his poison and sting.[54]

In *The Man Shakespeare and His Tragic Life Story*, Frank Harris's hopelessly spoiled masterpiece (1909), he avers emphatically, "The chief academic critics, such as Professor (Edward) Dowden and Dr. (Georg) Brandes, take pains to inform us that Biron in *'Love's Labour's Lost'* is nothing but an impersonation of Shakespeare." Dowden did not dare to go so far; he claimed only that Berowne was "the exponent of Shakspere's (*sic*) own thought," speaking out against the illusions of culture which look down on passion and the flesh. "Not that Shakspere is hostile to culture; but he knows that a perfect education must include the culture, through actual experi-

ence, of the senses and of the affections."[55] Dowden believed that
the Stratford rabbit-robber, the elder Anne Hathaway's seducer or
else seducee, "had graduated in the school of life" before he set to
work on his comedy of Court conversation. Brandes, also taking
seriously the play's pretense that the Court of Navarre would be
turned into libraries and laboratories, agrees that Shakespeare pleads
"Against this life of unnatural constraint... with the voice of Nature,
especially through the mouth of Biron, in whose speeches, as Dowden has rightly remarked, not infrequently we can catch the accent
of Shakespeare himself."[56] Neither of these critics dreamed that the
dramatist intended Berowne as an image of himself. Like Walter
Pater, the university recluse, they saw the play as a satire on Euphuism, its affectation and foppery of speech, the fashion of showing
off learning, which Pater discerned "had some fascination for the
young Shakspere himself": "he is the analyst of its curious charm in
Biron," the scholar said; "and this analysis involves a delicate raillery
by Shakspere himself at his own chosen manner." The arrogant
Harris never quoted Pater's recognition that there are "certain of his
characters in which we feel that there is something of self-
portraiture," and "Biron, in *Love's Labour's Lost*, is perhaps the most
striking of this group. In this character, which is never quite in
touch, never quite on a perfect level of understanding, with the
other persons of the play, we see, perhaps a reflex of Shakespeare
himself, when he has just become able to stand aside from and estimate the first period of his poetry."[57] Harris remarked that Samuel
Taylor Coleridge had said the same thing nearly a century before,
and said it better. Moreover, Harris added, Coleridge declared the
whole comedy revealed the writer "as in a portrait taken of him in
his boyhood."[58]

The writings of Coleridge on Shakespeare are brief yet more illu-
minating than all the critics I have quoted here. Consider, for instance, his question: "Where, from observation, could he learn the
language proper to Sovereigns, Queens, Noblemen, or Generals?
yet he invariably uses it." Quoting the speech by Othello in which
he declares, "I fetch my life and being/From men of royal

siege" (1.2), Coleridge noted, "I ask where was Shakspere to observe such language as this? If he did observe it, it was with the inward eye of meditation upon his own nature."[59] In other words, the
poet had a kingly soul. Consequently Coleridge rejected with scorn
the popular conception of Shakespeare as a man who never underwent intellectual discipline, a jack-of-arts together with trades, in
quest of funds rather than fame.

> "And ask your own hearts," Coleridge exhorted, "—ask your
> own common-sense—to conceive the possibility of this man be-
> ing—I say not, the drunken savage of that wretched sciolist
> (Voltaire), whom Frenchmen, to their shame, have honoured
> before their elder and better worthies—but the anomalous, the
> wild, the irregular, genius of our daily criticism! What! are we to
> have miracles in sport?—Or, I speak reverently, does God
> choose idiots by whom to convey divine truths to man?" [60]

Poor Coleridge answered his own question by carefully refraining
from inquiry into the Stratford-on-Avon legend or lies. With his
own brain ruined by opium (prescribed for him by physicians in-
toxicated by the tales of miraculous medicine that the East India
Company magnates spread in the British press free of charge), he
could not work to unravel the real biography of the creator of
Berowne and Macbeth. Nevertheless, in 1802 Coleridge ventured an
arrangement of Shakespeare's plays in what he termed a
"psychological" order, which placed "The old Taming of the
Shrew," *Pericles*, *All's well That Ends well*, and *The Two Gentlemen of Verona*, even a "first draft" of Romeo and Juliet, earlier than *Love's Labor's Lost*.[61] Of course he would have included the *Comedy of Errors*
among the pioneer plays, if he had remembered it while privately
drawing up that "psychological" list. He lacked armor to maintain
the stand he took in 1802; academic clamor compelled him to retreat into the affirmation that *Love's Labor's Lost* must have been the
artist's earliest drama.

Still, the author of the *Ancient Mariner* and *Kubla Khan* realised,
"how strong a presumption the diction and allusions of this play

afford, that, though Shakspere's acquirements in the dead languages might not be such as we suppose in a learned education, his habits had, nevertheless, been scholastic, and those of a student. *For a young author's first work almost always bespeaks his recent pursuits*, and his first observations of life are either drawn from the immediate employments of his youth, and from the characters and images most deeply impressed on his mind in the situations in which those employments had placed him;—or else they are fixed on such objects and occurrences in the world, as are easily connected with, and seem to bear upon, his studies and the hitherto exclusive subjects of his meditation." (Emphasis added)[62]

Among the listeners to Coleridge's wonderful lectures on our poet was a gentleman named Henry Holgate Carwardine who came from Colne Priory, Essex. If only Coleridge could have listened to what Mr Carwardine could tell him about Colne Priory, and its ancient tombs of the Earls of Oxford, a short distance from the old Norman structure of Castle Hedingham, the birthplace of the seventeenth Earl, Edward de Vere. Would not the imagination of Coleridge have been wonderfully kindled to learn about this prodigy and his lyric gift, his enthusiasm for the theater, his three weird daughters and two sons (one illegitimate), and his untimely silence in 1604? We might not have had to wait a hundred years for the revelation of the true Shakespeare. Coleridge's hawkeyed friend Charles Lamb might have made it if he did not!

Any of the Elizabethan playwrights could have named a stage character Boyet after the Huguenot veteran of the civil wars, Captain Poyet, who served under Lodowick of Nassau under the Dutch flag, and for a short time became Governor of Mons. One need not have been a noble to learn that Henri of Navarre wrote his love letters with words pouring over margins, and some where his seal covers the script. Somehow our dramatist acquired this peculiar fact, and dropt it from the lips of his Princess in the play: "Writ o both sides the leafe," says she, holding up a sheet from her royal lover to her ladies, "margent and all, / That he was faine to seale on Cupids name" (5.2.). A few of the visually educated writers for the Tudor stage could have composed the line comparing Eros with "Signior Junios gyant dwarfe" (3.1.), which John Upton recognised as an error in 1746, since it could only refer to the picture of the bearded dwarf Gradasso that the painter Giulio Romano, Raphael's pupil, put, nearly naked and smiling under a crownlike hat, among the soldiers of Constantine on the wall of the Vatican palace. Giulio Romano is the single Renaissance artist named by Shakespeare in all his works. The Earl of Oxford saw marvels from his brush on the Gonzaga palace walls in Mantua when he visited that city in 1575, and again in 1576.

Others could have dared to include among the courtiers of Navarre a man of the house of "Dumaine," altho the actual Duc de Mayenne, Charles de Guise, was one of the fiercest Catholics against Navarre. Mayenne indeed was the son of Queen Mary Stuart's uncle. King Henri wrote of his relief in 1576 because "Monsieur de Guise and Monsieur du Maine do not budge but with me." Mayenne attacked him in May 1580 when he tried to take Cahors. Shakespeare's Dumaine is entirely of his own making, like the Captain Dumaine whom he set as a comrade of Count Bertram in *All's well*.

What however stimulated the dramatist to write the little dialog in which Rosaline remarks to Katherine about Cupid, "You'll nere be friends with him; a kild your sister." And Katherine comments: "He made her melancholy, sad, and heavy, and so she died: Had she beene Light like you, of such a merrie nimble stirring spirit, she might a bin a Grandam ere she died. And so may you: For a light heart lives long" (5.2 13-18). Walter Pater pointed to these lines as "one of the most touching things in older literature." And H. C. Hart, in his edition of the drama, inquired: "Does not this passage point to some historical source of the plot, some undeveloped portion of a parent-tale?"[63]

We owe the discovery of Shakespeare's source to the rare scholarship of Abel Lefranc (1863-1952) who collected details of Queen Marguerite's journeys in 1578 to her brother in Belgium and her husband in Gascony, and showed how well acquainted Shakespeare was with these events. (Yet Professor Lefranc fondly adhered to the theory that William Stanley, Earl of Derby, Oxford's son-in-law, was the real William Shakespeare. The fact that Stanley was only seventeen when the events inspiring *Love's Labour's Lost* occurred hardly troubled him, altho he remained a lifelong student of the De Vere theory.)

Lefranc discovered that in June 1577 a young lady named Helene de Tournon, in the retinue of Marguerite de Valois, died when they were encouraging Alencon in Brabant. The bruit ran that she died of a sharp disenchantment in love.[64] So enchanted was Lefranc with her tragedy that he missed the prophecy in the little dialog, that Rosaline, that is, the lady she stood for in the comedy, would survive all arrows of Eros that reached her heart. For this is the same Rosaline who, in *As You Like It* (4.1), affirms: "Men have died from time to time and worms have eaten them, but not for love," without breathing a word about woman's fate in such affairs.

Perhaps the most personal tones in the comedy can be heard in these rimes of Rosaline (5.2.60-68):

> That same Berowne Ile torture ere I goe.
> O that I knew he were but in by th'weeke,
> How I would make him fawne, and begge, and seeke,
> And wait the season, and observe the times,
> And spend his prodigall wits in booteles rimes,
> And shape his service wholly to my hests,
> And make him proud to make me proud that jests.

The following line contained in the quarto text a word, "perttaunt," that no scholar could interpret intelligibly to our satisfaction until Leon Kellner wrote his ingenious scrutiny of Shakespeare's handwriting as demonstrated in the oldest editions of the dramas. Kellner's chirographic work, *Restoring Shakespeare* (New York 1925) proposed (on page 9) to change the queer word, a printer's blunder, to Partlet. And there was light.

> So Partlet-like would I o'resway his state,
> That he should be my foole, and I his fate.

The pun on fool and fowl proves Kellner correct; the line refers to Dame Partlet the hen, beloved by the bird Chanticleer in Chaucer's famous Canterbury Tale. Edward de Vere and Edmund Spenser were among the rare Englishmen who esteemed Chaucer's solitary art. Gabriel Harvey must have listened to them extolling the old poet for his "wit, pleasant vein, variety of poetical discourse, and all humanity. I specially note," said he, his "Astronomy, philosophy and other parts of profound or cunning art."[65]

When Rosaline commands Berowne to devote a whole year to amusing sick folk "With all the fierce endeavour of your wit" (5.2.587), her admirer promises, "Ile iest a twelvemonth in an Hospitall." To detect the joke in his assurance, you would have to know that Berowne was meant to represent the Earl of Oxford, who resided in the Savoy Hospital. He supported John Lyly in an apartment there. A short walk westward by the Thames river would bring him to Yorke House where the cynical soldier Rowland Yorke lived, whom Lord Burghley certainly knew was a ringleader among Oxford's "lewd friends" who had "enticed him to be a stranger to his wife." Incidentally, Queen Bess never seems to have objected to Oxford's treatment of poor Countess Anne; and none of the aristocrats in our comedy represents her.

V

Mary Stuart in her castle captivity heard the gossip of the Court, and rebuked Elizabeth for keeping Earl Edward and his grieving mate apart. The form of the fact that reached her ears was recorded in a letter to Elizabeth: "Even the Earl of Oxford doesn't dare to reconcile with his wife for fear of losing the favor that he expects to receive by making love to you."[66] De Vere was indeed making oblique love to her Majesty: the amorous rimes in our comedy bear abundant witness to his expectations. And it is not by chance that the dramatist contrived to mask Berowne in the role of Navarre's King to play the lover for the Princess or "Queen" from the north.

Nevertheless, the fire of love in Berowne's heart turns most in-

tensely and above all toward the lady Rosaline, "The heire of Alan-
son" (2.1.). For *Love's Labor's Lost* Shakespeare drew the portrait of
the woman who seems to be almost the demidivinity of his life with
words that "sparcle still the right promethean fire" (4.3.325).
Berowne upbraids himself for adoring her:

> Nay, to be periurde, which is worst of all:
> And among three, to love the worst of all,
> A whitely wanton, with a velvet brow,
> With two pitch bals strucke in her face for eyes.
> I, and by heaven, one that will doe the deede,
> Though Argus were her Eunuch and her garde.
> And I to sigh for her, to watch for her,
> To pray for her, go to: it is a plague
> That Cupid will impose for my neglect,
> Of his almighty dreadfull little might. (3.1.191-200)

This pallid lady with the black orbs is portrayed as equal to Berowne
in duels of wit. After some brief and fast talk about a time they
danced together, he complains, "Your wit's too hot, it speeds too
fast, 'twill tire." Promptly she replies, "Not till it leave the Rider in
the mire" (2.1.120). When he taunts her for predilection to "the
deed," wishing her "many lovers," she dismisses him with a curt
"Amen, so you be none." Later, when Berowne confesses to the
King that in her beauty he sees "the Sunne that maketh all things
shine," Ferdinand exclaims, "By heaven, thy Love is blacke as
Ebonie." "Is Ebonie like her?" Berowne wonders. "O word divine!
A wife of such wood were felicitie" (4.3.243-245). But he keeps
quiet when Dumaine remarks, "I never knew a man hold vile stuffe
so deere." The slander aids us in identifying Rosaline, for we hear
the charge thru all the years, and they were long, Anne Vavasor
lived.

Shakespeare would have seen at once that the last two syllables
of her name spelt backward yielded the name Rosa. But what could
he contrive out of Vav? The problem appears to have been solved
before he encountered her, by the great British poet Edmund

Spenser. In October 1579 Spenser assured Gabriel Harvey that his *Shepherd's Calendar* had been "made in honor of a private Personage unknown, which of some ill-willers might be upbraided not to be so worthy, as you know she is." Harvey gave away part of the secret in *Three Proper and Witty Familiar Letters, lately passed between two University men*, in 1580. Here Harvey repeated a letter he sent to Spenser on April 24, 1579, enclosing a poem he wrote for his friend to one whose "deserts are such," he warbled, "That no one in this world can love thee too much." To Spenser he sent cold comfort: "you charge me somewhat suspiciously with an old promise; to deliver you of that jealousy. I am so far from hiding mine own matters from you that lo, I must needs be revealing my friend's secrets, now an honest Country Gentleman, sometimes a Scholar: At whose request I bestowed this palting bungerly rime upon him, to present his Mistress withal. The parties shall be nameless: saving that the Gentlewoman's true, or counterfeit Christian name must necessarily be bewrayed." So the pedant addrest his drastic verses to "my good Mistress Anne: the very life of my life, and only beloved Mistress."[67] In the same letter Harvey chatters concerning Spenser: "Gentle Mistress Rosalinde once reported you to have all the Intelligences at commandment, and (at) another time christened you her Signior Pegaso."[68] Now what inspired Spenser to call Mistress Anne "Rosalind"?

He too naturally would have observed how the reversal of "asor" made poetry of the girl's name. In his juvenile pursuit of erudition Spenser learnt more than enough of the Hebrew language to know that its letter *Vav* was drawn as a mere line. Therefor he would have converted Vavasor to Rosaline in a flash, since he was well aware that the line in England signified the lime or linden tree, one particularly precious to lovers who believed that its leaf verily looked like a heart. In medieval folklore about the tree Jesus emerges imposing on the harlot Mary Magdalene a penance of long lying supine on linden leaves, eating them for her nurture, and drinking only their dew.[69]

The Earl of Oxford would have been interested also to hear that

Anne Vavasor came from Copmanthorpe near Hazlewood, a very old village in Yorkshire, on the little stream called Cock opposite the battlefield of Towton, where Edward IV in 1461 defeated the Lancastrian warriors led by Queen Margaret of Anjou. He certainly knew that her family cherished Roman Catholic sympathies, and had joined the Percys and Fairfaxes in the middle of May 1568 when they rode to welcome Mary Stuart at Carlisle when she crossed the Solway in flight from the Protestant Scots. Anne was not yet seven years old when her father rode to greet Queen Mary. Two years later she may have glimpsed the young Earl of Oxford, twenty years old, riding by the side of the Earl of Sussex in the latter's cruel drive from his headquarters in York to crush the Catholic rebels in the north, and instruct their friends in Scotland to quiver with terror when invited to war against the Tudor dynasty.

According to Eva Turner Clark's research in the records of Yorkshire, Anne's mother Margaret was the daughter of Sir Henry Knevitt of Charlton, Wiltshire. According to Edmund K. Chambers, the authority on Shakespeare, mother Margaret Vavasor was the daughter of Henry Knyvet of Buckenham, Norfolk.[70] Whichever lineage is correct, Anne Vavasor on both her father's and mother's side may have been a kinswoman of Edmund Spenser. For her sister Margaret married Miles Southwell, the son of Barbara Spencer; and mother Margaret's sister Katherine married Lord Henry Paget, whose mother was a Spenser. In 1573 Edmund Spenser obtained the Bachelor of Arts degree from Pembroke Hall, Cambridge University, where he won the affection of the student Gabriel Harvey, whom he calls Hobbinol in the *Shepherds' Calendar*. Himself he named in the pastoral poems Colin Clout. The first writer of commentary on the *Calendar*, who called himself E. K. (which I interpret to mean Edward Knight), said that Hobbinol hunted for Colin's love every day. This, he deplored, "seemeth to be some savour of disorderly love, which the learned call paederastice; but it is gathered beside his meaning."[71] Colin hands over to his beloved Rosalind the gifts of Hobbinol. This could not have happened in reality, for Spenser's romance with Rosalind began some time after he became a Master of Arts at Cambridge in 1576 and went north, to brood over his destiny, perhaps with relatives. The January eclog of the *Calendar* already laments "his unfortunate love, being but newly (as semeth) enamoured of a country lasse called Rosalinde."

> I curse that carefull hower,
> Wherein I longed the neighbour towne to see ...
> I blesse the stoure,
> Wherein I sawe so fayre a sight, as shee.

The "stour" (stir, misfortune) that Spenser refers to, I imagine was a funeral in Anne Vavasor's family. The April poem speaks of Rosalind as "the Widdowes daughter of the glenne." E. K. warns the reader to beware of mistaking her for a rustic wench. "For it is well knowen, even in spighte of Colin and Hobbinoll, that shee is a Gentle woman of no meane house, nor endewed with anye vulgare and common gifts both of nature and manners." The January Gloss informs us that Rosalind is "a feigned name, which, being wel ordered, wil bewray the very name of hys love and mistresse, whom by that name he coloureth." Colin regrets that she scorned his pastoral verse, altho he modeled the poems in the fashion of the French master-artist Pierre Ronsard in his *Amours*.

> She deignes not my good will, but doth reprove,
> And of my rurall musick holdeth scorne,
> Shepheards devise she hateth as the snake,
> And laughes the songes, that Colin Clout doth make.

To "color" the beloved more and steer the readers astray from her identity, Spenser, singing "Who knows not Rosalind?" gave her "golden locks" in the June rimes. But the main purpose of this month's poem was to mourn over her seduction by Menalcas—whoever he was—and subsequent diversion to scandalous affairs: "her floure is woxe a weede," Spenser grieves.

> And thou Menalcas, that by treacheree
> Didst underfong my lasse, to wexe so light,

Shouldest well be knowne for such thy villanee.

Underfong means "deceive by false suggestion." The word "light" here reminds me of its usage in the last act of *Love's Labor's Lost* where Katherine remarks to Rosalind, "a light heart lives long," and the dark lady challenges her, "What's your darke meaning, mouse, of this light word?" Katherine replies, cryptically, "A light condition in a beauty darke," which forces Rosalind to pursue the duet: We need more light to finde your meaning out.

> *Katherine.* You'll marre the light by taking it in snuffe:
> Therefore Ile darkely end the argument.

But Rosalind will not let her go so blithely. "Look what you doe, you doe it stil i' th' darke. So do not you," says Katherine, "for you are a light Wench" (5.2.24-25).

I consider Menalcas to have been in actuality a distant cousin of Anne Vavasor and Edward de Vere, the treacherous courtier Charles Arundel, who became several years after this romance of Rosalind an agent on the payroll of Spain. I believe that she is the Lady to whom Arundel wrote a letter on May 1 of an uncertain year, vowing a passion perfect for her, summarised centuries later as follows: "Sorry he has not oftener had occasion to express his love and friendly disposition toward her, which is now in that degree of perfection that it cannot take any increase. His love to her has led him to deal with her sister (Frances, a younger girl, who became a royal Maid of Honor), that she might utter his mind to her."[72]

Hobbinol in the *Calendar* pleads with his disillusioned friend, "Forsake the soyle, that so doth thee bewitch." And E. K. noted that the poet, "for speciall occasion of private affayres (as I have bene partly of him selfe informed) and for his preferment removing out of the North parts came into the South, as Hobbinoll indeede advised him." Evidently Spenser left York about the autumn of 1577 and went down to Kent where the Bishop of Rochester may have employed him for a year. Harvey alluded to such service in a letter of April 1579 telling Spenser, "Imagine me to come into a goodly Kentish garden of your old Lord."[73] When Spenser arrived in London he set to work on the *Shepherds' Calendar* and dedicated it to Sir Philip Sidney, who praised it in his *Defense of Poetry* thus: "The Shepherds' Calendar hath much poetry in his Eclogues, indeed worthy the reading, if I be not deceived. That same framing of his style to an old rustic language I dare not allow, since neither Theocritus in Greek (pastoral), Virgil in Latin, nor Sannazar in Italian did affect it." Luckily for literature, Spenser did not consult Sidney while warbling the Eclogues in their delightful Lancashire dialect, evidently his native tongue. His friend E. K. produced an introductory letter to Gabriel Harvey for the book, dated April 10, 1579. We have no idea of the date of Anne Vavasor's arrival in London to enter the service of the Queen as a Gentlewoman of her Majesty's Bedchamber. When Colin Clout began singing love lyrics again, twelve years later, the lady of his song was extolled as "The floure of vertue and pure chastitie."[74]

Between the fall of 1578 and August 1580, when Spenser traveled to Ireland, the luminous comedies by the poet whom he hailed as "Our pleasant Willy" were gracing the London stage. (See the Thalia section of his *Tears of the Muses*.)

Anne Vavasor unquestionably enjoyed the different modes by which the Queen's courtiers attempted to sever her virgin zone. From the start of her Bedchamber employment she found a protector in her uncle, Sir Thomas Knyvet, a man who comprehended how to take advantageous care of his person and purse. As early as 1576, he successfully appealed to the Lord Treasurer and the Privy Council that they should exempt him, on account of business considerations, from having to captain a company of volunteers in the Low Countries.[75] Knyvet or Knevet appears in our play, as Thomas Looney observed, in the role of Boyet, "honey-tongued Boyet," whose name recalls the old English word Knave meaning boy. Shakespeare described him at length: He is wit's pedlar, "can carve too, and lisp," a "most tender-smelling knight," he smiles on everyone, but likes best to "pin the wenches on his sleeve, an old lovemonger." When he gambled he chided the dice in nearly reverential terms. But he sang "meanly," prefering to whisper rumors, "carry-tale" and "mumble-news" When he makes fun of the Nine Worthies, however, Berowne applauds him in the last words he pronounces to Boyet: "Well said, old mocker, I must needs be friends with thee." (5.2.545)

Knyvet and his niece were probably present when Sir Philip Sidney and his mother presented New Year's day gifts to the Queen (January 1, 1578), Lady Sidney bringing her perfumed gloves, which were introduced from Italy to England by the Earl of Oxford. "In odd contrast was her son Philip's present of a cambric smock, the sleeves and collar wrought with black work, and edged with a small bone-lace of gold and silver."[76] The idea of giving the Queen a smock must have struck Oxford as funny enough to pull into our play; for a moment Boyet was made to seem like Sidney. Berowne predicts to Boyet: "Die when you will, a smocke shall be your shrowd" (5.2.480). The lines that follow,

> You leere upon me, do you? There's an eie
> Wounds like a Leaden sword.

the prototype of Boyet would not forget after he heard them at Court. A few years after, his sword wounded Edward de Vere almost fatally, in a notorious duel rumored to be a "quarrel of Bessie Bavisar."[77]

The New Year's present of Sidney reminds me of the gift Berowne gives the "Queen" (5.2.), a "jewel on her sleeve." It recalls the jewel that Oxford gave Queen Elizabeth on Shrovetide night (March 3, 1579) at Greenwich palace during some shows, mentioned by the Earl of Shrewsbury's son in a letter to his father: "The chiefest was a device presented by the persons of the Earl of Oxford, the Earl of Surrey (Philip Howard), the Lords Hayworth (Howard), and Windsor (the son of Oxford's half-sister Katherine). But the device was prettier than it had hap to be performed; but the best of it, and I think the best liked, was two jewels, which were presented to her Majesty by the two Earls."[78]

Richard Eden's *Travels in the West and East Indies*, printed in 1577, told of savages who worshipt the sun. Shakespeare remembered the description when he wrote Berowne's rhapsody about the black-complexioned Rosaline:

> Who sees the heauenly Rosaline,
>
> That (like a rude and sauage man of Inde),
>
> At the first opening of the gorgeous East,
>
> Bowes not his vassall head, and strooken blinde,
>
> Kisses the base ground with obedient breast? (4.4. 217-221)

The word "vassal" here reminds us that Vavasor meant a chief of vassals.

On January 11, 1579, the Queen and her Court attended a "double mask," which Eva Turner Clark sadly erred in regarding as the original of *Love's Labour's Lost*. It was not a comedy but a costumed recital, "A Maske of Amasones," in which one of the armored women delivered "A Table with writings" and a speech to her Majesty. Expenses for the show included payment to Petruchio Ubaldino "for the translating of certen speaches into Italian to be used in the maske..." Then they beheld "An other Maske of knightes." The records of the Queen's Revels inform us: "The Amazons and the Knights had danced awhile with ladies before her Majesty, did then in her Majesty's absence fight at barriers." A "Mask of Moors" was intended for the night of March 3, which may have given our poet his device for the fifth act of our comedy in which, says a stark stage direction, "Enter Black moores with musicke, the Boy with a speech, and the rest of the Lords disguised."[79]

The Greenwich entertainment of March 3 was intended primarily for the pleasure of Alencon's embassy, headed by the clever and cruel Jean Simier. Among the festivities at Whitehall the same evening, beside a "grand ball," " there were comedies and many inventions," one entitled *Murderous Michael*, which has been deemed the original of the anonymous tragedy *Arden of Feversham*, said by some to be Shakespeare's work. *Love's Labor's Lost* could have been one of the comedies, perhaps played by the same troop that presented *Murderous Michael*, the Earl of Sussex's actors commonly called the Lord Chamberlain's men.

The maskerade of the Navarre nobles in the fifth act of our play, dressed like men from Moscow, was conceived by the dramatist remembering the feast at Angers on April 15, 1578, where Alencon and his malcontents were amused by soldiers clad in the manner of Muscovy. This mummery may have reminded the Earl of Oxford of the time in 1520 when, at the French court in Ard, "certain young honorable lords of England, appareled after the manner of Russland or far Eastland," wearing visards, engaged French ladies in a dance.[80] Edward's grandsire John perhaps was one of those lords. The elaborate triviality of the four in Russian robes with vizards encountering the four ladies recalls the strange tale of how "Elmont, Milord of Oxfort," appeared as one of "great worthies" in a *Tirata*, a mock-tournament, of Italian ladies against knights. Clad in violet, on a fawn-colored horse, carrying a big sword, Oxford flaunted a falcon device and a motto from the Roman comedian Terence— *Tendit in ardua virtus.* He tilted with Alvida, "the Countess of Edemburg," and they overthrew each other at the same time, striking their faces in the dust.[81] This could have occurred before Edward Webbe witnessed in Sicily the Earl's invitation to chivalry combats and tournaments: "no man durst be so hardy to encounter with him, so that all Italy over he is acknowledged the only Chevalier and Nobleman of England."[82]

In May 1578 Oxford invested fervently in the voyage of Captain Martin Frobisher to the northwest frost in search of a waterway to China. Frobisher returned at the end of September with a cargo of worthless ore, making bitter contrast with the riches in furs and so forth that the Muscovy Company brought by way of the Baltic Sea. Oxford's Rosaline would have seen him in that season looking as if he was in truth "Sea-sicke, I thinke, comming from Muscovie" (5.2.394). On January 26, 1579, the English Court heard that the Czar had protested against Frobisher's intrusion in lands proclaimed by Ivan the Terrible to be part of the Russian empire. Frobisher had also offended the Czar by taking on board his ship three Siberians, a man, woman and child. (The man died soon after their arrival in London.)[83]

On January 27, 1579, by the way, William Davison informed the secretkeeper Sir Francis Walsingham that he had done for Mr Knevet, "a man devoted to the Secretary," what the latter had desired Davison to do between his own duties in the Netherlands. We learn about Knyvet's job there from a letter of January 29, indicating that he took pains to decipher intercepted Spanish letters.[84] Early in February, Knyvet came back to the Court, and the care of his niece.

The sarcasm about Sir Jerome Horsey's mission to Moscow—"a message well simpathis'd, a Horse to be embassadour for an Asse" (3.1.)—was plainly added to our comedy in or after 1590 when Horsey had to return from Russia, where the Czar had refused to see him, accused of illicit commerce and "malversation." We can guess what Oxford reflected, in view of Horsey's disgrace, remembering Thomas Randolph's visit to Ivan IV, which he would have heard about when Randolph came to the Queen in July 1578 during her Progress, after the stay at Theobalds where Burghley had invited the ambassador to dine, saying, "percase you may see as much to content you as in Muscovia (that barbarous country)."[85]

We have one contemporary allusion to the performance of *Love's Labor's Lost*. It occurs in the nearly forgotten *Honest Excuses* of Thomas Lodge, printed in 1580, where he casually mentions "your Muscovian straungers, your Scithian monsters wonderfull, by one *Eurus* brought upon one stage in ships of Sheepeskins." Literally, Eurus is ancient Greek for an east-southeast wind. But what Lodge intended by the name, I fancy, is an impersonation of the obsolete English adjective "eurous" (from the French heureux) meaning fortunate. (William Caxton's *Game of Chess* defines it: "As long as a man is eurous and fortunate he hath many friends.") *Honest Excuses* contains a lament by Lodge against the icy censorship of drama by the Privy Council, noisily sustained by the London burgesses, who hired Stephen Gosson to write *The School of Abuse* (registered in July 1579) and Anthony Munday's *Second and Third Blast of Retreat from Plays and Theatres* (1580). Munday called Gosson's tract the "first blast." Lodge declared, "surely we want not a Roscius (a great actor), neither are there great scarcity of Terence's profession, but yet our men dare not nowadays presume so much as the old Poets might. And therefore they apply their writing to the people's vein ... If in the beginning they had ruled, we should nowadays have found small spectacles of folly."[86]

Edward de Vere never tired of protesting against "art made tongue-tied by authority." And you can hear his genuine voice in Berowne's avowal,

> I will sweare to studie so,
> To know one thing I am forbid to know. (1.1.59-60)

To recompense the public for what it lost at the hands of imperial horror over art, scribes like Tom Churchyard poured out pamphlets, such as his 1579 gloating, "The Miserie of Flaunders, Calamitie of Fraunce, Misfortune of Portugall, Unquietness of Ireland, Troubles of Scotland: And the Blessed State of England." Shakespeare felt so guilty of perjury in his submission to the official crippling of creativity that almost every scene of his play rings with the concept. "Necessity will make us all forsworne" (1.1.). "Ile lay my head to any good mans hat, / These oaths and lawes will prove an idle scorne." Which prompts Costard to protest, "I suffer for the truth, sir" (1.1.). In the most lyrical peak of the play, in soliloquy Berowne declares, "Well, I doe nothing in the world but lye, and lye in my throat" (4.3.). Even in the exposure of the Muscovite mummery, he beholds a heavenly penalty. "Thus poure the stars down plagues for periury." He struggles to break up the cloud of blame on his soul, accusing womanhood for the falsehood of men:

> We to our selves prove false,
> By being once false, for ever to be true
> To those that make us both, faire Ladies, you.
> And even that falsehood in it self a sinne,
> Thus purifies it selfe, and turnes to grace. (5.2.762-766)

What dart of self-mockery could be acuter than Shakespeare's derision of the motto of Edward de Vere—*Vero nihil verius*, Nothing
truer than truth—by presenting Don Adriano de Armado lauding his
Jaquenetta with the words, "truer than truth it selfe" (4.1)? Hearing
this, we remember the King's avowal, "I love to heare him lie" (1.1).
Yet the master-minstrel was determined, in his sole way, to keep his
word, even at the cost of the eminence he coveted in the government. He inwardly resolved to tame and train himself to join what
he afterward called in *King Lear* "God's spies." He concealed himself, like his beloved lord Berowne:

> All hid, all hid, an old infant play;
> Like a demie God, here sit I in the skie,
> And wretched fooles secrets heedfully ore-eye. (4.3)

Of course the censorship of Cecil and his colleagues permitted the
powerless to be made targets of hilarity in the theater. Gabriel Harvey surely detected the mirror of his mind that Shakespeare held up
in Holofernes. I hear him complaining about it in a letter to Spenser
from the summer of 1579: "I suppose thou wilt go nigh hand
shortly to send actors from the troops of Leycester, Warwick, Vaux,
or my Lord Rich's players, or some other fresh startup comedians
unto me for some new devised interlude, or some malconceived
comedy fit for the Theater, or some other painted stage, whereat
thou and thy lively copesmates in London may laugh their mouths
and bellies full for pence or twopence apiece." It certainly was not
Spenser he attacked when he wrote: "you have prejudiced my good
name forever in thrusting me thus on the stage to make trial of my
extemporal faculty, and to play (Robert) Wylson's or Tarleton's
part."[87] To what else could this refer if not the "extemporall Epitaph" that Holofernes proudly declaims (4.2.) on the Princess and
the Pricket? The wretched rimes play on the name of the river Sore
that runs by the city of Leycester. Exactly when Harvey enlisted
among Leycester's myrmidons in opposition to the faction of Sussex and Oxford, which favored the marriage of Elizabeth and Alencon for the sake of concord between England and France, we do

not know. The earliest document of Harvey's political allegiance is the letter of April 24, 1579, from Trinity Hall, Cambridge, which I have already quoted. In it the pedant confided to Spenser, "this little body of mine carrieth a great mind towards my good lord"—Robert Dudley—and offers "to attempt and endure any kind of travail (either at home or abroad, by speaking, writing, or doing, one way or other)" in Leycester's service.[88] This explains why the Pedant shows up in the last scene of our comedy in the role of Judas, meaning Maccabeus, but damned immediately as if he stood for Iscariot, despite his denial. Berowne calls him "A kissing traitor." The part could have been given to Parson Nathaniel, "the hedgepriest," easily interpreted as a traitor to the Anglican church. But I believe with Eva Turner Clark, "The caricature of Harvey in *Love's Labour's Lost* impelled the victim in his turn to caricature Lord Oxford" in his scurrilous verses called *Speculum Tuscanismi*, sent to Spenser in April 1579. Harvey claimed, "this bold Satirical Libel (was) lately devised at the instance of a certain Hartfordshire Gentleman, of mine old acquaintance."[89] He invited Spenser's opinion of the poem, but alas, it never came to our light. Sometime in 1580, when Harvey publisht his epistles to Spenser, "Another company of special good fellows would needs forsooth very courtly persuade the Earl of Oxford, that something in those Letters, and namely, the Mirror of Tuscanismo was palpably intended against him; whose noble Lordship, I protest, I never meant to dishonour with the least prejudicial word of my tongue, or pen, but ever kept a mind full of reckoning of many bounden duties toward the same."[90] He blamed nobody more than John Lyly for the charge; "Pap-hatchet," as Harvey nicknamed Oxford's servant, because Lyly wrote a polemic on the Puritans named *Pap With a Hatchet*, "desirous for his benefit, to curry favor with a noble Earl... some years since provoked me."[91] However, Harvey insisted that Oxford did not change his jovial and amiable attitude toward him. This is not denied by Thomas Nashe, who pictured Harvey in a satire, without provocation, throwing up "certain crude humours of English hexameter verses that lay upon his stomach; a noble-man stood in his way, as he was vomiting, and from top to toe all-to-berayed him with Tuscanismi." Nashe added, in defense of Lyly, that "he hath written something too in your praise, in *Pap-hatchet*, for all you accuse him to have courtly incenst the Earl of Oxford against you."[92]

I wonder whether Edward de Vere's sisters saw their images in the characters of Katherine and Maria? Their personalities are not delineated clearly enough. Still I imagine Lord Longaville an idealised sketch of Peregrine Bertie, Lord Willoughby, who married Lady Mary de Vere.

The clown Costard, I do not consider a figure standing for any statesman, unless he was drawn to represent the Belgian Gastel, whom Don John sent to London (he arrived on December 1, 1577, and left on the 9th) to deny that he intended to invade England; Gastel reminded the English government of their long dormant treaty with Spain. But Costard calls Berowne "a good master of mine" (4.1). This makes me think of Oxford's servant Gastrell, a brave swordswinger.[93] Possibly he was an ancestor of the Reverend Francis Gastrill, who tore down the Shakspere house in Stratford and chopt away the mulberry tree there, whose wood, planted by the "Bard" himself, was sold to tourists in miraculous quantities.

As for the minor personage, the constable Anthony Dull, I have a suggestion or rather a suspicion: that he was the primitive portrayal in drama of the printer, actor, spy on Papists, translator of French romances, and miscellaneous playwright Anthony Munday. Anthony Dull has the distinction of being the sole character in our comedy (unless we except the taciturn Jaquenetta) with loyalty to the commonplace literal and aversion to the mythic and metaphysical. When he appears for the last time in the play he volunteers to play a tabor for the Nine Worthies show, but his name was left out of the last act. So the little we are shown of his nature conforms with the figure of Anthony Munday, whose "hardy and venturous" version of *Gerileon of England* was registered for the press in May 1577, when he was only sixteen; its mistakes compelled the publisher to delay printing till the next year. In November, the lad's (lost) book entitled *Defense of Poverty* was licensed by John Lyly's printer, Cawood. And on August 2, 1578 the printer John Allde was fined for issuing from his press, without a license, the apprentice Anthony Munday's "Dream." This may have been the month when he abruptly quit his trade and, encouraged by the Earl of Oxford himself, went to Italy. He traveled to the capital of Popery and entered a school for training English missionary priests, apparently as an apostate, not a spy. But the "English Roman Life," as he afterward reported, wearied and disgusted him. By July 1579 he was back in London, writing Puritan propaganda against playhouses, but soon proudly announcing himself a servant of Oxford.

On April 9, 1604, less than a twelvemonth after King James appointed him a liveried servant of the Crown company of players, the name of William Shakespeare appeared for the last time on a list of the King's company. On June 24, 1604, Edward de Vere died. The effect of the Earl of Oxford's death on the theater seems to have been disastrous at first. Sometime in 1604 his brother-in-law Robert Cecil, Viscount Cranborne, instructed Walter Cope, his father's usher, to find him a new play for production at Queen Anne's court. Cope replied: "I have sent and been all this morning hunting for players, jugglers, and such kind of creatures, but find them hard to find. Wherefor leaving notes for them to seek me, (Richard) Burbage is come, and says there is no new play that the Queen has not seen; but they have revived an old one called *Love's Labour Lost*, which for wit and mirth he says will please her exceedingly. And this is appointed to be played tomorrow night at my Lord of Southampton's [Oxford's loving young friend] unless you send a writ to remove the *corpus cum causa* to your house in the Strand. Burbage is my messenger, ready attending your pleasure.—From your library."[94] Collegiate craniums employed to instruct our youth in classics of English literature will continue to teach that an indefinite number of Shakespeare's plays were brand new late in 1604 and after.

In the summer of 1604 Anne Vavasor, to the best of my knowledge, was the busy mistress of Sir Henry Lee, the veteran warrior twenty years older than Oxford. Lee had been a resident of the Savoy when the Earl and Lyly worked together at the "Hospital," and

may have met her there. In 1605 Lee gave John Finch, a merchant
active in the trade with Russia, an annuity of sixty pounds. Finch
later was listed as one of Anne's fiercest lovers. We are unaware
when Sir John Harington wrote the lubricous tribute to her called
"Of Lelia," but it was probably circulating among his friends at this
time. The academic editor of Harington's rimes evinces no sign of
understanding this epigram about Lee's lady.[95]

> When lovely Lelia was a tender girle,
>
> She hapt to be deflowred by an Earle;
>
> Alas, poore wench, she was to be excused,
>
> Such kindnesse oft is offered, seld refused.
>
> But be not proud; for she that is no Countesse,
>
> And yet lies with a Count, must make account this,
>
> All Countesses in honour her surmount,
>
> They have, she had, an honourable Count.

References

1   Oscar James Campbell, ed. *The Reader's Encyclopedia of Shakespeare* (New York; Crowell, 1966) 470.

2   Ibid. (v).

3   E. K. Chambers, *The Elizabethan Stage* (Oxford, 1923) iv, 165.

4   Campbell, op. cit. 612.

5   Edmund Lodge, *Illustrations of British History, Biography & Manners* (London; John Chidley, 1838) ii, 256, derived from Talbot Papers, G, 263.

6   Eva Turner Clark, *The Satirical Comedy Love's Labour's Lost* (New York; William Farquhar Payson, 1933) surpasses all commentaries on the comedy.

7   John Lothrop Motley, *The Rise of the Dutch Republic* (New York; Harper & Brothers, 1855) iii, 339. Burghley's journal, concerning Don Juan and the French pox, is copied in *A Collection of State Papers Relating to Affairs in the Reign of Queen Elizabeth*, ed. William Murdin (London; William Bowyer, 1759) 745.

8   Frederick Chamberlin, ed. *The Sayings of Queen Elizabeth* (London; John Lane) 29.

9   *Relations Politiques des Pays-Bas et de l'Angleterre, sous le Regne de Philippe II*, ed. Joseph Kervyn de Lettenhove (Brussels; Hayes, 1882 1900) x, 629.

10 George Gascoigne quoted in Edward Arber's *An English Garner* (London; 1896) viii, 142.

11 Chamberlin, *op. cit.* 153, translating *Recueil des Depeches, Rapports, des Ambas-*

sadeurs de France en Angleterre, ed. Charles Purton Cooper (Paris; 1838) 1, 198.

12 J. B. Black, *The Reign of Elizabeth* (Oxford; Clarendon, 1936) 125.

13 Roger Williams, *The Actions of the Low Countries*, ed. Peter Manwood (London; Matthew Lownes, 1618) 56f. The English volunteers called Charles Chester's "Ruyters," described in July 1573, were different radically. An observer named S. Jewks wrote to London that they rode over their own men; he wished, "God send them old beer, that they may be more stabler, and not to shit in their breeches and run away as often they have done." (Lettenhove, *op. cit.* vi, 792.)

14 George Gascoigne, *The Fruits of War or Dulce Bellum Inexpertis*, in his *Works*, ed. J. B. Cunliffe (Cambridge; University Press, 1907) I, 160.

15 *Ibid.* I, 194.

16 Gabriel Harvey's *Marginalia*, ed. G. C. Moore Smith (Stratford-on-Avon; Shakespeare Head, 1913) 165.

17 Conyers Read, *Mr Secretary Walsingham* (Oxford; Clarendon, 1925) II, 260f.

18 Sir Robert Naunton, *Fragmenta Regalia* (London; Edward Arber, 1870) 33.

19 *Tarlton's Jests*, ed. James Orchard Halliwell (London; Shakespeare Society, 1844) xxix.

20 Clark, *The Satirical Comedy Love's Labour's Lost*, op. cit. 91, 1 12; and 210 in Ruth Loyd Miller's incandescent edition of Clark's *Hidden Allusions in Shakespeare's Plays* (Jennings, LA, Minos Publishing Co, 1974).

21 Harvey, *Marginalia*, op. cit., 21 f.

22 Bernard Mordaunt Ward, *The Seventeenth Earl of Oxford* (London; John Murray, 1928) 80-3.

23 Ibid. 157-8.

24 *The Zurich Letters, or The Correspondence of Several English Bishops and Others, with some of The Helvetian Reformers, During the Reign of Queen Elizabeth.* ed. Hastings Robinson (Cambridge; University Press, 1846) 508.

25 Ward, op. cit. 33.

26 Harvey, *Four Letters*, in Huth edition of his *Works*, I, 184.

27 Sir Thomas Smith died in 1577. In the next year Gabriel Harvey published his Latin obituary, Smitheius vel Musarum Lachrymae. Let me add here that Mary Dewar's biography of Smith confuses the life of Edward de Vere with that of his father John (p. 80).

28 Motley, *History of the United Netherlands* (New York; Harper, 1880) 11, 27.

29 Rabelais, *Gargantua and Pantagruel* (1535) Book I, Chapter XIV.

30 On Bishop Bonner's trial, see John Foxe's *Acts and Monuments*, ed. S. R. Cattley & G. Townsend (London; 1841).

31 Thomas Churchyard, *Discourse of the Queenes Maiesties Entertainement in Suffolk and Norffolk* (London; Henry Bynneman, 1578).

32 Idem.

33 Harvey, Commonplace Book, in *Marginalia*, 97; Ibid. 151.

34 F. W. Fairholt, ed. *The Dramatic Works of John Lilly, (The Euphuist.)* quoting *Euphues and His England,* (London; John Russell Smith, 1858) I, xi.

35 On De Vere in the Savoy, see William John Loftie, *Memorials of the Savoy; the Palace, the Hospital, the Chapel* (London; Macmillan, 1878) 125. On Bernard Hampton, appointed Clerk of the Privy Council for life, 12 November 1553, see the Calendar of State Papers Foreign: 1560-61 pp 63, 89, 135, 249.

36 Harvey, *Works,* ed. Alexander B. Grosart (London; Huth Library, 1884) II, 124.

37 Harvey, *Marginalia,* 161.

38 Ward, *The Seventeenth Earl of Oxford,* op. cit., 85.

39 John Lyly, *Complete Works,* ed. R. Warwick Bond (Oxford; Clarendon, 1902) 11 209 153 31.

40 Albert Feuillerat, *John Lyly: Contribution a l'Histoire de la Renaissance en Angleterre* (Cambridge; University Press, 1910) 77: "entra au service du plus brillant, du plus littre, du plus leger aussi des seigneurs de la Cour d'Elizabeth."

41 Walter W. Greg, "The Authorship of the Songs in Lyly's Plays," *Modern Language Review* (Oct. 1905) I, 46-7.

42 See Fairholt, op. cit. I, xxx-xxxii. Greg, op. cit. 51.

43 J. Thomas Looney, *"Shakespeare" Identified in Edward de Vere, Seventeenth Earl of Oxford* (London; Cecil Palmer, 1920). See 3rd edition ed. Ruth Loyd Miller (Jennings, LA, Minos Publishing Co. 1975) I, 246-8.

44 Ward, op. cit. 61.

45 *Depeches de la Mothe Fenelon,* ed. Cooper, IV, 186.

46 A letter by John Ross, Bishop of Leslie, Mary Stuart's adviser, dated October 11, 1570, affirms: Sir William Cecil, "The Secretary (of State) hath told me secretly he could like well of the Duke of Norfolk's marrying her, but now is no time to speak of it." (British Museum: Cotton Ms. Cal. C 111 f.102 102v).

47 The French envoy reported on December 22, 1571: "le Comte d'Oxford ung peu broiller ez affaires du Duc de Norfolc" hence it was deemed advisable to bind him by matrimony to a family faithful to the Crown and its church.—Correspondance Diplomatique de Bertrand de Salignac de la Mothe Fenelon, Ambassadeur de France en Angleterre, de 1568 a 1595 (Paris, 1840) IV, 315.

48 G. C. Moore Smith, in *Notes & Queries,* Series 11 (1911) 111, 261. see Harvey's *Marginalia,* 137f.

49 See the chapters on these plays in Clark's *Hidden Allusions in Shakespeare's Plays,* ed. Ruth Loyd Miller (1974) and the chapters on the earlier plays in this volume.

50 Public Record Office (London): State Papers Domestic, 1581, cli, 45.

51 Calendar of State Papers Foreign, 1575-77, p. 565.

52 E. Partridge, *Shakespeare's Bawdy* (New York; Dutton, 1960) 53.

53 Calendar of State Papers Foreign, 1575-77. Note by Percy Allen, *The Plays of*

Shakespeare & Chapman in Relation to French History (London; Denis Archer, 1933) 75. This volume is a pathetic example of Allen's hasty-wasty style of scholarship when he would not spare time for "sessions of sweet silent thought," too eager for the glory of a discoverer.

54 Ward, op. cit. 244, quoting Lansdowne Mss. 39:22.

55 Frank Harris, *The Man Shakespeare* (New York; Mitchell Kennerley, 1909) 160, misquoting Edward Dowden's *Shakespeare: A Critical Study of His Mind and Art* (1875), Dowden's first book, which is quoted at length in the Furness Variorum edition of L.L.L., 362.

56 Georg Brandes, *William Shakespeare* (New York; Macmillan, 1924) 45, first published in Danish (Copenhagen 1896), translated to English (London, 1898).

57 Walter Pater, in MacMillan's Magazine (December 1885), copied by Furness, op cit 364, 365; also in Pater's *Appreciations* (New York; Macmillan, 1908) 171, 172, 174, 175.

58 Samuel Taylor Coleridge, *Lectures and Notes on Shakespeare,* ed. T. Ashe (London; George Bell, 1890) 283. Harris depicted Biron's boyhood in Chapter XIV of his book, where we are told, "It was lucky for Shakespeare (sic) that his father's increasing poverty withdrew him from school early, and forced him into contact with life." (Harris, op. cit 354.) A butcher boy's life, in "low company."

59 Coleridge, op. cit 88. (Conceived in 1812).

60 Ibid 230. (Delivered in 1818).

61 Ibid 247. ("Classification attempted, 1802"!)

62 Ibid 287. (1818). The material about H. H. Carwardine comes from *Notes and Queries* (2 April 1870), ibid. 179f.

63 Pater, *Appreciations, op. cit.,* 168. H. C. Hart, ed. *Love's Labour's Lost* (Indianapolis; Bobbs-Merrill, 1906) 123f.

64 Abel Lefranc, *A la Decouverte de Shakespeare* (Paris 1945-50), the ultimate version of his Sous le Masque *de William Shakespeare, William Stanley, VF Comte de Derby* (Paris; Payot, 1919), II, 17 f. See Motley on Marguerite's tour of Brabant, in *The Dutch Republic, op. cit.* III, 339.

65 Quoted by Caroline Spurgeon, *Chaucer devant la critique* (1911), amplified in her *Five Hundred Years of Chaucer Criticism and Allusion* (1357-1900), Chaucer Society, Second Series, No. 56.—There is not a word about Kellner in Campbell's *Encyclopedia.*

66 Literally translated from *Lettres, Instructions et Memoires de Marie Stuart,* ed. Alexandre Labanoff (London; Charles Dolman, 1894), III.

67 Harvey, *Works,* ed. Grosart, I, 96, 97.

68 We have no difficulty in fancying why Rosalind would call the poet her winged steed.—Harvey, *Works,* I, 81.

69 Spenser learnt Hebrew at the Merchant Tailors School in London, studying

with the wise teacher Richard Mulcaster. Concerning the legend of the Line leaves, see (Wolfgang?) Menzel, *Christliche Symbolik.*

70 E. K. Chambers, *Sir Henry Lee* (Oxford; Clarendon, 1936) 153f. Eva Turner Clark, *The Man Who Was Shakespeare* (New York; Richard R. Smith, 1937) 287.

71 E. K. (Edward Knight?), Gloss of January Eclogue in *The Shepherds' Calendar,* all editions of Spenser's works.

72 Calendar of State Papers Domestic: Elizabeth, CXLIX, 2.

73 On Spenser's departure from the North, see the June eclogue and its Gloss.—Harvey's *Works,* ed. Grosart, I, 81.

74 Edmund Spenser, *Colin Clout's Come Home Again,* dedicated to Raleigh from Ireland, December 1591. The end of the poem praises Rosalind, for fear of divine punishment, as Greek poets were alleged to have been blinded for their harsh opinions of Helen of Ilion!

75 Acts of the Privy Council, ed. Dasent, VII, 121.

76 Burghley's servitor William Camden made an effort to deprive Oxford of credit for the perfumed gloves: he claimed that one Marquis Frangipanni introduced the wearing of these. (Remains of a Greater Work Concerning Britain, London 1605, containing what Camden called "rubbish.")—On the Sidney gifts, see H. R. Fox Bourne, *Sir Philip Sidney* (London; Putnam's Sons, 1891) 140. Possibly the idea of the "Queen's" gift of "A Lady wal'd about with Diamonds" (5.2) struck the poet on New Year's Day 1579, when Philip's father, Sir Henry, brother-in-law of Oxford's dear friend the Earl of Sussex, gave Elizabeth "a fair jewel of gold, wherein is Diana fully garnished with diamonds." (Fox Bourne, 171).

77 Ward, op cit 227.

78 Edmund Lodge, op cit. II, 146.

79 *Documents Relating to the Office of the Revels in the Time of Queen Elizabeth,* ed. Albert Feuillerat (Louvain; A. Uystpruyst, 1908) 286-7 301, 308. Eva Turner Clark relied for her information from this book on Mary Susan Steele's *Plays and Masques at Court* (New Haven; Yale University Press, 1926).

80 The "comedies and many inventions" of March 1579 are mentioned in the Calendar of State Papers Spanish for that year, II, 655. The Russian or Asiatic mummery in France of 1520 is recorded in Raphael Holinshed's *Chronicles of England, Scotland, and Ireland* (London 1587) III, 860.

81 Exhumed by Julia Cooley Altrocchi, for the *Shakespeare Authorship Review* (London, Autumn 1959) from Andrea Perrucci, Dell' Arte Rappresentativa Premeditata ed all' Improviso (Napoli 1699). See Ruth Loyd Miller, ed. *Hidden Allusions ...* (1974) 134-5.

82 *The Travels of Edward Webbe* (1590), cited by Ward, *op. cit.* 112.

83 Calendar of State Papers Foreign, 1579, CXXIX, 19.

84 Kervyn de Lettenhove, *op. cit.* X, 254, 262, 280.

85 John Nichols, *The Progresses and Public Processions of Queen Elizabeth* (London;

Nichols, 1823) II, 104. — Compare F. Sorenson, "The Masque of the Muscovites," *Modern Language Notes* (1935) L, 499f.

86 Thomas Lodge, *Works* (London; Hunterian Club, n.d.) 20; also in the Shakespeare Society's Papers (London 1845) II, 163.

87 Harvey, Works, I, 125f.

88 Quoted in the superb chronicle by E. F. Tenison, *Elizabethan England* (Leamington; The Author, 1930-9) V, 152f. Unluckily the scarcest as well as the most accurate history of the age of Shakespeare.

89 Harvey, *Works*, I, 83, 84f. Clark, *The Satirical Comedy*, 156.

90 Harvey, *Works*, I, 183.

91 Ibid 11, 122.

92 Thomas Nashe, *Works*, ed. Ronald B. McKerrow (London; Sidgwick & Jackson, 1910) 111, 295, 300.

93 About Gastrell, see for example, Clark, *Hidden Allusions* ... (1974) 462.

94 Salisbury (Cecil) Mss. at Hatfield House: Calendar, XVI, 415.

95 Sir John Harington, *Letters and Epigrams*, ed. Norman Egbert McClure (Philadelphia; University of Pennsylvania Press, 1930) 269.

Chapter 9—SHYLOCK OF LONDON

There is always a compulsory personality in the books that
we write, for what could we put into our books if it were not
for the experience of our lives?

George Sand

Nulla poena sine crimine

Roman Maxim

Prolog

We are all aware that the mastery of any art is revealed by the concealment of the artistry. It is the duty and the divine joy of the artist
to entrance us into forgetting the maker when we see or hear the
work, in precisely the same way that most of us, in the presence of a
sunrise or a waterfall, if enraptured by its beauty or grandeur, fail to
remember God. From the magic spell of absorption in art, great
critics have concluded that the genuine artist always endeavors to
disappear in, to keep self out of the masterpiece, a feat, a miracle!
which other observers have pronounced impossible. For every wonder our hands produce could only come from those hands, the joys
and sufferings, the adventures or vicissitudes of our singular hearts
and heads. In my own experience of the world's literature I have
encountered only one writer who succeeded in obliterating his identity from his everlasting artifacts. That is the utterly mysterious master whom researchers in the sacred scriptures of the Jews designate
as I because he regularly spells the name of God IHVH. His pieces
have been familiar to millions, especially the stories of Jacob's and
his mother's deception of his blind father, Joseph the dreamer and
his interpretation of dreams, and other beloved legends that have
never induced the majority of their readers to wonder what kind of
man carved them so beautifully? We can say but one thing concerning him with certainty: his soul burned with a love of justice which
made him see it as the road of God, blazed by truth, which could
never be divided from freedom of speech. He was the kind of crea-

tive writer who dared to imagine the lonely and landless Abraham challenging the Almighty with the question, Shall not the Judge of all the earth do justice?

James Russell Lowell, having unconsciously cherished from childhood the literary standard of the chief genius of the Bible, maintained that "Shakespeare, the truest of artists, is also nothing more than a voice. We seek in vain in his plays for traces of his personal character or history."[1] Under the influence of such teaching, Walt Whitman told his friend William Douglas O'Connor, who believed that Francis Bacon, Lord Verulam, composed the sublime dramas of "William Shake-speare," that English poetic art has "nothing to do with the poet's special personality, nor exhibiting the least trace of it—like Shakspere's great unsurpassable dramas."[2] A year later (in 1884) Whitman affirmed "the impressions of my early years, that the distinctiveness and glory of the Poet reside not in his vaunted dramas of the passions, but those founded on the contests of English dynasties, and the French wars... Conceiv'd out of the fullest heat and pulse of European feudalism," said the democratic bard, "—personifying in unparallel'd ways the medaeval aristocracy, its towering spirit of ruthless and gigantic caste, with its own peculiar air and arrogance (no mere imitation)—only one of the 'wolfish earls' so plenteous in the plays themselves, or some born descendant and knower, might seem to be the true author of those amazing works—works in some respects greater than anything else in recorded literature."[3] No matter what you may think of Whitman's opinion about "What Lurks Behind Shakspere's Historical Plays," you will consent that he surpassed all the celebrated American interpreters of the plays in courage of imagination. Nor can it be denied that Walt's vision had winged far from the old view that the dramas did not exhibit the least trace of personality. On the contrary, he almost perceived in the century-powdered pages the very man who made them, with blue veins throbbing exultantly to music of aristocracy, pulsing with the blood of earls.

Please observe that Whitman blindly followed academic authority in spelling the poet's name as Shaksper never did. The scholastic skulls of his day were determined to fix in the pantheon of all peoples their image of the dramatist, their idol William Shakspere the malt dealer and miser of Stratford-on-Avon. They desired to impress on every brain the belief that the longing to create literature could live in peace with the lust for property, money and mortmain, in the same soul. "There seems to have been no clash," declared Professor Hazelton Spencer, "between his acquisitiveness and his art."[4] There certainly was no conflict in the customary college cranium between the conception of Shakespeare as a drudge devoted to greed, to the pursuit of petty debts, and the various portrayals of him as the maker of *The Merchant of Venice*.

In the prime of Lowell and Whitman, in the boyhood of Hazelton Spencer, "The most popular of Shakespeare's comedies, the one most widely known, the one by means of which most abundant success has been obtained on the stage, is *The Merchant of Venice*."[5] In the period Mark Twain called "the gilded age," commercial mentality, capitalism, found none of Shakespeare's works so delightful as the drama of Shylock the Jewish moneylender and the merchant Antonio, his enemy. Altho the play was listed in the first collection of Shakespeare's dramas, the folio of 1623, as a comedy, it is not a fantasy of fun. Neither is it the near-tragedy that sentimental mercantile gentlemen of Jewish origin, like the extravagant stage profiteer David Belasco, tried to make it. In 1922 Belasco treated the play as "wholly a figment of fancy."[6] He presented Shylock's first scene with a synagog on the stage, close to the Jew's house; melody of godly adoration rises from the Jewish church; a cantor and quire sing Hebrew. While the religious service goes on, Shylock conducts his loan business with Antonio. Belasco's version of the play stayed faithful to the mangling of it by the actor Edwin Booth, adding what the critic John Corbin termed "perversion" of his own: "He has made Shakespeare's story fit the needs of his scenery."[7] Belasco explained his treatment of the drama: "A diamond is always a diamond," he remarked, "but cut, polished and placed in a suitable and lovely setting, it always shows to better advantage than when left, rough and imperfect, imbedded in clay."[8] To the best of my knowledge, there was hardly a voice lifted in American Jewry to repel this gaudy mud insult to the religion and the race.

While the versions of *The Merchant of Venice* favored by Edwin Booth in America and by Henry Irving in Britain, presenting Shylock as an almost tragic hero, a champion of Jewish piety fighting infidels, an instrument of divine vengeance! enthralled thousands on both sides of the Atlantic, a humble English pedagog named John Thomas Looney nearly learnt the play by heart.

"For several years in succession," (Looney informs us) "I had been called upon to go through repeated courses of reading in one particular play of Shakespeare's, namely *The Merchant of Venice*. This long continued familiarity with the contents of one play induced a peculiar sense of intimacy with the mind and disposition of its author and his outlook upon life. The personality which seemed to run through the pages of the drama I felt to be altogether out of relationship with what was taught of the reputed author and the ascertained facts of his career. For example, the Stratford Shakspere was untravelled, having moved from his native place to London when a young man, and then as a successful middle-aged man of business he had returned to Stratford to attend to his lands and houses. This particular play on the contrary bespoke a writer who knew Italy at first hand and was touched with the life and spirit of the country. Again the play suggested an author with no great respect for money and business methods, but rather one to whom material possessions would be in the nature of an encumbrance to be easily and lightly disposed of: at any rate one who was by no means of an acquisitive disposition."[9]

The teacher's faith in the orthodox ideas about England's greatest artist had already been undermined by similar collision of facts. He did not have the craving for mental anchorage in myth that drives hosts of customers every year thru the Stratford shrine. Some while before those myriads followed their leaders into the bloodpits of the summer of 1914, John Thomas Looney went to work on the quest that led him to write *"Shakespeare" Identified in Edward de Vere, Seventeenth Earl of Oxford*, which could not be published before 1920.

Twelve years later I read the book and acquired the faith of the author, serene and unwavering thru countless hours of research.

The following essay might be termed the breviary of a volume I could have written for commentary on *The Merchant of Venice*. It represents an effort to do justice to the attractive and repulsive qualities of the characters in that romance. But above all I have dealt justly with their creator, holding ever in view the plea of the Israelite prophet to keep an eye of compassion on the ordeals of mortality.

I

We start with the well known fact that *The Merchant of Venice* was founded on an Italian tale that the runaway from Stratford-on-Avon could never have read. Shakespeare found it in a fourteenth-century anthology entitled *Il Pecorone* (The Blunderer) by Giovanni Fiorentino, printed in Italy in 1558, but not turned into English in Shakspere's time. In this childishly plotted fairytale the hero Giannetto, youngest of three sons, becomes the darling of his dead father's friend Ansaldo, a merchant of Venice, who lets him spend lavishly on dinners and tournaments, steeds and ladies. Then Ansaldo trusts him to take a ship carrying rich merchandise to sea, bound for Alexandria. However in the harbor of Belmonte the gallant Giannetto hears that the port belongs to a widow lady, "who has ruined many gentlemen... she is a beautiful and capricious woman, and makes this law, that anyone (sic) who arrives must sleep with her, and if he possesses her he can take her for his wife and become lord of the port and all that country. But if he fails, he loses everything that he has." Giannetto resolves to win the whimsical princess, but when they are preparing for bed she persuades him to drink a potion that permits him to sleep late alone. In the morning he is compelled to leave his unloaded vessel and return to Venice on a horse the lady lends him. He makes excuses for his loss to Ansaldo, who forgives him, and provides a second ship of costly wares. The stupid hero exchanges the vessel for another narcotic slumber in the Belmonte woman's home. Returning to Venice, he learns that his squanders have ruined Ansaldo, "who was the greatest and richest of the Christian merchants." Giannetto vows to retrieve his Venetian benefactor's fortune by making a third voyage to Belmonte. The imbecile Ansaldo stript his house and self of all he owned to furnish the third ship. Apparently bereft, not only of his wits, but of all credit with his Christian compatriots, he goes to borrow ten thousand ducats from "a Jew at Mestri." The Jew exacts an agreement for the loan, "that if he had not repaid the debt by the feast of St John in the following June, the Jew might take a pound of flesh from any part of his body he pleased."

Back at Belmonte the idiot Giannetto is led by the lady's hand at bedtime to her chamber and invited to hearten himself for the night's enchantment with a drink. One of her damsels takes sudden pity on him and counsels him not to drink. He understands! and secretly pours the usual wine "into his bosom." Soon after the princess undresses for bed he stops his show of snoring and embraces her. At last he enjoys "the bliss of holy matrimony, and all night long she did not leave his arms." So overjoyed was the lady that the next morning she "knighted" Giannetto and put him on the throne. After the wedding festival he gives away his cargo of silken commodities and other treasures. "He showed himself a strong ruler, and made himself respected by administering right and justice to all sorts of people." In the very next breath the story-teller reveals how seriously this praise of our hero was meant. "He thus dwelt some time in joy and gladness, and never cared nor gave a thought for poor Messer Ansaldo..."

On the day Ansaldo's debt is due, Giannetto wakes up to realize the peril of his old friend. His princess speeds him to Venice with "a hundred thousand ducats." Meanwhile Ansaldo is arrested by the Jew demanding his pound of meat. He grants the old merchant a delay of a few days. "All Venice talked about the affair; everyone was grieved at it, and many merchants joined together in offering to pay the money, but the Jew would not have it, for he wished to commit this homicide (*sic*) in order to be able to say that he had put to death the greatest of the Christian merchants." You know the rest of the romance: how the nameless lady followed her lover to Venice disguised as a lawyer, who rescues old Ansaldo by insisting that the Jew must cut off one pound from his body, no more, no less, yet shed not a single drop of blood, because the loan bond did not say that he was to have any blood beside the flesh; how the nameless Jew frustrated and enraged tears up the bond; how the cunning lawyer gets her hero's ring as reward and later, confronting the fool in her royal gown, taunts him for giving it to some female charmer, and so on. *Il Pecorone* does not go so far as Shakespeare in piling insult on injury to its Israelite usurer by wrenching him away from his "sacred nation," forcing him to submit to baptism. Nor did Fiorentino adorn his story with the romance of the Jew's daughter who robs and deserts her father for a Gentile lover. The love-story of the melancholy merchant whom Shakespeare named Antonio and the merry fortune hunter Bassanio also came from the dramatist's unique mint.[10]

Shakespeare probably got his notion of the choice caskets in the courtship of his lady of Belmont, Portia, from the medieval volume of odd fiction called *Gesta Romanorum*, rendered in London 1577 by one Richard Robinson. In the same book there was a tale remotely resembling his flesh-bond plot; however no Jew appears among its personages. But Richard Robinson left that story out of his edition of the *Gesta*. So where could the supreme thaumaturge of the theater have seen the raw material of his romance? A common answer of the college conjurors is that he may have had the good luck to handle the very text of an old play, which they unanimously assume has since been lost, dealing with the caskets and the bond. In the summer of 1579 an Oxford University youth, Stephen Gosson, who had explored his histrionic talent on unknown stages and tried to win applause if not shillings by scribbling plays, issued a book entitled *The School of Abuse*, "containing a pleasant invective against Poets, Pipers, Players, Jesters and such like Caterpillars of a Commonwealth." The polemic appears to have been paid for by municipal burgesses, amorists of money, who hated to see theaters prospering and poets eating better. Gosson, who slavishly imitated John Lyly's style of Euphuism, was careful not to sweep all contemporary poets into damnation. He admitted, "some of their Plays are without rebuke: which are as easily remembered as quickly reckoned. The two prose Books played at the Belsavage, where you shall find never a word without wit, never a line without pith, never a letter placed in vain." I venture to guess that they were from Lyly's pen, perhaps his *Mother Bombie* and *Campaspe*. But let us go ahead with Gosson:

> The Jew and Ptolme, shown at the Bull, the one representing the greediness of worldly choosers, and bloody minds of Usurers: the other very likely describing how seditious estates, with their own devices, false friends, with their swords, and rebellious commons in their own snares are overthrown: neither with Amorous gesture wounding the eye: nor with slovenly talk hurting the ears of the chaste hearers.[11]

In the Spring of 1881 the scholar Edward Scott discovered that correspondence between the poet Edmund Spenser and the rhetoric instructor Gabriel Harvey during the year 1579 was full of allusions to plays they had seen. One of Harvey's letters enclosed a fancy bond for his friend, and Spenser cheerily replied pronouncing himself "fast bound unto thee in more obligations than any merchant in Italy to any Jew there."[12] It seemed evident to Scott that the two friends had been to the Bull inn and enjoyed *The Jew* as cordially as Stephen Gosson did. Their remembrance of the play, Scott concluded, supports the opinion that it was the prototype of Shakespeare's romance.[13] Unexplained, therefor, remains the shyness with which academic commentators avoid noticing Scott's discovery while constantly quoting Gosson's reference to the allegedly lost *Jew*. They are all of course acquainted with the fact that James Roberts applied for a license to print Shakespeare's play on July 22, 1598, under the title of *The Merchant of Venice* "or otherwise called the Jew of Venice." The Stationers Register noted, it should not be printed "by the said James Roberts or any other whatsoever without licence first had from the Right honorable the lord Chamberlain," evidently meaning the patron of Shakespeare's own actors. The little book came from the Roberts press in 1600, without any words on the titlepage about the company that performed *The Merchant* or *The Jew*. The university experts on Shakespeare are commonly ignorant of the fact that the phrase "Lord Chamberlain" meant two different men to Elizabethan Londoners: the Lord Chamberlain of the Queen's Household and the Lord Chamberlain of England. In 1579 the former, Thomas Radcliff, Earl of Sussex, kept a troup of splendid players, headed by the comedian John Adams, who performed at the royal court "prototypes" of dramas that Looney and his followers claim for Edward de Vere, Lord Chamberlain of England.

Eva Turner Clark surmised that *The Jew of Venice* delighted Elizabeth and her ladies and courtiers on Tuesday night, February 2, 1580, when, according to their Revels record, "*The history of Portio and demorantes* (was) shewen at whitehall on Candlemas daie at night enacted by the Lord Chamberleyns seruants wholly furnyshed in this office whereon was ymployed for scarfes garters head Attyres for women & Lynynges for hattes vj ells of Sarcenett A Cytie a towne & vj payre of gloves." The Revels office apparently transcribed the title of the play wrongly from a notice made by one of the Chamberlain's men. Eva Clark suggested that its title at the Court had been "Portia and the merchants."[14]

The year 1580 saw the publication of Anthony Munday's *Zelauto, the Fountain of Fame*, "Erected in an Orchard of Amorous Adventures, containing a Delicate Disputation gallantly discoursed between two noble Gentlemen of Italy, given for a friendly entertainment to Euphues, at his late arrival into England." Munday dedicated his book to the recently returned from Italy Edward de Vere, proudly designating himself a servant of the Earl of Oxford. *Zelauto* includes the tale of Truculento, a Christian usurer, who lends four thousand ducats to two gentlemen who pledge to pay him, if they forfeit the debt, their lands and their right eyes. When they fail to redeem the loan, their brides—one of whom is the moneylender's daughter, disguise themselves as lawyers, and plead for mercy to Truculento, exhorting him not to act like a "Turk." But he cries for justice; "no more, wherefore I will have it." The lady Cornelia argues that no blood may be shed in removal of the eyes, and the usurer is consequently driven to ordain his son-in-law Rodolfo to be his heir. After spinning this yarn Munday promised, "You shall have the rest as possibility can permit me," but he printed no more of the story. This manifest mimicry of *The Merchant of Venice* induced Janet Spens into thinking that Anthony Munday was the author of *The Jew*.[15]

In contrast to the play produced by the Earl of Sussex's men, his chief political antagonist, the Earl of Leycester, sponsored a morality drama, *The Three Ladies of London* by Robert Wilson, beloved comedian of Leycester's company. Lady Lucar, representing the root of all evil, in this play, seduces the world, above all England, with her agents, Usury, Fraud, Dissimulation, and stains the face of Lady Conscience with cosmetic "abominations," and degrades Lady Love to scortatory affection. Apart from these embodiments of abstraction, the comedy shows us Mercadorus, an Italian merchant, corrupting the English people by taking their precious exports to Turkey and giving them gaudy stuff and trifles in trade. A Jew named Gerontus resident in Turkey lends the Italian money which Mercadorus carries away from the country, and refuses to pay back. Gerontus appeals to law for the loan. The Italian finds a way to elude the Jew: Turkish law liberates every convert to the creed of Muhamad from prior obligations. But the Jew, astonished and horrified by the greed which is willing to throw away the faith of the merchant's parents, lowers the amount he demanded and then yields his legal rights. Mercadorus immediately refuses to become Moslem and merrily departs; the cheated Jew urges him to pay his debts in the future. Their judge remarks, "One may judge and speak truth, as appears by this, Jews seek to excel in Christianity, and Christians in Jewishness." No Turk of the time would have thus flattered the creed of the grand German financiers, the Fuggers and Welsers, and Thomas Gresham, the founder of the London stock exchange, famous for his doctrine that bad money is bound to expel from currency good cash. Nor would the Turkish magistrates have insulted Jewishness, which they knew better than the Britons since multitudes of Jews had found refuge in Turkey from the cruelty of Christian Spain.

Wilson's comedy aimed to instruct his countrymen that the merchants of their church set deplorable and putrid examples in commerce and finance. Yet *The Three Ladies of London* had sunk into stage oblivion before the well-named John Wolfall tortured fellow Londoners by means of his moneylending, and Will Shakspere commenced his series of lawsuits for petty debts. Wolfall is hardly remembered except as a nuisance in the career of the poet and playwright George Chapman. Wilson's master, Robert Dudley, Earl of Leycester, admired and valued Jews who escaped from the Catholic Inquisition of Portugal to the charity of England, where they joined Protestant churches and practised their skills in trade and medicine while secretly continuing ancient customs of their parental religion. The Earl of Oxford lived close to their houses and surely viewed with wonder their courage, wide-ranging intelligence, wit and charm, but, I suspect, he regarded them with nearly conscious dread. It is simply absurd to contend, as many Jewish historians still do, that Shakespeare "probably had never laid eyes on a living exemplar of the Jewish faith." Compare this opinion with the verdict of Cecil Roth on the poet's lore about Shylock: "Shakespeare's intuition has enabled him to sketch in trivial details with such remarkable fidelity as to render it quite conceivable that (as has been conjectured) he knew Italy at first hand..."[16] Poor Roth, whether environed by British university ivy or the cloisters and minarets of Jerusalem, did not dare to suppose that our poet knew Jews in the English metropolis.

Let us go back to the time before the performance of *The Jew* at the Bull, the days out of whose sights and thoughts our dramatist evolved the adventures, laughter and lyric speeches of *The Merchant of Venice*.

It will be recalled, on April 12, 1576, George Gascoigne finished his preface to *A Discourse of a Discovery for a New Passage to Cataia*, by Humphrey Gilbert, written to promote investment in the voyage that Captain Martin Frobisher, Gascoigne's cousin, engaged to make into the frozen north beyond Canada, hopeful of finding a way to the wealth of China. I am unaware of any connexion between this expedition and "A note," made by one of Lord Burghley's secretaries, "of the manor of Badlesmere in Kent, late belonging to Lord Oxford, now to Sir Hump. Gilbert in right of his wife, 1576."[17] Oxford did not invest in the voyage, which was mainly sponsored by Leycester's brother Ambrose, the Earl of Warwick. On June 7, 1576, Frobisher's two ships, the Gabriel and the Michael, sailed for the northwest region of perpetual winter. On this day, I have conjectured, Edward de Vere worked on the play which became *The Comedy of Errors*, which contains the enigmatic line, "the bark Expedition put forth tonight" (IV, iii) and declares that "Lapland sorcerers inhabit" the Greek scene of the comedy. Among the minor characters we find an Italian goldsmith named Angelo, clearly made in the image of Baptista Agnello the alchemist employed by Warwick and his fellow "adventurers" to search for gold in the earth Frobisher would bring them. The Michael deserted him before the crew came in sight of Greenland. From the Gabriel Captain Frobisher and his men explored the coast of Baffinland, and attempted to teach the Eskimos economic exchange. On October 2 the Gabriel entered the harbor of Harwich bringing black pyrites believed to contain gold. The stones were first handed over to the merchant Michael Lock, an enthusiast for the northwest enterprise. He gave them to Agnello to assay; the latter claimed to have discovered gold ore in them. Naturally they were chagrined by the outcome of their chemistry. Michael Lock appears to have been hurt the most hard; he purchased nearly half the shares of the expedition.

The rest of the 1600 pounds it cost were paid by Sussex, Leycester, Burghley, the Lord Admiral Edward Fiennes de Clinton (Earl of Lincoln), Francis Walsingham, Philip Sidney, and a few other believers in Lock's illusions. The Earl of Oxford surrendered to his spell and invested in the company while Agnello's allurement and Lock's talks began a gold fever in London that financed the second northwest voyage of Frobisher. In May 1577 he sailed for Baffinland with the Gabriel, the Michael, and the Aid, piloted by Andrew Dyer. During their absence the Queen bestowed land worth 250 pounds a year on Oxford, "our faithful cousin," for services not specified. Lord Burghley had arranged for a favorite Italian banker in London, Benedict Spinola, to pay over 3000 pounds in Italy and France to the Earl for his travel costs from the sale of Oxford estates. On 25 September Frobisher returned with about two hundred tons of Arctic ore. Dr John Dee, the astrologer and alchemist, insisted that he found silver in it. The Cathay Company ardor was not dampened by disappointing tests at her Majesty's Mint. Michael Lock or Lok expected a profit of forty pounds from each ton. His ardor inspired fresh purchase of shares in the third Frobisher voyage. Meanwhile Walsingham gained promotion to the post of Chancelor of the Order of the Garter at Windsor Castle on April 23, 1578, St George's day, the anniversary on which we celebrate the birth of William Shakespeare nowadays.

On April 26 the Stationers guild licensed publication of the earliest English book dealing with a Jewish theme, a sermon by the renowned writer of Protestant history, John Fox, on the baptism of a convert to the Anglican creed. Nathaniel Judah Menda turned up first in British records in 1572 when the town of Ipswich paid six pence "For whipping of a Jewish man"—three times the amount paid for whipping a Welshman.[18] The miserable Menda went down to London where he dwelt in peace at the Domus Conversorum (home for converts) founded by King Henry III in 1232. That building had never been empty of Jewish stragglers who wanted to become true-blue Britons. The conversion of Menda seems to have been welcomed almost as a signal for the advent of Christ. After six years of royal charity he underwent baptism in ceremony of pomp. The preaching of John Fox over him certainly attracted more curiosity than the translation of Lambertus Danaeus's *The Wonderful Workmanship of the World* by Thomas Twyne, one of Oxford's ardent admirers. Twyne's work was also registered for printing on April 26.

De Vere wrote to the Cathay Company Commissioners of the third Frobisher expedition on 21 May 1578, offering his investment of a thousand pounds, which "upon your certificate of admittance, I will enter into bond, shall be paid for that use unto you upon Michaelmas day next coming (September 29)." On May 25 he bought shares from Michael Lock valued at two thousand pounds, altho London goldsmiths were skeptical about the prospects of the enterprise. Captain Frobisher embarked at Harwich on May 31, leading fifteen ships toward the straits that entered Hudson Bay. Eva Turner Clark enjoyed the honor of having been the first to perceive how these three thousand pounds the Earl of Oxford owed inspired Shakespeare to make the debt of his Venetian merchant to Shylock three thousand ducats.[19]

In 1578 the Earl may have examined the Thomas Rogers translation of *A General Discourse Against the Damnable Sect of Usurers*, by Philippus Caesar, dedicated to Oxford's foe Sir Christopher Hatton, who prefered to invest his money in the voyages of Francis Drake against the Spaniards transporting silver from the Americas. Those were the days when British wits tried to cut down Spanish pride by deriding the caballeros of Castile as men of Moorish and Jewish blood, not Europeans. A French tract, anonymous, *L'Anti-Espagnol*, denounced Castilians in this manner: "bastard Catholics, half-Jews and half-Moors, recently sprung from the Synagogue and the Qoran."[20] The satirist Rabelais echoed similar accusations when he pointed out that his hero Gargantua owned a "sword not from Valencia, nor his dagger from Saragossa, for his father could not endure these *hidalgos borrachos maranisados como diablos*."[21] Spanish nobles were not only considered drunkards; they were marinated like the devils called in Christian Spain "Marranos," meaning literally a sort of swine, but usually the crypto-Christians who had converted from Judaism but only gave lip-loyalty and the patience of their posteriors to the Church.

On August 4, 1578, Abdul-melech, the emperor of Morocco, encouraged by the government of Queen Elizabeth to make war on Portugal, met brave Sebastian, the king of that country, in a skirmish trap. In the battle of Alcazar the young king fell to death. Don Antonio, the bastard nephew of King John III by a beautiful Jew named Violante Gomez, claimed the throne of Portugal, and the English government supported his aspiration. The popularity of the son of King John's brother Luis sustained his cause until August 25, 1580, when King Felipe of Spain, demanding the throne of the Portuguese by obscure right of his mother Isabella, the daughter of King Manoel I, defeated the army of Antonio at the battle of Alcantara. Antonio fled from his homeland to the shelter Queen Elizabeth opened for the King of Portugal. He was always called thus in her age; later historians entitled him Pretender. Some scholars have fancied that Shakespeare derived the name of his protagonist in *The Merchant of Venice* from King Antonio.[22]

It is easier to tell where he obtained the name of Bassanio, the dearest if not the sole friend of Antonio. On July 27 Cambridge University adored and bored the Queen, tiring her with speeches and debates. Certain musicians helped to rehearse a comedy for this occasion. It is reasonable to suppose they included her masters of music, the trio of Arthur, Andrew and Jeronimo Bassano.[23] At St Helens church in Bishopsgate, on December 28, 1588, Jeronomy Bassano had the happiness of seeing baptised a son named Edward, whose godfather may be guessed. In 1579 another Bassano, Antonio, from Venice, received from the royal treasury payment of twenty pence a day for his "good service" in the "science or art of music."[24] Shakespeare gives no inkling of knowledge that the Italian town of Bassano heads the list of cities whose names were given to Italian Jews by tax authorities. The Gentiles of Bassano were once notorious for exciting their bishop's fury by their fondness for attending the weddings of Jews.[25] One of the academic disputes the Queen heard, which apparently lingered in the memory of the man who wrote

> The quality of mercy is not strain'd.
> 'Tis mightiest in the mightiest, it becomes
> The throned Monarch better than his Crowne, (4.1.182-187)

and so forth, for all the world like a prophet of Israel, centered on the question, "Whether clemency was more laudable in a prince than severity?" During her Majesty's "progress" from Cambridge to Saffron Walden the Public Orator of the University accompanied her to his hometown. Gabriel Harvey recited encomiums to her and the Earl of Leycester, then to William Cecil, Lord Burghley, and his son-in-law, the Earl of Oxford. We do not know how Burghley received the declamation calling him "Sicilides." Presumably Harvey intended to allude to Cecil's claim that his ancestors were Sitsilts of Wales, tho we know of no Sitsilt who hailed him as kinsman. The unfortunate spelling of Cecil's name in Harvey's poem would have reminded the Lord Treasurer of the Romanist contention that he was an offshoot of Sicilian stock, perhaps descended from the Italian financiers who swarmed into England to take the places of the Jewish moneylenders expelled with all the rest of English Jewry in 1290 by King Edward I. The effect of this imperial act on the English people may be estimated from the deathbed warning Robert Grosseteste, the philosopher, bishop of Lincoln, gave his flock in 1253, "to shun the Christian usurers because they were all without mercy, and to resort to Jewish ones instead."[26] After 1290, "it was said that Jews sometimes disguised themselves as Italian moneylenders in order to gain admittance to countries, like England, from which they had been expelled."[27]

Quite plausible is the proposition of James Russell Lowell, when he served as United States minister to Great Britain, that among those Jews who came from Sicily to settle in Lincolnshire, converting to Christians for corporeal profit and comfort, were "the Cecils, including Lord Burleigh and Lord Salisbury; he cited some old chronicle in which he had cornered one Robert de Caecilia and exposed him as an English Jew."[28] The Cecil family cannot be traced before David Cecil, a prosperous tavern owner in their home town Stamford, which once tolerated a large community of Jews. When the Jews were banished in 1290, Stamford held a tremendous sale of their goods, including numerous Hebrew manuscripts. They had lived there for about a century, especially energetic at the Lent Fair of the town, where Crusaders enjoyed slaughtering and looting them after listening to Easter agitation of priests and friars in 1190.

Among the documents of the house of Cecil currently called the Lansdowne Manuscripts there is a solitary record of one Reyne, a Jewess, wife of David, who rented a house in All Saints parish, Stamford, for which she regularly paid one Gilbert of Chesterton.

In the year the Earl of Oxford was born, 1550, Michael Angelo Florio, the son of an Italian Jew turned Christian, escaped from Valteline persecution by Catholics who hated him for quitting the Franciscan fraternity. He left Italy, became a Protestant, and settled in England, befriended by Burghley, who aided in his elevation to the pulpit of chief preacher to the Italian congregation in London. In 1553 he became the father of the famous linguist and translator John Florio, whose version of the *Essays* by Michel de Montaigne, another descendant of brilliant Jews, shines among the gems of Elizabethan literature. John married Rose Daniel, the daughter of a musician, John, whose son Samuel earned a high place among the poets of the age. Another daughter of John Daniel married Francis Meres, the scholar whose *Wits Treasury* is a major source of our knowledge of Shakespeare. For reasons not entirely clear, Michael Florio was forced to leave England in 1559. He did not win many friends by the history he wrote about Queen Jane Grey, whom he had served as tutor. He spent his final months in obscurity in Soglio, Italy, knowing nothing of the role his son would play in the English theater, travestied as the coward soldier Parolles, wizard of tongues.

But we have strayed too distant from our main theme. Let us return to the fleet of Captain Frobisher, which came back to Britain in September 1578. From the Cornish coast he transported the ore he had collected to London, stopping to inform the Court at Richmond of his arrival. Dr George Baker, who had served the Countess Anne of Oxford as physician, a gentleman skilled in the Spanish language, examined Frobisher's minerals and discovered they were worthless.[29] The angry Captain quarreled with the Treasurer of the Cathay Company, Michael Lock, who could not pay him his salary, despite the commands of the Privy Council. On September 29, Michaelmas day, Edward de Vere found himself in desperate straits facing his creditors of the Meta Incognita partnership. Frobisher's fury conveyed forty men after him on November 20, when he came to Lock's house and loudly told the town that Lock was "a false accountant to the company, a cozener to my Lord of Oxford, no venturer at all in the voyages, a bankrupt knave."[30] Lock informed Francis Walsingham that Captain Martin "entered into great storms and rages with him like a mad beast, and raised on him such shameful reports and false slanders as the whole Court and City were full of." Believing that Lock had known the ore would be worthless when he sold Cathay shares, the Privy Council locked him in the Fleet prison. He protested to Walsingham on January 14, 1579, that he had paid his "adventure" in Frobisher's last voyage. And he desired that the Earl of Oxford might be called upon for 450 pounds, the residue of the sum required from him.[31] Poor Lock, who had lost at least three thousand pounds in the voyage, at last obtained pity from the Council. On March 25 he submitted an account of abuses by Frobisher in directing affairs entrusted to him by the "Adventurers," for fetching ore and discovering new lands, together with a list of his slanders against "Lok." On the same day Lock pleaded for relief from his expenses, for the sake of himself, his wife, and their fifteen children.[32] The Cathay Company declared itself bankrupt on April 25, and Michael Lock got most of the blame.

Eva Turner Clark correctly explained the origin of the name Shylock. Shakespeare prefixed the word "shy" to the name Lock, because of the former's colloquial meaning, "of questionable character, disreputable, shady," discerning perhaps at once how the epithet Shy Lock punned upon the Hebrew name Shelach (in Genesis, X, 24). The Bible avers that Shelach was the ancestor of the Hebrews. Shakespeare may have learnt in his brief acquaintance with Hebrew that the word shalakh stood for the cormorant, the bird that fed on fish (*Leviticus*, XI, 17). No such name as Shylock has been located in the archives of Venice.[33]

II

Nobody has ever suggested that Michael Lock was a "Marrano" or even of Jewish genes. Alexander Grosart traced his pedigree back to Thomas Lok, a modest burgess who died in 1507. His son William (1480-1550), the father of Michael, became Sheriff of London and a knight in 1548. As a London merchant he traveled on the continent, and was able to send Thomas Cromwell, the revolutionary counselor of Henry VIII, "intelligence" from Antwerp. In 1541 he went to Paris in the service of Edward Seymour, Earl of Hertford, who received notice in April 1544, "Mr Locke desires that he may receive his money within 7 days, as he tarries here for no other cause."[34] Five years after Sir William died, his son Michael had the satisfaction of seeing his name next to Richard Eden's on the titlepage of their translation of Peter Martyr's *De Novo Orbe*, englished as *The Decades of the New World or West Indies.* In 1570 Michael Lock took the place of John Broke as London agent of the Muscovy Company, organised for commerce with the Russian empire. His brother Thomas was a charter member of the firm. Michael held the Muscovy post until 1576. We do not know what relation of consanguinity or matrimony existed between Michael and Humphrey Lock, the builder and architect whom the Muscovy Company employed to go to Russia and serve the Czar Ivan IV, usually called the Terrible, in 1567. Years later they heard from Humphrey, as usual lamenting his inability to go home.[35] From whatever angle we look at Michael Lock and his close fellow-workers, we will find it impossible to thrust him into the narrow class of souls whose mental horizon is restricted to money exchange and the tides of trade. He proclaimed himself a man intensely interested in the variety of cultures on our planet, one who had "traveled thru almost all the countries of Christianity."[36] He served not only as treasurer but also as "governor" of the Cathay Company. We have seen him as a translator of Spanish narrative of West Indian exploration. We can understand why Humphrey Gilbert, the soldier, and Dr John Dee, the occult scientist, would be glad to join him in April 1575 to discuss the project of a northwest passage to China. Richard Eden, the expert in geography, who had served William Cecil as secretary before 1562, when he journeyed to the continent and traveled there until 1573, would have collaborated with Lock if he had not died in 1576. I am unable to tell how the admiral John Lock, with whom Martin Frobisher sailed to Guinea in 1544, was connected with Michael.

Michael reported to his superiors in politics that he was "well placed in the business of the Company of Moskovia, which I did execute quietly, and for the doings thereof I had of them a pension of cc (200) marks by the year, besides my house rent free and other things well worth to me ccl (200 pounds) by the year."[37] After Burghley and his cronies released him from the Fleet jail, his credit proved strong enough to win him appointment by the Levant Company to be their consul at Aleppo from 1592 to 1594. We have no record of his conclusion; nor have his fifteen offspring been traced. However we know that his nephew Henry, a graduate of Oxford University, became a poet of humble fame. His *Ecclesiasticus* (1594), dedicated to the Earl of Essex, demonstrates his learning and refined taste. Perhaps to compensate for having devoted himself in this book mainly to Jewish morality and poetry, he "annexed sundry Sonnets of Christian Passions." He gave a copy of the work to the Earl of Oxford with a sonnet extoling

> Your blood's, your mind's, your body's excellence,
> and asking for his kind scrutiny of the verse,
>> for work's proper sake,
> Which treats of true felicity's essence...
> Whereof your own experience much might say,
> Would you vouchsafe your knowledge to bewray.[38]

Early in 1601 Henry Lok appears to have been a servant of Sir Robert Cecil, and acted as a messenger between him and Edward de Vere, Cecil's brother-in-law. Henry's mother, Anne Vaughan, was a Welshwoman, a member of the family of the poet Henry Vaughan, whose immortal lyric beginning "They are all gone into the world of light" is well known to all lovers of English poetry. Henry married

Anne Moyle of Cornwall, whose ancestors had romantically defended the claim of young Perkin Warbeck to the throne usurped
by Henry Tudor, King Henry VII. These Loks lived at the inn sign
of the Lute in the Strand, close by the residence of the Cecils.[39] I
have long believed that from Henry's loins or his uncle Michael's
came the seed of John Locke, the philosopher of religious tolerance
and liberal statecraft, but his lineage record is confined to Dorset-
shire.

It seems to be pretty clear that Shakespeare conceived of his
drama about melancholy Antonio's debt to the Jew Shylock of three
thousand ducats on account of the three thousand pounds the Earl
of Oxford owed for his Cathay shares, money which could also be
said to have been lost at sea, like Antonio's fortune. But why did
our dramatist imagine his monstrous creditor as a Jew? The answer
to this question is only partly supplied by Thomas Nashe in his
Christ's Tears Over Jerusalem (1593), where he urges his countrymen,
"Let us leave off the proverb which we use to a cruel dealer, saying,
Go thy ways, thou art a Jew, and say, Go thy ways, thou art a Londoner. For than Londoners are none more hard hearted and
cruel."[40] I believe that Edward de Vere had always, since his childhood at Castle Hedingham, imagined the Jews, not as the nation
created by God to convey his messages to mankind, but as a people
cursed, because they had been the first to hear the gospel of the
Galilean called Christ and dared to spurn it. They clung to their ancient covenant which allowed no man into their sanctuary unless his
body carried the mark of the sexual sacrifice of circumcision, a ritual
which must have amazed and terrified our poet, whose adoration of
his body, in particular the main organ of masculinity, all his writings
testify. The legend of the pound of flesh that the Jew wanted alludes
to nothing else. Shakespeare was thinking of this when he made Costard the Clown in *Love's Labour's Lost* (3.1.) call the little boy Moth,
"My sweet ounce of man's flesh, my in-conie Jew." For "in-conie"
plainly puns on the popular word for a rabbit (familiar in America
as bunny) and the old English term for the vagina, the organ our
poet regarded with awe because it convinced him that his comfort-

ing rod and staff could be verily lost, maybe conjured away, by witchcraft. In his intellect Jewry was the nucleus of witchcraft, not merely because his church preachers condemned the Jews as children of Satan; he identified them as followers of the Fiend just as his Bible, in the version of John Calvin's Geneva, glossed "Conjurers" for the reference in *Acts of the Apostles* (XIX, 13) to "vagabond Jews, exorcists" who competed with Paul in healing the delirious in Ephesus. He remembered that passage when he wrote *The Comedy of Errors*, depicting Ephesus like a pandemonium. Very early in his life father John de Vere, a lover of histrionics and bloody sports, probably carried him to see the folk plays at fairs and marketplaces called "miracles" and "moralities." Of them all none were more lurid in his remembrance than the shows about the Jewish king Herod and his mythical massacre of innocent children, among whom, we are told by the *New Testament* alone, he was seeking a male child born to take from his dynasty the throne of Israel or Judea. We find nightmare visions of the stage horrors of Herod in Shakespeare's *Henry the Fifth* (3.3), where the English monarch warns the French town of Harfleur to surrender lest they be forced to see

> Your naked infants spitted upon pikes,
> Whiles the mad mothers with their howls confus'd
> Do break the clouds, as did the wives of Jewry
> At Herod's bloody-hunting slaughtermen.

The poet could not locate in his colossal lexicon a finer metaphor for a scoundrel: "What a Herod of Jewry is this! O wicked, wicked world!" (*The Merry Wives of Windsor*, 2.1) When he made Hamlet plead for an end to actors' shrieking and thundering constantly, he shielded his ears because "It out-Herods Herod: pray you, avoid it" (3.2). We may be sure he connected the myth of the massacre of the innocents with the tale told by the Prioress in his beloved Chaucer's *Canterbury Tales* concerning the sainted child who, she recited, was murdered by merciless Jews but managed to get them punished by chanting to the Virgin Mary despite his cut throat. Shakespeare

knew that story well and never forgot its "Jewerye / Sustained by a
lord of that contree / For usury and lucre of felonye." And when
Edward, Viscount Bulbeck, was told that the star on the Vere crest
commemorated a heavenly revelation over an ancestor's head during a Crusade, he engraved in his soul an image of the "nova" over
Bethlehem together with the burial place of Jesus (furnished by the
forgotten Jew Joseph of Arimathea):

> The sepulcher in stubborn Jewry
> Of the world's ransom, blessed Mary's son   *Richard the Second,* 2.1

During the conversations that Edward de Vere surely had with
Lock, the "Cathayan," he heard about Lock's visit to Venice, re-
freshing the Earl's memories of the time he spent there. "When I
was at Venice," Lock wrote to Sir Robert Cecil on January 29, 1603,
"I spoke divers times with some of the chief nobles there touching
the state of that commonwealth, and the traffic of our nation into
all Levant."[41] The Earl of Oxford arrived in the city in the summer
of 1575. Clemente Paretti, a financier, informed his father-in-law,
on September 23,

> I am sorry that afore this time I could not, according to duty,
> write to your honour of my Lord's success and good disposition
> in this his travel. But my daily and continual service about my
> Lord hath rather hindered than furthered my good intention and
> service which always hath been and is employed to obey your
> honour's commandment. At this present your honour shall un-
> derstand my Lord's better disposition, God be thanked, for now
> last coming from Genoa his Lordship found himself somewhat
> altered by reason of the extreme heats; and before, his Lordship
> hurt his knee in one of the Venetian galleys, but all is past with-
> out further harm. Of any other reports that your honour hath
> understood of my Lord, no credit is to be given unto.[42]

What the Earl did or said or saw in Venice remains unknown to us
since the house of Cecil, which took charge of all the letters he
wrote to his Countess and the Queen during his tour of Europe,
were painstakingly determined to deprive us of them.[42]

We may fancy that the English newcomer in Venice usually acted like Ben Jonson's buffoon Sir Politick Wouldbe on entering the city of *Volpone*:

I had read Contarene, took me a house,
Dealt with my Jews to furnish it with movables. (4.1)[43]

Of course he had heard, like Robert Greene, "that of all the cities in Europe, Venice hath most semblance of Venus' vanities."[44] And naturally the chief nobles, including the Doge Nicola da Ponte, would have spoken to him sooner and more freely than with Michael Lock. He must have invited their sea veterans to tell him about the great naval battle of Lepanto in 1571, where Don John of Austria had led the champion sailors of Christendom to triumph over the Turkish fleet. Perhaps the Venetians were ashamed to tell him how the Turks had nevertheless conquered the island of Cyprus. Then they heard a rumor that the Sultan Selim had promised his Jew Joseph Nasi, whose wisdom he valued more than pearls, that he would be crowned King of Cyprus; he already was Duke of Naxos. On December 14, 1571, the Venetian Senate agreed to expel all Jews in their jurisdiction, "the foes of the faith," in alleged thanksgiving for the Lepanto victory in October. This decree violated a treaty granting the Jews rights of dwelling and business which did not expire until two years later. On March 7, 1573, Venice made a peace treaty with Turkey, promoted by the Sultan's Jewish physician, Solomon Ashkenazy, a clever rival of Joseph Nasi. Dr Ashkenazy was a native of nearby Udine and had kin in Verona. Perhaps his Italian influence was instrumental in the Senate's repeal of the law banishing the Jews on July 7. Burghley's Italian correspondent in Paris, Pietro Bizarro, sent him a report describing how cordially Venice had greeted the Jewish doctor.[45] During Oxford's journeys to the marvels of art and technology in northern Italy, he may have also heard about the sensational rumor widespread among the Jews there that the year 1575, according to the Hebrew calendar dating from the creation of Eden, 5335, would see the Doomsdays of the evil world and the rise of the *Messiah*, the Anointed man, destined to be their king.[46]

Evidence of the Doomsdays coming was seen in the pestilence that struck Italy in 1575, and raged for three years. It killed about fifty thousand people in Venice, nearly one-third of the town. The Earl of Oxford's fever indicates that the epidemic grazed him. But there were a legion of Jews capable of laughter at the dreams of the Messiah, full of confidence in the durability of Christendom. A group of these founded in 1575 the Scuola Italiana in Venice, a synagog for the Sefardi (Spanish) ritual of the Jews. Shylock would not have belonged to this synagog, for, as Cecil Roth conclusively maintained, he was created in the image of the Jew adhering to the Ashkenazy (Teutonic) ritual.[47] Shakespeare would have been interested in the architecture of the Scuole Italiana, and other structures in the first of Europe's ghettos—named after the ghetto, the Venetian iron foundry, where the Jews were compelled to cluster. He would have been surprised as Thomas Coryat was when that English traveler walked thru the Ghetto of Venice and beheld there "elegant and sweet-featured" persons, "some as beautiful as ever I saw," surpassing the countesses of England in grace of garments and servant-girls.[48] Shakespeare's Jessica must have been modeled after one of the Jewish damsels viewed in Venice.

On September 24, 1575, Benedetto Spinola wrote to Burghley that he had "sent his Lordship's letter by the ordinary post to Venice to be delivered into the hands of the Earl. No letters have come from thence for six weeks on account of the great pestilence at Trent, thru which place the post has to pass, so that it is no marvel that the Countess has not heard from her husband." Oxford arrived in Venice in the summer of 1575, and soon became familiar with the cathedral of St Mark, gondolas, the Tranect, "the common Ferrie, / Which trades to Venice," mentioned in *The Merchant of Venice* once (3.4.53-54), and the granite pillar by the bridge of the city's main mercantile traffic, on which the Republic announced her decrees; at the base of this pillar stood a figure of stone popularly called Il Gobbo di Rialto. Gobbo means a humpback, but Shakespeare nowhere indicates that he intended his Clown in the romance to have one. Young Robert Cecil's feelings might have been severely hurt, if he had been nicknamed Lancelot Gobbo; he suffered enough when the Queen called him her dwarf.

Benedict Spinola congratulated Burghley on October 6 for the safe arrival of his son-in-law from Milan at Venice. He added that Pasquale, his brother, would soon go there to pay his respects.[49] Pasquale wrote from Venice on December 11, "The Earl of Oxford is in good health, and is resolved to see the rest of Italy if he can travel with safety, and will leave tomorrow for Florence." Yesterday, Pasquale added, he paid Il Conte all the money which he had been directed to deliver, keeping part for himself, and substituting "letters of Cambio" (exchange credit) for different towns.[50] The Earl appears to have enjoyed especially his sights of Mantua, the magnificent palace of art erected by the Gonzaga dynasty, the tomb of Baldassare Castiglione, whose *Book of the Courtier* he treasured and wrote introductory praise for when his tutor at Cambridge, Bartholomew Clerke, translated it into Latin. The painter and sculptor Giulio Romano constructed the tomb. This pupil of Raphael was the sole artist to have the honor of being named in a Shakespeare play (*The Winter's Tale*). He is the Signior Julio whose painting of a dwarf is mentioned in *Love's Labor's Lost*. But you will not find a line about him in Professor Oscar Campbell's *Readers Encyclopedia of Shakespeare*, because the Professor could not explain how his Stratford hero became acquainted with Giulio Romano. Nor will you find reference to Pietro Aretino, whose poems of nude ladies with paramours Romano drew illustrious pictures for. Aretino's play *Filosofo* was not translated to English in our dramatist's time, nor scarcely known in England. Yet Shakespeare certainly read it. Its simile for a woman beautiful and shameless (5.8), "*una sepoltura di fuor dorata, e di dentro verminosa,*" appears to be the source of the line in *The Merchant of Venice* (2.7.69) wrongly printed as

> Guilded timber doe wormes infold,

which Samuel Johnson mended: Guilded *tombes* (without knowing Aretino). Edmund Malone supported the correction, quoting in its favor Shakespeare's Sonnet CI, "It lies in thee/To make thee much outlive a gilded tomb." Possibly from Aretino's play *Orazia*, where

Publio cries to a crowd for mercy to his son, came inspiration for Portia's declaration: "And earthly power doth then shew likest Gods / When mercie seasons Iustice" (4.1.194-195). Aretino wrote: "So those come close to God, who, always merciful, arm us against the errors of others; thus in the act of pardon man becomes divine." Incidentally the Italian's comedy *Marescalco* contains a scene in which a juvenile Gentile sarcastically salutes a Jew named Abram (3.1). But otherwise Shylock's portrait bears no resemblance to Aretino's Jew.

Shortly after De Vere left Italy, Guglielmo the Duke of Mantua received instruction from a legate of Pope Paul IV which inspired his decree for strict segregation of the Jews in his City. His obedience to the Papal bull *Cum nimis absurdum* prohibited the Chosen People to give lessons in Latin or grammar in return for different learning; also forbidden were Jewish lessons in music and dancing. Yet a few years later Mantua became the first government in the West to exalt a Jew to nobility; the Duke made Joseph da Fano, a favorite servant of his court, Marquis of Villimpenta.

When Oxford returned to London in April 1576 he found the royal court mildly excited by the tricks and devices of an Italian magician, Dionisio alias Scoto of Mantua, who I suspect was a Jew making a precarious livelihood as some of his religion and race became famous for in Italy. The English ambassador in Paris, Valentine Dale, informed Burghley about him in March: "There is one Scotto, an Italian, that playeth such knocks as Feates doth upon the cards, who cometh to show the Queen's Majesty some of his toys." Oxford's cousin Lord Henry Howard never forgot Dionisio: "I was present myself," he wrote in 1583, "when divers gentlemen and noblemen, which undertook to descry the finest sleights that Scotto the Italian was able to play by Leiger du main before the Queen, were notwithstanding no less beguiled than the rest."[51]

Lord Harry Howard was himself a trickster of the first magnitude. His lies and calumnies concerning the Earl of Oxford nearly eclipsed the facts of his biography for centuries. From his mint of mendacity, I maintain, James Augustus St John, once celebrated for his book about Borneo, acquired the vicious nonsense he put into his tome on Sir Walter Ralegh in 1869, about Edward de Vere's appointment to command English troops in Flanders which he dated prior to the Earl's tour of Europe!

Dislodged from this position by the Queen's order, he returned to England; but, after a brief stay, again repaired to the Continent, crossed the Alps, and in the quarrels of Genoa, this ancestor of the renowned Captain Lemuel Gulliver proceeded to Venice, by whose priests and courtesans he appears to have been equally fascinated.[52]

If the Earl of Oxford had direct dealing with Benedict Spinola after his homecoming, he would have found wonderful the new dwelling the banker had built in the parish of St Bartolph outside Aldgate. The Queen granted the financier the land for it on January 29, 1575. Spinola's Pleasure, people called it. At an unknown date he sold this property to Oxford, who died the owner of "a messuage or tenement called the Gate House, with its appurtenances, and a garden commonly known as the Great Garden alias the Covent Garden of Christ church, and in addition newly constructed buildings in the aforesaid Great Garden..."[53]

In those days northern Portsoken Ward included Spinola's Pleasure facing Hog Lane, where Thomas Watson and Christopher Marlowe crossed swords with a ruffian named William Bradley in 1584. "In this Hog Lane... lying on the Back-side of White chapel, were eight acres of Land, which about the year 1574 (*sic*) were in the possession of one Benedict Spinola," at least until 1584.[54] Nearby on Bishopsgate Street bustled the Bull Inn, where *The Jew* was first performed. In Whitechapel were the Boar's Head tavern and the Blue Boar Inn, the latter named after the savage beast which the Earls of Oxford emblemed in their livery. Hog Lane stretched northward to the hospital of St Mary outside Bishopsgate, between rows of elm trees, from Houndsditch in the west up to east Whitechapel. Houndsditch extended from Aldgate northwest to Bishopsgate and in Tudor times was crowded with brokeries of old clothing and the shops of usurers. Before 1572 when Oxford's genial cousin, Thomas Howard, Duke of Norfolk, lost his head under the royal ax prepared for him by a labyrinthine plot of Lord Burghley, the Duke used to delight the citizens beyond Aldgate by riding with his Duchess thru Bishopsgate Street to Leadenhall, past the church of St Catherine Cree to the site still called Duke's Place. People long recalled how superb he looked, attended with a hundred horses bearing his livery, a company of his gentlemen riding ahead, their coats edged with velvet. Four heralds went before his horse, into Bevis Marks, once the gardens of the abbots of Bury and therefor named Bury's Marks originally. Duke Street there is believed to have been the location of a secret Jewish meetingplace in Elizabethan days.[55] On the same ground, Bevis Marks, many decades after those Jews had been driven out of England (except the few who could not bear the penalty of exile and embraced Christianity) Portuguese Jews accepted Oliver Cromwell's invitation to come and enrich his country, and they built on the earth of the old synagog a grand new structure for their faith. The synagog named the Holy Assembly of the Gates of Heavens (*Kahal Kadosh Shaarei Shamaim*), I am told, stands on land once owned by the Pointz family, formerly the Priory of Holy Trinity in Aldgate. Next to it bloomed the garden of Sir Thomas Heneage, who married the Countess Mary of Southampton. In 1692 German and Polish Jews erected here, near Gracechurch Street, a synagog devoted to their Ashkenazy ritual, Shylock's mode of adoration of his God. The Sefardi synagog now adorning Duke's Place with its ornate Italian style was built in 1838, but is scarcely used today.

A family named Gobbo, by the way, lived at Titchfield in Hampshire, the hometown of the Earls of Southampton, Oxford 's unfortunate friends.

There is nothing to prove that Benedick Spinola, as the banker was occasionally called, bore the brand of Abraham on his sex. He was "naturalised" in London on March 10, 1552.[56] He lived in Langhorne ward, before he built his Pleasure, and was a member of the English church named St Gabriel Fenchurch.[57] Benedick the Genoese acted as executor of the last will and testament of the antiquarian William Lambard's father.[58] The name Lambard of course came from the Lombard bankers who swarmed into England after Edward I exiled the Jews. Near Benedick's residence lived a fugitive from Portugal, Dr Hector Nunez, physician, merchant, and chief informant to Lord Burghley on Iberian business and secrets of state. Dr Nunez was the secret leader of the Jewish community in London.[59] In 1564 Elizabeth appealed to the Czar Ivan that one Raphael Barberini should be permitted to hunt debtors in Russia. His real purpose was to win trade privileges for his Antwerp firm, his employers Francis and Nicholas Spinola, and Francis Berty, perhaps an Englishman. We have no document of communication between Dr Nunez and Spinola. Presumably Benedick and his brother Pasquale in Venice suffered from the calamity which, in December 1570, caused the bankruptcy of Pedro Francesco and Pedro Christophoro Spinola of Genoa. They were stricken in Antwerp. In November Tommaso Spinola went bankrupt in Lyons.[60] In 1571 Giraldo Despes, the Spanish ambassador in London, urged the Duke of Alba to arrest "Hieronimo Salvago, Genoves," ostensibly engaged in commerce in the Low Countries, connected with "Spinola;" the envoy accused Jerome Salvago of opening cipher mail from the Queen of Scots.[61]

In 1575 Francesco Giraldi, ambassador from Portugal, complained to Burghley that Hebrew Bibles were being sent from England to the Jews in Morocco. To discuss the matter, the Lord Treasurer noted, "I appointed him Spinola's house in his garden near Shoreditch," Spinola's Pleasure.[62] On June 18, 1578, Dr Roderigo Lopez, the multitalented physician, a distant relative of Michel de Montaigne's mother, petitioned Burghley for the payment of twenty pounds owed by Mr Henry Howard, son of the Viscount Bindon, to Mr Spinola. On June 27 Cecil made a note about Howard's creditor: "not paid any thing at all, D. Lopes. Benedict Spinola £20."[63] This can be taken as evidence of Jewish blood in Spinola's veins only if you agree with Francis Bacon that money lending is a peculiarly Jewish undertaking. In the first logical defense "Of Usury" ever written, Bacon joked that "Usurers should have orange-tawny bonnets because they do Judaise."[64] Jews had been commanded by

Popes to wear orange-colored caps in order to identify them as proper targets for Christian mud and rocks.

Allow me to complete the London record of the Spinolas so far as I have traced it. In August 1578 Baptista Spinola, a banker of Antwerp, a creditor of the Queen, visited the English metropolis. In September he and William Faunt, a servant of the Lord Treasurer, sailed to the Netherlands to meet her Majesty's ambassadors there, we know not what for.[65] On July 27, 1580, an unknown mourner arranged for publication of a lost Epitaph on the Death of Benedick Spinola. His initials are R. B. The name of Spinola is commonly coupled with Nigroni among the bankers from whom the Spanish despot Philip borrowed. He owed them more than any other financiers.[66]

I conjecture but am unable to bear adequate witness that Shakespeare's picture of the strength, pride and dignity of Shylock resulted from personal acquaintance with Benedict Spinola as well as Michael Lock, and maybe Hector Nunez. There is manifestly not a man in the drama who is Shylock's equal in courage, intellect, and devotion to ideals. But this did not become clear to Europe until the Irish actor Charles Macklin revived Shakespeare's own work for the London stage in 1741. He put an end to the ridiculous and vulgar version of *The Merchant of Venice* made by George Granville, Viscount Lansdowne, which the histrionic profession favored for forty years. Macklin's Jew was almost a monster, bordering on tragic heroism. The German scholar E. C. Lichtenberg saw his performance in 1775 and remarked: "It is not to be denied that the sight of this Jew suffices to wake at once, in the best ordered mind, all the prejudices of childhood against this people." However, after witnessing Edmund Kean's portrayal of Shylock as a passionate believer in his law, the German observed that the vulgar conviction that the Jew "has but one idea is not true; he has more ideas than any other person in the play." Lichtenberg correctly concluded, "The stage is not, in general, the best place to study our author's characters in... things rank and gross do merely gender in it!" And too seldom, "genius comes once an age to clear away the rubbish to make it fruitful and wholesome."[67]

III

When our dramatist composed *The Merchant of Venice* his mind was not on justice but on pity, particularly self-pity. You have only to open the romance at the first page and listen to his protagonist, the merchant, Antonio, amuse his friends with his reflections on the invisible mirror of his ego, to see what concerned our author thru the entire work:

> In sooth I know not why I am so sad,
> It wearies me: you say it wearies you;
> But how I caught it, found it, or came by it,
> What stuffe 'tis made of, whereof it is borne,
> I am to learne:
> And such a Want-wit sadness makes of mee,
> That I haue much ado to know my selfe. (1.1.1-7)

Shakespeare in this mood would not give a fig for the facts about usury, or the truth about the Jews. He needed a convenient object, a scapegoat, on which to throw the blame for his gloom. He knew himself well enough to perceive that money or the necessity of it was not the root of his sorrow. Yet he saw in the giant he imagined as incarnation of Jewish jurisprudence, avarice and revenge, a worthy target for the anger of his barely conscious greed which turned inward became melancholy.

Strange as it may seem, De Vere was proud of having Hebrew blood, or vain of genealogical reveries that, like his cousin Percival Golding, derived the pedigree of the Veres from Serug, the great-grandfather of Abraham. Edward de Vere preferred such Biblical charts of his lineage to the inquiries that Francis Peto described for Burghley in a letter from Milan dated March 31, 1576, where Peto told how he had inscribed "a perfect genealogy of all the marriages and affinities between the houses of England and Scotland, and also in what wise the said houses are allied with divers foreign families, the greatest of all Christendom... Meant to have shown this designment to the Earl of Oxford when he passed this way, but was always refused to be spoken with."[68]

Certainly he would not have cared to learn that his ancestors came to Britain more than two hundred years after Jews settled there. Shakespeare would have been more interested to observe how a renegade Jew named Theobald of Cambridge, a monk of Norwich, in 1144 accused the Jewry of that town of kidnapping a Christian lad named William and draining his blood for magical employment in their ritual. Nobody knew better than this fugitive from Judaism that Jews never used blood in ritual or diet. The Norwich monk Thomas of Monmouth wrote about the alleged martyrdom of William, showing how flimsy was the case against the Jews and how malignant was the sycophant Theobald. Edward de Vere may have taken in such East Anglican legends with his mother's milk. He would have been inclined to overlook the uprisings against the Jews led by gentry eager to burn records of the money they owed the Jews. I assume he was ignorant of the way in which Christian moneylenders combined in debt the principal of loans with fixt interest charges not depending on the duration of debt. Matthew of Paris about 1255 affirmed: "This is worse than the Jew's conditions; for the Jew will still receive the principal courteously whenever thou shalt return it, with only such interest as is proportionate to the time for which thou holdest it in hand." Matthew noted that the English king Henry III, patronising loan-leeches from Lombardy, "extorted from the Jews whatever visible property those wretched people possessed, not only, so to say, skinning them merely, but also plucking out their entrails."[69] Nearly fifty years before Edward's decree of expulsion, Jews begged King Henry for freedom from his dominion: "No hope remains to us of breathing freely, the Pope's usurers have supplanted us; therefor permit us to depart, and we will seek another abode somewhere or other."

When they were banished from England, King Edward made all debts owed them debts to the Crown, and strove to keep accurate ledgers of the Christian bonds. But many a family with hands cunning or strong for the task was able to gain access to the royal chests that held the documents of these debts, and get rid of the evidence against them. The lists of bonds for money or commodities, mainly wool and corn, owed Jews of seventeen towns are missing, including those for York, Bedford, Ipswich, Stamford, Colchester and London. There is not even a note of the delivery of an arca, a chest, of the bonds from Stamford. Thus testimony of the presence and business of the Cecil family in their home city may have been removed.

During De Vere's travels in Germany in the spring of 1575 he could have encountered Jewish merchants visiting the fairs and heard how many of them had been given by comic tax-collectors family names bearing the syllable "Gold." This might have induced him to wonder about the derivation of his mother's name, Golding, which her kin tradition claimed to be originally from Denmark. The idea that the Goldings could have been converts to Christianity when they first emerged in England was bound to be disquieting. The night's sleep that King George II lost after attending Charles Macklin's production of *The Merchant of Venice* would have been a trifle by comparison with the nightmare the Earl of Oxford would surely have suffered on suspecting that his mother had Jewish blood. It might have explained for him the attraction of Protestant heresy exhibited by his beloved uncle Arthur Golding, who reacted with nearly physical revulsion against the Catholic authority which the Earl believed that the Popes got from Simon Kephas, called in Greek Peter. At all events the Earl displayed a remarkable lack of curiosity about the ancestry of the Goldings. So did William Cecil, his father-in-law, who knew that John Golding, Oxford's grandfather, had served as an auditor in the Tudor treasury.

At the same time that the English people taught their children that Jews were offspring of the Devil, their clergy manifested a peculiar fondness for calling their country "Israel." Buried in ancestral oblivion were stories of the sailors from the land of Canaan who developed the tin mines of Cornwall and probably built the sun-shrine named Stonehenge. But "Elizabethans believed themselves to descend from the Ten Lost Tribes" of the Israelites. In a theological tract of 1598 the Queen herself was hailed as "the light of Israel." Fulk Greville spoke of the doom of Lord Essex as "the fall of this great man in Israel." Sir Robert Cecil liked to glorify her Majesty's court in this fashion, "Who in Israel did not know...?"[70] The eminent scholar Leonardo Bruni of Arezzo condemned the study of Hebrew as a waste of time and work, not necessary for knowledge of God. "What comparison is there," he inquired furiously, "between the erudition of the Greeks and the crude scholarship of the Jews?" Adoring the pagan Hellenic and Roman lore, he appealed for exclusion of Judaic study from European schools. It was plain to him that the people of the Psalms, the kinsmen of Ecclesiastes, the oracles of the Bible "have no philosophers, no poets, no orators!"[71] Nevertheless the great teacher Richard Mulcaster persevered in urging the children in his care to learn Hebrew. In 1572 the boys there were publicly tested in reading the Psalms. Edmund Spenser underwent Mulcaster's training. The author of the most memorable Sonnets ever written made them with the Hebrew Psalms gleaming in his mind. He was familiar with opinions of Leonard Aretine, for Arthur Golding had translated the latter's history of "the wars between the Imperials and the Goths for the possession of Italy" (1563), dedicated to Sir William "Sicill," a year after Edward de Vere entered Cecil's household as a royal ward. Golding finished his translation at Cecil's home in the Strand, and submitted it to the "Master of her Highness' Court of wards and liveries."

I believe it was from Golding, not Cecil, that young De Vere learned the phrase "stubborn Jewry." Golding profoundly admired John Calvin and on October 20, 1571, dedicated to "his very good Lord Edward de Vere" *The Psalms of David and Others. With M. John Calvin's Commentaries.* Concerning the text of Psalm 22 (verse 17) Calvin suggested a change, and remarked with bitterness: "I do not labor here in order to convince the Jews, whose stubbornness is indomitable to the ditch (ad rixandum). I merely wish to show how unjustly they have troubled Christian minds because of their different reading of this passage."[72] I will not trouble my readers with this textual problem. Nor will I deny that the poet of *The Merchant of Venice* disputed in 1579 against the contention of Arthur Golding and John Calvin: "There is no difference of the Jews or Gentiles,

Greeks or Barbarous, learned or unlearned, before God, but that whosoever serveth him faithfully and unfeinedly, the same is accepted of him as his dear child, notwithstanding that he seem not to be within the bounds of the visible Church."[73]

Young Oxford may not have known that the city of Geneva, with Calvin's approval, sanctioned the practice of lending money, setting the rate of interest at 5%. He would have found far more interesting the report of Calvin's prosecution of Miguel Servetus, the wandering Spaniard, who discovered the circulation of the blood, and tangled his discovery in wild webs of religious controversy, which infuriated Christians of almost all varieties. Servetus was too vain of his reasoning power, and revolted against the concept of the Trinity, the union in a single being of the Heavenly Father, his immaculately conceived Son, and the Holy Ghost (*Sanctus Spiritus*). At the trial in Geneva in 1553, they searched for the source of his obsession with unity, which led him to see the arteries and capillaries running as parts of one system, and also drove his pen to the notes he made for Ptolemy's *Geography*, printed in Latin at Lyon in 1535. A lawyer challenged the poor physician, demanding to know if his father had been Jewish, or any of his ancestors. Proudly he replied, "O no! They were Christians of ancient lineage, living as nobles." However Calvin understood that Spanish warlords had mingled their breeds with the Jews whom they regarded as aristocrats in the years before the Roman church inquisition took charge of justice in Spain. He did not go so far as Pope Paul IV, who denounced Spaniards for being "no better than renegade Jews."[74] Nor would Calvin have endorsed the extravagance of Erasmus, who asserted in a letter of March 1518, "Jews are very numerous in Italy; in Spain there are scarcely any Christians."

The miserable Miguel attacked Calvin for claiming to cling to the "irrational, impossible, tyrannical law" of Moses, instead of adopting the posture of the Apostle Paul toward that code which forbade the eating of pigs, rodents, and reptiles, forbade laboring on the Sabbath, and exacted justice as more desirable than charity or love. Servetus demanded that the Presbyterian patriarch should stop "twisting that law to apply to us, violently agitating for its observance, as if you were dealing with a Jew." *"Tu vero judaico quodam zelo scandalizaris!"* He actually called Calvin himself a Jew! Even to the present day Geneva has displayed little remorse for burning the Spanish physician on October 27, 1553. Servetus died at the stake for heretics not for his fantasies in law, mathematics, medicine, or astrology, but simply for "Judaising," insisting on the singularity of God.[75]

Practically every sage of the period, including those who called themselves humanists, delighted with Calvin and Servetus in detesting the Jews, the curst nation that could not imagine liberty without law. Erasmus wrote to the Catholic inquisitor Jacob Hoojstraten, "Who among us does not heartily dislike this race of men? If it is a Christian matter to hate Jews, all of us are sufficiently Christian." His devout friend, Saint Thomas More wrote a book in defense of the burning of heretics, beside the juvenile volume he completed for his mentor Cardinal John Morton teeming with lies about King Richard the Third.[76]

At the beginning of the sixteenth century, the Spanish ambassador to England interrupted festivity at the marriage of Prince Arthur Tudor and Catherine of Aragon to complain, "there are in England and Flanders many heretics who have come from Spain, and people who have fled from the Inquisition, who speak ill of Spain, and wish to excite hatred against her." King Henry VII consoled him. "He laid his hands on his breast and swore, 'by the faith of his heart,' that if anyone (without mentioning those cursed exiles) of his best beloved subjects should say anything against the King and Queen of Spain, he would not esteem him, or any longer treat him as his friend. He promised to punish soundly any Jew or heretic to be found in his realms."[77] In the same year, 1501, the fugitive Jew Juan Lopez died in London without leaving a will. He was a kinsman of the great skeptic and peacemaker of France, Montaigne, and of Dr Roderigo Lopez, Queen Elizabeth's charming physician, who was accused of poisoning her.[78]

In 1512 the fugitive family of Mendes settled in Antwerp and began the business which nearly attained for them a monopoly of the pepper market in Europe. Not long after, the houses of Mendes managed loans for the English treasury. Their beauty Dona Gracia Mendes, sometimes named Beatrice de Luna, became the Queen of the secret hives of Judaism that flourished and perished in this century. She came to England in 1535 with her nephew Joao Miguez, the future Duke of Naxos, whom Kit Marlowe held plainly in view when he invented his *Jew of Malta*. Three years before, the commercial rivals of Diogo Mendes in Antwerp accused him of the crime of "Judaising." His wife Brianda was Gracia's sister. The Holy Office of Antwerp imprisoned Diogo, and King Henry VIII personally intervened for his liberty. Diogo was able to spend his last ten years peacefully assisting in the rise of Antwerp as the world-market city, and in the private covenant of his creed.[79]

An obscure connexion of the Mendes family seems to be the clan of Jorge Anes of Valladolid who made his home in London about 1521. His son Francis became the secret agent of Sir Francis Drake in the Azores, later commanded the English garrison in Youghal, Ireland, holding down Irish rebellion. Francis's brother Dunstan imported supplies for Elizabeth's household and the Portuguese king Antonio made him his financier. A daughter of Dunstan married Dr Roderigo Lopez. It was not long before her clan became accustomed to being named Ames; they turned true Christian, entered the service of the earldom of Oxford; and among their descendants in America none appeared prouder of his Jewish heritage than the brilliant theatrical director Winthrop Ames.

These clandestine Jewish families held regular religious services in the house of Alvares Lopes, a cousin of Diogo Mendes, in London. Two uncles of Michel de Montaigne belonged to the little community, which had less than forty householders in the capital and other cities, notably Bristol. The Catholic Inquisition of Milan discovered these outlaws, and informed the Privy Council during the Christmas jollities of 1541. The Holy Office of Milan enjoyed a terrific reputation. In March 1575 the Earl of Oxford confessed, "For fear of the inquisition I dare not pass by Milan, the Bishop whereof exerciseth such tyranny."[80] A certain Gaspar Lopez, nursing an unknown grudge, informed the Inquisitors about his English relatives. The royal Council ordered the arrest of the "Merchant Strangers... suspected to be Jews," and sequestered their property. At the request of Margaret of Austria, the Queen Regent of the Netherlands, who assured the English prosecutors that the colony in London consisted of good Christians, they were freed. They dispersed, leaving only about seven in the British metropolis.[81] At Bristol a larger group, headed by the physician Henrique Nunez and his wife Beatriz Fernandes, continued to worship in their old way. The lady Beatriz baked *mazos*—unleavened bread—for their Passover holidays, and sent the festival disks of dough to London, to the Anes home, their inlaws of the Simon Ruiz family, and Doctor Hector Nunez. Nunez belonged to the Corporation of Italian Merchants. His brother-in-law Bernaldo Luis Freire was a member of the Florios' Italian Reformed Church. But Freire's sister Grace was buried on January 17, 1574, at the church of St Dunstan in Stepney. Dr Nunez requested in his will to be buried by her side, altho he had joined a different church. When the Jews returned to England at the invitation of Oliver Cromwell, they purchased ground there in Stepney for a cemetery.

By the way, we ought to note that the Lomellini family, of which Lord John Lumley, Oxford's cherished friend, was a scion, had no kin in the Italian church. They had arrived in England before the Protestant insurrection, and the Catholic Church had no more loyal son than Lord Lumley, whose fascination by the arts, especially medicine, never drew him into heresy. He does not seem to have sustained a tie with his relatives in Portugal.[82]

Under Henry VIII, in 1543, the parliament repealed all early English legislation against usury. Ten per cent was permitted as a rate of interest, with harsh penalties for tricks to increase rates. But Edward Seymour, the Duke of Somerset, guardian of the boy King Edward VI, believed that Bible rejection of interest-taking on loans between Israelites applied to Britons too. He repealed the first formal permission of usury in England, condemning it, "by the word of God utterly prohibited as a vice most odious and detestable."[83]

In 1567 Pope Pius V outlawed money lending for interest in his realm. On February 26, 1569, his bull *Hebraeorum gens sola* banished all Jews from dominions of the Church, excepting Rome and the seaport of Ancona, threatening them in Italy and France with loss of property and slavery. In this year 1569 the English humanist Thomas Wilson finished his *Discourse on Usury*. It was not published until 1572, a year after Parliament, under the Cecil tutelage, allowed the taking of interest or usance at the rate of 10%, while declaring the act of interest taking a sin.

Burghley's cousin, the Reverend Henry Smith, known to all London as "silver-tongue" Smith, preached at his pulpit in St Clement Danes, "the name of usury shall be fulfilled as it signifieth biting, so when it hath bitten other it shall bite the Usurer too, and never rest biting." Thomas Wilson's *Discourse* assured his gullible public that "for this cause" the Jewes "were hated in England, & so banished worthily, with whom I would wish all these Englishmen were sent, that lend their money or other goods whatsoever for gain, for I take them to be no better than Jews. Nay, shall I say: they are worse than Jews."[84] There you have one of the morals that Shakespeare clearly hoped his *The Merchant of Venice* would impress on every mind attending his play.

When Shakespeare presented Shylock muttering at the sight of Antonio "I hate him for he is a Christian" (1.3.39), he betrayed the infantile origin of his rage against Jews. If he had been acquainted with any Jews, he would have soon learnt that Christians were hated only when they earned reputation as oppressors, malignant antagonists of Jews. No Jew would hate because somebody believed in the trinity of Divinity, or the virgin birth of God's Son as carnal middle-class man, or the salvation of the soul from mortality by eating divine brawn in the shape of a wafer and drinking God's blood transmuted to wine. Nor would a Jew have despised Antonio

> for that in low simplicitie
> He lends out money gratis, and brings downe
> The rate of usance here with us in Venice. (1.3.40-43)

Such a saintly merchant would have had no effect at all on the rate of interest where strangers to Antonio needed to borrow, and the "Want-wit" was not always available, particularly when all of his vessels were somehow at sea. Need we call attention to the fact that, while Antonio disdains "making" or "breeding" money "By taking, nor by giving of excess," he is not averse to gleaning profit from merchandise, nor collecting rent from "real" estate? He may be a hero of fairytale ideals, but he is not absolutely incredible. What Shakespeare cannot possibly persuade us to believe is that this prodigy of loving-kindness and good-will—"the best condition'd and unwearied spirit in doing courtesies"—is the same saintly creature who "spit upon (Shylock's) gabardine," voided his rheum on the old Jew's beard, spurned him with his foot, in short, behaved with childish brutality to a man who could hardly punish him as he deserved. It is difficult to believe that the gentleman who treated the Jew like this would have been gentle, patient, generous to anybody else he may have felt free to abuse as a figure he unreasonably feared. We must not forget that Shakespeare never protested against the brutality of the state toward heretics. We can be confident that the Earl of Oxford would have said nothing to disturb his Queen's rigor of righteousness when, on 22 June 1575, she ordered two Dutch Anabaptists to be burned for declining to go her primrose road to Paradise, preferring their own path of thorns. And I am sure his contempt for Sir Francis Walsingham was not diminisht when she denounced him, on October 7, 1579, as "fit for nothing but to be a champion of heretics."

IV

Edward de Vere enrolled as a student of law at Gray's Inn, on February 1, 1567, when he was sixteen years old. Here he was taught that the foundations of English law and order, therefor of civilisation in his native land, were made of ancient pagan tribal customs, to whose vestiges the common folks clung in the "common law," sometimes ludicrously literal, and the old Roman commandments which Christian states had practically sanctified.

So he would have learnt little of such nonsense as modern schools repeat like parrots, about Occidental culture being based on the "Old Testament." He would have seen that the Roman rules of the *Twelve Tables* were dearer to Western civilisation than the *Ten Commandments* of the Jews. But his brain would not have been granted liberty to linger over the difference between the *Leviticus* handling of loans and debts and *Tabula Tertia*, which decreed: "If the creditor is not paid after the third market day, he may either put his debtor to death, or sell him to any stranger resident beyond the Tiber: but if there be two or more creditors of the same insolvent debtor, and if, after the third market day, his debts to them be yet unpaid, the creditors may cut their several portions off his body. If they cut too much or too little, let that be no wrong."[85] The Twelve Tables allowed ninety days or three months for the repayment of loans. The young Earl of Oxford could have verified from his perusal of the Latin classics and early Christian writings around Rome that this law was literally observed.[86] Ancient Norwegian and German laws upheld the Roman frigid ferocity.[87] Our dramatist pulled stale European wool over his wits and pretended that exacting human flesh for a lost loan was a Jewish idea. He knew that Shylock was telling the truth when he protested, "O father Abram, what these Christians are,/Whose owne hard dealings teaches them suspect/ The thoughts of others" (1.3.158-160), yet obstinately stuck to his delusion implied in the humorous remark of Antonio, "This Hebrew will turne Christian, he growes kinde." How kind the countrymen of Antonio were, we are shown in this very scene, where the merchant, presumably after fulfilling the promise he made to his friend Bassanio in the first scene, to "Try what my credit can in Venice doe," is forced to turn to the Jew he despises for financial aid.

There is little value in going over the ridiculous trick by which Shakespeare cheated Shylock of the pound of flesh close to Antonio's heart that the latter and all his friends knew had been lawfully forfeited. When the Venetians who contracted for the Jew's ducats to be paid for, in case of Antonio's failure to redeem his loan as promised, by surgery, went to a notary to draw up the bond, that

invisible official uttered not one word about the bond's violation of
the law of Venice. Not until Act 4 do we hear Shylock warned concerning the forfeit, "But in the cutting it, if thou dost shed / One
drop of Christian bloud, thy lands and goods / Are by the Lawes of
Venice confiscate / Unto the state of Venice." (4.1.307-310) Portia
promises to show the Act ordaining such a penalty, but of course
she could not do it, because Venetian law would never have admitted that any flesh alive might be legally cut without allowing along
with it the blood, the lymph, and so forth.

A Jewish lawyer, Harris Jay Griston, who absurdly dated the action of the fantasy before the year 320, when the Emperor Constantine abolished seizure of a debtor's body for an unpaid loan, lamented that Shakespeare had stooped to "low cunning" and
evinced a ghastly disrespect for justice in *The Merchant of Venice*:
"does chicanery cease to be chicanery because practised in the name
of humanity?"[88] The name of humanity is gestured in the drama
perversely and in vain; Shylock is punished for his frank effort to rid
the world of Antonio for insulting him cruelly by compelling him to
become a Christian, contrary to his conscience. Shakespeare strips
him of all his possessions, without letting the spectator know that
this deprival was the normal reward for an Italian Jew's relinquish-
ing the creed of his kin. Thomas Coryat the traveler explained in his
Crudities (1611):

> Pitiful it is to see that few of them (the Jews) living in Italy are
> converted to the Christian religion. For this I understand is the
> main impediment to their conversion: All their goods are confis-
> cated as soon as they embrace Christianity; and this I heard was
> the reason, because whereas many of them do raise their for-
> tunes by usury, in so much that they do sometimes not only
> shear but also flea many a poor Christian's estate by their griping
> extortion; it is therefor decreed by the Pope and other free
> Princes in whose territories they live, that they shall make a resti-
> tution of all their ill-gotten goods, and so disclog their souls and
> consciences when they are admitted by holy baptism into the
> bosom of Christ's Church.

Students of the play who care deeply for justice have always felt that Shylock's principle of revenge violated the spirit of his religion, which teaches that vengeance should belong only to God. Nevertheless, justice was not done in the case of the Jew. "I crave the law," he cries. "To what mighty great dimensions does not the weak man grow, when he speaks those words!... The eminently tragic interest which we feel in Shylock, I find to have its basis precisely in the fact that justice is not done him; for this is the conclusion to which the lawyer must come." So wrote Rudolf von Ihering in *The Struggle for Law* (1872).[89] It is the conclusion that any fair inquirer into the point and purpose of Shakespeare's plays eventually comes.

Why did the poet distort justice in his romance of Venice? That is the question we have to answer. Our reply naturally is bound to be personal, concerning the creator of this so-called comedy alone. One scholar, Graham Midgley, has seen that Shakespeare intended his play to contrast dynamically the polar personalities of Antonio and Shylock, loading his dice against the latter by making him a caricature of the Children of Israel, and exalting Antonio, not in the image of the Lamb of the Lord crucified, but as "a tainted Wether of the flocke, / Meetest for death" (4.1.114-115) because he is glad to die for the sins of his kind, specifically for the lust and luxury of his beloved Bassanio. Antonio is presented to us as a man innocent of ugly transgressions, the opposite of the Jew. But the honesty of the artist permits more than a glance at the vileness in Antonio's nature. He is guilty of more than ugly manners toward the Jew. Shakespeare dared not name his sin. Yet we can detect it, as Graham Midgley did, in every act of the play. Our dramatist failed, just as the loan-leeches of his age did, when they substituted the term "interest" for usury, in the art of swindling God. Lefevre, the tutor of King Louis XIII, called the casuistry of the French financiers *l'art de chicaner Dieu.*

Vero nihil verius: Than truth nothing truer. This motto of the greatest poet among Queen Elizabeth's courtiers, engraved in his brain forever by a passion for understanding the universe unrivaled in the realm, could not be eclipsed by the lies he piled alp-lofty to win forgiveness for his vices. He wished to blame Michael Lock, maybe Benedick Spinola, for his misfortunes with money. I accept the opinion of Gerald Phillips that he covertly attacked William Cecil, Lord Burghley, in *The Merchant of Venice*, hiding his father-in-law's character in the monstrous miser, Jessica's father. The Lord Treasurer indeed was Oxford's chief creditor, since he endeavored to collect from the Earl's estates a mountain of money De Vere was alleged to owe the "Crown" for the nine years he lived with Cecil, the Master of the royal wards. There could be no better exemplar for Shylock's thrift than the father of Anne Cecil. On January 1, 1567, the wily William gave his girl a New Year's gift with some rimes that were fortunately preserved:

> As years do grow so cares increase
> And time will move to look to thrift,
> These years in me work nothing less
> Yet for your years and New Years gift
> To set you on work some thrift to feel
> I send you now a spinning wheel.
> But one thing first I wish and pray
> Lest thirst of thrift might soon you tire,
> Only to spin one pound a day
> And play the rest as time require
> Sweat not (O fy!) fling work in fire
> God send, who sendeth all thrift and wealth
> You long years and your father health.[90]

You can easily tell that the composer of these rimes was no lover of music or poetry. But they give us a gratifying glimpse of the wheels spinning in his brain, for avarice, for exploitation of children, for selfishness. The comedian Richard Tarlton called Burghley's house in the Strand, near the Savoy hotel, "the Lord Treasurer's Alms gate, because it was seldom or never opened."[91] But William Cecil is more plainly to be seen in Juliet Montague's father and in the Lord Chamberlain Polonius than in our Venetian Jew.

Jessica calls her home a hell. And Shylock's Christian servant, the clown Lancelot Gobbo, declares that he is fed stingily by the Jew. Yet the daughter retains an unchilled personality, good humor and generosity as well as native intelligence, in her father's house. The clown talks mere Christian commonplaces about his master's character, while showing how he too remained merry and convivial under the alleged miser's roof. Shylock's daughter is perhaps the warmest hearted woman in the drama; and Shakespeare failed to account for her character. He betrays to us how blind his Judeophobia made him to true Jews by allowing glimpses of the flesh and blood that constituted the man he modeled his moneylender after. The real Shylock was a loved bridegroom, and must have been a father lavishing affection on the beautiful child that always reminded him of her mother. When the Jew (3.1.111-114) hears that Jessica in Genoa gave one of Antonio's creditors a ring in exchange for a monkey, he groans: "Out upon her, thou torturest me, Tuball, it was my Turkies (turquoise), I had it of Leah when I was a Batchelor: I would not have given it for a wildernesse of Monkies." But Shakespeare understood his Jewess. In headlong flight from her mother's religion, the rebel gives away the ring for an animal mimic of humanity, just as she threw herself away on the wastrel and parasite Lorenzo, a mere ape of a man. Jessica's intelligence collapses before the temptations of her social-climbing; and no Christian lass would envy her the love-life she is doomed to lead with the gallant fellow she momentarily enriched with her father's stolen property.

Gerald Phillips noted that Shylock swearing (as no Jew would) by Jacob's staff (2.5.36) reminds us of Burghley's fondness for wielding a processional staff. His Lordship also liked to wear a gaberdine cloak.[92] However it is Gratiano who vows to "Weare prayer bookes in my pocket, looke demurely," like Cecil did (2.2.180). There the resemblance between old Shylock and the shrewd Lord Treasurer of England ends.

The elegant picture that Shakespeare drew of "Lorenzo and his infidel" (3.2) represents, in my judgment, the poet's wish that his wife could have been faithless to her father. He extols Jessica as "wise, faire, and true," while showing her as false to her father and questionably committing "pretty follies" for a lover whose testimony of having a "constant soule" comes from none but himself

(2.6). It is not by chance that he and his comrades wear masks in contriving her elopement. Her running away from home in a page's costume is flimsily explained by any necessity of speed or disguise, for Shylock would not have power to capture her from any house of Lorenzo's aristocratic ring. Venetian law gave no Jewish father the right to recover a child who had found a lover outside the ghetto and converted to the church of the state. Shylock voices a kind of pride in being a resident of Venice, where Jews had "privileges,"—they could not be called rights, since no Jew could be a citizen. He could have compared his luck with the predicament of Jews in Mantua. In 1569, as Oxford would have been fascinated to learn when he visited the capital of the Gonzaga dukes, a judge maintained that any Jew caught copulating with a Christian female should be killed. Another judge declared that Mantua had never done this to Jews before. Two other doctors of law contended that the best penalty would be cutting off the culprit's testicles, "a most beautiful spectacle for a Carnival." In 1577 the death penalty and confiscation of all property were ordained in Mantua, by the Inquisition courts, for every Jew discovered copulating with a Christian.[93]

At the time (early spring—perhaps April? 1579) when our dramatist wrote *The Jew* or "Portia and the Merchants," he must have been suffering from sexual anxiety. He was living in virtual divorce from his wife. I feel sure that the young lady his heart had chosen for a paramour, the Queen's Bedchamber maid Anne Vavasor had steadily spurned his blandishments and temptations, his gifts of precious things, and his songs. She may have been profoundly entertained by her portrayals in the plays we call today *All's Well That Ends Well* and *Love's Labor's Lost*, where she clearly emerges in the roles of the seductive virgin Diana and the "whitely wanton" with "two pitchballs" in her eyesockets, Rosaline. But she would have fiercely enjoyed keeping up her resistance to the wooing of the Earl of Oxford, whom she must have deemed wicked for the way he had deserted his wife, and her child Bess. The fury of his frustration would have been driven under his skin by the demands of the Queen for romance and lovesong from him. The forcing inward of his fury caused, according to my diagnosis, the strange melancholy that his protagonist Antonio obtrudes in the opening speech of *The Merchant of Venice*. The melancholy would have deepened if, as Graham Midgley seems to imply, Antonio's author endured hallucinations of homosexuality before he wrote the play. To be precise, Midgley's judgment is that Antonio, like Shylock, is an outsider, solitary and uncompromising, but the former lives not for the love of commodities but of men: "he is an unconscious homosexual."[94] Shakespeare himself was not isolated from ladies, and the supreme passion of his life flowed for no Bassanio.

The man who composed *The Merchant of Venice* certainly indulged in more than daydreams of desire for bodies that mirrored his own adored one. We know from the charges hurled at the Earl of Oxford by Lord Harry Howard and Charles Arundel in 1581, after his attempt to expose their treason in the presence of Elizabeth and the French ambassador broke down, that he had experimented with homosexuality. The evidence is too drearily detailed to rehearse here.[95] Analytic psychology upholds the conviction that the play was conceived in a mental struggle over his guilt-agony for yielding to the allurement of buggery. The poet punished himself by having his *alter-ego* Antonio threatened with a symbolic castration, staged by what Freud designated the displacement upward of the suffering spot. In addition the dramatist left himself pathetically alone at the end of the drama, his dearest companion departing to bed with a strange woman desirous of raising a family where his temperament would not be welcome.

How utterly absorbed the author was with himself can be observed, as if thru patches and tatters, in the deliberately comic scenes, the efforts of fun-relief from the perversity and gloom of the romance. Every student of the Looney hypothesis not only recognises the dramatist's trademark in the speech

> I hold the world but as the world, Gratiano,
> A stage, where every man must play a part,
> And mine a sad one. (1.1.77-79)

We know what the poet saw in his mind's eye when he wrote, afterward,

> Why should a man whose bloud is warme within
> Sit like his Grandsire, cut in Alabaster? (1.1.83-84)

The relief of Edward de Vere's grandsire John, the fifteenth Earl of Oxford, still lives, "cut in alabaster," on his tomb in St Nicholas Church at Castle Hedingham village. But who would dream of probing under the garb and organism of Shylock's servant-clown Lancelot Gobbo for a revelation of the dreamer who created them? Well, permit me to point out that our poet named him, not Lancelot, as commonly printed, but Lancelet, a word signifying *small spear*. If this is not perceived as a reference to the poet's castration complex, I will not dispute. I will follow Percy Allen and quote from the Howard-Arundel gossip the passage about Edward de Vere's stepfather appearing to him like a ghost: "Tyrrell appeared to him with a whip, which had made a better show in the hand of a carman than of Hob-Goblin."[96] I agree with Allen that Hob-Goblin was transformed by the artist into Gobbo, not a fantom but a fragile little mortal, a buffoon. His mother's second husband turns up again as Lancelet's "fiend," urging him to "budge" and run away from conscientious employment, just as De Vere wanted to escape from England to serve what her Majesty deemed the Devil, that is the Spanish empire or the French in war. The Clown confesses, "my Father did something smack, something grow to; he had a kinde of taste" (2.2). This oral allusion to malevolence reminds us of the persecution of John de Vere, the sixteenth Earl of Oxford, by Edward Seymour, Duke of Somerset. The latter, on the first of February 1548, "did, under colour of justice, convent before himself for certain criminal causes, John Earl of Oxenford, and did so terrify him, that to save his life he was obliged to alienate to the said Duke by deed" nearly all his wealth in landed property.[97] Actually what Somerset arranged was the marriage of his son Henry to the Earl's heiress, Katherine Neville de Vere, who was thirteen when his son Edward was born. However William Cecil did not think it worth while to safeguard for posterity those proofs of crime.

The seventeenth Earl of Oxford, "the yong gentleman, according to fates and destinies, and such odde sayings, the sisters three, & such branches of learning," must have heard rumors or testimonies about his sire's sins that made him realise he was indeed John's son. They made him wonder, I believe, why he had ever fancied himself the son of a superior man, a king or an emperor: "it is a wise Father," says Gobbo the younger, "that knowes his owne childe." That is a thrust against the sex which most deeply disappointed Edward de Vere. I wish I could explain Lancelet's confiding to his blind father: "Well, old man, I will tell you newes of your son, give me your blessing, truth will come to light, murder cannot be hid long, a man's son may, but in the end truth will out." (2.2.72-75) If we could date this passage after March 23, 1581, when Edward Vere, the illegitimate son of Edward, Earl of Oxford, uttered his first protest against the world's wintry disposition, we might construe it as a reference to the new Vere's advent. However I cannot see its relation to Lord Edward's life. Immediately clearer is the sudden avowal of the Clown, "I am sure Margerie your wife is my mother." (2.2.83) Lord Edward had exactly the same assurance when he wondered about the bond of nature and fortune between him and his father. Unquestionably he was Margerie Golding's child. When Lancelet and Jessica talk about bastardy (3.5) and she reflects on the likelihood of her mother's sins being "visited" upon her, the poet was probably remembering how his elder sister Kate had insisted by lawsuit that he and his sister Mary were bastards until Arthur Golding succeeded in clearing their mother's name. Edward, Baron Windsor, who married the terrible-tongued Kate, left this charge as a heritage to the Windsors. Baron Thomas, his great-grandson, asked the House of Lords to brand the house of Vere with the bar sinister, because he believed he could prove that Margerie Golding had never been the lawful wife of Lord John de Vere. The vigilant Burghley protected his daughter's title of Countess, and the titles of her daughters, claiming that he cleared Margerie's name: "I prefered his title to the Earldom, the Lord Windsor attempting to have made him illegitimate."[98] The record of the Windsor assault and the Golding defense has yet to be made public for popular justice.

V

Graham Midgley observed that *The Merchant of Venice* had a peculiar symmetry or balance of its pictorial settings and duets: "a remarkably steady alternation of scene between Venice and Belmonte, giving the whole of Act IV to Venice and the trial scene, and the whole of Act V to Belmonte, with Shylock apparently forgotten."[99] Stephen Gosson noted the moral features of this balance of the stage conflicts. What neither of these sharp-eyed and keen-eared critics detected was the way in which Shakespeare's perversity and inward driven anger undermined his pretty architecture.

First, like his Italian plot-provider Fiorentino, he had no clear idea of the location of Belmonte and its distance from Venice. [Thanks to the brilliant scholarship of Dr. Noemi Magri, Belmont has now been been firmly identified as the Villa Foscari, ten miles from Venice, on the river Brenta.—W.H.] It has been suggested that he meant Montebello, which is not far from Genoa, where Lorenzo and his "infidel" fled from her father. Someone discovered a fishing village named Belmonte on the northern coast of Sicily. The mystery of Portia's domain is deepened if you see her name, as I do, meaning only the princess of the port.[100] She is outstanding among the handsome females of the drama because of her regal behavior and her blondness.

> For the foure windes blow in from euery coast
> Renowned suitors, and her sunny locks
> Hang on her temples like a golden fleece ... (1.1.168-170)

The disciples of John Thomas Looney made short merry work of the problem of Portia's identity, altho few of them gave adequate notice to his detection of traits from Mary the Queen of Scotland in the beauty of Belmonte. In the main we may consent that Portia stands for Queen Bess. Our poet leaves little doubt when he made

Portia sigh about her suitors, "I may neither choose whom I would, nor refuse whom I dislike; so is the will of a liuing daughter curb'd by the will of a dead father" (1.2.21-24). Her Majesty's notion of a desirable husband had been subjected from girlhood to the last testament of Henry VIII. Elizabeth's ambition chimed with his imperial designs quite cheerily, and we all know how Portia's prediction came true for the Virgin Queen: "I will die as chaste as Diana," if the "princely suitors" do not satisfy her father's demands.

Ruth Loyd Miller has demonstrated how Shakespeare made sport of the Austrian Don Juan's aspiration for the throne of England in describing the Neapolitan Prince who courted Portia. The Don's half-brother Philip of Spain was king of Naples. The suspicion of Portia that "his mother plaid false with a Smyth" alludes to the bastardy of Don John, whose mother, Barbara Blomberg of Ratisbon, is said to have denied that the Emperor Charles the Fifth was his father.[101]

In the person of "the County Palatine," our author, I think, intended a satire on Hans Casimir, the Count Palatine of Germany, whose armies often served English policy for pay both in the Low Countries and France. "He doth nothing but frowne... He heares merrie tales and smiles not... I had rather to be married to a deaths head with a bone in his mouth." (1.2.45-49) Casimir came to London on 22 January 1579 seeking money for his mercenaries, and Sir Thomas Gresham gave the guest at least the drink he craved at his home in Bishopsgate Street, shortly before Gresham died. Shakespeare produced a double for the County Palatine in "the yong Germaine, the Duke of Saxonies Nephew," simply in order to denounce his drinking. Casimir was actually the son-in-law of the Duke of Saxony. He left London after the Queen's farewell on February 12.

Admiral Hubert Holland was able to identify the source of the caricature, "the French Lord, Mounsier Le Bonne," whom Portia laughs at because, "if a Trassell sing, he fals straight a capring." Holland remarked that the French word for a throstle is *mauvis*, making Portia's allusion plain, since the French ambassador in 1579 was

Michel de Castelnau, the Seigneur de Mauvissiere. The English word mavis means a kind of thrush.[102] There is perhaps more of the Frenchman Jean de Simier than of the sedate Castelnau in Monsieur Le Bon. Simier was the envoy courting the Queen for his master Hercules d'Alencon, Duc d' Anjou. The Queen was nearly spellbound by Simier's versatility. Not only was he a wizard with swords (Le Bon in the play "will fence with his own shadow"); he was a master of mimicry, and inevitably acquired from her the nickname, punning on the suggestion of the Simian in his name, Ape. "If I should marry him," Portia asserts, "I should marry twenty husbands." Simier made the French alliance joyously attractive to Queen Bess, and she liked Lord Thomas Radcliff, the Earl of Sussex, more than ever because he favored her marriage with the prince of France. Sussex's filial friend, the Earl of Oxford, quarreled with Philip Sidney over possession of a tennis court ostensibly, but the real reason was the antagonism of Sidney, the Earl of Leycester's nephew, to the alliance with Alencon. Once Leycester blurted to the French ambassador Fenelon, that Cecil did not want the Queen to marry at all; he preferred to remain king himself.[103]

Shakespeare made Bassanio on the surface a surrogate for Hercules d'Alencon. For hardly another reason does Portia behold, on hearing triumphal music, "the flourish (of trumpets), when true subiects bowe / To a new crowned Monarch" (3.2). She also is reminded by the presence of Bassanio of "yong Alcides, when he did redeeme / The virgin tribute." To emphasise the classic allusion, she encourages her Venetian lover thus: "Goe, Hercules, / Liue thou..." Later she hails him "her Lord, her Gouernour, her King," feeling no longer "Queene ore my selfe."

Scrutiny of the character of Bassanio convinces us that the poet intended him to represent no French stranger but a familiar Briton. Unlike the Duke of Anjou, Bassanio is a scholar as well as a soldier. Indeed he is a light-hearted double for the love-starved soul Antonio, and appears before us with barely more individuality than our dramatist endowed his ordinary merry lovers with. It seems to me that his name was selected for no better reason than that it recalled to Shakespeare's ear the French imperative *Baissons nous!* (Let us kiss). Since Antonio depicts the sober sad, if not sadistic, side of Edward de Vere himself, Bassanio may be viewed as equal and opposite, the shining side of his moon. When Portia's Messenger declares that he has "not seene / So likely an Embassador of loue," what Shakespeare saw in his mind's orb was not Jean de Simier but Will Shakespeare; the very next line proves it to me: "A day in Aprill neuer came so sweete" (2.9.92). If these lines were not written on the anniversary of Oxford's birth, they were certainly composed in the season. The ill luck of the Earl in the Northwest Passage affair could not overdarken his evidence of the Queen's affection for him, and he could still dream extravagantly of winning an imperial place by her side. On January 27, 1579, Edward Seymour, Earl of Hertford, met her Majesty, at eleven o'clock in the morning, walking with the Earl of Oxford in her garden. This is the only testimony we have of their going alone together.[104] But Gilbert Talbot, the Earl of Shrewsbury's son, also recorded the "love matters" between De Vere and the Queen, at which her Lord Treasurer "winked." None but the Earl would have presented Bassanio admitting "such confusion in my powers" as when "the buzzing pleased multitude" changes "to a wilde of nothing, save of ioy," by listening to "some oration fairely spoke / By a beloued Prince" (3.2.178-180).

The story of Bassanio's selection of the leaden casket instead of the gold and silver, Shakespeare got from the *Gesta Romanorum*, where a girl has to choose between three metal boxes of the same values to win an emperor's son. Sigmund Freud composed one of his most beautiful essays in explaining this theme of gold, silver and lead. "If we had to do with a dream," he remarked in telling the tale of the young Venetian's choice, "it would at once occur to us that caskets are also women, symbols of the essential thing in woman, and therefor of a woman herself, like boxes, large or small, baskets, and so on." The psychoanalyst interpreted the folktale transformed by our poet as a legend of a man's *trilemma*, having to pick one of three women (womb-men). Freud was reminded of the myth of Paris of Ilion who was invited to pick the most charming of three goddesses, and chose the third. Freud also remembered how Shakespeare's King Lear resolved to live his last days with the youngest of his three daughters. She is shown as a woman extremely modest, "unassuming as lead," Freud says; "she remains dumb, she 'loves and is silent.'" In the same way, the analyst noted, the Venetian lover caresses the lead casket saying,

Thy paleness moues me more then eloquence. (3.2.106)

Freud was drawn to the opinion of savants who rejected the "paleness" of the Quarto and Folio copies of the play in favor of "plainness," which I take to be a distortion. Paleness is more proper in Freud's interpretation of the scene. He translated the quality of the casket metal and its equivalence to muteness as meaning "an unmistakable symbol of death." If the third of the women our hero has to choose his mate from is Sister Death, then it is plain that the three deities are the Fates of yore, the Moirai, or Parcae, or Norns, who spin man's destiny. Human vanity invented a reversal of the truth in the ancient tale: "Choice stands in the place of necessity, of destiny. Thus man overcomes death, which he has recognised in his thought. No greater triumph of wish-fulfilment is conceivable. Just where in reality he obeys compulsion, he exercises choice; and that which he chooses is not a thing of horror, but the fairest and most desirable thing in life."[105]

Freud did not comment on Shakespeare's perception in handling the old legend. In my belief he almost consciously composed Bassanio's selection scene. For he knew that a leaden casket clearly represented a coffin, that Portia signified "carrier," and Bassanio *bisigno* or necessity. Concealed in the love-story of Belmonte was the craving of Antonio, Bassanio's double, for death. The latter's last words express happiness over the news "that my ships / Are safelie come to Rode," which some fancy means a harbor-road, and others read as Rhodes—the red haven.

The Earl of Oxford wrote a lyric or lullaby proximal to the theme of the three choices, which I quoted in my chapter on *The Two Gentlemen of Verona*. Permit me to repeat it here:

Were I a king I might command content;
   Were I obscure unknown would be my cares,
And were I dead no thoughts should me torment,
   Nor words, nor wrongs, nor love, nor hate, nor fears;
A doubtful choice of three things, which to crave,
A kingdom or a cottage or a grave.

Sir Philip Sidney wrote a reply to this little song, perhaps after his quarrel with the Earl over occupation of a tennis court, in the presence of the Frenchmen who were striving to win Elizabeth for a marital alliance with their prince Francois Hercules d'Alencon. Sidney, you know, was absolutely opposed to her marriage with the "Frog."

Wert thou a King yet (ye'd?) not command content,
   Since empire none thy mind could yet suffice,
Wert thou obscure still cares would thee torment;
   But wert thou dead, all care and sorrow dies:
An easy choice of these things, which to crave,
No kingdom nor a cottage but a grave.

It was Looney who discerned the relation between these rimes and the August eclog in Edmund Spenser's *Shepherds' Calendar*, registered for the press on December 5, 1579, which describes a riming duel between two competitors named Willie and Perigot. Spenser disguised as the shepherd Cuddy acts as their arbitrator, remarking "What a judge Cuddy were for a king."[106]

When our author idealised Elizabeth in the image of his lady of Belmonte, he conceived of her as more than majestic. The speech he put on her tongue about mercy concentrates on clemency in the royal. But in other passages he ventured to glorify her as divine. First he had his Jessica play with the thought: "Why, if two gods should play some heauenly match, / And on the wager lay two earthly women, / And Portia one: there must be something else / Pawned with the other, for the poore rude world / Hath not her fellow" (3.5.72-75). In the last act he uttered rapture about this virgin-mother-love, appealing for melody to "wake Diana with a hymne... And draw her home with musicke." Jessica's reply to this appeal: "I am neuer merry when I heare sweet musique," reminded my psychoanalytic instructor Dr Theodor Reik of the young man who questioned Franz Schubert, why was all his music sad? The melody master's answer was, Is there any other kind? Lorenzo's reply to his virgin Jew is the famous declaration,

> The man that hath no musicke in himselfe,
>
> Nor is not moued with concord of sweet sounds,
>
> Is fit for treasons, stratagems, and spoyles,
>
> The motions of his spirit are dull as night,
>
> And his affections darke as Erebus,
>
> Let no such man be trusted. (5.1.83-88)

As I have already remarked, I consider William Cecil the prime target of this bitterness, which is not necessarily true. Likening England's Queen with the Roman goddess of the woods continues with a lyric clause from Portia herself: "Peace, now the Moone sleeps with Endimion, / And would not be awak'd." (5.1.109-110) The identity of this Endymion is clarified only when we examine John Lyly's play *Endimion*, written for the Earl of Oxford's boy-players.[107]

Lorenzo's lines in praise of music have been traced in France to a source I have not seen named in all editions of *The Merchant of Venice* known to me. In a once celebrated novel about a symphony composer occurs the following quotation:

> He who does not rejoice to hear a sweet concord of instruments,
>
> or the sweetness of the natural voice, and is not
>
> moved by it, and does not tremble from head to foot with
>
> its sweet ravishment, and is not taken completely out of
>
> himself, does thereby show himself to have a twisted,
>
> vicious, and depraved soul, and of such a one we should
>
> beware as of a man ill-born.

"I know that," said Christophe. "It is my friend Shakespeare." "No," said Arnaud gently. "It is a Frenchman who lived before him, Ronsard."[108]

Shakespeare was meditating not only on the poetry of Pierre Ronsard when he worked on this romance. Stephen Gosson correctly lauded *The Jew* for not "wounding the eye" with erotic gesture, "nor with slovenly talk hurting the ears of the chaste hearers." Until the end of the romance our dramatist did conscientiously avoid mingling the amorous with the hilarious. However, he could not resist the temptation offered by the perplexity of Graziano over his darling Nerissa's ring. Before Graziano can go tranquilly to bed with her he has to learn the lesson that Hans Carvel in Rabelais's epic comedy *Gargantua and Pantagruel* is compelled to learn in honor of his wife's ring, which the great French humorist plainly employed as an emblem of her sex. So we can comprehend why the love-starved writer concluded his romance with the couplet,

> Well, while I liue, Ile feare no other thing
> So sore, as keeping safe Nerrissas ring. (5.1.306-307)

The uxorious joke ought not to be left the last words of the play. One would rather hear Nerissa repeat the words of Portia on seeing the light burning in her hall:

> How farre that little candell throwes his beames,
> So shines a good deed in a naughty world. (5.1.90-91)

Apropos de rien, I wonder if Anne Vavasor knew and ever told her ravenous lover Edward de Vere that her family's ancestral hall of Hazlewood in Yorkshire had been given by King Henry III as pledge for a loan to the Jew Aaron of York, who gave it to her forefather John de Vavasour when the latter redeemed the royal debt.

References

1   J. R. Lowell (1846) in *The Round Table* (Boston 1913) 189.

2   Bliss Perry, *Walt Whitman* (Boston 1906) 238-9.

3   Walt Whitman, *November Boughs*, or *The Critic*, 27 Sep. 1884; in *Complete Prose Works* (Boston; Small, Maynard; 1898) 390.

4   H. Spencer, *The Art and Life of William Shakespeare* (New York 1940) 51.

5   William Winter, *Shakespeare on the Stage* (New York 1911) I, 129.

6   David Belasco, *The David Belasco Arrangement of Shakespeare's The Merchant of Venice* (New York; Privately printed, 1922) 8.

7   John Corbin in the *New York Times*, 21 Jan. 1922.

8   Belasco, op. cit. 15.

9   J. Thomas Looney, *"Shakespeare" Identified in Edward de Vere, Seventeenth Earl of Oxford*, ed Ruth Loyd Miller (Jennings, LA; Minos Publishing co, 1975) 1, 2.

10 Geoffrey Bullough, ed. *Narrative and Dramatic Sources of Shakespeare* (London 1966) 1, 454-5.

11 *A New Variorum Edition of Shakespeare: The Merchant of Venice*, ed. Horace Howard Furness (Philadelphia 1886) 320.

12 Ibid. 322; Gabriel Harvey, *Letter Book*, ed. Edward J. L. Scott (London; Cambridge Society, 1884) xiii.

13 Idem.

14 Eva Turner Clark, *Hidden Allusions in Shakespeare's Plays*, ed. Ruth Loyd Miller (Jennings, LA; Minos Publishing Co, 1974) 331; Albert Feuillerat, ed. *Documents Relating to the Office of the* Revels in the Time of Queen Elizabeth (1908) 321.

15 Janet Spens, *Shakespeare and Tradition* (1916) 16f. Bullough, op. cit. 452f, 486-490.

16 Salo Wittmaier Baron, *A Social and Religious History of the Jews* (New York, 1969) xi, 21 1. Cecil Roth, in *Review of English Studies* (1933) and *Personalities and Events in Jewish History* (Philadelphia 1953) 241.

17 Lansdowne Ms. 22, f. 74. (British Museum).

18 Historical Manuscripts Commission: ix, Appendix, 249b.

19 Bernard M Ward, *The Seventeenth Earl of Oxford* (London 1928) 238f.

20 Lillian Winstanley, *Othello, as the Tragedy of Italy* (1924) 63f.

21 Francois Rabelais, *Gargantua and Pantagruel*, Book I, chapter viii.

22 Geoffrey Bullough (*op. cit.* 445) confused King Antonio with Antonio Perez, the Madrid courtier notorious for his moral crookedness.

23 Calendar of Salisbury (Cecil) Ms. at Hatfield, xiii, 519.

24 John Stowe, *Survey of London* (London 1618) viii, 69. In 1568 Anthony Bassano and his wife Helen were residents in the parish of All Hallows Staining. NOTE: Anthonio is the poet's preferred spelling probably because the poet

enjoyed seeing Italian transformed, Greekwise, by the word antho, signifying flower.

25 Cecil Roth, *The History of the Jews of Italy* (Philadelphia 1946) 173, 184, 359. Compare Baron, *op. cit.* xiv, 120, 351. Roth also indicates how popular among Italian Jews was the surname Graziano (op. cit. 398 483); see Baron, about the playwright Lazaro di Graziano Levi whose piece on Queen Esther was staged in Venice in 1558.

26 Lee Max Friedman, *Robert Grosseteste and the Jews* (1934) 12f, 23f. The greatest pupil of Grosseteste, the pioneer scientist Roger Bacon rejoiced about 1260: "there is no lack of teachers. There are Hebrews everywhere."—*Opera,* ed. J. S. Brewer, 391.

27 Louis Israel Newman, *Jewish Influence On Christian Reform Movements* (New York 1925) 202.

28 Anon. "Conversations with Mr. Lowell," *Atlantic Monthly* (Jan. 1897); Horace Elisha Scudder, *James Russell Lowell* (Boston 1901) II, 303.

29 Acts of the Privy Council of England, ed. Dasent, X, 147.

30 Calendar of State Papers Colonial (1578) 50: 64. H. R. Fox Bourne, Sir Philip Sidney (New York 1891) 161.

31 Calendar of State Papers Domestic (1579) CXXIX, 12.

32 Ibid. CXXX, 17, 18.

33 Eva Turner Clark, op. cit. 355-6. Roth, "The Background of Shylock," *Review of English Studies,* 9 (Apr. 1933) 149. Shakespeare invented the name Jessica, turning into his Italian the Hebrew Iscah (niece of Abram in Genesis xi:29). Her name means "She who looks out," like Jessica. Originally it may have been an epithet for the moon-maid.

34 Calendar of Seymour Ms., Bath Longleat Ms. iv, 82, 119.

35 T. S. Willan, *The Early History of the Russia Company* (Manchester 1956) 92f. E. M. Tenison, *Elizabethan England* (Leamington; Privately printed, 1953) x, 324.

36 "Lok, Michael." Article in *Dictionary of National Biography,* xxxiv, 92.

37 *The Three Voyages of Martin Frobish*er, ed. Richard Collinson (Hakluyt Society) 339.

38 Bernard M. Ward, *op. cit.* 298. Henry Lok, *Poems, 1593-1597.* With Memorial-Introduction and Notes, ed. Alexander B. Grosart (Blackburn, 1871) 346.

39 Calendar of Salisbury (Cecil) Ms. xii, 280.

40 Nashe, *Works,* ed. Ronald McKerrow (1904) xi, 159.

41 Calendar of Salisbury (Cecil) Ms. xiii, 622.

42 Ibid. xi, 114.

43 In an essay on Jonson's Fox lost in an editorial office in Holland about 1950, I argued that Sir Politick Wouldbe pictured for us cartoonwise Sir Walter Cope, the agile agent of Lord Robert Cecil.

44 Robert Greene, *Complete Works in Prose and Verse,* ed. Grosart (London; Huth Library, 1886) viii, 221.

45 Calendar of State Papers, Foreign Series . . Elizabeth, 1572-74, no. 1085, p. 386. Cecil Roth, *The House of Nasi: The Duke of Naxos* (Philadelphia 1948) chapter vi.

46 Cecil Roth, *Revue des Etudes Juives* (1925) lxxx, 7 If.

47 Cecil Roth, *Personalities and Events in Jewish History*, 239-242.

48 Coryat's *Crudities* (1611), quoted by Roth, idem. 246.

49 Calendar of State Papers, Foreign Series, 1575-77, no. 368; cv, 50.

50 Ibid. no. 495.

51 Calendar of Salisbury (Cecil) Ms, ii, 129; Henry Howard, *Defensative Against Supposed Prophecies* (1583). There are allusions to Scoto in Thomas Nashe's novel *Jack Wilton, The Unfortunate Traveler* (1594) and Ben Jonson's *Volpone* (1606). Compare Cecil Roth's chapter on Abraham Colorni the magician of Mantua in *Personalities and Events* .

52 J. A. St John did us the kindness of not repeating the putrid joke about Oxford's departure from his country which the antiquary John Aubrey converted to a paragraph that is called "biography" by editors of his miscellany they entitled *Brief Lives* (1813). Aubrey stretched the time of Oxford's travels to seven years.

53 Margaret Sefton Jones, *Old Devonshire House by Bishopsgate*, 67 f., quoted by Gwynneth Bowen in the *Shakespearean Authorship Review* (Summer 1973) 3, 6. She also provided the following reference.

54 Robert Seymour, *Survey of London and Westminster* (1734) I, 269.

55 Charles J. Sisson, "A Colony of Jews in Shakespeare's London," *Review of English Studies*, and Essays and Studies, xxiii (1938) 49.

56 *Letters of Denization and Acts of Naturalization for Aliens in England*, 1509-1603, ed. William Page (Lymington; Huguenot Society Publications, 1893) 1, 224.

57 Ibid. 1, 352, 389.

58 John Strype, *Annals of the Reformation* (London; John Wyat, 1709) IV, 271.

59 Huguenot Society, op. cit. I, 384. Lucien Wolf, "Jews in Elizabethan England," *Transactions of the Jewish Historical Society of England*, 1926, xi, 7f. Willan, The Early History of the Russia Company, 87.

60 *The Fugger News-Letters*, ed. Victor Klarwill (1926) I, 13.

61 *Relations Politiques des Pays-Bas et de l'Angleterre...* ed. Kervyn de Lettenhove (Brussels 1900) VI, 194.

62 Calendar of State Papers, Foreign Series (1575) XII, 105-45. See Shillington and Chapman, *Commercial Relations of England and Portugal*, 141.

63 Calendar of State Papers Domestic (1578) CXXIV, 38, 49. Incidentally, Sir Sidney Lee (born Lazarus Levi), in "The Original Shylock," Gentlemen's Magazine (Feb. 1880) boasted, "What we may fairly claim to have proved is, that Jews were residing in England in Shakespeare's day, and that the Jew of Venice bears evidence of having had a contemporary prototype." But his nomination for the prototype was Dr Roderigo Lopez, a fellow extremely

unlike Shylock. Lopez was a victim of vanity, whose political meddling cost him his life, in 1594.

64 Francis Bacon, "Of Usury," *Essays* (1625), xli.

65 *Relations Politiques des Pays-Bas... op. cit.* x, 530, 736. Acts of the Privy Council, *op. cit.* x, 323.

66 *Fugger News-Letters*, ed. Klarwill, II, 288.

67 E. C. Lichtenberg, *Vermischte Schriften* (Göttingen 1867) III, 266f.

68 Percival Golding's manuscript pedigree of the Veres remains in the British Museum Harleian Ms., 4189. Peto's letter to Burghley on the "perfect genealogy" he made is reported in Calendar of State Papers, Foreign Series (1576) no. 707.

69 Matthew of Paris, *Chronica Majora* (1259), published by Archbishop Matthew Parker in London 1571, edited by H. R. Luard in 7 vols. (London 1883).

70 Tenison, *op. cit.* XII, 732. Greville, *The Life of the Renowned Sir Philip Sidney* (Oxford; Clarendon Press, 1907) xv, 185.

71 Leonardo Bruni, *Epistolae*, ed. L. Mehus, ii, 160f. Compare H. B. Wilson, *The History of the Merchant-Taylors School* (London 1814) 40; Alexander C. Judson, *The Life of Edmund Spenser* (1945) 14.

72 Calvin, *Opera* (Brunswick 1900) xxxl, 228.

73 Arthur Golding, dedication to Leycester of *Sermons of Maister John Caluin upon the Booke of Iob* (London 1579).

74 Calvin, Opera, viii, 763f. Calendar of State Papers, Venetian (1556) vi, i, 587. Thomas Stafford, in Queen Mary Tudor's day, heard Spaniards swear they would rather live with Jews and Moors than the English. John Strype, *Ecclesiastical Memorials*; Oxford 1822; iii, 515.

75 Servetus, *Christianismi Restitutio* (Geneva 1553). Three copies escaped the Presbyterian church pyre, but manuscripts survived.

76 Erasmus, quoted by Baron, *op. cit.* xiii, 179, 189. On More, the Platonic saint, see any biography. None have so far attempted to reconcile More's ferocity on religion and his Utopia, his communism.

77 Calendar of British State Papers (Spanish: 1484-1525) I, 164.

78 On Juan Lopes, the London Probate Registry Office at Somerset House so testifies. See Roth, "The Jewish Ancestry of Michel de Montaigne," in *Personalities and Events*, 218f. Sir Sidney Lee discovered the more remarkable "Magister Hernando Lopez," whom the Spanish ambassador introduced to Henry VIII as "a most distinguished doctor," recommended by King Ferdinand of Aragon, in 1515. He may be the unlucky Ferdinando Lopez of St Helens parish, Bishopsgate, a physician "Jew born," who was found guilty of obscure immoral behavior.—Lee, op. cit. supra.

79 Cecil Roth, *The Duke of Naxos*, passim. See Theophile Malvezin, *Michel de Montaigne, son origine, sa famille* (Bordeaux 1875) 108f. On the Anes or Ames family, see Lucien Wolf, op. cit., and Edna Ferber, *A Peculiar Treasure* (New

York 1939).

80 Bernard M Ward, op. cit. 102.

81 Cecil Roth, *A History of the Marranos* (Philadelphia 1932) 254.

82 V. Rau, "A Family of Italian Merchants" in *Portugal in the XVth Century*, the Lomellini, Studi in onore di Armando Sapori, I, 715-726.

83 William Hartpole Lecky, *History of Rationalism in Europe* (London 1925) II, 256. J. L. Cardozo, review of Thomas Wilson's *Discourse on Usury*, in *English Studies* (1925) VII, 149.

84 Wilson, *Discourse on Usury* (1572) f. 37b; ed. Richard H. Tawney (1925).

85 Andrew Stephenson, *A History of Roman Law* (Boston 1912) 128.

86 M. Ortolan, *The History of Roman Law*, trans. Pritchard and Nasmith (London 1871) 127.

87 Frederick Parker Walton, *The Early Roman Law* (London 1916) 192-6.

88 Griston, *Shaking the Dust from Shakespeare* (New York; Cosmopolis Press, 1924) xvi, 5. Originally printed as an Introduction to *The Merchant of Venice* (Cleveland 1921), this humorless work tries to defend the Jews from the poet's charge of hardheartedness, instead of chastising the poet for sadism. Mario Praz might have written about Shakespeare's cruelty a better book than *The Romantic Agony* (1933).

89 Ihering, *The Struggle for Law* (Chicago 1879) 81, 82.

90 Lansdowne Ms. civ, 193. Gerald W. Phillips, *Lord Burghley in Shakespeare* (London 1936) 191 f.

91 John Manningham's *Diary* (Jan. 1602), ed. Bruce, 16.

92 Phillips, *op. cit.* 191.

93 Baron, op. cit. XIV, 352.

94 G. Midgley, "The Merchant of Venice: A Reconsideration," *Essays in Criticism* (April 1960) X, 125.

95 State Papers Domestic (1581) cli, 45: "To report at large all the vices of this monsterous Earl were a labor without end." Also cli, 46-49: Henry Howard on "the botches and deformities of (Oxford 's) misshapen life."

96 Percy Allen, *The Life Story of Edward de Vere as "William Shakespeare"* (London; Cecil Palmer, 1932) 136.

97 Philip Morant, *History and Antiquities of the County of Essex* (1768) II, 293f.

98 Calendar of Salsbury (Cecil) Ms. II, 170. Bernard M Ward, *op. cit.* 124.

99 Midgley, *op. cit.* 119.

100 Bordering on delirium is Professor Sigurd Burchardt in his article, "The Gentle Bond," *English Literary History* (Sep. 1962) vol. 29, when he affirmed, "Brutus speaks the tragic epilogue to *The Merchant of Venice*: 'Portia is dead.'" (p. 262). The rest of the lecture is on the same intellectual plane.

101 Ruth Loyd Miller, in Clark's *Hidden Allusions...* 342-3.

102 H. H. Holland, *Shakespeare, Oxford, and Elizabethan* Times (London 1933) 14-18.

103 *Depeches de La Mothe Fenelon,* ed. Cooper, III, 462.

104 Calendar of Seymour Ms. IV, 186.

105 Freud, "The Theme of the Three Caskets," in *Collected Papers,* (London 1925) IV, 144f.

106 J. Thomas Looney, *"Shakespeare" Identified* ... ed. Ruth Loyd Miller, op. cit. 1, 596-7.

107 Josephine Waters Bennett, "Oxford and Endimion," *Publications of the Modern Language Association,* 1942, lvi, 354-369.

108 Romain Rolland, *Jean-Christophe in Paris,* trans. Gilbert Cannan (New York; Henry Holt, 1911) 411. The passage was brought to my attention by my son Owen.

Chapter 10—MALVOLIO OF ILLYRIA
OR WIT YOU WELL

I

Before falling asleep yesternight, on the brink of oblivion, my memory and reason went randoming, as Mark Twain called it, free and baresarc, among some facts from the life and scriptures of Edward de Vere alias William Shake-speare. I recalled John Thomas Looney's perception that the genius of comedy whom Edmund Spenser called Willie in "The Tears of the Muses" (*Complaints*, 1591) appears like a shepherd in Spenser's *Shepherds Calendar* (1579), also called Willie, and clearly the same humorist. I had figured out, several moons ago, that the name signified not only desire, in the sense of our poet when he described himself in the *Two Gentlemen of Verona* as "a votary to fond desire," but primarily a *spring*, in the ancient English meaning of the word will (specialised and preserved in well), for Ver in the Latin language meant the season *Spring*, and our poet could never resist a pun so pontifical. (Originally in the Roman tongue that adjective signified simply bridge-building.) The question danced in my head, Did he deliver his comedies and interludes or romances under the naked name Willie? or did he add a surname, some word of irony, using a signature like Will Whit or Willie Witlass (to compare with cutlass while seeming to suggest a wittol)? I remembered that William Wright registered with the Stationers office in London on September 7, 1580, a book called "William Wit, Wits Will, or Wills Wit, Choose You Whether." The phrase "Willy Nilly" was not known before the end of the sixteenth century. However, there could be no doubt that our pleasant Willie intended a contrast between himself and the personage of power whom he chose to satirise under the name Malvolio, meaning Ill-will, the chief target of his comedy *Twelfth Night or What You Will*. That personage has long ago been identified as the well-known and wealthy statesman Sir Christopher Hatton (1540-1591). The contrast between him and Edward de Vere, Earl of Oxford, who turns up in

Twelfth Night without individuality, divided indeed into several characters for drollery's sake distinct, has yet to be drawn.

Esther Singleton, a modest authority on Shakespeare's horticulture, one of the first Americans to be convinced by Looney's reasoning, beheld in the phrase "the fortunate unhappy" (2.5.151), almost always printed by modern editors with capital letters, a plain allusion to Kit Hatton, who used the Latin tag *Si fortunatus infoelix* to sign mediocre amorous rimes in *A Hundreth Sundrie Flowres* (London; Henry Bynneman, 1573). The Cambridge instructor in rhetoric Gabriel Harvey noted in his copy of *The Posies of George Gascoigne* (1576) that *Fortunatus infoelix* had been "lately the posy of Sir Christopher Hatton."[1] In the summer of 1578, when the court of Queen Elizabeth arrived in Saffron Walden, or rather at Audley End nearby, Gabriel Harvey, who came from the former town, welcomed them with a set of Latin eulogies, in one of which he hailed Sir Christopher Hatton, "the honorable and brave knight, counselor to the Queen's Majesty, concerning his emblem *Foelix Infortunatus*."[2] Harvey also extoled Hatton as "nobly born." None of these praises, in my estimation, can be reasonably applied to the captain of the Queen's "Gentlemen Pensioners," her bodyguard, the Vice-Chamberlain of her household, and later the Chancelor of her government. Miss Singleton left her discovery to be developed in *Shakespeare's Plays in the Order of Their Writing* by her friend Eva Turner Clark (London; Cecil Palmer, 1931). But Mrs Clark made the mistake of taking seriously the nickname of "Sheep" which the Queen gave Hatton, and his subsequent claim, "The Sheep, he hath no tooth to bite."[3] At first the Queen apparently called him "Mutton," because of the assonance to his name, and then animated the meat-reference on account of Sir Kit's crafty softness of manner with her, his skill in pulling wool over people's eyes to make invisible the wolf underneath his golden fleece. Out of the two biographies covering his career, he strikes my vision as a paragon of greed and political ambition, who battened on hating his moral superiors.

So I have no hardship in embracing Eva Clark's decision that "A pleasant Conceit of *Vere*, Earl of Oxford, discontented at the Rising of a mean Gentleman in the English Court, circa MDLXXX," which Francis Peck found in the manuscripts of the Elizabethan scholar Abraham Fleming (1552?-1607) was in fact the prototype of *Twelfth Night*.[4] Unfortunately Peck never fulfilled the promise he made in *Desiderata Curiosa* (London 1732-35) to publish the manuscript, "Now ready for the Press; & will be Printed on the same Letter & Paper with this Book," tho he lived and labored on until 1743. But I can find no date more comfortable than 1580 for the first performance of *Twelfth Night*. And there was no Gentleman in the English Court more "mean" than Kit Hatton, the model for Malvolio. When King James's company played it for his Court on Candlemas, February 2, 1622, they called it *Malvolio*.[5] The year 1623, remember, saw the production of the First Folio of Shakespeare's plays, the first publication of *Twelfth Night*.

Ever since John Manningham recorded in his *Diary*, on February 2, 1602, how his fellow lawyers of the Middle Temple arranged for a Candlemas performance of the comedy, students have been familiar with the fact that our play was "much like the *Comedy of Errors*, or *Menechmi* in Plautus, but most like and near to that in Italian called *Inganni*,"[6] to be exact, *Gli Ingannati* (The Deceived). The Academy of the Intronati, the Thunderstruck, enacted that play on the last day of the Catholic Carnival in Siena in 1531, and publisht it in 1537. No translation from the Italian saw daylight in England in Shakespeare's lifetime. Charles Estienne translated it into French (*Les Abuses*, 1543), but no sign of knowledge of this work is visible in English until the appearance of the First Folio. Our dramatist certainly had read the Italian text. The book *Il Sacrificio* (1537) containing the comedy of deceived lovers preluded it with sonnets, madrigals and monologs for an altar to Love, including the lament of one Agnol Malevolti, bringing a carved Cupid, the gift of his lady, and singing how he had been tricked by Love's illusions of felicity. Geoffrey Bullough pointed out, while the name Malevolti seems to suggest Malvolio, the actual meaning of the former ("ache-faces") indicates the origin of Sir Andrew Aguecheek.[7] The Italian Prolog announced, "The story is new, never seen nor read," derived by the writers from "their own industrious skulls like your prize tickets are groped for and gripped out on Twelfth Night," *la notta di Beffana*. In 1566 the boys of Trinity College in Cambridge played Plautus's *Menaechmi*, and the future author of the *Comedy of Errors* and *Twelfth Night*, a former pupil at St Johns College in Cambridge, may have been among the blissful in the audience.

The Viscount Ned de Vere would not have been able to witness the entertainment provided by the law students of the Inner Temple from January 6, Twelfth Night, 1562, until Sunday, January 18, at Westminster. Edward did not live at Cecil's house in Westminster then. We have a vivid description of the Christmas pleasures of the Inner Temple men. Their leader, the "Master of the Game" introduced a huntsman in the Mall of their show, who fetched along a fox and a cat, "both bound at the end of a staff; and with them nine or ten couple of hounds, with the blowing of hunting horns. And the fox and cat are by the hounds set upon, and killed beneath the fire."[8] The bloody sport exhilarated all who saw it, including those who crowded into the Mall windows. The "Master of the Game" next proceeded to demonstrate his versatility in the dancing that ensued. On New Year's Eve the law students staged a play, believed to be the tragedy *Gorboduc* or *Ferrex and Porrex* by Thomas Sackville (the future Lord Buckhurst) and Thomas Norton, and a maskerade. The tragedy stiffly and stridently lectured to England against feuding political factions that threatened to upset autocracy. We do not know if the "Master of the Game" also acted in the play. However, "It was presumably at the mask of 18th January that Hatton danced his way into Elizabeth's heart."[9] We have the word of Sir John Perrot, Queen Bess's bastard brother, that Kit Hatton first gained her glances of esteem "by a galliard."[10] Sir John seems to have felt honored by the hostility of Hatton, who strove with all his ingenuity to snare him to a traitor's death. But Perrot was perhaps the only man among all of the Queen's environers whose honesty could have been seen without the lantern of Diogenes. Strange as it may seem, the word galliard (for a quick gay dance in triple time much enjoyed by the Elizabethan court) is found in but one play by Shakespeare beside *Twelfth Night, Henry the Fifth*.[11] In our comedy Sir Toby Belch pronounces the foreign word three times in Scene 3 of the first act. When his dupe Aguecheek—whose name in Italian might be Malevolte—boasts, "I am a fellow o' th' strangest minde i' th' world: I delight in Maskes and Reuels sometimes altogether," Sir Toby inquires:

> What is thy excellence in a galliard, knight?
>
> *Andrew.* Faith, I can cut a caper.
>
> *Toby*... Wherefore are these things hid? ... Why dost thou not goe to Church in a Galliard, and come home in a Carranto? My verie walke should be a ligge: I would not so much as make water but in a Sinke-a-pace: What dooest thou meane? Is it a world to hide vertues in? I did thinke by the excellent constitution of thy legge, it was form'd under the starre of a Galliard. (1.3.112-125)

Altho enlightened listeners to the dialog would have been likely to take it as merriment at the tall Kit Hatton's expense, hinting that his lucky star was merely a sky symbol for a libidinal leg, the dramatist deliberately made the name and talent of Sir Andrew Aguecheek bewildering, for he was never intended to stand for Sir Christopher, whose soul likeness, but not his leg, is discovered in Malvolio alone.

On June 30, 1564, the Queen appointed Hatton a Gentleman Pensioner, equipt with armor and ax to protect her from the enemies who haunted her slumbers. He pleased her Majesty not only with his capering and cunning and skill in tilts and tournaments, but even more by his refusal to be involved in court affairs of love. He pretended bachelor devotion to her in a sort of travesty of her posturing as the Virgin Queen. She may have been acquainted with the facts of hidden sexual excursions. He had at least one illegitimate son. And Shakespeare had him in mind, I believe, when he made Mistress Quickly in *The Merry Wives of Windsor* boast that her house was no ordinary brothel: "There have been Earls, nay, what is more, Pensioners here."

The literary covetousness of Sir Christopher Hatton wrung from him in 1568 the fourth act of a tragedy named *Tancred and Gismund*, "compiled by the Gentlemen of the Inner Temple," and enacted before Elizabeth. In 1591 a Robert Wilmot issued the play "newly revived and polished according to the decorum of these days," that is in blank verse. Each of the acts was "compiled" by a student of law at the Temple, dramatising a story from Boccaccio's *Decameron*. I will emulate all the historians of British literature I have consulted, and say nothing to suggest that I have read the tragedy. Silently they all sustain the judgment of Edmund Gosse when he declared about Philip Sidney's *Apology for Poetry*, that it "labours under but one disadvantage, namely, that when it was composed in 1581, there was scarcely any poesy in England to be defended." Gosse had in view the dominance in England of such metrical cudchewing as *Tancred and Gismund*, or Gabriel Harvey's "Speculum Tuscanismi," and the verses of *Fortunatus Infelix*, in *A Hundreth Sundrie Flowres*.

On Mayday 1571 the Earl of Oxford, followed by Lord Charles Howard, Sir Henry Lee and Sir Christopher Hatton, challenged other courtiers to a "solemn Just at the tilt, turney and barrier," the chivalric collisions on horseback between the "knights" to take place at Westminster before her Majesty. Riding as a red knight, De Vere headed the other three challengers respectively arrayed in white, green and black, against the Gentleman Pensioner George Delves, Oxford's friend Thomas Bedingfield, his brother-in-law Thomas Cecil, and the uncle of the girl he desired terribly, Thomas Knyvet, along with Burghley's agent Ralph Lane, and twenty-two other defendants. All the fighters "did very valiantly, but the chief honour was given to the Earl of Oxford."[12] He broke thirty-two lances and scored three attaints—direct hits on chest or head. The Queen awarded him the prize of a tablet of diamonds. To Hatton she gave a gold bell and chains. George Delves remarked that the Earl's performance was "far above the expectation of the world."[13] People were always being surprised by the abilities of Edward de Vere. On August 15, 1571, Burghley wrote to Edward Manners, Earl of Rutland: "by dealing with him, I find that which I often heard of your Lordship, there is much more in him of understanding than any stranger to him would think. And for my part I find that whereof I take comfort, in his wit and knowledge, grown by good observation."[14] Rutland had been an orphan ward of the Crown in Cecil's care, and thus became almost intimate with the little laughter-loving Earl, the Lord with odd learning and strange tongue.

In May 1572 the Queen appointed her "Mutton" Captain of the royal guards. Thomas Churchyard dedicated to Hatton a plodding translation of Ovid's elegies, *De Tristibus*. And in July, during the Queen's "progress" or summer tour, he got the privilege of lodging at the Cecil estate of Theobalds in the tower chamber above the Earl of Leycester's room, which was above the apartment of the Queen. After three days the Court journeyed on to the estate of the Bacons, Oxford's cousins by marriage, with their curious stream named Ver. The "progress" ended at Windsor in September, and Captain Hatton found himself acridly dissatisfied with his progress up the scales of his ambition. He inquired for advice from the traditional author of "My Mind to Me a Kingdom is," Edward Dyer. [A case now has been made for Oxford as the poem's potential author—W.H.] Dyer's October reply was deemed deserving of preservation in Hatton's privy letterbook:

> The best and soundest way ... is to use your suits toward her Majesty in words, behaviour, and deeds: to acknowledge your duty, declaring your reverence which in heart you bear, and never seem to condemn her frailties, but rather joyfully to commend such things as should be in her, as though they were indeed: hating my Lord Ctm in the Queen's understanding for affection's sake, and blaming him openly for seeking the Queen's favour. Marry, thus would I advise you to remember, that you use no words of disgrace or reproach toward him to any; that he being the less provoked, may sleep, thinking all safe, while you do wake and attend to your advantages.[15]

While every investigator of Captain Hatton's correspondence agrees that "my Lord Ctm" could be none other but the Earl of Oxford, they admit they are baffled by the cryptic abbreviation. Some maintain that it should be read as "Chn," meaning Chamberlain, refering to Oxford's title of Lord Great Chamberlain of England. Since no other mistake in spelling has been detected in the Hatton letters, carefully copied in his book, I reluctantly abandon the suggestion and hunt for another explanation. But the one which occurs to me, others will probably loathe. It strikes me as a shortcut for Catamite, alluding to the "Ganymede" complex of Edward de Vere, which Dyer would have despised as a recluse in Southwark rooms among the Bishop of Winchester's "geese"—the girls whose pimps paid fat rent to the Bishopric on the south side of the Thames.

One of Burghley's innumerable spies reported to him in January 1573 that William Saunders of Northampton, Hatton's maternal uncle, had become virulently vocal about the obstacles to Kit's advancement at the Court and exultant about his abettors, the gentry who "in all their doings prefer Mr Hatton above the Lord Treasurer" and looked forward to the day when "Mr Hatton should have one step before him and give him the glike"[16] (Shakespeare pronounced the latter word "gleek"; it meant a joke at somebody's expense.)

Hatton's efforts to prove to the richest and robust proprietors of the empire that he could do as good, if not a better job as their prime minister in the Privy Council, than William Cecil were mainly obstructed by his excessive sweetness of sycophancy and the sordid social-climbing of his kin and kind. Apparently in vain he wrote to the Queen in October 1572 to repel charges of covetousness and ingratitude that had caused her displeasure; he swore that "most entirely he loved her person and service," and had vowed his whole life "everlastingly," his freedom and his fortune, to serve her; and signed the letter, "Your despairing most wretched bondman."[17] Meanwhile he circulated among friends certain poems celebrating his prowess in seduction of ladies in Northampton, his home country. However, late in March 1573, a domestic disaster in London afflicting close relatives threw an ugly cloud over his tall gallant veneer. A merchant tailor, George Browne, murdered George Saunders, first cousin of Hatton's mother, for the love of his wife Anne, and nonchalantly went to Greenwich Palace to mingle with the courtiers. On March 28 Browne was arrested, underwent severe questioning for several days, and finally confessed the crime. On April 17 he endured a trial that ended in condemnation to a frightful death. He tried to save Anne Saunders from charges of complicity up to his ultimate consciousness before execution at Smithfield, on April 20. On May 13 the widow Saunders and her bosom friend Anne Drury suffered their extinction in Smithfield for encouraging the killing of George Saunders. The Earl of Oxford's uncle Arthur Golding wrote a pamphlet of horror and morality concerning the affair, printed in 1573 by Henry Binneman, servant of Christopher Hatton. Unknown years later, the anonymous haunting tragedy *A Warning for Fair Women*, based on the passions of Anne Saunders and George Browne, spellbound Londoners for a little while. The affair seems to have sickened Kit Hatton.

On May 11, 1573, Gilbert Talbot wrote to his father, the Earl of Shrewsbury:

"My Lord of Oxforthe is lately grown in great credit, for the (Queen's Majesty) deliteth more in his personage, and his dancing, and valiantness, than any other. He presented her Matie with a rich jewell, which was well liked. I think Sussex doth back him all that he can; if it were not for his fickle head, he would pass any of them shortly. My Lady Burghley unwisely hath declared herself, as it were, jealous, w(hich) is come to the Queen's ear; whereat she hath been not a little offended with her, but now she is reconciled again. At all these love matters my Lo Treasurer winketh, and will not meddle any way.

Hatton is sick still: it is thought he will very hardly recover his disease, for it is doubted it is in his kidneys: the Queen goeth almost every day to see how he doth. Now are there devices (chiefly by Leycester, as I suppose, and not without Burghley's knowledge) how to make Mr Edward Dyer as great as ever was Hatton; for now, in this time of Hatton's sickness, the time is convenient ... These things I learn of such young fellows as myself."[18]

On May 29 the Queen granted her "Lids" permission "to pass over the seas for recovery of his health."[19] She sent her Doctor Julio to travel with him to the acid fountains of Spa, twenty miles southeast of Liege. I suspect that he enjoyed himself immensely at the Spa, even tho his letters to Elizabeth wail about his loneliness and longing for her. During the summer months of his vacation Henry Binneman's press groaned for his delectation with *A Hundreth Sundrie Flowres*, evidently arranged for the press by the unemployed soldier and scholar George Gascoigne.

One of the funniest of Captain Hatton's epistles to her Majesty, duly filed with the royal correspondence among her state documents, informed her: "Your Mutton is black ... I love your self. I cannot lack you God bless you for ever. The branch of the sweetest bush I will wear and bear to my life's end: God witness I feign not. It is a gracious favour most dear and welcome unto me; reserve it to the Sheep, he hath no tooth to bite, where the Boar's tusk may both raze and tear."[20] The "Boar" of course was his rival Edward de Vere, whose livery was familiar to all England bearing the emblem of a blue boar.

Hatton made his summer at the Spa politically useful by cultivating certain tenebrous relations with the Roman Catholic authorities of the region. Cardinal William Allen wrote happily about Hatton that he was one English statesman who had no doubt of the veracity of the Catholic creed. He seems to have met in Antwerp the Papist poet George Turberville, who mailed him on June 26 a shortened version of *A Treatise of Treasons*, the pamphlet attacking the Protestant exploiters of England led by the Cecils and Bacons, which the Queen proclaimed in September a slanderous tract of which all copies caught were to be surrendered to the Privy Council.[21]

A Hundreth Sundrie Flowres came from Binneman's shop in the shape of a collection publisht by one H. W. (Henry Wotton?) adverse to the wishes of his friend G. T. Almost blatantly Hatton hoped to get Romanist flanking in his maneuvers for upheaval of Lord Burghley from the summit of the Tudor monarchy.

When he returned to London, eager to go down on "the knees of his heart" to the Queen, a Puritan patriot, Peter Byrchet, determined that Hatton would have to die, because he was "a wilful Papist, and hindereth the glory of God so much as in him lieth." Byrchet's weapon injured the popular sea-captain John Hawkins, whom the Puritan mistook for the Queen's Captain.[22] For this failure of his dagger, Byrchet, who also studied law at the Inner Temple, was hanged.

In the following year, on May 24, Gilbert Talbot wrote to his father, the Earl of Shrewsbury, about Court talk of a royal Progress to Bristol, despite the deplorable weather: "her Majesty's great desire is to go to Bristow. Mr Hattoun, by reason of his great sickness, is minded to go to the Spaw."[23] For heavily shaded reasons the Queen became pensive and sad in June. Hatton got leave to visit the Spa with Dr Julio again, altho she granted it unwillingly. Burghley received her command to wait on her at Woodstock, but abruptly Francis Walsingham indicated that he should delay in London. The Lord Treasurer, surprised, did as he was ordered.[24] Elizabeth behaved as if apprehensive of some danger. Her spirit lightened by the time her "progress" arrived at Croydon in July to visit the Archbishop of Canterbury's palace. She found amusement in his problems of chambering the guests. The grooms of the privy chamber had no other way to their quarters but thru the apartment where the Countess of Oxford was placed. And there was bewilderment about where to put Mr Hatton.

The Countess Anne de Vere had to endure the pity of the courtiers because her husband had suddenly left his "country Muses of Wivenhoe" on the coast of Essex in a flight to Flanders, where it was alleged he intended to volunteer for military service with the Spaniards, or else to engage in conspiratorial talks with English fugitives faithful to the Catholic church. Bishop Cox of Ely had Oxford mainly in mind when he asserted on July 20, 1574, "Certain of our nobility, pupils of the Roman pontiff, either weary of their happiness or impatient of the long continued progress of the Gospel, have taken flight, some into France, some into Spain, others into different places, with the view of plotting some mischief against the professors of godliness."[25] Early in August, after Thomas Bedingfield came to De Vere in the Low Countries, carrying a message from her Majesty, the Earl sailed back to Britain and joined the Progress of the Queen, quickly winning her forgiveness. Tom Churchyard described her entertainments on this trip in *The First Part of Churchyard's Chips* (1574) dedicated to Hatton, the author's "tried and worthy friend," a book worthy of usage for Billingsgate commodity wraps, fish and chips.

At the end of January 1575 George Gascoigne undertook full responsibility for *A Hundreth Sundrie Flowres*, claiming that they were mostly products of his pen alone, and printed without his consent ("I being in Holland in service with the virtuous Prince of Orange"). Henry Binneman printed *The Posies of George Gascoigne* with his new dedication "To the reverend Divines," with a wish for their "quiet in conscience" from a poet "professing arms in the defense of God's truth" [26] Kit Hatton was then busy with a private crusade in Parliament for the fiercer prosecution of Jesuits landing illegally in England. In early March 1576 he delighted Elizabeth with a splendid feast at Eltham, "*avec force musicques et comedies.*"[27] Her pleasure fortified Hatton's influence in the government. He secured for the grocer William Tipper the revival of the law of "hosting," which obliged foreign merchants in England to lodge with local traders. Tipper got a Crown grant to host merchant-strangers in all the realm except Italians and Germanic traders of the Steelyard, the importers of exotic Baltic sea-food. Netherlanders protested against Tipper's monopoly and his lust for lucre. Sir Thomas Smith told Hatton the grocer's "patent" was illegal: "Indeed, I like not monopolies, for they be to the Monopolyer tyrannical, to all other servitude and bondage." Hatton ignored Oxford's boyhood tutor, and went on his profitable primrose path. He must have been instrumental in obtaining for Edward Dyer in January a monopoly of tannery licenses. So he was well prepared to appreciate the dedication to him of Arthur Golding's translation of the Roman savant Seneca's book *On Benefits* in 1577.

II

There is an allusion in the second act, scene five, of *Twelfth Night* which continues to frustrate every effort of professors of Elizabethan erudition to account for it. Malvolio is overheard daydreaming about his future fortune, wedlock with the Countess Olivia and lordship over her estate. "There is example for't," says he: "The Lady of the *Strachy* married the yeoman of the wardrobe." (2.5.36-37) Robin Greene seems to have remembered the rhythm of this; in *The Card of Fancy* (1584), the first of his writings revealing theatrical imagery, dedicated to the Earl of Oxford, he lilted the line: "The duchess of Malphey (Amalfi) chose for her husband her servant Ulrico." Many inquirers are inclined to fancy a connexion between Malvolio's words and William Strachey of Saffron Walden, who invested after 1606 in the Blackfriars playhouse, where David Yeomans was a tailor or guardian of the actors wardrobe. This Strachey wrote a letter about the wreck of a ship bound for Virginia in 1609 which is believed by many to be the source of *The Tempest*. But his letter was not printed until 1625, two years after Shakespeare's plays appeared in Folio, long after the dramatist died, and more years after *The Tempest* was composed. His father may have been the William Strachey, sheep farmer, who witnessed, in the summer of 1557, the will of John Smith of Walden, Essex, the father of Sir Thomas, Edward de Vere's first unforgettable teacher.

The Strachey family, which has adorned the shire of Essex and the precincts of Bloomsbury in London for centuries, donating to English literature a notorious pervert of renown, a fascist philosopher and statesman, a psychoanalytic editor and translator of Freud, and some eminent women better known by their husbands' names, cannot illuminate the reference. I am aware of but one remark concerning Stracheys by a neighbor who knew them well that might help us crack the nut. Gabriel Harvey noted in his *Marginalia* under the date 1577 (perhaps in September) the following quotation.[27]

"Lay your cares in a narrow room: Mistress Strachie to her husband."

We do not know the lady whom Harvey thus quoted, but we may imagine her as a woman of homely wisdom, comforting her mate with advice as old as the human race on how to escape from anxiety. Maybe future research will inform us if she was a sister or cousin of the Strachey who wedded the wardrobe yeoman.

Naturally our poet could not present the more illustrious example of a lady marrying a man of lower class, the instance of Katherine Willoughby Brandon, the Duchess of Suffolk, who took for husband her gentleman-usher Richard Bertie. In *The Taming of the Shrew* Shakespeare portrayed the love of her son Peregrine for the Earl of Oxford's sister Mary. We shall behold these fighting lovers once more in *Twelfth Night*. Of course our dramatist could not strengthen the daydream of Malvolio with any allusion to the love of John de Vere, the sixteenth Earl of Oxford, for Margaret Golding the daughter of John, an auditor of the royal Exchequer.

On November 11, 1577, the Queen lifted Hatton to the office of Vice-Chamberlain of her household. In this post he would have power over the production of the Court Revels; the Lord Chamberlain, Radcliff of Sussex, Oxford's oldest friend, no longer had the strength to arrange them in his wise cosmopolitan way. The spirit of Hatton manifested itself in the peculiar economy and censorship of the Revels. He was a mercurial spendthrift on furniture and costumery, but exhibited a remorseless avarice of the soul in matters of essential art. One of the forms in which this miserliness appeared was the clerical mode of defining the plays performed before the Queen. Before Hatton's appointment the clerks of the Revels almost always recorded the names of the dramas presented at the Court. On December 29, 1577, the dictation ran tersely, "A play before the Queen" acted by the Children of Paul's Church. The old fashion did not yield rapidly to the new while he was distracted from these affairs of what he surely considered folly by his new position in the Privy Council, four days before Francis Drake started his voyage around the globe. Hatton invested heavily in Drake's enterprise. That is why the flagship was named the Golden Hind—in honor of Hatton's family crest. Drake confided that the Queen had commanded him, "of all men my Lord Treasurer should not know" the true purpose of the voyage. For Burghley did not relish plots to raid the rich traffic of Spain on the western coast of South America, particularly from the mines of Peru. The Treasurer dreaded the rage of the Spaniards, who ruled not only the oceanic empire and the Low Countries but exerted profound influence in the Romanist dukedoms of France. The Queen however could not resist the temptations opened for her by Hatton, and in fact the profits from Drake's plundering in the Pacific amounted to four thousand percent.[29] She exalted Hatton to knighthood on December 1, 1577.

While deep in plans of provocation of the Spanish empire, Sir Christopher encouraged his servant Barnabe Rich, a veteran soldier, to write *Alarm to England*, "foreshowing what perils are procured where the people live without regard of Martial law." Christopher Barker, the Queen's own printer, issued Rich's book in 1578, dedicated to his master. On April 24, one Zacharias Jones reported to the espionage masters of the state a prison conversation he had with one Gifford, a Catholic enthusiast who implicated Hatton in Papish politics.[30] Evidently Sir Christopher had developed his skill in double-masking with the church parties to the point where none could tell in what godliness he believed. A clew to his real cult can be detected in the letter John Aylmer, Bishop of London, sent him on June 8, declaring, "I trust not of God, but of my Sovereign, which is God's lieutenant, and so another God unto me... will you throw down him whom you have set up yourself?"[31] I have never bothered to find out what troubled the Bishop. He interests me only as the chief target of the rebels against English ecclesiastic law and ordure who wrote the pamphlets of "Martin Marprelate," and sanctified the gallows by their martyrdom. Hatton hounded these Bible-embracers with the same ferocity that he dogged the Jesuits. In both he saw subverters of the Tudor state without which his own estate was defenseless against the fighters of famine, the poor, the base of society.

The pursuit of his political career was never separate in his soul from the infinite courtship of the Queen. When Robert Dudley of

Leycester went north for his health, to the well of Saint Ann at Buxton which English patriotism prefered to the Belgian Spa, Sir Kit wrote to him, on June 18, 1578, "Since your Lordship's departure the Queen is found in continual and great melancholy: the cause thereof I can but guess at, notwithstanding it bear and suffer the whole bent of her mislike in generality. She dreameth of marriage that might seem injurious to her: making myself to be either the man or a pattern of the matter."[32] Henry Bynneman printed for his employer Gabriel Harvey's *Walden Greetings*, including a Latin eulogy of the Earl of Oxford, merely because it carried a flood of flattery for Hatton and the Queen. Five years later the poor printer had a load of a hundred copies of Harvey's verses valued at less than a halfpenny each.[33] But in 1578 Binneman enjoyed better luck with Captain George Best's account of Frobisher's expedition to coldest Canada, *A True Discourse of the late Voyages of Discovery for the finding of a passage to Cathaya, by the North-west.* (South of Frobisher Bay, you can still see the headland named Hatton.) Because of the large funds lost in the Cathay Company's attempts to find a frost-way to China, a Cathayan came to mean a confidence-gamester. Therefor Sir Toby Belch affirms (2.3.70-72) that the lofty Olivia, "My Lady's a *Catayan*, we are politicians, Malvolios a Peg-a-ramsie, and *Three merry men be wee.*" We have the tune of "Peg-o-Ramsey" but no idea of the damsel it deals with, probably a wench of poor repute. Ideas of the Frobisher expedition sparkled in our poet's head as he wrote the comedy, and easily gave rise to figures of speech like these: "you are now sayld into the North of my Ladies opinion, where you will hang like an ysickle of a Dutchmans beard" (3.2.23-25). To a cognate interest doubtless belongs the allusion in Maria's report of the metamorphosis of Malvolio: "He does smile his face into more lynes, then is in the new Mappe, with the augmentation of the Indies" (3.2.72-74).

I do not exclude the likelihood that the passages quoted, concerning Dutch endeavors in the Arctic ocean and the fresh map expanding the Indies, were added to our comedy during revision which appears to have taken place after October 7, 1594, when

Francis Vere, Oxford's first cousin, informed Burghley of Captain Willem Barents's attempt to cross the northwest ice to "Chinay." The Dutchman De Veer's account of the Barents voyage, describing mariners' beards icicled, came out after the death of the great sailor in the frozen north on June 20, 1597. A map with "augmentation of the Indies" appeared in London in 1598.[34]

Before the Cathay Company started its attempts to open an oceanic path to the Orient, the Muscovy Company had succeeded in extending commercial activities beyond Moscow southward, penetrating Persia. Shakespeare indicates his awareness of the Persian expeditions in the speech of Fabian (2.5.172-173), "I will not giue my part of this sport for a pension of thousands to be paid from the Sophy," and Sir Toby's pretense that Cesario is "a firago" of a swordsman: "They say, he has bin Fencer to the Sophy" (3.4.266-267).

Eva Clark elucidated references in *Actus Quintus, Scene Prima*, to ships disturbing the shores of Illyria:

Orsino, this is that Anthonio
That tooke the Phoenix, and her fraught from Candy,
And this is he that did the Tiger boord,
When your yong Nephew Titus lost his legge. (5.1.57-60)

She proved that in 1577 a ship called Phoenix of London troubled the southwest coast of England "in warlike manner," and seems to have been suspected of piracy. On July 17, 1579, while Elizabeth made a merry Progress thru Essex and Suffolk, the Irish noble James Fitzgerald and his militant priest, Father Nicholas Sanders, launched a battle for their church and country at Smerwick Bay in Kerry on the western coast of Ireland. They had Papal and Spanish troops, and King Philip and King Sebastian promised support, but in a short struggle they soon learned they had only the Irish peasantry and fishing folk to depend on. Lord Arthur Grey of Wilton attacked their Castle of Smerwick, employing in his fleet a ship named the Tiger, and drove the revolutionaries into a desperate retreat.[35]

We have testimony of Edward de Vere's strong sympathy for the Irish insurgents in the polemic that Charles Arundel scribbled against him in the year 1581. Arundel's charges included "His often wishing that Dr Saunders were Pope, for he went into the quick; the rest were but hedge-priests; that he would give a thousand pound for such a chaplain.

That the Viscount of Baltinglasse (James Eustace, the rebel chief who died in Spain in 1585) wrote the bravest letter to the Deputy (Baron Grey) that ever was, putting great difference between the Queen and Christ's mother, whom notwithstanding he would never make supreme head." (Oxford quoted Lord Baltinglas, Arundel avers: "he said that the Queen would challenge the primacy which Christ would never give in to his own mother.") The Earl was furthermore accused of "daily spreading of Irish intelligence."[16]

The only signs of our dramatist's compassion for the Irish in his play that I can find are his use of the names Sebastian and Antonio for two heroes, and the generosity shown by the Duke Orsino to the sea warrior Antonio, who fought against the Duke's fleet. Among the eighty men that Fitzgerald and Sanders led to their valiant defeat in Smerwick were Sebastian de San Josepho, an Italian, and Don Antonio Ortega of Biscaya. There were also a Josefo Fabian and Fabian Lucas, who could have furnished Shakespeare with another name for his comedy.[37] Of course he would have found more attractive the name of the King of Portugal, Sebastian, who died in battle against the Moors in the summer of 1578, and Sebastian's kinsman Antonio, the illegitimate son of the Jewess Violante Gomez, whose claim to the Portuguese throne England upheld. In August 1579 Fitzgerald died fighting the English at Munster. The Smerwick fort of the *bisognos* inspired by the Jesuits under Father Sanders' leadership surrendered to Lord Grey and Walter Ralegh in November, who freed the officers that paid ransom and killed the other soldiers. The poet Edmund Spenser was in the service of Ralegh when he conducted the massacre, but left no memorial of the event.

Eva Clark suggested that King Antonio's mother may have been in our author's imagination when he made Viola's brother Sebastian, her twin, tell Captain Antonio, "my father was that Sebastian of Messaline, whom I know you haue heard of" (2.1.16-17). For nobody has been able to tell us where this Messaline was located, but Mrs Clark supposed that the poet got the name from wandering Semite fanatics called Messalians who drew adverse attention by their beggary in towns of Asia Minor.[38] She imagined that Shakespeare might have invented the place-name from reflection on the half-Hebrew king of Portugal who came to Britain a beggar for aid against his Spanish enemies.

Meditating on the Irish revolt against English colonial cruelty, I am reminded of a letter that Lord Burghley received from Ireland seven years later from a colonist named Andrew Trollop. "From the 10th to the 21st year of her Majesty (1568-1579)," Trollop said, "I was deputy to Thomas Gent, Esquire, then steward of the manors of the right honourable the Earl of Oxford, and during all that time being privy, not only of his public dealings but also of his private doings and secret intents, found and knew him endued with special piety, perfect integrity, great care to discharge all trust reposed in him, and no less desire to do good in the commonwealth."[39] Another witness to the Earl's truly religious love of his country was the soldier Geoffrey Gates, who dedicated to Oxford on December 23, 1578, *The Defence of Military Profession*, "Wherein is eloquently showed the due commendation of Martial prowess, and plainly proved how necessary the exercise of Arms is for this our age." Gates appealed to De Vere, "that under the shield of your noble favour and judgment it may stand in grace before our nation, to some good effect."

August 1579 elevated Sir Christopher Hatton closer to his heart's desire. In that month the French envoy Jean Simier, wooing Elizabeth for the double-nosed Duc d'Alencon or Anjou, discovered that Robert Dudley of Leycester had secretly married the year before the widow of Walter Devereux, Earl of Essex. The Queen's fury against Robin, whose ears she had delighted in tickling for years, found no outlet dignified enough. She banished him from the Court, and for three days suffered "extreme regret and many tears." According to rumor that reached Queen Mary Stewart in captivity, Hatton too had indulged in clandestine wedlock. The Queen signed the passport for Alencon's entrance into England. Leycester's nephew, Philip Sidney, searched his world for some way to express his outrage at his uncle's dismissal and the subsequent joy of the advocates of the French alliance. One August day he found himself confronting the Earl of Oxford in a tennis court where Sidney and some friends were playing, and the Earl requested him to quit the net for his Lordship's sport. Sidney refused; in the following dispute De Vere called him a "puppy." Philip challenged the Earl to a duel, but her Majesty rebuked him for transcending the bounds of blood or rank. The defender of Dudley honor received encouragement from Kit Hatton. On August 28 he wrote to Hatton: "As for the matter depending between the Earl of Oxford and me, certainly, Sir, howsoever I might have forgiven him, I should never have forgiven myself if I had lain under as proud an injury as he would have laid upon me; neither can anything under the sun make me repent it, nor any misery make me go one halfword back from it. Let him, therefor, as he will, digest it. For my part, I think tying up makes some things seem fiercer than they would be." The last sentence puts you in visionary presence of a pepper-tempered puppy? Sidney reinforced the picture in his *Arcadia*, after he too went into "exile" in his sister Mary's mansion at Wilton for writing against the union of England and France. "See whether any cage can please a Byrde," he cries in *Arcadia*, "or whether a Dog grow not fiercer with tying."

"Philip always had a touch of the self-righteous about him," remarks the biographer of his friend Edward Dyer, "which frequently nauseated those with whom he had to deal."[40]

Hatton's hypocrisy is usually excused as the compromise tactics of a patriot. The vicious streak in his character is not even seen by most examiners of Elizabethan ethics. Customarily he is remembered as Sir John Harington portrayed him by quotation of his mock-lamentations: "The Queen did fish for men's souls, and had so sweet a bait that no one could escape her net-work." So "she caught many poor fish who little knew what snare was laid for them." He spread his saccharin so lavishly that even ladies who admired Edward de Vere long extoled Sir Kit as "benign" and deservedly loved by multitudes.[41] It was exactly this deception of the surface-satisfied populace that Shakespeare selected for his target in picturing Malvolio. Your political science would designate him an opportunist: Maria calls him "constantly but a time-pleaser, an affection'd Asse, that cons State without booke, and utters it by great swarths. The best perswaded of himselfe: so cram'd (as he thinkes) with excellencies, that it is his grounds of faith, that all that looke on him, loue him: and on that vice in him, will my reuenge finde notable cause to worke." (2.3.136-142) Let us hope that English historians do not neglect too long the description of Hatton by John Clapham, the secretary of Burghley, left for centuries in posthumous dust: "very passionate and being provoked a violent and implacable enemy."[42]

In August 1579 the Puritan champion John Stubbe delivered to the press his *Discovery of a Gaping Gulf*, exhorting Elizabeth to spurn the allurements of France to marriage with the youngest of the Valois. He appealed to her Majesty to sacrifice felicity for the sake of what he trusted would be a godlier England. Hugh Singleton, who printed Edmund Spenser's *Shepherds Calendar*, where Bishop John Aylmer was derided as "Morell" and the friend of Puritans, Edmund Grindal, Archbishop of Canterbury, was applauded as "Algrind," printed John Stubbe's booklet, and William Page broadcast copies from his bookstall. Sir Christopher Hatton severely questioned the writer, the printer and the publisher in their prison, but he delayed the judgment of their dooms until he had unearthed from the Tudor archives a law condemning persons responsible for books presuming to make judgments on Majesty to the loss of their right hands. Not until November did the prisoners learn their fate. On October 16 the Queen shrewdly informed the French ambassador, "in the end," the Puritans "would want to recognise neither God nor King."[43]

On November 3, the right hands of John Stubbe and William Page were cut off under the law Hatton discovered in the parchments of Queen Mary Tudor and her consort Philip of Spain. Perhaps you are acquainted with the story of Stubbe's heroic raising of his hat afterward with the cry, "God save the Queen!" and swooning from his loss of blood? Burghley took pity on the "*scaeva*" left-handed patriot in September 1580 and helped him economically. But Stubbe's best friends were Lord Willoughby, Peregrine Bertie, and his valiant wife, the Earl of Oxford's sister, who took the Puritan martyr into their employment and home. They did not mind meeting his brother-in-law, the Puritan agitator Thomas Cartwright. Here I refrain from telling the story of Sir Kit's feud with Sir John Perrot, an infinitely finer man, whom the dancing Chancelor contrived to trap in the Tower of London, and failed to fetch under the royal ax only because death arrested him. These facts illuminate what malice our dramatist held in his mind's eye when Malvolio uttered his last words in the play: "Ile be reueng'd on the whole packe of you!"

III

The mood in which our poet wrote *Twelfth Night* or *What You Will* resembled the temper in which he composed the *Comedy of Errors* so intensely that he felt inspiration to write a play very like it in Plautine plot. However the image of his deserted mate no longer dominated his fantasy. Instead of her body appearing in the shapes of two sisters, he presented the figure of his desire as two different women, one so unlike the other that she could fool people into believing her a boy. So he reformed the Plautine plot under the influence of the girl disguised as male whom he had starred in the *Two Gentlemen of Verona*. But when he wrote that play he still fancied this girl in the form of his abandoned wife, modified by his lust for a young lady of the Queen's service who rejected his offers of affection and told him to return to the mother he had left. I have given my reasons for supposing that he drew the nonpareil Silvia in the semblance of his Queen. I shall assume that the lady Olivia in *Twelfth Night* represents her Majesty, tho there is hardly anything to prove this but the fact that the Duke Orsino desires her for his

bride, and Feste calls her "my princess" (5.1.294). Orsino I take for
a picture of Oxford; the poet permitted a slip of his pen to remain
in the manuscript, where Sir Andrew Aguecheek remarks, "the
Count himselfe here hard by wooes her," and Sir Toby too calls the
Duke of Illyria "the Count." A Count, you know, was continentally
what the English called an Earl. Moreover the name Orsino meaning bearlike would suggest to our dramatist a suitable substitute for
the Oxford whose emblem was a beast with a similar name. He
might have located his Greco-Italian romance in Illyria merely because that name reminded him of the misery of his music or poetry,
under the spell of his unrequited love for Anne Vavasor and the
fruitless wish for the heart of Queen Elizabeth. The result of his
enforced celibacy was a straining of his internal barriers to wishes
for rapture with his own sex. These feelings aroused his oldest passion, the paramount lust of his life, which identified the amorous
with nourishment, excitement of his mouth.

> If Musicke be the food of Loue, play on,
> Giue me excesse of it: that surfetting,
> The appetite may sicken, and so dye. (1.1.1-3)

The lines were recalled when he made Cleopatra speak of music,
"moody food of us that trade in love." The Duke of the sick lyre
unites in his thought both love and death. Life, he declares, lowers
values and spoils; only fancy, illusion, keeps things quiet and permanent. In this introversal vein Shakespeare's unconscious plays tricks
that betray the singular learning of this creator: he puns on heart
and hart, thinking of himself in the place of the hunted animal, torn
by desires "like fell and cruell hounds," as Actaeon was hunted and
destroyed in Ovid's poem, for daring to intrude by the bathing pool
of the goddess Diana. But venery does not interest Orsino, nor falconry, tho he goes to ancient vocabulary of the bird's soaring for his
metaphor "validity and pitch," which makes me remember Hamlet's
expression "enterprizes of great pitch and moment." The idea obtrudes in my imagination that Shakespeare chose the name Orsino
for his hero in remembrance of Orson, the hero of medieval ro-

mance, twin brother of the hero Valentine, whose name he had given the almost faultless protagonist of the *Two Gentlemen of Verona.* Orsino's first messenger to his Countess is named Valentine.

Twelfth Night blends a Renaissance romantic plot with mild political satire and a revery about the poet's predilection for loving girls who reminded him of boys, the self-reflecting bodies that attracted his soul, and the mystery of his bisexuality. Remembrance of the Greek novels he had devoured produced Antonio's phrase "The gentlenesse of all the gods" (2.1.40) and the twitching of Greek passion added Antonio's outburst, "But come what may, I do adore thee so, / That danger shall seeme sport, and I will go." (2.1.43-44) The adoration is for an absent idol, the future lover of Olivia, whose name Shakespeare deftly turned into Viola, standing for the adored man's twin sister, his feminine self. When Olivia falls in love with Viola disguised as Cesario, and mistakes Sebastian for that ideal, Shakespeare's oblivion evolved his confession thus that what he loved most was the body mirroring his colossal ego in miniature. In such terms do I translate the splendid incantation of the Duke:

> Get thee to yond same soueraigne crueltie:
> Tell her my loue, more noble then the world,
> Prizes not quantitie of dirtie lands,
> The parts that fortune hath bestow'd vpon her:
> Tell her I hold as giddily as Fortune:
> But 'tis that miracle, and Queene of Gems
> That nature prankes her in, attracts my soule. (2.4.80-86)

Soon after this lyric beauty comes the expression of the writer's monstrous buccal fervor, his avowal that love in him "is all as hungry as the Sea, / And can digest as much."

Nearly every editor of our comedy has noted the Greek source of Orsino's lines in the last act, meditating the murder of "Cesario" because Olivia loves his servant:

> Why should I not, (had I the heart to do it)
> Like to thy' Egyptian theefe, at point of death
> Kill what I loue? (a sauage iealousie,
> That sometime sauours nobly). (5.1.114-117)

Shakespeare was thinking of Thyamis, the Egyptian robber in the *Ethiopica* by Heliodoros, who fancied that he killed his beloved Chariclea to prevent her from being captured by his enemies. "If the barbarous people be once in despair of their own safety," declared the Hellenic novelist, "they have a custom to kill all those by whom they set much, and whose company they desire after death." These editors usually observe that Heliodoros's novel was translated by Thomas Underdowne in 1569. But they invariably neglect to note that Underdowne dedicated his version to the poet and dramatist Edward de Vere.

In calmer frame of mind, our poet portrays Orsino far less physically. He drops from Olivia's lips the praise of his intellectual and moral merits: "of fresh and stainlesse youth; / In voyces well divulg'd, free, learn'd, and valiant." (1.5.248-249) This contrast between the spirituality of the masculine and the carnality of the feminine may have been an outcome of the discovery that Shakespeare made in psychology, which the wizards of modern science have not even glimpsed :

> For, boy, howeuer we do praise our selues,
> Our fancies are more giddie and vnfirme,
> More longing, wauering, sooner lost and worne,
> Then womens are. (2.4.32-35)

Implicitly the poet here admits the superiority of woman's intelligence to the common man's, whose perception of actualities must work its way thru wishful thinking of crass kinds. This probably makes the male *il miglio fabro*—the better mechanic, mathematician, and musician.

The phrase "miracle and queen of gems" that Shakespeare applied to the beautiful female body of his dreams consorts in my mind with the marvelous line from the opening scene of *Troilus and Cressida*: "Her bed is India: there she lies a pearl." Both metaphors remind me of the words of laudation Laertes utters for the Frenchman Lamord, who is only heard of in *Hamlet*, words converting him to an Englishman: "I know him well, he is the Brooch indeed, / And gemme of all our Nation."

I have the impression that *Twelfth Night* was the first of our writer's plays to display prominently a habit of his speech and scripture which may be deemed the art-mark of his mind. I refer to his magnetic delectation for coupling of concepts and metaphors in short, powerful, lyrical spans. If Shakespeare kept his attraction to this form of phrase consciously covert in earlier plays, he exultantly cast off the restraint in our comedy. This may be the undercurrent reason for his naming the play *Twelfth Night*, in honor of the feast on January 6 that commemorates the coming of the Magi, the three astrologers from the East, to the manger of the baby named Savior in Hebrew, bringing crowns. The feast is named Epiphany because it rejoices in the earthly revelation of the divine in human shape. Perhaps on January 6, 1580, Edward de Vere experienced thrills of self-discovery, realising that he had been born the "gem" of the English nation for literature and theater. Up to that time he could have contented himself with the notion that he merely played with the quill, like Philip Sidney, none of whose writings were allowed publication in his lifetime, since ink-work was not really worthy of a warrior and statesman. Our poet's epiphany revealed to his eyes the divine mission of his life, to become the race's supreme dramatist. And he evidently celebrated it by making Orsino, Duke or Count of Illyria, sound "non-pareil," like none but the Earl of Oxford. The peculiar coupling of concepts emerges in the first speech of Orsino in the deliberate rhythm of the invocation, "O spirit of Loue, how quicke and fresh art thou," submerges for a moment in the terseness of "validity, and pitch" followed by "abatement, and low price," then leaps into the simile light of "my desires like fell and cruell hounds." It shows up again in Viola's admiration of her captain's "faire and outward charracter," later in her allusion to "Natures owne sweet, and cunning hand," which seems to reverberate in Olivia's line "And in dimension, and the shape of nature." But I like more Olivia's phrase "inuisible, and subtle stealth," and Orsino's "these most briske and giddy-paced times," in the dialog with Viola alias Cesario where he rises to the incandescence of "that miracle, and Queen of Gems." (2.4.85)

Priority of observation in print of this Shakespeare trait honors the English poet William Empson, whose misanthropy and aversion to life-learning seem to have made him a myopic yet minute scrutiniser of poetic texts. His *Seven Types of Ambiguity* (London 1930) first called our attention to that "linguistic form common in Shakespeare's verse, and typical of his method," which Empson mistakenly regarded as a pairing of nouns to qualify another noun.[44] The earliest example he quoted came from *All's Well That Ends Well* (5.3), and has not a breath of the magic and music evinced in the coupling of concepts that ensued: "Th' inaudible, and noiselesse foot of time." Long before I glanced at any of Empson's compositions, I had noticed the phraseology in the letters of Edward de Vere that the Cecils did not destroy, and considered it "The effect of composing stage blank-verse for years."[45] Now I view it as the inclination of his intellect to condense different images for conveyance of one idea, his favorite rhythm of association of lineage of concepts. When he perceived the practice in his artistry, he might have seen it as the art-mark of his muse, the epiphany of his genius, and spontaneously thought of the subtitle of his comedy *What you Will* as a challenging pun, Wot You *Will*.

In a similar spirit, the comedy introduces the couplet mocking Malvolio and luring him into delusion of grandeur, which Queen Elizabeth could be tempted to take as the poet's conjuration of her love for him. "I may command where I adore," it begins, and ends: "M. O. A. I. doth sway my life." (2.5.100-105) We know how the letters were designed in the play to be "crushed" by Malvolio to signify him. But the anagram simply affirms the equivalence of the vowels, I AM O, not only the initial of Oxford but the vocable of all emotion (a word, by the way, not to be found in Shakespeare's works, altho it entered the language in 1579). Hence Sir Toby's echo "O I" and his prayer, "O shall end, I hope."

It should be possible, by the way, to date our comedy by determining when the word "element" was so favored by the fashionable, it became an annoyance. While we hear the voice of the Earl of Oxford's earliest printed poems in the Duke of Illyria's declaration, "I myselfe am best/When least in companie" (1.4.37-38), it is easier to recognize the Earl in Sebastian (and therefor in his sister Viola or Cesario). Not only are we shown his customary melancholy manner ("My starres shine darkely ouer me"—2.1.3-4); we see him, shortly after his shipwreck, looking at Illyria precisely like his soul-brothers Antipholus of Syracuse and Valentine of Verona, desirous above all in a strange city to behold the wonders of the place: "What's to do?/Shall we go see the reliques of this Towne?" (3.2. 18-19) "I pray you, let us satisfie our eyes/With the memorials, and the things of fame/That do renowne this City." (3.3.22-24) More-over Sebastian and his Viola are the sole persons in the play who lost a father at the age of thirteen. So our poet presented them as orphans when they were about nine months older than he was when his father died. In this connexion it is noteworthy that the young lady Maria assures us, "My name is Mary" (1.3). Feste the clown calls her "mistris Mary," and makes the first anticipation in the play of her marriage with Olivia's uncle Toby Belch (1.5). Inci-dentally, Feste's remark about the latter, "One of thy kin has a most weake *Pia-mater*" leads me to wonder if Shakespeare believed that brains were maternal heritage? Viola calls Mary the Countess's "giant" in this scene, and our poet plainly delighted over the small stature of the "wren," "the little villaine," as Toby hails her rejoicing over her ingenuity in practical joking. Eva Clark had no difficulty in demonstrating that she and her Toby comically represented exactly the same two persons that Petruchio and his Kate caricatured in *The Taming of the Shrew*.[46] Aguecheek calls Mary "fair Shrew" (1.3).

The portrayal of Peregrine, Lord Willoughby, as a nobleman ca-pable of saturating his wits with wine, and thus falling short of the standard of desirability set by little Mary for the man she would adore, would strike especially risible those persons acquainted with the complaints of Peregrine's mother about them. Kate Bertie, Duchess of Suffolk, wrote to Burghley on March 12, 1578, request-ing his help "for a more unthankful person—in counsel may I say it for my daughter Mary, and her husband, who will in any wise use a house out of hand, and I fear will so govern it as my husband and I shall have small comfort of it and less gain; for what disorder may make, we must pay for it, but neither the young folk nor my husband so considers of it yet. That my Lady loves wine, who knows her that knows not that? ... and my son hates it not ... my suit therefor is, if it shall not mislike you, or that you may do it, to grant them impost for two tuns of wine to be taken at Hull or Boston, and I dare better be bound to you that it shall be all drunken quickly in their house than orderly or well spent."[47] The young Berties were residing at Grimsthorpe in Lincolnshire, an estate granted to the Duchess's father, Lord William Willoughby, and his bride Maria de Salinas, the dearest friend of Queen Catherine of Aragon, when Maria married. They obtained the land on condition that its occupant, the Dowager Countess of Oxford, should live there until her departure. The Willoughbys married in 1516, and their child, the future Duchess Katherine, was born at Parham Old Hall in Suffolk, where they went to live until the Countess Anne (born Howard), childless widow of the wretched John, fourteenth Earl of Oxford, died in 1559.

What helps us to identify the original or prototype of Toby is more than the combination of the last syllable of Bertie with the last syllables of Willoughby; it is the testimony Shakespeare makes of his religion. Peregrine Bertie became the English commander whom the Spanish army in the Netherlands feared like they dreaded the Devil, because of his courage rooted in parental religion. He was a passionate Protestant. So we hear Sir Toby defy the king of hell when he goes to encounter the stranger at the gate: "Let him be the diuell and he will, I care not: giue me faith, say I" (1.5.123-124). He proclaims his trust in salvation of his soul from hell by faith, rejecting the Catholic's confidence in "good works," or sacraments, penances and charities. When Aguecheek asserts that, for being "a kind of Puritane," Malvolio would deserve to be beaten like a dog, Toby inquires: "What, for being a Puritan? thy exquisite reason, deere knight?" (2.3.132) In the precise vein of her lover's piety, Maria takes her stand contrary to the Romanist persuasion: "there is no christian that meanes to be saued by beleeuing rightly" (3.2.66-67)

denotes her creed. Yet Lady Mary Vere, like her lover Lord Willoughby, would have chuckled, far from being offended, at the
question put on the tongue of Sir Toby, "Shall wee rowze the night-
Owle in a Catch, that will draw three soules out of one
Weauer?" (2.3.55-57) They were cosily acquainted with the fondness
of Protestant refugees from the Netherlands, who swarmed in the
industrial towns of East Anglia, the homeland of the Veres, for the
trade of textile manufacture in which they could frequently be heard
chanting psalms and other songs, especially in groups, like the melodious guildmasters of Nurenberg. And university-trained brains in
Shakespeare's audience would have found extremely funny the idea
of applying the Aristotelian doctrine of the three souls—vegetal, animal and rational—to an ordinary laborer, a lowly theologian of the
loom. Malvolio denounces their songs as "Coziers Catches," using
an old French term for tailors.

When Toby turns on Malvolio, the self-enamored, with the
query: "Art any more then a Steward? Dost thou thinke because
thou art vertuous, there shall be no more Cakes and Ale?" the
clown Feste chimes in, "Yes, by S. Anne, and Ginger shall bee hott
y' th' mouth too." The reference to Saint Anne is not accidental or
haphazard. Shakespeare was thinking not only of the medieval ma-
tron-saint who furnished virgins with husbands, the mother of Jesus's mother. He had in mind the fantom of Anne, his virgin of the
Vavasors, bride of his heart. He coupled her with ginger, which his
countryfolk credited with being aphrodisiac. Naturally, the rustic
reference made our poet remember Essex where Mary's vow to gull
Malvolio "into an ayword" would ring familiar. In Essex and Suffolk people employed "nayword" to mean "a laughing-stock."[48]
Toby tells the steward, "Goe, sir, rub your Chaine with
crums." (2.3.110-111) This may be an indication that Sir Kit Hatton
habitually wore one of the chains the Queen gave him for a prize
after the tournament of 1571.

In portraying the daydream compulsion of Malvolio to toy with
objects like chains and watches, Shakespeare revealed his insight
into the unconscious masturbatory habits of narcissic characters like

himself. He must have watched Sir Christopher Hatton innumerable times before he sketched him indelibly as Olivia's subchamberlain. But the psychology of the daydreamer evinced in *Actus Secundus, Scena Quinta*, is in the fringe of perfection. Half-awake he beholds himself, "Calling my Officers about me, in my branch'd Veluet gowne: hauing come from a day bedde, where I haue left Olivia sleeping." (2.5.44-46) To imagine himself making love to her would have been a deed of altruism beyond his moral might. He shifts to the happier plane of fantasy where nobody but Malvolio needs payment of attention: "I frowne the while, and perchance winde vp my watch, or play with my—some rich Iewell." That is how it is printed. I suppose that Shakespeare personally intervened to discuss with the comedian of the role that interval between "my" and "some" which churns the cream of the jest. In my judgment, the essence of the fellow is unveiled in his reserve about "quenching my familiar smile with an austere regard of controll." The poverty of sense and humor thus betrayed covers an even deeper cavity of conscience. He can see in the mortals surrounding him nothing but stumbling-devices or instruments; the communion of culture for such a man is mere make-believe.

Our dramatist relieved the grimness of his portrait of Sir Christopher Hatton by having fun with the sort of lechery that the knight discharged. Shakespeare may never have seen the epistles in which Hatton hinted to her Majesty of his hallucinations about her breasts. But he could have conjectured that Sir Kit indulged in reveries of intimacy less chaste, and so allowed himself to fool with the venereal puns in the passage concerning the letter Maria forged: "By my life, this is my Ladies hand: these bee her very C's, her U's, and her T's, and thus makes shee her great P's. It is, in contempt of question, her hand." The poet's wish to punish Hatton in this manner must have sprung from the same hurt that inspired, not only Viola's avowal, "they that dally nicely with words, may quicklely make them wanton," but Feste's complaint about official confinements of the liberty of literature: "But indeede, words are very Rascals, since bonds disgrac'd them" (3.1). "A sentence," the clown lamented, "is but a cheu'rill gloue to a good Witte; how quickely the wrong side may be turn'd outward." (3.1.11-13)

Reflecting on the writer's whirligig of revenge, I am struck again by the way in which he connects Malvolio with the image of a bird. When the steward sees the letter on the garden walk, Fabian hiding in the box tree blurts, "Now is the Woodcocke neere the gin" (2.5). And when Malvolio is subjected to the treatment of a madman, the counterfeit Curate Sir Topas tests his intellect by asking, what Pythagoras taught "concerning Wilde-fowle?" Immediately Malvolio answers, "That the soule of our grandam, might happily inhabite a bird," an opinion which he condemns, because he deems it a degradation of the soul. The concealed Clown however insists he will have to remain in his dark cell until he alters his philosophy to consent that a woodcock might contain the soul of his grandmother (4.2). One is induced to wonder if one of Kit Hatton's grandmothers was a Woodcock? The year 1580 saw him earnestly urging the royal college of heraldry to draw up for him a preposterous pedigree, inventing for his first English ancestor a Norman named Ivon, who (the claim ran) came over with William the Bastard, now known as the Conqueror.

I should have mentioned, in relevance to the Clown's sorrow over censorship, on July 24, 1579, the Queen appointed Edmund Tylney Master of the Revels, the first formal censor of the British theater. Who would be surprised to learn that Hatton proposed this appointment, setting the stage in bondage? It certainly extended the distance between him and the histrionic Duttons, the Earl of Warwick's players who formed Oxford's own company in 1580. They sprang from the loins of the Duttons of Cheshire who had tangled with Hattons in matrimony.

The Clown's song in *Actus Quartus* (2) mocking Malvolio for his Lady's alleged unkindness, I take to be a taunt to smite both Hatton and Robin Dudley, Earl of Leycester. Listen to it, recalling how she banished the lordly lover to his castle Kenilworth for marrying Leticia Knolles Devereux, listen, in the light of our knowledge of Hatton's own aspirations:

Clown. Hey Robin, jolly Robin, tell me how thy Lady does.
Mal. Foole.
Clown. My Lady is unkind, perdie.
Mal. Foole!
Clown. Alas, why is she so?
Mal. Foole, I say.
Clown. She loues another. Who calles, ha? (4.2.72-79)

There is nothing in our Hatton records resembling the sport of Malvolio's yellow stockings and cross-gartering. But I believe that Eva Clark guessed rightly when she related this jest of costume to Hatton's chagrin when the Queen grew angry at the sight of his gold-buttoned coat. About November 1584 Queen Mary Stuart reported to Elizabeth some venomous gossip collected by the notorious "Bess of Hardwick," Countess of Shrewsbury:

> As for the said haton (she said) that you ran him hard showing so publicly the love that you bore him that he himself was constrained to withdraw from it and that you gave a box on the ear to [William] Killigrew for not having brought back the said haton to you after he had been sent to recall him having departed in anger from you for some insulting words you had said to him because of certain gold buttons which he had on his coat.[49]

Eric Brooks explained the incident by reason of a gift the Scottish queen had given Sir Henry Goodere of gold buttons which he wore on his doublet and cap, and became in the English Queen's eyes a flaunt of disloyalty to her. Elizabeth never forgot that the Cecils and the Hattons were creatures who, long before Sir Robert Walpole, maintained that every man had his price. Burghley did not bother to hide his dogma that old nobility meant ancient riches, and peerage was empty pomp without property. In short, they prized only "quantities of dirty" estates, and shielded her crown because Roman Catholic authority denied, not merely her legitimacy, but their right to lands once stolen from the Church.

If *Twelfth Night*, a story of mistaken identities, may be regarded as a study in hypocrisy superficial and profound, its moral lesson may

be found in the wisdom of Feste, falsely called "fool." Disguised as
the clergyman Topas he tells Malvolio, "as the old hermit of Prage
that neuer saw pen and inke, very wittily sayd to a Neece of King
Gorboducke, that that is, is" (4.2.12-14). Thus he cheerfully contra-
dicts the remark he makes to Sebastian believing him to be Cesario
(Viola in male vesture): "Nothing that is so, is so" (4.1.8). Shakespeare seconds the latter motion when Orsino (whose name suddenly strikes me as anagram for Orison, a word for prayer dear to
the dramatist) seeing Sebastian next to Viola, cries, "A naturall Per-
spectiue, that is, and is not" (5). The very same view of society compels Olivia to sigh, " 'Twas neuer merry world,/Since lowly feigning
was call'd complement" (3.1.97-98). Viola warns her, "I am not
what I am," yet proudly declares, "I haue one heart, one bosome,
and one truth." (3.1.157) Anne Cecil de Vere might have pronounced this, conscious of her father's motto, *Cor unum, via una*, and
her husband's, *Vero nihil verius*.

Among the more curious testimonies of our comedy that things
are not what they seem, we are struck by contradiction of the economic argument of *The Merchant of Venice* against the right of moneylenders to collect a surplus from the use of their supply. Feste inquires about Viola's gift of "expences" (3.1.43): "Would not a paire
of these haue bred, sir?" She answers, quite soberly, "Yes, being
kept together, and put to use"—exactly Shylock's excuse for his
"interest." But we do not need this proof that our poet's enmity to
the Jew sprang, not from economics, but from reason of ritual, his
code of holiness.

IV

The evidence that Sir Andrew Aguecheek theatrically caricatures
that valiant and talented gentleman Sir Philip Sidney was assembled
conclusively in Charles Wisner Barrell's humorous fiction "Matinee
at the Swan" (in the *Shakespeare Fellowship Quarterly*, January 1944).
Barrell pointed out that when Belch signals to Maria to speak Spanish—"*Castiliano vulgo*: for here comes Sir Andrew Agueface," the
poet was reminding his public that the pattern of chivalry approach-

ing had been the godson of the Spanish king Philip, when Mary Tudor acquired her brother's throne. The knight in the comedy is named Andrew because Sidney's birthday was November 30, Saint Andrew's day. When Toby replies, "Were we not borne vnder Taurus?" to Andrew's question, "Shall we fit about some Reuels?" the poet did not have Sidney's birthday nor Peregrine Bertie's in view (Mary Vere's mate was born on October 12, 1555, a year after Sidney's first autumn). He was thinking as usual of Edward de Vere, born in mid-April, under the constellation of the Bull, under whose imaginary sway babies arrive with earthy strong-willed souls, most energetic, the star-sages say, in legs and thighs.

Before Sir Andrew enters the stage, we are told that Toby brought him to become a wooer for wedlock with the lady Olivia, which would recall to all acquainted with Sidney and Oxford how warmly the knight's father had striven to win Anne Cecil for his son's wife. We are next told that Aguecheek is tall, prodigal with money, "playes o' th' Viol de-gamboys, and speaks three or four languages word for word without booke, & hath all the good gifts of nature." Maria caps the compliment with derision: "he's a great quarreller: and but that hee hath the gift of a Coward, to allay the gust he hath in quarrelling, 'tis thought among the prudent, he would quickely haue the gift of a graue." A personal grudge snarls in the lines, for Sidney was no coward; his efforts to force Thomas Butler, Earl of Ormonde, his father's Irish enemy, into a duel testify to his audacity. Barrell also notes the letter Philip sent Sir Henry Sidney's secretary Edmund Molyneux, threatening him with the son's dagger for reading Sir Henry's mail from home. Of course the direct cause of this comic distortion of Sidney's nature was his tennis-court quarrel with Oxford and the rimes he rumbled in reply to Oxford's lyric about his obsessional vision of having to choose for his fate "A kingdom, or a cottage, or a grave."

Our comedy even contains terms of opprobrium reminiscent of the tennis court dispute, particularly of Oxford's insults. Sir Toby invites Andrew and Feste to join him in a noisy trio. Aguecheek gleefully agrees: "And you loue me, let's doo't: I am [a] dogge at a

Catch." The clown, doubtless in remembrance of some puppies, remarks: "By'rlady, sir, and some dogs will catch well ... I shall be constrain'd in 't, to call thee knaue, Knight." Aguecheek is undismayed: " 'Tis not the first time I haue constrained one to call me knaue" (2.3.59-64). His adventure in writing a challenge for a duel with Cesario, and subsequently being beaten by Sebastian, simply vents a gust of the grievance that Oxford nursed against Philip Sidney. We gladly forget his bloodshedding for the sake of the fun Shakespeare got from writing Sir Andrew's self-revelation: "mee thinkes sometimes I haue no more wit than a Christian or an ordinary man has: but I am a great eater of beefe, and I beleeue that does harme to my wit" (1.3.79-82). Sir Philip, a devout friend of Huguenot sages and fighters, probably spoke of himself often in this fashion. He certainly begged the Archbishop of Canterbury for a special dispensation to eat beef during Lent, even while he worried over his weight. His hair too declined to curl, and hung "like flax on a distaffe."

Sidney's principles of reform of Christendom were somewhat fiercely Calvinist. So we hear his authentic opinion from the tongue of Aguecheek when the latter affirms that he prefers valor to policy: "it must be with Valour, for policie I hate: I had as lief be a Brownist, as a Politician" (3.2.28-29). The Brownists were the forerunners of modern Congregationalists—democratic republicans, you might call them, of the churches which had long been accustomed to monarchy and aristocratic oligarchy. They called themselves Separatists because they did not want to be members of churches organized unlike the original group of the Galilean's followers. Thomas Browne, their patriarchal teacher, came from Stamford and Cambridge University, like his cousin Burghley, who tried to protect him from the fury of British bishops, who resolved on silencing Browne and his brethren at the dawn of 1581, when they saw the magnetism of Browne's preaching in the eastern counties of the kingdom.

Finally Barrell pointed out that Sir Philip was a "knight dubb'd with vnhatch'd Rapier, and on carpet consideration" (3.4). In June

1577 a London rumor reported to Don John of Austria said that Sidney would marry a daughter of Prince William of Orange and become governor of Holland and Zeeland. But not until 1585 did he get the chance for demonstrating heroism in the Low Countries. However when Prince Hans Casimir of Germany came to England in 1579, the Queen granted her mercenary the privilege of the Garter, with her own hands fastening the badge of the Order on his leg. But Casimir could not wait for his formal installation on St George's day (April 23) in the chapel at Windsor castle. He chose his "very dear friend" Sidney to serve as his proxy, and that was how Master Philip got his knighthood. But he had to wait until January 8, 1583, for the ceremony; the anniversary of her Majesty's coronation, on January 13, required that he should be qualified with the accolade, for none below the rank of knight could act as proxy then.[50]

Barrell neglected to note the peculiar likeness of the merry Andrew's mode of speech to that of Abraham Slender in *The Merry Wives of Windsor* (1.1). Master Slender wishes for a beloved volume: "I had rather than forty shillings I had my Book of Songs and Sonnets here." Aguecheek wishes he could sing well: "I had rather then forty shillings I had such a legge, and so sweet a breath to sing, as the foole has" (2.3.18-20). But nobody ever recorded Philip Sidney's way of wishing.

I cannot leave this review of Sir Toby Belch's dupe and the unstaged love affair between Toby and his "Mettle of India, the youngest Wren of nine," without suggesting that a stage direction may well be inserted in the scene (2.3) that honors Saint Anne (whose festival fell on July 26). When Malvolio talks of Olivia's willingness to have her uncle depart, Toby turns to Maria chanting a pastoral fragment, "Farewell, deere heart, since I must needs be gone." Maria responds, "Nay, good Sir Toby." Feste chants, "His eyes do shew his dayes are almost done." The Folio text then makes *Mal.*, not *Mar.*, ask, "Is't euen so?" Toby trumpets, "But I will neuer dye." At this point I picture him aiming an amorous gesture at her and falling to the floor. The next line is the Clown's: "Sir Toby, there you lye."

It is regrettable that Shakespeare was unable to let us learn what he thought about Sidney's grandsire, the vaulting John Dudley, Duke of Northumberland, who made his son Guildford temporary monarch of England by enthroning his daughter-in-law, Jane Grey, as young King Edward's successor. When Elizabeth observed the lack of Northumberland nerve in her darling Robin Dudley, she touched on the fatality of character that accounts for Leycester's failure to attract even one biography comparable to those scribbled about his inferiors in the realm. "I am a Dudley in blood," Sidney asserted, "that duke's daughter's son... I do acknowledge, I say, that my chiefest honor is to be a Dudley... England can boast of no nobler" blood.[51] He disdained answering the charges against his uncle: "Dissimulation, hypocrisy, adultery, falsehood, treachery, poison, rebellion, treason, cowardice, atheism, and what not..."[52] Sidney made the list in 1584, the year to which I trace the composition of *Hamlet*, where in the opinion of many, you may behold the soul of the Earl of Leycester in the frame of the King of Denmark, Claudius. Thereby hangs a tale for a different tome.

Late in the year 1580 Sidney is believed to have written his *Apology for Poetry*. The dominant idea of this treatise is that the art in question merits more than our tolerance because it purposes moral reform; it is "medicine with cherries." Evocation of beauty would have seemed to Sidney almost a wicked purpose. He clung to beliefs of venerable antiquity. And in this fidelity to the past he and his narrow ring of friends resolved that poetry should obey in Britain the rules of classic meter, renouncing forever the tradition of the island's language and balladry, which, Sidney confessed, rang in his blood like a clarion. Gabriel Harvey joyfully joined them. In October 1579 he wrote to Edmund Spenser, who modestly attended the group's conversations, eager to learn all he could about the craft to which he would devote his life: "Master Sidney and Master Dyer, they have me, I thank them, in some use of familiarity... And now they have proclaimed in their Areopagus a general surceasing and silence of bald rymers and also of the very best too." The Cambridge instructor in rhetoric informed his friends and foes: "let me rather be epitaphed, The Inventor of the English Hexameter."[53] To make Sidney and Dyer merry and earn the patronage of the Earl of Leycester, the gay Gabriel attempted a sort of hexametric retching, doggerel which he entitled *Speculum Tuscanismi*, but friends and foes called the "Mirror of Tuscanismo." He publisht the poem in *Three Proper and Witty Familiar Letters*, "lately passed between two University men: touching the Earthquake in April last, and our English reformed versifying," in June 1580.

Here I merely record Harvey's elaborate apology for his satire, which he called "patcheries and fragments," with commentary by Thomas Nashe. "Another company of special good fellows," Harvey affirmed over a decade later, headed by De Vere's secretary, John Lyly, "would needs forsooth very courtly persuade the Earl of Oxford, that something in these Letters, and namely, the Mirror of Tuscanismo, was palpably intended against him, whose noble Lordship, I protest, I never meant to dishonour with the least prejudicial word of my tongue, or pen, but ever kept a mind full of reckoning of many bounden duties toward the same."[54]

Whatever his goal was in penning the poem, one public effect would surely have been loud laughter at Leycester House at the spectacle of their scholar showering Oxford with hexametric excrement, bewraying him, as Nashe said, with "Tuscanism" from top to toe. Nashe explained the piece as primarily political: "whereas two great Peers being at jar, and their quarrel continued to bloodshed, he would needs, uncalled and when it lay not in his way, step in on the one side, which indeed was the safer side (as the fool is crafty enough to sleep in a whole skin) and hew and slash with his hexameters; but hewed and slasht he had been as small as chippings, if he had not played Duck Friar and hid himself eight weeks in that Nobleman's house for whom with his pen he thus bladed."[55] But Oxford did not take the lampoon seriously, Harvey insisted: "the noble Earl, not disposed to trouble his Jovial mind with such Saturnine paltry, still continued like his magnificent self."[56] Nashe considered the Cambridge don's judgment of Italianate taste in the arts paltrier: "he casts Tuscanism, as a horrible crime, in a Noble-man's teeth, and almost in the same wind the finest Tuscanism in grain."[57] Nashe was then a student at St Johns College in Cambridge, and had observed Harvey "in the pantofles of his prosperity, as he was when he libelled against my Lord of Oxford."[58] But he got an impression that the rhetorician had gone to jail for writing brutal satire, and Harvey denied it. Privately he admitted that Sir James Croft, a statesman with a stubborn Spanish orientation, had seen in his *Speculum* an attack on Dr Andrew Perne, Dean of Ely, and locked him in the Fleet prison near Ludgate after he failed to obtain refuge in a noble's house.[59] Harvey hated Perne for blocking his academic ambition.

The title of Harvey's burlesque possibly inspired Anthony Munday to name his new book, licensed for printing on October 10, 1579, *Mirror of Mutability*. He signed the dedication to the Earl of Oxford several days before, with a flourish of Tuscanism, "*humilissimo, e Divotissimo, e sempre esservandissimo Vasallo e Servitore.*" In it he indicated that the Earl had suggested he should travel and learn languages to "reap some commodity." Munday apologised for "having not so fully comprised such pithiness of style as one of a more riper invention could cunningly have carved," but, knowing Oxford's generosity to apprentices in prose as well as verse, "I rest, Right Honourable, on your clemency, to amend my errors committed so unskilfully." His teacher of French, the Huguenot schoolmaster Claudius Hollyband, his cousin William Hall (who usurped immortality by becoming the only procurer of Shakespeare's *Sonnets*) and the invalid scholar Edward Knight, the E. K. of Spenser's *Calendar*, wrote commendatory meters for the *Mirror*. The book is of no importance, dealing tritely with the seven deadly sins, illustrated by Bible people, common Christian vices and virtues, all handled in the same dreary didactic verse. Munday promised a third part but never produced it.

The Earl manifested his pleasure in Tuscan wit and artistry in the comedy of Illyria. Take, for example, the lines of Viola's approval of Feste's frolic speech: "This fellow is wise enough to play the foole, / And to do that well, craues a kinde of wit" (3.1.59-60). The source of the praise has been found in Pietro Aretino's comedy *Filosofo* (Act 3). Just after the First Thief advises the hero, "Make a virtue of necessity!"—a line that Shakespeare used in *Two Gentlemen of Verona*, the Second Thief says, "Come with us as a third, I say with us, who are masters of that which, to do well, requires skill, wariness, firmness, nimbleness," and so on.[60] When our poet has Viola tell how she would woo Olivia with sonnets and nocturnes, he may have been recalling Aretino's prolog to the *Marescalco*, where the speaker predicts, "I shall have madrigals composed in her praise, and have songs made about her by Tromboncino." Viola's promise that she would "Write loyall Cantons of contemned loue" (1.5.259) is meant to convey sadness, not hilarity, but its Italian tone appears in the word "Cantons." It evokes for me the music of the song "O Mistris mine" (2.3) where the line "What's to come, is still unsure" recalls the last line of *Il Trionfo di Bacco e di Adrianna* by the Florentine Lorenzo the Magnificent:

Di deman non c' e certezza.

There is one contemporary document bearing witness that Edward de Vere was renewing his knowledge of the Tuscan tongue about this time. On April 23, 1582, the English ambassador in Paris, Sir Henry Cobham, reported to Walsingham: "I have lately been intreated by letter from the Abate del Bene to recommend Bartolomeo Spatafora the Sicilian, who has, as he says, some time served the Earl of Oxford. I have given him a letter to yourself only, being since informed he has spoken with the Pope's nuncie."[61] We have no record of the fact, but it follows that Oxford was acquainted with the music of Sebastiano Festa, and Cattaneo, the violinist of Mantua, entertainer at the court of Vincenzo Gonzaga, father-in-law of the more famous opera composer Claudio Monteverde.

There is a passage in Sidney's *Apology for Poetry* which prompts me to the confidence that he had seen *Twelfth Night* on the stage. It presents the first scene of Act 2 and the first scene of Act 3 in reverse order, but the critical reference is clear: "Now ye shall have three Ladies," Sidney offers in illustration of the absurdity of English theater, "walk to gather flowers, and then we must believe the stage to be a Garden. By and by, we hear news of a ship wreck in the same place, and then we are to blame, if we accept it not for a Rock."

In February 1581 Captain Barnabe Riche's *Farewell to Military Profession* was registered at the Stationers guild. This collection of tales mostly for ladies, without a spark of wit or scintilla of insight in human perplexities, has been embraced by every adherent of the Stratford idolatry as a book from which Shakespeare took the love plot of *Twelfth Night*. They must, of course, make their Stratford idol a borrower and copier—never an innovator—for otherwise their dating of the dramas would be exploded. They ignore Riche's plainly stated acknowledgment that he himself borrowed plots for the book from the contemporary stage: —

> Gentle Reader, now thou has perused these histories to the end, I doubt not but thou wilt deem of them as they worthily deserve, and think such vanities much fitter to be presented on a stage (*as some of them have been*) [emphasis added] than to be published in print.

Riche did not take the trouble to tell his readers that "Of Apolonius and Silla" was one of the borrowed plots, but evidently he assumed his readers would recognize theme and plots recently or currently on stage.

Captain Riche called Sir Christopher Hatton "My very good Lord and upholder," and took pains in his nugatory novelets to make fun of the Earl of Oxford's Francophile fashions.[62] Just as Oxford's fetching from Italy in April 1576 of perfumed gloves and other pleasantries commenced a tide of Tuscanism in his country, his devotion to the cause of union with France appears to have inspired both trivial and spirit-scouring political passions. The magazine wizard William Gifford noticed that the arrival of Francois Hercules de Valois, Duc d'Alencon and Anjou, in November 1579 to win Elizabeth as a bride, seems to have been viewed by English dramatists as the opening of an epoch. For instance, Ben Jonson in

Cynthia's Revels (1600) marks an episode by the words, "when Monsieur was here." Thomas Dekker recalled "the year when Monsieur came in" for his *Seven Deadly Sins of London* (1606), and Thomas Middleton remembered difference of things "in Monsieurs days" in *A Mad World, My Masters* (1608). Gifford failed to observe that the epoch thus dated in British literature is the same as the phase of Euphuism, the popularity of which is usually dated from the printing of John Lyly's *Euphues: The Anatomy of Wit*, in 1579, but may better be dated from the publication, at the beginning of 1580, of *Euphues and His England*, dedicated to the Earl of Oxford. Poor Tom Churchyard's pedestrian writings were fast forgotten on the bookstalls at Paul's Churchyard under the deluge of emulations of Lyly. Churchyard's *Choice: A General Rehersal of Wars*, registered in August 1579, netted him little more than the pittance he got from Sir Kit Hatton for the dedication.

Early in 1580 Anthony Munday published *Zelauto: The Fountain of Fame*, "Erected in an Orchard of Amorous Adventures, containing a Delicate Disputation gallantly discoursed between two noble Gentlemen of Italy, given for a friendly entertainment to Euphues, at his late arrival into England." This book, dedicated to Oxford, shows everywhere the influence of Will Shake-speare, the enchanter really responsible for the literary revolution which is customarily credited or blamed on the author of *Euphues*, "the minion Secretary," as Harvey called him. *Zelauto* exhibits not only the impact of *Two Gentlemen of Verona*; it imitates *The Jew* or *The Merchant of Venice*. But it lacks Lyly's talent for lighthearted talk, and its characters are unlike those in *Euhpues and His England*, about whom we are told, "They are too expert in love, having learned in this time of their long peace, every wrinkle that is to be seen or imagined."[63] The Stratford cult comedians have long described the greatest artist—"not of an age, but for all time!"—as a pupil of Lyly, ignoring the testimony of Gabriel Harvey on Lyly's oracle, and nucleus of light. They have never reflected enough on the pithiness of the difference in Shakespeare's epigrammatic manner from the style of Lyly. Compare Viola's equivocation in *Twelfth Night* (2.4.120-121), "I am all the daughters of my Father's house, / And all the brothers too," with the coy Phillida's saying in Lyly's *Gallathea*: "My father had but one daughter, and therefore I could have no sister" (3.2). The difference is not between sadness and subtlety merely; there is an abyss here between educated ears, quick to pick up tricks, and "the modesty of nature," a voice from what Orsino names "the booke euen of my secret soule" (1.4.14).

There appears to have been upheaval in the London theaters "when *Monsieur* came in." On September 26, 1579, James Burbage, builder of the playhouse beyond Bishopsgate named the Theatre, and one John Brayne mortgaged it to John Hyde. Brayne was Burbage's brother-in-law, and always a miserable partner in the perilous enterprise. His morose disposition to the mummery and Popery of the players worsened under the rains, "the great abundance and superfluity of waters that fell shortly after Michaelmas," September 29.[64] And on December 27, the boys of the Chapel Royal acted for the last time under the direction of Richard Farrant, the founder of the indoor Blackfriars theatre. They played something called "A History of Alucius" at Whitehall. Not long after, Farrant died, leaving the Blackfriars lease to his widow Agnes, who persuaded his Chapel colleague William Hunnis to continue the boys' performances. If they acted in *Twelfth Night*, we cannot locate the Revels record of it.

Early in the year 1580 Edward de Vere organised his own theatrical troup. The actors John and Lawrence Dutton left the histrionic service of Leycester's brother, the Earl of Warwick, and donned Oxford's livery. A buffoon of a rival outfit, perhaps Dick Tarleton who seems to have belonged to Leycester's company, wrote some rimes about it, preserved in a manuscript as follows:

> The Duttons and theyr fellow-players forsakying the Erle of Warwycke theyr mayster, became followers of the Erle of Oxford, and wrot themselves his COMEDIANS, which certayne Gentlemen altered and made CAMOELIONS. The Duttons, angry with that, compared themselves to any gentleman [remember, they were relatives of Hatton]; therefore these armes were devysed for them.
>
> "The fyeld, a fart durty, a gybbet cross-corded,

A dauncing Dame Flurty of alle men abhorred;
A lyther lad scampant, a roge in his ragges,
A whore that is rampant, astryde with her legges,
A woodcocke displayed, a calfe and a sheepe,
A bitch that is splayed, a dormouse asleepe;
A vyper in stynche, *la part de la drut*,
Spell backwarde this Frenche and cracke me that nut.

Parcy per pillory, perced with a rope,
To slythe the more lytherly anoynted with sope;
A coxcombe crospate in token of Witte,
Two eares perforate, a nose wythe slytte,
Three nettles resplendent, three owles, three swallowes,
Three mynstrellmen pendent on three payre of gallowes,
Further sufficiently placed in them
A knaves head, for a difference from alle honest men.

The Wreathe is a chayne of Chaungeable red,
To shew they are vayne and fickle of head ;
The crest is a lastrylle whose feathers ar blew,
In signe that these fydlers will never be trew;
Whereon is placed the horne of a gote,
Because they ar chast, to this is theyr lotte,
For their bravery, indented and parted,
And for their knavery innabulated.

Mantled lowsy, wythe doubled drynke,
Their ancient house is called the Clynke;
Thys Posy they beare over the whole earthe,
Wylt please you to have a fyt of our mirthe?
But reason it is, and heraultes allowe welle,
That fidlers should beare their armes in a towelle."[65]

Obscene sadism in rime did not satisfy the critics of Oxford 's company. On April 10, 1580, a brawl occurred at the Theatre. Two days later the Lord Mayor of London wrote about the fray to Sir Thomas

Bromley, the Chancelor, expressing his hope that the Privy Council would take decisive steps to prevent such fights, especially on Sundays. The next day the Council sent Robert Leveson and Laurence Dutton, servants of the Earl of Oxford, to Marshalsea jail for having rioted against students from the Inns of Court (fellows faithful to the Dudley game in the state). The sequel documents concerning the case are bereft of light for us; they tell us that on May 26 the Theatre riot was refered to three judges, and on July 18 Thomas Chesson, "sometimes servant" of Oxford, was released on bail.[66] Meanwhile, on June 21, John Hatcher, vice-chancellor of Cambridge University, informed Burghley that he had received the recommendations of the Lord Treasurer, the Chamberlain Sussex, and the Chancelor Bromley, that Oxford's men should be allowed to "show their cunning in several plays already practised by them before the Queen's majesty." Hatcher added, in view of pestilence and the need for student industry at commencement time, a prior refusal to Leycester's troup, and a Privy Council order of 1575 against "open shows" and assemblies in Cambridge, he had deemed it better to give the company with the blue boar emblem on their sleeves twenty shillings and send them away.[67] And so the whirligigs of England went their spinning ways.

V

Sometime in 1580 Susannah, the daughter of an obscure kinsman of the Earl of Oxford, Hugh de Vere, died in Castle Hedingham parish, and was buried in St Nicholas churchyard. I am unaware of a connexion between this pathetic event and the persistence in our poet's memory of a ballad of Susannah, the heroine of the Hebrew *Apocrypha*, who resisted the seduction and blackmail of dirty old men in Judea long long ago. When Sir Toby inquires aloud about his relation to Olivia, "Am not I consanguinious? Am I not of her blood? tilly vally," he recalls the ballad: "Ladie, *There dwelt a man in Babylon, Lady, Lady*" (2.3.72-74). Fragments of the same song recur in *Romeo and Juliet* and *The Merry Wives of Windsor*. Shakespeare would have remembered the song when he composed *The Merchant of Venice*, for he often mentioned in that romance the wise young Daniel who rescued Susannah from the elders when she came to trial.

Lechery certainly flared in our dramatist's brains when he composed *Twelfth Night* during the winter of 1579 and the first months of 1580. To this very time I attribute the poem printed anonymously in William Byrd's *Songs of Sundry Natures* in 1589, which rises in loveliness from stanza to stanza, and reminds me of one sweet singer alone:

> From Citheron the warlike boy is fled
>> And smiling sits upon a Virgin's lap,
>> Thereby to train poor misers to the trap,
> Whom Beauty draws with fancy to be fed:
> And when Desire with eager looks is led,
>> Then from her eyes
>> The arrow flies
> Feather'd with flame, arm'd with a golden head.
>
> Her careless thoughts are freed of that flame
>> Wherewith her thralls are scorched to the heart:
>> If Love would so, would God the enchanting dart
> Might once return and burn from whence it came!
> Not to deface of Beauty's work the frame,
>> But by rebound
>> It might be found
> What secret smart I suffer by the same.
>
> If Love be just, then just is my desire:
>> And if unjust, why is he call'd a God?
>> O God, O God, O just! reserve thy rod
> To chasten those that from thy laws retire!
> But choose aright (good Love, I thee require)
>> The golden head,
>> Not that of lead!
> Her heart is frost and must dissolve by fire.[68]

You can hear the outcry "O God, O God," in Hamlet's first soliloquy, which some editors change to read, more metrically, "O God, God!" In the tragedy and in the song the outcry is related to thoughts of lust.

We have met stage personalities representing the object of the Earl of Oxford's desire, Diana Capilet in the play many believe was once entitled *Love's Labors Won*, and Rosaline in *Love's Labor's Lost*. (The name Capilet, incidentally, turns up in *Twelfth Night* as the name of a gray horse coveted by Sir Toby Belch, owned by Sir Andrew. See 3.4.) I am pleased with Eva Clark's surmise that the young lady was Edmund Spenser's Rosaline in the *Shepherds Calendar*, and her real name was Anne Vavasor, which I have suggested was converted to Rosaline by being read backward—Rosavav, the latter syllable being the Hebrew letter made by a strait line. According to the gossip of John Aubrey, who may have heard it from the poet and playwright John Dryden, Spenser's girlfriend was a kinswoman of the wife of Sir Erasmus Dryden, the poet's father.[69] The Vavasors were ardent Catholics of Yorkshire, and their name appears frequently in the Jesuit records of the seminary of Rheims and at Rome. Anne's reputation, however, has been described best in the *Sonnets* of Shake-speare concerning his "Dark Lady."

In April 1579 Gabriel Harvey wrote to Spenser about her in his habitual circuitous prose: "You charge me somewhat suspiciously with an old promise; to deliver you of that jealousy, I am so far from hiding mine own matters from you that lo, I must needs be revealing my friend's secrets, now an honest Country Gentleman, sometimes a Scholar: At whose request I bestowed this palting bungerly rime upon him, to present his Mistress withal. The parties shall be nameless," says Harvey: "saving that the Gentlewoman's true, or counterfeit Christian name must necessarily be bewrayed."[70] We need not waste time over his poem, the quality of which is adequately shown by its declaration, "thy deserts are such,/That no one in this world can love thee too much." The poem is addrest to "my good Mistress Anne: the very life of my life, and only beloved Mistress."[71] In October 1579 Spenser let the world know by letter to Harvey that his *Calendar* had been "made in honor of a private Personage unknown, which of some ill-willers might be upbraided not to be so worthy, as you know she is."[72]

I suppose the main source of the vilification of Anne Vavasor was *The Copy of a Letter*, "Written by a Master of Arts of Cambridge, to his friend in London, concerning some talk past of late between two worshipful and grave men, about the present state, and some proceedings of the Earl of Leycester and his friends in England." This ugly polemic, manufactured by Charles Arundel and his comrades of the English Catholic circle in Paris in 1584 singled out for slander Arundel's cousin, "Anne Vaviser." Thus her name appears in the margin of a report, said to be Robert Dudley's own confession, "(so little shame he hath) that he offered to another of higher place, an hundreth pound lands by the year with as many Jewels as most Women under her Majesty used in England: which was no mean bait to one that used traffique in such merchandise: she being but the leavings of another man before him, whereof my Lord is nothing squeamish, for satisfying of his lust, but can be content (as they say) to gather up crumbs when he is hungry, even in the very Laundry itself, or other place of baser quality."[73] The Gentlewoman of the Queen's Bedchamber never recovered from the publicity of the calumny pamphlet, commonly named "Leycester's Commonwealth." She was never mentioned in Sidney's posthumous *Defence of the Earl of Leycester*, apparently written in 1584.

On July 10, 1584, we ought to note, Hercules de Valois, Duke of Anjou and Brabant, died at Chateau Thierry, extinguishing the last hope of continuance of the Valois dynasty. Henri de Bourbon, King of Navarre, became the heir presumptive to the French crown. Nobody made an epitaph for "Monsieur" more accurate than Navarre's judgment that the Duke was "as double-minded and malicious as he is ill-formed in body." He seems to have carried from England to France a tale that Elizabeth had revealed to him why she would have to die a virgin queen. According to Amelot de la Houssaie, who admitted, "I know not whether all that has been said or written concerning the loves and the lovers of Queen Elizabeth be quite true; but it is certain that she had no vulva, and that the same

reason which prevented her from marrying hindered her from having any coitus." She told Alencon, "she did not believe that her subjects cared so little for her as to wish her in the grave before her
time."[74]

In 1596 a scholar named Johannes de Witt sailed from Holland
to visit London. Among the results of his voyage, described in a
document he left to the University of Utrecht, is the only contemporary picture of a playhouse familiar to Shakespeare, the Swan
theatre. His drawing has been used as an illustration of Elizabethan
theatrical architecture in hundreds of volumes, but not until Eva
Turner Clark unveiled its secret was the drama De Witt had seen at
the Swan identified. She pointed to the fourth scene of Act 3 of
Twelfth Night as the sole conceivable source of De Witt's drawing, in
which we behold Olivia's steward strutting with his staff before her
(seated on a garden bench) while the mischievous Mary behind her
queries, "Why, how doest thou, man? What is the matter with
thee?"[75] By the time of this performance at the Swan, the fruit of
the love-union of Edward de Vere and Anne Vavasor was fifteen
years old. She surrendered to Oxford's importunity and poetry at
the end of Spring 1580. Perchance he vanquished her wonderfully
armored mind by an appeal that kindled recollection of these lines
from *Twelfth Night* (1.5.231-232), drifting on a rivulet of oblivion in
her:

> Lady, you are the cruell'st shee aliue,
> If you will leade these graces to the graue,
> And leaue the world no copie.

References

1   See Eva Turner Clark, *Hidden Allusions in Shakespeare's Plays* (Jennings, Louisiana; Minos Publishing Company, 1974) 367; also Bernard M Ward, *A Hundreth Sundrie Flowres*, ed. Ruth Loyd Miller (Jennings, Louisiana; Minos Publishing Company, 1975) 17f.

2   *Idem.*

3   Ward, *op. cit.* 40.

4   Clark, *op. cit.* 364; Ruth L Miller, *op. cit.* 369.

5   Maureen Grice, in *The Reader's Encyclopedia of Shakespeare*, ed. O. J. Campbell (New York; Crowell Company, 1966) 904.

6   *The Arden Shakespeare: Twelfth Night*, ed. Morton Luce (London; Methuen, 1918) xi.

7   Maruice Hewlett the novelist hinted the meaning of the name and its Italian origin to Morton Luce, *ibid.* 180.

8   Gerard Legh, *Accedens of Armory* (London, 1562).

9   Edmund K. Chambers, *The Elizabethan Stage* (Oxford; Clarendon Press, 1923) 111, 457.

10   Sir Robert Naunton, *Fragmenta Regalia* (1653) ed. Edward Arber (London, 1870) 41, 42.

11   Kenneth Muir asserted, the four words, "coisterell, garragascoynes, pavion, and galliard are to be found in *Twelfth Night* and in no other of Shakespeare's plays."—*Shakespeare's Sources* (London; Methuen, 1957) 70.

12   John Stowe, *Annales, Or, A General Chronicle of England* (London; Richard Meighen, 1615), 669. Bertrand de Salignac, Marquis de la Mothe-Fenelon, *Correspondance*, iv, 88. Calendar of Rutland Manuscripts, i, 92.

13   Rutland Manuscripts, *loc. cit.*

14   Calendar of Rutland Manuscripts. i, 95.

15   Harris Nicholas, *Life and Times of Sir Christopher Hatton* (London; Richard Bentley, 1847) 18.

16   Calendar of Salisbury (Cecil) Manuscripts at Hatfield, ii.

17   Calendar of State Papers, Domestic Series (1572) lxxxix, 47.

18   Edmund Lodge, *Illustrations of British History* (London; John Childey, 1838) 11, 17-19, from the Talbot Papers, vol. F, folio 79.

19   Acts of the Privy Council of England, ed. J. R. Dasent (London; Eyre and Spottiswood, 1907) viii, 108.

20   Calendar of State Papers, Domestic (1573) xcii, 16; Nicolas, *op. cit.* 28. See Eric St John Brooks, *Sir Christopher Hatton, Queen Elizabeth's Favourite* (London; Jonathan Cape, 1946), for more details.

21   Brooks, *op. cit.* On Hatton's communication with George Turberville, see Bernard Ward edition of *A Hundreth Sundrie Flowres*, 2d. ed. Ruth Miller, 75-89.

22   Ward, *op. cit.* 85.

23 John Nichols, *The Progresses and Public Processions of Queen Elizabeth* (London; Nichols, 1823) 1, 388.

24 Nichols, *op. cit.* i, 389.

25 *The Zurich Letters...* ed. Robinson (Cambridge; University Press, 1846) 475.

26 *A Hundreth Sundrie Flowres*, ed. Miller. 23f. *The Works of George Gascoigne*, ed. John W. Cunliffe (New York 1910) 1, 3.

27 *Relations Politiques des Pay-Bas et de l'Angleterre* ed. Kervyn de Lettenhove (Brussels; F. Hayez, 1900) viii, 221.

28 Gabriel Harvey, *Marginalia*, ed. G. C. Moore Smith (Stratford; Shakespeare Head, 1913) 139.

29 Conyers Read, *Mr Secretary Walsingham* (Oxford; Clarendon, 1925) iii, 395-6.

30 Calendar of State Papers, Domestic Series (1578) cxxii, 33.

31 Nicolas, *op. cit.* 59.

32 E. M. Tenison, *Elizabethan England* (Leamington; Author, 1933) iii, 160.

33 Mark Eccles, "Bynneman's Books," *The Library*, 5th Series (June 1957) xii, 81f.

34 C. H. Coote, "Shakspere's New Map," *New Shakspere Society Transactions* (London 1871-79) p99.

35 Clark, *op. cit.* 378f. See *The Shakespeare Fellowship News-Letter* (New York, April 1941) ii, 35.

36 State Papers Domestic (October 1581) 12/151: 46 and 50.

37 See Clark in *The Shakespeare Fellowship News-Letter* (August 1941) ii, 64, and the *Fugger News-Letters*, ed. Victor Klarwill (London) ii, 47.

38 Clark, *Hidden Allusions* ... ed. Miller, 378-79.

39 Calendar of State Papers: Ireland (1587) 424.

40 Ralph Sargent, *At the Court of Queen Elizabeth* (London; Oxford University Press, 1935) 55. Compare Bronson Feldman, "Othello in Reality," *The American Imago* (Summer 1954) vol. 11, 165-66.

41 Compare Katherine Eggar in the *Shakespeare Fellowship News-Letter* (London, Spring 1955) p. 12.

42 John Clapham, *Elizabeth of England*, ed. E. and C. Read (Philadelphia; 1951).

43 Read, *Walsingham*, ii, 260n.

44 William Empson, *Seven Types of Ambiguity* (New York; New Directions, 1966) 90. Harold W. Patience independently discovered the habit of "double description" in Shakespeare and in Oxford's correspondence. (*Shakespearean Authorship Review*, Autumn 1971, 19-20.)

45 Bronson Feldman, "The Confessions of William Shakespeare," *The American Imago* (Summer 1953) vol. 10, 147-48.

46 Clark, *Hidden Allusions* ... ed. Miller, 368.

47 Salisbury Manuscripts at Hatfield House, 160/1 19.

48 Robert Forby, *The Vocabulary of East Anglia*, ed. Turner (London 1830).

49 Clark, *op. cit.* 374, quoting Frederick Chamberlin's *The Private Character of Queen Elizabeth*.

50 H. R. Fox Bourne, *Sir Philip Sidney* (London; G. P. Putnam's Sons, 1891) 281.

51 *The Miscellaneous Works of Sir Philip Sidney, Knt.*, ed. William Gray (Boston; Burnham, 1860) 314.

52 *Ibid.* 310.

53 Harvey, *Works*, ed. Grosart, i, 182.

54 *Ibid.* 183.

55 Nashe, *Works*, ed. Ronald McKerrow (London; Sidgwick and Jackson, 1910) iii, 69, 78.

56 Harvey, *op. cit.* supra, i, 184.

57 Harvey, *Pierce's Supererogation* (London; John Wolfe, 1593).

58 Nashe, *Have With You to Saffron Walden* (London; John Danter, 1596).

59 Harvey, *Marginalia*, ed. Smith, 32.

60 See John M. Lothian, "Shakespeare's Knowledge of Aretino's Plays," *Modern Language Review* (October 1930) vol. 25, p. 416, 7.

61 Calendar of State Papers, Foreign Series (1581-82) 700.

62 Bernard M. Ward, *The Seventeenth Earl of Oxford* (London; John Murray, 1928) 193-4.

63 John Lyly, "Euphues and His England," in *Works*, ed. R. Warwick Bond (Oxford; Clarendon, 1902) ii, 153.

64 Harvey, *Works*, i, 43.

65 Thomas Wright and James Orchard Halliwell, *Reliquiae Antiquae* (London, 1845) ii, 122.

66 E. K. Chambers, *The Elizabethan Stage*, ii, 100.

67 *Idem.*

68 *Lyrics From the Song-Books of the Elizabethan Age*, ed. A. H. Bullen (London; John C. Nimmo, 1889) 17. William Byrd, *Collected Vocal Works*, ed. Edmund Fellowes (London; Stainer & Bell, 1937-50) xiii, xiv.

69 John Aubrey, *Brief Lives*, ed. Oliver Dick (Ann Arbor; University of Michigan Press, 1957) 242.

70 Harvey, *Works*, i, 96.

71 Ibid. 96, 97.

72 *Idem.*

73 *History of Queen Elizabeth, Amy Robsart and the Earl of Leicester*, ed. Frank Burgoyne (London; Longmans, Green, 1904) 49-50.

74 Amelot de la Houssaie, ed. Lettres de le Cardinale Offat, 1595, iii, 399, quoted in Pierre Bayle's *Dictionnaire historique et critique*, 5th ed. (1734) ii, 720.

75 Clark, *The Man Who Was Shakespeare* (New York; Richard R. Smith, 1937) 188-9.

Chapter 11—EXPERIMENT IN TRAGEDY

> In men as in a rough-grown grove remain
> Cave-keeping evils that obscurely sleep.
>
> *The Rape of Lucrece.*

I

Most inquirers into the development of the artist who, Alexandre Dumas declared, after God, created the most, have agreed that the earliest of his tragedies was probably *Titus Andronicus.* Some contended that the poet, so often extolled by his contemporaries as a "gentle" personality, could not have written this extremely brutal play. They nominated one or two other Elizabethans as men more likely to compose a series of horrors such as we are shown in this work. But the inclination of testimony in favor of William Shakespeare's authorship, single-handed, is too strong.

When Edward Ravenscroft in 1686 changed the old tragedy to a piece more palatable to the elegant, allegedly classical taste of his time, he reported that he had been told, "by some anciently conversant with the Stage, that it was not Originally" from the pen of Shakespeare, "but brought by a private Author to be Acted, and he only gave some Mastertouches to one or two of the Principal Parts or Characters." This, added Ravenscroft, "I am apt to believe, because 'tis the most incorrect and indigested piece in all his Works. It seems rather a heap of Rubbish than a Structure."[1] You see, the theatrical idolatry of Shakespeare had already advanced so far by 1686 that popular English playwrights even found it incredible that the demigod ever produced one drama replete with blemishes. Later English learning attained the charitable insight that *Titus Andronicus* was a juvenile effort of the divine Will, indeed his first play in the tragic vein, bearing not only his "mastertouches" but characteristic apprentice faults.

Scholars are fond of pointing out that just as he had gone to the Latin comedian Plautus for material and inspiration to write his earliest comedy, so he had applied to the Latin tragedian Seneca for guidance in the production of his first tragedy. Their prevailing opinion is that Shakespeare decided to write *Titus Andronicus* because he wanted to attempt a tragedy and naturally looked to ancient Rome for a model to work by. All intellectual roads led to Rome in his day when Occidental culture still labored under the impressions of the Roman Catholic Church. The only Roman drama the scholars found showing any resemblance to the plot of *Titus Andronicus* was Seneca's *Thyestes*: the climax of both plays is a scene of cannibal banqueting, the spectacle of a parent eating unaware the flesh of children who were killed and cooked for the sake of revenge. In the Latin play a father is made to devour his sons by a brother whose wife he had seduced. In Shakespeare's work a mother is made to eat her boys' bodies by one not her kin, whose daughter had been raped by her sons. Why did our dramatist choose this particular plot for his first experiment in tragic poetry?

The monstrous meal is what distinguishes *Titus Andronicus* from the mass of theatrical butcheries which were so fashionable in Shakespeare's period. Professor Joseph Quincy Adams said that our poet "could hardly have had a genuine artistic interest in the bloody *Titus*, but his business shrewdness showed him the opportunity of turning it into a great money-maker for his company."[2] Professor Adams was a devout believer in the notion that William Shakespeare the money-lender of Stratford-on-Avon was the same Shakespeare who wrote *The Merchant of Venice* and other polemics against the business of money-lending. So the sole motive he could conceive for the bard lending his hand to the production of *Titus Andronicus* was the acquisition of cash. Plays of murder and massacre were tremendous magnets for the pence of the people in the reign of Queen Elizabeth (the bloody Bess). To get a pile of their pennies, what else must the reign's greatest writer do but write to drown his stage in blood? But if we grant that Shakespeare was tempted to compose the tragedy by this vulgar goal, and really lacked an artistic interest in the plot, how are we to explain the play's anthropophagy, the eating of human meat? Were numerous murders, the rape, and the cutting off of three hands not enough to satisfy his public's appetite for atrocities? Why did he feel compelled to revive for his theater the cannibal theme from Seneca?

To break the silence of scholarship on this question William H. Desmonde has written a striking paper tracing the savage feats of our play to primitive rituals of child sacrifice and other performances of ancient religious cruelty. It seems to me that Desmonde has proved this point conclusively. However I am unable to follow him when he claims that *Titus Andronicus* was derived from some Roman play or myth.[3] He proposed to demonstrate that the tragedy had such a source but his article contains no evidence of it. Shakespeare may have borrowed his cannibal feast from Roman drama but he took the raw materials of his tragedy from Greek myth as seen thru the prism of his dearest poet Ovid, the epic bard of the *Metamorphoses*. Desmonde is certainly correct in deriving the rape of the daughter of Andronicus and the tearing out of her tongue from Ovid's book. The Latin poet's story of the rape of Philomela also includes a feast of anthropophagy. Philomela's sister Procne obtains vengeance on the royal ravisher Tereus by killing his son and serving the lad's flesh at the table of the king. The legend of the two sisters and Tereus actually plays a part in Shakespeare's play. By indicating the pages where it appears in a volume of the *Metamorphoses* the tongueless Lavinia helps her father and brother understand the terrible things that happened to her. Yet why did Shakespeare base his first tragedy on these frightful scenes from Ovid? Why in fact should he have turned to writing tragedy at all? Excellent dramatists have lived, earned immortality and died without daring a tragic story. Samuel Johnson sagely observed that the deity of British theater appeared to repose in his comedies and to toil in his plays of terror and pity: "his tragedy seems to be skill, his comedy to be instinct."[4] There is more truth in Johnson's remark than meets the casual eye. Anyhow, we are justified in inquiring what motive or motives spurred the best of playwrights to make the jump from comedy and romance to tragedy—and enter the tragic stage with a banquet of bestialities like *Titus Andronicus*. Desmonde abstained from treating "the relation of this tragedy to the playwright's personality." Nevertheless, that is exactly what "the psychoanalytic study of the play's origin," which he set out to make, demands from us. The job becomes especially bewildering when, like Desmonde, one yields to the insistence of veterans of Professor Adams's authority that Shakespeare did not write the play, merely tailored it for his troup.

Titus Andronicus was originally published without an author's name in 1594. Shakespeare's powerful friends, who delivered the first collection of his plays to the press in 1623, included it, and were never challenged about its right to be there until Edward Ravenscroft tried to dramatize the rape of Lavinia a second time. Francis Meres, a well-informed scholar in Shakespeare's own day, listed the play among the poet's outstanding tragedies in his book *Palladia Tamia* in 1598. These facts, together with internal evidence of language, portraiture, and psychological peculiarities, determine the true authorship beyond the shade of doubt.

We have a singular advantage in the scientific interpretation of *Titus* because the dramatist created the framework of its events out of original fantasy. There is no foundation in history for the imaginary Romans and Goths of this tragedy. He put the scenes of his story in a Rome that never existed; its vestiges of old chronicles, the names of imperial personages and the background of Gothic war, perhaps a few hints of characters, came from Greek or rather Byzantine history. (There was an Eastern Roman monarch named Andronicus, whose queen, like Shakespeare's Tamora, had a son by secret meetings with him. Queen Theodora was taken prisoner with her two sons. Emperor Andronicus ended his short bloody reign in a revolt of his people who tortured him to death. Two other Andronici became kings in Constantinople, weaklings both; one of them was driven from the throne by his grandson. Any comparison of these historic figures with the characters in our play would be farfetched.) Therefore we may be confident that analysis of the happenings in *Titus Andronicus* will reveal for us the very terrors that were ravaging Shakespeare's imagination prior to his conception of the tragedy. This labor of creation produced his own dramatic catharsis, discharged from his mind certain agonies and deadly moods, without the exalted reflection necessary for the real work of art.

II

Shortly after the opening of the drama at the tomb of the Andronicus family, the poet presents a scene of sanctimonious murder. The old protagonist Titus—"Patron of virtue, Rome's best champion"— hands over to his sons the first-born son of Tamora, Queen of the Goths, for a sacrifice to appease the blood-thirst of the ghosts of their brothers, all of whom died in battle with the Goths. Mother Tamora pleads for her young man's life in vain: "O cruel, irreligious piety!" Her son Chiron wonders how these bloody Romans can claim to be civilised. "Was ever Scythia," he asks, "half so barbarous?" (1.1.134)

In the reference to Scythia I see one of the touches that point for us the identity of the hand that penned this tragedy. Of all the things concerning the Scythians which the poet had read in records of antiquity, one fact remained traumatically fixed in his memory, that they were cannibals. To Shakespeare the thought of Scythia went forever linked with the idea of eating human flesh. Surely he had the Scythians in remembrance when he made Othello speak of his travels among "the cannibals that each other eat, / The Anthropophagi." Shakespeare planted this association in the brains of younger playwrights. Thus Thomas Dekker arrived at the definition: "Anthropophagi are Scythians, that feed on men's flesh."[5] In what may have been the last of Shakespeare's tragedies, *King Lear*, he again refers to "The barbarous Scythian, / Or he that makes his generation messes / To gorge his appetite." The mention of man-consuming Scythia at the beginning of *Titus Andronicus* foreshadows the ghastly supper at the end. I think it was Tomyris, the queen of Scythia, that our poet was recalling when he named his queen of the Goths Tamora. He alludes to Tomyris in *Henry the Sixth, Part One* (2.3) where a French countess plans to capture and slay the English hero Talbot:

> The plot is laid; if all things fall out right,
> I shall be as famous by this exploit
> As Scythian Tomyris by Cyrus' death.

Parallel to this passage we may set the lines of the answer made by Demetrius, another son of Tamora, to brother Chiron's question about Scythia. "Oppose not Scythia to ambitious Rome," mutters Demetrius,

>   but hope withal
> The self-same gods, that arm'd the Queen of Troy
> With opportunity of sharp revenge
> Upon the Thracian tyrant in his tent,
> May favor Tamora, the Queen of Goths (1.1.135-142)

We shall see later how this memory of the cannibal queen Tomyris came to haunt the dramatist's mind.

Old Titus unconsciously assists Tamora and her sons to gain revenge on him. He refuses the crown of the Roman empire offered him by the tribunes of the people in gratitude for his services in war. He hands it over to Prince Saturninus, who had furiously threatened him a moment before if he ventured to accept the crown. The sole reason of Titus for this election is that Saturninus was the eldest son of the former emperor of Rome, and the prince was capable of pouring for the old man such soothing syrup as the phrase, "Titus, father of my life!" Titus hopes that the impatient youth will make a good autocrat and welcomes his promise to marry Lavinia, his daughter, altho he knows that she was engaged by rights of love to Prince Bassianus, the new emperor's brother. Bassianus carries the girl away with drawn sword, aided by Titus's sons, one of whom their father stabs for blocking his road of pursuit. Saturninus refuses to chase his brother for Lavinia's sake; his heart has already inclined to raise Tamora from prisoner to empress. Titus indignantly notes that he is not invited to their wedding. But his courtier's spirit is soon appeased by Tamora's hypocritical reconcilement of her husband and the house of Andronicus. Then he invites the emperor to go hunting with him at dawn.

Incidentally it is likely that Shakespeare took the name of his young emperor from Saturninus the Roman tribune, who murdered a rival in his election, strove for sharper laws against treason, caused the murder of another political antagonist, and was finally killed in a popular uprising. Bassianus is a more famous name in Roman history. He was a high priest of the sun in Syria, rumored to be the bastard of the murdered emperor Caracalla. He appealed to the Roman army to help him get vengeance for his father's death and was proclaimed emperor. He then named himself Heliogabalus. A lover of luxury, he spent the rest of his brief life in wantoning with his eunuchs; for love of one parasite he drest as a lady and officially married the man. Among his crimes was the ravishing of a vestal virgin. At last Bassianus was violently put to death, his corpse dragged thru the streets of Rome and thrown into the Tiber river. Shakespeare may have been particularly interested in this priest of the sun, since he too is alleged by some critics to have suffered from a predilection for pederasty, and he wrote his most glorious play with the theme of vengeance for a father's death.

The second act of *Titus Andronicus* introduces the queerest character in the drama, Aron the Moor. (So the name is spelt in the dialog directions of the old text.) We learn that this black scoundrel has been the lover of blond Queen Tamora, and now expects to use her siren quality to destroy the whole Roman commonwealth. He sees her two sons, Demetrius and Chiron, quarreling because they both wish to seduce Lavinia and cuckold her lord Bassianus. He persuades them to join in "policy and stratagem" to rape her instead.

> Come, come, our empress, with her sacred wit
> To villany and vengeance consecrate,
> Will we acquaint with all that we intend;
> And she shall file our engines with advice. (2.1.120-123)

(In the course of this dialog the curious Moor alludes to "The House of Fame," a poem by Shakespeare's favorite English bard, Geoffrey Chaucer.) The brothers go off gleefully. Aron meets Tamora, already weary of the dawn deer-chasing, and she summons him to her arms. But he prefers plotting and bloodshed. He lets her into the secret of Lavinia's coming doom, and adds that they will murder Bassianus. Then he leaves her just as the latter appears with his bride. Lavinia and Bassianus have witnessed the amorous parting of the Goth and the Moor; they ridicule Tamora for her strange passion while assuring her that Saturninus will be told of all they had seen. Demetrius and Chiron enter. Their mother states that Lavinia and her lover had enticed her to the place where they stand, "A barren detested vale," unpenetrated by the sun, and had shown her a certain pit swarming with snakes. Here, she cries, they had sworn to tie her to a yew tree and leave her waiting for death. Her boys believe her instantly. They stab Bassianus and throw him into the pit. "This is the hole where Aaron bid us hide him." Next they drag Lavinia away. Tamora warns them, "make her sure," and departs in search of her "lovely Moor."

But Aron is still diligently carrying out his plot. He brings Quintus and Martius, two sons of Titus, in quest of a panther which he says he had seen in "the loathsome pit." The suddenly sleepy Martius falls into it. Quintus, whose eyes are strangely dimmed, stares after his brother wondering,

> What subtle hole is this,
> Whose mouth is cover'd with rude-growing briers,
> Upon whose leaves are drops of new-shed blood
> As fresh as morning's dew distill'd on flowers?
> A very fatal place it seems to me. (2.3.198-202)

Aron hurries to fetch the emperor. Martius calls to his brother for help, declaring that he has fallen on "the dismall'st object" ever seen. Quintus's nerve fails him. He cannot lift Martius "From this unhallow'd and blood-stained hold." He protests: "ne'er till now / Was I a child, to fear I know not what." Martius informs him that he had dropped on the body of Lord Bassianus, lying like "a slaughter'd lamb, / In this detested, dark, blood-drinking pit." He recognized his lordship by a ring he wore, bright enough to illumine the hole. The sight reminds him of the legend (in Ovid's *Metamorphoses*) of the lovers Pyramus and Thisbe.

So pale did shine the moon on Pyramus
When he by night lay bath'd in maiden blood. (2.3.231-232)

This allusion to virgin's blood confirms the impression which must have been growing in every analytic reader of these lines, that the "subtle hole" of the scene represents an unconscious vision, which the poet had preserved from his childhood, of the female genital at menstruation time. Sexual symbolism becomes almost manifest in the following metaphor, when Quintus utters his terror of being "pluck'd into the swallowing womb / Of this deep pit, poor Bassianus's grave." (2.3.239-240) Of course we can only conjecture what vision burned in the dramatist's brain when he rang so many variations on this theme of the bloody abyss. There may have survived in his unconscious memory a sudden sight of his mother wearing a menstrual cloth, which provoked an infantile incest fantasy and anxiety about losing his maleness, perhaps dying, in that sanguine place. If he did not imagine the vagina as equipt with teeth, he still conceived it as an infernal mouth capable of eating man's flesh. To Shakespeare the "subtle hole" where Bassianus bled to death is no passive earth but a live and hungry thing; a "fell devouring receptacle," Martius calls it, "As hateful as Cocytus' misty mouth," one of the gateways to the Greek hell. (2.3.23) It exudes a magic atmosphere that weakens men and drives them mad. Martius has no strength to climb out of it, and when Quintus takes his brother's hand to help him up he drops down by his side.

Whatever unconscious memory of trauma stirred at the making of this symbol of the womb-pit, with its proximity to the offstage violation of Lavinia, there can be little question that the poet in writing the scene had at least on the threshold of his consciousness a remembrance of deflowering some girl. He must have recalled the shock of seeing maiden blood for the first time. Why this should be preying on his mind at the time he composed *Titus Andronicus* is a problem I shall try to answer later.

Saturninus comes on the scene with Aron at his heels. The emperor wonders at once, "what hole is here," and questions the first man he sees in "this gaping hollow." Martius informs him of the murder of Bassianus. The empress appears holding a letter that was left on the ground nearby. It requests an unknown "Sweet huntsman" to slay Bassianus for a reward which is concealed among the nettles by the elder tree overshadowing the mouth of the pit. Aron uncovers this reward, having hidden it there himself—a bag of gold.

(The analytic student will not miss the significance of this gold, ancient symbol of excrement, placed so closely to the symbols of pubic hair and the poet's parent—the elder.) Saturninus leaps to the conclusion that the two sons of Andronicus down in the hole were the authors of the loose letter and have somehow been caught redhanded by their victim. He orders them jailed until he can think up "Some never-heard-of torturing pain for them." He rejects their bewildered father's plea for bail. But Tamora promises Titus that she will plead for him.

III

The scene changes to the forest place where Tamora's sons had perpetrated their lust on Lavinia. She is shown "ravished; her hands cut off, and her tongue cut out." Her uncle Marcus finds her and discovers how "A craftier Tereus" had deprived her fingers, "That could have better sew'd then Philomel," of the power to name her mutilators. (2.4.43) He laments the loss of her hands, which he had often observed trembling, "like aspen leaves, upon a lute." He grieves over her wounded mouth, whose "heavenly harmony" might have made Cerberus, the watchdog of hell, fall peacefully asleep, as he had once done when Orpheus sang. Marcus takes her away to her father convinced that the spectacle will "make thy father blind."

The episodes of sadism that come rapidly after contain several relieving flashes of Shakespearean poetry and wit. Titus Andronicus casts himself on the street to beg the Roman tribunes for his condemned sons' lives, and when his son Lucius tells him that the judges have gone and he is entreating nothing but stones, the old man replies, "Why, 'tis no matter, man; if they did hear, / They would not mark me, or if they did mark, / They would not pity me, yet plead I must... Therefore I tell my sorrow to the stones;" (3.1.33-37) at least they do not repulse his tears. The revelation of his daughter's ruin is drowned in mere rhetoric: the poet shows his early developed mastery of speech, not his future unsurpassed comprehension of human nature in deepest distress. So we are not displeased to see the Moorish monster interrupt the flood of grief phraseology. Aron brings a promise from the emperor that the lives of Martius and Quintus can be ransomed by the sacrifice of a hand by one of the Andronici. "O gentle Aaron!" Titus exclaims, "Did ever raven sing so like a lark, / That gives sweet tidings of the sun's uprise?" (3.1.157-159) Brother Marcus and son Lucius will not let his hand be chopped off. They hurry to get an ax to sacrifice one of their own hands. As soon as they are gone Titus eagerly asks the Moor, "Lend me thy hand, and I will give thee mine." Aron is glad to oblige and goes away with his prize evincing the grin on his conscience: "O how this villany / Doth fat me with the very thoughts of it." He knows that Saturninus will respond to the Andronicus sacrifice with the heads of his doomed sons. The old man's hand is returned. In the midst of his desolation he stands as if in a dream inquiring, "When will this fearful slumber have an end?" (3.1.252)

It does not take the old warrior long to ascend from gloom bordering on madness to the resolution of revenge. Since Lucius has been doomed to exile for attempting to rescue his brothers with his sword, the silver-haired veteran of countless patriotic wars commands his son to go to the Goths and raise an army among them to overwhelm his fatherland. The readiness of Shakespeare's heroes to carry out this sort of treason (witness *Coriolanus* and *King Lear*) is a peculiarity that has not been sufficiently examined by the patriots among his international audiences.

The second scene of Act 3 was left out of the 1594 quarto edition of the play. It has been suspected that the actors who used that text could not bear to perform it because tragedy here strayed too close to the brink of the ludicrous. Uncle Marcus kills a fly and Titus grieves for it, abruptly breaking into a fury at the insect on hearing that "it was a black ill-favour'd fly,/Like to the empress' Moor." The pathos and the music of the patriarch's regret—

> But? how if that fly had a father and a mother?
> How would he hang his slender gilded wings
> And buzz lamenting doings in the air!
> Poor harmless fly,
> That, with his pretty buzzing melody,
> Came here to make us merry! (3.2.60-65)

the pathos and music of these cadences barely save the scene from laughter, particularly when the old statesman exults with a knife over the dead fly as if it was his black foe. Such extrusions of fantasy, elaborate and frigid—worse than the typical punning of the poet over the ruined Lavinia, calling her dear and deer—compel us to believe that his rage against the obscure person represented by Aron did not run very profound. Still we would be sorry to lose the conclusion of the third act. It ends with lyrical rhythms that could have come from no voice but our dramatist's, melancholy, delicate, loving the songs of his own sadness.

> Lavinia, go with me:
> I'll to thy closet: and go read with thee
> Sad stories chanced in the times of old.
> Come, boy, and go with me: thy sight is young,
> And thou shalt read when mine begins to dazzle. (3.2.81-85)

Literary allusions fly thick as autumn leaves thru the whole drama, allusions first of all to the beloved Ovid, then Vergil (especially to his tale of Aeneas to Queen Dido, which moved Hamlet so much in dramatic form) and Seneca and other classic models of our dramatist.

He opens the fourth act with an emotional tribute to Latin literature. Lavinia is seen pursuing her nephew, the child Lucius, who carries an armful of books. Titus tells him not to be scared of her.

> Ah! boy; Cornelia never with more care

Read to her sons [the Gracchi] than she hath read to thee
Sweet poetry and Tully's Orator. (4.1.12-14)

Young Lucius guesses that his noble aunt is crazy: "And I have read
that Hecuba of Troy/ Ran mad through sorrow." Titus beseeches
the desperate girl, "take choice of all my library, / And so beguile
thy sorrow." With her maimed arms she turns up the treasure of his
library.

> *Titus*: Lucius, what book is that she tosseth so?
> *Boy*: Grandsire, 'tis Ovid's Metamorphoses;
>   My mother gave it me.
> *Marcus*:   For love of her that's gone,
>   Perhaps she cull'd it from among the rest. (4.1.41-44)

Titus assists her in finding the page she wants, apparently well
known to his daughter. It is the very poem and the page that Imogen was reading in *Cymbeline* before she fell asleep and the sneak
Iachimo beheld her with the open book in bed.

> This is the tragic tale of Philomel,
> And treats of Tereus' treason and his rape.(4.1.47-48)

Reading the Latin magician's evocation of Philomela's downfall in
"ruthless, vast, and gloomy woods," he suddenly recollects the dell
where his daughter was tortured: "See, see: Ay, such a place there is,
where we did hunt. / O! had we never, never hunted there,— Pattern'd by that the poet here describes, / By nature made for murder
and for rapes." Old Marcus chimes in challenging the blue sky:

> O! why should nature build so foul a den,
> Unless the gods delight in tragedies? (4.1.54-60)

There ensues the device by which Lavinia learns to name her ravish-
ers by writing in sand with a staff held in her mouth.

Who can be unmoved by the personal message, the outcry, of
Titus and his brother in reading the description in Ovid of the fall
of Philomela? Do their words not clearly inform us that the dramatist himself had undergone some terrible metamorphosis in a for-

est,—something that drenched his imagination in blood a brief while before he wrote this play?

One result of that forest transformation appears to have been his determination to gain a great revenge, even tho in the effort he shook all Britain to its bedrock. In the first heat of this endeavor he wrote his first tragedy. As if in some black corner of his unconsciousness, our dramatist's prophetic soul could glimpse the drama that would follow, he gave the heroine of *Twelfth Night* a seal depicting the Roman lady Lucrece, apparently committing suicide after her rape, and later sang the simile, "But silence, like a Lucrece knife." (*Twelfth Night*, 2.5) He vowed that he would bring his enemies down from imperial pride to bloody dust, just as one of the Roman heroes he worshipt once swore in revolt against the tyranny of the Tarquins: "Lord Junius Brutus sware for Lucrece's rape," Titus remembers, kneeling with Lavinia and his grandson Lucius; and he promises "Mortal revenge upon these traitorous Goths," including the Moor Aron and the Roman Saturnine. Little Lucius declares that if he was a man,

> Their mother's bed-chamber should not be safe
> For these bad bondmen to the yoke of Rome. (4.1.108-109)

To herald his vengeance Andronicus sends the boy with a bundle of weapons as presents to Tamora's sons together with a scroll quoting Horace's famous ode about the soul upright and purified that need not fear the Moorish javelin. Chiron recognizes the Latin: "O! 'tis a verse in Horace; I know it well: I read it in the grammar long ago." (The lines were familiar to all schoolboys in Shakespeare's day.) But Chiron is blind to the verse's significance for Andronicus. Aron perceives it. Nevertheless he feels only scorn for Titus and his literary insinuations.

The Moor is quickly distracted by the entrance of Tamora's nurse bearing "a blackamoor child." The empress sent it to her Moorish lover, its father, insisting that he "christen it with (his) dagger's point." To guard the baby from the anger of its half-brothers, Demetrius and Chiron, Aron has to seize his offspring and threaten them. He kills the nurse, closing one mouth that might betray his adultery to the emperor, and arranges to murder the midwife too. Opportunely he recalls that a countryman of his named Muli has just been presented with a baby as light-skinned as its mother, and he schemes to transfer Muli's child to the arms of Tamora and her lord. "To calm this tempest whirling in the court.... Then let the ladies tattle what they please." (4.2.161-169)

Sardonic Aron leaves the stage to make way for the caprice of Titus. The old man has become nearly delirious and in this temper turns, Lear-like, playful. He has arrows shot toward the sky, the zodiac, to deliver protests to the gods who have delayed the justice that he believes is due him. Among the arrows he sends heavenward is one shot by the boy Lucius which his grandfather asserts will land in the "lap" of the zodiac sign called the Virgin. Into this mockery of old religion and astrology, bordering on Christian blasphemy, steps abruptly one of those curious products of Shakespeare's dialectical humor which he found irresistible in the midst of tragedy, this time a Christian clown. Andronicus hails him as a messenger from heaven. The clown expostulates, "From heaven! sir, I never came there. God forbid I should be so bold to press to heaven in my young days." If there was any Elizabethan brain beside Shakespeare's capable of conceiving this odd irreverent dialog, I am unacquainted with it. These lines alone should prove that his was the mind that engendered *Titus Andronicus*. It is strange that James Joyce's marvelous memory failed to retain the Clown's pretense of poor hearing which permits him to mistake the sound of "Jupiter" for "Jibbet-maker." (Jibbeter?) Else Joyce would not have missed the chance to associate that ghastly pun with his own gallows-laugh at the Deity in his chapter about Shakespeare in Ulysses. "The most Roman of catholics," he remarks, meaning the Papal apologist Joseph De Maistre, as well as the common folk of the Eternal City, call the Heavenly Father (Jupiter in Latin) "dio boia, hangman god."[6]

For carrying a letter from Titus to Saturninus charging the latter with unjust butchery, the poor Clown is condemned to be hanged.

He accepts his fate with usual humor, swearing by the Virgin Mary, "By'r Lady, then I have abrought up a neck to a fair end." (4.4.50)

Before the emperor can wreak his anger on Andronicus he learns that the Goths have risen against him headed by the son of his enemy. Immediately Saturnine is deprest: "'Tis he the common people love so much," he grieves (precisely like King Claudius envies Hamlet's popularity). The masses, we hear, "have wish'd that Lucius were their emperor." Queen Tamora consoles her forlorn despot, firmly believing that she can twist old Titus any way she pleases with her "golden promises."

IV

The last act brings in Lucius with his Gothic legions confident of victory. A soldier captures the Moor Aron and his baby—in a monastery: The villain, eager to save his child, declares that he will confess the "murders, rapes, and massacres," the treason plots he has had a lusty hand in if Lucius will spare his son. "I know thou art religious," he tells young Andronicus,

> And hast a thing within thee called conscience,
>
> With twenty Popish tricks and ceremonies,
>
> Which I have seen thee careful to observe. (5.1.74-77)

Thus Shakespeare lets us know that the hero Lucius is a Roman Catholic altho his father is a Roman of the older creed. Aron is indifferent. He has noticed, "An idiot holds his bauble for a god, / And keeps the oath which by that god he swears." He will cheerfully exploit the religion of Lucius for his own purposes. The Catholic general swears to protect the infant Moor, and its father proceeds to boast how he had incited the slaying of Bassianus, the ravishing of Lavinia, the mutilation of Titus, and other crimes, all of which he immensely enjoyed. Lucius orders him to be held gagged for a lingering frightful death. And that is the last we see of the monstrous Moor until he is brought on stage at the end of the drama to hear his doom—burial breast-deep in the earth, famishing to death—which he meets remorseless.

The next scene shows us the empress Tamora masquerading like an allegorical personage in Seneca's plays, the goddess Revenge (Nemesis). In that guise she visits Titus convinced that he has been driven insane by his woes. Her sons accompany her; she calls them her ministers. Titus calls them Rape and Murder. She sees no sign of reason in his sarcasm and prosecutes her own fantasy, persuading the old man to send for his son Lucius and prepare a banquet for him. There, Revenge assures him, the emperor, his wife and her sons will fall on their knees before him. Apparently delighted with the prospect he sends the invitation, and the vanity-drunk queen departs, but Titus insists on keeping Demetrius and Chiron as his guests. No sooner has their mother gone than he summons servants to bind them both, and goes to bring his daughter to witness their punishment. Exultantly he announces the festive offerings he will concoct from their bodies after he has cut their throats. Their mother shall eat morsels of their baked heads. So she did.

The cannibal feast scene may be spoiled for idolaters of the Bard by his fancy of costuming old Andronicus as a cook. Some may also be outraged by his spilling of Lavinia's blood because of the barbarous Roman principle, approved by Saturnine, that "the girl should not survive her shame, / And by her presence still renew (her father's) sorrows." (5.3.41-42) Thus Titus sacrifices with his own hand a second child. He employs his final strength to tell Tamora what she has done and eaten, and knifes her too. Her husband kills him and Lucius kills the emperor. In the tumult that ensues this regicide, Marcus the brother of Titus and their partisans ascend to another stage, the balcony, where the tribune and his nephew pacify the people and restore unity to Rome with the choice of Lucius as their autocrat.

V

To understand how our poet was brought to the depicting of these brutalities we must first retrace the theatrical history of *Titus Andronicus.*

We have already remarked that the drama was printed without an author's name in 1594, when it was acted twice in June by Shakespeare's own troup, the Lord Chamberlain's men. It was licensed for publication on February 6, along with a ballad on the same plot. The titlepage affirmed that it had been played by three companies, the servants of Lord Strange and the players of the Earls of Pembroke and Sussex. On January 23 the Sussex men performed it at the Rose theater claiming it was a new play. By "new" they evidently meant renovated, revised. That seems to have been their last performance in London; they did not succeed with "Titus and Andronicus," as the owner of the Rose called it. Yet we know that the story exerted a chronic attraction for the crowd. As late as 1600 English actors touring in Germany staged "A Lamentable Tragedy of Titus Andronicus and the Arrogant Empress," which was most likely an adaptation of Shakespeare's work in its older shape. Among the chief characters is the warrior Vespasian, whose place is taken in the later version of the drama by Lucius the elder. The name Vespasian is found in the title of the tragedy as it was recorded in documents prior to the play's appearance in English print. On April 11, 1592 *Titus and Vespasian* was acted at the Rose by Lord Strange's company. They collected a pile of shillings from its frequent performances, and yet the play was an old one in their repertory. Ben Jonson made fun of its popularity in his *Bartholomew Fair*, acted in 1614: "He that will swear Jeronimo or Andronicus are the best plays yet shall pass unexcepted at here as a man whose judgment shows it is constant, and hath stood still these five-and-twenty or thirty years." We therefore have to look back to 1589 or 1584 to find the earliest theatrical triumph of *Titus and Vespasian*.

Parenthetically perhaps we should mention that George Peele's poem 'The Honour of the Garter' issued in 1593 contains numerous phrases and concepts which also appear in our play. The English scholar who first pointed out these parallels was confident that William Shakespeare had copied them from Peele. Other experts argued that Peele wrote most of *Titus Andronicus*, revising an older work by an unknown hand.[7] All these learned men were hamstrung in their researches by the necessity of keeping faith in the chronology of Shakespearean drama created by the cult of Stratford-on-Avon, which could not conceive its adored one writing tragedy shortly after he had mastered the alphabet. If *Titus Andronicus* was an old play before their demigod came to London, then they reasoned it must have been written by somebody else. Reluctantly or cheerfully they set to work depicting the greatest of all dramatists learning his art by tinkering with other folk's vehicles, reshaping trash for cash. It appears to me more palatable to describe him as a worker making his own mistakes, learning from them as well as alien faults, and evolving his plays like palimpsests, ever returning to his old offspring to renew their youth in the light of another age.

George Peele was capable of writing a comedy like *A Knack to Know a Knave*, which was played at the Rose in June 1592, and included among its contemporary allusions a reference to the conquest of the Goths by Titus and the chance he was offered to wear the imperial diadem.

The years 1584-1589 were times of high patriotic fervor in England. The people lived always on the alert for outbreaks of war with Spain. To maintain their love of the island and hate of the Spanish empire at a militant pitch, the theaters were arrayed in the service of Queen Elizabeth's government. And *Titus and Vespasian* was viewed as the strongest contribution to her warlike endevors. Enlightened gentlemen of London and even the provinces had no difficulty detecting in the emperor Saturnine the insolent and bloody Philip II, the despot of Spain. King Philip was nicknamed Saturn among politicians in England and France.[8] No spectators of the drama would have missed the resemblance between Tamora, Queen of the Goths, and Mary, Queen of the Scots.

The poet caricatured Mary of course, stressing exclusively her diplomatic and amorous traits. The Scottish queen died under the ax of Elizabeth on February 8, 1586. It is extremely hard for me to imagine Shakespeare insulting her fallen and isolated majesty. (I have no hardship imagining him in the act of reviling Jeanne of Arc, for she was a fighting peasant. Mary was a forlorn queen.) So I seek the origin of *Titus Andronicus* or rather *Titus and Vespasian* in prior years.

VI

In August 1585 Elizabeth's secretary of state, Sir Francis Walsingham, learnt from an agent in France that King Philip had planned to send an army into England headed by English Catholic fugitives, and the man selected to lead the invading troops was Charles Arundel. This expedition never set sail, but Charles Arundel continued to dream of subduing Protestant Britain and placing Mary the Scot on the English throne.[9] Perhaps Arundel also dreamt of becoming her paramor. Of one thing we may feel certain and that is the theatrical identity of Arundel and Aron the Moor.[10] The English Catholic rebels against Elizabeth were often denounced as Moors. Thus in 1570 Sir Thomas Gargrave reported to William Cecil that the Spanish Duke of Alba was rumored to be providing ships "to assist our Moors in England," the Catholic insurgents of the north.[11] In a similar spirit Anthony Munday's tract *The Masque of the League and the Spaniard Discovered*, translated from Huguenot French, and authorised for printing on June 5, 1591, calls the Spaniards Goths.

But what impelled Shakespeare to portray Charles Arundel as the "Chief architect and plotter of these woes" in *Titus Andronicus?* The man was merely an energetic member, not a leader, of the Tudor court faction that advocated the return of England to the bosom of the Roman Church. As a politician he assumed no major part in treason or any business of state. We can only conclude that when the dramatist painted him as the chief contriver of his drama's tragic events, he was not thinking of Arundel as a public figure but a villain in privacy. Political crimes were less on the poet's mind than murder and rape—or deeds equivalent to these in his morality. When he created the character of Aron he had in mind a dell where Arundel had contrived something as horrible to him as the violation of Lavinia and the slaying of her husband Bassianus. The word dell, Eva Turner Clark observed, denotes a deep hole, a pit, a woodland hollow or vale, and all these words with the exception of dell are employed by Shakespeare for the scene of the two atrocities, and he added "den." Somewhere in the poet's experience there must have been such a fatal place.

What was Charles Arundel to William Shakespeare, or what did Arundel do to the dramatist that he should hate him so?

Arundel ran away from England early in November 1583, protesting that he fled for the liberty of worshiping as he wished. He also complained that he had to escape "for fear, having enemies," altho he enjoyed the political shelter of Sir Christopher Hatton, the Queen's sweet courtier. We are acquainted with only one man in the world who hated Arundel so intensely he could spill his blood with joy. This was the noble poet and playwright Edward de Vere, Earl of Oxford, in whom more than one inquirer in Tudor literature has discerned the genius and the guilt of William Shakespeare. None of Oxford's plays has ever been singled out from the anonymous shelves of Tudor theater. For plenty of reasons he kept his name off the title pages of plays. "It is ridiculous for a lord to print verses," said the learned lawyer John Selden, under a later and more tolerant reign. "He may write them to please himself, but to publish them is foolish." In the days of De Vere it was worse than foolish; it raised the question in minds of all classes whether the lord had not actually tainted his blood by toiling with common ink, especially for the theatrical profession, one that ranked in the eyes of aristocracy and the law with vagabonds and rogues. Nevertheless Lord Oxford could not resist the allurement to unpack his heart with words thru stage paint and pageantry. He felt exactly like Titus Andronicus in his mood of grief: "my bowels cannot hide (my) woes, / but like a drunkard must I vomit them."

> Then give me leave, for losers will have leave,
> To ease their stomachs with their bitter tongues. (3.1.232-233)

To a certain dangerous extent De Vere did relieve his woe and wrath by direct speech. But this relief was perforce less than he desired. When his brain inflamed with longing for revenge on Charles

Arundel and his colleagues of the Court, he naturally turned to histrionic weapons to spurt in fantasy the blood he was unable to spill in reality.

Until the summer of 1580 Oxford and Arundel appear to have been inseparable companions, going to playhouses and taverns together, drinking, sporting, laughing together at all hours everywhere, and attending the forbidden Roman rituals in secret at their Catholic kinsmen's homes.

When the Jesuit Father Edmund Campion entered London in June 1580, disguised as a jewel merchant, he stirred the heart of De Vere profoundly with his sermons pleading for fidelity to the mother-church. On June 29 at a hall near Smithfield rented by Lord Thomas Paget, the passionate Jesuit preached on the New Testament text that contains the pun on Saint Peter exalting the apostle to the office of founder of the Christian church. The Earl of Oxford was always quick prey to the enchantment of a daring pun. Campion's text and his eloquence exerted on him the spell of an epiphany. Joyously he joined the Popish young gentlemen, his cousins, Henry and Philip Howard (the Earl of Arundel), Francis Southwell, and the others who clustered around the outlaw evangelist. These enraptured gentlemen, wrote Campion, "embrace me, reapparel me, furnish me, weapon me, and convey me out of the city." A warrant was issued for the Jesuit's arrest; "great persons at Court" warned him of his peril and he went into rural hiding.

Meanwhile the Roman Catholic statesmen of the Court were undergoing a cleavage of belief about the right course to steer in continental history. On the surface they were all advocates of alliance with France; they favored the marriage of Elizabeth and the French king's brother, Francois Hercule, Duke of Anjou, often called by his earlier title of Alencon. In defending the policy of solidarity with the French they necessarily took a stand of antagonism to the imperial game of Spain. This position appealed less and less to the cleverest leaders of the Catholics. They saw no hope for the downfall of Protestantism and its bourgeois bulwarks except in the supremacy of the Spaniards over Christendom. So Lord Henry Howard attacked Anjou to the Earl of Oxford for lacking religion and constancy in his diplomacy and his war-making, since he slaughtered Huguenots in his native land and shielded their fellow Calvinists from the Spanish army in the Netherlands. Lord Howard despised the French prince as a man whom his best friends could not trust.

Look at the way he betrayed Bussy d'Amboise, his most devoted comrade in arms. Howard no longer expected the divided lords of France to redeem the English from their commercial reformation of Christianity. "For his part," he told De Vere, "he had long given over that course and taken another way, which was to Spain." The piety and the wealth of Madrid, asserted Charles Arundel, would make King Philip the monarch of the world—"and all should come to one faith."[12] Since a pro-Spanish policy meant treason in England, Howard and Arundel confided their change of opinion to none but the intimates of their family. Officially they remained supporters of the Queen's union with France.

Edward de Vere's bewilderment and depression at the sight of this two-faced statecraft of his cousins, the Howards and Arundels, inspired them merely to mirth. He began swearing to several friends that "the Howards were the most treacherous race under heaven." But Charles Arundel dated the beginning of the break in their friendship from July 11, 1580 when the royal court followed Elizabeth in her summer progress from Nonesuch Palace to Oatlands, where she desired to hunt deer. The cause of Oxford's malice against him, Arundel declared, "began with friendly warning of his drunkenness at the Queen's remove from Nonesuch to Oatlands."[13] The drunken poet left a permanent memorial of her hunting Oatlands game and his adventures in the woods in the vivid pages of *Titus Andronicus*.

Somewhere in those woods, I conjecture, the Earl of Oxford obtained access to the womb of Anne Vavasor, the stalwart lady of her Majesty's bedchamber, whose power and glory in wittily frustrating seducers the poet had celebrated in his *Two Gentlemen of Verona*, *Love's Labor's Lost*, and *All's Well That Ends Well*.[14] The event of her yielding to his love was certainly not as merry as he imagined it would be. He must have felt compelled to vanquish her by rude force so that the result seemed a rape. Nine months after—to be exact, March 21, 1581—"On Tuesday at night Anne Vavysor was brought to bed of a son in the maidens' chamber"—close to where the Virgin Queen slept. "The Earl of Oxford," wrote Sir Francis Walsingham to the Earl of Huntingdon, "is avowed to be the father, who hath withdrawn himself with intent, as it is thought, to pass the seas. The ports are laid for him." He passed instead to a dismal chamber in the Tower of London for two months. Arundel and Howard, and another former friend of Oxford, Francis Southwell, were at that time leniently treated prisoners in the custody of different courtiers. Walsingham conducted inquisitions about their dealings with agents of the Pope. He and his master William Cecil had to resort to forgery because they could not get their hands on a single letter like the one Tolomeo Galli, Cardinal Secretary of State for the Vatican, sent on December 12, 1580, to Philip Sega, Bishop of Piacenza, the Pope's Nuncio at Madrid, justifying the assassination of Elizabeth, "Since that guilty woman of England usurps two such noble kingdoms of Christendom and is the cause of so much injury to the Catholic faith, and the loss of so many millions of souls, there is no doubt that whoever sends her out of the world with the pious intention of doing God service, not only does not sin, but gains merit, especially having regard to the sentence pronounced against her by Pius V of holy memory. And so, if these English nobles decide actually to undertake so glorious a work, your Lordship can assure them that they do not commit any sin."[15]

VII

Between the summer of his Oatlands escapade and his summer captivity in the Tower the Earl fell from the splendor of Elizabeth's love for him, like Lucifer, never to rise again. In this precipitous descent of his star his intellect found itself for the first time at home in the realm of tragedy. The months of his imprisonment in the Tower would have served perfectly for the composition of a play like *Titus*

Andronicus (or *Titus and Vespasian*). Consciously he designed the drama to unmask the traitors who had concealed themselves in the "Trojan horse" of pretended devotion to their ancestral religion.

> Tell us what Sinon hath bewitch'd our ears,
> Or who hath brought the fatal engine in
> That gives our Troy, our Rome, the civil wound. (5.3.85-87)

Every literate Londoner could perceive in these verses at the close of the tragedy a reference to his metropolis, for like Rome it traced its origin to fugitives from the Sinon-sold city of Troy. In medieval poetry London is called "Troynovant." All who watched the play could discern in its Queen of the Goths a furious portrait of the Queen of Scots, whose endless conspiracies against the Queen of England are still believed to have led to the beheading of Oxford's beloved cousin, the Duke of Norfolk, and nearly entangled Oxford himself. Some observers of the play probably discerned in Tamora's feeding on her sons' heads a reminiscence of Tomyris, Queen of Scythia, who commanded the head of King Cyrus, her enemy, to be immersed in human blood. This command is found in only one English classic of the period, the *Histories of Trogus Pompeius, abridged by Justin*, translated by Arthur Golding, the uncle of Edward de Vere. The tale of Queen Tomyris is told in its opening chapter. Golding published it in 1564 with a dedication to his legend-loving nephew, who was then fourteen years old. A third edition appeared in 1578. Golding seems to have gone to work on the *Trogus* right after he finished, at the house of Sir William Cecil where he was then tutoring the boy De Vere, a translation of another Latin volume that contributed to the making of *Titus Andronicus*. In April, 1563, a week before his nephew Edward's birthday was celebrated, Golding completed *The History of Leonard Aretine, Concerning the Wars Between the Imperials and the Goths for the Possession of Italy*. However, Shakespeare evidently took from Leonardo Bruni's chronicle only the bare fact conveyed in Golding's title. The rest of the Roman history in *Titus* is the poet's own fabrication, political propaganda mingled with mythology.

His recollection of the Aretine's narrative was possibly stimulated by Robert Greene's novel *Mamillia* which came out in October 1580. Its background is one of fancied war between Italians and Goths. The idea of introducing a Moorish conspirator into ancient Rome was perhaps linked in our playwright's mind with his memory of the play *Scipio Africanus* which was acted by Oxford's favorite troup of children, the quire-boys of St Paul's Cathedral, in January 1580. The Earl would also recall in this connexion the *Mask of Moors* rehearsed for the royal entertainment in March 1579. On the third of that month De Vere himself performed a theatrical "device" for her Majesty, but nobody knows what it was. His conception of a Moorish lover for his Gothic queen might have been inspired by the fact that Don Juan of Austria, bastard of Emperor Charles V, came to make war on the Low Countries disguised as a Moorish slave. Don Juan's desire to marry the Queen of Scots and set her on the English throne was common knowledge on both sides of the Channel. Shakespeare made sport of it in *Love's Labor's Lost*.

The amorous adventures of Mary of Scotland formed a staple of gossip at the court of Elizabeth. In October 1565 the court whispered insinuations of incest against Mary, alleged to explain why she hated her bastard half-brother, Lord Murray. Murray in person entered the life of Oxford by spending the night of October 22 at the house of Cecil, the orphan Earl's guardian. De Vere was surely thrilled by his meeting with the sinister Scot, whose shadow may still be seen in *Macbeth*. Less than two years later London heard the horrible news of the murder of Mary's husband by her lover Bothwell, whom she promoted to the dukedom of Orkney. The duke swiftly divorced his first wife and married Queen Mary. The next year she indicated her approval of a plan to divorce Bothwell, knowing that Thomas Howard, Duke of Norfolk, wished to marry her. Norfolk was the son of Oxford's aunt Frances, and a very affectionate friend of the young Earl. Consequently he knew what he was saying when he informed a Papal spy that De Vere belonged with the nobles who wished for Norfolk's wedding with the Scottish queen. De Vere was then (1571) listed at the Vatican among the leading Englishmen "well affected toward Catholics." Queen Eliza-beth was anything but well affected toward Norfolk's marital ambi-tion, and he literally lost his head for allegedly plotting with the ex-iled Queen of Scots. Oxford strove desperately to save his kinsman from the royal ax. Cecil, his father-in-law, now Lord Burghley, who has been charged with contriving the Duke of Norfolk's downfall, acted as if he considered the execution of Norfolk necessary for the welfare of the state. He listened pitilessly (like the potentates of Rome to Titus Andronicus) to De Vere's arguments and plea. Hence the rumor spread among Papists in the Low Countries, re-ported to Burghley in March 1572, that young Oxford "has con-ceived some great displeasure against you for the same, whereupon he hath, as they say here, put away from him the Countess his wife."[16] This rumor swelled into the story that De Vere had sworn to avenge his cousin by reducing Burghley's daughter to beggary. He did mistreat her, but there were other, more tenebrous reasons for his decline in gallantry. He continued to try to convince his fa-ther-in-law that he remained faithful to him. When the Protestants were massacred in Paris in August 1572 he wrote to Cecil how anx-ious the news had made him. He expressed a fear that Cecil's own life was in danger of Catholic cruelty. "I am bolder with your Lord-ship than my custom is..." he said, "to admonish you, as one with whom I would spend my blood and life, so much you have made me yours."[17]

Not long after this letter the wayward Earl evinced a readiness to spend his blood and life in the camp of his father-in-law's deadliest foes. He sailed away from England to become a student of the art of war with the Spanish army in the Netherlands. The Queen com-manded him to return home without delay. He returned, made a handsome apology and she restored him to her sunshine. In August 1574 he rode beside her hunting stag, and neglecting his pregnant wife.

On the Sunday after Christmas that year Philip Howard, Earl of Arundel, Norfolk's son, amused himself with an effort to ravish Mercy Harvey, the sister of Gabriel Harvey the scholar. In his game with the girl Lord Arundel toyed with the pseudonym of "Don Jamy," in which a far-fetching fancy may descry a basis for Shake-speare's use of the name Demetrius for one of the brothers who ravished the daughter of Andronicus. The Greek name's first two syllables would easily be pronounced like Jamy by an Elizabethan tongue. The Earl of Arundel has attained posthumously the title of Venerable for his loyalty to the Roman Church and is on the way to sainthood. He was equally devoted to the politics of Mary of Scotland and the saturnine emperor of Spain. If the rapist Demetrius stands for him in the tragedy of Andronicus, then brother Chiron may well stand for Lord Henry Howard, his uncle, a frosty-blooded treacherous politician, worthy of representing Murder incarnate. (Shakespeare afterward endowed his Iago with the temperament and intellect of this lord.) A "dangerous intelligencing man, and no doubt a subtle Papist inwardly," Francis Bacon's mother described him. "I have long known him and observed him, for he, pretending courtesy, worketh mischief perilously." Her description fits Chiron, whose name I surmise to be a rough anagram for Henry (Honric); its meaning seems to be "handy," quite apt for one who so adroitly eluded the penalty of treason and lived to become Earl of North-ampton under King James I.

Those scions of the house of Howard labored most subtly and got the greatest pleasure from sundering the Earl of Oxford and his wife. They aimed at breaking her father's spirit, to bring old Cecil in sorrow to his grave. He admonished his son-in-law that Countess Anne's "grief is the greater and always shall be... because she cannot or may not, without offense, be suffered to come to your presence, as she desireth, to offer the sacrifice of her heart."[18] We witness in the killing of Lavinia one of the dramatic forms in which Will Shakespeare carried out the sacrifice of his wife's heart. For Lavinia is fundamentally an image of Anne De Vere, just as Titus Androni-cus superbly represents her father, with the same temper, humor, slyness, and eagerness for ruling his family and serving the state. The disgrace of Lavinia is a fierce distortion of the shame of Count-ess Anne, whom Oxford accused of playing false and bearing a child that was not of his seed. Our poet named her Lavinia, I suppose, not only because he pictured her like the Latin beauty who became the bride of Trojan Aeneas after he defeated her lover Turnus in battle, but also because he was thinking of his country estate of Lavenham when he created her stage surrogate. On November 4, 1580 the Earl sent a warrant from Vere House in London for the payment to Lady Oxford of 200 pounds a year out of his rents from Lavenham Park. What motivated this outburst of generosity, we do not know. On December 7, 1581 his wife was still pleading to learn "what you would have me do in my power to recover your constant favor, so as your Lordship may not be led still to detain me in calamity without some probable cause, whereof, I appeal to God, I am utterly innocent."[19] We learn from the same letter that Anne had reason to hope that poor Edward would have compassion for her. In the last summer (when *Titus and Vespasian* was first composed) he began to behave with kindness to her again: "you made me assured of your good meaning, though you seemed fearful how to show it by open address." But then a long silence fell and early in the winter of 1581 she heard "that your Lordship is entered into misliking of me without any cause in deed or thought." He was in fact madly in love with Anne Vavasor, Charles Arundel's amazing Catholic cousin.

I have mentioned Sir Christopher Hatton as one of the chief politicians who befriended Charles Arundel. Hatton detested the Earl of Oxford from the bottom of his exquisitely servile soul and did everything in his power to turn the Queen against him, but never openly. The character of Sir Christopher was lucidly exposed in his handling of the prosecution of John Stubbe, the Puritan pamphleteer who wrote against the Queen's project of matrimony with a French Catholic. In October 1579 Stubbe was arrested for scribbling what her Majesty damned as sedition; Hatton took charge of the inquisition concerning Stubbe and his little book. The chill severity of his examination of the prisoner foreshadowed Stubbe's punishment. An old statute of the reign of Mary Tudor and her husband Philip of Spain was resurrected to condemn the Puritan patriot and William Page his bookseller to lose their right hands under the royal ax. Stubbe begged for clemency but Hatton and Elizabeth stayed deaf to his appeals. The sentence was carried out on 3 November 1579. Who can ever forget how the brave Stubbe, after the chopping off of his hand, took off his hat with the left and cried, "God save the Queen" before he fainted? I feel sure that Shakespeare witnessed this tragedy of her Majesty's attack on the freedom of the press. He conveyed his disgust and horror in the scenes of *Titus Andronicus* where Lavinia and her father are bereft of their hands. There is no need to point out what complex was agitated in him by the mutilation of John Stubbe. In the play he made the figure representing his father-in-law the victim of a doom which he unconsciously expected Cecil to inflict on him for writing against the powerful old man. The brave Stubbe found a lifelong friend in Peregrine Bertie, Oxford's brother-in-law, and became an honored member of Mary Bertie's household.

VIII

At this epoch Edward de Vere stood, in the words of Fulke Greville, an opponent of his, "superlative in the Prince's (that is Elizabeth's) favor." In the summer of 1580 the Earl touched the zenith of his incandescent rise in her esteem. I nearly forget to draw your attention to the fact that *Titus Andronicus* takes place in the torrid season: No doubt, the artist produced it at white heat with more anger than art. He wished to lay bare before English eyes the depth of Charles Arundel's deceit as he had fathomed it in the months following the July revelations at Oatlands. "I remember well," Arundel affirmed in January 1581, "that, being at the Earl of Oxford's lodging at Westminster, we fell in talk of travel and travelers that would travel." (The style of this statesman illustrates the epigram of Talleyrand, that language was invented to hide thought.) At one time this would have signified the revival of Oxford's chronic desire to escape from England, to discover what new landscapes, especially those of the Mediterranean, could do toward the healing of his soul

malady. This time the Earl was urging Arundel to fly to France or
Spain to escape prosecution for his allegiance to Papal imperialism.
Otherwise he, De Vere, would be dutybound to unmask him before
the Queen. "I told him," Arundel testified, "that if he persisted in
his wicked purpose, I would lay open all his treachery. And now
most specially hath he turned... on me." Among the servants of De
Vere were some ungodly guys whom Arundel termed his "cutters."
He accused Oxford of employing these fellows in plots of
"butcherly bloodiness," but the examples he presented for Elizabeth's eyes are threats, not deeds, and more fantasies than threats,
worthy of the author of the carnage in *Titus Andronicus*. "By devising
tales and lies," said Arundel, "he would set one man to kill another,
and hath sought my life by sundry devices."[20] Evidently nobody in
the government took these charges seriously; the strong men
around the Queen were perfectly aware that Oxford's tongue was
sharper than his teeth. They were probably provoked to hilarity by
Arundel's assertion, "the world never brought forth such a villain-
ous monster." The Earl however seems to have been tragically
moved by his enemy's statement that he had "damned himself to
the pit of hell."[21]

In his first tragedy the poet indeed doomed himself to be killed
in a pit. For none but he could stand as model of Prince Bassianus,
if Lavinia represents Anne Cecil de Vere. We know that her father,
like old Andronicus, would have preferred her to marry another—
Philip Sidney (if a worthwhile fortune had been offered with him)
or Gilbert Talbot, son of the Earl of Shrewsbury, or Edward Manners, Earl of Rutland. We know that the lords Philip and Henry
Howard, like Demetrius and Chiron in the play, would have happily
witnessed the violent off taking of Oxford, whose wife they had
slandered with whispers. They were certainly active in the promotion of enmity between De Vere and Sir Thomas Knyvet, a kinsman
of Charles Arundel and uncle of Anne Vavasor, enmity that reached
its climax in their bloody duel of March 1582. In the murder of Bassianus the dramatist seems to be telling us that his wife was treach-
erously deprived of his love by the traitors of the house of Howard

(servitors of Mary Stuart). He resurrects the martyred prince in the person of the militant Lucius (formerly named Vespasianus) who acquires the crown that Bassianus only coveted, and heals the wounds of their country.

In attempting to decipher the name Bassianus I am struck by its likeness to Bassanio, the romantic hero of *The Merchant of Venice*, a lover in whom the poet clearly mirrored himself. In both names I detect one of those puns to which his genius was so prone. ("A quibble," Samuel Johnson remarked, "was to him the fatal Cleopatra, for which he lost the world, and was content to lose it.") The pun in question is a poor twist of vowels, but it is easy to see how Shakespeare might have found it tempting. My guess is that he meant Bassanio and Bassianus to signify Bess's scion. *The Merchant of Venice* and *Titus Andronicus* were both written in a spirit of almost conscious appeal to her Majesty, Queen Bess, to nourish and protect him like a mother. Had he not been her darling ward from the age of twelve to twenty-one? In the case of the Venetian romance he craved her help against "Jewish" money lenders. In the case of the Roman tragedy he craved her help against other Semitic enemies, "Moorish," i. e. pro-Spanish conspirators. It is even possible that he chose the name Vespasian for his hero, and Titus for the hero's father, because the Roman generals and emperors, Vespasian and his son, Titus, were most famous for their victories in wars against the Jews as well as the ancient Britons. Emperor Titus had also distinguished himself by fervent love for the Jewish princess Berenice.

The tragedy was originally entitled *Titus and Vespasian*, after the Romans who became Caesars by subduing the pride of the Jews to the yoke of Rome. It may be that in the original version Aron was not a Moor but a Jew. The list of crimes he brags about at the end of the play parallels closely the catalog of crimes ascribed to Barabas the protagonist in Christopher Marlowe's aborted tragedy, *The Jew of Malta* (which was written, I guess, in 1588). Presumably the reason that Shakespeare did not make his Aron of the younger seed of Abraham is that his contemporaries simply could not conceive of

any Jew on the stage except as a grotesque, contemptibly comic figure. Marlowe's endevor to raise his Barabas to a graver pose col-
lapsed in absurdity. Marlowe's master wisely restricted the tragic
gestures of his Shylock to sophistic argument on his rights to financial interest and revenge. Shakespeare retained the brand of Abraham, nevertheless, in the villain of *Titus and Vespasian*; he who rejoices in the cutting off of hands lacks a foreskin. Oddly enough,
the scoundrel is the sole major character in the play who does not
pay for his bloody deeds before the public eyes. In the poet's impotence to determine a death worthy of the monster he fails to provide us the catharsis of terror that Aron's cruelty seems to demand.
One cannot help observing in this dramatic failure the survival in
the playwright of his peculiar tenderness toward Charles Arundel, a
vestige of perverse love.

IX

On Christmas day in 1580, "the Earl of Oxford," Arundel afterward
reported to the Privy Council, "desired a secret conference with me.
We met by means of my cousin Vavasour, with whom he had secret
talk, and then after assurance of secrecy, he unfolded his treachery
to me, offering me 1000 pounds to practise against Lord Harry and
Francis Southwell, and affirm that they were reconciled (to Rome)
by Stevens, a priest. I dissuaded him, saying I never heard of such a
thing. He said Stevens was taken and racked, and had confessed,
and advised me to leave the realm. I said I was free from offense,
but he said Southwell had betrayed all; he offered me to remain at a
house of his in Norfolk or Suffolk, till I could get over the sea,
when I should have 1000 pounds, or bills for so much, from the
Ambassador of Spain, on his account, and further said he would
send me money over, and sell land of 100 pounds a year rather than
I should want. I refused his counsel.

"He then told me that he had confessed to the Queen that he
was reconciled (to the Roman Church), and had got his pardon, and
would save me, if I would be ruled by him. He said no man could
do him harm but myself. I judged that he wished my flight, that he

might be freed of his monstrous dealing, and others brought into suspicion. I asked time to think of it....

"As to Stevens, I set down in writing what I have before told you, that a few years since, the Earl being grieved in conscious desired conference with some learned man, and I brought one to him."[22]

On this same Christmas day the Ambassador of Spain, Bernardino de Mendoza, informed his king: "Milord Harry Howard... heard that the Earl of Oxford had accused him and one Francis (Southwell and Charles) Arundel of being reconciled to the Holy Roman Church. For this the Queen had given secret order the other day for his arrest, and they were advised of this by a Councilor, a friend of milord Harry. What with their close correspondence with the Ambassador of France, and their fears of being committed to the Tower, and so losing their lives, they did not dare at this emergency to trust him, nor to go to their home. But coming to my house at twelve in the night, tho I had never spoken to them, they told me the danger in which they found themselves of losing their lives, unless I would hide them. As they were Catholics I so entertained them that no one in my house knew it except one of my men, until their friend the Councilor gave them notice that they would only be confined in the house of a gentleman; and in view of this they immediately showed themselves in public.

"Milord Harry, in gratitude for the good will with which I received him, and with a care that I can hardly describe, has informed me and informs me of everything he hears which is of service to your Majesty, and recognizes my favor, no little novelty for an Englishman to do. He has very good qualities and intelligence, and such friendship with the ladies of the Privy Chamber, who inform him exactly what happens indoors... To touch on the greatness of the affection with which he occupies himself in the service of your Majesty is impossible."[23]

The Catholic financiers of the house of Fugger learnt from Antwerp on January 1, 1581, "The last letters from England report that the Queen has thrown the brother of the Duke of Norfolk and two of the nobility into prison for conspiring against her."[24] A more accurate account was despatched on January 11 from London to the King of France by Michel de Castelnau, Seigneur de Mauvissiire, the French Ambassador:

> "I must not omit to tell your Majesty that some days before the Noel festival the Count of Oxford declared that, about four and a half years ago, on his return from Italy, he had professed fidelity to the Catholic religion with several gentlemen, his relatives and best friends, and sworn, as he says, and signed with them a pledge that they would do everything they could for the advancement of the Catholic religion. Now he has accused them to your good sister the Queen of England, and for his part he asked pardon, saying that he sees clearly he had done wrong, and wants to blame them, who have loved him most, and defended and companioned him in his recent quarrels. He said that they had conspired against the state by making a profession of the Catholic religion, and he seeks to do them all the harm he can think of. This has deeply distressed the Queen, your good sister, for she was marvelously fond and showed a great deal of favor to most of those whom the Count of Oxford has accused, like milord Henry Howard, brother of the late Duke of Norfolk, and Charles Arondel, who is greatly devoted to your Majesties, and to my lord your brother (Alencon, the prince desirous of marrying the Queen of England), both being good advocates of the marriage; on account of their activity for the cause, which pleased the lady, they received many expressions of her goodwill. It was therefore with great regret, as she herself told me, that she was constrained to put them under guard in the hands of some Councilors, namely, the Chancelor (Sir Thomas Bromley) in charge of milord Henry, Sir Hatton in charge of Charles Arondel, and Sir Walsingham in charge of Southwell.

> "Having been questioned about the Count of Oxford's accusation that they had plotted against the state, they cleared themselves very well; as far as the Catholic religion is concerned, they are known to have always held it in strong affection, with no

other near it in their hearts, precisely like the greater part of the nobility in this kingdom. The Queen knew this, and my Lord Howard, Arondel and Southwell, altho ardent Catholics, are nevertheless esteemed and favored by the Queen, your good sister, seeing that they and their friends have always been for the marriage and the alliance with France. The Count of Oxford found himself all alone as accuser and witness, losing his credit and honor, being abandoned by all his friends and all the ladies of the court for his wish to hurt some of the men most favorable to my lord your brother. So the Count stands covered with shame, and remorse, having lost all countenance, with nobody to support his cause.

"However the Queen has been trying up to this hour to extract all she can about the business, for she told me a few days ago that she perceived they were lunatics, they did engage in secret practices, inspired from afar; and she much regretted seeing them involved who were so well affected toward France and so favorable to the marriage. She added that tho some evil may be discovered in them, she would shut her eyes to it as far as possible in view of their attitude to the marriage. She is sorry that such incidents should occur here at this time.

"The Count of Oxford has begged the Queen, and went down on his knees several times to implore her, seeing that he could offer no testimony but his own, to ask me to tell her and to learn from me if I did not know of a Jesuit who had celebrated the mass about four years ago and then had led them back to the Roman Church. Also if I had not aided in saving the Jesuit in France at the request of the said Count of Oxford. On hearing this the Queen earnestly begged me to tell her the facts, not to do them any harm but to help her know the truth. She said that I was well aware of her regard for the Catholics who did not set their consciences at odds with the state, and she made a great urgency and prayer to obtain some knowledge from me.

"I denied knowing anything about the business; I had never even heard any talk of it, nothing at all. Seeing which, the Count of

Oxford again threw himself on his knees before her in my presence pleading with her to pray me for the truth. And he begged
me at the same time that I should do him the kindness of remembering something that concerned him a good deal, and that
was how he had sent a message to me requesting and begging me
to help rescue that Jesuit to France and Italy, and when he was
gone in safety, he (Oxford) had thanked me for it. I spoke out
decisively to the Queen, that I knew nothing about this, that I
had no information nor memory of such a thing. Thus in the
presence of his mistress the Count found himself quite confused."

The reader of this timorous letter will easily recall how Titus Andronicus knelt to the Roman tribunes and afterward to the stones of
the street to plead for some gesture of pity.

The Earl persisted in begging the French ambassador to tell what
he did remember. "I bade him speak no more. Evidently he is trying
to sicken those who were earnest on the side of the marriage. Perhaps he is jealous of the others, or belongs to the Spanish faction."[25]

De Vere tried in vain to convince Castelnau that he was a true
friend of France. It may have been in honor of the ambassador that
he selected the names he gave the two heroes of his tragedy, the
names by which the play was first known. Castelnau had two brothers named Titus and Vespasian. If he saw the play he should have
recognized its plea for salvation from the masquerading enemies of
Tudor England and Valois France. But how could the rather obtuse
Frenchman tell that the subtle Howard and adroit Arundel were
disgusted with the French courtship of their Queen and had resolved on a new political path—subservience to Spain?

To this very day, despite the revelation of Lord Howard's name
and Charles Arundel's on the payroll of the Spanish secret service,
the life and personality of the man who strove to unmask them are
recorded in official biography from their point of vantage and calumny.

X

Oxford's failure to convict his cunning kinsmen of disloyalty to England appears to have been eclipsed in the mind of her Majesty by the revelation of his triumph over the virginity of Anne Vavasor. On Thursday, March 23, 1581, Walsingham informed Henry Hastings, Earl of Huntingdon, "On Tuesday at night Anne Vavaser was brought to bed of a son in the maiden's chamber. The earl of Oxeforde is avowed to be the father, who hath withdrawn himself with intent, as it is thought, to pass the seas. The ports are laid for him and therefor, if he have any such determination, it is not likely that he will escape.

"The gentlewoman, the selfsame night she was delivered, was conveyed out of the house and the next day committed to the Tower. Others that have been found any ways party to the cause have also been committed. Her Majesty is greatly grieved with the accident, and therefore I hope there will be some such order taken as the like inconvenience will be avoided." Agents of the German bankers of the firm of Fugger supplied them with more news, distorted, on April 29: "the brother of the last Duke of Norfolk and the two knights are still in prison. This is taken very ill in the country. There is a suspicion too that they have been plotting against the crown and realm of England. But, as hitherto nothing has been brought against them, they remain in prison, simply because they are in bad odor. The Earl of Oxford, also arrested but seen at liberty, is again in the Tower for forgetting himself with one of the Queen's Maids of Honor, who is in the Tower likewise. This in spite of his having a pretty wife, daughter of the Treasurer. But he will not live with her."[26]

Elizabeth's fury over the procreation of the child named by his mother Edward Vere—who grew to be one of England's finest and least famous soldiers and scholars—diminished under the cares of her government. She gave Secretary Walsingham a message for the Earl after his captivity, "First, that she would have heard the matter again touching Henry Howard, Southwell, and Arundel. Secondly, that she understood, he meant to cut down all his woods, especially about his house. Which she did not so well like of. Also, that he should sell so many lands elsewhere, as he had done a great many before. And lastly, that she had heard that he had been hardly used by some of his servants during the time of his commitment. Wherein she promised her aid so far as she could with justice to redress the loss he had sustained thereby."[27]

In the agony of his frustration Edward de Vere applied himself as usual to theatrical poetry for relief. He craved vengeance and granted it to his cause in stage disguise. Characteristically his craving assumed at once an oral form, a wish to consume his enemies in the flesh. Among the counter-charges of Charles Arundel there is a note recalling that De Vere had once spoken "of his tasting blood in his infancy, which almost prefigured a damnation."[28] The only way the poet could master his thirst for the blood of his adversaries was to revel in fantastic details of their blood being ignorantly drunk by their spiritual mother on the stage. Unconsciously perhaps this represented the reversal of a wish from his own childhood passion for his mother Margery, the wish to eat of her breast and drink of her blood. He paid in advance emotionally for the vicarious fulfilment of this wish by having his dramatic image bitten with the fang of a dagger and perish in a hole symbolic of the bleeding matrix. Naturally for the lyric impulse to write out his fantasies he turned to the book he held dearest of all his library, her brother's translation of Ovid.

'Tis Ovid's Metamorphoses;
My mother gave it me.

The remembrance of his kind uncle comforted him as he wrote. In Act 4, Scene 3, he suddenly mentioned an uncle of Titus Andronicus, named Publius, as mourning over the old warrior's loss of sanity, just as Arthur Golding must have grieved over his nephew's distracted wits.

For the plot of his tragedy young Shakespeare appears to have recollected an old story in song printed about 1570, "A Lamentable

Ballad of the Tragical End of a Gallant Lord and of his Beautiful
Lady." Then he drest the plot in a fabric of his own spinning from
memories of Roman, actually Byzantine, history. The product still
bears the odors of dusty books. It was composed, in my opinion, in
June 1581, when the Queen confined the dramatist in a chamber of
the Tower of London, where he was certainly permitted the companionship of his beloved classics. Here he made believe that he
was back in the solitude of his home,

> his study, where they say he keeps,
> To ruminate strange plots of dire revenge. (5.2.5-6)

He gives old Andronicus a study like this, and pictures him resent-
ing the intrusion of anyone. Summoned to his window the hero
wonders who would dare to "molest my contemplation?" It is not
simply contemplation that absorbs his energy in the room; he also
writes there, schemes and decrees, "And what is written shall be
executed." The name of the first company that 'executed' *Titus and
Vespasian* has been lost. My surmise is that the Earl of Derby's men
were the first to stage the tragedy, having already won much glory
and profit from the performance of *Jeronimo: The Spanish Tragedy*,
another bloody play concerning a father's revenge. The son of
Derby, Lord Strange, was the patron of the troup whose name appears first of the actors known to have staged *Titus Andronicus*. Incidentally I offer a surmise on the time when Shakespeare changed
his drama's name and the names of its chief persons. In 1584 Edward Hellowes published a translation of the *Familiar Epistles of Antonio Guevara*, a courtly work well known to the dramatist. In it he
would have noticed the tale of one Andronicus who did a kindness
for a lion and was rewarded by the lion's paying him homage in a
show presented before the Emperor Titus. A few months before
the publication of this story Charles Arundel fled from London to
Paris to escape Walsingham's rack and the royal ax. Lord Henry
Howard was arrested again, charged by a spy at the French embassy
with being a chief agent of the Queen of Scots. The vindication of
Oxford's claims against these men did little to raise him in the eyes

of Elizabeth, altho she was gracious enough to improve his economic position by a grant of money each year paid from her secret-service fund. At any rate the year 1584 probably saw the revision of *Titus and Vespasian* into the play we now hold in our hands. You will remember that Ben Jonson indicated this year as marking the beginning of the fame of *Titus Andronicus*.

What the original drama was like may still be guessed from the Dutch and German adaptations made of it by writers working under the spell of English tragedians who toured Europe in Shakespeare's lifetime. In 1641 a glass-maker of Amsterdam, Jan Vos, published a play called *Aran en Titus: of Wraak en Weerwraack* (Aran and Titus: Vengeance and Countervengeance) and which is said by critics among Vos's countrymen to display "een barbaarschen genius."[29] The playwright named Shakespeare's Lavinia "Rozelyna," a name dear to Shakespeare himself but always employed for characters resembling his mistress Anne Vavasor. The Dutchman's drama features four choruses. However scholars find at least twelve details in his work which could not have come from any source but Shakespeare's tragedy or English versions prior to the first quarto printing of *Titus Andronicus*. In 1650, a German author, Georg Greflinger, planned to translate a Dutch tragedy of "Andronicus mit dem Aaron." The German version contains elements of Shakespeare's story that are not in the Dutch, notably Lavinia's engagement to the emperor and its breaking; the episode of the black baby and the capture of the Moor; the business of the arrow-shooting; the Moorish villain's confession at the end. One orthodox researcher has ventured to date the origin of our drama as far back as 1586, but naturally he dares not ascribe the composition to the Will Shaksper of Stratford who in that year was hardly more than a rustic ruffian.[28] The scholars would rather put on our poet the brand of the plagiarist, the patcher of other men's works of art.

To me it appears more necessary for mental economy to put the credit and the blame for *Titus Andronicus* on the sole dramatist of the sixteenth century who could have identified himself with the clan of Andronicus and proudly placed his family tomb on the stage:

This monument five hundred years hath stood....
Here none but soldiers and Rome's servitors
Repose in fame. (1.1.353-356)

The family tomb of the Veres was erected at Colne Priory by their ancestor Alberic about 1080, five hundred years before the production of *Titus Andronicus.* Yet while identifying himself with the noblest of Romans, our dramatist was also capable of one moment of sympathy with an outcast and criminal like Aron the Moor. When Aron is presented with his "first-born son and heir," the child is condemned by aristocratic rascals as a bastard, but he protects it lovingly.

My mistress is my mistress; this myself:
The vigor and the picture of my youth. (4.2.107-108)

He vows to bring the baby to a foreign nation (the Goths) who, he dreams, will "bring you up/ To be a warrior, and command a camp." I can conceive no other Elizabethan mind in which these lines and the episode of the unwanted infant could have been born but the mind of Edward de Vere, Earl of Oxford, who on 21 March 1581 became, by his dark lady Anne Vavasor, the father of a bastard whom their Queen abhorred, but who grew up to be a warrior among the English volunteers in the Low Countries, and the commander of a Dutch camp in the war against Spain.

References

1   *The Shakespeare Allusion-Book*, ed. Munro (London, 1932) ii , 319.
2   J. Q. Adams, *A Life of William Shakespeare* (Boston, 1925) 135.
3   W. H. Desmonde, "The Ritual Origin of Shakespeare's Titus Andronicus," *International Journal of Psycho-Analysis*, xxxvi (Jan. 1955) 61.
4   S. Johnson, Preface, *The Plays of William Shakespeare* (London, 1793) ii, 92.
5   T. Dekker, *The Wonderful Year* (London, 1803) in Grosart's edition of Dekker's prose, vol. 1, p. 103.
6   James Joyce, *Ulysses* (New York, 1934) 210.
7   Charles Crawford, in *Jahrbuch der Deutschen Shakespeare-Gesellschaft*, (1900); J. M. Robertson, *Did Shakespeare Write Titus Andronicus?* (London, 1905).
8   Martin Hume, *The Courtships of Queen Elizabeth* (London, 1898) 232.

9 Calendar of State Papers Domestic: Elizabeth (3 Aug. 1585) Addenda, xxix, 39.

10 The likeness between Aron and Arundel was first pointed out by Eva Turner Clark in *Hidden Allusions in Shakespeare's Plays* (New York, 1931) 46.

11 Calendar of State Papers Domestic: Elizabeth (4 Jan. 1570) Addenda, xvii, 5.

12 J.A. Froude, *History of England* (London, 1865) xi, 345. State Papers Domestic: Elizabeth (Ms.) 1581: cli, 42.

13 State Papers Domestic (Ms.) 1581: cli, 46.

14 E.T. Clark, *Hidden Allusions in Shakespeare's Plays*, 162-179; E. T. Clark, *The Satirical Comedy Love's Labour's Lost* (New York, 1933) 74-82. P. K. Angell, "Light on the Dark Lady," *Publications of the Modern Language Association*, iii (1937) 652ff. See also Frank Harris, *The Man Shakespeare* (any edition) for references to "Rosaline", the "Dark Lady" of the Sonnets.

15 J. W. Bennett, "Oxford and Endimion," *Publications of the Modern Language Association*, lvii (1942)), 354ff. See Philip Hughes, *Rome and the Counter-Reformation in England* (London 1944)

16 State Papers Domestic: Elizabeth (1572) Addenda 21: 23.

17 Harleian Manuscripts (British Museum) 6991: 5.

18 The Howard-Harvey affair is described by Moore Smith in *Notes & Queries*, series 11 (1911) iii, 261. Cf. J. H. Pollen's *Philip Howard, Earl of Arundel*, vol. xxi of the Catholic Record Society. Cecil's letter is in the Lansdowne Manuscripts (British Museum) 238: 129.

19 Lansdowne Mss. 104: 63.

20 State Papers Domestic: Elizabeth (1581) cli, 46. Cp. Calendar of State Papers Foreign (1583) no. 602.

21 State Papers Domestic: cli, 43.

22 State Papers Domestic: Addenda, xxvii , 46.

23 Documentos Ineditos para la Historia de Espagna, ed. Fuensanta del Valla et al. (1888) xcii, 220, quoted by Pollen, op. cit. 30-31.

24 *Fugger News-Letters, op. cit.* 47.

25 British Public Record Office: Transcripts from Paris (xxvi ii, ff. 304-306, Depesche 304) quoted by Pollen, *op. cit.* 29-30. CP. Les Memoires de Messire Michel de Castelnau, Sei neur de Mauvissiére (Paris, 1659) i, 199-201.

26 Calendar of Hastings Manuscripts, II, 29-30. *Fugger Newsletters*, Second Series, Klarwill (London 1926) 55.

27 John Strype, *Annals of the Reformation* (London: John Wat, 1709) iii, 58.

28 State Papers Domestic: Elizabeth, cli, 46.

29 W. J. Hofdijk, *Geschiedenis der Nederlandsche Letterkunde* (Amsterdam, 1872) 156; H. E. Moltzer, *Shakspere's Invloed op het Nederlandsche Tooneel der Zeventiende Eeuw* (Groningen, 1874) 34-41.

30 H. D. Fuller, "The Sources of Titus Andronicus," *Publications of the Modern Language Association*, xvi (1901) 47, 63.

Appendix 1—From a Report about the Fifth National Conference of the Shakespeare Oxford Society in Philadelphia, October 18, 1982

The final report was by Dr. A. Bronson Feldman, entitled "Early Shakespeare," it dealt with his forthcoming book of that title, which is also a pun: Earl E. Shakespeare. Dr. Feldman's book is to be published in 1982 and its author said that a fourth of the work is in galleys. In his presentation, Dr. Feldman referred frequently to the one preceding his own by Dr. Louis Marder. He characterized the latter's approach to the Stratfordian case as one of fragmentation, in which each link in the Oxfordian argument is attacked singly—without regard for the whole case. He contrasted this to the Oxfordian argument, which is one of synthesis. Feldman said that Marder and the Stratfordians do not come to grips with the question of what kind of man Shakespeare was. What we know about Shakspere of Stratford is primarily that he was a money-lender. In addition to the other acknowledged evidence of this Shaksperian trait in the Stratford records, Dr. Feldman cited the first indication we have of Shakspere in London is a loan he made in 1592 to one John Clayton. Eight years later the record shows that Shakspere sues the latter to recover the debt. Such a man, Dr. Feldman asserted, is not in the great company of Keats and Shelley. Nor can the author of *The Merchant of Venice* be an encloser of commons and a hoarder of grain. The speaker mentioned J. Thomas Looney's list of the author's characteristics, which were both special and general, and he has not seen Looney's argument from these characteristics refuted. No Stratfordian scholar has yet explained, said Dr. Feldman, how Shakespeare could have dared to present a prime official (Burleigh) on the stage, kill him, and then speak contemptuously of his corpse.

In "Early Shakespeare," the author tries to establish the context of the sequence of events leading Shakespeare to write the plays the way he did. The book is a psychological, historical, and biographical study. Feldman had investigated several of the plays, starting with Eva Turner Clark's analyses (but correcting her at several points). One orthodox contention was neatly disposed of by Dr. Feldman when he cited reasons against the popular notion that Shakespeare wrote his plays as "pot-boilers." All of his plays "belie the stage" and "overflow the boundaries" of conventional stagecraft, Feldman said.

One new fact was claimed by the speaker. He had assumed, along with earlier Oxfordians, that Malvolio was the only representation of Christopher Hatton in Shakespeare. Was this the only play to portray Hatton? Feldman finds this official in the characters of Lucio in *Measure for Measure* (the Luce was Hatton's coat-of-arms, since he was a member of the Lucy family) and Angelo in the same play as representing Hatton's more "angelic" posture. Also the notorious hand-cutting scene in *Titus* is a reference to Hatton's having cut off John Stubbe's hand for the latter's pamphlet against the Queen. Dr. Feldman said that he was certain Stratfordians would have an answer for each single detail of his argument in his forthcoming book, but he would like them instead to answer to the case.

In an exchange with Dr. Marder following his presentation, Dr. Feldman mentioned an hypothesis presented by the late C. W. Barrell: Cyril Tourneur, a Jacobean playwright for whom no biography can be found, was apparently a soldier in Sir Francis Vere's army. Barrell contended that this Cyril Tourneur was really Sir Edward Vere, natural son of the 17th Earl of Oxford by Anne Vavasour.

Appendix 2—Chart of Dates

1550 April 12: Birth of Edward de Vere, Viscount Bulbeck, at Castle Hedingham, Essex, only son of John de Vere, 16th Earl of Oxford, and Margaret (Golding).

1558 November: Enrolment of Edward de Vere as fellow-commoner in Queens College, Cambridge University. Sir Thomas Smith was evidently his first tutor.

Elizabeth Tudor became Queen of England. Lord John de Vere served as Great Chamberlain at her enthronement; his Countess Margery was appointed a Maid of Honor.

1561 August 14: The Earl of Oxford entertained the Queen and her Court at Castle Hedingham for five days with hunting and hawking, and his musicians and actors.

1562 July 28: John de Vere made his will, appointing his son one of his executors.

1562 August 3: Death of Lord John at Castle Hedingham.

September 3: Edward, Earl of Oxford, left his widowed mother and rode to London to enter the house of William Cecil, Master of the Court of Wards, in Westminster. His uncle Arthur Golding seems to have accompanied him as tutor, assisted by Lawrence Nowell.

1563? The Countess of Oxford married Charles Tyrrell.

1564 August 10: The boy Earl of Oxford received from Cambridge the degree (honorary) of Master of Arts.

1566 September 6: Oxford University granted him the Master-of-Arts degree.

1567 February 1: He enlisted to learn law at Gray's Inn.

July 23: While Earl Edward and a tailor named Edward Baynam were exercising with fencing blades, in the backyard of Cecil House in the Strand, Thomas Brinknell, undercook in the Cecil kitchen, drunkenly attacked Oxford and was killed, by a thigh wound. The coroner's inquest called the homicide *felo de se*. Among the jurors sat the historian Raphael Holinshed.

1568 December 2: Margaret Golding Vere Tyrrell died. Her husband buried her at Earl's Colne, Essex, a short ride from her
Castle.

1569 November 24: Oxford wrote to Cecil for permission to enlist
in the army headed by Thomas Radcliff, Earl of Sussex, for
crushing a Roman Catholic revolt in the north. He reminded
his guardian how he always wished to experience "the wars
and services in strange and foreign parts," and to win honor
by "service of my Prince and country."

1570 Spring: Charles Tyrrell, Esquire, died.

1571 March 30: Cecil reported, "the Queen's Majesty sendeth at
this present the Earl of Oxford into the north parts to remain
with my Lord of Sussex, and to be employed there in her Majesty's service."

1571 April 2: Edward, Lord Great Chamberlain of England, entered the House of Lords and observed the Parliament at
work.

1571 May 1: The Earl of Oxford won "the chief honor" in tournaments of chivalry held for three days at Westminster. July:
Edward's engagement to marry Mistress Anne Cecil, daughter
of William, Master of the royal wards, whom the Queen promoted to the Lordship of Burghley so that his girl would be
meet for the match. Cecil had desired her wedlock with Master Philip Sidney but Sidney's family failed to satisfy Cecil's
demands for money and land.

December 19: Edward and Anne married in Westminster Abbey. The Queen was the prime guest at the wedding and the
feast at Cecil House.

1572 January 5: For *De Curiali sive Aulice*, the Latin translation by
Bartholomew Clerke, Oxford's Cambridge teacher, of Baldassare Castiglione's classic work *The Courtier*, the Earl wrote a
Latin Greeting to the Reader. The volume was issued from
the press of John Day.

January: Thomas Howard, Duke of Norfolk, aspirant for marriage with the exiled Queen Mary of Scotland, was sentenced

to death by the House of Lords for alleged plotting to destroy the State and Church. The Earl of Oxford strove in vain to win his freedom from the charges and imprisonment contrived by plotting of William Cecil, Lord Burghley.

June 2: Oxford's aunt Frances's son, the Duke of Norfolk, was beheaded.

1573 Spring: For the translation of Girolamo Cardano's *De Consolatione* by Oxford's friend Thomas Bedingfield of Suffolk, the Earl wrote a letter of introduction "From my new country Muses of Wivenhoe," and a poem on the pains and rewards of literary labor. *Cardanus Comforte, translated into Englishe. And published by commaunde ment of the right honourable the Earle of Oxenforde. Cum privilegio.*

1575 January 7: Earl Edward, licensed by the Queen to travel in Europe for a year, having arranged for the payment of his enormous inherited debts to the Crown and the disposal of his estates to prevent his sister Mary from acquiring "the ancient Earldom," leaving certain lands for the sons of his uncle Geffrey Vere, Francis, Robert and Horace, said farewell to Elizabeth, and sailed for France.

March 17: In Paris he heard from Burghley that Countess Anne was going to make him a father. He "wrote to his wife, and sent her his picture and two horses," Burghley noted, without telling what he did with the letter.

1575 March-May: Oxford visited Germany, making a friend of Johannes Sturm, the great educator who trained boys by production of plays.

May: De Vere arrived in Padua.

July: He stayed in Venice, learning there that on July 2 his wife had delivered a daughter, named of course Elizabeth.

December 12: He went to Florence.

1576 January 3: He wrote to Burghley from Siena.

February? At Palermo, Sicily, he challenged "all manner of persons whatsoever," to meet him in tournaments, barriers, or combats, but none ventured to encounter him.

March: Apparently he sailed up the Rhone river to Lyons, politely spurned an invitation to review troops of Hans Casimir, Prince of the Palatinate serving as mercenary for the French King, and came to Paris before March 31, when Valentine Dale, the English ambassador, wrote to Burghley about the Earl's arrival.

April 4: Calumny against Countess Anne came to his ears and flared his temper against her and all the Cecils. The slanders appear to have started from the tongue or pen of Lord Henry Howard, the Duke of Norfolk's brother, and a soldier attendant on Oxford, Rowland Yorke. We do not know if cousin Francis Vere and the Welsh warrior Roger Williams were with Oxford in Paris at this time or in March of 1575.

April: Dutch and Flemish pirates attacked his ship in the Channel passage and robbed him. Brother-in-law Thomas Cecil rode to welcome him at Dover, but De Vere would not land there. Instead he and Yorke sailed up the Thames to London, met Burghley and poor Anne and rejected their appeal for a talk on April 20. Having made arrangements for temporary residence at Yorke House, he went to salute the Queen.

May? The Earl arranged for publication of *The Paradise of Dainty Devices*, aptly furnished, with sundry pithie and learned inventions: devised and written for the most part, by M. (Richard) Edwards, "sometimes of her Maiesties Chappel: the rest, by sundry learned Gentlemen, both of honor, and worshippe, viz. S. Barnarde. Iasper Heywood. E. O." and other Catholic poets. "Imprinted at London by Henry Disle... 1576." E. O. is Edward (or Earl) of Oxford.

June 7: Captain Martin Frobisher sailed with two tiny barks in search of the northwest passage across the Arctic to Asia. *The Comedy of Errors* marks the historic moment: "the bark Expedition put forth tonight" (4.3).

1576 August? The romance finally named *Pericles, Prince of Tyre* was prepared for the stage.

1577 January 1: The Children of St Paul's Cathedral played *the History of Error* for the royal court.

February 17: The Lord Chamberlain's servants acted for the Queen *The History of the Solitary Knight: Pericles*.

March? Conception of the romance now named *Cymbeline, King of Britain*.

July: Mary Vere, Oxford's sister, promised to marry Peregrine Bertie, Lord Willoughby, despite the cursory predictions of his mother Katherine and the angry opposition of her brother.

December? Prototype of the comedy *The Taming of the Shrew*.

1578 March? Prototype of the comedy *Two Gentlemen of Verona*.

Summer? Original composition of the romance *All's Well That Ends Well*, later entitled *Love's Labors Won*.

October? Original composition of the comedy *Love's Labor's Lost*, for which there is no definite record of performance until 1598.

1579 January 1 Children of Paul's performed *A Moral of the Marriage of Mind and Measure* (*The Taming of the Shrew*) at the royal Revels.

Spring? *The Jew* was performed at the Bull Inn, presumably by the Sussex troup.

Summer: Tennis court quarrel of Philip Sidney and Edward de Vere—over the prospect of marital union with France.

December 26: Lord Chamberlain Sussex's men acted *A History of the Duke of Milan and the Marquis of Mantua* (*Two Gentlemen of Verona*) for the Queen.

1580 February 2: The Sussex company played *The History of Portia and the Merchants* for her Majesty.

February 14: The Earl of Derby's players performed for the Court *The Soldan and the Duke of Rhodes* (known nowadays as *Soliman and Perseda*)—by Thomas Watson?

Spring? Original composition of the comedy *Twelfth Night or What You Will*.

June: Conception of Edward Vere, illegitimate child of Edward de Vere and Anne Vavasor. The parents were put in the Tower of London, for a short period.

December? The boys of Paul's Cathedral played John Lyly's *Alexander and Campaspe* for the Queen?

December 22? The Earl of Oxford accused Lord Henry Howard and Charles Arundel of conspiring for the restoration of Papal power. They applied for refuge at midnight in the house of Bernardino de Mendoza, Ambassador of Spain, until they learned they would be held in temporary custody of Hatton and Walsingham.

1581 January 1: The Derby troup performed *The Story of Hieronimo* (*The Spanish Tragedy?*) at the royal court. (By Thomas Watson?)

June? *The tragedy of Titus and Vespasian (Andronicus)* written for the Earl of Sussex's company? Oxford again in the Tower for interrogation.

Autumn? First endeavour to write the romance of *Measure for Measure*.

December 26 or January 6? Paul's Cathedral boys performed *Twelfth Night* at the Court?

1582 February 2: Quire boys of Paul's played John Lyly's *Endimion* for the Queen?

Summer: Prototype of the tragedy *Romeo and Juliet*.

Autumn: Original composition of the comedy *Much Ado About Nothing*.

556

A Bibliography of Publications on Tudor Literature by A. Bronson Feldman*

(1947)   "Shakespeare's Jester—Oxford's Servant," *Shakespeare Fellowship Quarterly*," Volume VIII, No. 3, Autumn, 1947

(1951a)   [Letter about] *"Greene's Groatsworth of Wit," Shakespeare Fellowship Newsletter (English)*, April 1951

(1951b)   "The Man Who Might Have Been Shakespeare," *The Critic and Guide*, June, 1951

(1952a)   "Othello's Obsessions," *American Imago*, 9, June, 1952

(1952b)   "Who is Shakespeare? What Is He?" *Shakespeare Newsletter*, Volume II, September, 1952

(1953a)   "The Confessions of Will Shakespeare," *American Imago*, 10, Summer, 1953

(1953)   "Shakespeare Worship," *Psychoanalysis*, 2, Summer, 1953

(1954)   "Othello in Reality, " *American Imago*, 11, Summer, 1954

(1955a)   "Shakespeare's Early Errors," *International Journal of Psycho-Analysis*, xxxvi, April, 1955 (Chapter 1 of this book is a revision of this article.)

(1955b)   "Imaginary Incest: A Study of Shakespeare's Pericles, " *American Imago*, 17, Summer, 1955 (Chapter 3 of this books is a revision of this article.)

(1959)   "Portals of Discovery," *American Imago*, 16, Spring, 1959 (Chapter 2 of this book is a revision of this article.)

(1963)   "The March of Hamlet," *Shakespeare Newsletter*, Volume XIII, December, 1963

(1966)   "Psychoanalysis and Shakespeare," *Psychoanalytic Review*, 53 (1966)

(1968)   "Shakespeare's First Tragedy," *Love Lore*, Winter, 1968 (*Love Lore* was a journal privately published and circulated by A. Bronson Feldman and his friend Stephen Karpowitz. Feldman used the pen name Obadiah B. Morse as the author of this article. Chapter 11 of this book is a revision of this article.)

(1972)   *Secrets of Shakespeare: Four Chapters from a Subversive History*, (Philadelphia: Lovelore Press, 1972) This privately published and circulated book contains early versions of Chapters 6 and 7 of this book.

(1977a)   "Thomas Watson, Dramatist," *The Bard*, Volume I, No. 4, 1977

(1977b)   *Hamlet Himself* (Philadelphia: Lovelore Press, 1977)—A reprint of this book appeared in 2010 from iUniverse.

(1979a)   "Noblesse Oblige," *Shakespeare Oxford Society Newsletter*, Winter, 1979

(1979b)   "A Preface to *Arden of Feversham*," *The Bard*, Volume 2, No. 3, 1979

(1980a)   "A Tyrant's Vein," *The Bard*, Volume 2, No. 4, 1980

(1980b)   "The Marlowe Mystery," *The Bard*, Volume 3, No. 1, 1980

(1981)   "Bunk and the Bust," *Shakespeare Oxford Society Newsletter*, Spring, 1981

(1982a) "The Secret Verses of Edward de Vere," *The Bard,* Volume 2, No. 3, 1982

(1982b) "Oxford's Sole Acrostic," *Shakespeare Oxford Society Newsletter,* Spring 1982

(1982c) "A Decalog for Idolators," *Shakespeare Oxford Society Newsletter,* Summer, 1982

(1983) "Shakespeare and Patriotism," *Shakespeare Oxford Society Newsletter,* Winter, 1983

(1984) "Amendments to Bernard Ward's *The Seventeenth Earl of Oxford,*" *The Bard,* Volume 4, No.2, 1984

* Some of these articles have been reprinted at various times in various places. For details, please consult the indispensable *An Index to Oxfordian Publications,* James Warren, editor.

Index